Sustainable Value Chain Management

There are these rare moments when musicians together touch something sweeter than they've ever found before in rehearsals or performance, beyond the merely collaborative or technically proficient, when their expression becomes as easy and graceful as friendship or love. This is when they give us a glimpse of what we might be, of our best selves, and of an impossible world in which you give everything to others, but lose nothing of yourself.
Ian McEwan, Saturday

Sustainable Value Chain Management

A Research Anthology

Edited by
ADAM LINDGREEN, FRANÇOIS MAON,
JOËLLE VANHAMME AND SANKAR SEN

Routledge
Taylor & Francis Group

LONDON AND NEW YORK

First published in paperback 2024

First published 2013 by Gower Publishing

Published 2016 by Routledge
4 Park Square, Milton Park, Abingdon, Oxon OX14 4RN

and by Routledge
605 Third Avenue, New York, NY 10158

Routledge is an imprint of the Taylor & Francis Group, an informa business

Publisher's Note
The publisher has gone to great lengths to ensure the quality of this reprint but points out that
some imperfections in the original copies may be apparent.

Gower Applied Business Research
Our programme provides leaders, practitioners, scholars and researchers with thought
provoking, cutting edge books that combine conceptual insights, interdisciplinary rigour and
practical relevance in key areas of business and management.

British Library Cataloguing in Publication Data
Sustainable value chain management : a research anthology.
  1. Business logistics. 2. Social responsibility of
  business. 3. Sustainability.
  I. Lindgreen, Adam.
  658.7-dc23

Library of Congress Cataloging-in-Publication Data
Lindgreen, Adam.
  Sustainable value chain management : a research anthology / by Adam Lindgreen, François
  Maon, Joëlle Vanhamme, and Sankar Sen.
    pages cm
  Includes bibliographical references and index.
  ISBN 978-1-4094-3508-2 (hardback) -- ISBN 978-1-4094-3509-9 (ebook) -- ISBN 978-1-4094-
  7134-9 (epub) 1. Industrial management--Environmental aspects. 2. Sustainable development.
  3. Industrial procurement--Environmental aspects. 4. Purchasing--Environmental aspects. I.
  Maon, François II. Vanhamme, Joëlle. III. Title.
  HD30.255.L55 2013
  658.7--dc23

                                                                                    2013000318

ISBN: 978-1-4094-3508-2 (hbk)
ISBN: 978-1-03-283690-4 (pbk)
ISBN: 978-1-315-61158-7 (ebk)

DOI: 10.4324/9781315611587

Reviews for Sustainable Value Chain Management

From the garment factories of Bangladesh to the mines of Peru, today's globally colossal value chain raises critical and thorny questions about its sustainability. Conflicting objectives, stakeholders at cross-purposes, implementation and assessment conundrums: modern managers are in dire need of thoughtful and actionable guidance in their quest to do right by the people, planet, and profits that inspire and make possible their businesses. This book rises to this urgent challenge by providing a comprehensive, thorough, and deep look into what makes value chains sustainable. Through the collective contributions of over fifty sustainability thought leaders from around the world, this book sheds welcome light on what it means for a company to have a truly sustainable value chain as well as, importantly, how best to achieve it. In that, this book is a stand out in the increasingly crowded realm of sustainability thought. It is required reading for practitioners, scholars, and students of sustainability alike.

Prof. CB Bhattacharya, E.ON Chair Professor in Corporate Responsibility and Dean of International Relations, European School of Management and Technology

This important book shines a clear light into the darkest shadows of contemporary business: the global value chains of multi-national corporations that stretch into the deepest recesses of developing countries. What the book reveals is an extensive series of questionable practices relating to human rights, labour standards and environmental impact. In a practical and informed way the work tackles the issue of corporate social and environmental responsibility in remote supply chains where it is most difficult to accomplish effective and lasting reform. The book connects up the engaging statements on social and environmental responsibility of international corporations, and tests them in lengthy and complex value chains to discover if they have any practical meaning. This definitive analysis is infused with insights on how sustainable value chains may be recognised, gauged and evaluated. The design of collaborative and inclusive value chains is authoritatively examined. A comprehensive survey and integration of theoretical and policy perspectives on responsibility in the value chain is offered, together with a range of sectoral and industry strategies. This book sets a new benchmark for the advance of understanding and policy on sustainable value chain management, and will prove an invaluable tool in the effort to raise the standards of employment and environmental practices among communities who are the most vulnerable in increasingly complex and inter-connected global value chains.

Prof. Thomas Clarke, Director, Centre for Corporate Governance, UTS Sydney

The last two decades have seen the growing recognition in business that social and environmental problems are increasingly business problems. Initially, it was in the sectors most obviously affected, such as the resource-extraction industries, now it is becoming widely taken for granted as businesspeople in many sectors come to see how their companies affect and are affected by forces such as climate change, resource scarcity, and population growth. As this research anthology makes amply clear, value chains are key to an effective response by companies to many of these sustainability challenges, and organizations are now starting to give attention to sustainability in managing their value chains. Drawing on a wide range of different geographical and industry perspectives, this rich collection of articles provides a basis for deeper understanding of both the sustainability challenges in value chains and the business opportunities.

N. Craig Smith, INSEAD, Fontainebleau Cedex, France

Contents

List of Figures

List of Tables

Foreword and Acknowledgment

The way organisations manage their value chains has changed dramatically in the past decade.[1] Today, not only do they account for economic issues, but organisations also adopt a broader perspective on their overall purpose, leading them to express their interests in and devotion to social[2] and environmental[3] issues.

Despite a global spread, however, sustainable value chain management remains an uncertain, poorly defined ambition, with few absolutes.[4] The social and environmental issues that organisations confront might easily be interpreted as omnipresent, including virtually everything. Current literature on the topic seeks to understand the effects and management of initiatives that work to address concerns about diversity, human rights, safety, philanthropy, community, and the environment.[5] However, the integration of social and environmental considerations into value chain management represents a sort of "desire lacking reality", such that the idea has had only "patchy success".[6]

The objective of this research anthology is therefore to investigate multiple angles from which to consider sustainable value chain management. Together, the chapters fill gaps in prior research, but they also explore and expand new fields. The book's 27 chapters constitute five sections:

i.   Sustainable value chains: context, drivers, and barriers
ii. Sustainable value chains: managing activities
iii. Sustainable value chains: managing networks and collaboration
iv. Sustainable value chains: integrative perspectives
v.   Sustainable value chains: specific sectorial and industry perspectives

Sustainable Value Chains: Context, Drivers, and Barriers

Sustainability has garnered notable attention in the popular press, but its appearance in academic literature is less consistent Research thus far has not been able to explicate the actual drivers of and barriers to adopting environmentally sustainable practices within organisations – particularly in relation to their implementation in the purchasing and supply management function, where sustainability remains an emerging topic. Accordingly, the chapters in this section review both the challenges that remain to implementing sustainability in the supply chain and the features, both external and internal, that encourage it.

For example, to clarify the scope of sustainability in purchasing and supply chain fields, "Environmental sustainability in the supply chain: a review of past literature and discussion of potential drivers and barriers" by Robert E. Hooker, Diane Denslow, and Larry C. Giunipero provides a review of prior literature on the topic of sustainability. It also reports on the early stages of development of a framework of purchasing and supply management sustainability, related to potential drivers and barriers faced by both government and industry. The review and framework, offered in the early stages of the development of a wider understanding of sustainability as it relates to purchasing and supply management, is critical for advancing research in the field.

Helen Walker and Stephen Brammer consider the roles and commitment of managers and their effects on organisational dedication to social and environmental issues in "Sustainable procurement, institutional context and top management commitment: an international public sector study". Using institutional and managerial choice theory views, the authors note the relationships among sustainable procurement practices, an institutional policy context, and senior management commitment. They developed their sustainable procurement questionnaire by drawing on extant purchasing social responsibility, socially responsible buying, and environmental attitudes scales. The resulting survey, designed to assess the extent to which sustainability influences public procurement practices, was conducted with a sample of more than 280 public procurement practitioners from 20 countries, whose collective expenditure responsibilities reached $45 billion. With multiple regression, the authors develop a model to show that both the institutional context and top management commitment influence the extent and nature of sustainable procurement practices. However, if policymakers need to decide which aspects of sustainable procurement to prioritise, they should focus on senior managers' commitment to sustainable procurement, because practices are likely to follow.

In "Environmental research and development, public policy, and value chain management: a competitive advantage perspective" John T. Scott situates environmental research and development (R&D) within the context of research into corporate social responsibility and value chain management. In so doing, he explains how public policies aimed at improving environmental performance create opportunities for socially responsible corporate investments in environmental R&D. Thus, an organisation's managers can find profitable opportunities for environmental R&D if public policy in their surroundings focuses on the environmental performance of the activities that constitute the organisation's value chain. Although public policy creates opportunities for profitable R&D, the general expectation that socially responsible investments create sustainable competitive advantages for the organisation is unwarranted. Investments instead appear necessary simply for the organisation's survival in the post-policy environment. Finally, in describing actual corporate behaviour towards environmental R&D, this chapter corroborates the validity of theoretical lessons about socially responsible corporate behaviour.

Beyond environmental R&D needs, concerns about economic globalisation have led to continuing efforts to regulate the activities of multinational corporations and ensure respect for human rights globally. The nature of globalisation suggests that such efforts must include both nation-states and multinational corporations, separately and in cooperation, though they often are initiated by global organisations. In "Human rights in the value chain", Emily F. Carasco and Jang B. Singh examine five global codes of ethics published by global organisations to address human rights: the UN Center for Transnational Corporations' Draft Code, the OECD Guidelines for MNEs, the ILO's Tripartite Declaration of Principles Concerning Multinational Enterprises, the Global Compact, and the Norms on the Responsibilities of Transnational Corporations and Other Business Enterprises with Regard to Human Rights (Norms). Particular emphasis is placed on the last code, which is also the latest and, in many ways, the most promising effort to promote human rights in the value chain. The authors examine corporate codes of ethics as organisation-specific instruments in this quest, too.

But multinational corporations also continue to come under pressure to adopt private regulatory initiatives, such as supplier codes of conduct, to address poor working conditions in their global supply chain factories. Moving beyond the drivers and outcomes of such monitoring schemes among large organisations, "The growth of private regulation of labor standards in global supply chains: mission impossible for Western small and medium-sized organisations?" by Jette Steen Knudsen focuses on the growing integration of small and medium-sized enterprises into global supply chains. Focusing on the Business for Social Compliance Initiative (BSCI), the author examines the positions of private actors who demand and supply private regulation, as well as the positions of smaller organisations that are the targets of such schemes. As membership of the BSCI has grown, small and medium-sized enterprises increasingly face demands to meet its requirements in global supply chains. Complete compliance, unfortunately, appears to be a mission impossible for many smaller organisations, and as a result, the private regulatory system is under growing strain.

Organisations come under increasing pressures from stakeholders, too, to incorporate the triple-bottom line of social, environmental, and economic responsibility considerations into their operations and supply chain management strategies. In "Supply chain themes in corporate social responsibility reports", Wendy L. Tate, Jon F. Kirchoff, and Lisa M. Ellram use content analysis software to perform centring resonance analysis and examine corporate communications to stakeholders through corporate social responsibility reports. Their goal is to determine how supply chain strategies factor into the triple-bottom line for 100 socially and environmentally responsible global companies. This research compares and contrasts influential terms in the corporate social responsibility reports across a range of industries, organisational sizes, and geographical regions. The content analysis reveals 10 themes that describe how top global companies integrate and improve their triple-bottom line in internal operations and external supply chains. Although institutional pressure drives the integration of sustainable practices in supply chain management, companies emphasise different facets of social, environmental, and economic responsibility internally and externally, upstream and downstream, throughout their supply chains.

Sustainable Value Chains: Managing Activities

Once organisations determine that sustainability is a critical requirement of their supply chains, as well as a viable goal for them, the next step involves actions taken to achieve the goals. Some supply chains turn to sustainability certification; others seek to adopt closed-loop systems or rely on information technology (IT) resources to enhance their sustainability. Regardless of the method chosen, the organisation must manage these sustainability actions throughout its supply chain. Therefore, the seven chapters in this section offer a broad range of possible management approaches that supply chain members can adopt and implement.

Organisations that seek more sustainable practices or products through their supply chains often struggle to recognise the variety of goals and practical limitations that exist. Dayna Simpson and Damien Power highlight the importance of goal definition and alignment with value chain activities in "Aligning goals and outcomes in sustainable supply chain management". As they note, many organisations' intentions are distant from the realities of sustainable supply chain management (SSCM). The poor alignment of sustainability goals with sourcing requirements or key relationship investments limits organisations' SSCM capabilities, whereas better alignment across suppliers, focal organisations, and customers should improve the likelihood of success.

One method of ensuring such alignment might rely on "cradle-to-grave" or life cycle approaches that feature closed-loop supply chains. For sustainable innovation in a value chain, a life cycle assessment might help practitioners and researchers overcome the challenges of balancing the pressures of organisation-level economic performance against environmental and social responsibilities. In "Setting a framework for life cycle assessment in sustainable technology development", Stelvia Matos and Jeremy Hall propose a life cycle assessment that includes economic, environmental, and social variables and their interactions to identify potential issues with technology development. Their multilevel perspective stems from complexity theory, stakeholder theory, and supply chain literature, and their case investigation of biomass-processing technologies reveals the key requirements for undertaking a life cycle assessment that provides useful information in this context. They conclude with a framework for conducting a life cycle assessment for sustainable innovations and paths for further research.

In "Creating socially responsible and environmentally sustainable IT-enabled supply chain", Ian M. Langella, Jerry Carbo, and Viet Dao also examine varying definitions of sustainability in sustainable management research. True sustainability comprises economic profit, environmental concern, and social justice, yet sustainability literature often eschews the latter rung. To overcome this narrow focus, this chapter conceptualises sustainable and responsible supply chain management as a process in which products are produced from sustainable inputs gained from responsible suppliers, manufactured in a sustainable and responsible manner, and marketed and distributed by responsible distributors and retailers. To enable such supply chains, information must flow seamlessly within and among supply chain partners. For example, information about the sustainability of suppliers can be brought to bear on selection, evaluation, and development decisions. Distribution and retail partners can be preferred or rejected based on their environmental and social performance. Regardless of the method used, IT resources must be integrated into the development of a socially and environmentally sustainable supply chain.

Socially responsible employment practices also can help organisations attract, develop, and manage employees, who represent investments. Creating socially responsible and sustainable employment practices helps organisations meet current needs without compromising their ability to meet future needs, according to Wendy S. Becker and Richard Smith in "Social and environmental responsibility, sustainability, and human resource practices". In this sense, sustainable employment practices have strategic implications for the organisation, and unsustainable practices create long-term risks. The use of unsustainable employment practices when times are tough limits success during better times. The authors thus examine three broad functions of employment practices: attracting, developing, and managing employees. In their proposed framework, socially responsible practices contrast with short-term, unsustainable practices, and industry examples demonstrate the challenges of creating sustainable value chains through employment practices.

In contrast, in supply chains, contracts and trust coordinate processes across actors, even though these contracts are often incomplete, and trust takes time to develop. Francesco Ciliberti and Job de Haan suggest "Using codes of conduct to help small and medium-sized enterprises manage supply chains: the case of SA8000". Their literature review documents how codes of conduct (in particular, Social Accountability 8000) can help manage supply chains (especially those involving small and medium-sized companies) by solving the problem of incomplete contracts, replacing trust in new partnerships with respect to intangible performance indicators, and solving principal–agent problems. The chapter also includes a case summary of a real organisation that has used a code of conduct throughout its supply chain.

It is not only small organisations that struggle. Developing countries are particularly affected by the mounting environmental problems that result from mass production. Environmental standards that pertain to the entire supply chain offer a response to these challenges, for instance the Forest Stewardship Council (FSC), the Programme for the Endorsement of Forest Certification Schemes (PEFC), the Marine Stewardship Council (MSC), and ISO 14001. This response is based on the assumption that standards increase legitimacy among stakeholders and generate value for the shareholders, but the positive effects may be questionable. In "Environmental standards and certification in a value chain perspective: NGOs' views on the legitimacy of the process", Martin Müller, Stefan Seuring, and Virginia Gomes dos Santos examine why certification might not convert into wider benefits and whether environmental standards really are the best instrument to assure value in supply chains. A poll of 22 representatives from NGOs reveals high variance among the standards; a comparison of these reveals some interesting weaknesses and strengths. Using the concept of normative legitimacy, the authors argue that it is possible to improve the legitimacy of standards in supply chains.

At the same time, organisations and their partners need to make business cases for the development and implementation of sustainable supply chains and networks. Such networks have substantial tangible and non-tangible costs and benefits, some of which are easy to define, though others are not so easily determined. Central to the business case is the need for performance metrics and measures, made readily available to organisations and their partners. For example, Joseph Sarkis, Aref Hervani, and Marilyn Helms, in "Applying economic non-market valuation for sustainable supply chain performance measurement and evaluation", seek to propose ways that organisations can use ecological economics literature, related to the non-market valuation of natural eco-systems, to integrate valuation methodologies into sustainable, or green, supply chains. The authors provide an overview and review literature on the valuation of sustainable supply chains and environmental and social programmes associated with them, before summarising key methods, philosophies, and tools from economics literature that explain the non-market valuation of social goods (e.g., natural eco-systems). Their discussion features examples of how the tools can be used internally in organisations, as well as descriptions of the substantial opportunities for analytical, methodological, descriptive, and critical analyses.

Sustainable Value Chains: Managing Networks and Collaboration

Broader concerns in relation to sustainable value chains can span networks as well as nations. The six chapters in this section therefore address more expansive, innovative versions of sustainability that are not limited to a single organisation. Whether the value chains comprise green purchasing, cotton sales, local food sources, or biofuels, the chapters in this section reveal the imminent need for creative management methods and reliable tactics to ensure their success. Two key options for doing so include codes of conduct and enhanced resilience in complex networks.

An overriding sustainability concern pertains to green supply chains for purchasing, although this topic remains underresearched. With "Green offerings and buyer–supplier collaboration in value chains", Paul Matthyssens and Wouter Faes contrast suppliers' efforts to augment their offerings with green value against buyers' reactive and/or proactive strategies. Using a multiple case study methodology, they scrutinise various forms of "green" collaboration across partners in a supply chain. To develop path-breaking green solutions, the network of all supply chain partners must collaborate very closely, though the initiative can be taken by any partner and is not the sole responsibility of the buyer. If the partners are not at the same level of green development or technical expertise, mutual aid can move lagging partners up the "value ladder" (which implies green co-evolution in industrial markets). Customer ideas and supplier capabilities are particularly important inputs for this process. Finally, the authors acknowledge that green purchasing offers a signal of increased "purchasing maturity" in industrial settings.

Similar multistakeholder initiatives also involve combinations of private sector companies, NGOs, and public sector agencies, largely aimed at making value chain management more sustainable. Research attention has centred on studying the political evolution of these initiatives or assessing their impact on producers, workers, and the environment, though without connecting these two streams. The chapter, "Multistakeholder initiatives in cotton value chains: towards a theoretical framework and a methodology", contributes to filling this gap by developing an analytical framework of the political evolution and impacts of multistakeholder initiatives in developing countries. Using a case study of cotton value chains in West Africa and South Asia, Peter Lund-Thomsen introduces the methodology to use when conducting fieldwork with the proposed analytical framework and studying multistakeholder initiatives in real-world, developing country contexts.

Moving to another geographic context, Martin Hingley and Adam Lindgreen examine local and regional food organisations and their networks in the context of sustainable development in "Barriers and facilitators to developing sustainable networks: UK local and regional food". Several key influences prevent or facilitate organisational and network development in this setting, including governmental, commercial, and voluntary agencies that support local and regional food. The empirical analysis draws on three UK cases (two successful local networks and one regional network that thus far has failed to establish itself). Using a market mapping approach, the authors identify the roles of organisations and surrounding networks, as well as of the enabling environment. Although support structures and funding bodies offer useful assistance, they can overlap and are bureaucratic in their operation. Local and regional business assistance cannot account for the market barriers to development that emerge due to power plays and blocking tactics of actors interested in channel control. Rather, facilitating actions tend to come from supportive channels, network members, and the focal organisations. Therefore, organisations and their networks, in addition to evaluating their own business strengths and capabilities, should devote greater attention to blocking and facilitating specific agents and determining the importance of their vested interests, which may have positive (or benign) or negative effects on the success of sustainable local and regional food.

Recent policies in Brazil instead have tried to encourage impoverished farmers to participate in the growing biofuels sector. "Incorporating impoverished communities in sustainable supply chains" examines the challenges of trading with impoverished communities for improved sustainable supply chain management; the authors, Jeremy Hall and Stelvia Matos, draw on sustainable supply chain literature, transaction cost economics, and base of the pyramid discourse. Using interview data collected with supply chain stakeholders, policymakers, NGOs, and farmers in Brazil – an emerging economy and leader in biofuels production that still grapples with poverty – they find considerable challenges associated with sourcing raw materials from farmers. Brazilian policymakers may recognise the importance of providing opportunities in the biofuels supply chain, but the often illiterate farmers lack basic business knowledge and distrust industry and government policy.

Farmers cannot be forced to act in a certain way, but codes of conduct set for supplier factories offer a private way to regulate workers' rights. The merits of codes of conduct have been debated intensely. Niklas Egels-Zandén suggests that both proponents and detractors are correct in their assessments in "Learning to improve or deceive? Chinese supplier responses to multinational corporations' codes of conduct". This study determines what Chinese toy suppliers have learned from their exposure to codes of conduct. Suppliers initially learn to deceive auditors rather than improve workers' rights, by decoupling their symbolic and substantive actions. Subsequently, though, they may learn to recouple symbolic and substantive features and even improve workers' conditions.

Similar to codes of conduct, external forces can disrupt engineered systems, which suggests the need to reconsider sustainability by moving beyond the identification and reliable prediction of risks. Uncertainties are inherent to complex systems; in "Understanding resilience of complex value-chain networks", Jeryang Park, Thomas P. Seager, and P. Suresh C. Rao propose resilience as an essential characteristic that enables an engineered system to continue functioning, even in the face of uncertainties and unexpected shocks. Modern value chains should be understood as complex networks, whose efficiency-driven strategies might reduce their resilience and create a risk of failure due to unpredicted events (shocks). Rather than being a state variable, however, resilience in a complex network may constitute an emergent property, the outcome of a recursive process of sensing, anticipating, adapting, and learning. By focusing on adaptation across these processes, the authors derive a modelling framework for designing resilient value chains. Furthermore, in addition to conventional metrics for evaluating the robustness of complex networks (e.g., topological measures, loss of services from non-specific and specific disruptions), this chapter proposes autocorrelation and spectral analysis as quantitative methodologies for incorporating underlying stochastic processes into disruptions and system responses. These analyses also can improve the memory of a complex network, which in turn supports anticipation of low frequency but high consequence events (i.e., shocks). The Lorenz inequality analysis provides a learning method that can evaluate the extent to which a system's functionalities depend on certain nodes/links, as well as diagnose the system's adaptive state. These various methods all can be applied to clarify the resilience of value chains and develop adaptive strategies for designing and managing value chains as complex adaptive networks.

Sustainable Value Chains: Integrative Perspectives

Corporate social responsibility has been on the corporate, public, and academic agenda for several decades. Over this period, the responsibility demands of corporations have evolved, such that organisations today are held responsible for things that they have not done themselves but to which they are connected. Accordingly, research into corporate social responsibility needs to evolve as well, and such an evolution is possible by combining insights from various theories and field of research. The three chapters in this section each exemplify that effort.

The first chapter, "Ever expanding responsibilities: upstream and downstream corporate social responsibility" by Judith Schrempf-Stirling, Guido Palazzo, and Robert A. Phillips, reviews the expanding corporate responsibilities that extend both up and down the value chain. For example, corporations are held increasingly responsible for worker and human rights violations within and beyond their supply chain. Such corporate social responsibility demands cannot be understood according to a liability approach; rather, a social connection approach to corporate social responsibility can better examine the legitimacy of various corporate social responsibility demands up and down the value chain. That is, this social connection approach can assess the responsibility demands that arise from various relationships.

The growing awareness of corporate social responsibility also highlights the need for its systematic management. However, literature on systematic approaches to implementing corporate social responsibility remains underdeveloped. Muhammad Asif, Cory Searcy, and Olaf A.M. Fisscher elaborate on the meta-management of corporate social responsibility by detailing how to organise its implementation at a high level of abstraction. The essentials of the meta-management of corporate social responsibility appear in an original framework, which they propose in "Meta-management of corporate social responsibility". The starting point is a stakeholder-oriented approach that proceeds through dynamic processes of sensemaking, stakeholder interaction, and structural and infrastructural changes for organisation-wide corporate social responsibility integration and continual improvement. To illustrate their meta-management, the authors present a case study of Shell.

Natalia Aguilar Delgado and Luciano Barin Cruz, in "When the social movement and global value chain literatures meet: the case of Fair Trade", propose an analytical framework derived from social movement literature to examine the evolution of global value chains. The transformation of governance modes for global value chains is manifest in the shifts in key characteristics proposed by social movement literature (i.e., field opportunities, mobilising structures, and framing processes). To illustrate this proposal, the authors use the case of the Fair Trade movement. When the field (not particular organisations) is the unit of analysis, different actors mobilise structures and frame claims without acting in isolation. Therefore, considering social movement literature elements from a field perspective can not only reconstruct the linkages among actors but also reveal how these elements interact to explain the governance modes that appear in global value chains literature.

Sustainable Value Chains: Specific Sectorial and Industry Perspectives

The final section in this book reflects the ways we can understand the broadened, expansive concepts associated with sustainability by taking a specific instance as an example. By studying in detail the value chains for coffee, banks, Greek food, Tanzanian biofuels, and humanitarian organisations, the chapters in this section elucidate new and specific insights that cut a path for further research, while also offering key implications for supply chain managers in these and similar industries and sectors.

First, in "Contributing to a more sustainable coffee chain: projects for small farmers instigated by a multinational company", Ans Kolk presents an empirical, practical case study of the move towards a more sustainable coffee chain. Small coffee farmers in developing countries undertook projects instigated by a multinational company (Sara Lee's international coffee and tea division) through its DE Foundation. The consumer goods giant established this foundation as part of its overall commitment to ensuring sustainable coffee in the mainstream – an objective that remains far from reality thus far. The hindrances fall largely outside its sphere of influence, such as insufficient certified coffee on the market, lack of widespread consumer interest, and confusion related to standards for and approaches to sustainable coffee. The author introduces the broader context of the coffee sector and the strategy adopted by the multinational enterprise, but he also offers a rather practical overview of five projects for small farmers on three continents (South America, Africa, and Asia). Beyond their basic characteristics, this chapter reveals the results, lessons, and implications for multinational enterprises and sustainable supply chains.

Second, in "Corporate social responsibility in the bank value chain", Bert Scholtens analyses what banks do and why, in an effort to determine how their actions connect to their corporate social responsibility. The author argues that banks engage in financial risk transformation, which represents their main economic and societal value. As intermediaries, they affect the size and direction of economic development, which implies that their activities are inherently connected to human, social, and economic development. As a service industry, banking has a relatively small social and ecological footprint, however, such that banks' impact stems only from their economic role as financial intermediaries. The proposed theoretical framework offers a means to assess bank activity; the chapter also provides an example of international banks' corporate social responsibility.

Third, the chapter "Sustainability in value chains: empirical evidence from the Greek food sector" by George Maglaras, Michael Bourlakis, and Christos Fotopoulos sheds light on the various sustainability outcomes within an extended Greek food value chain that includes dairy, fruit, meat, and vegetable food products. The key members (growers, manufacturers, wholesalers, and retailers) help to illustrate which stages of this value chain underperform with regard to their sustainability value outcomes, and to identify best practices. The results of a survey of 1,042 food companies showed that the Greek food value chain has many characteristics of a traditional chain that undermine its sustainability, including product conservation time, quality of packaging, and traceability. Organisations that deal with vegetables simply lack a sustainability orientation. The authors identify specific sustainability weaknesses and strengths for every food product and every value chain in every stage, leading to explicit directions for improvements and benchmarking opportunities.

Fourth, standards and certifications, as "scientific" governance instruments, have recently emerged to ensure environmental and social sustainability of renewable energy global value chains. In "Standardising sustainability: certification of Tanzanian biofuels smallholders in a global value chain", Henny Romijn, Sanne Heijnen, and Saurabh Arora detail a pilot certification project aimed at thousands of Tanzanian smallholders who cultivate Jatropha oilseeds as a source of bio-kerosene. The authors study the tense encounters between a universal biofuel sustainability standard, designed in an ostensibly participatory process in the Netherlands, and the socio-ecological realities of smallholders in Tanzania. In these encounters, many provisions in the standard and certification protocols had to be modified to align with the local realities, but the changes initially were resisted by the standard's designers. Other frictions, both similar to and unique from those discussed in the chapter, are bound to crop up as the proposed, adjusted standard travels to different localities. Therefore, the authors call for regional or niche standardisation strategies and reject the notion of globally applicable standards. A niche standardisation strategy is better poised to facilitate the smallholders' abilities to benefit from the sustainability of their existing practices, even though they cannot afford to prove it "scientifically".

Fifth, in "Sustainability in humanitarian organisations", Ira Haavisto and Gyöngyi Kovács seek to increase understanding of sustainability in humanitarian organisations, which exist solely to help society, and especially vulnerable people. Multiple sustainability aspects appear in humanitarian operations, ranging from their impact on local economies, to questions of the long-term effects of aid, to their social and environmental impacts in the long and short runs. This chapter pays particular attention to operationalising sustainability in a humanitarian context and thus focuses on logistics and supply chain management. The proposed framework illustrates various perspectives on sustainability and identifies unique aspects in the humanitarian context through a content analysis of the annual reports of the largest humanitarian organisations. Generally, they feature little consideration of sustainability, though recent developments, such as GRI reports by humanitarian organisations and the UNDP's consideration of climate change in its agenda, indicate increasing attention to these aspects. This trend is likely to persist in the future.

Closing Remarks

We extend a special thanks to Gower Publications and its staff, who have been most helpful throughout the entire process. Equally, we warmly thank all of the authors who submitted their manuscripts for consideration for this book. They have exhibited the desire to share their knowledge and experience with the book's readers – and a willingness to put forward their views for possible challenge by their peers. Finally, we thank Elisabeth Nevins Caswell for her superb editorial assistance.

There are companies that have built themselves entirely around delivering on their social and environmental responsibilities and have been remarkably successful, yet as the chapters in this book demonstrate clearly, there is still a lot we do not know about sustainable value chain management. We are hopeful that the chapters in this book help fill some knowledge gaps for readers while also stimulating further thought and action pertaining to sustainable value chain management issues.

Professor Adam Lindgreen
Cardiff, Wales

Dr. François Maon
Lille, France

Professor Joëlle Vanhamme
Roubaix, France

Professor Sankar Sen
New York, US

1 June, 2013

Notes

1   Carter, C.R. & Rogers, D.S. (2008), "A framework of sustainable supply chain management: moving toward new theory", *International Journal of Physical Distribution and Logistics Management*, Vol. 38, No. 5, pp. 360–387; Sarkis, J. (2001), "Manufacturing's role in corporate environmental sustainability: concerns for the new millennium", *International Journal of Operations and Production Management*, Vol. 21, No. 5/6, pp. 660–686; Svensson, G. (2007), "Aspects of sustainable supply chain management (SSCM): conceptual framework and empirical example", *Supply Chain Management*, Vol. 12, No. 4, pp. 262–266.

2   Campbell, T. (2006), "A human rights approach to developing voluntary codes of conduct for multinational corporations", *Business Ethics Quarterly*, Vol. 16, No. 2, pp. 255–269; Carter, C.R. & Jennings, M.M. (2002), "Logistics social responsibility: an integrative framework", *Journal of Business Logistics*, Vol. 23, No. 1, pp. 145–180; Royle, T. (2005), "Realism or idealism? Corporate social responsibility and the employee stakeholder in the global fast-food industry", *Business Ethics: A European Review*, Vol. 14, No. 1, pp. 42–53; Van Tulder, R., Kolk, A., & Van Wijk, J. (2009), "From chain liability to chain responsibility: MNE approaches to implement safety and health codes in international supply chains", *Journal of Business Ethics*, Vol. 85, No. 2, pp. 399–412.

3   Carter, C.R. & Ellram, L.M. (1998), "Reverse logistics: a review of the literature and framework for future investigation", *Journal of Business Logistics*, Vol. 19, No. 1, pp. 85–102; Peattie, K. (2001), "Towards sustainability: the third age of green marketing", *Marketing Review*, Vol. 2, No. 2, pp. 129–146; Plante, C.S. & Bendell, J. (2000), "The art of collaboration: lessons from emerging environmental business-NGO partnerships in Asia", *Greener Management International*, Vol. 24, pp. 91–104; Tibben-Lembke, R.S. (2002), "Life after death: reverse logistics and the product life cycle", *International Journal of Physical Distribution and Logistics*

Management, Vol. 32, No. 3, pp. 223–244; Van Tulder, R., Kolk, A., & Van Wijk, J. (2009), "From chain liability to chain responsibility: MNE approaches to implement safety and health codes in international supply chains", *Journal of Business Ethics*, Vol. 85, No. 2, pp. 399–412; Yang, C.-L. & Sheu, C. (2007), "Achieving supply chain environment management: an exploratory study", *International Journal of Technology Management*, Vol. 40, No. 1, pp. 131–156.

4   Lindgreen, A., Maon, F., & Swaen, V. (2009), "Corporate social responsibility in supply chains", *Supply Chain Management*, Vol. 14, No. 2, pp. 71–74.

5   Carter & Jennings, *op. cit.*

6   Kakabadse, A., Kakabadse, N., & Middleton, R. (2006), "CSR penetrating the supply chain: desire lacking reality", in Kakabadse, A. and Kakabadse, N. (eds.), *CSR in Practice: Delving Deep*. Basingstoke: Palgrave Macmillan, pp. 46–71; Roberts, S. (2003), "Supply chain specific? Understanding the patchy success of ethical sourcing initiatives", *Journal of Business Ethics*, Vol. 44, No. 2, pp. 159–170.

About the Editors

Adam Lindgreen

After graduating with degrees in chemistry, engineering, and physics, Dr. Adam Lindgreen completed an MSc in food science and technology at the Technical University of Denmark. He also finished an MBA at the University of Leicester, as well as a one-year postgraduate programme at the Hebrew University of Jerusalem. Professor Lindgreen received his Ph.D. in marketing from Cranfield University. He has been Professor of Marketing at Hull University's Business School (2007–2010), the University of Birmingham's Business School (2010), and the University of Cardiff's Business School (since 2011).

Professor Lindgreen has been a visiting professor with various institutions, including Georgia State University, Groupe HEC in France, and Melbourne University, and is currently a visiting professor with Bradford University's Business School, Hull University's Business School, and Lincoln University's Business School. His recent publications have appeared in *Business Horizons, California Management Review, Industrial Marketing Management, International Journal of Management Reviews, Journal of Advertising, Journal of Business Ethics, European Journal of Marketing, Journal of Business and Industrial Marketing, Journal of Marketing Management, Journal of the Academy of Marketing Science, Journal of Product Innovation Management, Psychology & Marketing*, and *Supply Chain Management: An International Journal*; his most recent books are *A Stakeholder Approach to Corporate Social Responsibility* (2012, with Kotler, Vanhamme, and Maon), *Managing Market Relationships, Market Orientation, Memorable Customer Experiences, The Crisis of Food Brands, The New Cultures of Foods*. The recipient of the Outstanding Article 2005 award from *Industrial Marketing Management*, Professor Lindgreen also serves on the board of several scientific journals; he is the joint editor of *Journal of Business Ethics* for the section on corporate responsibility. His research interests include business and industrial marketing management, experiential marketing, and corporate social responsibility.

Adam Lindgreen has discovered and excavated settlements from the Stone Age in Denmark, including the only major kitchen midden –Sparregård – in the south-east of Denmark; because of its importance, the kitchen midden was later excavated by the National Museum and then protected as a historical monument for future generations. He is also an avid genealogist, having traced his family back to 1390 and published widely in scientific journals related to methodological issues in genealogy, accounts of population development, and particular family lineages.

François Maon

Dr. François Maon is Associate Professor of Strategy and Corporate Social Responsibility at the IESEG School of Management, Université Catholique de Lille (LEM-CNRS). Dr. Maon received his Ph.D. from the Louvain School of Management, Université Catholique de

Louvain. He has been a visiting researcher at the Haas School of Business, University of California Berkeley. Dr. Maon has published in *California Management Review, International Journal of Management Reviews, Journal of Business Ethics, and Supply Chain Management: An International Journal*, among others. His most recent book is A Stakeholder Approach to Corporate Social Responsibility (2012, with Lindgreen, Kotler, and Vanhamme). His main research interests include corporate social responsibility, organizational culture, organizational change processes, and corporate branding. Dr. Maon serves on the review board of Journal of Business Ethics.

Joëlle Vanhamme

Dr. Joëlle Vanhamme is Professor of Marketing at the Edhec Business School. Dr. Vanhamme received her Ph.D. from the Louvain School of Management, Université Catholique de Louvain. Previously, she was a Research Fellow with the Belgian National Fund for Scientific Research, an Assistant Professor at the Rotterdam School of Management, Erasmus University, and Associate Professor at the IESEG School of Management, Université Catholique de Lille (LEM-CNRS). Dr. Vanhamme also has been a Visiting Scholar with Delft University of Technology, Eindhoven University of Technology, Hull University's Business School, and the University of Auckland's Business School. Dr Vanhamme's research has appeared in journals including *Business Horizons, California Management Review, Industrial Marketing Management, International Journal of Research in Marketing, Journal of Advertising, Journal of Business Ethics, Journal of Consumer Satisfaction, Dissatisfaction and Complaining Behavior, Journal of Economic Psychology, Journal of Marketing Management, Journal of Retailing, Psychology & Marketing, Recherche et Applications en Marketing*, and *Supply Chain Management: An International Journal*, among others. Dr. Vanhamme serves as editor of Journal of Business Ethics' section on corporate responsibility.

Sankar Sen

Dr. Sankar Sen is Professor of Marketing at Baruch College of the City University of New York. Dr. Sen received his Ph.D. in business administration in 1993 from the Wharton School at the University of Pennsylvania. Prior to Baruch College, he was an associate professor at the School of Management at Boston University and associate professor and Washburn Research Fellow at Fox School of Business, Temple University. Dr. Sen also has been a visiting scholar at Stern School of Business, New York University and Sasin Graduate Institute of Management, Chulalongkorn University. Dr. Sen's research lies at the intersection of consumer decision making, corporate social responsibility/ sustainability, and marketing strategy. In particular, he has spent the last several years examining when, how, and why consumers and, more recently, other key stakeholders respond to companies' corporate social responsibility and sustainability endeavours. His research has been published in leading marketing and economics journals, and has been cited in publications such as *Business Week, Harper's*, and *New York Times*. Dr. Sen has lectured extensively on these issues in academic and executive forums in North and South America, Europe, and Asia, and his book, entitled *Leveraging Corporate Responsibility:*

The Stakeholder Route to Maximizing Business and Social Value, was recently published by Cambridge University Press. Dr. Sen serves on the editorial review boards of *Corporate Reputation Review, Journal of Consumer Psychology, Journal of Consumer Research, Journal of Marketing, Journal of Public Policy and Marketing,* and *Sasin Journal of Management.*

About the Contributors

Saurabh Arora

Dr. Saurabh Arora is an assistant professor at the School of Innovation Sciences, Eindhoven University of Technology. He received his Ph.D. from Maastricht University in 2009 with a thesis focusing on networked politics of agricultural development in a South Indian village. Recent publications have appeared in the *European Journal of Economic and Social Systems, Habitat International, Journal of Sustainable Agriculture,* and *Organization,* among others. His current research adapts insights from actor-network theory to analyse governance of global value chains through sustainability standards and certification protocols.

Muhammad Asif

Dr. Muhammad Asif is an assistant professor at Prince Sultan University, Saudi Arabia. Dr. Asif received his Ph.D. from the University of Twente in the Netherlands. He has published in *Corporate Social Responsibility and Environmental Management, Journal of Cleaner Production, Total Quality Management and Business Excellence,* and *TQM Journal,* among others. His research interests include corporate sustainability, total quality management, and integrated management systems.

Wendy S. Becker

Dr. Wendy S. Becker is Associate Professor of Management at Shippensburg University, Pennsylvania. Dr. Becker received her Ph.D. in industrial-organizational psychology from the Pennsylvania State University. She publishes in *Forensic Science Policy and Management, Human Resource Development Review, Organizational Dynamics, Organization Management Journal, Organizational Research Methods, People and Strategy,* and *Research in Organizational Behavior,* among others. Her books (with W. Mark Dale) include *Applying Business Principles to Forensic Laboratory Management* (Taylor & Francis, forthcoming) and *The Crime Scene: How Forensic Science Works* (Kaplan, 2007). Professor Becker's research interests include team and organizational learning, social responsibility, and start-ups and she contributes to the literature in qualitative research methods. In 2012 Becker was elected to the executive board of the Metropolitan New York Association of Applied Psychology (METRO), the oldest professional applied psychology association in the US. She serves as reviewer for scholarly journals and conferences in the organizational sciences and recently completed a three-year term as editor of *The Industrial-Organizational Psychologist.*

Michael Bourlakis

Dr. Michael Bourlakis is Professor in Supply Chain Management at Brunel Business School. His articles have appeared in supply chain management, marketing, and business journals including *Environment and Planning D, European Journal of Marketing, International Journal of Logistics Management, International Journal of Logistics: Research and Applications, Journal of Marketing Management,* and *Supply Chain Management: An International Journal.* He has received funding in excess of £600,000 from various bodies and he is on the editorial board of six journals. Dr. Bourlakis' current research interests include retail logistics and food supply chain management, information technology/e-business and supply chain management, and food marketing channels.

Stephen Brammer

Dr. Stephen Brammer is Professor of Strategy and Associate Dean for Research at Warwick Business School. His research has been widely published in leading journals such as *Financial Management, Journal of Business Research, Journal of Management Studies, Organization Studies,* and *Strategic Management Journal.* His research lies principally in the areas of business ethics and corporate social responsibility. Specifically, his research explores firm–stakeholder relationships, the strategic management of these, and their impact upon company performance and reputation. He is a member of the Academy of Management and serves on the executive board of the International Association for Business and Society; he has served as a section editor at the *Journal of Business Ethics,* and is a member of the editorial boards of *Business Ethics Quarterly, Business and Society,* and *Journal of Management Studies.*

Emily F. Carasco

Dr. Emily F. Carasco is Professor of Law at the University of Windsor, Ontario, Canada. Dr. Carasco received her S.J.D. from the Harvard Law School. She has published in the *Business and Society Review, European Business Review,* and *Journal of Business Ethics,* among others. Her book on the rights of non-citizens is to be published in November 2012. Dr. Carasco's research focuses on human rights, both domestic and international, and is primarily about the rights of vulnerable groups such as women, children, and temporary workers.

Jerry Carbo

Dr. Jerry Carbo is Associate Professor of Management in the Grove College of Business at Shippensburg University, Pennsylvania. Dr. Carbo received his Ph.D. from Cornell University and his JD from the Penn State School of Law. He has published in *Journal of Strategic Information Systems, Journal of Workplace Rights,* and *Working USA,* among others. His research interests include socially sustainable business practices, workplace bullying, and union revitalization.

Francesco Ciliberti

Dr. Francesco Ciliberti is a business consultant at Intellego S.r.l. and a former research fellow in sustainable supply chain management at the Polytechnic of Bari's Department of Environmental Engineering and Sustainable Development. Dr. Ciliberti received his Ph.D. from Polytechnic of Bari. He has published in *International Journal of Production Economics, Journal of Cleaner Production, Operations and Supply Chain Management: An International Journal*, and *Supply Chain Management: An International Journal*, among others. Dr. Ciliberti has contributed to books such as *21st Century Management: A Reference Handbook* (SAGE, 2008) and *Ethics in Small and Medium Sized Enterprises* (Springer, 2010). His research interests include corporate social responsibility, supply chain management, and small and medium-sized enterprises.

Luciano Barin Cruz

Dr. Luciano Barin Cruz is Associate Professor of Management at HEC Montreal. Dr. Barin Cruz received his Ph.D. from Jean Moulin Lyon III University (France) and the Federal University of Rio Grande do Sul (Brazil). He is currently co-director of the Interdisciplinary Research Group on Sustainable Development at HEC Montreal. He has published in *World Development, Business and Society, Journal of Business Ethics*, and *Management Decision*, among others. His research interests include corporate social responsibility, sustainable development, and inclusive and social innovation. He serves as a reviewer of many journals, including *Journal of Business Ethics* and *Management Decision*.

Viet Dao

Dr. Viet Dao is Associate Professor of Management Information Systems at Shippensburg University of Pennsylvania. Dr. Dao received his Ph.D. in management information systems from the University of Oklahoma and his M.Sc. in Information Systems from the University of Leeds. His research has been published in journals including *Journal of Engineering and Technology Management* and *Journal of Strategic Information Systems*, among others. His research has also been included in proceedings and presented at various national and international conferences. His main research interests focus on IT and technological innovation management, the business and sustainability value of IT.

Job de Haan

Dr. Job de Haan is Associate Professor of International Production Management at Tilburg University's School of Economics and Management (TiSEM). Dr. de Haan received his Ph.D. from Tilburg University. He has published in *International Journal of Cleaner Production, International Journal of Production Economics, International Journal of Production and Operations Management*, and *Supply Chain Management: An International Journal*, among others. He has contributed to books such as *Entrepreneurship, Innovation and Economic Development* (Oxford University Press, 2011 edited by Adam Szirmai, Wim Naudé, and Micheline Goedhuys) and *A Stakeholder Approach to Corporate Social Responsibility* (Gower Publishing, 2012, edited by Adam Lindgreen, Philip Kotler, Joëlle Vanhamme, and François Maon). His research interests include corporate social responsibility, lean management, social innovation, and international production and logistics.

Natalia Aguilar Delgado

Natalia Aguilar Delgado is a Ph.D. candidate in strategy and organizations at McGill University, Canada. Her research interests include the role of civil society and business organizations coalitions in transnational regulation building, particularly in environmental and social arenas.

Diane Denslow

Diane Denslow is an instructor in entrepreneurship at the University of North Florida and a certified business analyst for the Small Business Development Center. She was previously on the faculty at Florida State University and served as the Associate Director for the Jim Moran Institute for Global Entrepreneurship. She has taught numerous university classes on entrepreneurship and management. Diane Denslow has published in *Industrial Marketing Management, International Journal of Entrepreneurship and Innovation Management, Journal of Entrepreneurship Education, Journal of Purchasing and Supply Management, Journal of Small Business Strategy*, and *Korean Small Business Review*, among others. Diane is the co-author of a text entitled *So You Need to Write a Business Plan*. She has research interest in purchasing and supply management, sustainability, and small businesses. Diane has over 20 years of experience consulting with businesses, specializing in small and family businesses. She previously owned ABN Group, Inc., a Jacksonville, Florida based consulting firm specializing in business plan development, strategies for growth, and financial analysis.

Niklas Egels-Zandén

Dr. Niklas Egels-Zandén is Associate Professor of Business Administration at the School of Business, Economics and Law, University of Gothenburg, Sweden. Dr. Egels-Zandén received his Ph.D. from University of Gothenburg. He has published in *Business Ethics: A European Review, Business Strategy and the Environment, Corporate Social Responsibility and Environmental Management, Journal of Business Ethics*, and *Journal of Corporate Citizenship*. His areas of research are international business and corporate social responsibility, especially in relation to private regulation of workers' rights and how sustainability issues become integrated in business strategy.

Lisa M. Ellram

Dr. Lisa M. Ellram is the Rees Distinguished Professor of Supply Chain Management at Miami University's Farmer School of Business in Oxford, Ohio. She is also a visiting professor at Cranfield School of Management, and Director of the A.T. Kearney-Institute for Supply Management Center for Strategic Supply Leadership. She has published in *Academy of Management Journal, California Management Review, Journal of Operations Management*, and *Journal of Supply Chain Management*, among others. She has co-authored numerous textbooks. Her research interests include sustainable supply chain management, services purchasing and supply chain management, cost and value management, and risk management. She is co-editor-in-chief of *Journal of Supply Chain Management* and is on the advisory, editorial or review boards for a number of other journals.

Wouter Faes

Wouter Faes is Assistant Professor of Marketing and Supply Chain Management at Hasselt University, Faculty of Business Sciences. He has published in *Industrial Marketing Management, Journal of Business and Industrial Marketing*, and *Journal of Purchasing and Supply Chain Management*, among others. His research interests include purchasing management, negotiations, and industrial marketing.

Olaf A.M. Fisscher

Olaf A.M. Fisscher is Professor of Organization Studies and Business Ethics at the University of Twente, in the Netherlands. After his master's degree in industrial engineering, Professor Fisscher received his Ph.D. in social sciences from Groningen University. The Leuphana University of Lüneburg (Germany) awarded him an honorary doctorate in 2009. He has published in *International Journal of Technology Management, Journal of Business Ethics, Journal of Product Innovation Management, R&D Management*, and *TQM Journal*, among others. Dr. Fisscher's research interests and teaching activities include innovation and change management, the quality of organization, business ethics, and corporate responsibility. Olaf Fisscher is Director Continuing Education at the School of Management and Governance at the University of Twente. He is involved in several scientific and professional committees and boards in the field of quality, innovation, and business ethics. Dr. Fisscher is editor of the international journal *Creativity and Innovation Management*, amongst others.

Christos Fotopoulos

Dr. Christos Fotopoulos is Professor of Marketing Management at the Department of Business Administration of Food and Agricultural Enterprises of the University of Western Greece. His current research interests include, but are not limited to, management, agribusiness, food marketing, total quality management, supply chain management, and aspects of contemporary marketing of agricultural businesses.

Larry C. Giunipero

Larry C. Giunipero is Professor of Supply Management in the Marketing Department at Florida State University. Dr. Giunipero's primary research, teaching, and consulting interests are in the area of supply management. He holds a Ph.D. from Michigan State University. He has published over 50 articles in various academic journals such as *Decision Sciences, Industrial Marketing Management, International Journal of Logistics Management, International Journal of Physical Distribution and Logistics Management, Journal of Supply Chain Management*, and *Sloan Management Review*, among others. He has performed consulting and training projects for number of different corporations in the US, Europe, Australia, Philippines, Saudi Arabia, and the Caribbean. He is also active in presenting programmes for various supply management professional associations. He has co-authored four textbooks on supply management, the latest entitled *Purchasing and Supply Chain Management*. His current research interests are focused on supply chain sourcing strategies, social media in supply management, managing supply chain risks, e-purchasing solutions, and supply management skills and competencies.

Virginia Gomes dos Santos

Dr. Virginia Gomes dos Santos started her business studies at the University of Applied Sciences in Wilhelmshaven, Germany. After that, she started her Ph.D. at Carl von Ossietzky University of Oldenburg, finishing it in 2010. Dr. Gomes dos Santos worked as a business consultant and now works as an executive assistant for a member of the board at AXA Konzern AG, situated in Cologne.

Ira Haavisto

Ira Haavisto is a Ph.D. student at Hanken School of Economics, Helsinki, Finland. She has a master's degree in supply chain management and corporate geography from Hanken School of Economics. Ira Haavisto has a background of working with development and environmental responsibility for a commercial logistics service provider. She is part of the Humanitarian Logistics and Supply Chain Research Institute (HUMLOG Institute) and her research focuses on humanitarian logistics. Her particular interest in humanitarian organizations' performance, and on sustainability and quality in humanitarian supply chains.

Jeremy Hall

Dr. Jeremy Hall (D.Phil., University of Sussex) is a professor at the Beedie School of Business, Simon Fraser University in Vancouver. He has published in *Business Strategy and the Environment, Ecological Economics, Energy Policy, Entrepreneurship: Theory and Practice, International Journal of Production Research, Journal of Business Ethics, Journal of Business Venturing, Journal of Cleaner Production, Journal of Management Studies, Journal of Operations Management, MIT Sloan Management Review, Research Policy*, and *Technological Forecasting and Social Change*, among others, with support from Genome Canada and the Social Sciences and Humanities Research Council of Canada. His research interests include the social impacts of innovation and entrepreneurship, sustainable supply chains, and strategies for sustainable development innovation. Dr. Hall is editor-in-chief of the *Journal of Engineering and Technology Management* and a board member of the *Journal of Business Venturing* and *Technovation*.

Sanne Heijnen

Sanne Heijnen worked as a researcher at the School of Innovation Sciences of Eindhoven University of Technology. She did extensive fieldwork in Tanzania during several projects on biofuels and sustainability. She received her engineering degree in innovation sciences at Eindhoven University of Technology, specializing in technology and development studies. Currently, she is a Ph.D. candidate at the Copernicus Institute for Sustainable Development at Utrecht University and the Agricultural Economics Research Institute (LEI) of Wageningen University. Her research topic is the socio-economic impact of bioenergy production on a regional level.

Marilyn M. Helms

Dr. Marilyn M. Helms is the Sesquicentennial Chair and Professor of Management at Dalton State College (DSC), Dalton, Georgia. Dr. Helms received her D.B.A. from the University of Memphis. She has published in *Competitiveness Review, International Journal of Business and Management Research, International Journal of Management, Journal of Business and Entrepreneurship, Journal of Business Strategy, Journal of Developmental Entrepreneurship, Journal of Education for Business, Journal of International Business and Entrepreneurship, Journal of the International Academy for Case Studies, Journal of Small Business Strategy, Quality Progress*, and *Thunderbird International Business Review*, among others. Her research interests include supply chain management, reverse logistics for recycling, quality, and strategic management. She serves on the boards of many journals and is a frequent manuscript reviewer.

Aref Aghaei Hervani

Dr. Aref Aghaei Hervani is Professor of Economics at the Chicago State University. Dr. Hervani received his Ph.D. from West Virginia University. He has published in *Corporate Social Responsibility and Environmental Management Journal, Journal of Agricultural and Applied Economics, Journal of Education for Business, Journal of International Business and Management*, and *Journal of Resources, Conservation, and Recycling*, among others. He has also published chapters in books including *Agricultural Policy for the 21st Century* (edited by Luther Tweeten and Stanley R. Thompson), *Voices from the Nueva Frontera: Latino Immigration in Dalton Georgia* (edited by Donald E. Davis, Thomas M. Deaton, David P. Boyle, and Jo-Anne Schick). His research interests include energy and environmental policy analysis, applied microeconomics, market failure and market structure analysis, green supply chain management, reverse logistics operation, reuse, recycling, and sustainability.

Martin Hingley

Dr. Martin Hingley is Professor of Strategic Marketing at University of Lincoln (Lincoln Business School). Dr. Hingley received his Ph.D. from the Open University (UK). He has published in *Industrial Marketing Management, Journal of Marketing Management*, and *Supply Chain Management: An International Journal*, among others. His books include three joint edited texts in the *Food and Agricultural Marketing* series recently published by Gower. Dr. Hingley has wide-ranging business experience in the international food industry and has spent some time in the provision of market and business analysis and industry-based training with the Institute of Grocery Distribution in the UK. He previously held a three-year fellowship with global retail chain Tesco Plc. Dr. Hingley's research interests are in marketing and supply chain management. His specialism is in food marketing and retailer–supplier chain relationships, and he has published and presented extensively on the management of power-dependency in retailer supply. He serves on the editorial boards of many influential journals.

Robert E. Hooker

Dr. Robert E. Hooker is Assistant Professor of Marketing at the University of South Florida's College of Business Administration. Dr. Hooker received his Ph.D. from Florida State University. He has published in a variety of outlets, including *Journal of Purchasing and Supply Management, Journal of Supply Chain Management*, and *MIS Quarterly Executive*, among others. His research interests span various marketing and supply chain topics including sustainability, open innovation in new product development, and immersive technologies impacting consumer behaviour and branding.

Jon F. Kirchoff

Dr. Jon F. Kirchoff is an assistant professor at East Carolina University in the Department of Marketing and Supply Chain Management. Dr. Kirchoff received his Ph.D. from the University of Tennessee. He has published articles in *International Journal of Physical Distribution and Logistics Management* and *Journal of Supply Chain Management*, and in proceedings from numerous academic conferences. Dr. Kirchoff's research interests include green supply chain management, demand and supply integration, and global supply chain strategy.

Jette Steen Knudsen

Dr. Jette Steen Knudsen is a Professor of Business in Society in the Department of Political Science at Copenhagen University. Dr. Steen Knudsen received her Ph.D. from MIT. She has published in *Business and Politics, Comparative Political Studies, Corporate Governance, European Journal of Industrial Relations, International Journal of Business in Society, Journal of Business Ethics, Journal of Public Policy, Journal of Public Policy* and *Regulation and Governance*, among others. Dr. Steen Knudsen's research interests focus on the interface between government regulation and business actions. Most recently she has explored the motivations and abilities of governments in economically advanced industrialized countries to promote social change in less developed countries by regulating home country companies and their social activities (e.g., by addressing human rights, labour rights, and anti-corruption issues). She is a recipient of several research grants, most recently (October 2012) a two-year research grant from the Danish Social Science Research Council.

Ans Kolk

Ans Kolk is Professor of Sustainable Management at the University of Amsterdam Business School. She has published many articles in international journals including *California Management Review, Harvard Business Review, Journal of Business Research, Journal of International Business Studies, Journal of Management Studies, Journal of World Business, Management International Review,* and *World Development*. She has also written many book chapters, and published *Economics of Environmental Management* (Financial Times Prentice Hall, 2000) and *International Business and Global Climate Change* (Routledge, 2009; with Jonatan Pinkse). Her research interests include corporate social responsibility and sustainability, especially in relation to the strategy and management of international business firms, and international policy. She serves on the boards of many journals including *Business and Society, Journal of Business Ethics, and Journal of International Business Studies*.

Gyöngyi Kovács

Dr. Gyöngyi Kovács is Professor of Supply Chain Management and Corporate Geography at the Hanken School of Economics in Helsinki, Finland, and Director of the Humanitarian Logistics and Supply Chain Research Institute (HUMLOG Institute). Dr. Kovács received her Ph.D. from the Hanken School of Economics. She has published in *International Journal of Cleaner Production, International Journal of Physical Distribution and Logistics Management, International Journal of Production Economics,* and *Journal of Business Logistics*, among others. She has edited a book called *Relief Supply Chain Management for Disasters* (IGI Global, 2012), and contributed to many others. Her research interests include logistics research and teaching methods, corporate responsibility in supply chains, reverse logistics, supply chain collaboration, and humanitarian logistics. Since January 2008, Gyöngyi has served as a (European) regional editor of *International Journal of Physical Distribution and Logistics Management* and, since its foundation, as the co-editor in chief of *Journal of Humanitarian Logistics and Supply Chain Management*.

Ian M. Langella

Dr. Ian M. Langella is Associate Professor of Supply Chain Management in the John L. Grove College of Business at Shippensburg University, Pennsylvania. He holds a BS from Maine Maritime Academy, as well as an MA and a Ph.D. from the University of Magdeburg in Germany. His research centres on sustainable and responsible supply chain management. He has authored one book and co-authored articles published in journals including *Computers and Operations Research, International Journal of Sustainable Engineering, Journal of Strategic Information Systems*, and *OR Spectrum*, among others. He has presented his work at many conferences including the *INFORMS* and *POMS* annual conferences, as well as the Closed Loop Supply Chain International Workshop. Dr. Langella has consulted on sustainability issues with several Fortune Global 500 companies including Volkswagen and Porsche.

Adam Lindgreen

Dr. Adam Lindgreen is Professor of Marketing at the University of Cardiff's Business School. Dr. Lindgreen received his Ph.D. from Cranfield University. He has published in *California Management Review, Journal of Business Ethics, Journal of Product and Innovation Management, Journal of the Academy of Marketing Science*, and *Journal of World Business*, among others. His books include *Managing Market Relationships* (Gower Publishing, 2008), *Memorable Customer Experiences* (Gower Publishing, 2009), and *A Stakeholder Approach to Corporate Social Responsibility* (Gower Publishing, 2012; with Philip Kotler, Joëlle Vanhamme, and François Maon). His research interests include business and industrial marketing, experiential marketing, and corporate social responsibility. He serves on the boards of many journals; he is the joint editor of *Journal of Business Ethics* for the section on corporate responsibility.

Peter Lund-Thomsen

Dr. Peter Lund-Thomsen is Associate Professor of Corporate Social Responsibility at the Copenhagen Business School and Visiting Fellow at the Smith School of Enterprise and Environment, University of Oxford in 2012–13. Dr. Lund-Thomsen received his M.Phil. in Environment and Development from the University of Cambridge and his Ph.D. from the Copenhagen Business School. He has published in *Development and Change, Geoforum, International Affairs*, and *Journal of Business Ethics*, among others. His research interests include corporate social responsibility in developing countries, industrial clusters, and global production networks. He serves on the editorial review board of *Journal of Business Ethics* for the section on corporate responsibility.

George Maglaras

George Maglaras is a Ph.D. candidate and research assistant at the Department of Business Administration of Food and Agricultural Enterprises of the University of Western Greece.

His current research interests include food supply chain management, food supply chain performance, food marketing, and consumer behaviour.

Stelvia Matos

Dr. Stelvia Matos is an adjunct professor at the Beedie School of Business, Simon Fraser University and a senior researcher on a Genome Canada funded project working on life cycle assessment of lignin-based products and technological, commercial, organizational, and social uncertainties. Dr. Matos received her D.Phil. in civil engineering (University of São Paulo, Brazil). She has published in *Harvard Business Review* (Latin America edition), *International Journal of Production Research*, *Journal of Business Ethics*, *Journal of Cleaner Production*, *Journal of Management Studies*, *Journal of Operations Management*, *Research Policy*, and *Technovation*, among others. Her research areas include engineering policy, sustainable development innovation, environment management tools, life cycle assessment, and social aspects of innovation dynamics. Her research involves agriculture, aquaculture, chemical, energy, forestry, and tourism sectors, with field studies performed in Brazil, Bosnia, Canada, China, Italy, the Netherlands, the UK, and the US.

Paul Matthyssens

Dr. Paul Matthyssens is Professor of Strategic Management at the University of Antwerp and at Antwerp Business School. He holds the PASCION Chair on Purchasing and Value Creation. Dr. Matthyssens has published in *Industrial Marketing Management*, *Journal of Business and Industrial Marketing*, *Journal of Purchasing and Supply Management*, and *Technovation*, among others. He is member of the Industry Council of the Flemish Minister-President. His research interests include business and industrial marketing, value innovation, global strategy, and purchasing strategy. He serves on the editorial boards of many journals.

Paul R. Murphy

Dr. Paul R. Murphy is Professor of Business Logistics in the Boler School of Business at John Carroll University, Ohio. Dr. Murphy received his Ph.D. from the University of Maryland, College Park. His most recent publications have appeared in *Journal of Business Logistics* and *Transportation Journal*. His books include *Contemporary Logistics* (10th edition, Pearson, 2010; with Donald Wood) and *International Logistics* (2nd edition, American Management Association, 2001; with Donald Wood, Daniel Wardlow, and Anthony Barone). His research interests include logistics social responsibility, international logistics, and third-party logistics. He serves on the editorial review boards of several journals including *International Journal of Physical Distribution and Logistics Management* and *Journal of Business Logistics*.

Martin Müller

Dr. Martin Müller is Professor of Sustainable Management at the University of Ulm. Dr. Müller received his Ph.D. from University of Halle-Wittenberg and in 2000 was awarded the L.V. Kantorovic Research Prize at Institute of Business Management Halle. He has published in *Business Strategy and the Environment, Ecological Economics, Journal of Business Ethics*, and *Journal of Cleaner Production*, among others. His research interests include sustainable supply chain management and corporate social responsibility.

Guido Palazzo

Guido Palazzo is Professor of Business Ethics at the University of Lausanne (Switzerland). He graduated in Business Administration at the University of Bamberg (Germany) and earned his Ph.D. in political philosophy (1999) from the University of Marburg (Germany). His research interests are in corporate social responsibility and unethical decision making. He is associate editor of *Business Ethics Quarterly* and *European Management Review* and member of the editorial board of *Academy of Management Review, Business and Society*, and *Journal of Management Studies*, among others. His work has appeared in journals such as *Academy of Management Review, Business Ethics Quarterly*, and *Journal of Management Studies*.

Jeryang Park

Dr. Park is assistant professor in the School of Urban and Civil Engineering at Hongik University, Seoul, Korea. He received his Ph.D. degree from the School of Civil Engineering at Purdue University, Indiana, USA. Dr. Park received B.Sc. and M.S. degrees in Department of Civil, Urban, and Geosystem Engineering from Seoul National University. He has published in *Atmospheric Environment, Landscape Ecology, Risk Analysis, Integrated Environmental Assessment and Management*, and *Environmental Technology*. His research interests include the emergent phenomena of stochastic resilience and tipping points in complex coupled systems. He applies the concepts in various case studies, including hydrological and ecological networks in wetlands, supply chain networks, biofuel manufacturing processes, and atmospheric deposition in urban systems.

Robert A. Phillips

Robert Phillips is an associate professor at the University of Richmond's Robins School of Business and has a joint appointment with the programme in Philosophy, Politics, Economics, and Law (PPEL). He received his Ph.D. from The Darden School at the University of Virginia. His work has appeared in *Business Ethics Quarterly, Business and Society Review, International Journal of Management Reviews, Strategic Management Journal*, and *Strategic Organization*, among others. He is the author of *Stakeholder Theory and Organizational Ethics* (Berrett-Koehler Publishers, 2003), co-editor (with R. Edward Freeman) of *Stakeholders* (Edward Elgar Publishing, 2010) and editor of *Stakeholder Theory:*

Impact and Prospects (Edward Elgar Publishing, 2011). His other research interests include reciprocity and bounded self-interest, ethics in network organizations, and private military contractors. He is a senior fellow at the Olsson Center for Applied Ethics at the University of Virginia's Darden School. He has served as associate editor for *Business and Society* and is past president of the Society for Business Ethics (2009).

Richard F. Poist

Dr. Richard F. Poist is professor emeritus in the College of Business at Iowa State University. Dr. Poist received his Ph.D., with a specialty in business logistics, from Pennsylvania State University. He has published in *International Journal of Physical Distribution and Logistics Management*, *Journal of Business Logistics*, and *Transportation Journal*, among others. His research interests include macro aspects of logistics, supply chain security, third-party logistics, and the education preparation of logistics executives. He serves on several editorial review boards, and was formerly the co-editor of *International Journal of Physical Distribution and Logistics Management*.

Damien Power

Dr. Damien Power is Professor of Management in the Faculty of Business and Economics at the University of Melbourne. Dr. Power received his Ph.D. from Monash University in Australia. He has published in *Decision Sciences*, *European Journal of Operations Research*, *International Journal of Operations and Production Management*, *Internet Research Journal of Business Ethics*, *Journal of Operations Management*, and *Supply Chain Management*, among others. He has published numerous book chapters and conference papers, and has edited or co-authored three books. His primary research interests include business-to-business e-commerce, supply chain management, and operations strategy. He serves on the review or editorial boards of many journals including *Journal of Operations Management* and *Journal of Supply Chain Management*.

Suresh C. Rao

Suresh C. Rao is the Lee A. Rieth Distinguished Professor in the School of Civil Engineering at Purdue University, Indiana. Before coming to Purdue, he was on the faculty at the University of Florida for 25 years. His inter-disciplinary research and teaching interests have covered a wide range of topics in environmental/ecological engineering and science, including hydrologic, biogeochemical and ecological consequences of anthropogenic impacts on landscapes; contamination and remediation of soils and aquifers; and resilience of coupled complex systems. He has been an invited speaker at international conferences in Europe, Australia, and Asia.

Henny Romijn

Dr. Henny Romijn is Associate Professor of Technology and Development Studies at Eindhoven University of Technology. She received her Ph.D. from the CentER of Economic Research at Tilburg University. She has published in *Cambridge Journal of Economics*, *Energy Policy*, *Industrial and Corporate Change*, *Journal of Development Studies*, *Research Policy*, and *World Development*, among others. Her most important book is *Technological Capability Building in Small Enterprises in Developing Countries* (Macmillan/St Martin's Press, 1999). Her current research interests include the role of technological learning in sustainable development, success and failure of renewable energy projects, and social and environmental sustainability impacts of biofuels in the South. Before embarking on an academic career, she worked at the International Labour Organisation in Kenya and India for several years.

Joseph Sarkis

Joseph Sarkis is Professor of Operations Management at Clark University's Graduate School of Management. Professor Sarkis received his Ph.D. from the State University of New York at Buffalo. He has published over 300 publications in a wide variety of outlets including peer review journals, book chapters, and conference proceedings. He has also edited a number of books focusing on business and the environment. His research interests include green supply chains, operations sustainability, and compassionate operations. He is currently editor of *Management Research Review*, departmental editor of the Social, Ethical and Sustainability Department for *IEEE Transactions on Engineering Management*. He has been special issue editor for a variety of international peer-reviewed academic journals. He has served as a visiting scholar at the Dalian University of Technology, University of Oviedo, Hanken School of Economics, Cardiff University, Central European University, and Lund University. He is an AT&T Industrial Ecology Fellow and a programme coordinator for the Greening of Industry Network.

Bert Scholtens

Bert Scholtens holds the J.L. Bouma Chair in the Economics of Sustainability and is professor in the Department of Finance of the University of Groningen in the Netherlands. Furthermore, he is a professor in finance at the School of Management at the University of Saint Andrews, Scotland, UK. His research is directed at international financial intermediation, corporate social responsibility, socially responsible investing, and environmental finance and economics. He has published in *Corporate Governance: An International Review*, *Ecological Economics*, *Energy Economics*, *Journal of Banking and Finance*, *Journal of Business Ethics*, *Journal of International Money and Finance*, and *World Development*. He currently teaches about portfolio management, corporate governance, and credit risk analysis, and coaches bachelor and master students in completing their thesis. He also supervises several Ph.D. students.

Judith Schrempf-Stirling

Dr. Judith Schrempf-Stirling is Assistant Professor of Management at the University of Richmond's Robins School of Business. She received her Ph.D. from the University of Lausanne, Switzerland. She has published in *Business Horizons, Business and Society*, and *Journal of Business Ethics*. Her research interests focus on corporate social responsibility, business and human rights, and ethical consumption.

John T. Scott

Dr. John Scott is Professor of Economics at Dartmouth College. Dr. Scott received his Ph.D. from Harvard University. He has published in *Review of Economics and Statistics, Economica, International Journal of Industrial Organization*, and *Research Policy*, among others. His books include *Purposive Diversification and Economic Performance* (Cambridge University Press, 1993 and 2005), *Environmental Research and Development: US Industrial Research, the Clean Air Act and Environmental Damage* (Edward Elgar Publishing, 2003), and *Public Goods, Public Gains: Calculating the Social Benefits of Public R&D* (Oxford University Press, 2011; with Albert N. Link). His research interests include industrial organization, the economics of technological change, and related public policies. He served as president of the Industrial Organization Society and as an associate editor and a member of the editorial boards of several journals.

Thomas P. Seager

Dr. Thomas P. Seager is an associate professor in the School of Sustainable Engineering and the Built Environment at Arizona State University in Tempe. He serves as an associate editor for the journal *Environmental Systems and Decisions* and on the editorial board of *Integrated Environmental Assessment and Management*. Dr. Seager has published nearly 100 articles in journals, books, and at conferences. He earned his Ph.D. at Clarkson University in the Department of Civil Engineering, and has previously been a faculty member at Hudson Valley Community College, the University of New Hampshire, Purdue University, and Rochester Institute of Technology. Dr. Seager conducts research related to the systemic environmental consequences of alternative energy nanotechnologies, network-based approaches to resilience, sustainability ethics, and science of team science.

Cory Searcy

Dr. Cory Searcy is an associate professor and Director of the Industrial Engineering Program at Ryerson University. Dr. Searcy received his Ph.D. from the University of Alberta. He has published in *Business Strategy and the Environment, Journal of Business Ethics, Journal of Cleaner Production*, and *International Journal of Production Economics*, among others. His research interests include sustainability reporting, sustainability indicators, sustainable supply chain management, and integrated management systems.

Stefan Seuring

Dr. Stefan Seuring is Professor of Supply Chain Management at the Faculty of Business and Economics at University of Kassel, Germany. Prior to that, he worked at Carl von Ossietzky-University of Oldenburg in Germany and University of Waikato in Hamilton, New Zealand. His publications have appeared in *Business Strategy and the Environment, International Journal of Physical Distribution and Logistics Management, International Journal of Production Economics*, and *Journal of Cleaner Production*, among others. His research interest cover supply chain management – particularly at the intersection with sustainability management, the application of management accounting tools, and strategic management. He is subject editor for sustainability and supply chain management for *Journal of Cleaner Production*.

Dayna Simpson

Dr. Dayna Simpson is Senior Lecturer in Operations Management at Monash University in Australia. She holds environmental science and environmental engineering degrees, as well as a Ph.D. from the University of Melbourne. Dr. Simpson has published in a variety of journals including *International Journal of Operations and Production Management, International Journal of Production Economics, International Journal of Production Research*, and *Journal of Business Ethics*, among others. She serves on editorial review boards for *Journal of Operations Management* and *Journal of Supply Chain Management*, as well as on the Executive Committee for the Academy of Management Operations Management Division. Her research interests cover sustainable operations and supply chain management, and sustainable innovation.

Jang B. Singh

Dr. Jang B. Singh is Professor of Business Administration and Research Leadership Chair in Business at the Odette School of Business, University of Windsor, Ontario, Canada. His research papers have been published in several scholarly journals including *Business and Society Review, Business Ethics: A European Review, European Business Review, Journal of Business Ethics*, and *Journal of World Business*, among others. While he has published in many areas his research focus is business ethics with particular emphasis on corporate codes of ethics.

Richard Smith

Richard Smith is a General Manager in the life sciences sector for Exel, Inc., a subsidiary of Deutche Post DHL. He gained an MBA from Shippensburg University in December 2011. Richard also holds a BS in Business Logistics from the Pennsylvania State University and a Certification in Transportation and Logistics from the American Society of Transportation and Logistics. Prior to his current position with Exel, Richard worked as a manager for seven years in the Less-Than-Truckload transportation sector in the US for two nationally renowned truck transportation companies.

Wendy L. Tate

Dr. Wendy L. Tate is an associate professor at the University of Tennessee in the Department of Marketing and Supply Chain Management. Dr. Tate's research and teaching interests include offshoring and outsourcing, services purchasing, the services supply chain, and environmental supply chain management. She has published articles in *California Management Review*, *International Journal of Physical Distribution and Logistics Management*, *Journal of Business Logistics*, *Journal of Operations Management*, and *Journal of Supply Chain Management*, among others. Dr. Tate also contributes to a variety of managerial outlets that provide insights to practising managers including *E-side Supply Management*, *Inside Supply Management*, *Supply Chain Management Review* and *CSCMP Explores*, and *CSCMP Supply Chain Quarterly*. She frequently attends and presents at a variety of forums including the National Association for Research and Teaching Symposium (NARS), the Institute for Supply Management (ISM) and Decision Sciences. Dr. Tate is a member of the Institute of Supply Management, Decision Sciences, Production and Operations Management Society, and the Council of Supply Chain Management Professionals.

Helen Walker

Dr. Helen Walker is Professor of Operations and Supply Management at the University of Cardiff's Business School. Dr. Walker received her Ph.D. from Bath University. She has published in *International Journal of Operations and Production Management*, *International Journal of Production Economics*, *Journal of Purchasing and Supply Management*, *Public Administration Review*, and *Supply Chain Management: An International Journal*, among others. She won the *Journal of Purchasing and Supply Management* Best Paper Award in 2008, the *International Purchasing and Supply Education and Research Association* Best Conference Paper Award in 2009, and the *International Journal of Operations and Production Management* Outstanding Contribution Award in 2012 for papers addressing sustainable purchasing and supply management issues. Her research interests include sustainable procurement and sustainable supply chain management, supply strategy, and corporate social responsibility. She was a member of the UK Sustainable Procurement Task Force and the Chartered Institute of Purchasing and Supply Sustainable/Responsible Procurement Group. She serves on the boards of several journals and is the guest editor of special issues in *Journal of Purchasing and Supply Management* on sustainable procurement and *International Journal of Operations and Production Management* on sustainable operations management.

Sustainable Value Chains: Context, Drivers, and Barriers

1

Environmental Sustainability in the Supply Chain: A Review of Past Literature and Discussion of Potential Drivers and Barriers[*]

ROBERT E. HOOKER,[†] DIANE DENSLOW,[‡] AND
LARRY C. GIUNIPERO[§]

Keywords

Sustainability, environment, corporate social responsibility, green, purchasing/supply management, supply chain management.

Introduction

Previous literature on sustainability was found not only to be lacking, but is also void of standards, academically or conceptually.[1] Much of the prior work, albeit limited, conducted in sustainability focuses on issues outside of the scope of supply management, and neglects the views of executives and managers whose explicit focus is on purchasing/ supply management (P/SM). We extend Berns et al.'s (2009) work by conducting a thorough review of past sustainability literature. A review of the research uncovered significant discrepancies in the definitions of sustainability, and a significant lack of understanding of the drivers and barriers in P/SM sustainability efforts.

[*] This research forms part of a multi-phased project examining supply chain sustainability. For more, please see Giunipero L.C., Hooker, R.E., & Denslow, D. (2012), "Purchasing and Supply Management Sustainability: Drivers and Barriers", *Journal of Purchasing and Supply Management*, December, special issue on sustainability.

[†] Robert E. Hooker, Ph.D., Division of Innovation Management, College of Technology and Innovation, University of South Florida--Polytechnic, 3343 Winter Lake Road, Lakeland, FL, 33803, USA. E-mail: rhooker@usf.edu.

[‡] Diane L. Denslow, MBA, MA, CBA, Management Department, Coggin College of Business, University of North Florida, 1 UNF Drive, Jacksonville, FL, 32224, USA. E-mail: ddenslow@unf.edu.

[§] Larry C. Giunipero, Ph.D., Department of Marketing, College of Business, Florida State University, 821 Academic Way, Tallahassee, FL, 32306-1110, USA. E-mail: lgiunipero@cob.fsu.edu.

This chapter also extends previous research by developing a framework of potential drivers and barriers of sustainability in the supply management function, and specifically from the vantage point of multiple P/SM executives. The results seek to help eliminate confusion among researchers and practitioners with regards to the most pressing issues of concern in supply chain sustainability. This is done to help lay the groundwork for future research to be conducted in this area.

Literature Review

INCREASING STRATEGIC VALUE OF SUSTAINABILITY

Over the past few years, global organizations have recognized sustainability as an increasingly important strategic goal.[2] Linton et al. (2007) propose that sustainability as an integrative concept is following the same trajectory as global warming by both the public and private sectors. The significance of this concept is shown by the global interest in sustainability as evidenced by the European Union (EU), which is a highly influential proponent of sustainability (Table 1.1).[3] Additionally, if the EU's earlier influence in the area of quality management and the global adoption of ISO 9001 certification is any indication, the EU's emphasis on sustainability is likely to be a strong harbinger of actions by others. The UK organizations Business in the Environment and the Chartered Institute of Purchasing and Supply developed guidelines for addressing environmental issues in the supply chain early in the 21st century.[4]

Table 1.1   European Union sustainability milestone timeline

Awareness	Sustainability Education	Strategy	Emissions	Strategy Revised	R&D Goals
1997	2000	2001	2004	2006	2010
Treaty of Amsterdam includes discussion of sustainability as a fundamental objective	EU-25 lifelong learning rate, of which sustainability is a topic, sees 7.5% increase	First sustainable development strategy at Gothenburg Summit	Pollutant emissions from transport reduced by 4.4% per year, since 2000	EU sustainable developemt strategy revised, due to enlargement of EU to EU-25	Target rate for percentage of EU-25 GDP on sustainable R&D set at 3%

CHANGING THEMES WITH REGARD TO SUSTAINABILITY

Over the years, businesses have come under increasing pressure to pay attention to the environmental and resource consequences of their products and processes.[5] Others researchers state that two common explanations of the emergence and study of "greening organizations" are: 1) that this development was the evolving outcome of the environmental and social movements that received considerable attention in the 1960s and 1970s; and 2) that the perception that organizational entities have or could have significant impacts on their respective ecosystems became widely held, providing various motivations for organizational change.[6] One aspect of these overall themes is green supply chain management issues, and how organizations can maximize the potential of their suppliers to adopt green supply chain management practices.[7]

Several key themes exist in the sustainability literature. Environmental compliance was considered a "fringe" issue in the 1960s and 1970s and elicited little discussion at executive levels.[8] In the late 1960s, with environmental protection gaining prominence on the political arena, producers of commodities focused on the externalities connected to their products by national and local governments with regulative approaches.[9]

The period from 1970 to 1985 saw the beginning of the integration of environmental concerns and business and marketing strategies. The beginning of a strategic and coherent approach to handling environmental concerns can be traced to this stage.[10] During the 1980s, research was conducted on the various aspects of organizational greening.[11] Several leading-edge firms started to change their corporate positions from ignoring or even resisting environmental pressures to trying to embrace, incorporate, and even profit from them.[12] In the late 1980s, evidence indicates that businesses began internalizing the concept of sustainability into their own value sets.[13]

Beginning in the 1990s, the sustainability focus shifted to "green marketing" to gain or maintain a competitive advantage.[14] One popular approach used in the 1990s was the argument that environmental sustainability could contribute to economic profitability as well as to competitiveness.[15] In the 21st century, overall sustainability issues moved into the supply chain. Researchers began to probe into consideration of product life cycle during material selection, the impact of green purchasing on a firm's supplier selection, into waste management, packaging, and regulatory compliance.[16] Table 1.2 highlights the coverage of sustainability research, and its various themes, throughout the years.

Table 1.2   Coverage of sustainability research

Time frame	Major theme(s)	Key references
1960s	Compliance with government regulation	Vermeulen and Seuring, 2009 Walton et al., 1998
1970s	Initial actions to integrate sustainability into business	Costanza et al., 1991 Gladwin et al., 1993 Hawken, 1993 Menon and Menon, 1997 Schmidheiny, 1992
1980s	Change of corporate position to embrace sustainability Focus on environmental and resource consequences of products and processes	Kleindorfer et al., 2005 Schot and Fisher, 1993 Starik and Marcus, 2000 Winn, 1995
1990s	Incorporating sustainability to provide a competitive advantage	Lash and Wellington, 2007 Porter and van der Linde, 1995 Schmidheiny, 1992 Stone and Wakefield, 2001 Wald, 2006
2000s	Proactive approaches to sustainability and the realization of the value of sustainability as a strategic goal in the supply chain	Closs et al., 2011 Hart, 2005 Min and Galle, 2001

LACK OF GLOBAL AGREEMENT

Although global organizations have recognized sustainability as an increasingly important strategic goal, there are many definitions, focuses, and business activities associated with sustainability. Berns et al.'s (2009) research found that there is not a single established definition for sustainability. Linton et al. (2007) define sustainability as "using resources to meet the needs of the present without compromising the ability of future generations to meet their own needs." This is the definition put forth previously by the World Commission on Environment and Development.[17] Others suggest that a sustainable company is one that creates profit for its shareholders while protecting the environment and improving the lives of those with whom it interacts.[18]

Sustainability in the supply chain has taken a number of different labels in the literature, including socially responsible purchasing, green supply chain, or closed loop supply chain.[19] The Institute of Supply Management describes socially responsible purchasing as "a framework of measurable corporate policies and procedures and resulting behavior designed to benefit the workplace and, by extension, the individual, the organization, and the community."[20] Green or closed loop supply chains incorporate similar aspects of social responsibility, by recycling and reusing as much as possible throughout the production and supply process, with a goal of minimizing waste. Other concepts used in the literature, such as corporate social responsibility (CSR), have similar definitions. A classic definition of CSR is "the firm's consideration of, and response to, issues beyond the narrow economic, technical, and legal requirements of the firm."[21] Others maintain that the responsibilities of a business go beyond a base level of economic responsibility, to include legal, ethical, and discretionary responsibilities.[22] Matten and Moon (2008) state that corporations have recently begun to adopt the language and practice of CSR, particularly in Europe, but also in Africa, Australia, South America, and Southeast Asia.[23]

An example that highlights this lack of consensus on the definition of sustainability is a discussion that took place in a workshop on business sustainability at an international business research conference in 2011. One of the topics included in this workshop was the issue of sustainability of diversity programs in corporate settings. More specifically, efforts to build a culture of inclusion that was not dependent on separate initiatives were discussed, showing that as recently as 2001, a drive toward consensus on sustainability is still being discussed. Despite these confusions in defining sustainability, Berns et al. (2009) found that businesses were unified in their view that sustainability will be a major force that will need to be dealt with. Further, they felt it that it will have a determining impact on the way their businesses think, act, manage, and compete. Therefore, sustainability may ultimately follow a path similar to other global standards being adopted, such as ISO 9001.

Research Approach

This research focused on an initial discovery of potential drivers and barriers that P/SM managers encounter in implementing sustainability. This is combined with a proper review of the literature on sustainability. The overview of such potential drivers and barriers provides an important base from which future research can be conducted. While past research has looked at various "triggers" and "barriers" of sustainability, much of this was performed before the global economic woes of 2007–2009.[24]

Purchasing and supply chain experts from three different organizations who were knowledgeable about sustainability were asked to submit their sustainability issues via interviews. At these face-to-face meetings, the experts were asked to describe each issue in detail. This helped to mitigate potential misinterpretation by the researchers if respondents provided the same issue, but used different terms.[25]

Discussion of Potential Drivers and Barriers

The sections which follow discuss the potential drivers and barriers brought forward by our industry experts during interviews. A review of pertinent literature on each potential driver or barrier is also provided. The identification of these potential drivers and barriers are important for building a foundation for future research on business-to-business (B2B) sustainability.

POTENTIAL DRIVERS

One of the objectives of this research was to discuss early steps taken to identify the drivers of P/SM sustainability efforts. The following is a review of the literature that addresses these drivers. Previous research identified motives for corporate "greening" such as regulatory compliance, competitive advantage, stakeholder pressures, ethical concerns, events, and top management initiative.[26]

Sroufe (2003) identifies growing environmental regulations, government pressures, international certification standards such as the International Organization of Standardization's ISO 14000 series, changing customer demands, and managers recognizing pollution as waste as reasons why firms must now develop environmental policies for their manufacturing plants and supply chain partners while being consistent with new regulations.[27]

Pederson (2006) groups the drivers of green technology into five groups, all of which play a major role in stimulating companies' interests in going green.[28] The leading drivers are environmental regulations, consumer sentiment, environmental non-governmental organizations, global warming concerns, and economics.

Top management involvement

Members of the top management team are instrumental in encouraging firms to evaluate their role in society and are responsible for the firm's environmental management leadership.[29] They are also a strong internal political force that can foster corporate environmentalism.[30] Bansal and Roth (2000) state that top management team members and company values are instrumental in encouraging these firms to evaluate their role in society.[31]

Banerjee et al. (2003) identified four antecedents to corporate environmentalism: public concern, regulatory forces, competitive advantage, and top management commitment. They found that corporate environmentalism is related to all four antecedents and that industry type moderates several of those relationships. The influences of regulatory forces, public concern, and competitive advantage were all significantly mediated by top management commitment and moderated by industry type.

Government regulation

Previous research has shown the importance of legislation as a driver for corporate ecological responsiveness.[32] Escalating penalties, fines, and legal costs have underscored the importance of complying with legislation.[33] Furthermore, firms can avoid expensive capital refits by keeping ahead of legislation.[34] According to Rondinelli and Vastag (1996), firms may be reacting to an increasingly difficult regulatory environment or responding to market pressure in adopting environmental management practices.[35] Pruess (2001) found the motivation for environmental initiatives in manufacturing companies to date, centers around compliance with legislation and cost or quality considerations.[36] Berns et al.'s (2009) research found that government legislation is the sustainability-related issue with the greatest impact on businesses.

Banerjee et al. (2003) indicate that environmental regulations get top management's attention. Additionally, top management's direct involvement in environmental issues is sometimes more prevalent in firms that perceive regulations as a major threat or whose customers come from the environmentally friendly segment. Environmentally friendly customers are simply those that personally identify with, or are conscious of, environmentally sustainable practices.

Financial benefits

Studies have concluded that corporate social responsibility does pay off financially. In examining such measures as return on assets and return on sales, Waddock and Graves (1997) concluded that corporate social performance and profitability are significantly and positively related. They posit that slack resource availability gives organizations the freedom to be innovative and take risks they might not otherwise have taken. Bansal and Roth (2000) examined why companies go green, and refined a model that explained corporate ecological responsiveness.[37] They identified three motivations that induce corporate ecological responsiveness: competitiveness (potential for ecological responsiveness to improve long-term profitability); legitimization; and ecological responsibility. They found that organizational self-interest, including elements of both competitiveness and legitimacy, was needed to fuel the movement toward eco-responsibility.

Given the public and political pressure on firms to turn green, Stone and Wakefield (2001) studied the orientation of firms toward environmental issues and their subsequent business performance. Their findings suggest that firms that are responsive to eco-oriented issues perform better in the marketplace.[38]

Economic opportunities drive corporate ecological responsiveness. By intensifying production processes, companies can reduce their environmental impact while simultaneously lowering the costs of inputs and waste.[39]

Pullman et al. (2009) found that current sustainability programs indirectly help the economic bottom line of the company. The ISO 14001 system may help prevent expensive environmental non-conformances, but it also has a company often go above and beyond the legal requirements of applicable regulatory agencies.[40] Ganesan et al. (2009) state that social responsibility perceptions affect the images of brands and firms, the propensity of consumers to buy specific brands and patronize certain retailers, and the financial performance of firms.[41]

The results of these studies seem to mirror samples taken from industry groups such as the Global Responsible Investment network, which has charted the efforts of companies making their Global 100 list of the world's most sustainable companies. Although their methodology is multi-factorial, during the period from February 1, 2005 to November 30, 2011, companies in their Global 100 list financially outperformed those on the MSCI All Country World Index by over 13%.[42]

Competitive advantage

An increasing number of firms are engaging in "green marketing" to gain or maintain a competitive advantage. Previous research found that excellence in protecting the environment created opportunities to achieve competitive advantage.[43] Walton et al. (1998) reviewed integrating environmental management with the day-to-day processes of the organization and concluded that purchasing and supply chain managers can have a major impact on the ability of a company to establish and maintain a competitive advantage through environmentally friendly practices.[44]

Orsato (2006) states that "managers need to identify circumstances that favor the generation of both public and corporate benefits of sustainability initiatives."[45] He further presents a framework to categorize types of competitive environmental strategies that can be utilized by managers to optimize the economic return on environmental investments and transform these investments into sources of competitive advantage. Orsato (2006) identifies four types of environmental strategies that are based on the structure of the industry in which the firm operates, its position within that industry, the types of markets the company serves, and its capabilities. These strategies include eco-efficiency, beyond compliance leadership, eco-branding, and environmental cost leadership. The four types of environmental strategies can be used as a basis from which they can prioritize environmental investments.

ISO certification

Handfield et al. (2002) found that the movement towards greater environmental responsibility is a result of several recent developments, including the introduction of the ISO 14000 certification standard, and the emphasis on waste reduction from external or governmental agencies is escalating.[46] They further state that the need to be environmentally friendly is beginning to influence decision making in product design, process design, manufacturing practices, and purchasing.

Montabon et al. (2007) found evidence in both extant literature and anecdotal experiences of firms suggesting that environmental management practices are becoming increasingly popular due to the release of voluntary and international environmental standards.[47] Since the release of the ISO 14001 standard there has been additional pressure on some industry supply chains to address environmental performance through the use of environmental management systems (Zuckerman, 2000).[48] In addition to ISO 14001, firms wishing to sell in the EU must comply with the Waste Electrical and Electronic Equipment (WEEE) and Restriction of Hazardous Substances (RoHS) directives laid down at the European level and then re-implemented at each country level (taken from www. buyusa.gov/europeanunion/weee.html, accessed 7–23–2011).

Customer demand

During the 1960s and 1970s the emphasis was mostly on political solutions to environmental and social ills (Wells, 1990); however, in the 1990s the focus was on consumer purchase behavior.[49] Roberts (1996) found that ecologically conscious consumers of the 1990s differ from their predecessors.[50] The consumers' belief that they, as individuals, can help solve environmental problems was found to be the best predictor of ecologically conscious consumer behavior.

Stakeholders have played a key role in increasing corporate responsiveness with regards to ecology. Customers, local communities, environmental interest groups, and even the natural environment itself encourage companies to consider ecological impacts in their decision making.[51] Berns et al. (2009) found that consumer concerns about sustainability were a significant impact on the businesses in their study. Additionally, consumer concerns were viewed as a more critical force in sustainability in companies outside the US and Europe.

POTENTIAL BARRIERS

Lack of consensus amongst CEOs

Berns et al. (2009) found a lack of clarity amongst business leaders regarding sustainability and what it means to an organization. Sharma (2000) found that in the Canadian oil and gas industry, environmental strategies were associated with managerial interpretations of environmental issues as either threats or opportunities and that the extent to which some of these firms went further in incorporating environmental concerns into decision making was heavily dependent on the degree to which their managers perceived these issues as opportunities and not threats.[52]

Such results, as well as the lack of consensus on sustainability are not altogether shocking, particularly given the global nature of the topic. For example, Okoye (2009) asserts that there are "certain concepts which by their very nature are inevitably contested." Weingaertner et al. (2011) seems to further support this contention while highlighting that knowledge of sustainability is fragmented. More recently, Connelly (2011) utilizes a sustainability definition from the Center for Sustainable Enterprise, but at the time of this writing, it is not yet clear how widely that definition has been accepted.[53]

Costs of sustainability

Many companies are convinced that the more environmentally friendly they become, the more the effort will erode their competitiveness. They believe it will add to costs and will not deliver immediate financial benefits, even if long-term financial benefits are possible.[54]

On a short-term basis, going green can be an expensive undertaking. A company that decides to initiate a green revolution will have to front the cost for a wide array of upgrades, from more energy-efficient machines to recycled printer paper. There are a variety of other related expenses especially when considering green changes, specifically to manufacturing processes. Green materials tend to be more expensive and raise the product's overall cost.[55]

Hoffman (2008) found that while three quarters of logistics contracts included environmental impact targets, only 46% provided for the cost of compliance. They further predicted that shippers will continue to require green initiatives, but also continue to transfer the cost to service providers.[56] We posit that more research in this area would be beneficial.

Lack of sustainability standards

Koplin et al. (2006) state that globalization allows supply managers to work with numerous suppliers and obtain raw materials and preliminary products. Each first-tier supplier often depends on a multilevel supply chain for their own production.[57] Such a structure makes it difficult for a company to handle the whole supplier network and thus increases the complexity of purchasing. They further state that the global nature of today's business environment requires large supply chains to adequately serve different markets on various continents. Each continent has different acceptable standards of sustainability, as do the varying countries that comprise it. Gaining cooperation from such companies could be difficult and not all suppliers will agree to the restrictions placed upon them, thus limiting supply options. The various regions of the world face their own unique challenges to building and sustaining a global supply chain because of different environmental circumstances. In addition, the cost of conducting business across multiple continents means that businesses often develop their own standards, such as happened on occasion with RoHS and ISO. Furthermore, it is difficult to monitor these companies to ensure they are complying with set standards.

Misalignment of strategic goals across a short-term and long-term basis

Berns et al. (2009) found a lack of understanding among business leaders as to what sustainability means to a company.[58] Reasons for this include: 1) managers lack a common fact base about the full suite of drivers and issues that are relevant to their companies and industries; 2) companies do not share a common language for driving sustainability, with definitions from very narrow to very broad, to none at all; and 3) the goal of efforts is often defined very loosely and not collectively understood within the organization. Additionally, there is often no understanding of how to measure progress once actions are undertaken.

Their research found that a majority of businesses did not have a strong business case for sustainability. This was attributed to: 1) difficulty in forecasting and planning beyond the one-to-five-year time horizon that is typical of most investment frameworks; 2) difficulty in gauging the system-wide effects of sustainability investments; and 3) planning amid high uncertainty conditions including regulation and customer preferences.

Economic conditions

Berns et al. (2009) provide a good indication that sustainability has staying power. Less than one fourth of their survey respondents indicated that they had pulled back on their commitment to sustainability during the downturn.[59] Given this finding, one can posit that organizations may transition towards the adoption of more sustainable business practices once the global economy recovers.

Conclusion

This research provided a thorough review of literature on the topic of environmental sustainability. This review spanned multiple disciplines, including business-to-consumer (B2C) and B2B marketing, purchasing and supply chain management, general management, and corporate and social responsibility, among others. In order to know how to move forward with research in the area of P/SM sustainability, it is critical to first chart what has already been done.

One of the things to emerge from this literature review is that little is known about sustainability from the vantage point of P/SM executives. Given this, the early stages of a framework targeting the potential drivers and barriers of sustainability, specifically from the perspective of P/SM managers, is discussed. Interviews were conducted with P/SM executives to help uncover potential drivers and barriers of sustainability in the current global business environment. More research must take place to gain a deeper understanding of these concerns, particularly in the form of providing a ranking of such concerns, so as to help prioritize the most important concerns in achieving sustainability on a global scale. Nonetheless, this research provides an important first step for researchers and practitioners alike in better understanding P/SM sustainability.

Notes

1   Berns, M., Townend, A., Khayat, Z., Balagopal, B., Reeves, M., Hopkins, M., & Kruschwitz, N. (2009), "The business of sustainability", *MIT Sloan Management Review*, pp. 1–82.
2   Closs, D., Spier, C., & Meachman, N. (2011), "Sustainability to support end-to-end value chains: the role of supply chain management", *Journal of the Academy of Marketing Science*, Vol. 39, pp. 101–116.
3   Linton, J., Kalssen, R., & Jayaraman, V. (2007), "Sustainable supply chains: an introduction", *Journal of Operations Management*, Vol. 25, pp. 1075–1082.
4   Preuss, L. (2001), "In dirty chains? Purchasing and greener manufacturing", *Journal of Business Ethics*, Vol. 34, pp. 345–359.
5   Kleindorfer, P., Singhal, K., & Van Wasenhove, L. (2005), "Sustainable operations Management", *Production and Operations Management*, Vol. 14, No. 4, pp. 482–492.
6   Starik, M., & Marcus, A. (2000), "Introduction to the special research forum on the management of organizations in the natural environment: a field emerging from multiple paths, with many challenges ahead", *Academy of Management Journal*, Vol. 43, No. 4, pp. 539–546.
7   Walker, H., Di Sisto, L., & McBain, D. (2008), "Drivers and barriers to environmental supply chain management practices: lessons from the public and private sector", *Journal of Purchasing and Supply Management*, Vol. 14, No. 1, pp. 69–85.
8   Walton, S., Handfield, R., & Melnyk, S. (1998), "The green supply chain: integrating suppliers into environmental management processes", *International Journal of Purchasing and Materials Management*, Vol. 34, No. 2, pp. 2–10.
9   Vermeulen, W.J.V., & Seuring, S. (2009), "Sustainability through the market – the impacts of sustainable supply chain management: introduction", *Sustainable Development*, Vol. 17, pp. 269–273.
10 Menon, A., & Menon, A. (1997), "Enviropreneurial marketing strategy: the emergence of corporate environmentalism as market strategy", *Journal of Marketing*, Vol. 61, No. 1, pp. 51–67.
11 Starik, M., & Marcus, A., *op. cit.*
12 Schot, J., & Fisher, K. (1993), "Introduction: the greening of the industrial firm". In J. Schot & K. Fischer (eds.), *Environmental Strategies for Industry*, Island Press, Washington, DC, pp. 3–33; Winn, M. (1995), "Corporate leadership and policies for the natural environment". In D. Collins & M. Starik (eds.), *Research in Corporate Social Performance and Policy*, Supplement. Vol. 1, JAI Press, Greenwich, CT, pp. 127–161; Starik, M., & Marcus, A., *op. cit.*
13 Vermeulen, W.J.C., & Seuring, S., *op. cit.*; Sharma, S. (2000), "Managerial interpretations and organizational context as predictors of corporate choice of environmental strategy", *Academy of Management Journal*, Vol. 43, pp. 681–697.
14 Stone, G., & Wakefield, K. (2001), "Eco-orientation: an extension of market orientation in an environmental context", *Journal of Marketing Theory and Practice*, Vol. 8, No. 3, pp. 21–31.
15 Porter, M., & Van Der Linde, C. (1995), "Green and competitive", *Harvard Business Review*, Vol. 73, No. 5, pp. 120–134; Schmidheiny, S. (1992), "The business logic of sustainable

development", *Columbia Journal of World Business*, Vol. 27, pp. 18–24; Lash, J. and Wellington F. (2007), "Competitive advantage on a warming climate", *Harvard Business Review*, Vol. 85, No. 3, pp. 94–103; Sharma, A., Gopalkrishnan, R., Mehrotra, A., & Krishnan, R. (2010), "Sustainability and business-to-business marketing: a framework and implications", *Industrial Marketing Management*, Vol. 39, pp. 330–341.

16   Kaiser, B., Eagan, P.D., & Shaner, H. (2001), "Solutions to health care waste: life-cycle thinking and "green" purchasing", *Environ Health Perspect*, Vol. 109, No. 3, pp. 205–207; Zhu, Q., Geng, Y. (2001), "Integrating environmental issues into supplier selection and management: a study of large and medium-sized state-owned enterprises in China", *Greener Management International*, Vol. 35, pp. 27–40; Min, H., & Galle, W.P. (2001), "Green purchasing strategies of U.S. firms", *International Journal of Operations & Production Management*, Vol. 21, No. 9, pp. 1222–1238; Sarkis, J. (2001), "Manufacturing's role in corporate environmental sustainability", *International Journal of Operations & Production Management*, Vol. 21, pp. 666–686.

17   World Commission on Environment and Development (1987), *"Our Common Future"*, Oxford University Press, Oxford and New York.

18   Savitz, A.W., & Weber, K. (2006), *"The Triple Bottom-line. How Today's Best-run-Companies are Achieving Economic, Social and Environmental Success – and How You Can Too"*, San Francisco, CA: Josey-Bass.

19   Bowen, F.E., Cousins, P.D., Lamming, R.C., & Faruk, A.C. (2006), The role of supply management capabilities in green supply", *Production and Operations Management*, Vol. 10, No. 2, pp. 174–189; Carter, C.R. (2004), "Purchasing and social responsibility: a replication and extension", *Journal of Supply Chain Management*, Vol. 40, No. 4, pp. 4–16; Seitz, M.A., & Peattie, K. (2004), "Meeting the closed-loop challenge: the case of remanufacturing", *California Management Review*, Vol. 46, No. 2, pp. 74–89; Guide, V.D.R., & Van Wassenhove, L.N. (2009), "The evolution of closed-loop supply chain research", *Operations Research*, Vol. 57, No. 1, pp. 10–18; Krause, D.R., Vachon, S., & Klassen, R. (2009). "Special topic forum on sustainable supply chain management: introduction and reflections on the role of purchasing management", *Journal of Supply Chain Management*, Vol. 45, No. 4, pp. 18–25.

20   Roberts, J.S. (2004), "Responsible business = good business", *Inside Supply Management*, May, 2–8.

21   Davis, K. (1973), "The case for and against business assumption of social responsibilities", *Academy of Management Journal*, Vol. 16, No. 2, pp. 312–322; Salam, M. (2008), "Corporate social responsibility in purchasing and supply chain", *Journal of Business Ethics*, Vol. 85, pp. 355–370.

22   Carroll, A.B. (1991), "The pyramid of corporate social responsibility: toward the moral management of organizational stakeholders", *Business Horizons* (July–August), pp. 39–48; Selem, M. (2008), "Corporate social responsibility in purchasing and supply chain", *Journal of Business Ethics* Vol. 85, pp. 355–370.

23   Matten D., & Moon, J. (2008), "'Implicit' and 'Explicit' CSR: a conceptual framework for a comparative understanding of corporate social responsibility", *Academy of Management Review*, Vol. 33, No. 2, pp. 404–424.

24   Seuring, S., & Müller, M. (2008), "Core issues in sustainable supply chain management – a Delphi study", *Business Strategy and the Environment*, Vol. 17, pp. 455–466.

25   Schmidt, R.C. (1997), "Managing Delphi surveys using nonparametric statistical techniques", *Decision Sciences*, Vol. 28, No. 3, pp. 763–774; Schmidt, R., Lyytinen, K., Keil, M., & Cule, P. (2001), "Identifying software project risks: an international Delphi study", *Journal of Management Information Systems*, Vol. 17, No. 4, pp. 5–36.

26   Bansal, P., & Roth, K. (2000), "Why companies go green: a model of ecological Responsiveness", *Academy of Management Journal,* Vol. 43, No. 4, pp. 717–736; Dillon, P.W., & Fisher, K. (1992), *Environmental Management in Corporations,* Tufts University Center for Environmental Management, Medford, MA; Lampe, M., Ellis, S.R., & Drummond, C.K. (1991), "What companies are doing to meet environmental protection responsibilities: balancing legal, ethical, and profit concerns", *Proceedings of the International Association for Business and Society,* pp. 527–537; Lawrence, A.T., & Morell, D. (1995), "Leading-edge environmental management: motivation, opportunity, resources, and processes". In D. Collins & M. Starik (eds.) *Research in Corporate Social Performance and Policy,* JAI Press, Greenwich, CT, pp. 99–126; Vredenburg, H., & Westley, F. (1993), "Environmental leadership in three contexts: managing for global competitiveness", *Proceedings of the International Association of Business and Society,* pp. 495–500.

27   Kleiner, A. (1991), "What does it mean to be green?", *Harvard Business Review,* Vol. 69, No. 4, 38–47; Porter, M., & Van Der Linde, C., *op. cit.*; Rondinelli, D.A., & Vastag, G. (1996), "International environmental standards and corporate policies: an integrative framework", *California Management Review,* Vol. 39, No. 1, pp. 106–122.

28   Pederson, E., & Andersen, M. (2006), "Safeguarding corporate social responsibility (CSR) in global supply chains: how codes of conduct are managed in buyer-seller relationships", *Journal of Public Affairs,* Vol. 6, pp. 228–240.

29   Anderson, L.M., & Bateman, T.S. (2000), "Individual environmental initiative: championing natural environmental issues in US business organizations", *Academy of Management Journal,* Vol. 43, No. 4, pp. 548–570; Lawrence, A.T., & Morell, D., *op. cit*; Winn, M. (1995), "Corporate leadership and policies for the natural environment". In D. Collins & M. Starik (eds.), *Research in Corporate Social Performance and Policy,* Supplement, Vol., JAI Press, Greenwich, CT, pp. 127–161.

30   Banerjee, S., Iyer, E., & Kashyap, R. (2003), "Corporate environmentalism: antecedents and influence of industry type", *Journal of Marketing,* Vol. 67 (April), pp. 106–122.

31   Bansal, P., & Roth, K., *op. cit.*; Anderson, L.M., & Bateman, T.S., *op. cit.*; Lawrence, A.T., & Morell, D., *op. cit.*; Winn, M., *op. cit.*; Buckholz, R. (1991), "Corporate responsibility and the good society: from economics to ecology", *Business Horizons,* Vol. 34, No. 4, pp. 19–31.

32   Lampe, M., Ellis, S.R., & Drummond, C.K., *op. cit.*; Lawrence, A.T., & Morell, D., *op. cit.*; Vredenburg, H., & Westley, F., *op. cit.*; Post, J.E. (1994), "Environmental approaches and strategies: regulation, markets, and management education". In R.B. Kolluru (ed.), *Environmental Strategies Handbook,* McGraw-Hill, New York, pp. 11–30; Bansal, P., & Roth, K., *op. cit.*

33   Cordano, M. (1993), "Making the natural connection: justifying investment in environmental innovation", *Proceedings of the International Association for Business and Society,* pp. 530–537.

34   Lampe, M., Ellis, S.R., & Drummond, C.K., *op. cit.*

35   Montabon, F., Sroufe, R., & Narasimhan, R. (2007), "An examination of corporate reporting, environmental management practices and firm performance", *Journal of Operations Management,* Vol. 25, pp. 998–1014; Rondinelli, D.A., & Vastag, G., *op. cit.*

36   Preuss, L. (2001), "In dirty chains? Purchasing and greener manufacturing", *Journal of Business Ethics,* Vol. 34, pp. 345–359.

37   Bansal, P., & Roth, K., *op. cit.*; Waddock, S., & Graves, S. (1997), "The corporate social performance: financial performance link", *Strategic Management Journal,* Vol. 18, pp. 303–319.

38   Stone, G., & Wakefield, K., *op. .cit.*

39   Cordano, M., *op. cit.;* Lampe, M., Ellis, S.R., & Drummond, C.K., *op. cit.*; Porter, M., & Van Der Linde, C., *op. .cit.*

40   Pullman, M., Maloni, M., & Carter, C. (2009), "Food for thought: social versus environmental sustainability practices and performance outcomes", *Journal of Supply Chain Management*, Vol. 45, No. 4, pp. 38–54.

41   Ganesan, S., George, M. Jap, S., Palmatier, R., & Weitz, B. (2009), "Supply management and retailer performance, emerging trends, issues, and implications for research and practice", *Journal of Retailing*, Vol. 85, No. 10, pp. 84–94; Luo, X., & Bhattacharya, C.C. (2006), "Corporate social responsibility, customer satisfaction, and market value", *Journal of Marketing*, Vol. 70 (October), pp. 1–18.

42   Global Responsible Investment Network (2012), "Global 100 financial performance report".

43   Starik, M. (1995), "Research on organizations and the natural environment: Some paths we have traveled, the 'field' ahead". In D. Collins & M. Starik (eds.), *Research in Corporate Social Performance and Policy – Sustaining the Natural Environment: Empirical Studies on the Interface between Nature and Organizations.* JAI Press, Greenwich, CT, pp. 1–42.

44   Walton, S., Handfield, R., & Melnyk, S., *op. cit.*

45   Orsato, R. (2006), "Competitive environmental strategies: when does it pay to be green?", *California Management Review*, Vol. 43, No. 2, pp. 127–143.

46   Handfield, R., Walton, S., Sroufe, R., & Melnyk, S. (2002), "Applying environmental criteria to supplier assessment: a study in the application of the analytical hierarchy process", *European Journal of Operational Research*, Vol. 141, pp. 70–87.

47   Montabon, F., Sroufe, R., & Narasimhan, R. (2007), "An examination of corporate reporting, environmental management practices and firm performance", *Journal of Operations Management,* Vol. 25, pp. 998–1014.

48   Zuckerman, A. (2000), "Ford, GM set ISO 14000 requirements", *Iron Age New Steel*, Vol. 16, No. 3, pp. 58–60; Gordon, P. (2001), "Making EMS companies 'lean and green'", *Circuits Assembly*, Vol. 12, No. 9, pp.S2.

49   Wells, R. (1990), "Environmental performance will count in the 1990s", *Marketing News*, March 19, p. 22.

50   Roberts, J. (1996), "Green consumers in the 1990s: profile and implications for advertising", *Journal of Business Research* , Vol. 36, pp. 217–231.

51   Berry, M.A., & Rondinelli, D.A. (1998), "Proactive corporate environment management: a new industrial revolution", *Academy of Management Executive*, Vol. 12, No. 2, pp. 38–50; Buckholz, R., *op. cit.;* Lawrence, A.T., & Morell, D., *op. cit.*; Starik, M. (1995), *op. cit.*

52   Sharma, S. (2000), "Managerial interpretations and organizational context as predictors of corporate choice of environmental strategy", *Academy of Management Journal*, Vol. 43, pp. 681–697.

53   Okoye, A. (2009), "Theorising corporate social responsibility as an essentially contested concept: is a definition necessary?", *Journal of Business Ethics*, Vol. 89, No. 4, pp. 613–627; Weingaertner, C., & Moberg, A. (2011), "Exploring social sustainability: learning from perspectives on urban development and companies and products", *Sustainable Development*, October; Connelly, B.L., Ketchen, D.J., & Slater, S.F. (2011), "Toward a 'theoretical toolbox' for sustainability research in marketing", *Journal of Academy of Marketing Science*, Vol. 39, pp. 86–100.

54   Nidumolu, R., Prahalad, C.K., & Rangaswami, M.R. (2009), "Why sustainability is now the key driver of innovation", *Harvard Business Review*, September, pp. 57–64.

55   Koplin, J., Beske, P., & Seuring, S. (2007), "The use of environmental and social standards by German first-tier suppliers of the Volkswagon AG", *Corporate Social Responsibility and Environmental Management,* Vol. 15, No. 2, pp. 63–75.

56   Hoffman, A. (2008), *From Heresy to Dogma,* New Lexington Press, San Francisco, CA.

57   Koplin, J., Seuring, S., & Mesterharm, M. (2006), "Incorporating sustainability into supply management in the automotive industry – the case of the Volkswagen AG", *Journal of Cleaner Production,* Vol. 15, No. 11–12, pp. 1053–1062.

58   Berns, M., Townend, A., Khayat, Z., Balagopal, B., Reeves, M., Hopkins, M., & Kruschwitz, N., *op. cit.*

59   Berns, M., Townend, A., Khayat, Z., Balagopal, B., Reeves, M., Hopkins, M., & Kruschwitz, N., *op. cit.*

2

Sustainable Procurement, Institutional Context and Top Management Commitment: An International Public Sector Study

HELEN WALKER* AND STEPHEN BRAMMER†

Keywords

Sustainable procurement, institutional theory, managerial choice theory, international survey, public sector.

Introduction

Governments are increasingly concerned with ensuring that the way they buy goods and services has beneficial impacts on economic, social and environmental sustainability. This approach has been termed 'sustainable procurement', which is the pursuit of sustainable development objectives through the purchasing and supply process, including environmental, social and economic aspects. It is the application of sustainable supply chain management[4] practices in the public sector. Whilst governments around the world are developing sustainable procurement policies,[5] the extent to which such policies are implemented by buyers in public sector purchasing departments remains unclear.

In recent years, top managers have been accused of paying 'green lip service' to sustainability issues,[6] such as having worthy sustainability or environmental policies on their websites that amount to little more than a PR exercise. Senior managers have the status necessary to influence organisational actions, and demonstrate compassion and corporate social responsibility in their operations. Several studies have identified

*   Professor Helen Walker, Logistics and Operations Management Section, Cardiff Business School, Cardiff University, Colum Drive, Cardiff, CF10 3EU, UK. E-mail: WalkerHL@cardiff.ac.uk. Telephone: + 44 2920876083 or + 44 2920874271.

†   Professor Stephen Brammer, Warwick Business School, University of Warwick, Coventry, CV4 7AL, UK. E-mail: Stephen.Brammer@wbs.ac.uk. Telephone: + 44 2476524541.

that top management commitment and an internal impetus can be key variables influencing organisational approaches to sustainability and social care issues,[7,8] especially on operations, purchasing and supply issues.[9-11] Reflecting these observations, this study investigates the relationship between the institutional context and the degree of top management commitment, and how these factors influence sustainable procurement impacts.

This chapter makes several contributions. First, we adopt institutional and management choice perspectives and find strong evidence of the influence of both the institutional context and top management commitment on sustainable procurement practice. We provide a theoretical framework for understanding and differentiating organisational responses to sustainable procurement. Rather than focusing on measuring one aspect of sustainability, such as the environment, we develop a questionnaire, using established scales, which measures five sustainability impacts: the natural environment, diversity, human rights, philanthropy and employee safety.

Second, few studies have investigated sustainable purchasing and supply issues internationally, with the majority of studies conducting investigations in a single country context,[2-13] or comparing two countries,[14-16] or focusing on a region.[17] This study has provided an opportunity to take an international multi-country perspective on sustainable procurement, comparing the institutional contexts for sustainable procurement and how top management commitment varies, and conducting a survey of 280 public procurement practitioners in 20 in different countries.

Finally, much of the work in international operations management research has been motivated by a desire to provide firms with an economic benefit.[18] There have been calls for research to also be directed at non-profit, governmental agencies with social and other measures.[19] The public sector is concerned with achieving value for money in the way it procures goods and services, but has other policy objectives as well, such as using public procurement to support sustainability objectives or as a lever for broader societal reforms. What may be good practice in a profit-making firm may not be so clearly applicable for not-for-profit and public sector organisations. This study presents an opportunity to investigate sustainability in the under-researched research context of the public sector. Finally, this chapter makes a contribution to sustainable operations management debates internationally[20] concerned with how management strategies can best support the sustainability agenda, by illuminating how both institutional context and top management commitment can greatly influence public sector buyers to adopt sustainable procurement practices.

The chapter is structured as follows. The literature review describes the theoretical approach to the study, and covers the institutional and managerial choice views, along with sustainable procurement. The methodology is presented, detailing the survey sample, the independent and dependent variables, and the analysis. The results follow, and the discussion considers the conceptual framework. We conclude by reflecting on our contribution to the field, and the implications for research and management practice.

Literature Review

THEORETICAL APPROACH: COMBINING INSTITUTIONAL AND MANAGERIAL CHOICE VIEWS

This section presents the theoretical foundations of the study, linking the institutional context, management commitment and sustainable procurement practices. Our first premise is that the governmental approach to sustainable procurement policy will influence sustainable procurement adoption and practices in public sector organisations. Governmental pressures form a significant element of the institutional environment of organisations.[21–22]

The institutional approach suggests that three mechanisms constrain organisations: coercive, mimetic and normative isomorphism.[21] Our focus here is on coercive isomorphism that stems from political influences, described in the following excerpt:

> *In some circumstances, organizational change is a direct response to government mandate: manufacturers adopt new pollution control technologies to conform to environmental regulations … .and organisations employ affirmative action officers to fend off allegations of discrimination. The existence of a common legal environment affects many aspects of an organisation's behaviour and structure. (p.150)[21]*

A number of studies have adopted an institutional view to investigate sustainability issues,[23–25] such as voluntary environmental initiatives,[26] a firm's environmental strategies in emerging economies[14,27] the diffusion of environmental practices,[28] corporate social responsibility,[29] and green supply chain issues.[13]

Whilst the policy environment in different countries will provide institutional pressure for public sector organisations to pursue sustainable procurement, the way that the policy is interpreted and implemented will be influenced by the extent to which top management is committed to environmental and social buying within organisations. In this study, a managerial choice perspective is also adopted[30–31] that emphasises the active role of management, both in responding to external pressures and in taking positive action on its own. Top management can act both proactively and reactively, exercising choice in addition to responding to real or perceived external expectations.

> *Strategic choice analysis recognizes both a proactive and a reactive aspect in organisation decision-making vis-à-vis the environment. Organisational agents are seen to enjoy a kind of 'bounded autonomy'. They can take external initiatives … and also make adaptive internal arrangements. At the same time, the environment within which they are operating is seen to limit their scope for action because it imposes certain conditions for their organisation to perform well. (p.53)[31]*

There is already some support for combining an institutional perspective (that organisations are subject to governmental pressures) and a managerial choice view (that organisations and their top managers have a proactive role in relation to their environment). Scott, in his book *Institutions and Organisations*,[32] conceives of institutions as having regulatory, normative and cognitive pillars. The normative and cognitive pillars (defined as norms, culture and ethics) and the managerial choice approach seem to be complementary. This provides further indication of the potential fit between institutional (or regulatory) and management choice (normative and cognitive) elements.

Previous studies have combined the institutional and managerial choice views to study environmental strategies,[14] corporate ethics programmes[33] proactive approaches to environmental regulation[34] and corporate environmental approaches.[3] A combination of the approaches seems appropriate, and literature relating to each aspect is presented below.

THE INSTITUTIONAL VIEW: SUSTAINABLE PROCUREMENT POLICY IN DIFFERENT COUNTRIES

The government policy environments regarding sustainable public procurement in different countries are likely to impose institutional constraints on sustainable public procurement practices. This section discusses the character of these frameworks for countries relevant to the subsequent empirical analysis, including the US and Canada and countries in the EU. The aim is not to be exhaustive, since a complete analysis of sustainable procurement policy lies outside the scope of this chapter. Instead, the aim is to provide a flavour of the variation in these important institutional contexts internationally.

In EU countries there is considerable variation both in the extent to which countries have developed and implemented sustainable public procurement policy, and in the character and focus of such policy frameworks where they exist. One study examined the state of development of national action plans regarding green or sustainable public procurement in the EU.[5] Of the 27 EU member states, analysis showed that only a third of governments had adopted an action plan for sustainable public procurement by April 2007, with a further five countries having a draft policy for sustainable public procurement that had not yet been adopted. Countries with relatively well-developed plans included the Netherlands, Denmark and the UK, while countries still in the early stages of developing national action plans included Germany, Greece, the Slovak Republic and Malta. The emphasis of much of the policy that has been implemented in the EU is environmental rather than social in character. For example, in Italy there is a mandate that 30% of goods purchased by public administration comply with ecological criteria; Denmark, France, the Netherlands and the UK have public procurement policies specifically for wood and paper products; and in Belgium there is an initiative to ensure that 50% of government vehicles comply with specific environmental criteria.

The European Commission has provided a 'status overview' of green public procurement in Europe,[35] focusing on the environmental aspects of sustainable procurement. This study analysed tender documents from member states and required personnel working in public procurement to complete a questionnaire about the inclusion of environmental criteria in purchasing, barriers to implementing greener public procurement, best practice and how policies are communicated within the organisation. The review revealed that there was significant cross-national variation in the degree of development of sustainable public procurement, with seven European countries standing out above the rest.[35] The seven outstanding countries were Austria, Denmark, Finland, Germany, the Netherlands, Sweden and the UK.

Sustainable procurement policy frameworks in the US, as well as requiring that agencies engage in environmentally preferable purchasing, have, consistent with the Constitution, a particular emphasis on avoiding discrimination and providing equal opportunities.[36] For the US, these issues have most clearly been crystallised in the development of federal policies that promote procurement from women and minority owned businesses, with some emphasis on purchasing from indigenous peoples.

Canadian public procurement policies focus on non-discrimination and ensuring procurement opportunities for aboriginal businesses. The Canadian federal government founded the Office of Greening Government Operations (OGGO) in 2005, which developed the Policy on Green Procurement in 2006. Through this policy, all government bodies need to formulate green procurement targets and all personnel responsible for procurement need to be trained in green procurement. The OGGO provides purchasers with a decision-making toolkit and a checklist on their website to encourage them to consider sustainability.

It is apparent that countries vary in the extent of sustainable procurement policy development, just as countries vary in the diffusion and adoption of social and environmental standards.[37-39] In addition, there seems to be considerable variation in the relative emphasis on social and environmental issues within sustainable procurement policies. We therefore propose the following hypotheses:

> *Hypothesis 1 (H1)*: The more a public sector organisation is institutionally constrained by its country's government's sustainable procurement policy, the more it will engage in sustainable procurement practices.

> *Hypothesis 2 (H2)*: The greater the institutional policy emphasis on different aspects of sustainable procurement buying (e.g. social, environmental), the more that organisational sustainable procurement practices will reflect this.

THE MANAGERIAL CHOICE VIEW: TOP MANAGEMENT COMMITMENT

If top managers are committed to sustainability, their staff and practices will follow. Managerial commitment is influenced in part by characteristics of the manager, and is important because these people have the status necessary to influence organisational actions.[40]

The environmental attitudes and concerns of senior managers have been found to influence corporate environmental approaches,[3,43,42,41] such as environmental strategic change over time[7] and motivating employees to improve environmental performance.[8]

Several studies of sustainability and ethical issues have focused on the influence of management commitment on the purchasing and supply process. Management commitment has been found to influence socially responsible buying in organisations in the apparel sector.[2] Another study investigated ethical behaviour among the National Association of Purchasing Managers (NAPM) in the US,[41] and found commitment was a key factor. A study of ethics in the food supply chain suggests the moral and ethical standing of the food industry is a reflection of the moral and ethical values of the executives who lead the organisations that constitute the industry.[42] A study of UK retailers investigated their managerial commitment to ethical trade, and found managerial commitment influences organisational approaches to social auditing in the supply chain.[43]

It is apparent from these studies that top management commitment has an influence on environmental and ethical approaches in organisations. More specifically, top management seems to play a role in influencing environmental and ethical purchasing and supply. This leads us to our third hypothesis.

Hypothesis 3 (H3): The greater the degree of top management commitment to sustainable procurement, the more the organisation will engage in sustainable procurement practices.

The conjunction of the institutional view and the managerial choice view in the context of sustainable procurement policy and practice points to four main scenarios, which are presented in the analytical framework shown in Figure 2.1. The institutional dimension of the framework concerns the level of policy development; this may be comparatively high or low. A low level of constraint does not necessarily suggest inadequate policy development; it may also derive from the limited effectiveness of policy enforcement. The other dimension concerns the level of top management commitment to sustainable procurement, which may be comparatively high or low.

Coherent (High policy / High commitment), in which organisations behave in an active manner consistent with sustainable procurement policies. They are proactive and respond well to well-developed aspirational sustainable procurement policies.

Proactive (Low policy / High commitment), in which organisations take the initiative to exercise leadership in sustainable procurement. They are proactive, go beyond compliance, and may be seen as leading sustainability initiatives in their sector, going beyond current policy development.

Reactive (High policy / Low commitment), in which organisations comply grudgingly to sustainable procurement policy. They do not go beyond compliance with policy and legislation, and are reactive rather than proactive.

Inactive (Low policy / Low commitment), in which organisations do not buy sustainably, and are not penalised for not doing so. There is neither internal management commitment nor a policy imperative to implement sustainability practices.

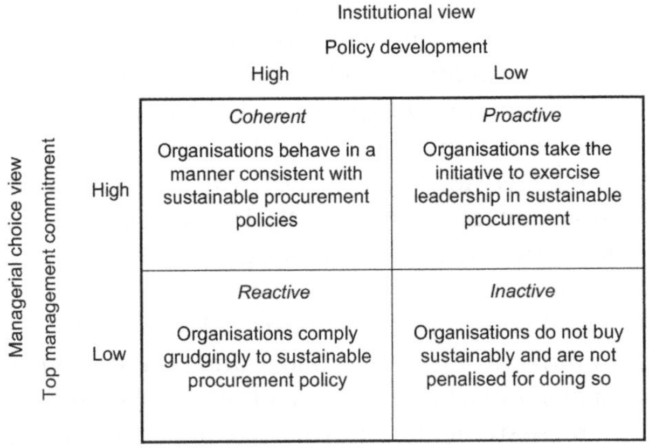

Figure 2.1   A conceptual framework of institutional constraint and managerial choice

Method

SAMPLE

Since there is no global database of public procurement professionals, the sampling strategy employed here began from a wide list of contacts in public procurement around the world encountered in earlier research. An initial approach was made to each contact asking them if they would be willing to forward the survey throughout their professional network, including contacts they had in other countries, and asking their contacts to do the same. This 'snowball' sampling strategy is not uncommonly used in contexts (such as in this study) that are characterised by there being relatively small numbers of appropriate respondents who are members of well-developed professional groups.[44] With the support of these contacts, the survey instrument was directly emailed to over 1,000 public procurement professionals in 25 countries. Given that there is no absolute certainty of how many purchasing professionals the survey ultimately reached, it is difficult to be precise regarding the final rate of response. However, after conducting some follow-up analysis it is estimated that the 283 responses drawn from 20 countries that were ultimately received represents an overall response rate in the region of 18%.

Table 2.1 provides a detailed description of the sample. Panel A describes the distribution of the sample across regions. A little more than a third of the sample comes from the UK, with the remainder of the sample comprising significant sub-samples of organisations from the US/Canada (18.4% of the sample), Western Europe (17.3%), Eastern Europe (12.7%) and Scandinavia (10.2%). A small group of observations came from the rest of the world. Panel B describes the sectoral composition of the sample, again broken down by country. General public service providers, typically local authorities or regional governments, make up the largest sub-sample of organisations in the sample, with bodies involved with education and healthcare also strongly represented. It is apparent that there is some variation in the composition of the sample across countries, with comparatively few organisations involved in 'other' aspects of the public sector in the UK, and relatively more in the Western European sub-sample.

As is often the case with survey research, the reliance on a single source for our evidence can lead to common methods biases whereby how respondents answer one question affects how they approach other questions, with the result that variables are spuriously correlated with each other.[45] While such problems are endemic in survey methods, it is possible to evaluate the likely impacts of them on our results using Harman's one-factor test and confirmatory factor analysis. We entered all our variables into an exploratory factor analysis in order to evaluate the number of factors that are necessary to capture the variance in the variables. Since no single factor emerged from the factor analysis and no single factor accounts for the majority of the covariance among the variables, we conclude that these potential sources of bias are not significantly affecting our results.

Table 2.1   Sample description

	UK	Western Europe	Eastern Europe	Scandinavia	US/ Canada	Rest of the world	All countries
Panel A – Geographic composition of sample							
Number of organisations	106	49	36	29	52	11	283
Percentage of sample	37.5%	17.3%	12.7%	10.2%	18.4%	3.9%	100.0%
Panel B – Sectoral composition of sample							
General public services	38.7%	35.4%	16.7%	51.7%	46.2%	36.4%	37.9%
Health	26.4%	10.4%	16.7%	3.4%	0.0%	0.0%	14.2%
Education	19.8%	8.3%	38.9%	17.2%	23.1%	0.0%	19.9%
Justice and public order	8.5%	0.0%	2.8%	0.0%	3.8%	0.0%	4.3%
Other sectors	6.6%	46.9%	25.0%	27.6%	26.9%	63.6%	24.6%
Total	100.0%	100.0%	100.0%	100.0%	100.0%	100.0%	100.0%

INDEPENDENT VARIABLES

Reflecting the conceptual discussion above, our key independent variables relate to the extent of top management commitment and the degree to which sustainable procurement is developed in different countries. A summary of the constructs and survey items is given in Table 2.2.

Top management commitment

In order to analyse top management commitment we drew on a study of corporate environmental strategies that investigated the environmental attitudes and concerns of senior managers,[3] and a study of socially responsible buying function and how it is influenced by top management commitment.[2] We name this construct TOPMGTCOMMIT, and survey items are shown in Table 2.2.

In Vastag et al.'s study[3] a company's environmental risks are analysed on two dimensions. One dimension, the endogenous environmental risks, arises from the internal operations of the company. The other dimension, the exogenous environmental risks, is determined by the company's external world. Four environmental management approaches are defined as a function of endogenous and exogenous environmental risks: reactive, proactive, strategic and crisis preventive. The framework was applied in a survey of 141 company representatives in Hungary. The study concludes that there is a relatively well-defined relationship between the environmental risks of companies and the nature of their environmental management approaches. The authors suggest a logical extension of the work would be to use an international data set, and focus on fewer industries. Our study follows their recommendations by conducting an international survey, and adopts the dimensions of general environmental attitude and key environmental concerns to explore senior management commitment.

In the study of socially responsible buying,[2] business ethics and attitude theories were adopted. The mail survey data obtained from buying/sourcing professionals in the US apparel/shoe companies were analysed using a Structural Equation Modelling technique. Socially responsible buying generally followed a cognitive decision framework and was partly influenced by the decision maker's affective reaction to peer buying/sourcing professionals' behaviours. Emotional reaction to top management, however, was not significant. The results suggest that changing the organisational environment where employees observe peers and providing standards of what is socially acceptable can improve socially responsible buying. In our study we adopt items from the top management scale to investigate top management commitment.

Table 2.2   Constructs and survey items

Authors	Variable name	Construct	Survey items/definition of construct
2	TOPMGTCOMMIT	Top management commitment	Top management behaves highly ethically and in a socially responsible manner There is frequent encouragement from top management on socially responsible buying Top management provides invisible, but value oriented support for socially responsible buying Overall, top management is highly committed to socially responsible buying Top management believes that higher financial risks are worth taking for social welfare
3			*General environmental attitude scale* The environmental challenge is one of the central issues in the 21st century Pollution prevention pays To avoid future (environmental) tragedies, we need a partnership between government, industry and academia
3			*Key environmental concerns scale* Complying with regulations Preventing incidents Enhancing positive image Integrating environment into corporate strategy
5,35	HIGHINSTPRESSURE	High institutional pressure	*Countries leading policy development* Austria, Denmark, Finland, Germany, the Netherlands, Sweden and the UK
	INDIGENOUSPOP	Indigenous population	*Indigenous population* Canada, US, Australia
	ENVPRESS	Environmental policy pressure	*Environmental policy pressure* All European countries

Table 2.2   *Concluded*

Authors	Variable name	Construct	Survey items/definition of construct
1	ENVLAB SOCIAL MINORITIES SMELOCAL	Purchasing social responsibility	Currently, our purchasing function: *Environmental purchasing* Uses a life-cycle analysis to evaluate the environmental friendliness of products and packaging Participates in the design of products for disassembly Asks suppliers to commit to waste reduction goals Participates in the design of products for recycling or reuse Reduces packaging material *Diversity* Purchases from minority/women-owned business enterprise (MWBE) suppliers Has a formal MWBE supplier purchase programme *Human rights* Visits suppliers' plants to ensure that they are not using sweatshop labour Ensures that suppliers comply with child labour laws Asks suppliers to pay a 'living wage' greater than a country's or region's minimum wage *Philanthropy* Volunteers at local charities Donates to philanthropic organisations *Safety* Ensures that suppliers' locations are operated in a safe manner Ensures the safe, incoming movement of product to our facilities *We added two additional items:* Purchases from small suppliers (<250 employees) Purchases from local suppliers

Institutional context: type and level of policy development

In order to assess institutional influences we analyse the degree to which sustainable procurement policy is developed in different countries, drawing on studies of sustainable procurement policy to identify countries that are seen as leading in policy development.[5,35] Because there is no existing scale relating to institutional pressures, we have categorised countries based on previous studies. These studies suggest seven outstanding countries in terms of sustainable procurement policy development are Austria, Denmark, Finland, Germany, the Netherlands, Sweden and the UK. We name this construct HIGHINSTPRESSURE. As well as the level of policy development, a further independent variable is the type of sustainable procurement policy. We have analysed studies that identify the differing social or environmental emphasis of sustainable procurement policies in different countries.[36] Such studies suggest that those countries with a large indigenous or aboriginal population (e.g. Canada, US, Australia) tend to use sustainable procurement to redress imbalances in society, and emphasise buying from minority-owned businesses (we name this construct INDIGENOUSPOP). In contrast, some countries emphasise first and foremost the environmental aspects of sustainable procurement, and often have regulation and legislation to relating to waste (e.g. WEEE Directive), packaging, etc. Countries that are part of the EU have a particular policy emphasis on green or environmental policy, and public sector organisations are under institutional pressures to respond to this agenda (we name this construct ENVPRESS).

DEPENDENT VARIABLES

Our dependent variables reflect the extent to which sustainability criteria are embedded in public procurement practice. In order to measure sustainable procurement practices, we took as our starting point Carter and Jennings' Purchasing Social Responsibility (PSR) scale items.[1] Carter and Jennings develop a scale consisting of 15 items that relate to five dimensions of sustainable procurement: the natural environment, diversity, human rights, philanthropy and employee safety. Their factor analysis, based on a sample of 201 US consumer product manufacturers, demonstrated that 12 of these 15 items can be reduced to a single factor (which they term *purchasing social responsibility*) that has a high degree of overall reliability and validity. In response to piloting the survey as outlined in the next section, we added two items that explored the importance of buying from small and local suppliers.

Consistent with best practice, our next step was to conduct an exploratory factor analysis of the 17 items using the maximum likelihood method with varimax rotation.[50,51] A total of four factors were identified with eigenvalues greater than unity, this being the most commonly applied threshold for retention of a factor.[53,50] Hair et al. (1998)[50] suggest that factor loadings on individual items greater than 0.5 in absolute value should be viewed as being of 'practical significance' in the interpretation of a given factor. With this in mind, Table 2.2 provides a detailed description of the factor loadings across the 17 individual items for the four retained factors. The detailed inspection of the factor loadings provided in Table 2.2 suggests that the six items that load most heavily onto the first factor relate to environmental improvements in the supply chain and to compliance in the domain of employee health and safety. In reflection of this, we name this factor ENVLAB. The second factor is comprised most heavily of four items, two of which relate to community aspects of sustainability, one of which relates to environmental improvements and one of which concerns labour rights. In light of the heavier loadings on the social items, we name this factor SOCIAL. The final two factors (respectively named MINORITIES and SMELOCAL) are more easily interpreted in that they each reflect only two underlying items that relate respectively to procurement from minority and women-owned businesses and to purchasing from small and local businesses. As a final check on the reliability of our factors, we calculated Cronbach's alphas for each, and all were in excess of 0.75.

CONTROL VARIABLES

The propensity of an organisation to embed sustainable procurement practices is likely to be related to a range of control factors. It may be that larger organisations may be more able and inclined to incorporate sustainability criteria into their procurement. In order to control for this possibility, we include an organisation's size (named ORGSIZE), as captured by the natural logarithm of the organisation's total purchasing expenditure, as an additional control variable.

PILOTING THE QUESTIONNAIRE

Given that our research is focused on public sector organisations, we first asked an expert panel of 10 public procurement professionals and policy makers to review the 15 PSR scale items in order to ensure the face validity and efficacy of the items. At their suggestion, and in order to reflect the breadth of the concept of sustainability as applied to the context of public procurement, we added two items that explored the importance of buying from small and local suppliers. Hence, we eventually elicited responses from sample organisations concerning the degree to which 17 sustainability practices were embedded in their current procurement practice. The panel suggested removing several survey items from the independent variable scales[2-3] that were focused on industrial processes or profits and would not be relevant in a public sector context. Examples of removed survey items include 'The industry will have to re-think its entire conception of the industrial process if it is to adapt profitably to an increasingly environment oriented world' and 'Top-management tends to concentrate profits and costs of each buying proposal and take it only if it is determined to provide high financial benefit'.

Findings

In this section, we present OLS regression results for econometric models of the influences on the propensity for organisations to implement sustainable procurement practices. Tests for econometric problems – Breusch-Pagan tests for heteroscedasticity; and the use of variance inflation factors (VIFs) for all model specifications, which are all below 4, to detect multicollinearity – provide no evidence of their presence. Nevertheless, as a precaution against undetected heteroscedasticity, we employ White's method to correct for any associated bias in statistical inference.

Table 2.3 reports the results of estimating eight models of the influences on aspects of organisational involvement with aspects of sustainable procurement. For each of the four dimensions (Environment & Labour; Social; Minorities; Small & Local Businesses), we estimate both a basic model that includes only organisational size as a control variable, and a full model that includes our measures of institutional pressure and managerial support for sustainable procurement. By so doing, we are able to shed light on the extent to which the influences we highlight contribute additional explanatory power over the base model (and, from this, provide an insight into the broad relevance of these variables for the aspects of sustainable procurement we identify).

Models 1 and 2 explore the influences on the extent to which an organisation is engaged in sustainable procurement practices oriented towards environmental and labour issues. Our findings show that organisational size plays no significant role in shaping this activity but, looking at Model 2, we show that the level of institutional commitment to sustainable procurement and the degree of management support in the organisation for sustainable procurement both have very substantial effects. This is also reflected in the very significant rise (of over 30%) in the explanatory power of Model 3 versus Model 1.

Models 3 and 4 focus on the drivers of participation in sustainable procurement practices oriented towards social issues. Again, our findings show that organisational size plays no significant role in shaping this activity but, looking at Model 4, we find that the degree of senior managerial support in the organisation for sustainable procurement, but not the general level of institutional commitment to sustainable procurement, has important effects. Overall, the addition of our variables of interest leads to a rise in the explanatory power of Model 4 versus Model 3 of over 12%. That the institutional variables appear to have no influence on engagement on social aspects of sustainable procurement is interesting and suggests, consistent with our discussion above, that the policy climate has tended to emphasise the natural environmental aspects of sustainability. In this context, only where substantial managerial discretion within organisations exists for social issues do such issues feature prominently in procurement practices.

Table 2.3   Regression results

	Environmental & Labour		Social		Minorities		Small & Local Business	
	Model 1	Model 2	Model 3	Model 4	Model 5	Model 6	Model 7	Model 8
CONSTANT	-0.150	-0.523	0.439	-0.013	0.117	-0.016	-0.783	-0.865
	(-0.439)	(-1.746)	(1.281)	(-0.038)	(0.341)	(-0.049)	(-2.302)*	(-2.423)*
ORGSIZE	0.009	0.022	-0.026	0.019	-0.007	0.014	0.047	0.045
	(0.459)	(1.082)	(-1.298)	(0.849)	(-0.350)	(0.644)	(2.334)*	(1.873)
HIGHINSTPRESSURE		0.533		0.101		0.134		0.171
		(3.170)*		(0.531)		(0.729)		(0.854)
INDIGENOUSPOP		-0.305		-0.336		0.650		0.239
		(-1.514)		(-1.480)		(2.953)*		(0.995)
ENVPRESS		-0.085		-0.463		-0.581		-0.010
		(-0.399)		(-1.927)		(-2.495)*		(-0.040)
TOPMGTCOMMIT		0.529		0.313		0.059		0.081
		(9.743)*		(5.099)*		(0.995)		(1.245)
R Square	0.1%	30.8%	0.7%	12.7%	0.0%	18.4%	2.1%	3.4%
Change in R-Square		30.7%		12.0%		18.4%		1.3%
No of Observations	257	253	257	253	257	253	257	253

Note: T-statistics are in parentheses, and * indicates p<0.05

Models 5 and 6 address the determinants of engagement with issues concerned with indigenous populations and minority communities as part of an organisation's sustainable procurement activities. As above, findings indicate that organisational size plays no significant role in shaping this activity but, looking at Model 6, we find that neither the presence of managerial support in the organisation for sustainable procurement nor the general level of institutional commitment to sustainable procurement have important effects. Instead, it is the particular issue orientation of the institutional environment that matters. In particular, we find that institutional environments characterised by a strong level of support for the rights of indigenous peoples and minorities, but a lower level of support for environmental issues, are more strongly oriented towards embodying such issues in procurement practices. Reflecting the importance of these factors, the addition of our key variables adds more than 18% to the overall explanatory power of Model 6 versus Model 5. These findings strongly suggest that, in addition to the importance of general institutional pressures for engagement in sustainable procurement, the particular ways in which countries configure their policy landscape and the issues that become enshrined in country policy are very important shapers of procurement activities.

Finally, we turn to Models 7 and 8, which explore the drivers of involvement in procurement of a focus on the importance of small and local businesses. In contrast to our other findings, we find that larger organisations are significantly more involved in this aspect of sustainable procurement. Concerning the role of the managerial context and institutional landscape, we find that these have no significant effect on organisational involvement with localised procurement initiatives. Reflecting this, the introduction of our key variables adds less than 2% to the overall explanatory power of Model 8 versus Model 7.

Discussion

This study adopted institutional and managerial choice theoretical perspectives to investigate organisational responses to sustainable procurement. We tested several hypotheses regarding the extent to which policy development and top management commitment influence sustainable procurement practice, and found broad support for these. Each hypothesis is discussed in turn below.

It was found that high institutional pressure had an influence on sustainable procurement practices (H1), particularly influencing environmental and labour issues, which are likely to be heavily regulated. Those countries leading in terms of policy development were found to have more advanced implementation of sustainable purchasing practices amongst practitioners. This affirms previous studies that have suggested that the institutional context can influence an organisation's environmental strategies.[14,27]

It was found that the institutional policy emphasis has an effect on the type of sustainable procurement practices (H2).[36] Particularly, those countries with indigenous populations that emphasise using public sector spend to redress imbalances in society are significantly more likely to practice public sector buying from minority-owned businesses. In addition, countries in Europe with more advanced sustainable procurement policies are more likely to conduct buying from minority-owned businesses.

We found strong support for the managerial choice view, that top management commitment has an influence on sustainable procurement practices (H3). This was particularly true for environment, labour and social aspects of sustainable procurement. This affirms studies that have found that managers have a particular influence on organisational actions,[40] particularly influencing organisational environmental approaches[7–8,45] and sustainable and ethical approaches amongst purchasing and supply practitioners.[2,41,43] Our study finds that top management commitment within public sector organisations has a strong influence on the extent to which sustainable buying takes place.

It is possible from our findings to begin to populate our analytical framework in Figure 2.2. In some instances we are extrapolating from our findings, as certain countries are under-represented in our sample.

Coherent (High policy / High commitment): We can see that in some countries organisations have a high policy context for sustainable procurement, such as emphasising social, minority-owned business and indigenous issues (Australia, Canada and the US), and emphasising environmental issues (Austria, Denmark, Finland, Germany, the Netherlands, Sweden and the UK). Some public sector organisations in these countries also have committed senior managers and implement sustainable procurement practices well, leading to coherent implementation of sustainable procurement policies.

Proactive (Low policy / High commitment): We did not have sufficient representation of countries with low policy development in our study to give examples, but possibly organisations that go beyond compliance to the low levels of sustainable procurement policy in developing countries could be represented in this part of the framework.

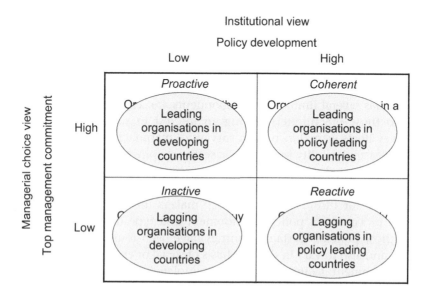

Figure 2.2   Conceptual framework with findings added

Reactive (High policy / Low commitment): Some countries have a high policy context, but public sector organisations have yet to fully embrace and implement sustainable procurement. This could include organisations in the EU where the policy context is high, but where some countries are lagging and are still in the early stages of developing national action plans, including Germany, Greece, the Slovak Republic and Malta.

Inactive (Low policy / Low commitment): Possibly lagging organisations in developing countries without policy development could be represented in this part of the framework

Our findings suggest it is beneficial to integrate the institutional context and management commitment views when considering the extent of sustainable procurement practice. The institutional approach in isolation may instil a sense of organisational passivity in approaching sustainability.[14] Even if institutional constraints are applied strictly, it has been suggested that organisations may be able to take adaptive action by being more innovative in all aspects of their operations, including the pursuit of greater resource productivity, in order to reduce the burden of compliance.[34] However, the managerial choice view in isolation may neglect the policy, regulatory and legislative context that organisations operate in. The implications of integration for policy and practice are discussed in the next section.

Conclusions

This study found that both the institutional context and the degree of top management commitment have an influence on the extent and nature of sustainable procurement practices amongst public sector organisations in different countries. Rather than focusing on measuring one aspect of sustainability, such as the environment, we develop a questionnaire, using established scales, which measures five sustainability impacts: the natural environment, diversity, human rights, philanthropy and employee safety. The study measures this range of sustainability impacts and observes that public sector organisations in different countries vary in their emphasis on different aspects of sustainability.

This study has several limitations. Respondents are self-selecting and likely to skew the sample to those practitioners having an interest in sustainable procurement. In addition, survey items were drawn from surveys of manufacturing organisations, which may have limited applicability in the public sector, despite our efforts in consulting with an expert panel to ensure the questionnaire was appropriate for the public sector.

There are several implications of the study for policy makers and public procurement practitioners, and for future research. Policy makers may need to consider the level of sustainable procurement policy development and type of sustainable procurement emphasis of those policies. Certain countries have been found to be leading in policy development, and also to vary in the emphasis of social or environmental policy and the regulatory environment. Countries starting to implement sustainable procurement may wish to emulate these leading countries and look closely at their policies. Conferences such as Ecoprocura (www.iclei-europe.org/index.php?id=ecoprocura2009) provide an opportunity for policy makers and practitioners in different countries to learn from one another.

For practitioners, there is a clear signal that if top management are committed to demonstrating compassion through sustainable procurement, purchasing and supply practice will follow. Previous studies have shown the importance of aligning organisational strategy with purchasing strategy, and of top management valuing the strategic contribution of the purchasing and supply function.[47-48] It seems from our study that top managers outside of the purchasing function can provide a strong lead that sustainability issues are important. There are those senior managers that already are supportive of sustainability issues, but what about the managers that are too busy or sceptical to provided an organisational steer on such issues?

Our research integrates institutional and managerial choice views in a conceptual framework, but in reality there still seems some way to go to integrate sustainable procurement policy and practice. We recommend that policy makers encourage effective commitment and support from managers. Suggested ways to increase top management commitment may be for policy makers and public administration to offer training to senior management, and to incorporate sustainable procurement measures in the annual reporting of public sector organisations. For example, in the UK sustainability dimensions are being incorporated into the national indicators for local government (www.communities.gov.uk/publications/localgovernment). Such performance measurement will hopefully ensure that senior managers attend to sustainable procurement issues. In addition, policy makers can invite senior managers and senior procurement staff to contribute to sustainable procurement policy development groups. Bottom-up feedback can also be provided to policy makers as sustainable procurement policy is implemented. At the organisational level, practitioners with an interest in sustainable procurement could lobby their senior management. Practitioners could provide top managers and directors of finance with business cases showing how sustainable procurement can be both economically viable and have positive sustainability impacts. Through such activities, the integration of sustainable procurement policy and practice can become a reality.

Future research into sustainable procurement may benefit from combining the institutional and managerial choice theoretical perspectives, which we have found to be of value in our research. The combination acknowledges both the institutional context and its interpretation by senior managers. It would also be useful to extend investigations of the influence of exogenous variables (e.g. the mimetic influence of other peer organisations, the market or sector context) and endogenous variables (e.g. having policy entrepreneurs or champions within organisations) on sustainable procurement. Qualitative studies would be of value to unearth the combination of personal characteristics and other factors that make up top management commitment to demonstrating compassion and addressing social and environmental issues in the supply chain. A more in-depth study of institutional pressures, how the policy context varies in different countries and how these differences came about would also be beneficial.

This study found that sustainable procurement policies are developing at different rates in different countries, and that top managers vary in their commitment to policy implementation. If the sustainability agenda requires international action,[49] this study suggests policy makers and practitioners may need to learn from those countries and senior managers that are embracing and supporting sustainable procurement.

References

1   Carter, C. & Jennings, M. (2004). The role of purchasing in corporate social responsibility: A structural equation analysis. *Journal of Business Logistics*, Vol. 251, 145–186.

2   Park, H. & Stoel, L. (2005). A model of socially responsible buying/sourcing decision-making processes. *International Journal of Retail & Distribution Management*, Vol. 334, 235–248.

3   Vastag, G., Kerekes, S. & Rondinelli, D. A. (1996). Evaluation of corporate environmental management approaches: A framework and application. *International Journal of Production Economics*, Vol. 432–3, 193–211.

4   Piplani, R., Pujawan, N. & Ray, S. (2008). Sustainable supply chain management. *International Journal of Production Economics*, Vol. 1112, 193–194.

5   Steurer, R., Berger, G., Konrad, A. & Martinuzzi, A. (2007). *Sustainable Public Procurement in EU Member States: Overview of government initiatives and selected cases*. European Commission, Brussels.

6   Greer, J. & Bruno, K. (1996). *Greenwash: The Reality behind Corporate Environmentalism*. New York: Apex Press.

7   Su, Y. L. & Seung-Kyu, R. (2007). The change in corporate environmental strategies: A longitudinal empirical study. *Management Decision*, Vol. 452, 196–216.

8   Govindarajulu, N. & Daily, B. (2004). Motivating employees for environmental improvement. *Industrial Management & Data Systems*, Vol. 1044, 364–372.

9   Klassen, R. D. (2001). Plant-level environmental management orientation: The influence of management views and plant characteristics. *Production and Operations Management*, Vol. 103, 257–275.

10   Bowen, F., Cousins, P., Lamming, R. & Faruk, A. (2001). The role of supply management capabilities in green supply. *Production and Operations Management*, Vol. 102, 174–189.

11   Chinander, K. R. (2001). Aligning accountability and awareness for environmental performance in operations. *Production and Operations Management*, Vol. 103, 276–291.

12   van der Vlist, A., Withagen, C. & Folmer, H. (2007). Technical efficiency under alternative environmental regulatory regimes: The case of Dutch horticulture. *Ecological Economics*, Vol. 63, 165–173.

13   Zhu, Q. & Sarkis, J. (2007). The moderating effects of institutional pressures on emergent green supply chain practices and performance. *International Journal of Production Research*, Vol. 4518/19, 4333.

14   Child, J. & Tsai, T. (2005). The dynamic between firms' environmental strategies and institutional constraints in emerging economies: Evidence from China and Taiwan. *Journal of Management Studies*, Vol. 421, 95–125.

15   Kaufmann, L. & Carter, C. R. (2006). International supply relationships and non-financial performance: A comparison of US and German practices. *Journal of Operations Management*, Vol. 24/5, 653–675.

16   Vachon, S. & Klassen, R. (2008). Environmental management and manufacturing performance: The role of collaboration in the supply chain. *International Journal of Production Economics*, Vol. 1112, 299–315.

17   Rao, P. & Holt, D. (2005). Do green supply chains lead to competitiveness and economic performance? *International Journal of Operations & Production Management*, Vol. 259–10, 898–916.

18   Prasad, S. & Babbar, S. (2000). International operations management research: Classification, analysis, and agenda. *Journal of Operations Management*, Vol. 182, 207–247.

19   Delmas, M. in *Production & Operations Management*, Vol. 10, 343–358 (Production Operations Management Society, 2001).

20   Kleindorfer, P. R., Singhal, K. & Van Wassenhove, L. N. (2005). Sustainable operations management. *Production and Operations Management*, Vol. 144, 482–492.

21   DiMaggio, P. J. & Powell, W. (1983). The iron cage revisited: Institutional isomorphism and collective rationality in organizational fields. *American Sociological Review*, Vol. 48, 147–160.

22   Meyer, J. W. & Rowan, B. (1977). Institutionalized organizations: Formal structure as myth and ceremony. *American Journal of Sociology*, Vol. 83, 340–363.

23   Shrivastava, P. (2004). Organizations, policy, and the natural environment: Institutional and strategic perspectives. *Academy of Management Review*, Vol. 291, 139–140.

24   Bansal, P. & Clelland, I. (2004). Talking trash: Legitimacy, impression management and unsystematice risk in the context of the natural environment. *Academy of Management Journal*, Vol. 471, 93–103.

25   Tijong, H. (2005). Institutional dynamics in environmental corporatism: The impact of market and technological change on the Dutch Polder Model. *Governance – An International Journal of Policy and Administration*, Vol. 181, 1–33.

26   Clemens, B. & Douglas, T. J. (2006). Does coercion drive firms to adopt 'voluntary' green initiatives? Relationships among coercion, superior firm resources, and voluntary green initiatives. *Journal of Business Research*, Vol. 594, 483–491.

27   Ghosal, S. (1988). Environmental scanning in Korean firms: Organisational isomorphism in action. *Journal of International Business Studies*, Vol. 191, 69–86.

28   Hoffman, A. J. (2001). Linking organizational and field-level analyses: The diffusion of corporate environmental practice. *Organization & Environment*, Vol. 142, 133–156.

29   Egels-Zanden, N. & Wahlqvist, E. (2007). Post-partnership strategies for defining corporate responsibility: The Business Social Compliance Initiative. *Journal of Business Ethics*, Vol. 702, 175–189.

30   Child, J. (1972). Organizational structure, environment, and performance. *Sociology*, Vol. 6, 1–22.

31   Child, J. (1997). Strategic choice in tbe analysis of action, structure, organizations and environment: Retrospect and prospect. *Organisation Studies*, Vol. 18, 43–76.

32   Scott, W. R. (2001). *Institutions and Organizations.* Thousand Oaks, CA: Sage.

33   Weaver, G. R., Trevino, L. K. & Cochran, P. L. (1999). Corporate ethics programs as control systems: Influences of executive commitment and environmental factors. *Academy of Management Journal*, Vol. 421, 41–57.

34   Porter, M. E. & Van de Linde, C. (1995). Green and competitive. *Harvard Business Review*, Vol. September–October, 120–134.

35   European Commission (2005). *Green Public Procurement*, europa.eu.int/comm/environment/gpp/background.htm#public.

36   McCrudden, C. (2004). Using public procurement to achieve social outcomes. *Natural Resources Forum*, Vol. 284, 257–267.

37   González-Benito, J. & González-Benito, Ó. (2008). Operations management practices linked to the adoption of ISO 14001: An empirical analysis of Spanish manufacturers. *International Journal of Production Economics*, Vol. 1131, 60–73.

38   Castka, P. & Balzarova, M. A. (2008). The impact of ISO 9000 and ISO 14000 on standardisation of social responsibility: An inside perspective. *International Journal of Production Economics*, Vol. 1131, 74–87.

39   Castka, P. & Balzarova, M. A. (2008). ISO 26000 and supply chains: On the diffusion of the social responsibility standard. *International Journal of Production Economics*, Vol. 1112, 274–286.

40   Finkelstein, S. & Hambrick, D. C. (1990). Top-management-team tenure and organizational outcomes: The moderating role of managerial discretion. *Administrative Science Quarterly*, Vol. 35, 484–503.

41   Baker, T. L., Hunt, T. G. & Andrews, M. C. (2006). Promoting ethical behavior and organizational citizenship behaviors: The influence of corporate ethical values. *Journal of Business Research*, Vol. 597, 849–857.

42   Manning, L., Baines, R. N. & Chadd, S. A. (2006). Ethical modelling of the food supply chain. *British Food Journal*, Vol. 1085, 358–370.

43   Hughes, A. (2005). Corporate strategy and the management of ethical trade: The case of the UK food and clothing retailers. *Environment and Planning. A*, Vol. 377, 1145–1163.

44   Kalton, G. & Anderson, D. W. (1986). Sampling rare populations. *Journal of the Royal Statistical Society*, Vol. 149A, 65–82.

45   Podsakoff, P. M., MacKenzie, S. B., Lee, J.-Y. & Podsakoff, N. P. (2003). Common method biases in behavioral research: A critical review of the literature and recommended remedies. *Journal of Applied Psychology*, Vol. 88, 879–903.

46   Banerjee, S., Bobby, I., Easwar, S. & Kashyap, R. K. (2003). Corporate environmentalism: Antecedents and influence of industry type. *Journal of Marketing*, Vol. 672, 106–122.

47   Paulraj, A., Chen, I. J. & Flynn, J. (2006). Levels of strategic purchasing: Impact on supply integration and performance. *Journal of Purchasing & Supply Management*, Vol. 123, 107–122.

48   Day, M. & Lichtenstein, S. (2006). Strategic supply management: The relationship between supply management practices, strategic orientation and their impact on organisational performance. *Journal of Purchasing & Supply Management*, Vol. 126, 313–321.

49   United Nations (2013). *The UN Global Compact*, www.unglobalcompact.org/. Accessed 13th March 2013.

50   Hair, J. F., Anderson, R. E., Tatham, R. L. & Black, W. C. (1998). *Multivariate Data Analysis* (5th edn.). Englewood Cliffs: Prentice Hall.

52   Kim, J. O. & Mueller, C. W. (1978). *An Introduction to Factor Analysis: What it Is and How to Do it*. Beverly Hills, CA: Sage.

53   Rietveld, T. & van Hout, R. (1993). *Statistical Techniques for the Study of Language and Language Behaviour*. Berlin: Mouton de Gruyter.

3

Environmental Research and Development, Public Policy, and Value Chain Management: A Competitive Advantage Perspective

JOHN T. SCOTT*

Keywords

Environmental research and development, R&D, value chain, corporate social responsibility, innovation, environmental regulation, sustainable technology development.

Introduction

This chapter discusses environmental research and development (R&D) in the context of corporate social responsibility (CSR) and the analysis of sources of competitive advantage in a corporation's value chain. Investment in environmental R&D is one way that socially responsible corporate behavior can lessen environmental degradation associated with the processes and products of industry. Environmental R&D investments can benefit both the public in general and the companies making the investments.

The chapter has the following structure. First, an introduction defines environmental R&D and explains how such R&D fits with the corporate behavior analyzed in the literatures about corporate social responsibility and about value chain management. Then, I use the theory of R&D investment to frame the research question that the chapter addresses, explains, and illustrates with examples. Namely: how does public policy to improve environmental performance make new investments in environmental R&D an effective corporate strategy? Next, to corroborate the theory that frames and explains the answer to the research question, I use evidence of actual environmental R&D investments in industry. The chapter's final section provides conclusions and discussion.

* Professor John T. Scott, Department of Economics, Dartmouth College, Hanover, New Hampshire 03755, USA. E-mail: john.t.scott@dartmouth.edu. Telephone: 1 603 646 2941. I am grateful to Adam Lindgreen, Troy J. Scott, and three anonymous referees for helpful criticism and suggestions resulting in many useful revisions.

ENVIRONMENTAL R&D

I define environmental R&D broadly to include any R&D aimed at reducing or controlling the effects of emissions that could potentially damage the environment; apart from the focus on solving problems of environmental damage caused by industrial operations, environmental R&D is no different than other types of industrial R&D. Such work could be research about the emissions themselves, or R&D for new processes that reduce emissions, or R&D for new products that will be cleaner when used in production by firms or for activities of consumers. The definition covers all types of emissions that damage the environment, and the evidence I discuss relates to a variety of emissions as described below and documented in more detail in the references cited.

Although my definition of environmental R&D is broad, such R&D is of course just a subset of the activities used by corporations to improve environmental performance. Industrial respondents report that much is done to clean up toxic emissions with routine engineering. Yet, R&D provides a different approach that is not simply moving down a learning curve for known processes or relegating new developments to routine engineering. Investing in R&D, the company accepts risky investments to develop new approaches, and it puts into play a part of the corporation with its identity and success bound up with the development of those new approaches rather than with incremental improvements to existing processes. Thus, my focus in this chapter is on a specialized type of behavior that some corporations can use to improve their environmental performance.

To illustrate such behavior, this chapter will present evidence from the economic history of the 1990s. Table 3.1 shows the mid-1990s environmental R&D intensity that I estimated, using primary data gathered about environmental R&D of all types, with an original survey administered at that time for the R&D performing firms in US manufacturing industries.[1] To set the stage for my subsequent discussion, observe that in the mid-1990s, even before the rapid development of widespread interest in environmentally friendly, socially responsible behavior, US industry was making substantial investments in environmental R&D. For the manufacturing companies responding to my survey, environmental R&D constituted about 24% of the industrial R&D they performed.[2]

Table 3.1   Environmental R&D intensity in US industry

Industry	Environmental R&D / sales (%)
Food	0.33
Textiles	0.46
Lumber	0.13
Furniture	0.10
Paper	0.25
Chemicals	0.88
Petroleum	0.15
Rubber & plastics	0.19
Primary metals	0.19
Fabricated metals	0.59
Industrial machinery	0.70
Electronics	2.15
Transportation	0.62
Instruments	1.00
Miscellaneous manufacturing	0.71

Environmental R&D in industry is associated with an economically and statistically significant effect on the reduction of toxic releases into the environment. With environmental R&D intensity measured as the estimated ratio of environmental R&D to sales in the broad industries as shown in Table 3.1 and with toxic releases measured by the percentage reduction in total on-site and off-site releases for those industries over the period 1988–1999 by the US Environmental Protection Agency, I estimate that for each one-tenth of a percentage increase in environmental R&D intensity, there was a reduction in toxic releases of between 2.1% and 2.9% in US industry over the period.[3]

SOCIALLY RESPONSIBLE VALUE CHAIN MANAGEMENT AND ENVIRONMENTAL R&D

A large body of literature has examined socially responsible corporate behavior in the sense of the expenditure of resources explicitly aimed at furthering "corporate social responsibility" (CSR). Lindgreen et al. have discussed corporate social responsibility as a part of managing the value chain and provided an overview of a collection of articles about the topic.[4] Here I shall place environmental R&D in the context of both CSR and value chain management. There are many different motives for CSR when managers work to create value.[5] Environmental R&D is a subset of CSR investments and will reflect those motives such as the goal of having processes compatible with doing no environmental harm, having competitive costs, and appealing to environmentally conscious consumers.

Although this chapter focuses on environmental R&D as socially responsible corporate behavior that is a source of value within a firm's value chain, the focus fits well in the context of the broader literature about the socially responsible management of corporate supply chains. Not all firms will do environmental R&D, just as not all firms will have active strategies about corporate social responsibility in the management of their supply chains. Such supply chain management strategies are more often pursued by large multinational corporations than by small and medium-sized enterprises (SMEs).[6] However, SMEs may well be able to manage their supply chain to encourage others in the chain to do R&D to improve the environmental performance of processes and the materials used, as well as to improve performance of the final products. Moreover, the larger corporations can be acknowledged leaders in their supply chains, bringing about changes that improve CSR of the supply chain practices.[7] Such acknowledged leaders could be the special set of firms that do environmental R&D, or leaders could encourage R&D initiatives by suppliers of materials. Managing the supply chain with the concern for ethical responsibility to ensure environmentally friendly materials obtained from innovative suppliers will add value to the firm.[8] Lee and Kim observe that "companies can contribute to building a sustainable economy by proactively innovating products and services that are not only commercially attractive and environmentally sound but also socially positive."[9]

Standards, in the form of codes of conduct for ethical issues underlying social accountability for corporate behavior and performance, can help with the coordination (perhaps spurred by an acknowledged leader) of desired environmental R&D throughout a supply chain for desired environmental performance throughout the chain.[10] Governments as well as private sector firms have a responsibility to achieve sustainable procurement.[11] Maon et al. explain that not-for-profit organizations providing disaster relief can benefit from socially responsible supply chain management, and an important

CSR initiative by the acknowledged corporate leaders in socially responsible supply chain management can be to share "supply chain and logistics expertise, technology and infrastructure."[12] In the context of this chapter's focus on environmental R&D, the procurement agencies in government, typical SMEs, and organizations coordinating disaster relief will not be investing in environmental R&D, yet with appropriate sharing of expertise by leading corporations, they can benefit from environmental R&D that is done in the corporate supply chains.

I shall model the value to corporations of socially responsible environmental R&D, and a key source of that value is avoiding the loss in corporate value that Andersen and Skjoett-Larsen identify, namely the erosion in the value of a manufacturer's brand because of negative publicity about environmental damage associated with operations within its supply chain.[13]

Environmental R&D and corporate social responsibility

Lindgreen et al. explain the multidimensional nature of CSR in the management of supply chains.[14] For my studies of environmental R&D, the perspective of McWilliams and Siegel about the CSR concept is particularly helpful.[15] They define corporate social responsibility, observing:

> *Managers continually encounter demands from multiple stakeholder groups to devote resources to corporate social responsibility (CSR). These pressures emerge from customers, employees, suppliers, community groups, governments, and some stockholders, especially institutional shareholders. With so many conflicting goals and objectives, the definition of CSR is not always clear. Here we define CSR as actions that appear to further some social good, beyond the interests of the firm and that which is required by law. This definition underscores that, to us, CSR means going beyond obeying the law.[16]*

The McWilliams and Siegel definition of CSR is particularly pertinent when thinking of corporate investment in environmental R&D as investments in CSR, because there is no law mandating that companies do environmental R&D. They choose to do it, and their investments in environmental R&D fit the definition of investments in CSR. Much of the environmental R&D that I have surveyed and used for the examples in this chapter is not directly related to compliance with existing regulations. Of the respondents to the surveys used in this chapter, 48% report that their environmental process R&D was not directly in response to an existing government mandate. For environmental product R&D, 38% reported no direct link to a government regulation. For background research about emissions, 83% of the respondents reported that the research was not directly responding to government mandates.[17] Such research that is not a direct response to a government regulation corresponds most directly to the McWilliams and Siegel definition of CSR investments as those going beyond simply obeying the law. Further, most environmental R&D, even when reported as a direct response to a government regulation, is voluntary in the sense that the regulations do not require R&D as the response.

Having considered the definition of CSR, environmental R&D investment is surely an example of socially responsible behavior by corporations. A priori, although the investments are undertaken because of society's concerns and interest in their results, I shall explain that the investments are grounded in the purposive, value-maximizing behavior of corporations. I shall explain the way that public policy to improve environmental performance creates profitable opportunities for investments in environmental R&D, discussing the theory and corroborating evidence.

Environmental R&D and value chain management

Lindgreen et al. discuss uses of the concept of a firm's value chain in the management of supply chains.[18] This chapter focuses on a special part of the general task of value chain management, and to place the focused discussion in the general context, I shall use the original statement of the value chain concept. Porter introduced the "value chain" as a tool for systematic examination of all of a firm's activities and their interactions in order to analyze the sources of the firm's "competitive advantage."[19] Porter explains, "The value chain disaggregates a firm into its strategically relevant activities in order to understand the behavior of costs and the existing and potential sources of differentiation. A firm gains competitive advantage by performing these strategically important activities more cheaply or better than its competitors."[20] The focal point for the contributions of R&D is in one of the activities supporting the primary activities in the firm's value chain – namely in the supporting activity of technology development, although Porter emphasizes that technology development is a much broader concept than R&D.[21] As he observes: "Technology development consists of a range of activities that can be broadly grouped into efforts to improve the product and the process. ... [T]his category of activities [is termed] technology development instead of research and development because R&D has too narrow a connotation to most managers."[22] Porter emphasizes and explains why it is "... important that a firm's technology strategy extend *beyond* product and process R&D as they are traditionally defined."[23] Of course, then, *environmental* R&D is an even narrower part of the supporting activity of technology development. That narrow part of technology development is the focus of this chapter. Nonetheless, that narrowly focused activity encompasses aspects of the technology development of materials, processes, and products.[24] Moreover, although in this chapter I focus on a firm's own investments in environmental R&D, improving the firm's environmental performance and thereby increasing the value created by the firm's products and services can be achieved by managing its supply chain to ensure that it purchases inputs associated with good environmental performance, both in their production and when used by the firm.[25] Through appropriate management of its supply chains, therefore, the firm may find profitable the use of inputs created with the environmental R&D of other firms.

Porter emphasizes and focuses on "desirable technological change," by which he means new technology that provides the firm with competitive advantage.[26] He explains "ways to recognize and exploit the competitive significance of technological change" and offers "tests for a desirable direction of technological change."[27] For Porter, desirable directions are those technological changes by a firm that create "sustainable competitive advantage," and he identifies circumstances where such advantage results; the key is that the technological change leads to changes in the firm's relative cost or differentiation, creating value that cannot be eroded by competition from other firms.[28]

Porter and Kramer explain how corporate social responsibility can be a source of competitive advantage for a firm that develops appropriate strategies using the analysis of its value chain.[29] Competitive advantage achieved with strategies developed from understanding the firm's value chain is of course exactly what Porter emphasized in his seminal book.[30] The keys are to look for ways that socially responsible behavior can create sustainable competitive advantage and hence sustainable value. Thus in the context of environmental performance, based on their careful observations of industry's responses to environmental regulation, Porter and Linde conclude that regulatory pressure motivates companies to innovate. They explain, and support with many actual examples, that government regulation of corporate behavior (that has negative impacts on the environment) stimulates innovation and may actually result not only in better environmental performance but additionally may coincide with greater profitability for the creative firms that exploit the opportunities created by regulation for creating sustainable competitive advantage.[31] Such privately valuable competitive advantages are created with socially responsible corporate behavior that improves environmental performance and social economic welfare. Importantly, when the behavior entails environmental R&D, it is not behavior that is mandated by law; it goes beyond the law because the law does not specify the use of environmental R&D to reduce environmental damage. Moreover, although not mandated by law and although social gains beyond the private gains for the firms are created, the behavior is in the private interest of the corporations that choose to use environmental R&D to solve environmental problems.

Thus, from the firm's perspective, ideally the innovations sought (whether with R&D or with technological development more generally) will create sustainable competitive advantage. Porter explains how the firm can develop a technology strategy to create technological change leading to competitive advantage.[32] However, the firm may not have the luxury of doing only R&D that creates competitive advantage. It may need to do R&D to survive in the post-innovation industry equilibrium, and that may be especially likely for environmental R&D in the context of emerging environmental regulations.

What I shall emphasize in this chapter are lessons from the economic theory of R&D investment about the circumstances – shifts in value and shifts in probability – when it would be profitable for a company to increase its environmental R&D investments. The theory explains why government regulations stimulate firms to make R&D investments. The result of such investments may well be sustainable competitive advantage, and certainly that would be ideal from the firm's perspective. However, it may be that the increased investments are profitable because they preserve the firm's place in industry, advancing its place only in the sense of advancement relative to what would occur without the investments, and what would occur without the investments may be a decidedly worse position than what the company enjoys at the time the investments are made. The post-innovation position of the firm with the investments must be compared with the benchmark of its post-innovation position without the investments. Circumstances may dictate that increased investments in environmental R&D are needed as a matter of survival in the industry rather than as a means to even a temporary competitive advantage over one's rivals, much less a sustainable competitive advantage. The investments may be necessary to keep pace with expected advances in technology. Certainly if alternative paths to a competitive technology can be ranked in terms of those more likely to create a sustainable competitive advantage, those more likely to create such advantage are the ones to choose, other things being the same. But firms may not have the luxury of choosing a strategy for such a supra-valuable outcome; instead, the strategy chosen may be one that is necessary to maintain the firm as a viable business.

My focus will be on how public policy creates new opportunity for profitable environmental R&D investment using the benchmark of the firm's profitability in the post-innovation equilibrium if it does not invest (evaluated as usual with present values at the time of the investment). As explained in the next section, profitable investment can be found when public policy or other forces have value-shifting or probability-shifting impacts on environmental R&D investments. From the standpoint of social economic welfare, more environmental R&D can be socially desirable even when from the private perspective of firms the new socially desirable equilibrium will entail lower profits for the firms. The new equilibrium investment in environmental R&D induced by environmental regulation can increase social economic welfare when the R&D reduces environmental damage that entailed social costs that had been external to the private firms.

Profitable Environmental R&D

Now, how is it that public policy towards environmental performance, whether explicit regulation or the discussions about the need to develop regulations, works to increase environmental R&D investment? The answer lies in the economics of investment in R&D – or innovative activity more generally. The answer entails more than the view of Porter and Linde that managers have very incomplete information, limited time and attention, and face many barriers to change.[33] In their explanation, there are many innovative opportunities that companies appear to be unaware of until they are pointed out by a regulator (such as the Environmental Protection Agency in one of their examples).[34] Good regulation, they explain, entails the public expression of concern about a problem – such as strict regulatory standards to be phased in over time – but allows for a flexible response by industry to find the innovations that will meet the standards.[35] But why does regulation cause firms to accept the challenge of environmental R&D investment?

The theory of R&D investment provides some insight into why the public concerns about environmental problems and regulation will stimulate environmental R&D and investments in innovation more generally. It may be that managers are unaware of innovative opportunities ("ten-dollar bills ... waiting to be picked up" in the metaphor used by Porter and Linde) until regulators point to the possibilities.[36] I do not know if that is the case. What I do know is that the theory predicts that even when managers do have complete information about innovative possibilities, do have sufficient time and attention and so forth, the public concern and regulation will stimulate more innovative investment. The reason is that the regulation, or even the anticipation of regulation, will change the incentives to invest in technological change. The theory's prediction provides a clear explanation for the observations of Porter and Linde, who report: "Our broader research on competitiveness highlights the important role of outside pressure in overcoming organizational inertia and fostering creative thinking."[37]

RELATIVE QUALITY OF R&D OUTCOMES

Profitability of R&D depends first on the *technical success* of the R&D program – achieving the technical goals of an R&D investment's output when it is embodied in products and services. Second, profitability depends on the *commercial success* when the ensuing final products and services are successfully marketed. When considering an R&D investment, both expected technical success and expected commercial success depend on the relative quality of a company's R&D outcome – that is, on the quality of its R&D outcome relative to the anticipated state of the art, given the current state of knowledge and the R&D of others, for the technology being developed.[38]

R&D investment generates a probability distribution over the *relative* quality, *x*, of technical outcomes from the investment. Relative quality reflects relative technical success – for example, the relative speed of an innovative computer that monitors emissions for process control, or relative strength and durability of an advanced material to replace materials that create environmental problems. More R&D shifts the probability distribution f(x) over *relative* technical success rightward, as shown in Figure 3.1. The commercial value, V, of the R&D output will increase with the *relative* technical quality of that output. Hence, we have the value function V(*x*) as shown in Figure 3.2.[39]

Now, with the foregoing description of R&D investment, how is it that public policy can increase the profitability of R&D investment? Government policies (such as regulation of emissions or taxes that are imposed until new environmentally friendly processes or products are introduced) toward environmental problems – in particular, policies that increase the anticipated state of the art and increase the commercial value of innovative solutions – will increase the marginal value of doing more R&D.[40]

VALUE SHIFTING AND PROBABILITY SHIFTING FACTORS

Assuming that policy is not so severe that it eliminates the prospect of at least a normal return, environmental policy will increase R&D (and ultimately improve environmental performance). It will do so by increasing the value of the firm's R&D results (as shown in Figure 3.2 with those results measured relative to the anticipated state of the art) and by shifting the probability distribution for the quality of its technical results (again, relative to the anticipated state of the art) from its R&D. Value increases as a function of the relative success of R&D's technical results. Public policy that makes improved environmental

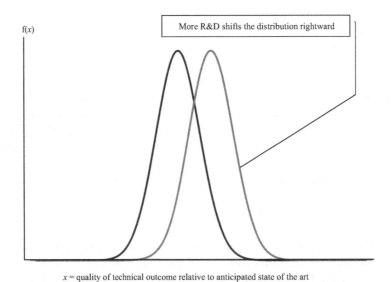

x = quality of technical outcome relative to anticipated state of the art

Figure 3.1   R&D investment generates a probability distribution over the relative quality of technical outcomes from the investment

performance more valuable shifts upward that value function. Public policy also changes the anticipated state of the art and shifts the probability distribution for the relative technical quality of a firm's R&D results. The anticipated state of the art will be greater; hence, the relative quality of any given R&D result will be less, shifting the distribution leftward. Thus, public policy toward environmental performance will have what I have termed value-shifting and probability-shifting effects on a firm's environmental R&D investments.[41]

Value-shifting effects of public policy

Public policy, whether explicitly mandating improved environmental performance or creating customers' awareness and willingness to pay for improved performance, increases the value of R&D induced improvements in performance relative to the anticipated state of the art. Thus, as shown in Figure 3.3, such policy increases the marginal value of doing more R&D to shift the probability distribution of relative technical success rightward over better relative outcomes.

Probability-shifting effects of public policy

Because of its spur to industry to begin technological development to improve environmental performance, public policy – for example, a new standard that must be met for emissions – also increases the state of the art expected from best practice technology. Hence, at the level of R&D that the firm would have chosen without the public policy, the promulgation of the policy will decrease the relative success (i.e., the quality relative to the anticipated state of the art) of any given technical outcome of a

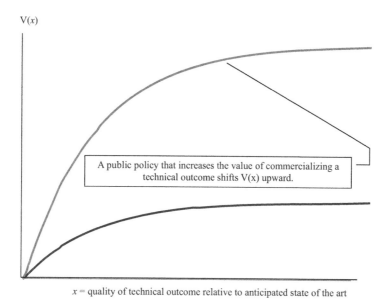

$V(x)$

A public policy that increases the value of commercializing a technical outcome shifts V(x) upward.

x = quality of technical outcome relative to anticipated state of the art

Figure 3.2   Commercial or market value of the technical outcome from R&D investment increases with the outcome's relative quality

Expected Profit $= \int V(x)f(x)dx - R \& D$ cost

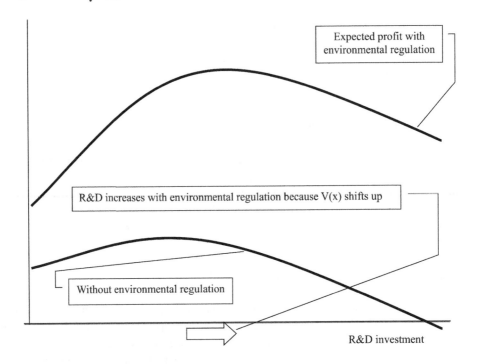

Figure 3.3   R&D investment and expected profits from R&D investment increase when regulation shifts V(x) up

firm's R&D. Thus the policy will increase the firm's marginal value of doing more R&D to improve relative technical outcomes. If the firm invested the same amount in R&D as it would in the absence of the public policy, the distribution over *relative* quality of technical outcomes will shift leftward because of the better anticipated state of the art. That leftward shift in the distribution increases the firm's marginal value of doing *more* R&D, as shown in Figure 3.4. More R&D is now valuable because without it the firm's relative position is less good.

Policy effects and market structure

Importantly, the R&D-increasing effects that are caused by a value-shifting and probability-shifting variable – here public policy toward environmental performance – pertain to both oligopolistic and competitively structured R&D environments.[42] The generality of the R&D-increasing effects of policy is important because the types of competition in innovation markets vary.

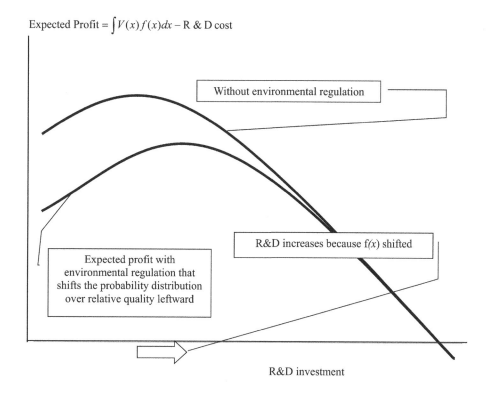

Expected Profit $= \int V(x)f(x)dx - $ R & D cost

Without environmental regulation

R&D increases because f(x) shifted

Expected profit with
environmental regulation that
shifts the probability distribution
over relative quality leftward

R&D investment

Figure 3.4   Increased R&D investment when regulation improves the anticipated state of the art and shifts f(x) for a given level of R&D leftward

THE LESSON FOR VALUE-CHAIN MANAGEMENT OF SOCIALLY RESPONSIBLE ENVIRONMENTAL R&D

With the increase in the value of new technology from environmental R&D and a leftward shift for the probability distribution of relative technical outcomes given the increase in the anticipated state of the art, both the value-shifting and the probability-shifting effects of public policy work together to increase the privately optimal R&D investment of the firm.

The lesson for sustainable, socially responsible value-chain management is that public concerns about environmental performance and the public policies associated with those concerns create opportunities for investment in environmental R&D. Corporations would be expected to find profitable opportunities for increasing environmental R&D in the supporting activity of technology development within their value chains. Shifts in public policies that strengthen emissions regulation theoretically make new investments in environmental R&D profitable. Of course, the appropriate expressions of public concern that bring about improvements in social welfare require responsible behavior by both industry and government. Maintaining the balance of responsible behavior is difficult and certainly cannot be assumed, given what at times becomes irresponsible lobbying by industry and irresponsible support of a partisan political agenda by politicians.

Importantly, the benchmark for comparison would be the firm's profitability in the post-innovation market if the new investments were not made. Thus, profitable environmental R&D investments may not create sustainable competitive advantage; moreover, the firm's profitability in the post-innovation equilibrium may well be less than it was before it invested in innovation. However, its post-innovation profitability will be greater than if it had not invested in technological change. The firm's environmental R&D investment may be necessary for its viability in the post-innovation market. Finding sustainable competitive advantage in that market is something to be desired, but avoiding investment that would merely keep the firm in the post-innovation game yet does not hold the prospect of an expected outcome of a sustainable competitive advantage may not be an option.

Because of transactions costs – such as bankruptcy costs – of exit and re-entry in a new activity, even when in its particular line of business a firm earns only a normal rate of return, it may be willing to do environmental R&D just to preserve that normal return despite the availability of similar alternative activities yielding that return. Among such firms will be some that have engaged in R&D, succeeded and survived in the industry, and with their past R&D expenditure viewed as a sunk cost, they are viable with revenues that exceed current operating costs. In the long-term view of such a firm – with its ongoing R&D in response to an ever-changing regulatory landscape and newly arriving information – we see the usual long-run equilibrium, with revenues equalling costs. There may be infra-marginal firms that have succeeded in carving out a niche of sustainable competitive advantage, whether through some facet of their environmental R&D agenda or otherwise, but that is not necessary for environmental R&D to be attractive. There will be marginal firms that choose not to cut costs by eliminating environmental R&D projects, because if they did so they would cease to be viable in the industry. There may be infra-marginal firms that choose to do environmental R&D not because they expect it to increase their already above-average performance but because they see it as a way of preserving a portion of that performance that would otherwise be eroded by evolving regulations or other shocks in the context of other firms' R&D performance. The environmental R&D is useful to preserve a good thing, even when it is not expected to create new sources of competitive advantage.

Corroborating Evidence

For evidence to corroborate the theory that public policy to improve environmental performance will open up profitable opportunities for socially responsible corporate investments in environmental R&D, I shall use information from my surveys of industrial environmental R&D investments.

The data on US industrial environmental R&D come from the first of my two surveys – one administered in 1993 and the other in 2001. Both surveys are provided in Scott (2003) and the samples and the data collected are carefully detailed there.[43] The 1993 survey was sent to parent companies in the *Business Week* R&D Scoreboard for that year. Scoreboard companies that year were companies with sales of at least $58 million and R&D expenditures of at least $1 million. The 2001 follow-up survey was sent to a representative group of respondents to the first survey and documented the stability of the environmental R&D investments observed. Among the firms responding to the 1993 survey, 71 reported environmental R&D with the goal of reducing toxic air emissions, and all but three of those 71 firms had R&D focused on chemicals targeted by Title III of the Clean Air Act Amendments of 1990. The information collected about the R&D that was focused on the Title III chemicals (along with information from the *Business Week* R&D Scoreboard, the US Environmental Protection Agency, the US Census, and other sources of information about industrial companies and their industries) was used to estimate the effects reported in Table 3.2. A subset of 47 of the firms also provided consistent information about the proportion of their total R&D effort devoted to all types of environmental R&D (i.e., not just to their air-emissions related R&D). The data about all types of environmental R&D were used to estimate the environmental R&D intensities reported in Table 3.1 to illustrate those R&D efforts.

I shall use rough estimates to suggest how the environmental R&D investments would change in response to six public policies. Table 3.2 uses corporations' responses to my survey to provide rough, suggestive estimates of the responsiveness of environmental R&D to the various public policies.[44] I have used an estimated model of environmental R&D as a function of variables that I associate with public policies. From the estimated model, for each policy, I then calculate in percentage terms the responsiveness of industrial environmental R&D to a specified change in the variable reflecting the policy. When the variable associated with the policy is measured continuously, the arc elasticity of the environmental response is estimated. It is the ratio of (1) the percentage change (on average over the range of the change) in predicted environmental R&D when the variable used to measure the presence of the policy is changed from low to high (i.e., from a standard deviation below its mean to a standard deviation above its mean) to (2) the percentage change (on average over the range of the change) in the variable measuring the extent of the policy. When the variable used to measure the presence of the policy is dichotomous, that dichotomous variable changes from 0 to 1 to predict the effects of its "low" and "high" values, and the percentage change in environmental R&D induced by the policy is observed. That is the natural experiment for policies represented by the qualitative (dichotomous) variables; a firm either has cooperative R&D or not, and so forth (although with sufficient information, for example about the proportion of a firm's R&D activity that is done in cooperation with other organizations, a continuous measure could be used in place of the dichotomous measure).

Details of the formulation of the estimates and their detailed interpretation have been published elsewhere.[45] Here I provide an overview, explaining why the estimates in Table 3.2 support the theoretical prediction that environmental R&D is stimulated by public policies that reflect public concern about environmental performance. It is important to observe that I am taking a broad brush and providing an admittedly impressionistic depiction of the effects of policies that could be aimed at environmental R&D. My estimates do not attempt evaluation of specific alternative policies such as conventional effluent taxes or cap-and-trade programs that my estimates do not encompass, and I certainly believe that the effects of such alternative policies are substantial.

Table 3.2   Estimated responsiveness of environmental R&D to public policies

Policies measured with a continuous variable	Elasticity of environmental R&D with respect to the policy (percentage change in R&D per unit percentage change in the measure of the policy)
Pre-innovation tax	1.0
Emissions regulation	1.1
Level playing field for imports	1.3
Policies measured with a qualitative (0/1) variable	**Percentage change in environmental R&D induced by the policy (%)**
Outside finance	200
Knowledge dissemination	180
Cooperative R&D	130

PRE-INNOVATION TAX

A pre-innovation tax, paid each period until a firm develops or acquires an innovation that achieves desired environmental performance, could increase environmental R&D.[46] Such a tax is a value-shifting variable; it increases the value of doing R&D and achieving an innovation. The value of the results of R&D will be greater the larger is the amount of the tax avoided by innovation.[47] Consistent with the theory, illustrated in Figure 3.3, for a value-increasing variable, the estimate of expected response of R&D to a pre-innovation tax is positive.

EMISSIONS REGULATION

Increasing the stringency of emissions regulation can increase environmental R&D. More stringent emissions standards increase the anticipated state of the art and shift leftward the probability distribution for relative performance of any particular R&D investment; they also increase the value of innovations that reduce the emissions. For both reasons, illustrated in Figures 3.3 and 3.4, environmental R&D then has a larger marginal benefit.[48] Again, the evidence of a positive response for environmental R&D supports the theory.

LEVEL PLAYING FIELD FOR IMPORTS

Porter and Linde explain one of the important roles for good regulatory policy: "To level the playing field during the transition period to innovation-based environmental solutions, ensuring that one company cannot gain position by avoiding environmental investments."[49] Diplomacy to encourage emissions regulations that are more uniformly stringent worldwide could increase environmental R&D. The value of environmental R&D outcomes is lowered when companies face import competition from firms facing less stringent environmental expectations in their home countries. A policy that levelled the playing field with regard to expectations about emissions performance would increase the value of environmental R&D, providing, as illustrated in Figure 3.3, an incentive to do more of it.[50] Consistent with the theory, the estimated response of R&D to such a policy is positive.

OUTSIDE FINANCE

Environmental R&D could be increased by policies to promote the availability and use of outside financing from other companies and from the public. Outside finance can enable investments that are both more valuable and more challenging by relaxing funding constraints faced by the investing firm and providing accompanying outside expertise and monitoring of the investments.[51] Greater value will increase R&D investments, as shown in Figure 3.3. More challenging investments are those for which the bulk of the probability distribution over relative quality is, for any given amount of R&D investment, positioned over a lower range of outcomes for relative quality. Thus, as shown in Figure 3.4, the optimal level of R&D investment will be greater. The estimated effect of outside finance on environmental R&D is positive, as predicted by the theory.

KNOWLEDGE DISSEMINATION

Promoting the dissemination of fundamental knowledge about emissions and of licensable emissions-reducing technology could increase environmental R&D. Public policy would promote the dissemination of emissions technologies, with appropriate compensation to innovators. Theoretically, as illustrated in Figures 3.3 and 3.4, the knowledge dissemination will increase environmental R&D if it increases the value of the R&D or makes possible more challenging R&D projects.[52] Supporting the theory that more knowledge will increase environmental R&D, the estimated effect for a knowledge dissemination policy is positive.

COOPERATIVE R&D

Policies promoting an increase in cooperative R&D (jointly performed R&D by two or more firms) could increase environmental R&D. Theoretically, cooperative R&D will increase the value of a company's R&D program if the cooperation improves appropriation of returns to innovation in the post-innovation markets. Further, cooperative R&D may enable more challenging projects for which the probability distributions over relative technical R&D outcomes are shifted leftward for given R&D investments. As illustrated in Figures 3.3 and 3.4, both the value-shifting and the probability-shifting effects of policies promoting cooperative R&D imply an increase in environmental R&D.[53] The estimated positive impact of cooperative R&D on environmental R&D supports the theory.

Discussion and Conclusions

In this chapter, I have first defined environmental R&D, used original data from the economic history of the mid-1990s to document its presence, and discussed it in the context of corporate social responsibility and sustainable value-chain management. Environmental R&D clearly is corporate behavior that conforms to the criteria for corporate social responsibility. It fits clearly within the value chain management literature about sustainable technology development.

Second, I have explained that public policies – such as more stringent emissions regulations, higher effluent taxes, diplomatic initiatives to make emissions regulation more uniformly stringent worldwide, initiatives to increase the availability of outside finance, increases in the dissemination of knowledge, and promotion of cooperative R&D – will, theoretically, increase a firm's opportunities for profitable investment in environmental R&D. Opportunities for profitable environmental R&D are created by public policy because there is greater value for R&D results and because a firm's relative environmental performance would fall without the additional R&D investments.

Third, I have presented some evidence that corroborates the theory by showing that the actual R&D investments of firms support the theory. Support is found in the interpretation of a model that estimates environmental R&D investment as a function of variables that could be associated with various public policies. For example, the presence of cooperative R&D is associated with greater investments in environmental R&D. Hence, public policies (such as the US National Cooperative Research and Production Act) that encourage such cooperative R&D activity are expected to increase environmental R&D. The evidence used to corroborate the theory is especially appropriate in the context of the perspective of socially responsible corporate behavior. It is especially appropriate because the environmental R&D investments used in the estimated model were aimed at reducing the emissions of the toxic chemicals identified in Title III of the Clean Air Act Amendments of 1990. In that legislation, the US Congress did not set out the regulations for the Title III chemicals, but instead it mandated that the US Environmental Protection Agency would develop such regulations and promulgate them in the future. Now, over two decades later, such regulations are still emerging. Yet, soon after the 1990 legislation, industry began investing in environmental R&D to reduce the emissions of the Title III chemicals. Clearly the investments were not required by law; they satisfy the definition of CSR that has been used in this chapter.

Fourth, the implication for sustainable value-chain management is that a company's managers should expect to find profitable opportunities for environmental R&D (conducted as a part of the supporting activity of the company's technology development more generally) when public policy focuses on environmental performance of the primary activities in the company's value chain. The implication follows from the fact that the public policy is expected to increase the value of the firm's environmental R&D results and to decrease its relative environmental performance in the absence of additional environmental R&D.

Fifth, the benchmark for determining the profitability of new investments in environmental R&D is the firm's profitability in the post-innovation market if it did not make the new investments. Thus, even when the new investments are profitable for the firm, socially responsible value-chain management that supports environmental sustainability with investments in environmental R&D may not create sustainable competitive advantage for the firm. Environmental R&D investment may be necessary for the viability of the firm in the post-innovation market. If while ensuring environmental sustainability it also provides a path to sustainable competitive advantage for the firm, so much the better; sustainable competitive advantage is to be wished for.

This chapter has used theory about R&D investment along with evidence taken from the economic history of the 1990s to explain that responsible public policy can create incentives for profitable environmental R&D that is in the social interest. Public policy can lead firms to make socially responsible corporate investments and reach the sustainable performance that responsible industrial and political leadership must define and articulate if environmental sustainability of industry is to be achieved.

Notes

1   Scott, J.T. (2003), *Environmental Research and Development: US Industrial Research, the Clean Air Act and Environmental Damage*, Edward Elgar, Cheltenham, UK, p. 114. There is quite a bit of variance across the firms in the intensity of their environmental R&D, as indicated by the fact that the model used to predict the average percentage for each industry shown in Table 3.1 explains about one-fourth of the variance in the observed environmental R&D to sales (significant at the 0.02 level) (*ibid.*, p. 42, p. 113). In this chapter I am taking an admittedly focused view of the literature about industrial environmental R&D. As I have defined such R&D here, documentation of it began with my working papers associated with seminar presentations in the early 1990s, as I worked to gather primary data from industry about "environmental R&D," and with the early publications about the data in Scott, J.T. (1996), "Environmental research joint ventures among manufacturers", *Review of Industrial Organization*, Vol. 11, No. 5, pp. 655–679, and Scott, J.T. (1997), "Schumpeterian competition and environmental R&D", *Managerial and Decision Economics*, Vol. 18, No. 6, pp. 455–469. Scott, 2003, *op. cit.*, provides a review of related and subsequent literature.

2   Scott, 2003, *op. cit.*, p. 36.

3   Scott, J.T. (2005a), "Corporate social responsibility and environmental research and development", *Structural Change and Economic Dynamics*, Vol. 16, No. 3, p. 322.

4   Lindgreen, A., Maon, F. & Swaen, V. (2009), "Corporate social responsibility in supply chains", *Supply Chain Management*, Vol. 14, No. 2, pp. 71–74.

5   *Ibid.*

6   Pedersen, E.R. (2009), "The many and the few: rounding up the SMEs that manage CSR in the supply chain", *Supply Chain Management*, Vol. 14, No. 2, pp. 109–116.

7   Defee, C.C., Esper, T. & Mollenkopf, D. (2009), "Leveraging closed-loop orientation and leadership for environmental sustainability", *Supply Chain Management*, Vol. 14, No. 2, pp. 87–98.

8   See Eltantawy, R.A., Fox, G.L. & Giunipero, L. (2009), "Supply management ethical responsibility: reputation and performance impacts", *Supply Chain Management*, Vol. 14, No. 2, pp. 99–108.

9   Lee, K. & Kim J. (2009), "Current status of CSR in the realm of supply management: the case of the Korean electronics industry", *Supply Chain Management*, Vol. 14, No. 2, pp. 138–148, at p. 145.

10   See Ciliberti, F., de Groot, G., de Haan, J. & Pontrandolfo, P. (2009), "Codes to coordinate supply chains: SMEs' experiences with SA8000", *Supply Chain Management*, Vol. 14, No. 2, pp. 117–127.

11   Walker, H. & Brammer, S. (2009), "Sustainable procurement in the United Kingdom public sector", *Supply Chain Management*, Vol. 14, No. 2, pp. 128–137.

12   Maon, F., Lindgreen, A. & Vanhamme, J. (2009), "Developing supply chains in disaster relief operations through cross-sector socially oriented collaborations: a theoretical model", *Supply Chain Management*, Vol. 14, No. 2, pp. 149–164, at p. 149.

13   Andersen, M. & Skjoett-Larsen, T. (2009), "Corporate social responsibility in global supply chains", *Supply Chain Management*, Vol. 14, No. 2, pp. 75–86.

14   Lindgreen et al., *op. cit.*

15   McWilliams, A. & Siegel, D. (2000), "Corporate social responsibility and financial performance: correlation or misspecification?", *Strategic Management Journal*, Vol. 21, No. 5, pp. 603–609;

McWilliams, A. & Siegel, D. (2001), "Corporate social responsibility: a theory of the firm perspective", *Academy of Management Review*, Vol. 26, No. 1, pp. 117–127.

16   McWilliams, A. & Siegel, D., 2001, *op. cit.*, p. 117.

17   Scott, 2003, *op. cit.*, pp. 48–50.

18   Lindgreen et al., *op. cit.*

19   Porter, M.E. (1985), *Competitive Advantage: Creating and Sustaining Superior Performance*, The Free Press, Macmillan, New York, p. 33.

20   *Ibid.*, pp. 33–34.

21   Porter provides a figure that provides a visual depiction of the generic value chain and the place of technology development within it. *Ibid.*, p. 37.

22   *Ibid.*, p. 42.

23   *Ibid.*, p. 179.

24   Scott, 2003, *op. cit.*, pp. 36–39.

25   Lindgreen et al., *op. cit.*

26   Porter, *op. cit.*, p. 169, p. 173.

27   *Ibid.*, p. 165, p. 171.

28   *Ibid.*, pp. 171–176.

29   Porter, M.E. & Kramer, M.R. (2006), "Strategy & society: the link between competitive advantage and corporate social responsibility", *Harvard Business Review*, Vol. 84, No. 12, pp. 78–92.

30   Porter, *op. cit.*

31   Porter, M.E. & Linde, C. v. d. (1995), "Green and competitive: ending the stalemate", *Harvard Business Review*, Vol. 73, No. 5, pp. 120–134.

32   Porter, *op. cit.*, pp. 176–200.

33   Porter & Linde, *op. cit.*, p. 127.

34   *Ibid.*

35   *Ibid.*, p. 129.

36   *Ibid.*, p. 127.

37   *Ibid.*, p. 128.

38   Scott, J.T. (2009), "Competition in research and development: a theory for contradictory predictions", *Review of Industrial Organization*, Vol. 34, No. 2, pp. 153–171.

39   *Ibid.*

40   *Ibid.*

41   *Ibid.*

42   *Ibid.*

43   Scott, 2003, *op. cit.*

44   Scott, J.T. (2005b), "Public Policy and Environmental Research and Development". In A.N. Link & F.M. Scherer (eds.), *Essays in Honor of Edwin Mansfield: The Economics of R&D, Innovation, and Technological Change*, Springer Science, New York, p. 121.

45   *Ibid.*, pp. 119–125.

46   Scott, J.T. (1995), "The Damoclean tax and innovation", *Journal of Evolutionary Economics*, Vol. 5, No. 1, pp. 71–89.

47   Scott, 2005b, *op. cit.*, pp. 120–122.

48   *Ibid.*, p. 123.

49   Porter & Linde, *op. cit.*, p. 128.

50   Scott, 2005b, *op. cit.*, pp. 123–124.

51 Scott, 2005b, *op. cit.*, p. 123; Link, A.N. & Scott, J.T. (2009), "Private investor participation and commercialization rates for government-sponsored research and development: would a prediction market improve the performance of the SBIR programme?", *Economica*, Vol. 76, No. 302, pp. 264–281.

52 Scott, 2005b, *op. cit.*, pp. 124–125.

53 *Ibid.*, p. 123. For examples of cooperative R&D, see Scott, J.T. (1988), "Diversification versus cooperation in R&D investment", *Managerial and Decision Economics*, Vol. 9, No. 3, pp. 173–186, and Scott, J.T. (2008), "The National Cooperative Research and Production Act". In Wayne D. Collins (ed.), *Issues in Competition Law and Policy*, vol. II, American Bar Association, Chicago, pp. 1297–1317.

4 *Human Rights in the Value Chain**

EMILY F. CARASCO† AND JANG B. SINGH‡

Keywords

Business and human rights, global codes of ethics, business ethics, ethics and the value chain.

Introduction

It is no longer enough for a firm to engage in ethical practices only in the functions it performs in the value chain of a product. The ethicalness of practices throughout the value chain should be of concern to all firms engaged in the production of goods or services. In a globalized world it is commonplace for various functions in a value chain to be performed in different parts of the world. How then does a firm ensure that human rights are respected by all players in the value chain, irrespective of their geographical location? In this chapter it is proposed that respect and promotion of human rights should be addressed in a manner that begins at the global level and moves to the firm level, from the general to the specific. After a discussion of the value chain from the global perspective, global codes of ethics will be examined. This will be followed by an examination of corporate codes of ethics. The aim of the chapter is therefore to examine some of the human rights instruments that may be relevant in the value chain.

Human Rights Responsibility and the Value Chain

According to Kaplinsky, "The value chain describes the full range of activities which are required to bring a product or service from conception, through the intermediary phase of production, delivery to final consumers, and final disposal after use."[1] The length of this chain would vary, depending on the production or delivery process. Moreover, the question of who bears responsibility for activities in the various links of the chain may not always be clear. As suggested by Phillips and Caldwell, the boundaries of the organization

* This is an extension of the authors' work on human rights in business (see "Human Rights in Business Ethics Codes," *Business and Society Review*, Vol. 113, No.3, pp. 347–374 and "Towards Holding Transnational Corporations Responsible for Human Rights," *European Business Review*, Vol. 22, No. 4, pp. 432–445).

† Professor Emily F. Carasco, Faculty of Law, University of Windsor, Windsor, Ontario, N9B 3P4, Canada. E-mail: ecarasc@uwindsor.ca. Telephone: 1-519-253-4232.

‡ Professor Jang B. Singh, Odette School of Business, University of Windsor, Windsor, Ontario,N9B 3P4, Canada. E-mail: jang@uwindsor.ca. Telephone: 1-519-253-4232.

are becoming increasingly blurry as stakeholder integration intensifies. Although value chains can be wholly domestic, it is global value chains that have become the focus of human rights analysts.[2] Perhaps the case that contributed the most to this development is that of Nike. The company is very heavily dependent on subcontractors in developing countries like Vietnam and at various times over the past two decades there have been public allegations that some of its subcontractors were violating the human rights of their employees. Nike initially denied responsibility for the actions of subcontractors that it viewed as being independent. However, in the face of negative public reaction Nike subsequently retreated from its position of having an arm's length relationship with its subcontractors.[3]

A number of contingency factors impact corporate human rights responsibility in the value chain. In situations where strong links exist among players the nature of the relationship would imply corporate responsibility for human rights throughout the chain. In other situations where the relationship to a supplier or end user is not proximate such responsibility may be minimal. However, depending on the situation, the corporation can influence the human rights policies of players in its value chain. Andersen and Skjoett-Larsen (2009) identify four contingency factors influencing corporate social responsibility (CSR) in supply chains (all of which are applicable to human rights responsibility): knowledge enhancing mechanisms for actors in the supply chain (e.g., training regarding code of conduct); knowledge controlling mechanisms aimed at incorporating CSR activities into performance evaluation (e.g., incorporating code of ethics conduct into performance evaluation); firm specific assets such as size; and corporate history on CSR.[4] Models of this type may be used in deciding the level of corporate human rights responsibility and guiding corporate response, as in the case of the electronics giant Apple as it grapples with acknowledged human rights abuses in its supply system in China.[5] When the corporation is aware of human rights abuse among its suppliers its actions may be guided by a decision matrix such as the one developed by the UN Secretary General Special Representative on Human Rights and Transnational Corporations and other Business Enterprises (see Table 4.1).

Table 4.1   Decision matrix on value chain human rights abuse

	Have leverage	Lack leverage
Crucial source / partner	• Mitigate the abuse • If unsuccessful	• Seek to increase leverage • If successful, mitigate abuse. • If unsuccessful, take steps to end the relationship; or be able to demonstrate efforts made to mitigate abuse, recognising possible consequences of remaining.
Non-crucial source / partner	• Try to mitigate the abuse • If unsuccessful, take steps to end the relationship	• Take steps to end the relationship

Source: United Nations, 2010, p. 4.

Global Codes and Human Rights

Ishay defines human rights as "rights held by individuals simply because they are part of the human species. They are rights shared equally by everyone regardless of sex, race, nationality and economic background. They are universal in content."[6] Perhaps the apex of the human rights chain is the Universal Declaration of Human Rights. The Declaration was the culmination of a campaign to establish human rights applicable to all of humanity that gained momentum during the early years of World War II and was adopted by the United Nations General Assembly on December 10, 1948. The United Nations urged all member countries to publicize the text of the Declaration and "to cause it to be disseminated, displayed, read and expounded principally in schools and other educational institutions, without distinction based on the political status of countries or territories".[7] The preamble of the document states that "the recognition of the inherent dignity and of the equal and inalienable rights of all members of the human family is the foundation of freedom, justice and peace in the world". Some of the prescriptions of the Declaration pertinent to global business include the following:

- All human beings are born free and equal in dignity and rights. They are endowed with reason and conscience and should act towards one another in a spirit of brotherhood.
- Everyone is entitled to all the rights and freedoms set forth in this Declaration, without distinction of any kind, such as race, colour, sex, language, religion, political or other opinion, national or social origin, property, birth or other status. Everyone has the right to life, liberty and security of person.
- No one shall be held in slavery or servitude; slavery and the slave trade shall be prohibited in all their forms.
- No one shall be subjected to torture or to cruel, inhuman or degrading treatment or punishment.
- Everyone has the right to recognition everywhere as a person before the law.
- All are equal before the law and are entitled without any discrimination to equal protection of the law. All are entitled to equal protection against any discrimination in violation of this Declaration and against any incitement to such discrimination.
- Everyone has the right to an effective remedy by the competent national tribunals for acts violating the fundamental rights granted him by the constitution or by law.
- No one shall be subjected to arbitrary interference with his privacy, family, home or correspondence, nor to attacks upon his honour and reputation. Everyone has the right to the protection of the law against such interference or attacks.
- Everyone has the right to own property alone as well as in association with others.
- Everyone has the right to work, to free choice of employment, to just and favourable conditions of work and to protection against unemployment.
- Everyone, without any discrimination, has the right to equal pay for equal work.
- Everyone who works has the right to just and favourable remuneration ensuring for himself and his family an existence worthy of human dignity, and supplemented, if necessary, by other means of social protection.
- Everyone has the right to form and to join trade unions for the protection of his interests.
- Everyone has the right to rest and leisure, including reasonable limitation of working hours and periodic holidays with pay.[8]

The Declaration provides the moral authority for the global codes discussed in this chapter and which apply to all human beings, irrespective of where they live or work. Donaldson and Dunfee see the development of such universal ethical standards as desirable.[9] They argue that any form of ethical relativism must be rejected and that moral free space and cultural diversity must be recognized. This means that there are overarching norms (hypernorms) that apply in all cultures but moral free space within cultures permit culturally specific practices; ethics requires a balance between the universal and particular and when the balance is lost, the moral game is up.[10]

Frederick views the invocation of human rights as a philosophical principle as being rooted in the Kantian belief that the human person has "inherent worth and dignity, as well as inalienable and equal rights and freedoms". He posits that the obligations and duties flowing from this leads to a "deceptively simple algorithm" that lays the moral foundation for prescribing rules of conduct for individuals, groups, governments and multinational corporations.[11]

Universal human rights ideals as overarching values influence global ethics codes. In discussing such universal values in an era of globalization, Hans Kung makes four propositions regarding globalization: a) globalization is unavoidable; b) globalization is ambivalent; c) globalization is incalculable; d) globalization can be controlled rationally. He suggests that that economic globalization and ethics globalization go hand in hand. Global ethics codes are a manifestation of this relationship.[12]

Concerns about economic globalization led to ongoing efforts during the last four decades to regulate the activities carried out by multinational corporations. Given the nature of globalization, states are widely seen as inadequate vehicles for the regulation of these corporations. Governments in the economically developed countries are often unwilling, and governments in the less economically developed countries are often unable, to constrain transnational corporations (TNCs).[13] In discussing a new definition of corporate citizenship, Matten and Crane suggest three situations that crystallize the role of corporations in administering citizenship rights (including human rights): where government ceases to administer them; where government is yet to administer them; and where the administration of those rights may be beyond the reach of the government. They suggest that the true definition of corporate citizenship is "the role of the corporation in administering citizenship rights for individuals".[14] Monshipouri, Welch and Kennedy (2003) analyse the globalization–human rights intersection and conclude that "given the many questions and controversies surrounding the operations of multinational corporations (MNCs), a case can be made for holding MNCs accountable to human rights standards and for pressuring MNCs to reorient their policies and practices".[15] Accordingly, various groups of individuals, non-state actors and groups of states have sought to devise global strategies for holding TNCs more accountable for their activities when they have an adverse impact on people and society.

The 1970s witnessed the birth of a number of voluntary codes, including the United Nations' abortive draft Code of Conduct for Transnational Corporations. These attempts to regulate TNCs failed because of a lack of support from states. The growing criticism of the negative impact of unfettered globalization led to a second phase of proliferation of global codes in the 1990s. This phase was also not successful in regulating the TNCs, and developing countries appeared to have abandoned their fervour for pursuing that goal. Much had changed in the international economic and political sphere since the 1970s. As Murphy suggests, though the story of the 1970s and 1980s may have been one of developing countries seeking to nationalize or expropriate foreign investment as a means of stemming post-colonial economic domination, the story of the 1990s was one of developing states seeking foreign investment and technology.[16] Inflows of foreign direct investment (FDI) to developing countries reached US$574 billion in 2010, representing slightly more than 50% of global inward FDI.[17] With regard to regulation, TNCs began to take over from where developing countries left off. During the 1990s, reacting to criticisms about their activities, a number of TNCs began to develop internal codes of conduct, and increasing numbers of TNCs have developed codes of conduct with a significant number of the larger TNCs participating in the development of global, group based or industry wide efforts to develop codes.

The effectiveness of the substantive provisions of global codes, five of which are discussed below, has largely focused on three categories: human rights, labour and the environment.

UN CENTRE ON TRANSNATIONAL CORPORATIONS' DRAFT CODE

An early attempt at introducing human rights in to the global operations of multinational corporations was made in the 1977 draft code of the United Nations Centre on Transnational Corporations (UNCTC draft code). The document was not endorsed by UN member states but its human rights content has been noted. For example, Frederick concluded that the incorporation of a general statement accepting the Universal Declaration of Human Rights provides explicit normative guides for the policies, decisions and operations of transnational corporations on basic human rights and fundamental freedom.[18]

OECD GUIDELINES FOR MULTINATIONAL ENTERPRISES

At about the same time that the UNCTC draft code was developed, the OECD Council of Ministers adopted the Guidelines for Multinational Enterprises (MNEs). This code has been revised several times. The latest revision was done in May 2011 when 42 OECD and non-OECD countries adhering to the Guidelines adopted, among other things, a new chapter on human rights. The updated provisions, reflecting the latest stance of the UN Council on Human Rights, include the following. States have the duty to protect human rights. Enterprises should, within the framework of internationally recognized human rights, the international human rights obligations of the countries in which they operate, as well as relevant domestic laws and regulations:

1. Respect human rights, which means they should avoid infringing on the human rights of others and should address adverse human rights impacts with which they are involved.
2. Within the context of their own activities, avoid causing or contributing to adverse human rights impacts and address such impacts when they occur.
3. Seek ways to prevent or mitigate adverse human rights impacts that are directly linked to their business operations, products or services by a business relationship, even if they do not contribute to those impacts.
4. Provide for or co-operate through legitimate processes in the remediation of adverse human rights impacts where they identify that they have caused or contributed to these impacts.[19]

The Guidelines are voluntary recommendations for business practices and every OECD member state appoints a "national contact point" (NCP), which has the responsibility to promote the Guidelines within the state's territory and to gather information regarding adherence to them. The OECD Guidelines, while non-binding, are officially endorsed by all the member states of the organization that created it. The Guidelines are also important because while currently just 42 states adhere to the Guidelines, those states are collectively the source of more than 85% of global direct investment flows.[20]

ILO'S TRIPARTITE DECLARATION OF PRINCIPLES CONCERNING MULTINATIONAL ENTERPRISES

Another global code adopted in the same period as the UNCTC draft code and the OECD Guidelines was the ILO's Tripartite Declaration of Principles Concerning Multinational Enterprises and social policy, which was adopted by The Governing Body of the International Body of the International Labor Organization in 1977.[21] The Declaration, aimed at MNCs, states, and employers' and workers' organizations, is intended to encourage the positive contribution which multinational enterprises can make to economic and social progress, and to minimize difficulties arising from their operations. The Declaration covers human rights related to the workplace and is voluntary for businesses, but the ILO Conventions contained within it are binding on state parties that have ratified those Conventions. Paragraph 8 of the Declaration stipulates that all parties concerned should respect the Universal Declaration of Human Rights and the corresponding International Covenants adopted by the General Assembly of the United Nations, while Paragraph 36 of the Declaration promotes the prohibition and elimination of child labour.

GLOBAL COMPACT

Another effort was launched at the United Nations in 1999 when the then Secretary-General, Kofi Annan, introduced the idea of a Global Compact. This was an initiative designed to bring businesses together with UN agencies, and labour and civil society organizations. In 2000, the Global Compact was launched in partnership with the International Chamber of Commerce. The United Nations describes the Global Compact in the following terms:

> *The Global Compact is a voluntary international corporate citizenship network initiated to support the participation of both the private sector and other social actors to advance responsible corporate citizenship and universal social and environmental principles to meet the challenges of globalization.*[22]

The principles address human rights, labour and the environment and are drawn from the Universal Declaration of Human Rights, the International Labor Organization's Fundamental Principles on Rights at Work, the 1995 Copenhagen Social Summit and the Rio Principles on Environment and Development. The following six principles in the Global Compact are related to human rights:

Human Rights

Principle 1:   Business should support and respect the protection of internationally proclaimed human rights.

Principle 2:   Businesses should make sure that they are not complicit in human rights abuses.

Labour

Principle 3:   Businesses should uphold the freedom of association and the effective recognition of the right to collective bargaining

Principle 4:   The elimination of all forms of forced and compulsory labour;

Principle 5:   The effective abolition of child labour; and

Principle 6:   The elimination of discrimination in respect of employment and occupation.

As of 2011, the Global Compact included some 6000 companies from all regions of the world, as well as 2000 other participants, including international labour and civil society organizations.[23] To assist participating firms in respecting human rights in their operations a matrix has been developed. "The matrix provides an approach for mapping and assessing the connection between business and human rights – including which human rights are relevant for business and what is regarded as 'essential', 'expected' or 'desirable' behavior".[24]

NORMS ON THE RESPONSIBILITIES OF TRANSNATIONAL CORPORATIONS AND OTHER BUSINESS ENTERPRISES WITH REGARD TO HUMAN RIGHTS

The United Nations Sub-Commission on the Promotion and Protection of Human Rights approved the Norms on the Responsibilities of Transnational Corporations and other Business Enterprises with Regard to Human Rights in 2003.[25] Mainly because they originated from the Sub-Commission on the Promotion of Human Rights, the Norms clearly identified specific human rights relevant to the activities of business and attempted to impose direct responsibilities on business entities "as a means of achieving comprehensive protection of all human rights – civil, cultural, economic, political and social".[26]

The obligations the Norms sought to impose upon transnational corporations and other businesses begin with the following general obligations:

States have the primary responsibility to promote, secure the fulfillment of, respect, ensure respect of and protect human rights recognized in international as well as national law, including ensuring that transnational corporations and other business enterprises respect human rights. Within their respective spheres of activity and influence, transnational corporations and other business enterprises have the obligation to promote, secure the fulfillment of, respect, ensure respect of and protect human rights recognized in international as well as national law, including the rights and interests of indigenous peoples and other vulnerable groups.

After this statement on the two-tiered responsibility for the promotion and protection of human rights, the Norms provide a comprehensive coverage of the following human rights issues: the right to equal opportunity and non-discriminatory treatment; the right to security of persons; rights of workers; respect for national sovereignty and human rights; obligations with regard to consumer protection; and obligations with regard to environmental protection.[27]

The Norms imposed specific obligations on TNCs and other businesses to adopt, disseminate and implement the principles contained therein. In an attempt to promote human rights in the value chain, the Norms did not limit the obligations on TNCs and other businesses to adopt them to their internal operations but extended the obligation to incorporate the principles into their contracts with business partners. A few corporations such as Novartis and British Petroleum initially supported the Norms but corporate support was generally weak. The influential International Chamber of Commerce and the International Organization of Employers lobbied against the Norms, arguing that they imposed obligations on corporations that should instead have been placed on states.[28] Strong lobbying by business interests and the prevailing view that the protection of human rights was a state responsibility contributed to the eventual failure of the Norms to receive approval from the UN Commission on Human Rights. Bachmann and Miretski attribute this failure to three factors:

> *Firstly, the fact that a large part of the Norms constituted a further development of existing international norms, rather than actual codification of existing international law. Secondly, the fact that the Norms assigned an important legal role to MNCs as direct addressees and not the States as the traditional addressees of international law blurred the distinction between international public and private legal frameworks, and thus undermined the central role of states as international law subjects. Finally, inherent contradictions within the Norms themselves and an overall vagueness in their overall nature and applicability helped to foster opposition against their adoption.[29]*

In 2005, when the UN Commission on Human Rights declined to proceed with the Norms it was not because human rights had faded as a concern in the value chain but because the thrust of the initiative had failed to garner the requisite level of support from business and states necessary for its implementation. In recognition of the continuing need to address what was a matter of global concern, the United Nations Secretary General appointed Harvard University professor John Ruggie as his special representative on the issue of human rights and transnational corporations and other business enterprises. This action breathed new life into the global push for the promotion and protection of human rights in business enterprises. However, it was not in the form envisaged by the working group that drafted the Norms.

In a report adopted by the United Nations Human Rights Council in 2011 Professor Ruggie described his work as progressing in three phases. His initial appointment for two years was seen as one to identify and clarify existing standards. In this phase a comprehensive description of the state of human rights in business globally was developed and disseminated to interested parties. The second phase of the Special Representative's mandate was for one year. In this period the Human Rights Council asked Professor Ruggie to make recommendations on the role of business and states in promoting human rights in business operations globally. In June 2008, Professor Ruggie's recommendation to support his "Protect, Respect and Remedy" framework was unanimously accepted by the Human Rights Council. In the third phase of his mandate, from 2008 to 2011, the Special Representative was asked to operationalize the framework, to provide concrete recommendations on implementing guiding principles on business and human rights. The adoption of the report to the United Nations Council on Human Rights (formerly the United Nations Commission on Human Rights) was the culmination of extensive stakeholder consultations by the Special Representative.[30] However, the Guiding Principles developed were seen not as the end of the process to standardize the protection and promotion of human rights in business globally but were described by Professor Ruggie as the end of the beginning of the process.[31]

What are the Guiding Principles adopted by the Human Rights Council? Before examining the principles, which are likely to heavily influence the management of human rights in business globally, it is important to heed the following comments by Professor Ruggie:

> The Guiding Principles' normative contribution lies not in the creation of new international law obligations but in elaborating the implications of existing standards and practices for States and businesses; integrating them within a single, logically coherent and comprehensive template; and identifying where the current regime falls short and how it should be improved. Each Principle is accompanied by a commentary, further clarifying its meaning and implications. At the same time, the Guiding Principles are not intended as a tool kit, simply to be taken off the shelf and plugged in. While the Principles themselves are universally applicable, the means by which they are realized will reflect the fact that we live in a world of 192 United Nations Member States, 80,000 transnational enterprises, 10 times as many subsidiaries and countless millions of national firms, most of which are small and medium-sized enterprises. When it comes to means for implementation, therefore, one size does not fit all.[32]

The report adopted by the Human Rights Council consists of 31 guiding principles grouped under three pillars. The first 10 principles focus on the first pillar, the state's duty to protect human rights. The next 14 address the second pillar, the corporate responsibility to respect human rights, while the final seven focus on access to remedy. While the principles do not create new legal obligations for states and businesses, they will lead to a more consistent approach to ensuring that human rights are respected globally and therefore chain-wide in the production of goods and delivery of services. As stated by Natour, companies' responsibility to respect human rights means: adopting a new human rights commitment; ensuring non-infringement through human rights due diligence; addressing any adverse human rights impacts the company was involved in; and measuring and reporting on performance.[33] This will clearly lead to more businesses formulating human rights policies. For example, the prevalence of human rights policies in the approximately 80,000 existing multinational corporations should be expected to rise considerably: it is estimated that only 271 currently have human rights policies.[34] Moreover, the requirement to ensure non-infringement through human rights due diligence puts a greater responsibility on corporations to monitor their value chain relationships.[35] Subsequent to the adoption of the Guiding Principles by the Human Rights Council a United Nations expert body was appointed charged with promoting and disseminating the principles.[36]

CORPORATE CODES OF ETHICS

At the specific level of the firm, respect for and promotion of human rights may be addressed through corporate codes of ethics. Langlois and Schlegelmilch define a corporate code of ethics as "a statement setting down corporate principles, ethics, rules of conduct, codes of practice or company philosophy concerning responsibility to employees, shareholders, consumers, the environment, or any other aspects of society external to the company".[37] The prevalence of corporate codes of ethics has been increasing globally.[38] KPMG's research on Fortune Global 200 companies reported in 2008 shows that 86% of them now have their own business code. This represents a progressive increase from 1970 when only a handful of these companies had a code and 1990 when the proportion had risen to 14%. In 2008 KPMG found the breakdown by region to be as follows: North America 100%, Asia 52% and Europe 80%.[39] Svensson et al., in surveys of the largest corporations in Australia, Canada and Sweden, have found a similar trend.[40]

A corporate code of ethics is the most important part of the ethics programme of a corporation. It sets the ethics standards for the corporation and is usually supplemented by measures such as ethics training, an ethics committee and support for whistleblowers. These supplementary measures are commonly found in large corporations.[41] The role that the various elements of an ethics programme play may be explained by looking beyond philosophically based ethics to social and cognitive factors, as done by Stajkovic and Luthans, whose social-cognitive theory seeks to identify factors influencing business ethics standards and conduct by proposing that a person's perception of ethical standards and subsequent behaviour is influenced by institutional factors (e.g., ethics legislation), personal factors (e.g., moral development) and organizational factors (e.g., ethics programmes). They posit that these antecedent institutional, personal and organizational factors triadically interact within the cultural context to influence standards.[42]

A survey of the world's largest corporations conducted in 2000 by the Ashridge Centre for Business and Society found that 44% of the responding corporations' codes make explicit reference to human rights, and for almost half that did not do so, an intention to do so was expressed. It was also found that 16% of the codes make reference to the Universal Declaration of Human Rights and 94% mentioned the prohibition of discrimination on the basis of specific grounds such as race and religion.[43] The Guiding Principles of the UN Human Rights Council can be expected to lead to a growing number of corporate codes of ethics covering human rights issues.

Conclusion

The effectiveness of corporate codes and voluntary global codes in enhancing human rights in business has not been clearly established. Singh (2006) reports that studies are not unanimous in finding that corporate codes of ethics are effective in influencing behaviours in organizations.[44] Compa (2008–2009) reports a change of heart on the effectiveness of corporate codes, arguing that they, global and multi-stakeholder codes could be effective in combination with strong enforced laws and strong, democratic trade unions.[45] Jenkins et al. (2002) agree with critics of voluntary codes who suggest that they serve as substitutes for statutory regulations and at the same time legitimize the absence of such instruments.[46] However, the prevailing global politico-economic environment does not seem to favour new statutory human rights legislation.

However, the extensive consultation that went into the formulation of the UN Guiding Principles and the subsequent appointment of the UN Working Group on Human Rights and Transnational Corporations and Other Business Enterprises provide hope that a path to a more robust system to promote respect for human rights and to remedy human rights abuses in business activity globally has finally been found. Only time will tell how successful this latest effort will be. Nevertheless, it is a most intriguing development: if, together with the other initiatives in the global business and human rights architecture, it succeeds, consumers will be reasonably assured that the value chains of the products and services they buy are free from human rights abuse.

Notes

1   Kaplinsky, R. (2000), "Globalisation and Unequalisation: What Can Be Learned from Value Chain Analysis?", *Journal of Development Studies*, Vol. 37, No. 2, pp. 117–146. See p. 121.

2   Phillips, R. & Caldwell, C. (2005), "Value Chain Responsibility: A Farewell to Arms Length", *Business and Society Review*, Vol. 110, No. 4, pp. 345–370.

3   *Ibid.*

4   Andersen, M. & Skjoett, T. (2009), "Corporate Social Responsibility in Global Supply Chains", *Supply Chain Management: An International Journal*, Vol. 14, No. 2, pp. 75–86.

5   Duhigg, C. & Barboza, D. (2012), "In China, the Human Costs That Are Built into an iPad", *The New York Times*, January 26: A1.

6   Ishay, M.R. (2004), *The History of Human Rights: From Ancient Time to the Globalization Era*. Berkeley: University of California Press. See p. 3.

7   United Nations (1948), *Universal Declaration of Human Rights*. Accessed February 24, 2007 at www.un.org/Overview/rights.html.

8   *Ibid.*

9   Donaldson, T. & Dunfee, T. (1999a), "When Ethics Travel: The Promise and Peril of Global Business Ethics", *California Business Review*, Vol. 41, No. 4, pp. 45–63.

10   Donaldson, T. & Dunfee, T. (1999b), *Ties That Bind: A Social Contracts Approach to Business Ethics*. Boston: Harvard Business School Press. See p. 41.

11   Frederick, W.C. (1991), "The Moral Authority of Transnational Corporate Codes", *Journal of Business Ethics*, Vol. 10, No. 3, 165–177. See p.169.

12   Kung, H. (1997), "A Global Ethic in an Age of Globalization", *Business Ethics Quarterly*, Vol. 7, No. 3, pp. 17–31.

13   Carasco, E. & Singh, J. (2008), "Human Rights in Global Business Ethics Codes", *Business and Society Review*, Vol. 113, No. 3, pp. 347–375.

14   Matten, D. & Crane, A. (2005), "Corporate Citizenship: Toward an Extended Theoretical Conceptualization", *The Academy of Management Review*, Vol. 30, No. 1, pp. 166–179. See p. 173.

15   Monshipouri, M., Welch, C. & Kennedy, E. (2003), "Multinational Corporations and the Ethics of Global Responsibility: Problems and Possibilities", *Human Rights Quarterly*, Vol. 25, No. 4, pp. 965–989. See p. 987.

16   Murray, J. (1998), "Corporate Codes of Conduct and Labor Standards" (Geneva, International Labor Organization Bureau for Workers' Activities). Accessed October 10, 2006 at www.itcilo.

it/english/actrav/telearn/global/ilo/guide/jill.htm#4.%20CASE%20STUDY%20-%20THE%20
SULLIVAN%20PRINCIPLES. See p. 397.

17   UNCTAD (2011), *World Investment Report*. New York and Geneva: United Nations.

18   Frederick, *op. cit.*, p. 167.

19   OECD (2011), *Guidelines for Multinational Enterprises*. Accessed January 8, 2011 at www.oecd.
org/dataoecd/43/29/48004323.pdf. See p. 33.

20   *Ibid.*

21   International Labor Organization (ILO) (2006), *Tripartite Declaration of Principles concerning
Multinational Enterprises and Social Policy*. Accessed March 4, 2007 at www.ilo.org.

22   United Nations Procurement Division (2005), The Global Compact. Accessed October 22,
2006 at www.un.org/depts/ptd/global.htm.

23   United Nations Global Compact (2011), Participants and Stakeholders. Accessed January 8,
2012 at www.unglobalcompact.org/ParticipantsAndStakeholders/index.html.

24   United Nations Global Compact (Undated). Accessed January 12, 2012 at www.
unglobalcompact.org.

25   United Nations (2003), *Norms on the Responsibilities of Transnational Corporations and other
Business Enterprises with Regard to Human Rights, Sub Commission on the Promotion of Human
Rights, E/CN.4/Sub.2/2003/12/Rev.2 (2003)*. Accessed January 12, 2012 at www1.umn.edu/
humanrts/links/norms-Aug2003.html.

26   United Nations (2005), *Report of the United Nations High Commissioner on Human Rights on
the Responsibilities of Transnational Corporations and Related Business Enterprises with Regard to
Human Rights,* Economic and Social Council, E/CN.4/2005/91. See p. 9.

27   United Nations (2003), *op. cit.*

28   Mantilla, G. (2009), "Emerging International Human Rights Norms for Transnational
Corporations", *Global Governance,* Vol. 15, No. 2, pp. 279–298.

29   Bachmann, S. & Miretski, P. (2011), "Global Business and Human Rights: The UN 'Norms on
the Responsibility of Transnational Corporations and Other Business Enterprises with Regard
to Human Rights' – A Requiem". Available at SSRN: http://ssrn.com/abstract=1958537 or
doi:10.2139/ssrn.1958537. See p. 6.

30   Human Rights Council (2011), *Report of the Special Representative of the Secretary General on the
Issue of Human Rights and Transnational Corporations and other Business Enterprises, John Ruggie
– Guiding Principles on Business and Human Rights: Implementing the United Nations "Protect,
Respect and Remedy" Framework*. Accessed January 21, 2012 at www.ohchr.org/documents/
issues/business/A.HRC.17.31.pdf.

31   *Ibid.*

32   *Ibid.*, p. 5.

33   Nantour, F. (2011), "UN Council Endorses Principles on Business and Human Rights", *Business
Ethics Magazine,* June 16, pp. 1–4. See p. 2.

34   *Ibid.*

35   "Business and Human Rights: Interview with John Ruggie" (2011), *Business Ethics Magazine,*
October 30, pp. 1–7.

36   United Nations (2011), Have your say! Help a new UN body ensure respect for human rights
by business. November 4. Accessed February 3, 2012 at /www.ohchr.org/en/NewsEvents/
Pages/DisplayNews.aspx?NewsID=11567&LangID=E.

37   Langlois, C.C. & Schlegelmilch, B.B. (1990), "Do Corporate Codes of Ethics Reflect National
Character? Evidence from Europe and the United States", *Journal of International Business
Studies,* Vol. 21 (Fourth Quarter), pp. 519–539. See p. 522.

38   KPMG (2008), *Business Codes of the Global 200: Their Prevalence, Content and Embedding*. The Netherlands: KPMG.

39   *Ibid.*

40   Svensson, G., Wood, G., J. Singh & M. Callaghan (2009), "Implementation, Communication and Benefits of Corporate Codes of Ethics: An International and Longitudinal Approach for Australia, Canada and Sweden", *Business Ethics: A European Review*, Vol. 18, No. 4, pp. 389–407.

41   Singh, J. (2011), "Determinants of the Effectiveness of Corporate Codes of Ethics: An Empirical Study", *Journal of Business Ethics*, Vol. 101, No. 3, pp. 385–395.

42   Stajkovic, A. D. & Luthans, F. (1997), "Business Ethics across Cultures: A Social Cognitive Model", *Journal of World Business*, Vol. 32, No. 1, pp. 17–34. See p. 32.

43   Wilson, A. & Gribben, C. (2000), *Business Responses to Human Rights*. Berkhamsted: Ashridge Centre for Business and Society.

44   Singh, J. (2006), "Ethics Programs in Canada's Largest Corporations", *Business and Society Review*, Vol. 111, No. 2, pp. 119–136.

45   Compa, L. (2008–2009), "Corporate Social Responsibility and Workers' Rights", *Comparative Labor Law and Policy Journal*, Vol. 30, No. 1, pp. 1–9.

46   Jenkins, R., Pearson, R. & Seyfang, G. (2002), *Corporate Responsibility and Labour Rights: Codes of Conduct in the Global Economy*. London: Earthscan.

5

The Growth of Private Regulation of Labor Standards in Global Supply Chains: Mission Impossible for Western Small and Medium-Sized Firms?*

JETTE STEEN KNUDSEN†

Keywords

Corporate social responsibility (CSR), small and medium-sized enterprises (SMEs), global supply chains, Business for Social Compliance Initiative (BSCI).

Introduction

Multinational corporations (MNCs) have come under pressure to adopt private regulatory initiatives in order to address poor working conditions in global supply chain factories.[1] As Levy and Kaplan[2] observe, it is indeed surprising how readily MNCs have adopted corporate social responsibility (CSR)[3] standards and reporting mechanisms, considering the lack of regulatory coercion. The emergence of private regulation as a component of global business regulation is primarily attributed to three related developments: economic globalization, the lack of inadequate regulatory mechanisms at both the national and international levels to govern global firms and markets, and a decline in state controls over business following privatization and deregulation.[4]

*   This chapter will also be published in *Journal of Business Ethics*. An earlier version was presented at the 2012 Society for the Advancement of Socio-Economic Studies (SASE) Conference at MIT where it was included in a mini-conference on sustainable supply chain management. I am grateful to the SMEs for sharing their insights with me although I cannot name then. I would also like to thank the BSCI for useful input. Asbjørn Klein provided valuable research assistance. The usual disclaimers apply.

†   Associate Professor Jette Steen Knudsen, Copenhagen Business School, Department of Business and Politics, Porcelaenshaven 24A, 2000 Frederiksberg, Denmark. E-mail: jsk.dbp@cbs.dk. Telephone: +44 2120 9295.

While the literature on responsible global supply chain management has focused on large brands and retailers, it has failed to think carefully about small and medium-sized enterprises (SMEs) as private regulators in *global* supply chains (though there are notable exceptions[5]). According to Moore and Spence,[6] "The research which has been conducted on responsible business practice and SMEs is almost entirely in developed western countries. While this is the same for the majority of research done on large firms, the gap is particularly pertinent since small firms are often a key part of the economy in developing countries" (see also Spence[7]). However, as SMEs too have begun to source from or produce in less developed countries,[8] many large buyers and retailers now demand that western SME suppliers document that they adequately control the social and environmental performance of their own suppliers in less developed countries.[9]

These demands pose significant challenges for many western SMEs.[10] First, most SMEs do not have the economic resources to ensure proper documentation and to follow up with each of their suppliers or license holders. Second, SMEs often lack political clout vis-à-vis their suppliers. They may be just one of many buyers and the incentive for the supplier to improve the social and environmental performance can therefore be limited.[11] Third, in recent years many MNCs have been consolidating their supply chain in order to increase efficiency so that they work with fewer and larger suppliers and some experts have therefore concluded that "there is a trend of pressuring and excluding SMEs from global supply chains."[12]

This chapter asks the following question: How does company size impact the willingness of western SMEs to engage in private regulation of labor standards in global supply chains?

This question is important from both a theoretical and a practical perspective. Theoretically, knowledge is lacking about how company size impacts the actions of western firms with respect to international private labor regulation. From a practical perspective SMEs are becoming more integrated into global supply chains, and responding to demands for private regulation is turning into an increasingly important competitive parameter for SME managers seeking to meet buyer requirements. Furthermore, from a societal perspective the international competitiveness of SMEs is a key issue. If large international suppliers increasingly avoid western SMEs, then many western economies could be negatively affected, since SMEs account for a significant proportion of the economy. In fact, 99 percent of all European businesses are SMEs, SMEs provide two out of three private sector jobs and they contribute to more than half of the total value-added created by businesses in the European Union (EU).[13]

I focus on the Business for Social Compliance Initiative (the BSCI) as a notable example of international private business regulation. The BSCI is a major international business-driven initiative governing working conditions in global supply chains. It has enjoyed tremendous growth in recent years and more and more MNC members demand that their suppliers – including SMEs – sign a contract stating that their production processes are in accordance with BSCI specifications. Furthermore, in the last 2–3 years more SMEs have joined the BSCI because large buyers and retailers have requested this. More than 700 out of close to 800 BSCI members have a turnover below €100 million.[14]

This chapter proceeds as follows. I begin by presenting my theoretical framework, which (following Büthe[15]) consists of three levels of analysis: a focus on rule-demanders, rule-suppliers and rule-takers. Next, I discuss my research methodology and case selection. I then proceed to a presentation of findings, which is followed by a discussion and conclusion.

Theoretical Explanations of Firm Interest in Private Regulation

The literature on CSR in large firms and the literature on CSR in small firms highlight distinctly different initiatives. The literature on large firms mirrors the internationalization process of companies such as Nike, GAP, Adidas and Hewlett Packard and how companies have had to deal with governance gaps as they operate outside their home countries.[16] The literature on CSR in SMEs reflects that these firms traditionally have been less likely to operate abroad. Most theoretical articles on CSR in SMEs examine initiatives at home. Examples include a focus on local community development in Ireland,[17] environmental sustainability in Catalonia,[18] social capital in Italy[19] and environmental performance in England.[20]

As my theoretical framework for analyzing the role of SMEs as providers of CSR in global supply chains, I follow Büthe's suggestion that an analysis of private regulation should include three major subsets of stakeholders. The first group of stakeholders consists of political-economic actors, who demand private regulation (*rule-demanders*). Frequently such demands are posed by third parties, who find that their non-material interests are negatively affected by missing or inadequate regulation. These actors can be social activists motivated by normative commitments that are altruistic (or perceived as such) and include, for example, non-governmental organizations (NGOs) or consumer organizations.[21] The second group of stakeholders consists of the private actors who write, maintain and disseminate regulatory rules for the global economy (*rule-suppliers*). As Büthe writes, "Why they supply private regulation needs to be explained because these activities are costly."[22] The third group consists of the political-economic actors whose behavior private regulations seek to affect (*rule-takers*). The interesting analytical question for the third group is about implementation and why they choose to comply with private regulation.

Concerning rule-demanders, my focus is on those actors who have demanded private regulation in the form of BSCI requirements. With respect to rule-suppliers, I address those large firms that impose BSCI requirements on key actors in the supply chain. Finally, with respect to rule-takers, I am interested in those firms that have to comply with BSCI requirements, in particular western SMEs.

Büthe suggests that this analytical approach is more useful than the application of economic models of demand and supply. According to Büthe, "In economic models of supply and demand, those who ultimately 'buy' a product or service are not only identical with those who subsequently 'use' it, they presumably purchase it in order to 'use' it".[23] These approaches work less well in political models of regulations because those who call for regulation may diverge from those who are supposed to act according to those rules. Below I present theoretical literatures associated with each of these three areas (demanding, supplying and taking rules), identify limits of this literature for explaining SMEs in global supply chains, and propose how my analysis will provide a theoretical extension of our current understanding of SMEs as private regulators in global supply chains.

RULE-DEMANDERS

A functionalist account of market demand emphasizes how market actors request regulation if the efficient operation of markets requires the existence of such a system of rules. A decline in or a lack of the public supply of rules will encourage private actors to create such rules instead. Motivations that drive private actors can be to lower transaction costs, increase reliability, achieve efficiency and ensure legitimacy.[24] Rule-demanders can be the participants of a commercial transaction but rule-demanders can also be a broader set of actors with an interest in rule-making. First, participants of a commercial transaction are key actors, who can demand rules or standard contracts that govern that transaction.[25] Second, governments may demand private regulation in order to substitute for costly and/or ineffective public regulation.[26] Finally, societal actors who are not party to a commercial transaction may also demand private regulation for material reasons.[27] Private actors such as NGOs, unions or the media may also demand private regulation for non-material reasons because they are motivated by values, norms or morals.[28] However, to the best of my knowledge this literature does not address SMEs as actors demanding private regulation.

RULE-SUPPLIERS

Developing and institutionalizing international private rules is costly.[29] Why then would private actors decide to supply regulation? One reason could be to preempt government regulation, while another could be to substitute for governance voids. First, private supply of regulation often occurs in the shadow of public regulation.[30] If the threat of less favorable regulation is credible then preempting more demanding public regulation can be a powerful incentive for the supply of private regulation.[31] Second, companies might prefer that the public sector provides regulation, for example as a way of creating a level playing field, but if governments are unable to do so private regulation can be adopted as a second-best solution.[32] While it is possible to have an ideal overlap between demanders and suppliers of private regulation this happens rarely.[33] It is more common that private regulation is supplied because companies expect this to lead to private gains. Regulation may, for example, protect the supplier from the risk of violating social and environmental rights in supplier factories and this may increase supplier legitimacy. International private rules can also lower the cost of compliance because rather than having to comply with numerous private codes of conduct, companies only have to comply with one standard. However, private regulation is supplied by large firms mainly. The literature on preemption and substitution does not address SMEs as suppliers of rules.

RULE-TAKERS

While a vibrant and strong literature exists regarding CSR in SMEs, this literature primarily addresses domestic CSR initiatives and is more or less silent about CSR initiatives by SMEs in global supply chains. For example, the theoretical literature does not address MNC demands for responsible behavior imposed on western SMEs in global supply chains. In an interesting study, Tencati, Angeloantonio and Quaglia[34] address the impact of demands by western SMEs on suppliers in less developed countries. The study shows that CSR demands imposed by western SMEs on their Vietnamese suppliers over time have become required for access to international markets and have in practice turned into a new kind of protectionism to the detriment of Vietnamese suppliers. However, the authors do not examine the role of MNCs as rule-demanders.

In another study Baden, Harwood and Woodward[35] find that for most SMEs the inclusion of social and environmental requirements as preconditions to supply goods and services increases their motivation to engage in CSR (82 percent for environmental criteria and 55 percent for social criteria). However, 25 percent would be put off tendering and 12 percent thought that such criteria would be counterproductive. However, this study does not distinguish between SME suppliers in advanced economic countries and less developed countries. Finally, Perrini, Russo and Tencati[36] observe a positive attitude among SMEs in managing CSR strategies along the value chain. They argue that the reason for this attitude is that SMEs differ from large firms in a number of key respects. SMEs have strong owner–manager relationships with their suppliers and customers, and these relationships seem to drive the integration of CSR strategies and corporate strategy. However, the authors focus on owner-managers' relationships with suppliers in Italy and do not consider international supply chains. In short, while a literature is emerging on the role of SMEs in supply chains, the focus is primarily on *domestic* supply chains.

In sum, I have presented a theoretical framework for analyzing the drivers behind the BSCI, why MNCs request that suppliers meet BSCI requirements, and why SMEs comply with this framework.

Case Selection and Methodology

CASE SELECTION

The BSCI is a business-driven initiative for companies committed to improving working conditions in the global supply chain.[37] It was created in 2003 by some of Europe's largest retailers in order to audit and monitor the social performance of their suppliers worldwide by utilizing a common system.[38] The initiative started as a sector-based solution for retail but has since spread to furniture, building material, importers, discounters and food companies.[39] The declared purpose of the BSCI is to implement ethical procurement practices and improve social standards in supplier countries on a voluntary basis in order to avoid duplication of monitoring efforts, confusion about requirements, lack of transparency and accountability, as well as high costs for companies and their suppliers.[40] The BSCI Code of Conduct is built on international conventions protecting workers' rights, notably the ILO Conventions and recommendations. All BSCI member companies agree to implement the Code in their supply chains. By signing the BSCI Code of Conduct companies commit themselves to the social and environmental standards of the Code. The BSCI approach focuses on three key activity areas: 1) monitoring social compliance in the supply chain; 2) empowering BSCI members and suppliers through capacity building; and 3) engaging with stakeholders. Supplier companies, in addition, must ensure that the Code of Conduct[41] is also observed by subcontractors.

The driving force behind the BSCI is the Brussels-based Foreign Trade Association (FTA), which is a lobby organization for European commerce that focuses on foreign trade issues and is opposed to "any form of new protectionism" (FTA press release, 5 May, 2004[42]). The FTA is opposed to the creation of binding rules on CSR and argues that a link between trade agreements and sustainability could serve as a trade barrier.

German retailers play an important role in the BSCI. They are organized in the Foreign Trade Association of the German Retail Trade (Aussenhandels Vereinigung des Deutschen Einzelhandel, AVE). The BSCI largely copied the AVE program called Sector Model Social Responsibility, a CSR initiative supported by retailers such as Karstadt Quelle, Otto Group, Metro Group and others. While NGOs such as the German Clean Clothes Campaign have argued that the BSCI program is an improvement over individual company approaches, they have criticized the lack of trade union and NGO influence in the verification process of the BSCI program. The only role for NGOs and unions is potentially through the BSCI Advisory Council. Its role is to advise member firms but it has no direct influence.[43] The German Clean Clothes Campaign has therefore declined an invitation to join the advisory council of the BSCI.

The BSCI has enjoyed strong growth since 2003. Between November 2009 and November 2010 the BSCI grew from 250 members to more than 600.[44] An overview of the growth of BSCI members is presented in Figure 5.1.

Since 2003 BSCI membership has changed in three ways. First, country representation has broadened from firms mainly from Germany, the Benelux countries and Switzerland to include firms from countries across Europe such as Austria, Denmark, France, Slovenia and the UK.[45] Second, while the BSCI primarily included retail as well as textile and apparel firms, members now come from a greater variety of sectors such as food, electronics, household goods and furniture.[46] Third, SMEs today outnumber large enterprises (more than 85 percent of members are firms with less than €100 million in annual turnover according to personal correspondence with the BSCI in February 2012). In 2005 seven firms were SMEs and 30 firms were large firms. In contrast in two months alone (January and February 2011) 21 SMEs joined the BSCI while only four large firms joined.

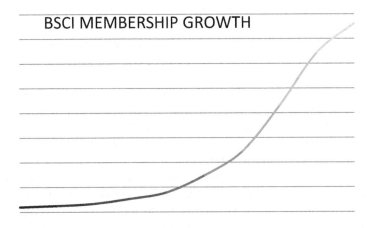

Figure 5.1   Increase in BSCI membership 2003–February 2012

Source: Author's own graph drawn from data in the BSCI Annual Reports 2004–2010 and www.bsci-intl. org/about-bsci/members

METHODOLOGY

The purpose of the research methodology was to gather information about three categories of actors and their positions on the BSCI: 1) rule-demanders, including business, civil society and governments; 2) rule providers in the form of large corporations that are members of the BSCI; and 3) SMEs as rule-takers faced with BSCI requirements. In order to obtain data about the positions of these different actors, a case-based approach was adopted,[47] which included the examination of public documents and newspaper articles. The case studies were explorative[48] and were not chosen to confirm or disconfirm a theory. The cases were used to answer research questions that addressed "how" and "why" size mattered as a determinant of key actor positions on the BSCI.

The positions of key actors were examined since the formation of the BSCI in 2003 and thus it was also possible to pinpoint how positions have evolved over time. A main purpose of the case studies was to be sensitive to temporal dynamics because regulation preferences can change over time. As Fransen and Burgoon have pointed out, "[T]he preference for private regulation from firms exercising power on others in the production chain (such as big retail firms) may, for instance, lead more dependent firms such as small brand firms to review their choices for regulation."[49] In addition, the investigation made it possible to track the size[50] of BSCI members over time. The BSCI allows SMEs to become members but it has a lower limit in terms of size. Companies with an annual turnover below €500,000 are not eligible for membership.

In order to determine the position of those who established the BSCI, publicly available documents were examined about the BSCI (academic papers, policy papers and internal documents). A number of interviews were also conducted with a BSCI representative, and publicly available documents were examined to obtain information about the position of key governments and civil society organizations.

Concerning the position of large retailers and buyers in the BSCI, two interviews were conducted with Danish retail companies that were named by several SMEs as major customers who demanded suppliers meet BSCI requirements. Their annual reports were consulted as well as the annual reports of some of the founding BSCI members (e.g., Otto Group).

Regarding SME positions, interviews were undertaken with 10 Danish SMEs that produced high-end (industrial designer) consumer goods. Five SMEs were selected that have been asked by their large buyers to meet BSCI requirements and five SMEs that have not met such requirements. The purpose was to determine if SMEs that did not follow BSCI requirements had found other alternatives or if they simply faced less pressure from buyers. All 10 firms were concerned about how to manage overseas suppliers in a way that satisfied large buyers and retailers.

Access to most of these SMEs was facilitated by the author's collaboration with several of these firms in a working group for SMEs on CSR in global supply chains. The author was approached initially by one of the SMEs to run a workshop with its license holders and suppliers about how to manage CSR in its global supply chain. This SME produced high-end designer goods and it was concerned that its license holders and suppliers might not be sufficiently aware of CSR requirements. At the same time the SME had begun to face BSCI requirements from large buyers and wanted to make sure that it could fulfill these demands. A working group of 10 SMEs in related sectors was subsequently established in order to explore how these emerging demands from large buyers could best be addressed. SMEs were included that sourced or produced in less developed countries (with the exception of two companies all companies operated in China). The group met four times and at each meeting members engaged in a frank discussion of challenges and opportunities for SMEs involved in managing CSR initiatives in global supply chains. In addition, individual interviews were held with each firm. All meetings and interviews were conducted in strict confidentiality with information only to be shared between participants. After each meeting the author wrote a summary of viewpoints (minutes), which was distributed to all members. The summary included a list of identified challenges in global supply chains, views on the BSCI and suggestions for alternative types of regulatory solutions in order to ensure responsible supply chain management. The distribution of the summary to participants served to enhance the robustness of key findings as it provided the opportunity to correct possible misunderstandings. Due to the sensitive business nature of the SMEs vis-à-vis their large buyers, the names and sectors of the SMEs could not be revealed to the buyers or to the BSCI.

The investigation only involved Danish SMEs. The author was not aware of other fora or venues in the EU that addressed the issue of SME regulation of social and environmental issues in global supply chains (the BSCI was consulted as well as the EU Commission's CSR Unit in Directorate General for Enterprise). Denmark was seen as a front-runner company for CSR[51] and thus Danish firms including SMEs were expected to have well-developed CSR policies. If Danish SMEs – which can be expected to be a sort of "best case" in terms of CSR – found it difficult to meet BSCI requirements then it is likely that SMEs in other countries will also have trouble meeting such demands. Table 5.1 provides an overview of the 10 Danish SMEs in the sample.

Table 5.1 Characteristics of sample companies

Company	Gross profit DKK (million)	Employees 2010	Ownership structure	Form of private CSR regulation
1	151,539	248	Private ownership	Self-assessment tool and NGO collaboration in the supplier country
2	72,003	66	Private ownership	Self-assessment tool
3	44,223	51	Private ownership	Self-assessment tool
4	n/a	7–8	Private ownership	Self-assessment tool
5	42,337	58	Private ownership	None
6	73,995	63	Private ownership	BSCI
7	29,184	60	Venture capital fund	BSCI
8	123,961	174	Foundation-owned	BSCI
9	220,400	181	Private ownership	BSCI
10	108,229	171	Private ownership	BSCI

Source: Green Database

Findings

RULE-DEMANDERS

Business demands

The Brussels-based Business for Social Compliance Initiative (BSCI) was launched in 2003 by the Foreign Trade Association (FTA) to establish a common platform for the various different European codes of conduct and monitoring systems and to lay the groundwork for a common European monitoring system for social compliance.[52] Founding firms included primarily large retail and textile and apparel firms from Germany, Switzerland and the Benelux countries. As they moved production overseas to less developed countries, these MNCs wanted to ensure that business was conducted in a responsible manner. Amongst the founding firms were companies such as the German Otto Group, which is the largest mail-order catalogue group in the world, and which has long been seen as a leader in driving the sustainability agenda in Germany (interview, BSCI 2009 and 2010). For example in 1996, Otto Group became the first mail-order company to sell carpets carrying the Rugmark seal, a labeling scheme launched by UNICEF to indicate that the product was not manufactured using child labor. One percent of the sale price went towards children's education in the country of manufacturing. In 2000, the company's commitment to social responsibility earned it the corporate ethics prize from the German Network of Economic Ethics.

Otto Group is a mail-order company with an extensive product portfolio and it relies to a large extent on imports from developing countries, particularly clothing and furniture. Otto Group has collaborated with the Council on Economic Priorities, a non-profit watch-group of corporate behaviour, to formulate a detailed set of measures for evaluating workplaces. The result was the international Social Accountability (SA) 8000 standard, modeled after the International Organization for Standardization (ISO) system. Other leading CSR companies were involved in this work, including, for example, Avon, Body Shop and J. Sainsbury (interview with BSCI, November, 2010).

The Charles Vögele Group, Switzerland's largest clothing retailer, is another example of a CSR leader that is a founding member of the BSCI. Already in 1996, Charles Vögele Group began issuing binding rules for its suppliers as part of its own Supplier Code of Conduct. Furthermore, since 2001 the Group has been a member of the New York-based human rights organization Social Accountability International (SAI), which publishes and administers the SA 8000 Social Standard.

Government demands

In 2003, when the BSCI was formed, EU governments did not focus on international CSR challenges but instead addressed domestic social and employment initiatives.[53] Only later did governments in CSR frontrunner countries such as Denmark and the UK adopt CSR action plans to enhance the competitiveness of firms.[54] Initiatives include endorsement of CSR (e.g., by creating a ministerial portfolio in the area), facilitation, whether by subsidies and tax expenditures (e.g., to companies or business associations), or partnerships by encouraging and joining with business and other actors in order to deliver public goods. Government initiatives can also mandate CSR, for example in the form of mandatory non-financial reporting. However, governments did not play a role in the creation of the BSCI.

Societal demands

Before the establishment of the BSCI, FTA members were approached by NGOs and consumer groups about creating a multi-stakeholder initiative rather than a business initiative. Several consumer groups promoted the British Ethical Trading Initiative. However, the FTA wanted a business-only initiative. Some of the FTA members had been criticized in anti-sweatshop campaigns, including Metro Group and Karstadt Quelle, and these members felt therefore that something had to be done to find solutions to social and environmental problems in the supply chain. However, companies hesitated to engage with NGOs that had recently criticized them (interview with BSCI, 2009). At the same time the EU had initiated discussions about how to create a CSR policy at the EU level that addressed international competitiveness issues.[55] By creating its own platform for compliance, the BSCI could simultaneously resist pressure from above by the EU and pressure from below by civil society groups. According to Merk and Zeldenrust, the FTA launched the BSCI "to establish a common platform for the various different European codes of conduct and monitoring systems and to lay the groundwork for a common European monitoring system for social compliance".[56]

RULE-PROVIDERS

A key driver for the establishment of the BSCI was that the EU Commission as part of the Doha Trade Round negotiations was considering the inclusion of sustainable development requirements (social clauses) in trade agreements. Furthermore, the European Commission promoted a European CSR Framework. MNCs wanted to avoid binding rules on CSR, as did the Foreign Trade Association of Brussels. The FTA's position was that "the broad spectrum of social issues connected with business cannot be controlled by legislation".[57] In short, a key driver for why MNCs and the FTA wanted to establish the BSCI was that they sought to preempt EU-level initiatives regarding CSR.

The founding members of the BSCI also wished to provide a solution to the "governance gaps" in their international supply chains in order to avoid damage to their brand if suppliers were found to be violating basic social and environmental rights (interview with BSCI, November 2010). However, while the founding members were CSR leaders, some of the recent large members have less experience with CSR (they are CSR followers rather than leaders). For example, the two large Danish retail buyers that were interviewed both operate in the low-price segment, and prior to joining the BSCI these companies did not have a history of working with social initiatives in global supply chains, in contrast to Otto Group and Charles Vögele Group. The new members ask their suppliers to meet BSCI requirements but do not work with them to ensure compliance. In contrast, Otto Group offers some limited assistance to SME suppliers to make sure that BSCI requirements are met (interview with BSCI, November 2011). According to the purchasing manager in one of the Danish retail chains, "at this current time SMEs are losing out. As buyers we are very demanding – all our suppliers irrespective of size must meet the BSCI requirements and preferably be SA 8000 certified. It is our suppliers' responsibility to ensure that they do so. It is in everybody's interest – including SMEs – that standards are raised overall" (personal interview by author, February 2011).

Most suppliers do not engage in capacity building with SMEs, nor do they pay a price premium for an SA 8000 certification. The Danish purchasing manager explains: "This is the way capitalism works. If companies want us to buy from them, then they must meet our requirements" (personal interview by author, March 2011). These large firms have increasingly shifted the responsibility for meeting BSCI requirements onto their suppliers. In this way large buyers expect to be "off the hook" if their suppliers are found to be violating basic labor rights.

This shift in responsibility appears to be characteristic of those MNCs that joined the BSCI late and that are more likely to be CSR followers rather than CSR leaders. The BSCI founders included several CSR leaders who viewed SME suppliers as an element of their own sphere of influence. While the CSR leaders see the BSCI as a government substitution strategy, followers are more likely to regard the BSCI as a low-cost risk management strategy. Several of the followers have joined the BSCI after facing media exposure for having a poor CSR performance. Examples include the low-end retailer JYSK and the supermarket chain Dansk Supermarked. Both were negatively portrayed in a critical television program aired on Danish television on 19 June, 2006.[58] The program heavily criticized JYSK and Dansk Supermarked for using Indian suppliers where working conditions were abysmal (e.g., they used child labor) and environmental working conditions were also very bad (e.g., workers were inhaling dangerous fumes). This program led to substantial public criticism of JYSK and Dansk Supermarked. Subsequently both companies announced that they would join the BSCI. As a result both companies now require that all their suppliers must meet BSCI requirements. Furthermore, all suppliers must accept regular visits from a third party accredited auditor.

RULE-TAKERS

The rule-takers are small companies with gross profits ranging from DKK 29 million to DKK 220 million[59] while the number of employees ranges from 7 to 248. Two companies are owned by capital funds, one is owned by a foundation, but most are privately owned with typically one or two owners. In sum, these are small companies and there is no clear pattern linking ownership structure to the choice of regulatory scheme. All 10 SMEs reported in interviews that social and environmental supply chain issues are becoming increasingly important elements of their competitive performance. However, the five firms that do not follow BSCI guidelines have only very limited production in less developed countries, although they expect that in the near future they will start outsourcing more production to China or India in order to save labor costs. These five firms also have a fairly narrow product range aimed at the high end of the market, which is less sensitive to price pressures. One SME collaborates with an NGO that is responsible for auditing suppliers in less developed countries, and this collaboration is quite successful (interview with SME, March 2011). This SME produces a quite limited range of high-price products and thus has fewer suppliers to manage. It can pay suppliers well and is therefore less sensitive to price pressures from large discount retail chains. Four SMEs have adopted a supplier self-assessment tool that overlaps with BSCI principles. They would like to be able to supply to large retail chains in Denmark and are therefore currently investigating if they should join the BSCI. One of these SMEs faces demands from public sector customers in Norway to document that it manages key social and environmental issues in its supply chain. So far it has managed to convince public sector customers that its self-assessment tool is adequate but is concerned that in the future customers will demand that it joins the BSCI or a similar international initiative. One SME has not adopted any initiatives in order to manage CSR issues in global supply chains.

Two SMEs reported that they send a local representative to visit their most important suppliers on a regular basis and also sometimes use external auditors. The SMEs also show up unannounced from time to time at supplier factory sites. They report that they always detect some violations, such as failure to wear protective clothing, a broken ventilation system, child labor or a roof that has fallen down. Local suppliers have their own suppliers as well and because these change often, it is difficult to ensure that CSR requirements are met.

The five firms that face BSCI requirements generally have a broader product portfolio and supply a relatively low end of the market where price is more important. These SMEs all face demands from buyers in large retail chains to pay for independent certification of their supplier companies in less developed countries. Several suppliers also reported that they have been asked to provide the names of their suppliers abroad. All SMEs stated that they would not reveal the names of their suppliers in less developed countries because they feared that their MNC customers would "side-track" them by approaching the suppliers directly.

Contractual requirements for SMEs regarding responsible supply chain management represent a new trend. For example, in a 2006 study of Danish SMEs and buyer requirements for CSR initiatives, at least one in three of the SMEs surveyed was subject to buyer requirements concerning environmental protection, health and safety, labor rights, human rights and corruption.[60] However, a majority of buyer requirements were neither contractual nor subject to verification.

The five SMEs that face BSCI requirements point out that their large customers are not willing to pay more for products or services even if SMEs undertake more costly initiatives such as increased external verification or unannounced inspections of supplier plants. The five SMEs find that they have to allocate substantial labor resources in order to meet BSCI requirements and this is time consuming. The first steps, such as screening the supply chain, raise many questions about how to proceed and they would like the BSCI to offer some assistance in order to coordinate initiatives with auditing companies and eventually with consultants and trainers. SMEs would also like the BSCI to develop a priority matrix to help them determine which suppliers to focus on first (distinguishing for example between products, countries and other key issues). They also find that a help desk function in major sourcing markets could be helpful in order to provide country-specific information and support.

Summing up, all 10 SMES report that they find it difficult to manage suppliers in developing countries owing to their limited resources, and express concern that it is impossible to control all suppliers.

Discussion and Conclusion

THEORETICAL IMPLICATIONS

The theoretical literature on CSR in SMEs focuses on domestic not international initiatives, while the theoretical literature on CSR in global supply chains focuses on MNCs not SMEs. This chapter seeks to remedy the gap in the literature by exploring how SMEs engage in private regulation of labor standards in global supply chains and in particular how they manage demands from large buyers. The case studies clearly show that a private solution such as the BSCI that is dominated by large firms does not work from the perspective of SMEs. While some of the founders of the BSCI, such as the Otto Group, have a long history of working with CSR issues and see the BSCI as a way to deal with the inadequate labor and environmental regulatory environment in the countries they source from or operate in, some of the more recent BSCI members are CSR followers not leaders. In contrast to companies such as the Otto Group, they have had less experience with CSR and view the BSCI as a low-cost risk management strategy. More and more large firms demand that SMEs join the BSCI. This way – to put it bluntly – large firms force their SME suppliers to bear the cost of living up to MNC supply chain requirements.

This development threatens to erode the societal benefits of private regulation as large buyers shift the burden of CSR demands onto SMEs, who are not able to meet these requirements on their own. A key finding is that both SMEs and the BSCI reported that large buyers need to be involved in helping SMEs meet buyer demands in order for long-lasting social change to take place. In short, buyers must collaborate with SME suppliers and assist them in meeting private regulatory demands in global supply chains. This conclusion is in line with ongoing work by Richard Locke and his research team at MIT.[61] Locke and his collaborators found that supplier codes of conduct, while important, do not offer a permanent solution. In fact, suppliers were found to be drifting in and out of compliance with code of conduct requirements from Nike, HP, Coca Cola, etc. One of Locke's key findings was that for sustained social improvements to take place, large buyers need to collaborate with their suppliers. In short, buyers need to take responsibility for the demands they impose on their suppliers rather than leave suppliers to work out solutions on their own.

PRACTICAL IMPLICATIONS

Focusing on SMEs and the BSCI, I now address some practical implications of these findings. First, what can SMEs do to improve their competitive situation when they operate in less developed countries? One possible solution is for SMEs to select suppliers that are already supplying other western MNCs and therefore have some experience in meeting such MNC demands. Furthermore, SMEs may benefit from engaging in networks with other SMEs where information about good suppliers can be shared (a challenge for SMEs is that such a strategy requires a high level of trust). SMEs can also sometimes share auditing costs. A second possibility is that SMEs lobby for mandatory regulation to ensure that large western firms assist SMEs in meeting BSCI requirements. For example, public procurement requirements could reward large firms that collaborate with SME suppliers to enhance CSR performance rather than simply impose demands on SMEs.

Second, what can the BSCI do to relieve organizational strain caused by: 1) a large influx of SMEs; 2) different views on how to manage CSR requirements in leading firms and follower firms; 3) the likely short-term nature of pushing the CSR responsibility onto SMEs; and 4) competition from alternative regulatory schemes?

It is difficult to achieve organizational coherence after receiving a huge increase in SME membership in the last 2–3 years (interview with BSCI, November 2010). While on the one hand it is a sign of success that membership is expanding, on the other hand it is problematic to have many members who are dissatisfied with the arrangement (interview with BSCI, November 2010). In Scandinavia SME membership of the BSCI has also grown. In Denmark 43 members (84 percent) are SMEs while 8 members (16 percent) are large firms. However, SMEs do not have a real choice whether to join or not. Most SMEs join because it is a requirement from large buyers and not because they see the BSCI as attractive.

The influx of low-end retailers with less CSR experience than the founding members creates tension between those members potentially interested in working with SMEs about how to meet BSCI requirements and those new members who leave the responsibility to the SMEs themselves.

Pushing CSR responsibility onto SMEs is not likely to be a viable solution in the longer term. A television image of a large buyer's extensive headquarters contrasted with an unassuming small western supplier factory or office could quickly illustrate to viewers the discrepancy in resources between a large buyer and a small supplier. The BSCI then risks being exposed as hypocritical.

Finally, business initiatives such as the BSCI that leave regulation to business actors can be criticized for leaving the fox to guard the henhouse, and the BSCI faces possible competition from multi-stakeholder initiatives. Multi-stakeholder initiatives such as the Ethical Trading Initiative (ETI) that award regulatory roles to societal groups build a watchdog and an empowerment element into the regulatory system[62] (though some argue that the ETI has led to improvements in outcome standards but little change in process rights for workers[63]). In terms of the stringency of private labor regulation, the ETI is stricter than the BSCI as it includes more control mechanisms.[64] Multi-stakeholder initiatives in the CSR field are believed to have the moral high ground over business-governed organizations and are expected to yield more positive results in the supply chain. According to the Clean Clothes Campaign, the BSCI represents an incomplete, minimalist model for compliance with labor standards that rely on weak auditing and is not accountable to the public.[65] In contrast to the BSCI, the ETI has not experienced a massive influx of SME members in recent years. For example, the Ethical Trading Initiative in the UK has nearly 60 members and most of them are large firms.[66]

The BSCI is therefore very interested in finding new ways to develop partnerships between front-runner MNCs and SME suppliers. So far the BSCI has developed two new initiatives: 1) A large retailer set up a program where a neutral third party (a well-known accountancy firm) certified that suppliers meet BSCI requirements but without revealing the identity of suppliers to large buyers. The idea was to ensure that retail customers could be certain that the accountancy firm had certified suppliers; however, the certification scheme did not work because of cooperation problems; 2) The BSCI also set up a supplier database with information about individual suppliers without disclosing this information to individual buyers. However, the cost involved in managing this project has been excessive.

Conclusion

A realistic assessment is needed about what global supplier codes of conduct can achieve and in particular how SMEs are affected. CSR in general[67] and supplier code of conducts in particular are seen as a magic wand by many consumers, governments, institutional investors and the media. For example, the Danish government declares that "companies must organize supply chain management based on an assessment of the risk of violations of basic rights and principles in the supply chain and target activities and purchases in areas where such actions will have the greatest impact. The companies will pose demands and establish a dialogue with suppliers about ongoing improvements including if necessary through monitoring of select suppliers' activities, cooperation, capacity building and / or education".[68] However, the Danish government's recommendation ignores the fact that large retail chains do not want to prioritize challenges but want suppliers to meet *all* BSCI requirements. This discrepancy needs to be addressed. Also, we should be careful in assuming that the presence of a supplier code of conduct equals a commitment to CSR.[69] Finally, codes do not always result in improvements of corporate social and environmental performance.[70] The challenges faced by SMEs in Denmark – a country known as a CSR leader – indicate that a frank discussion is needed concerning the limits of SMEs in managing labor standards in global supply chains and the possibility for cooperation between buyers and their SME suppliers and how to develop solutions that are sustainable in the long term.

There is no doubt that demands are increasing for social and environmental programs in global supply chains. Recently more and more governments have adopted non-financial reporting requirements focusing on CSR.[71] These demands have to be met by large firms, but as they struggle to meet the new requirements they also increasingly ask their SME suppliers to follow suit. Furthermore, public procurement in Denmark and in a growing number of countries also requires that suppliers, including SMEs, meet a range of social and environmental demands (often BSCI requirements or similar requirements). In order for SMEs to stay internationally competitive they therefore need to find ways to meet these new demands – cooperation with large buyers seems a promising way to go.

Notes

1   Bondy, K., Matten, D. & Moon, J. (2004), "The Adoption of Voluntary Codes of Conduct in MNCs: A Three Country Comparative Study", *Business and Society Review*, Vol. 109, No. 4, pp. 449–477; Bondy, K., Matten, D. & Moon, J. (2008), "MNC Codes of Conduct: Governance Tools for CSR?" *Corporate Governance: An International Review*, Vol. 16, No. 4, pp. 294–311; Locke, R. & Romis, M. (2010), "The Promise and Perils of Private Voluntary Regulation: Labor Standards and Work Organizations in Two Mexican Factories", *Review of International Political Economy*, Vol. 17, No. 1, pp. 45–74; Locke, R., Amengual, M. & Mangla, A. (2009), "Virtue out of Necessity? Compliance, Commitment and the Improvement of Labor Conditions in Global Supply Chains", *Politics and Society*, Vol. 37, No. 3, pp. 319–351; Locke, R., Qin, F. & Brause, A. (2007), "Does Monitoring Improve Labor Standards? Lessons from Nike", *Industrial and Labor Relations Review*, Vol. 61, No. 1, pp. 3–27.

2   Levy, D.L. & Kaplan, R. (2008), "Corporate Social Responsibility and Theories of Global Governance: Strategic Contestation in Global Issue Arenas". In A. Crane, A. McWilliams, D.

Matten & J. Moon (eds.), *Oxford Handbook of Corporate Social Responsibility*, Oxford University Press, Oxford.

3   The European Commission defines CSR as "the responsibility of enterprises for their impacts on society". European Commission (2011a), accessed 5 November, 2011 at http://ec.europa.eu/enterprise/policies/sustainable-business/corporate-social-responsibility/index_en.htm.

4   Vogel, D. (2008), "Private Global Business Regulation", *Annual Review of Political Science*, Vol. 11, pp. 261–282; Berger, S. (2000), "Globalization and Politics", *Annual Review of Political Science*, Vol. 3, pp. 43–62; Knudsen, J.S. (2011), "Company Delistings from the UN Global Compact: Limited Business Demand or Domestic Governance Failure?" *Journal of Business Ethics*, Vol. 103, No. 3, pp. 331–349. DOI: 10.1007/s10551-011-0875-0.

5   Andersen, M. & Skjoett-Larsen, T. (2009), "Corporate Social Responsibility in Global Supply Chains", *Supply Chain Management: An International Journal*, Vol. 14, No. 2, pp. 75–86; Ciliberti, F., Pontrandolfo P. & Scozzi, B. (2008), "Investigating Corporate Social Responsibility in Supply Chains: An SME Perspective", *Journal of Cleaner Production*, Vol. 16, pp. 1579–1588; Tencati, A., Angeloantonio, R. & Quaglia, V. (2007), "Unintended Consequences of CSR: Protectionism and Collateral Damage in Global Supply Chains: The Case of Vietnam", *Corporate Governance*, Vol. 8, No. 4, pp. 518–531.

6   Moore, G. & Spence, L.J. (2006), "Responsibility and Small Business", *Journal of Business Ethics*, Vol. 67, No. 3, pp. 219–226.

7   Spence, L. (2007), "CSR and Small Business in a European Policy Context: The Five 'C's of CSR and Small Business Research Agenda 2007", *Business and Society Review*, Vol. 112, No. 4, pp. 533–552, p. 543.

8   Petersen, T., Kirkelund, O., Knudsen, J.S., Andersen, R.K. & Pyndt, J. (2006), *Globalisering Starter i Danmark* (Globalization Starts in Denmark), Copenhagen Business School Press, Copenhagen.

9   Jørgensen, A. & Knudsen, J.S. (2006), "Sustainable Competitiveness in Global Value Chains. How Do Small Danish Firms Behave?", *Corporate Governance. The International Journal of Business in Society*, special issue, summer, pp. 449–462.

10   Raynard, P. & Forstater, M. (2002), Corporate Social Responsibility: Implications for Small and Medium Enterprises in Developing Countries. UNIDO's Small and Medium Enterprises Branch and the World Summit on Sustainable Development; Seuring, S., Sarkis, J., Müller, M. & Rao, P. (2008), "Sustainability and Supply Chain Management An Introduction to the Special Issue", *Journal of Cleaner Production*, Vol. 16, pp. 1545–1551.

11   Many MNCs also find that they do not have enough leverage to change supplier practices, especially when they only purchase a small share of a factory's overall production. However, MNCs have more resources than SMEs to follow up with suppliers, to influence local political actors and to obtain information and advice.

12   Jeppesen, S. & Thorsen, S. (2010), *Changing Course: A Study into Responsible Supply Chain Management*. Authored by GLOBAL CSR and Copenhagen Business School for the Danish Ministry of Foreign Affairs; Mayer, F. & Gereffi, G. (2010), "Regulation and Economic Globalization: Prospects and Limits of Private Governance", *Business and Politics*, Vol. 12, No. 3, Article 11.

13   European Commission (2011b), *Small Business Portal,* accessed 24 June, 2011 at http://ec.europa.eu/small-business/index_en.htm.

14   Business for Social Compliance Initiative, Frequently Asked Questions from Producers, accessed 29 February, 2012 at www.bsci-intl.org/.

15   Büthe, T. (2010), "Private Regulation in the Global Economy: A (P)Review", *Business and Politics*, Vol. 12, No. 3, Article 1.

16   Mayer & Gereffi, *op. cit.*; Locke, Amengual & Mangla, *op. cit.*; Locke, Qin & Brause, *op. cit.*; O'Rourke, D. (1997), *Smoke from a Hired Gun: A Critique of Nike's Labor and Environmental Auditing in Vietnam as Performed by Ernst and Young*, report published by the Transnational Resource and Action Center, San Francisco, CA, 10 November, 1997, accessed 24 April, 2011 at http://nature.berkeley.edu/orourke/PDF/smoke.pdf.

17   Sweeney, L. (2007), "Corporate Social Responsibility in Ireland: Barriers and Opportunities Experienced by SMEs when Undertaking CSR", *Corporate Governance*, Vol. 7, No. 4, pp. 516–523.

18   Murillo, D. & Lozano, J. (2006), "SMEs and CSR: An Approach to CSR in their Own Words", *Journal of Business Ethics*, Vol. 67, No. 3, pp. 227–240.

19   Perrini F. (2006), "SMEs and CSR Theory: Evidence and Implications from an Italian Perspective", *Journal of Business Ethics*, Vol. 67, No. 3, pp. 305–316.

20   Williamson, D., Lynch-Wood, G. & Ramsay, J. (2006), "Drivers of Environmental Behavior in Manufacturing SMEs and the Implications for CSR", *Journal of Business Ethics*, Vol. 67, pp. 317–330.

21   Büthe, *op. cit.*

22   Büthe, *op. cit.*, p. 8.

23   Büthe, *op. cit.*, p. 8.

24   Locke & Romis, *op. cit.*; Locke, Amengual & Mangla, *op. cit.*; Locke, Qin & Brause, *op. cit.*

25   Coase, R.H. (1937), "The Nature of the Firm", *Economica*, Vol. 4, No. 16, pp. 386–405; Williamson, O. (1985), *The Economic Institutions of Capitalism: Firms, Markets, Relational Contracting*, The Free Press, New York.

26   Moon, J, Kang, N. & Gond, P. (2005), "Corporate Responsibility and Government". In D. Coen (ed.), *The Oxford Handbook of Business and Government*, Oxford University Press, Oxford; Steurer, R. (2010), "The Role of Governments in Corporate Social Responsibility: Characterising Public Policies on CSR in Europe", *Policy Sciences*, Vol. 43, No. 1, pp. 49–72.

27   Mayer & Gereffi, *op. cit.*

28   Aguielera, R.V., Rupp, D.E., Williams, C.A. & Ganapathi, J. (2007), "Putting the 'S' Back in Corporate Social Responsibility: A Multi-Level Theory of Social Change in Organizations", *Academy of Management Review*, Vol. 32, No. 3, pp. 836–863; Brown, D., Roemer-Mahler, A. & Vetterlein A. (2010), "Theorising Transnational Corporations as Social Actors: An Analysis of Corporate Motivations", *Business and Politics*, Vol. 12, No. 1, DOI:10.2202/1469–3569.1302. Berkeley Electronic Press; Spar, D. & LaMure, L. (2003), "The Power of Activism: Assessing the Impact of NGOs on Global Business", *California Management Review*, Vol. 45, No. 3, pp. 78–110.

29   Keohane, R.O. (1984), *After Hegemony: Cooperation and Discord in the World Political Economy*, Princeton University Press, Princeton.

30   Büthe, *op. cit.*, p. 12.

31   Vogel, *op. cit.*

32   Jackson, G. & Apostolakou, A. (2010), "Corporate Social Responsibility in Western Europe: An Institutional Mirror or Substitute?" *Journal of Business Ethics*, Vol. 94, pp. 371–394; Matten, D. & Moon, J. (2008), "'Implicit' and 'Explicit' CSR: A Conceptual Framework for a Comparative Understanding of Corporate Social Responsibility", *Academy of Management Review*, Vol. 33, No. 2, pp. 404–424.

33   Büthe, *op. cit.*, p. 13.

34   Tencati, Angeloantonio & Quaglia, *op. cit.*

35   Baden, D.A., Harwood I.A. & Woodward D.G. (2009), "The Effect of Buyer Pressure on Suppliers in SMEs to Demonstrate CSR Practices: An Added Incentive or Counterproductive?", *European Management Journal*, Vol. 27, pp. 429–441.

36   Perrini, F., Russo, A. & Tencati, A. (2007), "CSR Strategies of SMEs and Large Firms. Evidence from Italy", *Journal of Business Ethics*, Vol. 74, pp. 285–300.

37   Egels-Zandén, N. & Wahlqvist, E. (2007), "Post-Partnership Strategies for Defining Corporate Responsibility: The Business for Social Compliance Initiative", *Journal of Business Ethics*, Vol. 70, No. 2, pp. 175–189.

38   Merk, J. & Zeldenrust, I. (2005), The Business Social Compliance Initiative (BSCI), A Critical Perspective. Clean Clothes Campaign, 1 June.

39   Business for Social Compliance Initiative, Annual Report 2009, accessed 5 October, 2011 at www.bsci-intl.org/.

40   Business for Social Compliance Initiative's contribution to the European Multistakeholder Forum on CSR, 29–30 November, 2010, Brussels, accessed 26 June, 2011 at http://ec.europa.eu/enterprise/policies/sustainable-business/files/.../bsci_en.pdf.

41   The goals of the BSCI Code of Conduct include: 1) respect for the freedom of association and the right to collective bargaining. In situations where the right to freedom of association and collective bargaining is restricted under law, the company shall allow workers to freely elect their own representatives; 2) prohibition of discrimination; 3) prohibition of child labor; 4) payment of legal minimum and/or industry standard wages; 5) a limit to working hours; 6) no forced labor and disciplinary measures; 7) workplace health and safety; 8) respect for the environment; 9) there is a policy for social accountability; and 10) there is an anti-bribery and anti-corruption policy (Business for Social Compliance Initiative Code of Conduct, accessed 29 February, 2012 at www.bsci-intl.org/our-work/bsci-code-conduct).

42   Merk & Zeldenrust, *op. cit.*, footnote 2.

43   Egels-Zandén and Wahlqvist, *op. cit.*

44   Business for Social Compliance Initiative, 2010, *op. cit.*

45   Business for Social Compliance Initiative, Annual Report 2008, accessed 7 November, 2011 at www.bsci-intl.org/.

46   *Ibid.* p. 4.

47   Eisenhardt, K.M. (1989), "Building Theories from Case Study Research", *Academy of Management Review*, Vol. 12, No. 4, pp. 532–550; Yin, R.K. (2003), *Case Study Research: Design and Methods*, *3rd edition*, Sage Publications, Thousand Oaks, CA.

48   Yin, *op. cit.;* Eisenhardt, K.M. & Graebner, M.E. (2007), "Theory Building from Cases: Opportunities and Challenges", *Academy of Management Journal*, Vol. 50, No. 1, pp. 25–32.

49   Fransen, L. & Burgoon, B. (2012), "A Market for Worker Rights: Explaining Business Support for International Private Labour Regulation", *Review of International Political Economy*, Vol. 19, No. 2, pp. 236–266, p. 240.

50   Firms are classified as SMEs that have an annual turnover of less than EUR 50 million (see also http://ec.europa.eu/small-business/policy-statistics/facts/index_en.htm).

51   Gjølberg, M. (2009), "The Origin of Corporate Social Responsibility: Global Forces or National Legacies?" *Socio-Economic Review*, Vol. 7, pp. 605–637.

52   Business for Social Compliance Initiative, Frequently Asked Questions from Suppliers, accessed 7 November, 2011 at www.bsci-intl.org/.

53   Bertelsmann Stiftung (2007), *CSR Navigator: Public Policies in Africa, the Americas, Asia and Europe*, accessed 10 February, 2011 at www.bertelsmann-stiftung.de/cps/rde/xchg/bst; Brown,

D. & Knudsen, J.S. (2011), "The Emerging Spread of CSR Initiatives in Multinational Firms: Do National Institutions and Government Policies Matter?" Paper presented at the SASE Conference in Madrid 23–25 June; Knopf, J., Kahlenborn, W., Hajduk, T. & Weiss, D. (2011), Final Draft CSR Compendium: Public Policies in the European Union, Adelphi, Brussels.

54 Brown & Knudsen, *op. cit.*

55 Doh, J.P. & Guay, T.R. (2006), "Corporate Social Responsibility, Public Policy, and NGO Activism in Europe and the United States: An Institutional-Stakeholder Perspective", *Journal of Management Studies*, Vol. 43, pp. 47–73.

56 Merk & Zeldenrust, *op. cit.*, p. 7.

57 Merk & Zeldenrust, *op. cit.*, p. 8.

58 "A Killer Bargain" produced by Tom Heineman, accessed 4 April, 2011 at www.youtube.com/watch?v=LZ0ylz1mguY.

59 1 Euro is worth approximately 7.5 Danish kroner (DKK).

60 Jørgensen & Knudsen, *op. cit.*

61 Locke & Romis, *op. cit.*; Locke, Amengual & Mangla, *op. cit.*

62 Fransen & Burgoon, *op. cit.*

63 Barrientos, S. & Smith, S. (2007), "Do Workers Benefit from Ethical Trade? Assessing Codes of Labour Practice in Global Production Systems", *Third World Quarterly*, Vol. 28, No. 4, pp. 713–729.

64 Fransen & Burgoon, *op. cit.*, Figure 5.1.

65 Clean Clothes Campaign, 24 November, 2005.

66 UK Ethical Trading Initiative (ETI), accessed 26 July, 2012 at www.ethicaltrade.org/.

67 Porter, M. & Kramer, M. (2002), "The Competitive Advantage of Corporate Philanthropy", *Harvard Business Review*, Vol. 80, No. 12, pp. 56–68; Porter, M. & Kramer, M. (2006), "Strategy and Society. The Link between Competitive Advantage and Corporate Social Responsibility", *Harvard Business Review*, Vol. 84, No. 12, pp. 78–92; Porter, M. & Kramer, M. (2011), "Creating Shared Value. How to Reinvent Capitalism—and Unleash a Wave of Innovation and Growth", *Harvard Business Review*, January–February, pp. 63–77.

68 www.raadetforsamfundsansvar.dk/sw63329.asp accessed 4 April, 2011, author's translation.

69 Bondy, Matten & Moon, 2008, *op. cit.*

70 Locke & Romis, *op. cit.*

71 Moon, J., Slager, R., Brunn, C., Hardi, P. & Knudsen, J.S. (2012), Analysis of the National and EU Policies Supporting Corporate Social Responsibility and Impact. Working Paper 2. Deliverable to "IMPACT Project" funded by the Directorate General for Research, European Commission (Framework 7 Program), accessed 27 July, 2012 at http://csr-impact.eu/documents/documents-detail.html?documentid=5.

6 Supply Chain Themes in Corporate Social Responsibility Reports*

WENDY L. TATE,† JON F. KIRCHOFF,‡ AND LISA M. ELLRAM§

Keywords

Centering resonance analysis, content analysis, corporate social responsibility reports, Crawdad software, global, operations, supply chain, sustainability, sustainable, supply chain management.

Introduction

Over the last several decades, consumers, shareholders, government regulatory agencies and other stakeholders have become increasingly aware of the impact world-wide industrial activity and global supply chains have on the natural environment and society.[1] As a result, firms are under pressure from stakeholders to incorporate social, environmental and economic responsibility considerations into their global supply chain management operations and strategies. Many companies have responded to stakeholder expectations by publishing annual corporate social responsibility (CSR) reports.[2] This chapter discusses issues related to CSR reports and how the information they contain can be an insightful source of social, environmental and economic actions, goals and performance outcomes of global firms' supply chain management functions.

CSR reports serve as a rich source of secondary data to understand better the company's intentions, strategies and activities, as well as the results of corporate social and environmental responsibility at supply chain level.[3] These reports often serve as a barometer of an organization's attitudes toward social and environmental responsibility,

* Parts of this chapter are adapted from the article, Tate, W.L., Ellram, L.M. & Kirchoff, J.F. (2010), "Corporate Social Responsibility Reports: A Thematic Analysis Related to Supply Chain Management", *Journal of Supply Chain Management*, Vol. 46, No. 1, pp. 19–44. first published by Wiley-Blackwell on behalf of the Institute for Supply Management. © 2011 Institute for Supply Management™. All rights reserved.

† Associate Professor Wendy L. Tate, College of Business Administration, University of Tennessee, 303 Stokely Management Center, Knoxville, TN. 37996. U.S.A. E-mail: wendy.tate@utk.edu. Telephone: +1 8659741648.

‡ Assistant Professor Jon F. Kirchoff, College of Business, East Carolina University, 3103 Bate Building, Greenville, NC. 27858. U.S.A. E-mail: kirchoffj@ecu.edu. Telephone: +1 2527374569.

§ Professor Lisa M. Ellram, Farmer School of Business, Miami University, Farmer Building, Room 2003, Miami, OH. 45056. U.S.A. E-mail: ellramlm@muohio.edu. Telephone: +1 5135299918.

current and planned sustainability activities, and their level of integration in the organization's economic strategic plans in supply chain management (SCM).

Nearly 60% of the top 200 global companies reported having CSR reports on their corporate websites and the use of CSR reports is growing among concerned stakeholders.[4] Investors, insurers and underwriters use the reports to gather information about socially and environmentally responsible business investments and possible risks such as fines for noncompliance. Safety information, such as the number of days lost due to injury, is looked at carefully by regulatory and non-governmental organizations (NGOs) to determine if firms are taking care of their own labor force. Consumers, government and NGOs use the information contained in the CSR reports to gauge involvement in and commitment to social and environmental issues by comparing the reports among firms and industries.

Despite interest from both academics and practitioners, there is limited research devoted to understanding how companies communicate supply chain social and environmental actions and strategies through CSR reports, how companies position CSR reports, and what the reports indicate about the companies publishing them. This chapter seeks to fill the void in the literature by addressing three different supply chain-related issues. First, by utilizing secondary data from the CSR reports, it seeks to provide insight into how companies are addressing social and environmental issues. Second, it looks at the interface between the issues companies emphasize in their CSR reports and their traditional SCM functions and strategies. Finally, it introduces Crawdad's content analysis techniques to the supply chain management literature.

This chapter begins with a discussion of the current literature streams related to CSR reporting, followed by a detailed description of the research methodology, Crawdad and centering resonance analysis (CRA). The research's results and implications are then explored. Finally, limitations and future research opportunities are identified.

CSR Reporting

Companies have a wide range of motivations for publishing information about corporate social and environmental responsibility. These include company-specific reasons such as corporate strategies and image, as well as regulation and societal aspects such as credibility and reputation.[5] The following streams of literature help explain what motivates companies to engage in socially and environmentally responsible activities, and include why and how these activities are reported by the organization to the public.

CORPORATE STRATEGIES

The development of corporate social and environmental strategies provides evidence of how businesses view their responsibilities to society, in relation to the overall strategies and goals of the firm; firms that engage in socially responsible behavior believe positive financial gains are possible in the process.[6] Specifically, firms that integrate corporate social and environmental strategies with economic strategies may gain economic benefits through cost savings from resource reduction and efficiency and through revenue generation from improved stakeholder relations and brand image.[7] Researchers predict that companies will realize the potential benefits of adopting social and environmental strategies that are more proactive, and deliberately move away from ones that are more reactive.[8]

Externally, stakeholders influence the development and expansion of corporate social and environmental strategies.[9] Consumers and shareholders insist the strategies are based on measurable financial goals, including cost reductions, increased market share, higher quality, improved manufacturing performance and continuous innovation.[10] Members of the upstream supply chain provide input, technology and information to customers to help construct and support corporate responsibility strategies.[11] Government also plays an important role in the development of corporate social and environmental strategies. The motivation of government regulation in inducing corporate social and environmental action has been widely recognized.[12] Furthermore, an organization's ability and willingness to work with government regulators can help create innovative strategies that potentially benefit the firm.[13]

CORPORATE IMAGE

Pressure from internal actors and external stakeholders strongly influences companies to maintain a positive, socially responsible image.[14] Control is often done through communication, described[15] as "deliberate attempts to influence public impression." Companies are aware of the positive link between an image of strong social responsibility and consumer preferences.[16] Research indicates that firms issue CSR reports as a marketing tool to enhance brand image among stakeholders.[17] Firms seek and obtain legitimacy from stakeholders by proactively discussing social and environmental responsibility and performance.[18] Legitimacy theory suggests companies publish CSR reports to benefit from an improved corporate image among stakeholders and other concerned parties.[19] While companies strive to project a positive image to stakeholders,[20] reputation is the stakeholders' actual view of the firm.[21] Thus, companies seek to enhance image in order to create a positive corporate reputation in the areas of social responsibility and contributions to social welfare. Improvements in social and environmental reputation have been correlated to higher long-term organizational performance, which suggests companies focus on reputation as a part of their overall corporate objectives and strategies.[22]

CORPORATE SOCIAL RESPONSIBILITY REPORTS

To make stakeholders aware of social and environmental activities and strategies, companies are increasingly issuing easily accessible CSR reports.[23] Use of these reports is growing among concerned stakeholders.[24] As indicated in earlier paragraphs, investors, insurers and underwriters use CSR reports to gather information about socially and environmentally responsible business investments and possible risks. Regulatory and watchdog groups watch the reportable injury rates and number of days lost due to injury. Many stakeholders assess the information contained in the CSR reports to gauge involvement in and commitment to social and environmental issues by comparing the reports among firms and industries.[25] Other concerned stakeholders examine the reports' language and statements to determine how proactive companies are in social and environmental actions.[26] For their part, firms recognize the importance of issuing

CSR reports. Nearly 60% of the top 200 global companies reported having CSR reports on their corporate websites.[27]

CSR reports also provide an outlet for firms to promote their focus on corporate responsibility and how it helps the communities in which the firm operates. CSR reports help legitimize firms' activities and operations in the eyes of stakeholders. Research supports the notion that the interaction of social and environmental responsibility and financial responsibility can be a beneficial relationship for the firm; published CSR reports are perceived to be a good indicator of the relationship between corporate responsibility reporting and firm performance.[28]

A concern among academics and practitioners is how statements in CSR reports compare with the actual corporate commitment to addressing social and environmental issues. Research has found that discrepancies may exist between actual practices of reporting firms and what is stated in CSR publications.[29] Furthermore, lack of CSR-mandated guidelines allows firms to avoid reporting negative or potentially harmful information, focusing rather on only positive sustainability actions and outcomes.[30] Conversely, other research has found CSR reports to be a good indicator of the relationship between corporate responsibility reporting and firm performance.[31]

Research Design

The research design used for this chapter was qualitative content analysis, given the subjective nature of the data and research purpose. Content analysis methodology is used to explore word usage in order to discover underlying meanings, patterns and latent themes in text data.[32] Content analysis was used to assess the information in the CSR reports of 100 carefully selected companies and was chosen for several reasons. First, it is well suited to efficiently and systematically evaluate complex and diverse recorded communications.[33] Second, content analysis allows researchers to synthesize texts with a large number of words into smaller categories.[34] Finally, this research uses CRA, a specific type of content analysis that allows for comparison and contrasting of influential words[35] in the CSR reports of firms from a range of industries, sizes and geographical regions.

ORGANIZATION SELECTION

Companies whose CSR reports were used in this study were first identified based on membership in the Global Environmental Manufacturing Initiative,[36] mentioned in the Global Reporting Initiative[37] and frequently mentioned in the media. Additional candidate companies were also identified using data from Roberts Environmental Center. Once identified, availability of the CSR reports was verified at the website corporateregister.com.[38] When possible, the level of sustainability activities and performance was verified using the scores posted at Roberts Environmental Center.[39] The scoring includes an evaluation of the firm's environmental and social intent, reporting and performance based on a set of predetermined criteria. When companies had similar scores, preference was given to those with frequent citing as good environmental citizens in academic and practitioner literature, as well as the media. The candidate companies were selected iteratively, until it appeared the database was saturated with companies that were actively engaged in sustainable practices in their supply chain management. This saturation occurred when it became difficult to identify additional firms in an industry based on mention in any of the above data sources. Companies from a cross-section of industries were chosen during the selection process in order to include a broad representation of companies in the study. Our sample contained firms from the following industry segments: consumer goods (15 firms in total), financial services (8), healthcare (13), industrial goods (14), materials (13), services (11), technology (15) and utilities (11). After the list of candidate companies was finalized, the most recent CSR report was downloaded from corporateregister.com.

CONTENT ANALYSIS

The CSR reports analyzed here averaged approximately 65 PDF pages for each organization. Therefore, content analysis was the appropriate methodology for examining over 6,500 PDF pages, categorizing the material into more manageable segments and analyzing the documents to determine what patterns existed. Content analysis is useful for gaining valid inferences and understanding the focus of written text in three ways:[40] inferences about the creator of the text, in this case the organizations whose reports are analyzed; inferences about the text itself, in this case what is said in the CSR reports; inferences about the audience of the message in the text, in this case stakeholders and members of the supply chain. Content analysis provides an empirical starting point for generating new research evidence about the nature and effect of specific communications.[41]

CENTERING RESONANCE ANALYSIS (CRA)

A recent and relatively sophisticated type of content analysis methodology is CRA.[42] Crawdad is an analytical software package developed specifically to perform CRA. CRA was chosen to analyze the reports because it interpreted the meaning of specific texts.[43] To interpret meaning, CRA uses a combination of linguistics, network theory and methodology that builds upon inference, position of words and representation of concepts.[44] CRA is a form of content analysis suitable for studying formal written communication[45] such as the published CSR reports. Using CRA, words and phrases are analyzed together in meaningful ways to form a network of nouns and noun phrases to represent main concepts, their influence and their inter-relationships.[46] Previous text analysis of codes has relied on frequency counts of words or phrases, which does not take into account the influence of words in relationship to other words. CRA considers a word to have more influence or prominence within a text if it ties other words together in the text network and facilitates meaning;[47] an influence score is assigned accordingly. For example, influence values of 0.01 are considered significant, while a value above 0.05 is considered very significant.[48]

TEXT ANALYSIS

The PDF files were first downloaded and converted into readable text documents. Then, each file was assessed for organization-specific terminology, such as organization name and specific brand names. A global search and replace was performed to insert words that were generic and common across all files. For example, a specific organization name was replaced with "Company." The PDF for each organization was cleansed and processed individually in the Crawdad system, and then they were processed together. Crawdad creates network maps of the words for each organization and then assigns influence values between 0 and 1 to words using the principles of CRA.

The parameters in Crawdad were set to identify the 300 most influential words that were common across the sustainability reports of two or more organizations. The goal was to identify the highly important words across the pool of 100 organizations. These influential words were then used to formulate factors or themes.

THEME DEVELOPMENT

Theme development commenced with an exploratory factor analysis (EFA). The themes that emerged during the EFA revealed some fairly coherent groups of words and provided a starting point for naming the themes and further latent coding. Using the initial EFA as a starting point, each researcher independently developed names for each theme. These names were compared and contrasted until the theme was well represented by the group of words associated with it. Then, rather than strictly relying on the results from the EFA, one of the Crawdad software developers recommended using additional latent coding. According to Neuman,[49] latent coding allows researchers to look for underlying implicit meaning in the text. The secondary latent coding used in this research helped to logically connect words to themes and strengthen the face validity of the theme. Crawdad links words rather than constructs[50] and looks at the relationship between words. Users of Crawdad have found that, because of the emphasis on influential words rather than on contextual phrases, complete reliance on traditional factor analysis does not provide a holistic and meaningful picture.

Using the consensus regarding the theme name, the researchers then independently performed latent coding and assessed the appropriateness of each word in that theme. Some words were eliminated (26.3% of total) due to very low loadings in the EFA. Words were also recoded from the original EFA loading to a different theme because of better interpretability and a logical fit, or to improve face validity.

Two of the initial themes, "Supplier" and "Supply Chain Inputs" were combined due to their similarity in focus. Because of the subjectivity involved in this phase of the coding process, the research team thoroughly discussed differences in interpretations until there was a high level of reliability and consensus. Ultimately, the themes were adjusted and the final analysis of the data yielded 10 major themes in the CSR reports. The amount of relative influence that each theme has on an organization or industry is reflected in its CSR report as one indicator of the firm's emphasis. The final themes and their associated words developed through the EFA and additional latent coding are shown in Table 6.1. The 10 themes are Supply Chain, Institutional Pressure, Community Focus, Consumer Orientation, External Environment, Risk Management, Measures, Energy, Health and Green Building.

Table 6.1   Themes and associated words

	Supply Chain		Institutional Pressure	Community Focus	Consumer Orientation	External Environment	Risk Management	Measures	Energy	Health	Green Building
1	Material	Lumber	Environmental	Program	Product	System	Emission	Year	Energy	Safety	Facility
2	Development	Farmer	Employee	Community	Management	New	Water	Percent	State	Health	Site
3	Supplier	Packaging	Business	City	Use	Global	Process	Good	Technology	Patient	Building
4	Store	Coffee	United States	Area	Equipment	Service	Waste	Report	Plant	Medicine	Reduction
5	Chemical	Cotton	Customer	Performance	People	Corporate	Information	Effort	Project	Pharmaceutical	Roofing
6	Standard	Home	Environment	Organization	Quality	Operation	Activity	Constraint	Gas	Disease	Construction
7	Forest	Supply	Group	Local	Consumer	World	Bank	Initiative	Power	Research	Office
8	Factory	Battery	Industry	Child	Substance	Responsibility	Policy	Goal	Nuclear	Care	Green
9	Seafood	Design	Sustainability	Center	Value	Data	Client	Time	Engine	Animal	Conservation
10	Food	Association	Financial	School	Way	Market	Social	Total	Fuel	Drug	
11	Training	Electronics	Discipline	Education	Nutrition	Award	Risk	Opportunity	Plan	Treatment	
12	High	Land	National	Park	Right	Fiscal	Issue	Need	Coal	HIV/Aids	
13	Resource	Tree	Compliance	Public	Brand	Diversity	International	Result	Cost	Healthcare	
14	Team	Ingredient	Stakeholder	Support	Director	Change	Country	Control	Electric	Life	
15	Aluminum	Natural	Sustainable	Habitat	Requirement	Sale	Air	Action	Refinery	Clinical	
16	Seedling	Potential	Commitment	Foundation	Fat	Innovation	Impact	Day	Oil	Vaccine	
17	Production	Benefit	Key	Member	Merchandise	Responsible	Number	Significant	Insulation	Medical	
18	Manufacturing	Sourcing	Economic	Student		China	Asbestos		Utility	Pain	
19	Practice	Farm	Leadership	Performed			Improvement		Electricity		
20	Paper	Computer	Environment	Protection			Investment		Efficiency		
21	Partner	Affiliate	Government	Loan			Carbon				
22	Resin	Source	Strategy	Partnership			Wastewater				
23		Recycling	Board	Family							
24			Approach	Charity							
25			Shareholder	Event							
26			Committee	Annual							
27			Council	Art							
28				Communication							

Theme Analysis

A strong institutional and stakeholder focus predominates all of the industries' CSR reports through the Institutional Pressure theme. Given this emphasis, it is not surprising that our findings are consistent with prior literature indicating that companies appear to be utilizing CSR reports as a means to enhance reputation[51] and to communicate positive social and environmental contributions. The positioning of these reports clearly emphasizes the firms' desires to meet external stakeholder demands.[52]

Looking beyond the dominant influence of institutional and stakeholder pressure, many of the themes developed through their emphasis in various industries based on specific industry concerns. For example, very industry-specific-dominated themes include sustainability themes such as Health in the healthcare sector, Energy in the energy sector and Risk Management in the financial sector. Even from a CSR perspective, these industries emphasize the areas that comprise the core focus of the business.

Other themes emerged as part of their importance in business functions, including the Supply Chain theme. In general, all of the themes that emerged from the data can be viewed through the lens of the triple-bottom line that defines sustainability in SCM.[53] The triple-bottom line refers to a holistic evaluation of a firm's overall performance, measured by the integration of its environmental, economic and social sustainability.[54] Furthermore, the data suggests that firms incorporate long-term sustainability strategies and vision throughout their supply chains. In many organizations, SCM participates in environmental sustainability more than any other function in the firm through a choice of suppliers, materials, technologies, manufacturing and transport modes. Financial sustainability is strongly influenced by SCM, particularly in manufacturing sectors such as automotive, consumer products and electronics, where 70% of the organization's value-added may be purchased from other organizations. Finally, SCM can influence social sustainability through selecting suppliers who meet the firm's employment, health and safety guidelines. Indeed, the role of suppliers in sustainability is gaining increased attention.[55] The 10 themes and their corresponding influential words listed in Table 6.1 provide evidence of how the firms in the study view and segment the different primary areas of communication in their CSR reports. They provide a snapshot of how top global companies integrate and improve the triple-bottom line in their internal and external supply chains. The amount of relative influence that each theme has on an organization or industry is reflected in its CSR report as one indicator of the firm's emphasis. SCM activities are present in all 10 themes that emerged from the data, and many companies specifically mentioned the importance of SCM in each of the themes. It was clear from the discussions in the reports, the role of SCM cuts across all aspects of sustainable practices and SCM was relied upon heavily to achieve triple-bottom line goals.

THE ROLE OF SUPPLY CHAIN MANAGEMENT

One aim of this chapter is to look at the interface between company-reported sustainable practices and their SCM operations and processes. To do this, additional analysis of the influential words for each theme was conducted to compare the focus of sustainability practices to the focus of traditional SCM practices. Traditional SCM has been used to describe the coordination of business functions and flows of information and materials across internal business units, and externally with suppliers and customers.[56] Accordingly, the research team independently analyzed the influential words of each theme in the context of the three primary facing areas in the supply chain: external upstream focusing on suppliers, external downstream focusing on customers, or internal facing focusing on the firms' internal supply chain and operations. Each researcher's results were compared and, when differences existed, a consensus was reached. The final results of the analysis show a definite integration among the themes and the three primary facing areas of SCM (Table 6.2).

Table 6.2 Definitions of themes

Theme	Definition	Facing		
		External – upstream	External – downstream	Internal
Supply Chain	Addresses sustainability issues and activities related to the members of the firms' upstream supply chain.	X		
Institutional Pressure	Addresses issues related to handling the internal and external pressure influences and expectations firms feel from stakeholders and institutions.	X	X	X
Community Focus	Addresses social issues and emphasizes showing concern for and doing good works in the communities in which the firms operate.		X	
Consumer Orientation	Addresses sustainability and customer service issues and activities related to the members of the downstream supply chain of the firm.		X	
External Environment	Addresses issues and activities that encompass the firms' global business environment and global corporate sustainability.		X	
Risk Management	Addresses potential risks related to policy and process and the impact of risk on the firms' physical and operating environments.	X		
Measures	Addresses issues related to how operations, outputs and impacts are measured, including those related to sustainability.			X
Energy	Addresses issues related to energy sources, consumption, usage, efficiency and by-products.		X	
Health	Addresses human health issues and the management of safe working environments in firms' operations.			X
Green Building	Addresses issues related to firms' internal operations in building construction, renovation and maintenance.			X

External – upstream facing

The upstream facing themes deal with inputs into the firms' supply chain and operations that are from external sources and include Supply Chain and Risk Management. The Supply Chain theme deals with issues related to "suppliers," "materials" and "inputs," "manufacturing," "development" and "sourcing," the way that firms interact with their suppliers, and the expectations firms have of their suppliers regarding social responsibility. The Supply Chain theme also addresses SCM and how managers deal with environmental issues in their supply chains and with their suppliers, evidenced by the words "partner," "practice," "recycling," "packaging" and "standards." The Risk Management theme deals with threats to the organizations' operations and supply chain. It addresses potential "risks" related to "policy" and "process" as well as risk associated with the firms' impact on the both the physical environment ("emission," "asbestos" and other "waste") and on its operating environment ("information," "client"). Risk also addresses scanning for risks in the external environment, related primarily to business continuity threats, addressing known risks and preparing for potential supply chain risks, and dealing with current and pending policies and requirements.

External – downstream facing

The downstream-facing themes also emphasize supply chain issues that are external to the firm, but not related to its inputs. Downstream themes focus mainly on the impact that the firms' outputs (products, operations, services) have on society, the business environment, the natural environment, and the way that the firms' outputs are viewed by stakeholders.

The themes here relate to energy, community, consumer and the external environment to the firm. The Energy theme focuses on concerns about sources of energy, as well as how the organization uses energy. The Energy theme includes "energy," "utility," "cost," "fuel" and "projects". Energy is a critical component of any supply chain and the management of energy sources, usage and by-products was found to be central to the discussions in the CRS reports analyzed. This is evidenced by the words "efficiency," "technology" and "plan." The Community Focus theme emphasizes thinking locally and includes "schools," "parks," "charities" and "habitats" with an emphasis on good works in the community. Community, as a part of the larger society, is one of the organization's key external stakeholder groups that are part of the social aspect of the triple-bottom line.

The Consumer Orientation theme focuses on the downstream supply chain, and includes the words "brand," "consumers," "products" and "quality." Consumer Orientation can be a marketing theme for firms as it emphasizes the firm's product end users. This is a critical group that supports the financial sustainability of the firm through their willingness to buy the organization's products and services at a price that allows the firm to remain profitable. Finally, the External Environment theme encompasses the firms' operating environment; it includes "global," "market," "world," "responsibility" and "system." This is the most expansive of the external-facing themes. Balancing global expansion and corporate responsibility is a challenging but imperative goal for firms with global supply chains.[57]

Internal facing

The internal-facing themes are related most closely to the firms' internal operations and supply chain. Included here are the three themes Health, Measures and Green Building. The Health theme encompasses "medicine," "healthcare," "safety," "drug," "care" and "patients." For firms outside of the healthcare industry, the focus is on the health and safety of the firm's workforce. This is also an important aspect of social responsibility. The Measures theme focuses on issues such as "reports," "goals" and "initiatives," "controls" and "results." While measures and outcomes are reported externally, ideally they are developed to inform and motivate the organization and its members regarding current and desired social, environmental and financial performance, and to generate the desired behaviors. The Measures theme also relates to how firms measure the management of sustainability in their supply chains, evidenced by "total," "need," "percent," "good" and "action." Finally, the Green Building theme includes "conservation," "building," "facility," "construction" and resource "reduction." Green Building is related to the firm's internal conservation efforts and operations regarding its own facilities. This theme relates primarily to the environmental aspect of sustainability and the triple-bottom line.

The Institutional Pressure theme is unique in that it can be considered both external and internal-facing. In general, Institutional Pressure focuses on handling pressure that the companies feel from "stakeholders" in their internal and external supply chains, which include "customers," "government," "employees," "shareholders," "board" and "industry." It also has a strong internal-facing component of planning through "strategy" and "approach" as well as an interest in a socially responsible corporate image. This is evidenced by the words "compliance," "environment" and "sustainability." The Institutional Pressure theme also addresses issues related to internal and external guidance as supply chain leaders and as focal firms in their industries. The words "leadership," "discipline," "committee," "council," "national" and "commitment" all reveal a sense of firms acting as leaders and role models in their industries and communities.

ADDITIONAL ANALYSIS: DIFFERENCES IN REPORTING AMONG FIRMS

The lack of uniform, mandated reporting standards for CSR reports creates great disparity in report formats. Despite this, there is a surprising level of similarity in the content among the firms' reports. To understand better the relationship between the themes and the companies in our sample, further analysis was performed on the Crawdad data. Two EFAs were run on the data by segmenting the organizations based on geographical location and revenue. Geographic location and organization size, as measured by revenue, have been associated with the type of information disclosed in CSR reports.[58] The first EFA compared organizational orientation by geographic location, comparing companies whose headquarters are located in the US, Western Europe and Japan. Companies in Western Europe and Japan were paired together due to similarities in their cultures and regulatory environments.[59] The second EFA compared the firms by revenue, dividing firms into two categories, smaller and larger. Because the mean annual revenue of the companies in the study was found to be US$22 billion, smaller companies were those that fell below the mean; larger companies were those that were above the mean. The analysis revealed some interesting underlying differences when the results were segmented by geographical location and firm size. The differences are evident in several ways.

First, among firms located in industrialized countries, US firms view responding to the institutional pressure of stakeholder's sustainability demands as a part of risk management, while Western European and Japanese firms view it as a part of community integration. This suggests that community integration in Western European and Japanese firms promotes a cooperative attitude among institutions, community and companies.[60] In the US, social responsibility is still linked to managing risks and some US companies react to institutional pressure by managing it as such.[61]

Second, among firms located in industrialized countries, US firms focus the measurement of sustainability on broad external operational issues such as globalization, whereas European and Japanese firms link measurement with more focused issues in the upstream and downstream supply chains. These findings suggest that for US firms, a primary goal is improving the corporate image in order to help build market share. In contrast, in Western Europe and Japan, firms' upstream and downstream supply chains are linked with measures in order to meet efficiency and effectiveness goals, along with customer expectations for environmental and social responsibility. This suggests a strong integration of the triple-bottom line into business strategies in Western European and Japanese firms.

Third, smaller firms, with fewer resources than large companies, view institutional pressure to adopt social and environmental strategies in supply chains as a risk to be managed, as opposed to larger firms who perceive it more as a routine business practice.

Finally, larger firms view measurement and reporting as an important way to deal with institutional pressure. This may be because larger firms, perceiving less risk from institutions than smaller firms, are able to work more collaboratively with institutions, using metrics to track joint CSR goals and performance indicators.

The results of the additional analysis of the companies in this study point to differences in how companies view social and environmental responsibility in the supply chain from the viewpoint of geographic location of the firm's headquarters and firm size. The analysis was not conducted to rank one firm's characteristics over another, but rather to reveal interesting differences in how firms in industrialized countries view social and environmental responsibility.

Implications, Limitations and Future Research

This chapter makes a number of contributions to research and practice. The original intent of this research was to determine what environmental and social issues companies are emphasizing in CSR reports and how those themes relate to SCM. A further purpose was to assess if there are differences in practice related to organizational location or size. The previous sections discuss how these research questions were addressed. The following sections discuss the impact of this research and then provide guidance for managers and researchers to continue to benchmark and build on these initial findings.

RESEARCH IMPLICATIONS

The findings from this research cut across academic disciplines while emphasizing the role of SCM. By applying inductive logic based on reviewing 100 corporate CSR reports, this research provides new insights into the far-reaching roles of SCM in sustainability at global corporations. Evidence of these expanded SCM roles are the findings that each theme faces a different part of the supply chain, external upstream, external downstream and internal. SCM spans across external boundaries, from raw material suppliers to end customers, and across internal functional boundaries within the firm.[62] Likewise, sustainability issues in SCM span the entire supply chain, both internal and external to the firm.[63] Furthermore, the findings provide evidence that firms report actions, strategies and outcomes of sustainability from the holistic view of SCM, something that is common in conceptual research in this area but unique in much of the empirical research.

This chapter also contributes to a greater understanding of the positioning of CSR reports. It provides a snapshot at a point in time and identifies current areas of emphasis in CSR reporting through the development of themes. As such, this research adds to the body of corporate reporting analysis. It enables researchers to better understand the themes being emphasized in regard to what companies are currently doing, or planning to do, relative to their social and environmental responsibility initiatives. This could be used as a barometer of future trends, as well as a starting point for a longitudinal study of CSR reporting practices.

Finally, this research contributes by applying Crawdad software and using CRA to analyze large amounts of publicly available narrative. The supply chain and operations literature has been highly reliant on survey work since the inception of these fields.[64] However, survey response rates are down; this allows a greater chance of biased and unrepresentative results, which ultimately affects validity.[65] At the same time, through the Internet and other sources, the wide availability of published data issued by companies, government agencies and other sources is at an all-time high. However, without access to good analysis tools the sheer amount of data can be overwhelming. Through the use of Crawdad and CRA, this research represents a relatively early effort to provide meaningful analysis based on publicly available data related to corporate social and environmental responsibility.

MANAGERIAL IMPLICATIONS

This research provides a number of insights for managers. Corporate social environmental reporting has become a critical and high-profile strategic initiative. This research can help organizations benchmark reporting of corporate sustainability practices and strategies. For example, the development and discussion of "themes" can be reviewed to help managers understand whether the organization is aligned with general and industry trends in reporting. This knowledge may also help organizations to improve the image being presented to various stakeholders. In-depth information regarding an organization's CSR report would also be extremely helpful for an organization that is early in creating, or is in the process of refining, its CSR report. Along the same lines, this research highlights the importance of not only having corporate social and environmental responsibility strategies and practices, but also of reporting these to stakeholders. This may help managers to see the economic and relationship-building benefits that have been realized by other organizations enacting strong social and environmental practices.

This study is also useful to SCM professionals because it analyzes the many roles of SCM across a broad range of corporate themes and industries. If an organization wants to implement innovative sustainability practices, or emphasize specific areas within corporate social and environmental responsibility, a review of these themes can provide an understanding of where other organizations are in these areas. If there is a theme that is highlighted in this research that is not influential in an organization's CSR report, the organization may want to reconsider its current social and environmental responsibility practices.

LIMITATIONS AND FUTURE RESEARCH

Some of the general limitations of secondary research using CSR reports are associated with the lack of standardization of the reports and possible biases in reporting. Selection bias in the CSR reports included in this study is another limitation to this research. The researchers selected organizations that are leaders in sustainability practices according to one or more possibly biased measures. In addition, because the PDF files had to be converted to text files, several desirable organizations were excluded from this analysis because embedded security controls prevented the conversion. Greenwashing –reporting unrelated activities in the light of sustainability and emphasizing extremely favorable cases – is also possible. A third limitation is the latent factor analysis. The initial EFA provided a clear preliminary view of the themes. However, there were words that "fit" better on alternative themes, did not fit any of the themes, or had low loadings. Based on the recommendation of the Crawdad software developers, these words were eliminated from consideration, which may bias the selection of themes.

There are a number of opportunities for future research. Content analysis can be suitable for longitudinal research so that the trends in corporate social and environmental responsibility can be better understood. This research provides a cross-organization comparison of CSR reporting at a particular point in time. Therefore, an analysis of whether the social and environmental policies of the organizations change over time would be useful. There is an opportunity to perform an in-depth longitudinal assessment of CSR reports. A number of proactive organizations have been publicly reporting on CSR since the late 1980s and early 1990s. Another opportunity is to use CRA to compare these environmental reports with other publicly posted information such as the annual reports. Most organizations are now required to report on certain aspects of corporate social and environmental sustainability. What similarities and differences exist between these two reporting documents? This analysis could also be used to explore practices in specific functional areas more directly. For example, many firms have a specific website section aimed at socially responsible supply chain practices for suppliers. Is there a strong relationship between supplier guidelines and the influence of supply chain management practices in the reports?

This is an exciting area of research with future opportunities for researchers who are interested in a developing phenomenon. This chapter provides not only a link in the emerging research of corporate communication, but also looks at it using an emerging scholarly methodology. Furthermore, with much of the research in corporate responsibility concentrating on US-based firms, this study incorporates international organizations and comparisons. This research shows that global perspectives are important and relevant in supply chain and operations social and environmental responsibility research.

Conclusions

CSR reporting remains an unregulated area that continues to grow. CSR reports cut across departments in global firms, while emphasizing the role of SCM. Reports indicate that SCM accounts for the majority of most firms' external spending, and has a large influence on the social, economic and environmental aspects of many areas of business. While there is not a great deal of similarity in the format of the CSR reports, despite the global reporting initiative, analysis of the data showed that there is actually a good deal of similarity in the overall message of these reports. Analysis of CSR reports enables a better understanding of the themes that companies are emphasizing in regard to what they are doing, or planning to do, relative to corporate triple-bottom line initiatives in their supply chains and throughout their operations.

Notes

1   Hart, S.L. (1995), "A Natural-Resource-Based View of the Firm", *Academy of Management Review*, Vol. 20, No. 4, pp. 986–1014; Carter, C.R. & Easton, P.L. (2011), "Sustainable Supply Chain Management: Evolution and Future Directions", *International Journal of Physical Distribution & Logistics Management*, Vol. 41, No. 1, pp. 46–62.

2   Esrock, S.L. & Leichty, G.B. (1998), "Social Responsibility and Corporate Web Pages: Self-Presentation or Agenda-Setting?", *Public Relations Review*, Vol. 24, No. 3, pp. 305–319.

3   Tate, W.L., Ellram, L.M. & Kirchoff, J.F. (2010), "Corporate Social Responsibility Reports: A Thematic Analysis Related to Supply Chain Management", *Journal of Supply Chain Management*, Vol. 46, No. 1, pp. 19–44.

4   Jose, A. & Lee, S.M. (2007), "Environmental Reporting of Global Corporations: A Content Analysis based on Website Disclosures", *Journal of Business Ethics*, Vol. 72, No. 4, pp. 307–321.

5   Tate, Ellram & Kirchoff, *op. cit.*

6   Carter, C.R. & Rogers, D.S. (2008), "A Framework of Sustainable Supply Chain Management: Moving Toward New Theory", *International Journal of Physical Distribution & Logistics Management*, Vol. 38, No. 5, pp. 360–387.

7   Hart, 1995, *op. cit.*; Hoffman, A.J. (2000), *Competitive Environmental Strategy: A Guide to the Changing Business Landscape*, Island Press, Washington, DC.

8   Porter, M.E. & van der Linde, C. (1995), "Green and Competitive: Ending the Stalemate", *Harvard Business Review*, Vol. 73, No. 5, pp. 120–134.

9   Handfield, R., Sroufe, R. & Walton, S. (2005), "Integrating Environmental Management and Supply Chain Strategies", *Business Strategy and the Environment*, Vol. 14, No. 1, pp. 1–19.

10   Russo, M.V. & Fouts, P.A. (1997), "A Resource-Based Perspective on Corporate Environmental Performance and Profitability", *The Academy of Management Journal*, Vol. 40, No. 3, pp. 534–559; Buysse, K. & Verbeke, A. (2003), "Proactive Environmental Strategies: A Stakeholder Management Perspective", *Strategic Management Journal*, Vol. 24, No. 5, pp. 453–470.

11   Handfield, Sroufe & Walton, *op. cit.*

12   Bansal, P. & Roth, K. (2000), "Why Companies Go Green: A Model of Ecological Responsiveness", *The Academy of Management Journal*, Vol. 43, No. 4, pp. 717–736.

13   Porter & van der Linde, *op. cit.*

14 Aguilera, R.V., Rupp, D.E., Williams, C.A. & Ganapathi, J. (2007), "Putting the S Back in Corporate Social Responsibility: A Multilevel Theory of Social Change in Organizations", *The Academy of Management Review*, Vol. 32, No. 3, pp. 836–863.

15 Hatch, M.J. & Schultz, M. (1997), "Relations Between Organizational Culture, Identity and Image", *European Journal of Marketing*, Vol. 31, No. 5/6, pp. 356–365, see p. 359.

16 Sen, S. & Bhattacharya, C.B. (2001), "Does Doing Good Always Lead to Doing Better? Consumer Reactions to Corporate Social Responsibility", *Journal of Marketing Research*, Vol. 38, No. 2, pp. 225–243.

17 Cerin, P. (2002), "Communication in Corporate Environmental Reports", *Corporate Social Responsibility and Environmental Management*, Vol. 9, No. 1, pp. 46–65.

18 Wilmshurst, T.D. & Frost, G.R. (2000), "Corporate Environmental Reporting: A Test of Legitimacy Theory", *Accounting, Auditing & Accountability Journal*, Vol. 13, No. 1, pp. 10–26; Cerin, *op. cit.*

19 Wilmhurst & Frost, *op. cit.*

20 Russo & Fouts, *op. cit.*; Esrock & Leichty, *op. cit.*

21 Brown, T.J., Dacin, P.A., Pratt, M.G. & Whetten, D.A. (2006), "Identity, Intended Image, Construed Image, and Reputation: An Interdisciplinary Framework and Suggested Terminology", *Journal of the Academy of Marketing Science*, Vol. 34, No. 2, pp. 99–106.

22 Fombrun, C. & Shanley, M. (1990), "What's in a Name? Reputation Building and Corporate Strategy", *Academy of Management Journal*, Vol. 33, No. 2, pp. 233–258.

23 Kolk, A. (2003), "Trends in Sustainability Reporting by the Fortune Global 250", *Business Strategy and the Environment*, Vol. 12, No. 5, September, pp. 279–291.

24 Solomon, A. & Lewis, L. (2002), "Incentives and Disincentives for Corporate Environmental Disclosure", *Business Strategy and the Environment*, Vol. 11, No. 3, pp. 154–169.

25 *Ibid.*

26 Wilmshurst & Frost, *op. cit.*

27 Jose & Lee, *op. cit.*

28 Montabon, F., Sroufe R. & Narashimhan, R. (2007), "An Examination of Corporate Reporting, Environmental Management Practices and Firm Performance," *Journal of Operations Management*, Vol. 25, No. 5, pp. 998–1014.

29 Cerin, *op. cit.*; Kolk, *op. cit.*

30 Solomon & Lewis, *op. cit.*

31 Montabon, Sroufe & Narashimhan, *op. cit.*

32 Weber, R.P. (1990), *Basic Content Analysis*, Sage Publications, Thousand Oaks, CA; Stemler, S. (2001), "An Overview of Content Analysis", *Practical Assessment, Research & Evaluation*, Vol. 7, No. 17, pp. 137–146.

33 Kolbe, R.H. & Burnett, M.S. (1991), "Content-Analysis Research: An Examination of Applications with Directives for Improving Research Reliability and Objectivity", *The Journal of Consumer Research*, Vol. 18, No. 2, pp. 243–250.

34 Weber, *op. cit.*

35 Corman, S.R., Kuhn, T., McPhee, R.D. & Dooley, K.J. (2002), "Studying Complex Discursive Systems: Centering Resonance Analysis of Communication", *Human Communication Research*, Vol. 28, No. 2 pp. 157–206; Corman, S.R. & Dooley, K.J. (2006), Crawdad Text Analysis System 2.0, Crawdad Technologies, LLC, Chandler, AZ.

36 Global Environmental Management Initiative (GEMI). Available at: www.gemi.org/gemihome. aspx, n.d. (accessed June 1, 2012).

37   Global Reporting Initiative (GRI). Available at: www.globalreporting.org, n.d. (accessed June 1, 2012).

38   CorporateRegister.com. Available at: www.corporateregister.com, n.d. (accessed June 1, 2012).

39   Roberts Environmental Center. Available at: www.roberts.cmc.edu/, n.d. (accessed June 1, 2012).

40   Weber, *op. cit.*

41   Kolbe & Burnett, *op. cit.*

42   Corman, Kuhn, McPhee & Dooley, *op. cit.*

43   Holsti, O.R. (1969), *Content Analysis for the Social Sciences and Humanities*, Addison-Wesley Reading, Reading, MA.

44   Lee, P.M. & James, E.H. (2007), "She'E'Os: Gender Effects and Investor Reactions to the Announcements of Top Executive Appointments," *Strategic Management Journal*, Vol. 28, No. 3, pp. 227–241.

45   Corman, Kuhn, McPhee & Dooley, *op. cit.*

46   Corman, Kuhn, McPhee & Dooley, *op. cit.*; Corman & Dooley, *op. cit.*

47   Canary, H. & Jennings, M. (2008), "Principles and Influence in Codes of Ethics: A Centering Resonance Analysis Comparing Pre- and Post-Sarbanes-Oxley Codes of Ethics", *Journal of Business Ethics*, Vol. 80, No.2, pp. 263–278.

48   Corman & Dooley, *op. cit.*

49   Neuman, W.L. (2000), *Social Research Methods*, Allyn and Bacon, London.

50   Dooley, K. (2007), Crawdad Technology, LLC, Personal communication.

51   Fombrun & Shanley, *op. cit.*

52   Hatch & Schultz, *op. cit.*; Aguilara, Rupp, Williams & Ganapathi, *op. cit.*

53   Tate, Ellram & Kirchoff, *op. cit.*

54   Elkington, J. (1998), *Cannibals with Forks: The Triple Bottom Line of 21st Century Business*, New Society Publishers, Stoney Creek, CT.

55   Pagell, M. & Wu, Z. (2009), "Building a More Complete Theory of Sustainable Supply Chain Management Using Case Studies of 10 Exemplars," *Journal of Supply Chain Management*, Vol. 45, No. 2, pp. 37–56.

56   Mentzer, J.T., Dewitt, W., Keebler, J.S., Min, S., Nix, N.W., Smith, C.D. & Zacharia, Z.G. (2001), "Defining Supply Chain Management", *Journal of Business Logistics*, Vol. 22, No. 2, pp. 1–26; Chen, I.J. & Paulraj, A. (2004), "Towards a Theory of Supply Chain Management: The Constructs and Measurements", *Journal of Operations Management*, Vol. 22, No. 2, pp. 119–150.

57   Handfield, Sroufe & Walton, *op. cit.*

58   Deegan, C. & Gordon, B. (1996), "A Study of the Environmental Disclosure Practices of Australian Corporations", *Accounting and Business Research*, Vol.26, No. 3, pp. 187–199.

59   Witt, M.A. & Redding, G. (2009), "Culture, Meaning, and Institutions: Executive Rationale in Germany and Japan", *Journal of International Business Studies*, Vol. 40, No. 5, pp. 860–885.

60   *Ibid.*

61   Delmas, M. & Toffel, M.W. (2004), "Stakeholders and Environmental Management Practices: An Institutional Framework", *Business Strategy and the Environment*, Vol. 13, No. 4, pp. 209–222.

62   Mentzer, DeWitt, Keebler, Min, Nix, Smith & Zacharia, *op. cit.*

63   Carter & Rogers, *op. cit.*

64   Carter, C.R. & Ellram, L.M. (2003), "Thirty-Five Years of The Journal of Supply Chain Management: Where Have We Been and Where are We Going?", *Journal of Supply Chain Management*, Vol. 39, No. 2, pp. 27–39.; Davis-Sramek, B. & Fugate, B.S. (2007), "State of

Logistics: A Visionary Perspective", *Journal of Business Logistics*, Vol. 28, No. 2, pp. 1–34; Calantone, R. & Vickery, S.K. (2009), "Using Archival and Secondary Data Sources in Supply Chain Management Research", *Journal of Supply Chain Management*, Vol. 45, No. 2, pp. 53–54.

65 Boyer, K.K. & Swink, M.L. (2008), "Empirical Elephants: Why Multiple Methods are Essential to Quality Research in Operations and Supply Chain Management", *Journal of Operations Management*, Vol. 26, No. 3, pp. 337–348.

Sustainable Value Chains:
Managing Activities

7 Aligning Goals and Outcomes in Sustainable Supply Chain Management

DAYNA SIMPSON* AND DAMIEN POWER†

Keywords

Sustainable supply chain, supply chain relationships, green supply chain, sustainable innovation.

Introduction

In the last decade, a growing number of firms have sought to involve their supply chains in projects that increase the sustainability of their activities. 'Sustainable' supply chain management (SSCM) is the coordination of activities at the extended enterprise level that seeks improvement of environmental or social performance, both in products and processes (Zhu and Sarkis, 2004; Mueller, dos Santos and Seuring, 2009). Motivations for SSCM have included new regulations for extended producer responsibility, consumer demands for increased supply chain transparency and competitive factors (Lamming and Hampson, 1996; Simpson, Power and Samson, 2007). Opportunities for cost reduction or potential for product-based risks, such as use of toxic materials, illegal labor practices, or banned substances by suppliers, have led firms such as Toyota and Hewlett Packard to pursue SSCM. Potential for improved sales through product innovations such as organic or recycled content have encouraged firms like Walmart and Nike to change their procurement practices. Regardless of the reasons for firms to engage in SSCM, however, many have experienced inconsistent success with its use. Like other supply chain scale performance initiatives, SSCM requires a coordination of activities, partners and skills, linking value chains between firms rather than focusing on those within individual firms. The relative infancy of SSCM activities for both firms and their customers further adds to the complexity of the management task (Parmigiani, Klassen and Russo, 2011).

* Dr Dayna Simpson, Department of Management, Monash University, Caulfield East, VIC, Australia. E-mail: Dayna. Simpson@monash.edu, Telephone: +61399032674.

† Professor Damien Power, Department of Management and Marketing, University of Melbourne, Parkville, VIC, Australia. E-mail: damien@unimelb.edu.au, Telephone: +61383443737.

For many firms, major gaps between the goals and practical implementation of SSCM exist. Firms have rushed to claim improved management of environmental or social impacts in their supply chain but without evidence of lasting change (King, Lenox and Terlaak, 2005; Delmas and Montes-Sancho, 2010). Notable examples include recent labor violations in the Adidas and Apple supply chains (Garside, 2012) and the Body Shop's now infamous but false 'animal-testing-free' campaign (Entine, 1994). In contrast to somewhat superficial attempts to implement SSCM other firms, such as Fedex, have invested significant resources in SSCM to attract environmentally conscious consumers only to be met with market ambivalence (US Government, 2007; Warner, 2008). Many green supply chain programs, although effective in principle, suffer from two major failures. First, although firms seek to involve their suppliers in SSCM, they often meet resistance (Simpson and Power, 2005). This has led to cases of poor uptake by suppliers (e.g. Starbucks) (Giovannucci & Ponte, 2005), or product failures (e.g. Seventh Generation and the Body Shop) (Entine, 2004; Goldstein and Russo, 2007). Second, firms that achieve success with SSCM often find a subsequent lack of interest in the marketplace (e.g. Fedex and sustainable wines) (Delmas and Grant, 2010). Both types of failure tend to de-motivate firms and their suppliers and discourage further SSCM investment.

As we describe in the discussion that follows, these failures have much to do with goal definition by firms. Firms' SSCM should focus on attainable goals, or goals that fit the capabilities of suppliers or existing strategies. Firms with a consumer base that is open to sustainable products, for example, should focus on activities that involve consumers, such as energy saving products or sustainable foods. However, firms in commodity markets or with more conservative consumers should consider focusing on more upstream SSCM activities. As we propose, firms should identify goals for SSCM that align with one or more major strategies of costs, risks or market.

SSCM is resource intensive, risky and requires inter-firm collaboration (Zhu and Sarkis, 2004; Kocabasoglu, Prahinski and Klassen, 2007). Like other supply chain performance projects, goals of cost and risk reduction are achieved in different ways to goals of product innovation. Each requires a different approach to investment, relationship management and skills development. Separating out the main goals of SSCM allows firms to achieve more consistent performance improvement on a value chain scale.

Background to Sustainable Supply Chains

SUPPLY CHAIN SUSTAINABILITY

Sustainability' has grown to become an important part of many firms' performance portfolios as they seek new sources of competitive advantage. Early definitions of sustainability captured practices that largely only impacted firms' individual environmental and social performance (Hart, 1995). In the last 10 years or so this has expanded into business partnerships and particularly supply chains as firms have sought to influence performance over upstream processes (Lamming and Hampson, 1996; Simpson et al., 2007). Outsourcing practices generally have reduced firms' overheads, and increased their capacity, labor flexibility and innovation opportunities. Outsourcing, however, has also led to a significant reduction in the ability to control the social and environmental impacts of production (Pagell, Wu and Murthy, 2007; Parmigiani et al., 2011). This has resulted in unexpected costs from ethical and environmental scandals (lost sales), pollution incidents (penalties and clean-up) or labor practice violations (plant closures and lawsuits) (Zhu and Sarkis, 2004; Mueller et al., 2009). As a result many managers within firms have become more concerned with the environmental and social performance of their suppliers.

The purpose of SSCM programs has evolved significantly in the past decade as new and valuable benefits have been discovered from its use (Bowen, Cousins, Lamming and Faruk, 2001; Simpson et al., 2007). Firms have used SSCM to manage legal concerns such as banned substances in products and processes (e.g. lead or CFCs), pollution control at suppliers' plants and monitoring of labor practices across international operations (Zhu and Sarkis, 2004). They have also sought to link SSCM to their product and financial performance by establishing specific supply chains for sustainable products (e.g. Nike and Keen) or creating closed loop systems (e.g. Fuji-Xerox) (Hardy and Hart, 1996; Toffel, 2003). Procurement practices have evolved such that many firms have developed policies for their purchasing staff and their suppliers that require the use of specific practices. These can include requiring suppliers to certify to environmental or social performance standards, reducing the chemical content of procured materials, or only sourcing locally (Bowen et al., 2001). Each is an example of an enterprise expanding its influence over its environmental and social performance to a supply chain scale.

Owing to the significant development of SSCM in recent years, it is difficult to categorize the field into one set of practices or outcomes. Instead, practitioners and researchers need to recognize that SSCM has many different forms, outcomes and implications for performance. Importantly, the structure of a firm's relationships with its suppliers will significantly influence the extent and success of an SSCM program.

SUPPLY CHAIN RELATIONSHIPS

Almost all products and services represent the efforts of a group of trading partners, each having added value at some point before a final product is sold. Most products also require a large number of firms to collaborate and to collectively coordinate their resources, production and distribution. Owing to the established connections of existing supply chains, most organizations have in place the foundation for even the simplest of SSCM programs. The connectivity provided by a firm's supply chain therefore offers a major resource for sharing knowledge, enforcing practices, and improving processes and products (Paulraj, Lado and Chen, 2008). Procurement, although traditionally used to ensure quality and lower costs, has the potential to also influence and promote more sustainable practices (Klassen and Vachon, 2003).

Procurement practices – the purchase of goods and services – have influencing power over other firms, particularly where procurement 'spend' is large or important to a firm's survival (Lamming and Hampson, 1996; Flynn, Huo and Zhao, 2010). Procurement directly influences specifications for goods production and distribution. Through purchasing, firms can control the method of production, the content of products and the willingness of suppliers to innovate. In this way, purchasing can either be detrimental to or facilitate the use of sustainable business practices. Procurement can be detrimental to sustainability where it severely limits the profit margins or raw material choices of suppliers. Small firms may be reluctant to innovate if their sourcing arrangement with a customer is tenuous or if their market is highly price sensitive. Most large customers have significant influence over the sustainable business practices of their suppliers (Kocabasoglu et al., 2007; Delmas and Montiel, 2009). For example, customers focused on low-cost competition are less willing to accept product changes that may be more sustainable but add cost to the product. Procurement, however, can actively facilitate more sustainable practices. Customers can require all suppliers to meet environmental or social performance criteria, arrange supplier networks for knowledge exchange or reward sustainable innovation (Mueller et al., 2009). At a minimum, procurement can be used to set standards for suppliers that cover pollution and safety. It can also, however, be used to establish more complex sourcing criteria that set targets for, or reward, related performance improvement (Klassen and Vachon, 2003).

Beyond simple contracting are partnering practices that involve suppliers more directly in the activities of customers. Innovation has been found increasingly to arise where customers and suppliers integrate their activities such that customers teach suppliers and suppliers take on greater responsibility (Liker and Choi, 2004). Integrated supply partnerships offer opportunities for novel ideas and solutions, shorter product-to-market cycles and can be a valuable store of collaborative knowledge (Droge, Jayaram and Vickery, 2004). Modular design, such as for the Boeing Dreamliner and tablet PCs, require customers and suppliers to work together on product design and delivery (Flynn et al., 2010). Learning networks and open innovation systems, such as the Toyota Production System, have been credited with major process and product advances for firms. Greater collaboration provides the necessary foundation for major performance improvement, complex knowledge exchange and advantageous innovation. The likelihood that customer–supplier collaboration would also facilitate SSCM is high, given its success in other performance domains. Collaborative arrangements, however, are time consuming and resource intensive for firms and open them up to risks such as intellectual property losses or inferior skills in one partner (Villena, Revilla and Choi, 2010).

Firms should identify the relationship requirements of their SSCM program during its design. Minor SSCM programs, such as material avoidance or risk reduction, can be managed through contracts. More complex programs, however, such as supply chain scale carbon emission reduction or specialized labor and manufacturing practices, require closer, more collaborative relationships. When deployed appropriately, procurement can therefore substantially improve the success rate of SSCM.

MARKETING ISSUES

A further factor in successful SSCM is the high volatility of markets for sustainable products and services. In most product markets, sustainable goods are highly novel, unregulated and used only by small or niche consumer segments (Delmas and Grant, 2010). Most consumers do not understand, trust or actively seek out sustainable goods (Ibanez and Grolleau, 2008). For some goods, such as re-manufactured product, their sustainable attributes can actually become a negative for consumers. Consumers also have shown general ambivalence toward sustainable goods in commodity markets such as greener power supply, biofuels and some organic produce. Fedex, for example, committed substantial resources to refit its fleet with more hybrid engine technology and reduce fuel use and emissions. The initiative, however, did not increase Fedex's sales or change consumer sentiment toward the firm (Gogoi, 2008).

Firms need to weigh the costs and benefits of how they market themselves and their products to downstream consumers. For one, not all SSCM activities are attractive to consumers nor do all firms' consumers care about sustainable products. For firms like Wal-Mart, for example, the consumer base is predominantly price conscious and conservative and not necessarily concerned with social and environmental performance. This should not preclude firms from considering the upstream marketing of sustainability and the value of unmarketable, but still beneficial activities, such as remanufacturing, recycling or preferred sourcing. Wal-Mart's SSCM goals, for example, could be better be directed toward upstream activities that reduce the company's costs rather than seek to enhance its reputation. In-store sustainability promotions may do little to influence consumer opinions of a retailer, may be costly, and may have a negligible impact on sustainability. For other firms whose supply choices matter significantly more to consumers, such as the sustainable grocer Wholefoods, their SSCM objectives should focus more on consumer facing characteristics such as product content.

Appropriate Strategies for Successful SSCM

SSCM offers multiple benefits for firms. These benefits, however, are derived from different program objectives. Goals of reputation enhancement or product design require a different SSCM approach to goals of cost or risk reduction. Such benefits also can often become counterintuitive. Innovative products require integrated relationships and funds for research and development rather than sourcing on price alone. Firms must establish early whether their SSCM program is aimed at lowering costs, at managing risks, or focused on reputation and sales (market focus).

COST FOCUS

SSCM offers firms new opportunities to lower costs across the supply chain. Several aspects of environmental and social performance improvement offer not just impact reduction but also operational and financial performance benefits. For environmental performance in particular, such benefits can be attained where firms reduce pollution (e.g. reducing disposal costs), increase resource use efficiency (e.g. recycling and reduction in energy and water use), optimize transportation, or remanufacture used parts and products (Porter and Van der Linde, 1995; Melnyk, Sroufe and Calantone, 2003; Jacobs, Singhal and Subramaniam, 2010). For social performance, better safety controls and employee investment have been associated with fewer liability costs, fewer safety violations and reduced employee turnover (Pagell and Gobeli, 2009).

To achieve cost reductions with SSCM, firms can begin by introducing waste and energy reduction targets into contracts. They can also require returnable packaging or co-location of suppliers to reduce transportation costs. As an example of this, Wal-Mart has recently encouraged waste reduction among its suppliers and asked them to look for cost saving opportunities that also reduce pollution (Plambeck, 2007). Wal-Mart's intentions, however, have been to 'encourage' change within a sourcing environment that has focused more on 'forced' change through the use of contracting. In Wal-Mart's case, its SSCM objectives do not appear to align with its sourcing arrangements and may not provide the benefits the firm expects. Equally, in highly cost-competitive environments, such as in commodity supply chains, suppliers may require assistance if they are to develop more sustainable business practices.

While simple contracting can be used to ensure that the right suppliers are selected to deliver sustainability goals, major innovation requires collaboration. In the global automotive industry, for example, several sustainable innovations that also reduce costs have been developed through partnerships between suppliers and customers. Tenneco built improved emission control and safety features into its products in cooperation with its customers. Tenneco's services were 'manufactured to fit' customers' products, making them cheaper over their life cycle and more desirable in the marketplace (Singh, 2010). In another example of partnering for sustainability, Toyota and Tesla formed a strategic partnership in 2010 to develop and commercially produce electric vehicles. Toyota plans to invest in Tesla's business and co-produce a range of low emission vehicle models (Welch, 2010). Both the Tenneco and the Toyota–Tesla alliance have sought to generate innovation that reduces the costs of production as well as reducing fuel consumption by end users.

At an industry level, several cooperative models have emerged that allow groups of firms to access new knowledge of sustainable practices and share ideas on pollution prevention. Cooperatives such as the Chicago Waste to Profit Network provide scope for networking among firms that are affiliated by industry and supply chain. Network events and regular forums allow firms to learn about recycling practices and waste reduction from their peers (Paquin and Howard-Grenville, 2009). This and similar industrial ecology networks have recently emerged as successful collectives for firms to source waste and cost reduction ideas and designs for remanufactured product (Chertow, 2007). Toyota also has in the past successfully used its existing supplier network associations to identify waste reduction opportunities that also reduce costs (Simpson and Power, 2005).

Simple contractual clauses as well as long-term strategic alliances can be used to force, encourage and generate innovative but sustainable cost reductions across a supply chain.

RISK FOCUS

A risk focus for firms' SSCM programs is appropriate where markets need assurances that certain practices or materials are being avoided during production. Risk reduction becomes most important where: a) customers and suppliers are separated by large distances; and b) the marketplace puts a premium on the use of sustainable business practices (Mueller et al., 2009; Nidumolu, Prahalad and Ranguswami, 2009). Risk reduction, particularly where distance complicates management, has become an increasing concern for some supply chains, particularly in textile and food industries. Risks typically include chemical spills at facilities, the use of illegal labor practices or the use of banned substances by suppliers. For these supply chains, past scandals or the prospect of scandal keep these issues high in the mind of consumers, potentially impacting sales (Klassen and Johnson, 2004). Risk reduction for these supply chains requires SSCM that focuses less on saving costs and more on avoiding costs through increased vigilance over supplier activities. Managers of firms involved in such supply chains must expect to invest funds if such a strategy is to be successful.

For risk-focused SSCM, two main options are available. In one, contractual clauses can be used to expand requirements for environmental, safety and worker welfare practices throughout the supply chain. The capacity to procure, particularly in large volumes or at high spend, provides a major opportunity to control supplier behavior (Delmas and Montiel, 2009). Both Toyota and Hewlett Packard force their suppliers to use environmental management systems (EMS) such as ISO 14001, as well as including their own additional EMS clauses in contracts. These provide procedures for hazard identification and control where distance presents a barrier to more collaborative performance improvement. Where generic standards are used, the onus typically lies with suppliers who are expected to implement new practices. Firms use fairly generic sourcing requirements for their suppliers in this way to protect themselves but keep the costs of risk management low. While it certainly provides firms with a level of comfort with regard to risk management within supply chains, such an approach does not always prevent incidents from occurring at supplier plants (Pagell and Gobeli, 2009; Gold and Casselman, 2010).

The second option requires firms to work more closely together in ways that cost more to implement but offer greater success. Where the costs of supply chain incidents are high, such as in industries where activist attention is significant or the issues are well known, firms can invest in independent standards and auditing. For Hewlett Packard and Nike, this has involved the use of auditing teams that regularly visit global suppliers to monitor compliance and provide assistance. Risk can be managed with greater inter-firm collaboration and by providing supply chain managers with assistance toward meeting new requirements. This approach is employed by Ford, which provides suppliers with assistance with ISO 14001 certification. Nike has also pioneered a joint design process whereby Nike and its suppliers work together to meet recycled content targets for products.

MARKET FOCUS

For a market focus, firms seek to create, market and sell commercially viable products or services. These tend to be goods that occupy niches (e.g. recycled outdoor clothing such as Keen shoes, or Fair Trade and organic coffee), or offer disruptive technologies and products. At the business-to-business level this can also include the use of specialized certifications by firms to improve their marketability to major customers, such as chemical-free food or safety standards. Significant investment in and strict control over suppliers is critical with this type of strategy. For niche products, the types of consumers that seek out such products tend to be highly loyal to an issue (e.g. Fair Trade) or a specification (e.g. chemical-free produce) (Giovanucci and Ponte, 2005; Gogoi, 2008). They are also highly critical of products that promise more sustainable practices but whose claims are later found to be fraudulent (Delmas and Grant, 2010). As a result, such programs require careful product design and supplier selection and a significant investment in supplier activities. Highly innovative products are typically based on disruptive innovations. They require greater integration of supply chain partners and ongoing investment in research and development (Liker and Choi, 2004). The Toyota Prius, for example, was a next generation product when it first arrived in the marketplace. The Prius required extensive supplier collaboration and was high risk. Its benefit to consumers, however, and its popularity have made it a highly successful product (Gertner, 2007).

One of the more successful but less well known examples of market-focused SSCM programs has been the development of food value chains (FVC). Predominantly a cooperative of firms within an industry or middle tier of a food supply chain, an FVC seeks sustainable outcomes for both the firms involved and consumers. In the Bend region of Oregon, for example, Country Natural Beef established a cattle growing cooperative based around an organic, non-intensive grazing system that sought to provide both a premium 'green' food product and a more sustainable farming business. The Country Natural Beef supply chain brought together a group of ranchers that wanted to separate from the price-sensitive and highly commoditized grocery chains and set their own higher prices with premium product (Pullman, Maloni and Carter, 2009). The supply chain, similar to Red Tomato in the US northeast, provides a successful example of a more sustainable food supply chain that is financially viable and competitive with more commoditized grocery chains. One of the major difficulties for food producers seeking to commercially develop and sell more sustainable produce (e.g. organic products) has been the amalgamation of grocery chains. High volume, low variety supply networks such as those operated by Tesco and Coles Australia have made it difficult for smaller suppliers to survive in many developed economies (Rigby and Vishwanath, 2006). These supply chains (or 'killermarts') amalgamate supplies to price out local suppliers and reduce diversity of supply over time. The formation of cooperatives that provide independent supply channels for small suppliers and sustainable produce or sustainable retailers such as Wholefoods offer a viable alternative to this increasingly unsustainable practice.

Closing Comments and Conclusions

Supply chains for traditional products and services are designed with outcome performance in mind. Sustainable supply chains should be no different and should be structured around intended product and process performance goals. Firms seeking cost reductions from their SSCM program require a focus on upstream practices and assistance for suppliers. Collaborative relationships provide some of the most significant opportunities for cost reduction as firms share knowledge and seek to improve products and processes that improve social and environmental performance but that also lower landed cost. For cost-focused SSCM, the end goal is toward lower costs or lower resource use rather than marketing or reputation management.

Supply chain relationships in all forms offer a significant opportunity for firms to control practices and share ideas that lead to more sustainable business practices. However, these relationships require time, effort and investment if they are to achieve significant performance outcomes. Most firms use procurement to contract with other supply chain parties in simple ways. Some firms utilize more sophisticated methods, such as preferred suppliers, joint projects and even joint innovation. Firms need to recognize that their procurement approach will significantly influence the performance outcomes of any SSCM program. The dynamics of SSCM are similar in many ways to other more traditional supply chain performance programs.

The fundamental dilemma confronting all firms, and all managers of firms, in the context of investing in SSCM initiatives is one of ethics versus economics. It is always attractive to pursue short-term economic benefit at the expense of the collective environmental or social good. In fact, 'rational' economists will argue that it is not the preserve of the manager to focus on factors that may only marginally be related to the profit motive. Further compounding this problem is the complexity inherent in managing across supply chains, and the associated risks. The challenge for stakeholders, firms and economies is to pursue growth alongside the objectives of sustainability. Where firms do not effectively align these two goals, or design SSCM programs for reputation alone, failure and cynicism are likely to ensue. Using approaches from other performance-focused supply chains, we highlight points of leverage that can be used to facilitate more successful SSCM. Aligning these mechanisms with appropriate SSCM goals and seeking more creative solutions should lead to more sustainable and innovative supply chains.

References

Bowen, F., Cousins, P., Lamming, R. and Faruk, A. (2001) The role of supply management capabilities in green supply. *Production and Operations Management*, Vol. 10, No. 2, pp. 174–89.

Chertow, M. (2007) Uncovering 'industrial symbiosis'. *Journal of Industrial Ecology*, Vol. 11, No. 1, 11–30.

Delmas, M. and Grant, L. (2010) Eco-labeling strategies and price-premium: the wine industry puzzle. *Business & Society*, Online First.

Delmas, M.A. and Montes-Sancho, M.J. (2010) Voluntary agreements to improve environmental quality: symbolic and substantive cooperation. *Strategic Management Journal*, Vol. 31, No. 6, 575–601.

Delmas, M. and Montiel, I. (2009) Greening the Supply chain: when is customer pressure effective? *Journal of Economics and Management Strategy*, Vol. 18, No. 1, 171–201.

Droge, C., Jayaram, J. and Vickery, S.K. (2004) The effects of internal versus external integration practices on time-based performance and overall firm performance. *Journal of Operations Management*, Vol. 22, No. 6, 557–573.

Entine, J. (1994) Shattered image. *Business Ethics*, September, 23–28.

Flynn, B., Huo, B. and Zhao, X (2010) The impact of supply chain integration on performance: a contingency and configuration approach. *Journal of Operations Management*, Vol. 28, No. 1.

Garside, J. (2012) 'Apple's Chinese factories to be audited after violation of working conditions.' *The Guardian*, January 24.

Gertner, J. (2007) 'From 0 to 60 to world domination.' *New York Times*, February 18.

Giovannucci, D. and Ponte, S. (2005) Standards as a new form of social contract? Sustainability initiatives in the coffee industry. *Food Policy*, Vol. 30, No. 3, 284–301.

Gogoi, P (2008) 'Is Fair Trade becoming "Fair Trade Lite"?' *Business Week*, June 18.

Gold, R. and Casselman, B. (2010) 'On doomed rig's last day, a divisive change of plan.' *Wall Street Journal*, August 26.

Goldstein, D. and Russo, M. (2007) *Seventh Generation: Balancing Customer Expectations with Supply Chain Realities, Environmental Management: Readings and Cases*, Sage Publications.

Hardy, P. and Hart S. (1996) *Deja Shoe: Creating the Environmental Footwear Company*. World Resources Institute.

Hart, S. (1995) A natural-resource-based view of the firm. *Academy of Management Review*, Vol. 20, 986–1014.

Ibanez, L. and Grolleau, G. (2008) Can ecolabeling schemes preserve the environment? *Environmental and Resource Economics*, Vol. 40, No. 2, 233–249.

Jacobs, B.W., Singhal, V.R. and Subramanian, R. (2010) An empirical investigation of environmental performance and the market value of the firm. *Journal of Operations Management*, Vol. 28, No. 5, 430–441.

King, A.A., Lenox, M.J. and Terlaak, A. (2005) The strategic use of decentralized institutions: exploring certification with the ISO 14001 management standard. *Academy of Management Journal*, Vol. 48, No. 6, 1091–1106.

Klassen R. and Johnson (2004) The green supply chain. In: S. New and R. Westbrook (eds.), *Understanding Supply Chains: Concepts, Critiques, and Futures*, Oxford University Press.

Klassen, R. and Vachon, S. (2003) Collaboration and evaluation in the supply chain: the impact on plant-level environmental investment. *Production and Operations Management*, Vol. 12, No. 3, 336–52.

Kocabasoglu, C., Prahinski, C. and Klassen, R. (2007) Linking forward and reverse supply chain investments: the role of business uncertainty. *Journal of Operations Management*, Vol. 25, No. 6, 1141–1160.

Lamming, R. and Hampson, J. (1996) The environment as a supply chain management issue. *British Journal of Management*, Vol. 7, S45–S62.

Liker, J. and Choi, T. (2004) Building deep supplier relationships. *Harvard Business Review*, Vol. 83, 104–113.

Melnyk, S.A., Sroufe, R.P. and Calantone, R. (2003) Assessing the impact of environmental management systems on corporate and environmental performance. *Journal of Operations Management*, Vol. 21, 329–351.

Mueller, M, dos Santos, V. and Seuring, S. (2009) The contribution of environmental and social standards towards ensuring legitimacy in supply chain governance. *Journal of Business Ethics*, Vol. 89, No. 4, 509–523.

Nidumolu, R., Prahalad, C.K. and Rangaswami, M.R. (2009) Why sustainability is now the key driver of innovation. *Harvard Business Review*, Vol. 87, No. 9.

Pagell, M. and Gobeli, D. (2009) How plant managers' experiences and attitudes toward sustainability relate to operational performance. *Production and Operations Management*, Vol. 18, 278–299.

Pagell, M., Wu, Z. and Murthy, N. (2007) The supply chain implications of recycling. *Business Horizons*, Vol. 50, No. 2, 133–143.

Paquin, R. and Howard-Grenville, J. (2009) Facilitating regional industrial symbiosis: network growth in the UK's national industrial symbiosis programme. In: J. Howard-Grenville and F. Boons, *The Social Embeddedness of Industrial Ecology*, Edward Elgar Publishing.

Parmigiani, A., Klassen, R. and Russo, M. (2011) Efficiency meets accountability: performance implications of supply chain configuration, control, and capabilities. *Journal of Operations Management*, Vol. 29, No. 3, 212–223.

Paulraj, A., Lado, A. and Chen, I. (2008) Inter-organizational communication as a relational competency: antecedents and performance outcomes in collaborative buyer-supplier relationships. *Journal of Operations Management*, Vol. 26, No. 1, 45–64.

Plambeck, E. (2007) The greening of Wal-Mart's supply chain. *Supply Chain Management Review*, Vol. 11, No. 5, 18–21.

Porter, M. and Van der Linde, C. (1995) Toward a new conception of the environment-competitiveness relationship. *Journal of Economic Perspectives*, Vol. 9, No. 4, 97–118.

Pullman, M., Maloni, M. and Carter, C. (2009) Food for thought: motivations to adopt sustainability practices and perceived outcomes. *Journal of Supply Chain Management*, Vol. 45, No. 4, 38–54.

Rigby, D. and Vishwanath, V. (2006) Localization: the revolution in consumer markets, *Harvard Business Review*, Vol. 84, No. 4, 82–92.

Simpson, D. and Power, D. (2005) Use the supply relationship to develop lean and green suppliers. *Supply Chain Management: An International Journal*, Vol. 10, No. 1, 60–68.

Simpson, D., Power, D. and Samson, D. (2007) Greening the automotive supply chain: a relationship perspective, *International Journal of Operations and Production Management*, Vol. 27, No. 1, 28–48.

Singh, S. (2010) 'Caterpillar looks for a few close friends,' *Business Week*, October, 2010.

Toffel, M.W. (2003) The growing strategic importance of end-of-life product management. *California Management Review*, Vol. 45, No. 3, 102.

US Government (2007) 'Transportation sector fuel efficiency, including challenges to and incentives for increased oil savings through technological innovation including plug-in hybrids.' Hearing before the Committee on Energy and Natural Resources, US Senate, January 30.

Villena, V., Revilla, E. and Choi, T. (2010) The dark side of buyer-supplier relationships: a social capital perspective. *Journal of Operations Management*, In-Press.

Warner, M. (2008) FedEx's Hybrid Truck Program Stalls. *Fast Company*, 129, October.

Welch, D. (2010) 'What Toyota sees in Tesla,' *Business Week*, July 2010.

Zhu, Q. and Sarkis, J. (2004) Relationships between operational practices and performance among early adopters of green supply chain management practices in Chinese manufacturing enterprises. *Journal of Operations Management*, Vol. 22, No. 3, 265–89.

8

Setting a Framework for Life Cycle Assessment in Sustainable Technology Development

STELVIA MATOS* AND JEREMY HALL†

Keywords

Life Cycle Assessment, sustainable development, stakeholder, supply chain, PF resins, biomass processing technologies.

Introduction

A number of authors have emphasized the importance of such tools as Life Cycle Assessment (LCA) as part of the sustainability efforts of many firms' operations (e.g. Krikke et al.,[1] Sarkis[2] and Sroufe et al.[3]). LCA is an analytical tool to assess the inputs and outputs of materials and emissions to air, water and land to and from the environment, over the life cycle of a product or service. LCAs can be used to assess the entire product life cycle (raw material acquisition, manufacture, transportation, use, maintenance and end-of-life), or focus on parts of a product life cycle.[4] The "cradle to grave" approach of LCA that extends the environmental assessment throughout the supply chain represents an evolution over environmental assessments focused on firm-specific impacts and end-of-pipe analyses, and is now part of a broader approach to sustainable development.[5] Such an approach is relatively easily implemented when key interacting variables and boundaries of responsibilities are well understood. However, the complexities and uncertainties of environmental systems,[6] imperfections of human reasoning and impossibility of ideal societal decisions lead to complications,[7] and it remains unclear for practitioners how LCA can help to overcome the challenges of balancing the often-conflicting pressures of firm-level economic performance versus environmental and social responsibility.[8]

According to Simon,[9] because of complexity, decision-makers are limited in what they can know (bounded rationality) and thus rational calculations cannot guarantee

*   Adjunct Professor Stelvia Matos, Beedie School of Business, Simon Fraser University, 8888 University Drive, Burnaby, BC, Canada, V5A 1S6. E-mail: smatos@sfu.ca. Telephone: + 1 604 294 3721.

†   Professor Jeremy Hall, Beedie School of Business, Simon Fraser University, 8888 University Drive, Burnaby, BC, Canada, V5A 1S6.E-mail: jkh5@sfu.ca. Telephone: + 1 778-782-5891.

an optional solution. These difficulties are exacerbated when dealing with novel and complex technologies because they may create new industry structures, require new regulatory frameworks, generate consumer uncertainty[10] and suffer from "liabilities of newness."[11] Hall and Martin[12] argue that in these situations, uncertainties about possible environmental, health and social impacts are more salient. When dealing with sustainable development, more complexities can be expected because it involves a higher number of interacting economic, environmental and social parameters.[13] According to Hall and Vredenburg,[14] innovating for sustainable development is also ambiguous, i.e. when it is not possible to identify key parameters or presents pressures that are sometimes conflicting or difficult to reconcile. They suggest that sustainability concerns frequently involve a wider range of secondary stakeholders, and decision-makers are thus likely to have significant difficulties in dealing with sustainable development.

Our objective is to examine how LCA can help identify sustainability "hot spots," i.e. key economic, environmental and social issues and their interactions during the development of more sustainable technologies. We draw from complexity theory, stakeholder theory and the supply chain literature to develop our arguments. We start by discussing the complexities of sustainable development innovation, including stakeholder management issues in the supply chain, a particular area that is often overlooked by LCA practitioners. Stakeholder theory has been well established in the sustainable development discourse, while more recently the complex and sometimes ambiguous nature of certain stakeholder relationships have exacerbated sustainable development efforts.[15] We then draw from the work of Matos and Hall[16] to show that LCA can help to identify potential areas of environmental, social and economic improvement during the development of biomass-based resins. The chapter concludes with a discussion of the implications of our work for LCA practitioners and academic research in sustainable development.

The Complexities of Sustainable Development

According to Simon,[17] complex systems are characterized by many interacting parameters, and because of these interactions, it is difficult to understand the entire system. Sustainable development can be conceptualized as an inherently complex system, as it requires the understanding and coordination among different problem solving techniques applicable to environmental, economic and social issues. For example, while environmental and economic issues can be analyzed using rational calculations, social issues require problem solving strategies not clearly systematized (i.e. high levels of bounded rationality) by managers. In addition, the interaction amongst environmental, economic and social issues may not be solved using science-based knowledge. Such difficulties may lead to considerable challenges during managers' decision-making processes, what we refer to in this chapter as complexities.

Hertwich et al.[18] suggest that environmental tools such as LCA should not be disconnected from social and economic facts (p. 15). The use of LCA explored in this paper differs from most studies, which discuss LCA while disregarding social issues.[19] We suggest that a key difficulty is the decision-maker's limitations to deal with complexities in the supply chain, i.e. the level of interdependence among the dimensions and the degree to which key input and output parameters cannot be determined or changed without compromising the technological and economic viability of the product. According to

Matos and Hall,[20] such abilities are generally inversely correlated to the degree of novelty and complexity of the product or process under analysis. Additional difficulties can be expected as interdependence (positive or negative) and intensity (interaction strength) alternate with time, as well as parameter importance.[21]

The importance of dealing with stakeholders and the inability to identify key actors and potential social outcomes are becoming increasingly important challenges, yet are insufficiently addressed in the literature.[22] This is particularly the case for sustainable development, where complexities may lead to difficulties in identifying not only interdependences among parameters but also the key parameters. For example, Hall and Vredenburg[23] argue that sustainable development pressures, especially social issues, can be conflicting or difficult to reconcile, particularly if the technology is based on new science or has radical impacts on those that use or are affected by the technology. The authors also suggest that sustainability often involves a wider range of stakeholders, many of whom are not directly involved with the organization carrying out an analysis.

Stakeholder theory makes the distinction between primary stakeholders, those with a direct interest in the organization, such as customers, shareholders, employees, suppliers and regulators; and secondary stakeholders, those that are not engaged in transactions with the organization but can affect, or are affected by the organization, such as academic researchers, non-governmental organizations (NGOs) and environmental activists.[24] The supply chain literature makes a similar distinction between "agents" (e.g. an individual, a project team, or even an entire organization) and the "environment" (e.g. end-consumer markets of products and services provided by the value chain members), which is directly or indirectly connected to the economic, cultural and the larger institutional systems.[25]

An important issue recognized by Freeman[26] and Clarkson[27] is that stakeholders are heterogeneous, and in particular, secondary stakeholder concerns are often interpreted differently than the focal firm. Mitchell et al.[28] recognize the dynamic and interdependent nature of stakeholder relations, where there are varying degrees of legitimacy, urgency and power, which according to Agle et al.[29], affect stakeholder salience, i.e. "the degree to which managers give priority to competing stakeholder claims" (p. 507). Such interdependencies suggest that stakeholders' concerns and decisions may change because of changes made by stakeholders with whom they are linked.[30] Levinthal and Warglien[31] argue that understanding interactions across organizations is a crucial mechanism to facilitate cooperation, and that it is important to ensure improvements and benefits are distributed amongst the stakeholders, because when actors only consider payoff implications of their local actions and ignore related effects in the supply chain, they only see artificial benefits. Empirical studies suggest that establishing cross-sector partnerships, such as corporate and NGO alliances, may lead to improved stakeholder integration and may contribute towards generating sustainable values and increasing cooperative behavior amongst stakeholders throughout the value chain.[32]

Integrating Environmental, Economic and Social Factors into LCA Studies

As discussed above, the literature has emphasized the increasing importance of sustainable development, but for many firms this has been a difficult task due in part to high degrees of complexity. According to Matos and Hall,[33] these circumstances make it difficult for decision-makers to fully understand the implications of how the parameters interact, leading to less-than-ideal options or compromises,[34] or increased political influences.[35] Environmental parameters will involve considerable complexities because of the very nature of ecosystem interactions;[36] conducting an LCA for sustainable development is that much more complex because it involves both scientific and non-scientific parameters due to interactions amongst economic, environmental and social factors.

In addition to complexity, Matos and Hall[37] suggest that it is also often difficult to identify key parameters, such as lobbyists or activist groups. Given that secondary stakeholders often have different rights, claims or interests than do primary stakeholders[38], conflicting or difficult-to-reconcile pressures may emerge.[39] Furthermore, given that secondary stakeholders are not involved in a transaction-based relationship, they may be difficult to identify at the early stages of technology development.[40] According to Matos and Hall[41] (p. 1091), "LCA for sustainable development is thus a rich mix of technical and non-technical issues," and disregarding interdependences may compromise LCA contribution to the sustainability performance of a new technology.

Although companies increasingly recognize that social factors may affect the development of new technologies or products, few studies provide guidance on how to deal with such factors. Matos and Hall[42] proposed an analytical framework that addresses LCA appropriateness in the evaluation of complex technologies for sustainable development. The framework is based on Elkington's[43] triple bottom lines of economic, social and environmental sustainability pressures and Hall and Martin's[44] TCOS framework for evaluating innovative uncertainties, i.e. technological, commercial, organizational and social uncertainties. They suggest that a technology can be conceptualized as a scientific experiment, or series hurdles that must be overcome before it is a successful innovation. The first is technological uncertainty, which is concerned with whether the potential innovation is technologically feasible, and is based on scientific and engineering heuristics and knowledge. Commercial uncertainty deals with whether or not it can compete successfully in the marketplace, and is based on marketing knowledge. Organizational uncertainty is concerned with whether the potential innovation is congruent with the firm's overall strategy and capabilities, and whether the firm possesses adequate intellectual property protection (e.g. patents) and complementary assets to appropriate the benefits of the innovation,[45] henceforth referred to as the "appropriability" regime. Social uncertainty is concerned with the societal impact of the innovation on or from diverse secondary stakeholders, and whether or not it will be resisted by civil society, and involves both social and environmental concerns. In analyzing LCA, Matos and Hall distinguished between environmental and social uncertainties, arguing that the underlying heuristics differ. For example, when conducting an LCA, environmental data, although often highly complex, is typically quantitative and generally accepted and understood within the scientific community (although the boundary definition is often debated), whereas social parameters are sometimes more ambiguous and based on less quantifiable data. Table 8.1 provides examples of economic, environmental and social parameters and the TCOS framework.

Table 8.1 **Examples of economic, environmental and social parameters to be considered during the identification of key variables and interconnections**

Economic			Environmental	Social
Technical	*Commercial*	*Organizational*		
• Raw material processing • Chemical reactions • Sub-products • Productivity • Processing time • Thermal properties • Reusability	• Markets, competition • Price structure • Earnings • Cash flow operations • Investment • Capital expenditures • Purchases (goods & services)	• Complementary assets (access to capital, market, internal expertise, economies of scale) • Firm competencies, capabilities intellectual property protection; other appropriability mechanisms	• Air emissions • Water discharge quality • Energy consumption • Water use • Waste management • Land disturbance and reclamation	• Jobs created • Knowledge enhanced/transferred to local communities • Health and safety (e.g. employees injuries, fatalities) • Health and safety of local communities • Equal opportunities and diversity (for women, aboriginals, persons with disabilities) • Potential negative side effect on or from secondary stakeholders • Stakeholders' engagement satisfaction

Source: Matos & Hall[46]

Under situations of low complexity and ambiguity (i.e. where variables and outcome probabilities can be estimated), Hall and Martin suggest that Popper's[47] scientific conjecture–refutation approach is appropriate. Under more complex and ambiguous situations such as social uncertainties, different heuristics are needed, such as Popper's[48] "piece-meal social engineering,|" Lindblom's[49] conceptualization of public decision-making as a process of "muddling through" and "mutual partisan adjustment," and Mintzberg's[50] argument that strategy is an emergent process, all of which acknowledge implicitly or explicitly the limitations of bounded rationality.

The Matos and Hall framework suggests that before conducting an LCA, practitioners should identify uncertainties by asking stakeholders about the key TCOS variables and how they may interconnect. For example, in order to list economic, environmental and social parameters, the authors suggest asking stakeholders the following question: "What parameters would you consider?" Similarly, in order to identify possible interdependences one should ask "If there are any changes made in a parameter (e.g. changing packaging material from plastic to cardboard), what other parameters will also be changed?"

Methodology

We draw from complexity theory, stakeholder theory and the supply chain literatures to examine how the LCA framework can help identify potential economic, environmental and social issues and their interactions related to the life cycle of emerging technologies. The replacement of phenol-formaldehyde (PF) resins with biomass-based (lignin) resins is used as our primary example to illustrate the framework that identifies which factors are key to undertake an LCA that provides useful information for the development of a more sustainable technology. Data was taken from technical papers drawn from the scientific literature.

Examining how an LCA framework can be used to identify issues related to emerging technologies required a research setting that allowed an analysis of how economic, environmental and social factors may influence the early stages of technology development. The development of lignin-based resins has several features that made it suitable for this purpose. First, this technology explores genomic technologies to transition from non-renewable to sustainable biomass feedstock, which provides links to environmental and social hurdles. Second, there are links to technological and commercial hurdles as the proposed technologies depend on scientific breakthroughs, and need to be compatible with deep-rooted traditional technologies, with established value chain infrastructure such as distribution networks and scale production.

Biomass-Based Resins: Economic, Environmental and Social Issues

Phenol-formaldehyde (PF) resins are synthetic polymeric materials mostly used to improve hardness and dimensional stability, as well as heat, moisture and chemical resistance of a number of products.[51] Examples of PF resin applications include panel boards, glass insulation binder, paper lamination, coating abrasives, phenolic foams and fiber-reinforced panels. The main structural panel applications for phenolic resins are plywood and oriented strand board (OSB). PF resins are amongst the most cost-effective type of adhesive and the building and construction industries account for 75% of PF resin demand in Canada and the US.[52] There are, however, some environmental and social concerns related to PF resins. For example, the use of formaldehyde in resins has raised issues regarding human and environmental health, as formaldehyde is a suspected carcinogen.[53] The emission of organic solvents is detrimental to air quality, and legislation that limits total volatile organic compounds (TVOC) emissions to indoor air from construction products is becoming increasingly stringent.[54] There are also concerns about limited product end-of-life opportunities to reuse, recycle and recover energy due to contaminants in reclaimed wood.

Studies on lignin-based resins have been motivated by a potentially attractive future market based on innovative technologies that could reinvigorate a somewhat stagnated pulp and paper market in North America. There is also the attraction of developing bio-resins technology that allows wood to be sent for composting, reuse or recovery of energy without any environmental or health and safety issues being compromised, plus reducing the use of fossil fuels.[55] Indeed, studies have shown a potential opportunity to replace part or all phenolic used in the PF resins production process with lignin.[56]

New lignin-based resins technology involves lower energy processes for lignin removal using biological pre-treatment as an alternative to the traditional energy-intensive thermochemical steam treatment at high temperatures and pressure. One promising method uses white-rot fungi as a natural lignin degrader.[57] and other studies suggest that an alternative and potentially effective method is to use soil bacterial enzymes, which .are easier to grow in large-scale fermenters.[58] While the results are promising, technological challenges remain, such as improving chemical reactivity, product quality or color compared to conventional resins.[59] One common difficulty in innovative processes involves the technical barriers of translating small-scale laboratory results into a large-scale economically viable process. Some of these technical challenges could be overcome with changes in the lignin separation process from wood processing. However, this may compromise the quality of cellulose, the most valuable product of the wood breakdown process; manufacturers may thus be reluctant to make changes that may compromise their economic returns.[60]

Environmental LCA studies on PF resins and related products have emphasized the importance of improving the environmental performance of formaldehyde-based resin both during its production process and as an input of other life cycle stages such as wood composites.[61] According to Wilson,[62] impacts due to the production of PF resins are small compared to the impacts related to its material resources such as natural gas and crude oil. For example, in order to produce 1kg of PF liquid resin, on-site energy use is 0.443MJ compared with 40.35MJ/kg resin for in ground resources. However, the same study reports that VOCs and formaldehyde emissions are 100% and 69% higher for on-site compared to in-ground sources. LCA studies on wood composites suggest that the use of lignin-based materials for the production of PF resins may significantly improve the product's environmental profile with regards to global warming, photochemical oxidant compound, acidification and eutrophication impact categories.[63] However, these studies do not address how practitioners and researchers can overcome the challenges of balancing process technical and economic performance with social and environmental improvements throughout the supply chain.

POTENTIAL ECONOMIC, ENVIRONMENTAL AND SOCIAL ISSUES OF BIOMASS-BASED RESINS

In this section, we use the Matos and Hall LCA framework to identify the sustainability hot spots of a new technology, in this case, the production and use of lignin-based resins. Table 8.2 summarizes these hot spots throughout the lignin-based resin life cycle compared to the conventional phenol-formaldehyde process. For each life cycle stage, we identify key economic, environmental and social challenges and opportunities. For example, input chemicals, fuels and electricity during the production phase is considered an area for further environmental and social improvements as all industrial processes aim to reduce emissions and use of fossil fuels. During the production process, there are, however, some technical challenges regarding molecular weight and viscosity control, oxidative stability, thermal stability, consistency in lignin properties, cure rate consistency and lignin color.[64] In terms of commercial and organizational issues, as the technology will provide a new process, patenting may not always provide strong protection from imitation,[65] although there are opportunities for trade secrets and vendor license agreements that may strengthen the appropriability regime. Such challenges may be compensated for by the potential environmental benefits derived from reduced use of toxic chemicals, which will reduce emissions to air when compared with traditional phenolic resins production. The last life cycle stages, use and reuse, may represent the highest potential environmental and social benefit related to lignin-based resins.

Table 8.2   Sample sustainability 'hot spots' throughout lignin-based resin life cycle when compared to the conventional phenol-formaldehyde process

Sustainability criteria / Life Cycle stages	Economic			Environmental	Social
	Technological	Commercial	Organizational		
Input materials: Chemicals, fuels, electricity and lignin	-	-	-	• Reduced GHG emissions and VOCs • Less dependence on non-renewable resources	• Improved health & safety issues (e.g. employees chemical exposure) • Potentially better stakeholders relations (e.g. NGOs, environmentalists)
Production: Lignin resin production process	• Challenges regarding reactivity, product stability, cure and colour	• New lignin-based resin process	• Relatively strong appropriability regime, mostly process innovation using trade secrets, vendor license agreements	• Reduced GHG emissions and VOCs • Less dependence on non-renewable resources	• Improvement on health and safety issues (e.g. employees chemical exposure) • Potentially better relations with stakeholders such as NGOs, environmentalists
Use: Resin applications in wood composites manufacturing	• Challenges with product quality and colour • Overcoming new building material regulatory framework	• New lignin-based product	• Relatively good appropriability regime; attractive future market	• Reduction of GHG emissions and VOCs from formaldehyde	• Potential new jobs creation • Improvement on health & safety issues (construction workers chemical exposure) • Potential better relations with stakeholders
Reuse: Wood resource reuse, recycle and recover energy	-	-	-	• Improved opportunities for reuse and recycle	• Improved health & safety issues (chemical exposure of end consumers) • Potentially better relations with stakeholders

The hot spots presented previously also describe how technological, commercial, organizational, environmental and social issues illustrate the interconnections between the life cycle stages. Such interactions point out the key opportunities for stakeholders' collaborations so that sustainability aspects of lignin-based resins can be accomplished. For example, primary stakeholders such as lignin feedstock providers may find higher incentives to cooperate with lignin resin producers if the market for more environmentally sustainable wood products is established. This may require the collaboration of the construction industry and demand from end users, which in turn may be shaped by secondary stakeholders such as environmental groups. In this case, these groups may have an important role as salient stakeholders, by influencing supply chain managers' decisions regarding the adoption of the technology.

The key point of this research is that the technology developers should engage with stakeholders at the early stages of the life cycle and supply chain, such as R&D researchers and mill operators, as well as interact with stakeholders at the end of the supply chain, such as building companies and consumers, environmental advocates and NGOs among others. The heuristics for understanding the needs of various stakeholders may differ, however. For example, LCA practitioners, scientists and engineers developing the new technology typically base their heuristics on scientific methodologies, whereas other stakeholders such as NGOs and social activists may be less dependent on purely scientific information. Such an approach is consistent with Popper's "peace-meal social engineering" strategy for dealing with complex situations and will be an effective mechanism to find more sustainable solutions for technical challenges. In addition, it will provide opportunities to identify environmental, economic and social benefits throughout the supply chain.

The technical challenges of translating small-scale laboratory results into large-scale production can be overcome through collaboration between researchers and stakeholders such as engineering companies that can provide important inputs related to the economic viability of a new product production. For example, scientists may favor research on soil bacteria enzymes over the fungi lignin pre-treatment process because the latter is more difficult to translate to large-scale production. Such a collaborative effort would provide a more efficient way of distributing the benefits of the technology throughout the supply chain, a crucial element when dealing with complex systems, as suggested by Levinthal and Warglien.[66]

One should expect stakeholder relations to change because the system is adapting and evolving as the agents, interactions and environments respond to changes in economic, environmental and social parameters. According to Ethiraj and Levinthal,[67] because of variance in nature (positive or negative) and intensity (interaction strength) of parameter interdependences and stakeholder salience, the system may be highly sensitive to some changes while robust to others. Although such variances in influence are difficult to predict, our framework allows *searching* for potential issues during the developmental stage of the technology where adaptations are easier to implement compared to later phases of project management and execution.[68] Further research is thus necessary to explore sensitiveness issues in terms of stakeholder salience for sustainable technologies.

Conclusions

Drawing on complexity theory, stakeholder theory and the supply chain literature, we identified key issues related to the development of lignin-based technology as a replacement for PF resins. As suggested by complexity theory, the interactions amongst many variables (in this case environmental, economic and social) represent a challenge for practitioners and researchers considering the sustainability context of new technologies. However, such a challenge also represents opportunities for improvements.

We added to the Matos and Hall framework by suggesting that practitioners should make efforts to qualitatively identify interconnections amongst economic, environmental and social variables for each phase of the product life cycle. This will allow for the examination of hot spots of opportunities for sustainable improvements. In addition, this will provide a better understanding of the interactions amongst stakeholders in the value chain, which may have significant positive implications for collaboration,

We concluded that by looking at the technological, commercial, organizational, environmental and social factors of each phase of the life cycle stages, we were able to identify hot spots for opportunities for improvements of the technology, particularly at the early phase of the technology's development. In addition, this approach allowed us to identify that stakeholders from different stages of the life cycle and supply chain that sometimes belong to different industry sectors were sometimes strongly interconnected, thus showing the importance of fostering collaborative work amongst them. Such an approach can provide the technology developers with useful insights for shaping the technology towards more economically, socially and environmentally sustainable options.

Our study aims to lay the groundwork for conducting an LCA for sustainable innovations and paths for further research. For example, further empirical work is needed to investigate how stakeholder interactions can be systematically integrated into LCA analytical procedures, as well as the financial and human resources required to do so. Empirical case studies would provide a way to investigate these issues because they would allow the identification and analysis of insights from the diversity of stakeholders involved, the complexity of their relations, as well as how such relations would affect technological, commercial and organizational factors. The message for practitioners and researchers is that the application of the LCA concept on innovated technology development represents a useful mechanism for the initial identification of major issues related to a product or process, allowing these issues to be explored in more detail as necessary.

Acknowledgements

This research would not have been possible without the financial support provided by Genome Canada and Genome BC.

Notes

1   Sarkis, J. (2001). "Manufacturing's role in corporate environmental sustainability". *International Journal of Operations & Production Management*, Vol. 21, No. 5/6, 666–686.

2   Sroufe, R., Curkovic, S., Montabon, F. and Melnyk, S.A. (2000). "The new product design process and design for environment". *International Journal of Operations & Production Management*, Vol. 20, No. 2, 267–291.

3   Krikke, H., Le Blanc, H. and Van de Velde, S. (2004). "Product modularity and the design of closed-loop supply chains". *California Management Review*, Vol. 46, No. 2, 23–39.

4   ISO (International Organization for Standardization) 14040 (1997). Environmental management: Life cycle assessment – Principles and framework. International Organization for Standardization, Geneva.

5   Mihelcic, J.R., Crittenden, J.C., Small, M.J., Shonnard, D.R., Hokanson, D.R., Zhang, Q., Chen, H., Sorby, S.A., James, V.U., Sutherland, J.W. and Schnoor, J.L. (2003). "Sustainability science and engineering: The emergence of a new metadiscipline". *Environmental Science & Technology*, Vol. 37, 5314–5324.

6   Allenby, B.R. (2000). "Implementing industrial ecology: The AT&T matrix system". *Interfaces*, Vol. 30, No. 3, 42–54.

7   Funtowicz, S. and Ravetz, J. (1992). "Three types of risk assessment and the emergence of post-normal science". In S. Krimsky and D. Golding (eds.). *Social Theory of Risk*. London: Praeger Publishers.

8   Matos S. and Hall J. (2007). "Integrating sustainable development in the extended value chain: The case of life cycle assessment in the oil & gas and agricultural biotechnology industries". *Journal of Operations Management*, Vol. 25, 1083–1102.

9   Simon, H. (1962). "The architecture of complexity: Hierarchic systems". *Proceedings of the American Philosophical Society*. December, 467–482; Simon, H. (1969). *The Sciences of the Artificial*. Cambridge, MA: MIT Press.

10   Ansoff, I. (1957). "Strategies for diversification". *Harvard Business Review*, Vol. 35, No. 5, 113–119; Martin, M. (1994). *Managing Innovation and Entrepreneurship in Technology Based-Firms*. New York: Wiley; Nelson, R.R. and Winter, S.G. (1982). *An Evolutionary Theory of Economic Change*. Cambridge, MA, Harvard University Press; Rogers, E. (1994). *Diffusion of Innovations* (4th edn). New York: Free Press; Utterback, J. (1994). *Mastering the Dynamics of Innovation*. Cambridge, MA: Harvard Business School Press.

11   Stinchcombe, A. (1965). "Social structure and organizations". In J.G. March (ed.), *Handbook of Organizations*. Chicago: Rand McNally.

12   Hall, J. and Martin, M. (2005). "Disruptive technologies, stakeholders and the innovation value chain: A framework for evaluating radical technology development". *R&D Management Journal*, Vol. 35, No. 3, 273–284.

13   Matos S. and Hall J. (2007), *op. cit.*

14   Hall, J. and Vredenburg, H. (2003). "The challenges of innovating for sustainable development". *Sloan Management Review*, Vol. 45, No. 1, 61–68; Hall, J. and Vredenburg, H. (2005). "Managing the dynamics of stakeholder ambiguity". *MIT Sloan Management Review*, Vol. 47, No. 1, 11–13.

15   Hall, J. and Vredenburg, H. (2003), *op. cit*; Hall, J. and Vredenburg, H. (2005), *op. cit.*; Matos S. and Hall J. (2007), *op. cit.*

16   Matos S. and Hall J. (2007), *op. cit.*

17   Simon, H. (1962), *op. cit.*

18   Hertwich, E., Hammitt, J. and Pease, W. (2000). "A theoretical foundation for life-cycle assessment". *Journal of Industrial Ecology*, Vol. 4, No. 1, 13–28.

19   Bovea, M and Wang, B. (2003). "Identifying environmental improvement options by combining life cycle assessment and fuzzy set theory". *International Journal of Production Research*, Vol. 41, No. 3, 593–609; Geyer, R and Jackson, T. (2004). "Supply loops and their constraints: The industrial ecology of recycling and reuse". *California Management Review*, Vol. 46, No. 2, 55–73; Mehalik, M.M. (2000). "Sustainable network design: A commercial fabric case study". *Interfaces*, Vol. 30, No. 3, 180–189; Mattheus, H.S. (2004). "Thinking outside 'the box': Designing a packaging take-back system". *California Management Review*, Vol. 46, No. 2, 105–119; Sarkis, J. (2001), *op. cit.*

20   Matos S. and Hall J. (2007), *op. cit.*

21   Ethiraj, S.K and Levinthal, D. (2004). "Modularity and innovation in complex systems". *Management Science*, Vol. 50, No. 2, 159–173.

22   Stone, M. and Brush, C. (1996). "Planning in ambiguous contexts: The dilemma of meeting needs for commitment and demands for legitimacy". *Strategic Management Journal*, Vol. 17, 633–652.

23   Hall, J. and Vredenburg, H. (2003), *op. cit.*

24   Freeman, R. (1984). *Strategic Management: A Stakeholder Approach*. Boston: Pitman.

25   Choi, T.Y., Dooley, K.J. and Rungtusanatham, M. (2001). "Supply networks and complex adaptive systems: control versus emergence". *Journal of Operations Management*, Vol. 19, 351–366.

26   Freeman, R. (1984), *op. cit.*

27   Clarkson, M. (1995). "A stakeholder framework for analyzing and evaluating corporate social performance". *Academy of Management Review*, Vol. 20, 92–117.

28   Mitchell, R., Agle, B. and Wood, D. (1997). "Toward a theory of stakeholder identification and salience: Defining the principle of who and what really counts". *Academy of Management Review*, Vol. 22, No. 4, 853–886.

29   Agle, B.R., Mitchell, R.K. and Sonnenfeld, J.R. (1999). "Who matters to CEOs? An investigation of stakeholder attributes and salience, corporate performance, and CEO values". *Academy of Management Journal*, Vol. 42, No. 5, 507–525.

30   Matos S. and Hall J. (2007), *op. cit.*

31   Levinthal, D.A. and Warglien, M. (1999). "Landscape design: Designing for local action in complex worlds". *Organization Science*, Vol. 10, No. 3, 342–358.

32   Sharma, S. and Henriques, I. (2005). "Pathways of stakeholder influence in the Canadian forest products industry". *Business Strategy and the Environment*, Vol. 14, 384–398; Perez-Aleman, P. and Sandilands, M. (2008). "Building value at the top and at the bottom of the value-chain: MNC-NGO partnership". *California Management Review*, Vol. 51, No. 4, 100–125; Dahan, M.N., Doh, J.P., Oetzel, J. and Yaziji, M. (2010). "Corporate-NGO collaboration: Co-creating new business models for developing markets". *Long Range Planning*, Vol. 43, 326–342.

33   Matos S. and Hall J. (2007), *op. cit.*

34   Frenken, K. (2001). "Understanding Product Innovation using Complex Systems Theory". PhD thesis, University of Amsterdam; Gatignon, H., Tushman, M., Smith, W. and Anderson, P. (2002). "A structural approach to assessing innovation: Construct development of innovation locus, type, and characteristics". *Management Science*, Vol. 48, No. 9, 1103–1122.

35   Rosenkopf, L. and Tushman, M. (1988). "The coevolution of community networks and technology: Lessons from the flight simulation industry". *Industrial and Corporate Change*, Vol. 7, 311–346.

36   Wolfenbarger, L. and Phifer P. (2000). "The ecological risks and benefits of genetically engineered plants". *Science*, Vol. 290, 2088–2093.

37   Matos S. and Hall J. (2007), *op. cit.*

38   Clarkson, M. (1995), *op. cit.*

39   Hall, J. and Vredenburg, H. (2003), *op. cit.*

40   Hall, J. and Martin, M. (2005), *op. cit.*

41   Matos S. and Hall J. (2007), *op. cit.*

42   Matos S. and Hall J. (2007), *op. cit.*

43   Elkington, J. (1998). *Cannibals with Forks: The Triple Bottom Line of 21st Century*. Gabriola Island, BC: New Society Publishers.

44   Hall, J. and Martin, M. (2005), *op. cit.*

45   Teece, D. (1986). Profiting from technological innovation. *Research Policy*, Vol. 15, 285–305.

46   Matos S. and Hall J. (2007), *op. cit.*

47   Popper, K. (1959). *Conjectures and Refutations* (5th edn). New York: Harper and Row.

48   Popper, K. (1945). *The Open Society and its Enemies*. London: Routledge.

49   Lindblom, C. (1959). "The science of muddling through". *Public Administration Review*, Vol. 19, No. 1, 77–88.

50   Mintzberg, H. (1978). "Patterns in strategy formation". *Management Science,* Vol. 24, 934–948.

51   Cetin, N.S. and Ozmen, N. (2002). "Use of organosolv lignin in phenol–formaldehyde resins for particleboard production I. Organosolv lignin modified resins". *International Journal of Adhesion & Adhesives*, Vol. 22, 477–480; Dewar, J. (2007). "Review of existing bioresins and their applications". Garston, UK: Forestry Government. Construction Division BRE. Retrieved December 1, 2011, from www.forestry.gov.uk/pdf/cr_existingBioresins.pdf/$FILE/cr_existingBioresins.pdf.

52   Global Insight (2005). "The economic benefits of formaldehyde to the United States and Canadian economies". Lexington, MA: Formaldehyde Council Inc. Retrieved November 1, 2011 from www.methanol.org/Methanol-Basics/Resources/The-Economic-Benefits-of-FA-to-the-US-and-Canadian.aspx.

53   Dewar, J. (2007), *op. cit.*

54   González-García, S., Feijoo, G., Heathcote, C., Kandelbauer, A. and Moreira, M.T. (2011). "Environmental assessment of green hardboard production coupled with a laccase activated system". *Journal of Cleaner Production*, Vol. 19, 445–453; Dewar, J. (2007), *op. cit.*

55   Moubarik, A., Pizzi, A., Allal, A., Charrier, F. and Charrier, B. (2009). "Cornstarch and tannin in phenol–formaldehyde resins for plywood production". *Industrial Crop Production,* Vol. 30, 188–193.

56   Cetin, N.S. and Ozmen, N. (2002), *op. cit.*; Hu L., Pan, H., Zhou, Y. and Zhang, M. (2011). "Methods to improve lignin's reactivity as a phenol substitute and as replacement for other phenolic compounds: A brief review". *BioResources*, Vol. 6, No. 3, 3515–3525; Jorge, F.C. (2010). "Reducing negative environmental impacts from the manufacturing and utilization of lignocellulosics-derived materials: An overview on research in 2007–2009". *Molecular Crystals and Liquid Crystals*, Vol. 522, No. 1, 28[328]–35[335].

57   Sena-Martins, G., Almeida-Vara, E. and Duarte, J.C. (2008). "Eco-friendly new products from enzymatically modified industrial lignins". *Industrial Crop Production*, Vol. 27, 189–195.

58   Ahmad, M., Roberts, J.N., Burton, K., Eastwood, D., Bending, G.D. and Bugg, T.D. (2010). "Development of novel assays for lignin degradation: Comparative analysis of bacterial and fungal lignin degraders". *Molecular Biosystems*, Vol. 6, 815–821.

59   Jorge, F.C. (2010), *op. cit.*

60   Graham, R.G. (2003). "Use of bark-derived pyrolysis oils as a phenol substitute in structural panel adhesives (Report)". Boston, MA: Department of Energy. Retrieved November 15, 2011, from www.osti.gov/bridge/purl.cover.jsp?purl=/828163-KecBKd/native/.

61   González-García, S., Berg, S., Gumersindo, F. and Moreira, M.T. (2009). "Environmental impacts of forest production and supply of pulpwood: Spanish and Swedish case studies". *International Journal of Life Cycle Assessment*, Vol. 14, 340–353; Wilson, J.B. (2010). "Life-cycle inventory of formaldehyde-based resins used in wood composites in terms of resources, emissions, energy and carbon". *Wood and Fiber Science*, Vol. 42(CORRIM Special Issue), 125–143.

62   Wilson, J.B. (2010), *op. cit.*

63   Athena Institute (2008). A cradle-to-gate life cycle assessment of Canadian softwood plywood sheathing. Retrieved January 15, 2012 from www.athenasmi.ca/publications/docs/CIPEC_Canadian_Plywood_LCA_Final_Report.pdf; González-García, S., Berg, S., Gumersindo, F. and Moreira, M.T. (2009), *op. cit.*; González-García, S., Feijoo, G., Heathcote, C., Kandelbauer, A. and Moreira, M.T. (2011), *op. cit.*

64   Holladay, J.E., Bozell, J.J., White, J.F. and Johnson, D. (2007). "Top value-added chemicals from biomass: Volume II – Results of screening for potential candidates from biorefinery lignin". Springfield, VA: Pacific Northwest National Laboratory (PNNL) and the National Renewable Energy Laboratory (NREL). National Technical Information Service, US Department of Commerce. Retrieved November 21, 2011, from http://www1.eere.energy.gov/biomass/pdfs/pnnl-16983.pdf.

65   Teece, D. (1986), *op. cit.*

66   Levinthal, D.A. and Warglien, M. (1999), *op. cit.*

67   Ethiraj, S.K and Levinthal, D. (2004), *op. cit.*

68   Clark, K.B. and Wheelwright, S. (1993). *Managing New Product and Process Development: Text and Cases*. Free Press, New York.

9

Creating Socially Responsible and Environmentally Sustainable IT-Enabled Supply Chains

IAN M. LANGELLA,* JERRY CARBO,† AND VIET DAO‡

Keywords

Environmental sustainability, social responsibility, supply chains, operations management, logistics, information systems.

Introduction

The exploration of sustainable operations management has received attention in both theory and practice ever since the term sustainability was defined by the Brundtland Commission in 1987. Companies such as Wal-Mart and GE often tout themselves as green companies due to their own operations or the products they sell. However, their focus on sustainability is often too narrow in scope and thus the term loses meaning, as companies may in fact be causing vast amounts of human and environmental destruction while purporting to be sustainable organizations.

First, organizations, and researchers too, often focus on a single component of sustainability, namely environmental sustainability. This focus ignores the broader conception that sustainability has three components, people, planet, and profit, and specifically impact on people and society. Even worse, many organizations have focused their sustainability efforts as a strategic tool to increase (or sustain, perversely) profits. This not only ignores the broader social implications of sustainability, it seems to refuse to accept any decision criteria outside of profitability on a fundamental level. Finally, organizations and researchers often focus on sustainability from a single unit of

---

* Associate Professor of Supply Chain Management, John L. Grove College of Business, Shippensburg University. E-mail: IMLangella@ship.edu.

† Associate Professor of Management, John L. Grove College of Business, Shippensburg University. E-mail: jacarbo@ship.edu.

‡ Associate Professor of Management Information Systems, John L. Grove College of Business, Shippensburg University. E-mail: vtdao@ship.edu.

operations, viewing a single firm as either sustainable or destructive. Unfortunately, this approach ignores the fact that sustainability – in order to be present – must be facilitated up and down the supply chain. Just as effective supply chain management can result in efficient multi-firm decisions, so responsible supply chain management can ensure that goods delivered to customers were produced in a responsible manner at each step of the supply chain.

In this chapter we will start by presenting some examples of a narrow focus on sustainability. We will then present a model for a broader view of sustainability that focuses on all aspects of the supply chain, paying particular attention to often-ignored social responsibility. This will lead to our conception of socially sustainable systems of supply chains that protect human rights and provide fair remuneration with human dignity while producing and delivering goods in a safe, clean, environmentally friendly manner. Finally, we set out some of the roles and responsibilities for different parts of the organization in achieving these socially sustainable supply chains. In particular, given the importance of information exchange within and across supply chain partners in developing such sustainable supply chains, our chapter also focuses on the role of IT resources in enabling the development of sustainable supply chains.

Sustainability and Examples of a Narrow Focus

In this section, we will start by examining various definitions of sustainability. This will lead us into an elaboration on some examples of narrowly focused sustainability, which will motivate a broader and more sophisticated manifestation of sustainable management.

SUSTAINABILITY

The idea that the responsibilities of businesses and organizations in general go beyond the merely financial is not a new one. The field of business and society emerged during the earliest periods of the New Deal era and has existed since.[1] In the early 1990s researchers such as Carroll,[2] Matten and Crane,[3] Mintzburg,[4] and others acknowledged that a socially responsible company must do more than simply make a profit. According to Carroll's model of sustainability, managers, corporations, and employers in general have four levels of responsibility: capital, legal, ethical, and philanthropic responsibilities.[5] Carroll also suggests that organizations owe these duties to a broad group of "stakeholders," which includes anyone with a "stake, claim or interest in the operations or decisions of the firm." For Matten and Crane corporations take on an added responsibility due to the power that they hold in the global economy and so are responsible for protecting and even assuring human rights are met.[6]

Likewise, Mintzberg, Simons, and Basu suggest that too many corporations operate on a series of "half-truths" that result in a sole focus on profits and that businesses should focus instead on their broader responsibilities to other stakeholders, including employees and communities.[7] As Hart and Milstein put it, "Increasingly, global capitalism is being challenged to include more of the world in its bounty and protect the natural systems and cultures upon which the global economy depends."[8] As a result, sustainability has increasingly become mainstream within management studies and practices. The most well-adopted definition of sustainability is that of the Brundtland Commission as "development that meets the needs of the present without compromising the ability of future generations to meet their needs."[9]

Over the last 15 years in particular the idea of sustainable operations has emerged as part of this broader business responsibility. Sustainability has become an important issue from both a business research perspective and a business practice perspective. This recent push can be attributed to the fact that while the last 15 years have brought much economic growth, there are many concerns surrounding both wealth disparity and natural resource depletion. These concerns are manifested in legislation expanding the responsibility of firms, the increasing focus on training managers in sustainable management, and the development of theory to support sustainable managerial decision making.[10] A perspective has emerged that defines sustainability to include three components: the natural environment, society, and economic performance.[11] This perspective is generally referred to as the "triple bottom line." The triple bottom line approach suggests that besides economic performance, organizations need to engage in activities that positively affect the environment and society while also looking to make a profit. However, the idea is that no one of these goals would trump the others, all three being of equal importance.

EXAMPLES OF NARROW FOCUSES

Despite this triple bottom line ideal, much of the current sustainability focus in both research and practice continues to focus on one or two legs of the model and thus never reaches true sustainability. In meeting such demands for sustainable development, focuses tend to either be centered on sustainable operations as a means to increase firm performance – in other words profits – or on the environmental perspective without explicit incorporation of the social aspects of sustainability.[12] Too often, both in practice and research, sustainability fails to focus on the requirement to meet all three components – sustainability of the planet, sustainable profits, and a sustainable life for all people of the planet such that they are afforded the opportunity to live the dignified life which makes one human.

While a great deal of work has been done in sustainability in the last decades, it seems that much of it is preoccupied with profit and that people and the planet are considered insofar as they lead to long-term profitability.[13] A survey of practitioners by the Economist Intelligence Unit found that revenue, profit, and cost were the top three reasons that respondents engage in corporate citizenship.[14] In another study, Springett found that for managers the term "viability" often replaced the term "sustainability." Managers were concerned with the ongoing ability of the organization to function and succeed. They were focused on eliminating waste, mainly for the profit motive. There was little concern for green initiatives to benefit society as a whole.[15]

Much like these practitioners, researchers often follow this same path of making profit the primary leg of the model. For some, the direct question becomes "Does it pay to be green?", as we see in Reinhardt's 1999 article.[16] In the field of supply chain and operations management research, Guide and colleagues, in a contribution on closed loop supply chain management, go so far as to suggest that "no rational firm will invest in environmental measures to save the earth."[17] Kleindorfer and colleagues focus on sustainable operations and look to sustainability to promote the "long term success" of businesses.[18] Citing Porter, they emphasize the long-term cost benefit of even environmental protection laws. Most recently, a piece on sustainable supply chains poses two research questions, the second of which is whether or not sustainability leads to long-term profitability.[19] In the IT literature, sustainability tends to focus on cost reduction.[20] Similarly in the sustainable HRM literature, sustainability seems to be just another strategic tool.[21] This further underscores that implied hierarchy of decision criteria.

When the people side of the issue is addressed, it is normally from the standpoint of meeting consumers' demands (again in order to increase revenues or to avoid the risk of consumer boycotts). Bansal and Clelland focus on sustainable operations as a way to gain legitimacy and observe increase in the firm's market value.[22] Even Elkington's own work in 1994 focuses on the marketing or PR push for sustainable operations.[23] The reasons to adopt these practices are not presented as protecting the planet or the people of the planet; instead they are presented as meeting the concerns of the customers and investors in a firm.

While the clear primary focus for researchers and practitioners of sustainability and corporate citizenship is clearly a strategic, profit-centered focus, it is also clear that the path to achieving this competitive advantage is an environmental focus rather than a people focus. Elkington discusses consumers' demands for a healthy planet, the IT literature focuses on the environment-based idea of "green IT," the operations literature discusses innovative techniques to cut down on environmentally harmful waste.[24] However, in each of these conceptions little or nothing is done to address the people of an organization. There is no discussion about whether current practices are sustainable for the employees or if they are destructive. There is little discussion of creating safe, dignified work that meets the basic human needs, addresses human rights and much less even considers the higher level needs and rights. Nowhere in the sustainable operations practice or research are concerns like the payment of a living wage or entitlement to paid time off (both listed as human rights under the Universal Declaration of Human Rights) discussed. There is no mention of assuring that the core labor rights under the ILO – freedom from slave labor, elimination of child labor, freedom from discrimination, the right to organize and engage in concerted activity – are adhered to as part of the sustainable practices. We fail to recognize that one component of sustainability is meeting the "needs" of today, including these human rights and the "needs" of all human beings as identified by Maslow. Further, when we talk about sustainability, there is a lack of discussion about whether the practices we engage in are creating a sustainable economy for all. There is little discussion of the destruction of the middle class in the US or the growing inequality and the resulting destructive nature of such inequality.[25] We see little concern as to whether business operations lead to the types of boom and bust cycles that have resulted in lost income for millions of working class and middle class citizens in the US and around the world. Without a more directed focus on the outcomes to all of the stakeholders of a business, we can never truly operate in a sustainable fashion.

The current conceptions of sustainability both in practice and research are profit centered. If this is to be the adopted conception of sustainability, then there is no need for a field of study of sustainability. Instead, sustainability becomes just another tactic within the field of strategic management. In the recent debate on global warming and international trade, Nobel prize winning economist Paul Krugman remarked that globalization and free trade do us no good if there is no globe.[26] While some conceptions of sustainability do at least consider planetary concerns as mentioned by Krugman, these conceptions at best are nothing more than environmentalism and again there is no real need for a new field. If we do not take care of the people of our planet then profit is meaningless and, at least for the people of the planet, environmental stewardship is also meaningless.

Now that we have examined sustainability and the need for a broader and complete understanding, we will turn our attention to discussing supply chain management and what it might offer the study of sustainability.

Responsible and Sustainable Supply Chain Management

In this section, we will begin by examining supply chain management as a field and particularly the fundamental insight of supply chain management, something called coordination, where the profit of two or more firms can be collectively increased by their combined actions. This will lead us to a discussion of how entire supply chains can be made sustainable and how individual firms and their supply chain partners can collectively contribute to a better world.

SUPPLY CHAIN MANAGEMENT

Almost every product we examine today is brought to us through the cooperation (in the narrowest sense) of several firms. The product was manufactured by a manufacturer and distributed by various parties to retail points of sale. Also involved were the suppliers of the manufacturer, and the suppliers' suppliers, and so on. As it became apparent that these firms could increase their combined profits through (now in a more broad sense) cooperation, the field of supply chain management emerged.

In an example of supply chain coordination, we can imagine a supply chain with a manufacturer, supplier, and retailer, in addition to the customary terminal member, the consumer. The end customer pays the retailer a certain amount of revenue for the purchase of the good. This revenue represents the sum of all of the revenue that the chain might gain from providing the product. Meanwhile, each part of the chain incurs a cost in providing its part of the value addition which takes place. Each partner sells the intermediate product to the next downstream product, receiving part of the revenue through the price. In the past, each partner would make decisions only in their own firm's profit maximizing interest. Suppliers would decide on the price of the input, the manufacturers would decide on the amount to order, each considering their own profit. Likewise, manufacturers would decide on the price to offer the retailers, and the retailer would decide on the amount to purchase. As an aside, this is exactly what we previously referred to as cooperation in the narrower sense, and this represents the status quo.

Under coordination, supply chain partners would share cost (and other) information to determine the prices and quantities at each stage which will result in the highest profit for the chain as a whole.[27] This typically involves some partners making disadvantageous (if viewed in their own isolated interest) decisions, decisions which potentiate even greater gains to other partners. Coordination concerns itself with calculating the optimal decisions and necessary payments between partners to allow for the coordination. In other words, those partners whose gains were large must subsidize the others, else the coordination would never take place. This is only one example which centers on procurement price and quantity decisions. Other examples of supply chain coordination where partners collaborate much more closely than traditional relationships held by two profit maximizing firms can be seen in areas like training and development and facility co-location.

Nowadays competition is not so much between firms and as between supply chains. It matters less what an individual firm does than that it is dependent on its partners. In today's more globalized world, supply chains are strewn across wide distances. This means we are moving ever increasing amounts of product around, creating more environmental demands. We are also less aware of the actions of supply chain partners which are further and further away. Just as successful demand fulfillment requires a supply chain approach where all of the actors are considered, having a sustainable supply chain will also logically require coordination between firms. After all, it does little good if a product is manufactured in an eco-friendly manner if the manufacturer's suppliers and distribution channels made large demands on the environment. Vachon and Klassen analyze green supply chains and provide some empirical insight.[28] Of course, supply chains are very different in different industries, a topic highlighted by the work of Pagell and Wu.[29]

In the following sections, we will discuss how an entire supply chain can be made sustainable. Just as it is our belief that the triple bottom line represents true sustainability, it is also our belief that in order for a product to be sustainable, the entire supply chain that produced it must be sustainable, from the supplier's suppliers to the retailers used to sell the product to consumers. We will start by examining the supplier and procurement, leading to manufacturing and production, and lastly marketing channels and distribution.

PROCUREMENT AND SUPPLIERS

In order to produce something, typically manufacturers will require many inputs from suppliers. These can range from raw materials like rubber or plastic to sophisticated components and modules. Suppliers are typically selected by the total landed cost, which is the cost including transportation and custom clearance and all costs necessary to land the goods at the buyer's door. While cost is important, since it influences profit and the firm must remain profitable, additional considerations are needed. As toymaker Mattel found out when its toys were found to be tainted with lead, having a complicated and global supply chain will not excuse a manufacturer from poor supplier performance.[30] Related to this, Foerstl and colleagues examine the role of sustainability risks using several firms in the chemical industry as a multi-case study.[31] While supplier codes of conduct might be a mechanism to align sustainability along the supply chain, as Jiang found suppliers under cost pressure will sometimes falsify numbers to obfuscate their triple bottom line performance.[32]

The firm can and should juxtapose the environmental burden caused by the production of the input. This would include the supplier's supplier (i.e. second tier) and subsequent tiers, and so would capture the entire supply chain environmental cost up to that point in the value adding processes. In this manner, a purchaser could compare several suppliers. The analysis should also include the supplier's use of recycled material and the end-of-use disposal environmental burden of inputs.[33]

Likewise, suppliers' people performance could also be measured and compared. While some suppliers offer a living wage and benefits to employees, others will seek to avoid these costs. Some firms will seek to be a good neighbor by investing in local communities over a long time horizon, while others will view the relationship in a short-term, arm's length manner without considering local communities more than immediately necessary. Carter and Jennings provide an interesting glimpse into the positive effects of purchasing social responsibility, showing that those firms which do this enjoy more fruitful buyer–supplier relationships and deeper commitment.[34]

A firm which believes in sustainability and the triple bottom line will naturally seek to do business with suppliers who are fellow believers. This might make it necessary for a firm to exert more control over suppliers than it might have otherwise have preferred, as in the Migros Palm Oil case.[35] Comparing suppliers based on cost, environmental, and social performance will contribute towards encouraging firms to offer consumers a truly sustainable product and to adopt a broader view of sustainability.

PRODUCTION AND MANUFACTURING

Traditionally, operations management, which fulfills the demand for a product, is the functional area where the majority of the costs are incurred. Producing goods requires labor, capital, and management in various proportions depending on the industrial context. Because of this, it is natural to presume that there might also be a large impact on sustainability by decisions made in production and manufacturing.[36]

A product's effects on the environment start with the design itself, and various design alternatives (product designs where the product has the same functionality) might differ greatly in the amount of material and energy needed to produce the products. Here, one must bear in mind that the weight and packaging of the product will affect the amount of energy needed to distribute it.[37] The choice of material is important, something that becomes essential when considering product recovery as we will soon discuss.[38] Likewise, hazardous materials can be utilized or avoided. Lastly, the same product with the same design can be produced in more than one manner, and production tooling will be another differentiating factor.

It is particularly relevant to mention the role of product recovery management (PRM) within the field of sustainability. In PRM, products which are at the end of their life or use, like engines which have failed or photocopiers returning from a lease, can be recovered by the manufacturer and used in some manner.[39] This might entail disassembling the returned products, inspecting the parts, and reassembling a good-as-new "remanufactured" product, as is done with engines at several large German auto manufacturers. In other cases, the recovered products can be recycled, decreasing the amount of material needed from the Earth. The issue of closed loop supply chain management is highlighted in the review by Seuring and Mueller.[40]

Manufacturing also impacts several groups of stakeholders, such as employees and communities. Employees are impacted by compensation, working conditions, and worker safety and health issues, for example.[41] Compensation should include not only remuneration, but also employee benefits and the like. Working conditions would include scheduling collaboration and training and development. Lastly, worker health and safety issues would protect employees' short and long-term health. The ISO 26000 norm has implicitly incorporated these aspects into reporting, as shown in Castka and Balzarova, for example.[42] It is easy to imagine situations where the firm would be under financial pressure to pay workers inadequately or ignore safety concerns, and true sustainable (and therefore responsible) management should seek to address also these concerns.

MARKETING CHANNELS AND DISTRIBUTION

Once produced, the product must be distributed to the market, and the channel used will generally depend on the product and geographic market served. Here too, different distribution options and partners will result in a more or less sustainable and responsible solution.

Environmental sustainability here would demand the incorporation of environmental costs in distribution network decisions, even in a multi-firm context.[43] When choosing retail partners, the environmental performance of the retail chains can be examined for suitability.

Arguably more interesting is to examine differences in the manner in which different retailers treat their employees. Here, there are a couple of good examples which will provide some illustration. In the US, Sam's Club competes against Costco in the wholesale market. Where Sam's Club compensates employees at minimum levels and resists unionization, Costco is known to pay its employees a living wage with benefits and takes a long-term view of its relationships with employees. Indeed, Costco financially outperformed Wal-Mart, providing support for those who believe that companies can do well by doing good, and that unethical decisions are by no means a prerequisite for success rather the seeds for failure.[44] In Germany, a similar juxtaposition can be made between Schlecker and dm in the retail drugstore market. Schlecker has been criticized for some time for wage levels, working conditions, and its attitude to unions. Schlecker maintained a list of employees which the firm considered important enough to "keep an eye on". The list, some 20 pages long, included union organizers, senior (and therefore expensive) employees, and other select employees.[45] German business magazine *Der Handel* also pointed out that employees (their person, clothing, and locker) were subject to search at any time and could be dismissed if an item was found which was sold at the store and if the employee was unable to prove that it was purchased. While Schlecker was traditionally stronger based on market share, dm has made substantial gains in the past few years both in number of outlets as well as in market share.[46] Although Schlecker made attempts to improve its employee relationships, it had gone out of business in the time between revisions of this chapter. While we cannot say that this is due to the company's lack of sustainability, it is arguable that its demise could have been prevented by a more employee friendly disposition. The above examples demonstrate that retail partners differ considerably, and more responsible and sustainable firms will seek to do business with retail partners who share their views. While it may seem odd to decide against some retailers or channels, and thereby sacrifice revenue, companies like Snapper correctly identify this as a moment to differentiate.[47]

It must be remembered that while these decisions might be difficult even in a domestic, single country context, making them will be even more challenging when considering multiple international markets which have resulted from globalization. In this case, there are a plethora of decisions to make, and information on performance (cost, social, environmental) will be more difficult to gather from geographically dispersed partners and candidates.

From Green to Sustainable: IT and Sustainability

As discussed, firms need to focus on sustainability both in their internal operation as well as in collaboration across their supply chain partners, and such sustainability activities could be enabled by information technology (IT) resources. This section discusses the contribution of IT resources to such sustainability activities, first looking at intra-firm (functional coordination) and then examining inter-firm (sectorial) supply chain cooperation.

IT AND SUSTAINABILITY WITHIN FIRMS

Over the last several decades, IT has increasingly permeated all aspects of business and played an increasingly important role in enabling business capabilities that help firms survive and thrive. As such, it is natural that IT plays an important role in enabling firms become more sustainable within their business operation.

As previously mentioned, while sustainability has gained increasing attention from academics and practitioners, sustainability research and practice have been traditionally over-concerned with the environment and under-concerned with people, especially the issue of employee wellbeing. This is particularly true with the current research and practice on IT and sustainability, where most research has focused on the role of IT in reducing the carbon footprint of firms' technical IT infrastructure through "green IT" initiatives. Research by the US Federal Environmental Protection Agency[48] has shown that data centers consume 1.5% of the US's electrical power, costing US$4.5 billion annually. However, a large percentage of such power usage is wasted and could be saved by optimizing energy consumption of these data centers by using virtualization, blade servers, etc. Additionally, by optimizing technology usage behaviors such as shutting down personal computers at the end of working day and enabling power saving features of servers and personal computers, firms could cut energy usage of computers by as much as 40%, saving them money and reducing IT infrastructure's environmental impacts.[49]

While green IT is important in helping firms become more efficient with their technology usage, recent research has started to recognize and argue for the contribution of IT towards sustainability beyond energy consumption reduction and to focus on IT's potential in improving firms' business strategy and activities towards more sustainable objectives. For example, Dao, Langella, and Carbo proposed an integrated framework of how IT resources could be combined with human and supply chain resources to help companies develop capabilities to deliver sustainable values and gain sustained competitive advantage at the same time.[50]

In addition to helping firms become more environmentally friendly with regard to technology usage, IT resources (including tangible technical components, human technical and managerial IT skills, and intangible IT-enabled resources such as knowledge, customer orientation, etc.) could be combined with other firm resources to develop specific sustainability business strategy and initiatives. For example, the application of IT resources that help firms automate certain business operations could help firms reduce costs and environmental impacts. Using digitized documents and e-filing systems, firms could automate different business activities, reducing costs of energy and paperwork processing. Additionally, automating business activities can free employees of mundane tasks and allows them time to focus on process improvements for sustainability objectives.

However, it is for the firms to decide whether such automated applications of IT allow them to cut their payroll or enable current employees to focus on more knowledge-intensive process improvement tasks. Therefore, human resource management activities such as hiring, training, and rewarding must be aligned with the application of automated IT resources to help firms develop sustainability capabilities in this field.

In another example, the application of technologies (such as sensors, RFID, etc.) that automate the collection and processing of sustainability operation information could help firms improve operational efficiency through automating organizational information processing ability.[51] The availability of such information would also help company managers with regard to employee management practices (rewards, engagement, etc.) and improve firms' environmental and social performance.

INFORMATION AND SUSTAINABILITY ACROSS THE SUPPLY CHAIN

As discussed, sustainability could not be achieved by the actions of a single firm. For sustainability to be truly effective, entire supply chains, not just individual partners, must operate in a sustainable manner. For example, if a manufacturer has strict environmental and labor management standards, its business is not truly sustainable if its suppliers exploit labor and have operations that have harmful impacts on the environment. As a result, implementing sustainability strategies requires firms to have a sound understanding of social and environmental impacts of the production as well as consumption of their products or services. These factors must be evaluated for their impact across the whole supply chain.

IT resources, when implemented within a supply chain context, can enable firms to collaborate to make the whole supply chain sustainable in different ways. First, in order to develop a sustainable supply chain, firms need to develop metrics of sustainability that could be used across the supply chain to measure the social and environmental impacts of business activities at different stages of the chain. Information systems can enable firms to standardize, monitor, capture, and utilize data and metadata that help evaluate economic, environmental, and social impacts of business activities, and communicate such information across the supply chain to help make the whole chain become more sustainable.

An example of this is Wal-Mart's Packaging Sustainable Value Network, a group of 200 leaders in the packaging industry. The network created a packaging scorecard with nine specific metrics that enabled suppliers to compare their own packaging materials, energy efficiencies, and environmental standards against their competitors'. Such metrics help suppliers focus on specific improvements towards sustainability. Such integration of information across a supply chain requires partners to develop capabilities to (1) share information, (2) optimize the staging and flow of materials by leveraging the visibility of resources, and (3) streamline interdependent financial operations such as billing and payments.

Information systems could also improve information flows among supply chain partners to help increase stakeholder involvement in the management of operations, increase employee training in environmental and matters, develop and facilitate cross-functional coordination, and monitor internal and external performance in financial, social, and environmental terms. For example, demands for information about a firm's social and environmental impacts from external stakeholders – e.g. consumers, regulators, non-governmental organizations or conscientious investors – have risen dramatically. While it is critical that sustainability practices must support employees being open and receptive to outside stakeholders, IT resources that enable such openness could help firms gain more legitimacy with regard to sustainability. For example, web portals could enable firms to provide transparent information about the social and environmental impacts of their products or enable collaboration with outside stakeholders such as potential employees and local communities.

In conclusion, IT resources that enable firms to develop capabilities to unbundle information flows from physical flows, and to share information with their supply chain partners and other stakeholders could have significant potential in enabling firms to coordinate with other supply chain partners and stakeholders to make the whole supply chain more sustainable.

Conclusion and Outlook

As we have seen, in order for a product to be truly sustainable, its entire supply chain should be sustainable. Because of the disparity in definitions of sustainability, and our belief that only the most broad manifestation, the triple bottom line, will adequately provide consistently sustainable global commerce, we call for this to be the universally accepted definition. In the contemporary global economy, it is difficult but necessary that all supply chain partners add value in a sustainable manner, protecting the environment as well as the often-ignored human rights of all stakeholders, regardless of where they live.

A sustainable supply chain starts with sustainable suppliers, supplier's suppliers, and so forth. A product which uses inputs produced by damaging the environment or stakeholders will be unsuitable for incorporation into any sustainable product. As value is added by manufacturing and production operations, the triple bottom line consequences must be followed closely, paying attention to stakeholders and the planet. Lastly, products which are sustainable should be marketed and distributed in channels which are also aware of their impact on the planet and stakeholders, and which seek to minimize adverse impact and positively contribute to the society which has enabled them to operate.

In order to create true sustainability, all functions within a firm must operate in such a way as to ensure the wellbeing of human and environmental stakeholders while still being financially feasible. Within the firm, this will require moving beyond just the operations and IS functions discussed in this chapter to explore the role of accounting, marketing, general management, HR management, and finance to name a few. Beyond the firm level, we must see this sustainable focus across the functions of each player in the supply chain. While these roles within each function must be further defined through research and practice, the IT framework we have introduced here[52] affords a path towards aligning and integrating these practices across entire supply chains that may span the globe.

In this realm, management information systems has much to contribute, more than just the decreased energy and material use that much of the literature seems preoccupied with. Within single firms, information systems can efficiently coordinate the actions of various functional units, gathering metrics in one corner of the firm and transporting them to other areas where decisions are being made. In geographically dispersed supply chains, the flow of information has an even more prominent role, and one that must take place over great distances. Here, information on a supplier's triple bottom line performance will be relevant not only in their selection, but also their evaluation and development. Lastly, information on distribution channels will prove useful in avoiding channels with poor social and environmental performance. As more firms embrace sustainability, it will become ever more difficult for firms to resist, if supply chains are made entirely transparent in this regard.

Notes

1   Marens, R. (2008), "Recovering the past: Reviving the legacy of the early scholars of corporate social responsibility", *Journal of Management History*, Vol. 14, No. 1, pp. 55–72.

2   Carroll, A.B. (1991), "The pyramid of corporate social responsibility: Toward the moral management of organizational stakeholders", *Business Horizons*, Vol. 34, No. 4, pp. 39–49; Carroll, A.B. (1998), "The four faces of corporate citizenship", *Business and Society Review*, Vol. 100, No. 1, pp. 1–7.

3   Matten, D., & Crane, A. (2005), "Corporate citizenship: Toward an extended theoretical conceptualization", *Academy of Management Review*, Vol. 30, No. 1, pp. 166–179.

4   Mintzberg, H., Simons, R., & Basu, K. (2002), "Beyond selfishness", *MIT Sloan Management Review*, Fall, pp. 67–74.

5   Carroll, 1991, *op. cit.*

6   Matten & Crane, *op. cit.*

7   Mintzberg, et al., *op. cit.*

8   Hart, S., & Milstein, M.B. (2003), "Creating sustainable value", *Academy of Management Executive*, Vol. 17, No. 2, pp. 56–67.

9   Brundtland, G.H. (1987), *Our Common Future*. In: *Report of the World Commission on Environment and Development*. Oxford: Oxford University Press.

10 Mintzberg, et. al., *op. cit.*; Hart & Milstein, *op. cit.*

11 Elkington, J. (1994), "Towards the sustainable corporation", *California Management Review*, Winter, pp. 90–100; Elkington, J. (2004), "Enter the triple bottom line". In: A. Henriques & J. Richardson (eds.), *The Triple Bottom Line: Does It All Add up?* London: Earthscan, pp. 1–16.

12 Carter, C.R., & Rogers, D.S. (2008), "A framework of sustainable supply chain management: Moving toward new theory", *International Journal of Physical Distribution & Logistics Management*, Vol. 38, pp. 360–387.

13 Hart, S., & Milstein, M.B. (2003), "Creating sustainable value" *Academy of Management Executive*, Vol. 17, No. 2, pp. 56–67.

14 EIU (2008), *Doing Good: Business and the Sustainability Challenge*. London: The Economist Intelligence Unit.

15 Springett, D. (2003), "Business conceptions of sustainable development: A perspective from critical theory", *Business Strategy and the Environment*, Vol. 12, pp. 71–86.

16 Reinhardt, F.L. (1999), "Bringing the environment down to earth", *Harvard Business Review*, July–August, pp. 149–157.

17 Guide, V.D.R., Harrison, T., & Van Wassenhove, L. (2003), "The challenge of closed-loop supply chains", *Interfaces*, Vol. 33, No. 6, pp. 3–6.

18 Kleindorfer, P.R., Singhal, K., & Van Wassenhove, L.N. (2005), "Sustainable operations management", *Production and Operations Management*, Vol. 14, pp. 482–492.

19   Carter & Rogers, *op. cit.*

20   Wagner, S., Hespenheide, E., & Pavlovsky, K. (2009), "The responsible and sustainable board", *Deloitte Review*, Vol. 4, pp. 60–71.

21   Colbert, B.A., & Kurucz, E.C. (2007), "Three conceptions of triple bottom line business sustainability and the role for HRM", *Human Resource Planning*, Vol. 30, No. 1, pp. 21–29.

22   Bansal, P., & Clelland, I. (2004), "Talking trash: Legitimacy, impression management, and unsystematic risk in the context of the natural environment", *Academy of Management Journal*, Vol. 47, No. 1, pp. 93–103.

23   Elkington, 1994, *op. cit.*

24   Elkington, 1994, *op. cit.*

25   Wilkinson, R., & Pickett, K. (2009), *The Spirit Level: Why Greater Equality Makes Societies Stronger*. New York: Bloomsbury Press.

26   Krugman, P. (2009), "Empire of carbon", *The New York Times*, May 14.

27   Hopp, W. (2007), *Supply Chain Science*. New York: McGraw Hill, pp. 129–146.

28   Vachon, S., & Klassen, R.D. (2006), "Extending green practices across the supply chain: The impact of upstream and downstream integration", *International Journal of Operations & Production Management*, Vol. 26, No. 7, pp. 795–821.

29   Pagell, M., & Wu, Z. (2009), "Building a more complete theory of sustainable supply chain management using case studies of 10 exemplars", *Journal of Supply Chain Management*, Vol. 45, No. 2, pp. 37–56.

30   Adenekan, D, & Calkins, M. (2009), "Mattel, Inc.: Lead tainted toys". In: E. Raufflet & A. Mills (eds.) *The Dark Side: Critical Cases on the Downside of Business*. Sheffield: Greenleaf, pp. 222–249.

31   Foerstl, K., Reuter, C., Hartmann, E., & Blome, C. (2010), "Managing supplier sustainability risks in a dynamically changing environment: Sustainable supplier management in the chemical industry", *Journal of Purchasing & Supply Management*, Vol. 16, pp. 118–130.

32   Jiang, B. (2009), "Implementing supplier codes of conduct in global supply chains: Process explanations from a theoretic and empirical prospective', *Journal of Business Ethics*, Vol. 85, pp. 77–92.

33   Epstein , M. (1996), *Measuring Corporate Environmental Performance*. Chicago: Irwin.

34   Carter, C.R, & Jennings, M.M. (2002), "Social responsibility and supply chain relationships", *Transportation Research Part E*, Vol. 38, pp. 37–52.

35   Hamprecht, J., & Corsten, D. (2007), "Purchasing strategies and sustainability: The Migros Palm Oil case study". In: J. Hamschmidt (ed.) *Case Studies in Sustainability Management and Strategy*. Sheffield: Greenleaf, pp. 123–142.

36   Kleindorfer, P.R., Singhal, K., & Van Wassenhove, L.N. (2005), "Sustainable operations management", *Production and Operations Management*, Vol. 14, No. 4, pp. 482–492.

37   Shedroff, N. (2009), *Design is the Problem: The Future of Design must be Sustainable*. Brooklyn: Rosenfeld.

38   Bhat, V. (1996), *The Green Corporation: The Next Competitive Advantage*. London: Quorum.

39   Guide, V., & Van Wassenhove, L. (2009), "The evolution of closed-loop supply chain research", *Operations Research*, Vol. 57, No. 1, pp. 10–18.

40   Seuring, S., & Mueller, M. (2008), "From a literature review to a conceptual framework for sustainable supply chain management", *Journal of Cleaner Production*, Vol. 16, pp. 1699–1710.

41   Cohen, E. (2010), *CSR for HR: A Necessary Partnership for Advancing Responsible Business Practices*. Sheffield: Greenleaf.

42   Castka, P., & Balzarova, M.A. (2008), "ISO 26000 and supply chains: On the diffusion of the social responsibility standard", *International Journal of Production Economics*, Vol. 111, pp. 274–286.

43   Langella, I.M., & Zanoni, S. (2010), "Eco-efficiency in logistics: A case study on distribution network design", *International Journal of Sustainable Engineering*, Vol. 4, No. 2, pp. 115–126.

44   Cascio, W.F. (2006), "Decency means more than "always low prices": A comparison of Costco to Wal-Mart's Sam's Club", *Academy of Management Perspectives*, Vol. 20, No. 3, pp. 26–37.

45   *Der Handel* (2011), "Spiegel: Schlecker führt Liste mit unliebsamen Mitarbeitern". May 1, 2011. In German.

46   *Der Handel* (2011), "dm Drogeriemarkt rückt Schlecker auf die Pelle". April 15, 2011. In German.

47   Fishman, C. (2007), "The man who said no to Wal-Mart". *Fast Company*. Retrieved July 30, 2011 from www.fastcompany.com/magazine/102/open_snapper.html.

48   Environmental Protection Agency (2007), *Report to Congress on Server and Data Center Energy Efficiency.*

49   Curtis, S. (2009), "Green IT Can Save Money, Too", *Business Week*. Retrieved November 30, 2009 from *www.businessweek.com/globalbiz/content/oct2009/gb20091030_246576.htm*.

50   Dao, V., Langella, I., & Carbo, J. (2011), "From green to sustainability: Information technology and an integrated sustainability framework", *Journal of Strategic Information Systems*, Vol. 20, No. 1, pp. 63–79.

51   Chen, A., Boudreau, M., & Watson, R. (2008), "Information systems and ecological sustainability", *Journal of Systems and Information Technology*, Vol. 10, No. 3, pp. 186–201.

52   see Dao, et al. *op. cit.*

10 Social and Environmental Responsibility, Sustainability, and Human Resource Practices

WENDY S. BECKER* AND RICHARD SMITH†

Keywords

Social responsibility, sustainability, human resource management, business ethics.

Introduction

Human resource practices have important long-term implications for social and environmental responsibility and sustainability in ways that may not be fully anticipated. *Socially responsible* human resource practices help organizations attract, develop, and manage employees while valuing them as investments.[1] *Sustainable* human resource practices help organizations "meet the needs of the present without compromising the ability to meet future needs."[2] *Environmental social responsibility* concerns the people, planet, and profit resources that lead to sustained competitive advantage.[3] Both social and environmental responsibilities concern the interconnectedness of human resource practices across organizations and industries. In this chapter, we explore the idea that the human resource practices used when times are tough can limit success during better times. Both irresponsible and unsustainable human resource practices can have unanticipated long-term impact, ultimately limiting organizational effectiveness.

During economic downturns, employees may be expected to increase productivity even while the organization is downsizing staff. But research has shown that over the long term, costs are not reduced through downsizing.[4] Employee productivity can be pushed only so far without detrimental effects such as increased turnover or reduced work quality. Recent economic data from the US Bureau of Labor Statistics illustrates this point. US output per hour rose steadily from 2009 and peaked during the first quarter of 2010. Throughout 2010, productivity began to trend down, with the first two quarters

---

* Professor Wendy S. Becker, John L. Grove College of Business, Shippensburg University, 1871 Old Main Drive, Shippensburg, PA 17257-2299 USA. E-mail: wsbecker@ship.edu. Telephone: +1 7174771410.

† Richard Smith. Exel Inc. 300 Salem Church Road, Mechanicsburg, PA 17050 USA. E-mail: rjsmith366@gmail.com. Telephone +1 7175761360.

of 2011 showing the first real decline in productivity since the credit crisis in 2008.[5] The downward trend in productivity cannot be explained by more employees entering the workforce, as the unemployment rate has stayed steady at around 9%. One hypothesis is that productivity has been maxed out in the current workforce because of employee fatigue. By sacrificing the long-term strength of the workforce in exchange for short-term cost reduction, employers eventually experience the real costs of human resource decisions. Sustainable, socially responsible human resource practices influence other areas in the value chain, such as productivity and product quality.[6]

A sole economic focus on short-term profit positions employees and the environment as expendable commodities, weakening organizations in at least three fundamental ways. First, a focus only on cost sets up a false dichotomy between profit and the environment. Second, a sole focus on cost positions employees and the environment simply as inventory without regard for longer-term consequences. Finally, a sole focus on cost does not acknowledge research relating employee knowledge and skills to the development of healthy and effective organizations, relevant to and imperative for a shift from traditional business practices to sustainable operations. Central to this argument is that motivated and engaged workers provide the innovations needed for social responsibility and sustainability – specifically with regard to the environment. The emphasis is on the *value* offered by employees as the intellectual capital of the organization. While costs to implement socially responsible initiatives may initially appear higher, ultimately society reaps greater benefits through sustainable development.

Three broad functions of human resource practices – attracting, developing, and managing employees – are examined in this chapter, using a framework that contrasts socially responsible practices with short-term, unsustainable practices (Table 10.1) often found in the US and increasingly adopted outside the US. Our position is that a sole focus on *cost* is not sustainable and sets up a false dichotomy between profit and the environment.[7] Importantly, 95% of CEOs agree that increasingly business must address social and environmental issues in society. Yet it is the *employees* who drive organizational efforts to attain sustainability through their knowledge and work experience.[8] Hence we view employee stakeholders as investments rather than as costs. Industry examples (primarily from the US) are used to demonstrate the challenges involved in creating sustainable value chains. We stress that global concerns for the environment will require thinking about people management at a higher level to explore how behavior is connected across organizations and industries.

Table 10.1 Contrasting short-term and socially and environmentally responsible, sustainable employment practices

	Short-term employment practices	Socially responsible, sustainable employment practices
Attracting	"Seat-of-the-pants" hiring due to extreme pressing need.	"Developing" candidates using job fairs, vocational schools, internships, job shadowing.
	No provision for job preview. Not being honest with applicants about the facts of the job.	Use of realistic job previews that make explicit good and bad aspects of jobs for applicants.
	Hiring employees with known skill deficits because of a short-term need.	Weighing both short-term and long-term human resource objectives.
	Overuse of short-term, temporary workers whose employment can be easily terminated.	Use of labor supply and demand forecasting to strategically plan for human resources.
Training and Development	"Trial-by-fire." Little or no training for new employees.	Using onboarding and frequent roundtables to provide consistent feedback.
	Overused on-the-job training may fail if employees are unwilling to codify or share specific job knowledge with peers.	Rewarding employees for developmental activities, such as helping, mentoring, and sharing knowledge with other employees.
	Online training systems used as primary training source.	Appropriate mix of online and remote delivery training methods with on-site classes so that employees can share experiences and issues with each other.
Managing	Over-outsourcing core employee skills.	Recognizing the value of employee core skills and people, planet, profit; allowing employees to bid on work scheduled to be outsourced; managing key partnerships with customers and contractors.
	Reducing benefits or increasing employee contribution share, limited benefit options, no employee input into benefit changes.	Long-term reward strategies; communicating the value of benefit packages to employees.
	Changing reward systems all at once (eliminating 401(k) match, base salary reduction, freeze on raises, increase in healthcare contributions).	Balanced strategy used when cost-cutting measures are needed. Creative strategies which still leave majority of workforce and their learned skills and experience intact.

Attracting Employees

Socially responsible and sustainable practices in the employment value chain result when organizations attract – and keep – the right employees. Making last-minute selection decisions due to unexpected and pressing demands represents short-term, unsustainable thinking that does not value employees as investments. In contrast, using validated employee selection practices creates value (similar to long-term capital investments in new technology) and demonstrates a socially responsible, sustainable approach to employment practices. The goal should be to maximize job fit and retention of valued employees.

Failure to anticipate the need for new personnel leads to poor selection decisions along with rushed initial training. The authors experienced an example of this in one US organization. High turnover led to placing new employees in front of customers before the employees were fully trained. This ultimately led to frustration, because while the newly hired employees wanted to do a good job, they could not because they were not given the training and tools they needed. They quickly became disengaged.

Not being completely honest with job candidates about challenges in the job also represents short-term thinking. Realistic job previews (RJPs) provide explicit information to applicants about the good and bad attributes of jobs before hire. Research has found RJPs to be a good tool for preventing turnover.[9] The influence that RJPs have on the reduction of turnover can be understood as an ethical underpinning of employer honesty.[10] Job fairs, vocational schools, job shadowing, and using retirees and part-time employees effectively can be used to attract the right people to the organization.

Honest Tea[11] is an organic beverage company that focuses on corporate social responsibility and sustainability in its employment practices. One-tenth of new employees start out as interns and 42% of job openings are filled from within,[12] a level of internal promotion that is quite high.[13] It will be interesting to see if Honest Tea retains these sustainable practices since being acquired by the larger firm Coca-Cola.

Staffing benches that have been emptied due to downsizing and other cost-control measures leave no slack for organizations to respond to unexpected and critical needs. Without a ready stream of internally developed candidates (as well as a database of high-quality external candidates) sub-optimal hiring decisions are made in the heat of the moment. Failure to allow for slack in the system can lead to a breakdown in the sustainable value chain of employees.

An example demonstrates the problem. A US trucking company replaced management personnel in one of its large terminals because of major operational failures. The entire management team from a small facility was promoted to leadership roles in the larger terminal. As part of this overhaul, a former supervisor was rehired because of his familiarity with company policies and systems and because he could begin working immediately with little lag time. However, the supervisor was known to have poor people skills. Rehiring the problem employee solved a short-term, pressing need for technical skills, but created a more serious long-term management problem. The new manager of the small terminal had to devote critical administrative time counseling the supervisor and documenting his performance problems; the supervisor was subsequently fired within the year. Hiring people with known skill deficiencies leads to long-term sustainability issues. Problem employees become entrenched in the organizational culture, and the effect of one bad hire can have unanticipated effects throughout the value chain. Poor performers cause morale problems with other employees and portray the company in a negative light with customers. The trucking company could have benefited by taking a longer term view of its human capital.

Organizations that focus on short-term cost savings to the neglect of sustainable human resources place their future growth and flexibility in jeopardy. The reputation of Amazon, the world's largest online retailer, suffered in one community when it hired only temporary, expendable staff. A steady supply of temporary workers kept the warehouse fully staffed despite difficult work conditions and without the expense of a permanent workforce and good benefits. Catherine Ruckelshaus, National Employment Law Project, stated that:

> They can get away with it because most workers will take whatever they can get with jobs few and far between. The temp worker is less likely to complain about it and less likely to push for their labor rights because they feel like they don't have much pull or sway with the worksite employer.[14]

Not planning adequately for staffing needs risks reduction in the overall quality of an organization's human resources over the long term. A more proactive, prosocial approach to workforce planning is demonstrated in Hershey's "future opportunity" job description posting:

> This job posting is for a "future opportunity" and does not represent a current vacancy. Job listings such as this allow The Hershey Company to proactively review and identify talent on an on-going basis before a position becomes available. We encourage you to submit your credentials today with the understanding that a real position does not exist and that you may not be contacted by a recruiter in reference to your resume submission. When an appropriate position opens that matches your profile, we will contact you to apply directly to the new position.[15]

In this way, the organization designates specific skills needed for the future using sustainable practices to develop talent pools. Job analysis can be used to determine which skills need to be brought into the organization and which skills can be developed. This is especially recommended for key positions.

Training and Development of Employees

Failure to proactively train and develop employees adversely impacts the value chain in socially responsible, sustainable employment practices. Traditional accounting procedures that fail to consider employee training and development as an asset or future benefit are detrimental to sustainable employment practices. Effective practices in this area can include employee skill inventories, performance feedback, job enlargement, job enrichment, and promoting from within. For example, team-based organizations such as Miller Beer and Harley-Davidson involve team members in all aspects of the employee selection, training, and development process.[16]

Once employees are brought into the organization, the challenge becomes how to train them in the processes and systems of the organization. Even highly skilled employees need a lead time before they become independent contributors. The challenge many managers face is the need to fill a critical vacancy as quickly as possible with newly hired employees. In organizations that lack a long-term sustainable view, these employees will primarily be trained on-the-job in a "trial-by-fire" fashion. While on-the-job training has the advantage of quickly filling a position and having the new employee learn by doing on their own, long-term negative factors can emerge for the organization. Some negative consequences of "trial-by-fire" training are ingrained bad habits that can be hard to change and a lack of customer service skills derived from improper training in company procedures; industry examples of these negative consequences can be seen later in this section.

Previously mentioned Honest Tea conducts "crew drives" in which newly hired personnel travel in teams to help launch the brand in a new market. This serves as a proactive employee development strategy that helps to forge both a strong team mentality and positive brand identity.[17] Forging a strong team fulfills a critical need for new employees by helping them build a network and support system within the new organization. Quickly building trust and a team mentality as Honest Tea does, allows new employees to feel comfortable asking questions to learn new skills. Established personnel are also more motivated to help new employees if they see everyone as part of the team. Through helping the new employees succeed the entire team can be successful.

A key management challenge to maintaining long-term sustainable value chains is encouraging the sharing of job-specific knowledge and skills between entrenched employees and new members of the organization. Current employees may feel threatened by newly hired personnel and may hoard information and resources in a misguided attempt to protect their own job. In addition to team-building initiatives to blend new and current employees as mentioned above, employers should also make mentoring and education of new employees part of the performance review process for current staff members. When current staff see that they are being evaluated on mentoring efforts, they are more likely to be open to sharing their specialized skills and knowledge with new employees. When all employees have access to a broader skill and knowledge set, human resource performance and value is increased throughout the value chain.

If an organization is not following sustainable practices in the area of attracting employees, problems may begin to surface in the initial employee development stage. Hiring practices that take a short-term approach may result in employees with lower levels of cognitive ability and employees that prove difficult to develop. Employees hired with lower skill levels cannot have the initial impact on organizational effectiveness and as a result slow down the speed at which newly hired staff reach their full capacity.[18]

Customer service is another key area of employee effectiveness that suffers with a lack of sustainability with regard to employee development. Staff members who are rushed into new positions with inadequate training and development can cause service-quality erosion.[19] An example from the trucking industry exemplifies this concern. Rapid growth in the industry created an increased demand for certified delivery drivers. New hires were sent out to make deliveries with only the minimum amount of training required by the US Department of Transportation. "Trial-by-fire" tactics helped the organization fill critical vacancies over the short term. However, these key employees who lacked knowledge of company and customer procedures led to an increase in customer complaints. In this case, pressing drivers into full service without proper training created additional long-term issues when the employees developed bad habits that required extensive retraining in order to bring them into policy compliance.

Short-term, unsustainable employment practices can also be detrimental to the health and welfare of employees themselves. Employees are most susceptible to on-the-job injuries within the first year of their tenure and when performing new or unusual tasks.[20] When employees are not given proper training in safety procedures, an already dangerous situation can become exacerbated because of a lack of safety knowledge. In the aforementioned trucking sector, this can result in an increase in preventable traffic accidents. In one facility alone, five new drivers were terminated because they each had more than three preventable traffic accidents within their first year of employment. In many cases, these drivers had been hired with less than desirable ability to learn and very limited training in order to fill a critical short-term staffing need.

The sustainable, long-term employment practice most suited to solve the issues caused by "trial-by-fire" training is the process of onboarding. Successful onboarding focuses on educating new employees in company culture and values instead of spending the first few days of employment filling out forms. United Water has recently taken proactive steps to streamline its onboarding process by sending a welcome packet to new hires and having them complete an online process to enter basic information and sign off on important human resource forms. The process takes about 45 minutes and clears the way for the employee to spend their first day learning about the company's strategy and vision as well as beginning the socialization process with their peers and their manager.[21] By focusing the initial onboarding process on socialization and enculturation, firms can enhance the initial employee experience and increase the chances of keeping that employee for the long term.

Not only is the pace and amount of training as well as the concept of onboarding important, the way in which training is delivered is also of critical importance in maintaining sustainable employment practices. Due to cost-cutting measures and the desire to standardize training presentations, as well as issues with geographical distance, many companies are shifting to online training delivery methods as opposed to in-person methods. The advances in internet bandwidth and the proliferation of low-cost computers have allowed many companies to create training presentations that can be produced at a central location and broadcast to all areas of an organization. This has allowed companies to cut back on training personnel as well as travel costs for those organizations with multiple off-site facilities.

The negative result of this technological advance is that employees lose important interaction time with experienced employees. Not only can questions be answered directly during a live presentation, but employees also begin to learn company culture through interaction with employees during live training. One large international transportation company moved to a near total online training experience for many groups of employees. Managers would often place newly hired dockworkers in a sequestered cubicle in an office until they had completed all of their online training modules. This often consumed the new employee's first two full days of employment; during this time they had almost no interaction with other employees, either those in their peer group or those managing them.

While good company information can be gleaned from the online training system, new employees may not fully integrate this knowledge when it is so clinically separate from actual operations. The first few days of training are critically important in the enculturation and development of employees. Having new employees completely isolated from any interaction except that provided by a computer screen can cause employees to form opinions of how the company operates that may be very different from reality. This can also lead to new employees becoming frustrated if they do not understand a portion of the training and do not have someone readily available to answer their questions. A long-term sustainable training delivery method can include online training, but a blended approach that also involves live interactive sessions provides the best training.

Related to proper levels of interaction during initial employee training, another sustainable human resource practice is to ensure that managers are interacting with employees and getting feedback on their attitude towards company practices as well as their ideas for improvement. One process that was well implemented at a large trucking company with multiple locations was the requirement that managers hold monthly roundtables with employees paid an hourly wage in order to get their feedback on company operations. Employees from each department were brought in, and the employees that attended the roundtable rotated each month to allow for a diversity of opinion and observation. Managers were expected to give employees information about recent facility performance, but the primary goal of the meeting was for the manager to record comments and concerns from the employees and work towards implementing possible solutions to problems raised.

Managing Employees

Human resource management practices can communicate sustainability or short-term thinking. For example, failure to match reward system metrics with reward strategy or changing multiple reward structures all at once can communicate the wrong message to employees. A more sustainable approach includes employees in reward system design. Honest Tea involves employees in the design of benefits, which include reimbursement for health-club membership, tuition assistance, paid leave for volunteer activities, subsidies for transportation, and recognition for maintaining healthy eating habits and quitting smoking. Honest Tea recognizes that the advantages of including employees in reward system design ultimately outweigh implementation costs. While difficult to quantify, employee perceptions of sustainable human resources is an important asset to Honest Tea.

Another common management practice – outsourcing – can lead to loss of core skills in the organization. Greenberg, Grunberg, Moore, and Sikora[22] describe Boeing's cost-cutting efforts to transform its business strategy from technical design expertise to one driven by finance. The effort left Boeing short of critical skills needed not only for production, but for oversight of subcontractors and second-tier suppliers. Boeing has since reversed course to exert more control over partnerships with customers and contractors in the global supply chain. A more sustainable approach would be to allow employees to bid on work scheduled to be outsourced when feasible.

In addition to losing core skills through outsourcing, the *management* of outsourced relationships ripples throughout the value chain. Apple Computer realized record profits for its popular electronics products by micro-managing supply partners in China to keep costs as low as possible. Apple's approach can be contrasted with a more sustainable approach at Hewlett-Packard:

You can set all the rules you want, but they're meaningless if you don't give suppliers enough profit to treat workers well. If you squeeze margins, you're forcing them to cut safety (former Apple executive).

Our suppliers are very open with us. They let us know when they are struggling to meet our expectations, and that influences our decisions (Zoe McMahon, Hewlett-Packard, Supply Chain Social and Environmental Responsibility Program).[23]

Slim profit margins compromise safety when employees must work extended hours to increase productivity. Even with the implementation of regular audits and the creation of a Supplier Code of Conduct, many Apple suppliers still have core safety violations yet remain an Apple supplier. In the more sustainable Hewlett-Packard model, suppliers realize more profits and have incentives to improve worker conditions.

During the economic downturn of 2008, one US national transportation company sought to save money by suspending the company match for tax qualified defined pension contributions indefinitely, increasing the amount that employees pay for healthcare coverage, suspending all raises for hourly and salaried personnel for one year, and cutting the salary of management employees by 5–10%. These cuts were made all at once without any sort of phase-in and were also done concurrent with a number of layoffs. The net effect had a major impact on morale and caused many employees to question their loyalty to the organization.

Making drastic changes to employee benefit systems such as those illustrated above represents short-term thinking that is not sustainable over the long term. While some changes to employee benefit systems can be positive, as we outline below, implementing drastic negative changes from the point of view of the employee leads to a lack of long-term human resource sustainability. When an employer needs to reduce costs, alternate methods can help to slow the growth of benefit costs while still giving employees sustainable incentive for high performance. Some examples are: split pay increase budget into increases and cash awards, replace future base pay increases with incentive potential, tie contributions to defined contribution plans to performance (defined contribution plans are alternatives to traditional pension plans and are becoming common in the US due to reduced cost to the employer).[24] In addition, if reductions in benefits are required, effort should be taken to implement reductions in the least painful way possible. In the example from the transportation company above, the pain could have been reduced if these reductions were not all implemented at once but rather phased in over time as necessary.

Companies can put into place employment practices that do not treat people as valued investments. For example, companies Netflix and Groupon have adopted former General Electric CEO Jack Welch's controversial performance management strategy of firing the lowest performing 10% of employees every year:

A company that bets its future on its people must remove that lower 10 percent, and keep removing it every year – always raising the bar of performance and increasing the quality of its leadership.[25]

Over the long term, this management strategy can create a situation in which *all* employees continually fear the loss of their jobs, including high performers. Treating employees as expendable commodities is not a sustainable practice.

In contrast, the construction supply company Marvin Windows and Doors exemplifies a more sustainable approach to managing employees. Despite a collapse in housing construction that resulted in a reduction of the industry workforce by one-third, Marvin did not close plants or lay off employees, as did its competitors. Rather, Marvin preserved jobs by distributing the economic pain across the entire company. All employees received a pay cut and perquisites such as tuition reimbursement and profit-sharing were eliminated. Susan Marvin, President of Marvin Windows and Doors, explained to employees that the company would not resort to short-term tactics because:

> You can't cut your way to prosperity. You can't grow if you are cutting your lifeblood – and that's the skills and experience your work force delivers.[26]

Similarly, Whole Foods Market cofounder and co-CEO John Mackey notes that management's job is to focus on all stakeholders for the long term, by making sure:

> that we hire good people, that they are well trained, and that they flourish in the workplace, because we found that when people are really happy in their jobs, they provide much higher degrees of service to the customers. Happy team members result in happy customers. Happy customers do more business with you. They become advocates for your enterprise, which results in happy investors. That is a win, win, win, win strategy. You can expand it to include your suppliers and the communities where you do business, which are tied in to this prosperity circle.[27]

Summary and Conclusion

The recent economic downturn worldwide has led to drastic industry cost-cutting measures used with the intent to drive profitability. Cost-cutting measures have a direct impact on employees such as those that result in layoffs, reductions in compensation, reduction in benefits, and demands for increased productivity. Reacting to economic downturns with a focus only on the short term to the detriment of long-term sustainable employment practices can have unanticipated effects. Human resource practices have strategic implications for organizations, industries, and the environment.

Without long-term sustainability, social and environmental responsibility practices may be perceived as simply public relations. Significantly, employees can tell the difference between intentions without action and long-term efforts.[28] Nike learned this the hard way. Unsustainable labor practices in the developing world ultimately hurt its business:

> The way it hurt our business was that it hurt our people. Individual employees at Nike started to wonder what kind of a company they were working for and what message was being sent about the people who worked there (Nike Vice President Maria Eitel).[29]

Attracting, developing, and managing employees can be achieved using socially responsible, sustainable practices. But focusing solely on cost neglects the employee stakeholder and sets up a false dichotomy between profit and the larger business environment. We demonstrate some of the challenges involved creating sustainable value chains in employment practices. A more global focus will require thinking about people management as interconnected across organizations and industries.

Socially responsible organizations reap sustainable benefits by attracting, developing, and managing employees. The industry supply chain has an advantage since the long-term view includes fairness and justice for employee stakeholders. This is all the more important in a new economy in which resources are depleted, operations are globalized, and where the right people make the difference between success and failure over the long term.

Notes

1   Bernardin, H. J. (2010), *Human Resource Management: An Experiential Approach*, 5th edn. McGraw-Hill Irwin, Boston, MA.

2   World Business Council for Sustainable Development (2005), *Driving Success: Human Resources and Sustainable Development*. The World Business Council for Sustainable Development Publication.

3   Hart, S. (1995), "A natural resource-based view of the firm", *Academy of Management Review*, Vol. 20, pp. 986–1014; Hart, S. (2005), *Capitalism at the Crossroads: The Unlimited Business Opportunities in Solving the World's Most Difficult Problems*. Wharton School, Upper Saddle River, NJ; Hart, S. L. & Milstein, M. B. (2003), "Creating sustainable value", *Academy of Management Executive*, Vol. 17, pp. 56–67.

4   Becker, W. S. (2011), "Are you leading a socially responsible and sustainable human resource function?", *People & Strategy*, Vol. 34, No. 1, pp. 18–23; Becker, W. S., Carbo, J. A. II, Esq. & Langella, I. M. (2010), "Beyond self-interest: integrating social responsibility and supply chain management with human resource development", *Human Resource Development Review*, Vol. 9, No. 2, pp. 144–168; Cascio, W. (2000), *Costing Human Resources*. South-Western, Cincinnati, OH; Cascio, W. & Boudreau, J. (2008), *Investing in People: Financial Impact of Human Resource Initiatives*. Pearson, Upper Saddle River, NJ.

5   United States Department of Labor, Bureau of Labor Statistics, www.bls.gov/news.release/pdf/.

6   Rogelio, O. & Sterman, J. D. (2001), "Cutting corners and working overtime: quality erosion in the service industry", *Management Science*, Vol. 47, No. 7, pp. 894–914; Maon, F., Lindgreen, A. & Swaen, V. (2009), "Designing and implementing corporate social responsibility: an integrative framework grounded in theory and practice", *Journal of Business Ethics*, Vol. 87, pp. 71–89.

7   Porter, M. E. (1991), "America's green strategy", *Scientific American*, Vol. 264, No. 4, p. 168.

8   Aaron, S. (2010), "Sustainability: harnessing the collective innovation of all employees", *People & Strategy*, Vol. 33, No. 1, p. 14; Boiral, O. (2009), "Greening the corporation through organizational citizenship behaviors", *Journal of Business Ethics*, Vol. 87, No. 2, pp. 221–236; Haugh, H. M. & Talwar, A. (2010), "How do corporations embed sustainability across the organization?", *Academy of Management Learning & Education*, Vol. 9, No. 3, pp. 384–396.

9   Cascio, *op. cit.*

10 Buckley, M., Fedor, D. B., Carraher, S. M., Frink, D. D. & Marvin, D. (1997), "The ethical imperative to provide recruits realistic job previews", *Journal of Managerial Issues*, Vol. 9, No. 4, pp. 468–484; Bernardin, *op. cit.*

11 "Honest Tea recognized by Inc. Magazine and Winning Workplaces as an exceptional workplace", BevNET, June 15, 2010. Available at: www.bevnet.com/news/newswire/2010/6–15–2010-honest-tea-inc-magazine/.

12 Choi, D. Y. & Gray, E. R. (2008), "Socially responsible entrepreneurs: what do they do to create and build their companies?", *Business Horizons*, Vol. 51, No. 4, pp. 341–352.

13 Cascio & Boudreau, *op. cit.*

14 Soper, S. (2011), "Inside Amazon's warehouse: Lehigh Valley workers tell of brutal heat, dizzying pace at online retailer", *The Morning Call*, September 18, 2011.

15 *Hershey Company* (2011), www.thehersheycompany.com/careers.aspx?ICID=HCOMP1006.

16 Becker, W. S. (2012), "Self-directed teams". In R. K. Prescott (ed.), *Encyclopedia of Human Resource Management, Key Topics and Issues*. Pfeiffer, San Francisco, CA.

17 Choi & Gray, *op. cit.*

18 Rogelio, O. & Sterman, J. D. (2001), "Cutting corners and working overtime: quality erosion in the service industry", *Management Science*, Vol. 47, No. 7, pp. 894–914.

19 *Ibid.*

20 Breslin, F. C. & Smith, P. (2006), "Trial by fire: a multivariate examination of the relation between job tenure and work injuries", *Occupational and Environmental Medicine*, Vol. 63, No. 1, pp. 27–32.

21 Arnold, J. T. (2010), "Ramping up onboarding", *HR Magazine*, Vol. 55, No. 5, pp. 75–78.

22 Greenberg, E. S., Grunberg, L., Moore, S. & Sikora, P. B. (2010), *Turbulence: Boeing and the State of American Workers and Managers*. Yale University Press, New Haven, CT.

23 Duhigg, C. & Barboza, D. (2012), "In China, human costs are built into an iPad", *New York Times*, January 25, 2012.

24 Greene, R. J. (2011), *Rewarding Performance: Guiding Principles, Custom Strategies*. Routledge, New York City, NY.

25 Bernardin, *op. cit.*, p. 227.

26 Martin, A. (2011), "In company town, cuts but no layoffs", *New York Times*, September 25, 2011.

27 Fox, J. (2011), "What is it that only I can do?", *Harvard Business Review*, Vol. 89, No. 1/2, pp. 118–123.

28 World Business Council for Sustainable Development, *op. cit.*

29 Willams, D. (2002), "Weaving ethics into corporate culture", *Communications World*, Vol. 19, No. 4, pp. 38–39.

11 Using Codes of Conduct to Help SMEs Manage Supply Chains: The Case of SA8000

FRANCESCO CILIBERTI* AND JOB DE HAAN†

Keywords

Corporate social responsibility, codes of conduct, supply chain management, Social Accountability 8000.

Introduction

Supply chain management (SCM) expands the relationships between business partners beyond mere market relationships. This is even more important in today's globalized business when partners are from different continents of the world and information asymmetry increases as a consequence. The responsibilities of the partners are also growing as companies are increasingly pushed by customers, non-governmental organizations (NGOs), pressure groups and the media to respect the human rights of workers and protect the environment, and to provide evidence that they do so. The consideration of these social and environmental issues in addition to economic ones is known as corporate social responsibility (CSR).[1] CSR increases the information asymmetry in supply chains even further. Search costs are often too high, owing to the number of partners involved and the intangible features that are included in CSR.

In order to integrate CSR issues into supply chains and reduce information asymmetry, contracts are not sufficient. Contracts are by definition incomplete, as they cannot, for example, regulate unforeseen circumstances. As contracts are not sufficient to govern supply chain relationships in a more transparent way, one would expect trust between partners to be the basis for governance. However, it takes time for trust to reach a level where it can facilitate governance between partners in a chain. In such circumstances, codes of conduct can be a useful tool. Codes of conduct are public statements published

*   Ph.D. Francesco Ciliberti, Polytechnic of Bari, Department of Environmental Engineering and Sustainable Development (DIASS), via de Gasperi, 74123 Taranto (Italy). E-mail: cilibert@poliba.it. Telephone: + 390994733218. Fax: +390994733304.

†   Professor Job de Haan, Tilburg University, Department of Organization and Strategy, Tilburg (The Netherlands). E-mail: J.A.C.deHaan@uvt.nl. Telephone: +31134662422. Fax: +31134668354.

by companies in which they commit to behavioural norms in a variety of areas of business ethics (e.g. environment or anti-corruption). Codes define rules for partners, and procedures to verify the implementation of such rules. Codes often represent only the first step in improving management processes. Subsequent steps include the implementation of management systems designed to promote ethical compliance.[2] In this chapter we refer to codes of conduct as codes that are preparatory to the implementation of a management system, which may or may not be certified by an independent third party. Widely used examples of these codes can be found in operations and logistics: ISO9000 for quality, ISO14000 and EMAS (European Eco-Management and Audit Scheme) for the environment to name but a few. Some codes are increasingly used by companies to explicitly deal with social issues in supply chains, for example Social Accountability 8000 (SA8000) for labour conditions and human rights.

This chapter presents a literature review on SCM and codes of conduct, and in particular SA8000. The aim is to show how SA8000 can reduce information asymmetry and solve the principal–agent problem, thus improving transparency and reducing transaction costs. Then we provide a case study of a company that has made use of SA8000 along its supply chain.

Supply Chain Coordination and the Principal–Agent Framework

Traditionally two extreme forms of supply chain coordination are distinguished: market and hierarchy. Market means a series of independent firms whereas hierarchy indicates a vertically integrated firm. However, over time hybrids emerged, such as chain directors.[3] A chain director is a partner that is properly informed about the demands of the final customers and is able to organize the supply and demand side of its chain in order to improve overall competitiveness.[4] An example of a chain director would be a retailer or producer of popular branded products. Related, though different, concepts are the focal company[5] and the supply chain leader:[6] the first concentrates on the supply side of the chain, whereas the latter emerged from a survey among senior supply chain managers. In a chain governed by market relationships the chain director can urge the other members of the chain to act in a specific way by using information about the final customers' demand to persuade chain members to collaborate in order to gain benefits, for example in terms of higher prices, higher number of products sold or long-term contracts. This collaboration is beneficial for the supply chain as a whole, and supply chain partners are more likely to be persuaded if they see that they will benefit individually as well. In this case, partners accept an incomplete contract and the related risk of opportunism in order to reduce the costs of negotiating a complete contract, but maintain flexibility in the relationship. Lack of transparency increases the likelihood of opportunism.

Supply chain partners may not live up to the expectations of the chain director, which may have consequences for both the chain director and the other partners. Consequently, all supply chain members would welcome an adequate safeguard against opportunistic behaviour by any one of them. This position resembles the principal–agent relationship in which one party (the principal) delegates work to another (the agent) who performs that work. The contract between the two parties should resolve both the agency and the risk problems. Partners are driven by self-interest, are prone to bounded rationality, have partially conflicting goals, and information is asymmetric. Because of these assumptions, agents can show moral hazard or adverse selection.[7] Both problems are caused by information asymmetry, which occurs when at least one party to a transaction has more or better information than the other(s). Moral hazard occurs when the *ex post* behaviour of the agent is not appropriate. In this case, the agent with more information about its actions has an incentive to behave not in line with the principal's interest. By contrast, in adverse selection models, *ex ante* information exchange is not appropriate. In such cases, the principal is not informed about a certain characteristic of the agent.

Agency theory assumes that individuals are self-interested creatures and addresses the problem of opportunism.[8] In order to avoid opportunism, it is necessary to provide the agent with incentives to act in accordance with the principal's interests. This can be done either by monitoring behaviour or rewarding outcomes.[9] Which of the two alternatives should be chosen depends on their effectiveness and related costs.

Despite the fact that agency theory adds to the understanding of the many dilemmas that exist in supply chains, applications of the theory in this field are scarce. This could be because agency theory is traditionally used in dyads, whereas in a supply chain there are a number of agents serving one principal. Existing literature emphasizes the potential goal incongruity in supply chains and the potential role of agency theory in mitigating such a misalignment.[10]

When applying the principal–agent framework to the supply chain context, the chain director can be considered as the principal and the other partners can be considered as agents. Indeed, the partners have partly conflicting goals as they all share an interest in creating more value collectively, but may want to get a larger part of that value themselves, or may want to put less effort in for the same reward as before. The overall results depend on the efforts of all partners but only to a certain extent, because uncertain external conditions also contribute. The partners can measure the actual outcomes of the supply chain and each of the partners individually with respect to costs, timeliness, quality, etc.[11] However, the amount of effort as such cannot be measured and is only known to the agent involved (i.e. asymmetric information). Some potential supply chain partners may promise more than they are able to produce (i.e. adverse selection), and/or may underperform once accepted as chain members, blaming limited output on external conditions (i.e. moral hazard). To solve these problems the chain director needs a monitoring device to learn about the agents' efforts. Codes of conduct can be used for this.

Codes of Conduct in Supply Chains

Firms can apply numerous codes to show their commitment to CSR issues and their fulfilment of stakeholder demands. Some examples are ISO14001 for the environment,[12] SA8000 for working conditions and human rights[13] and Occupational Health and Safety Assessment Series (OHSAS) for health and safety.[14] Each of these covers one or more aspects of CSR.

Several papers have addressed the use of codes of conduct in supply chains. A research study of 27 large US firms in the apparel industry found that monitoring the employee rights performance of suppliers is a major problem;[15] 22 of the codes analysed stated that the actions of suppliers would be monitored but relatively few specified how monitoring would take place. Furthermore, 16 of these 22 codes indicated that on-site visits could be made to verify compliance, and six of these companies required at least annual reporting by suppliers on their adherence to code provisions.

Roberts analysed the use of codes of conduct in three sectors: branded clothing and footwear, forest products and branded confectionery.[16] Comparing these supply chains revealed that four characteristics affect the propensity to introduce a code of conduct in a supply chain: (1) the number of links between members demanding a code of conduct and the stage of supply chain under scrutiny; (2) the diffuseness of the stage of supply chain under scrutiny; (3) the reputational vulnerability of different chain members; (4) the power of different chain members.

Salomone investigated the potential for integration between quality management systems (based on ISO9001), environmental management systems (based on ISO14001), occupational health and safety management systems (based on OHSAS18001) and social responsibility management systems (based on SA8000), by surveying a sample of Italian organizations.[17] A significant number of organizations stressed the difficulty of constantly monitoring the entire supply chain.

Finally, a step-by-step plan was developed by Cramer to implement CSR in international product chains.[18] Based on this study, how a company can organize global chain responsibility depends on four main factors: (1) the diversity of the chain in which the company operates; (2) the extent of the ambition to reach social and environmental standards; (3) the complexity of the chain; and (4) the power of the company in that chain.

Codes or third-party certification mean that an independent party sets the norms, audits suppliers and informs buyers. Such codes can be used to overcome information asymmetry[19] despite their limitations, which include a limited uniformity across codes, a lack of substantial detail, and a neglect of the areas of monitoring and enforcement.[20] In order to overcome such limitations, Emmelhainz and Adams suggested that managers should develop procedures for independent audits, conforming to SA8000 requirements, of their own performance as well as that of their suppliers.[21] In addition, Preuss found that economic issues affecting supplier firms are of little concern in codes of conduct.[22]

Codes of conduct are instruments that facilitate communication between parties in a network of indirect relationships. Manufacturers can inform final customers, NGOs or the general public about certain features of their products. These features are sometimes immediately visible for the other parties and relevant for them. However, these features often reflect (intangible) aspects of the processes from which they emerge, for example no child labour or no polluting emissions during the production process. Although producers can inform the other partners that this is the case, the others may not believe them. If an independent third party monitors whether the producer lives up to these claims and publishes publicly about the results, this will enhance credibility.

Codes of conduct and the way they are monitored can be included in contracts between supply chain partners. Such codes reduce information asymmetry (both *ex ante* and *ex post*) among supply chain partners because the way partners execute processes becomes more transparent. For example, the principal can be better informed about the compliance of both actual and potential suppliers with the rules defined in the code(s) of conduct.

When first-tier suppliers adopt the same third-party certification as the chain director, they are able to gather information for second- and third-tier partners. Certification of these partners thus enables the chain director to convince the final customer that promises will be met and facilitates the way the director can perform his role. In addition to third-party certification, first- and second-party certifications also exist of course. In first-party certification, a supplier sets its own norms and communicates them to its customers: brand names and labels are examples of this. In second-party certification, (large) buyers audit both potential and actual suppliers on whether the latter live up to norms set by the buyers themselves. Buyers using a second-party certification have been compared against those using a third-party certification regime:[23] due to additional agency costs that arise when second-party certification is used, third-party certification is preferred by buyers.

Social Accountability 8000 and Supply Chain Management

SA8000 is a voluntary accountability standard developed in 1997 by Social Accountability International (SAI), an international non-profit human rights organization, and mainly based on the principles of core International Labor Organization (ILO) conventions, the United Nations (UN) Convention on the Rights of the Child and the Universal Declaration of Human Rights.[24] The standard defines eight principles related to working conditions and human rights: (1) child labour; (2) forced labour; (3) health and safety; (4) freedom of association and the right to collective bargaining; (5) discrimination; (6) disciplinary practices; (7) working hours; (8) compensation. The ninth issue of the standard concerns the establishment of a social management system. SA8000 is in use worldwide: 2,606 facilities are certified in 62 different countries (Italy, India and China being the countries with the highest number of SA8000-certified companies) and 65 different industries. All together, these facilities employ over 1.4 million people.[25]

SA8000 was designed to fit into the ISO9001 and ISO14001 certification and performance audit process, because the management system elements in SA8000 follow the same logic as in ISO standards, and make it easier to implement the code at the operational level.[26] Like ISO9001 and ISO14001, SA8000 is formulated to allow a third-party certification body to audit and certify on behalf of SAI. A company can have a management system even if it is not externally certified; however, third-party certification facilitates communication to customers and requires a public description of the behaviour of the audited firm and the management systems implemented. Once certified, firms are monitored to ensure that they live up to SA8000 norms. An SA8000 certification lasts for three years and there are surveillance audits every six months during this period. The company itself should conduct internal audits to ensure that the system is being maintained, at least on an annual basis ('continuous monitoring'). Over the three-year period for which a certificate is valid, the total cost of certification would be between US$20,000 and US$40,000 per company. Consequently, many SMEs may find it difficult to achieve this standard.[27] By integrating SA8000 with other management systems (especially ISO9001 and ISO14001), companies (and especially SMEs) can achieve a cost reduction.[28]

The principles of SA8000 tend to create a supply chain effect, being used as a tool to manage suppliers. Organizations may consider the benefits of SA8000 certification in terms of improved public perception of their activities.[29] A company seeking certification must implement proper steps to ensure that its suppliers comply with the standard. This may happen through personal visits, documentation review or requirement for a second- or third-party audit. Auditors are not obliged to visit these suppliers, but to verify the steps taken by the company. As a first step, first-tier suppliers must provide the company with a written statement that expresses the supplier's commitment to conform to SA8000 requirements. The company can include such a clause in its purchasing contracts and ask suppliers to provide a written commitment that they will require the same from their sub-suppliers. In addition, suppliers and sub-suppliers should identify the root causes of possible non-conformances with SA8000, repair them and implement a plan to avoid them in the future, and inform the customer company about the steps taken to put this plan in effect. In this way, the supplier can prove it is making a reasonable effort to adhere to SA8000 norms and that it requires its sub-suppliers to do the same.

From a buyer's perspective, Henkle showed that SA8000 increases confidence in suppliers and leads to a lower risk of being associated with human rights violations.[30] A social management system based on SA8000 can be used to transfer socially responsible behaviour along the supply chain, even when SMEs are involved.[31] Every SA8000-certified company has to evaluate and select its suppliers on the basis of the fulfilment of SA8000 principles. It also has to invite its suppliers to adopt socially responsible behaviour. Consequently, SA8000 affects every node in the supply chain, resulting in a domino-like effect throughout the global supply chain.[32] This is especially important for second- and third-tier suppliers, particularly in developing countries, where the powers of governments and civil society are weak and poverty prevails.[33] Monitoring of suppliers becomes more critical in these cases, since opportunism is more likely to occur due to a number of reasons: lack of strict regulation or poor efforts to enforce what regulation there is by governments and local public authorities; difficulties in retrieving information on suppliers; differences in culture and language; and lack of adequate tools to communicate with suppliers.[34]

Mueller et al.[35] pointed out that only producers are actually certified, not their first- and second-tier suppliers, which means that certified companies do not accept full responsibility for the working conditions along their supply chain. SA8000 is site-centred, although the standard claims that the suppliers of the location will be SA8000-certified in the future. A certification of suppliers is therefore intended. However, the demands on suppliers are not very precise and no clear time period is stipulated for achieving such certification.[36]

From a supplier's perspective, lack of support from buyers has been identified as an obstacle to the implementation of SA8000.[37] Buyers do not share the costs incurred by suppliers to become compliant with the standard. In addition, there are no contracts to ensure that complying with standards represents a safe investment. Combining the standard's requirements while also maintaining attractive prices for the buyers is therefore difficult.[38] This is in line with the theory on bonding costs, i.e. the costs a party bears to show the outside world how they behave.[39] Bonding costs have the same purpose as monitoring costs, since both costs are incurred to collect information on the behaviour of the agent. The main difference is that bonding costs are carried by the agent and monitoring costs are carried by the principal.

In future, it is likely that SA8000 will be integrated into the ISO guidelines for CSR, ISO26000, which were released in 2010. ISO26000 offers guidance on socially responsible behaviour and possible actions. It does not contain requirements and, therefore, in contrast to ISO management system standards, is not certifiable. ISO26000 will help organizations contribute to sustainable development and encourage them to go beyond compliance with existing legislation. Such guidelines are not intended to be a substitute for CSR tools like SA8000.

The Case of SMEs

The implementation of codes of conduct can be costly and time-consuming, and the related potential benefits may not be clearly identified or may be unevenly distributed among supply chain partners.[40] This is even more important when SMEs are involved in the chain. In smaller businesses, ownership and control are typically merged, which reduces the incentive to make inefficient investments.[41]

The effects of agency relationships are most significant if the businesses are small.[42] In smaller firms there is a greater level of uncertainty in the estimation of risk,[43] since for such firms the problem of information asymmetry is greater. This happens because SMEs generally do not have adequate resources, in terms of time, money and personnel, to monitor the agents.[44] In particular, monitoring and bonding are likely to be more costly.[45] The implementation of codes like SA8000 requires major investment that can be difficult for SMEs to bear.[46] Reputation can emerge as a relevant way of securing commonality of interests when considering SMEs. However, reputation effects are less visible to end customers when the principal is an SME than when it is a larger company.[47] Because SMEs rarely have a brand name to protect, they are unlikely to suffer adverse effects of poor reputation on brand image.

Case Study

RESEARCH DESIGN

The research question this chapter addresses is how SA8000 can help a company to improve information flows through the supply chain, thus reducing information asymmetries, building trust among the different players and solving the principal–agent problem. The research question was articulated in several research propositions.

> *Proposition 1.* Codes of conduct can improve the communication flows about intangible aspects of business between partners within a supply chain and consequently reduce information asymmetry between the principal and the agents.

> *Proposition 2.* Codes of conduct can solve the adverse selection problem both when seeking new suppliers (selected from certified firms) as well as when negotiating intangible issues in new contracts with current suppliers.

> *Proposition 3.* Codes of conduct can solve moral hazard problems with respect to intangible aspects of business because monitoring improves communication on these issues, in particular in the case of third-party monitoring of all parties involved.

> *Proposition 4.* Agents can further reduce moral hazard problems when they apply bonding practices towards their partners, such as the principal, to support monitoring activities by a third party.

This section reports a case study of a garment-producing company located in Italy. The company has relationships with suppliers located in developing countries and is SA8000-certified.

The data collection activity aimed for triangulation: an interview and direct observation were used for primary data, and internal and external documents and websites were used for secondary data. A lengthy semi-structured interview was conducted with the person in charge of the social management system and the social report, so as to let the informant talk freely about the issues under investigation while addressing the research propositions.[48] To corroborate the information derived from the interview and increase construct validity, we analysed all the company documents relevant to the research objective, i.e. the SA8000 report and social report.

The interview and observations were transcribed and summarized, together with the documents, and the results were fed back to the interviewee to confirm the accurateness of the data. This report was then coded according to the literature review summarized in previous sections.

In the next sub-section we present a brief profile of the company and characterize its relationships with suppliers (especially in developing countries). In the Discussion section we show how SA8000 is used to address the research question.

CASE DESCRIPTION

Monnalisa was founded in 1968 as a sole trader, became a limited company in the 1980s and a joint-stock company in 1991. The firm is located in Central Italy. The founder and his wife (who designs the products) own the majority of the company shares. Currently Monnalisa is the core firm of a group of six companies. The firm makes unique, upmarket clothes for children that are good value for money. Products are sold in 41 countries (including Europe, Russia, the Middle East, North and South America, China and other Asian countries). Customers include boutiques, shops and large retailers.

Monnalisa obtained ISO9001 certification in 1999 and SA8000 certification in 2002. The company defines CSR as 'being aware of the role played by the company within the community and being responsible for this role in the community'. The owners decided to join SA8000 certification to show its commitment to considering social and environmental issues. Since 2002, Monnalisa has also published an annual social report, which includes the SA8000 report showing how the SA8000 principles are respected.

Monnalisa outsources most of its production activities to firms located in China, India, Tunisia and Turkey. It also sells its products in those countries. A licence agreement is defined with the Chinese supplier. Suppliers in developing countries are all medium-sized. Monnalisa procures from them a share of its total supplies, but the percentage of production sold by suppliers to Monnalisa is low compared with their total production. CSR is an order qualifier for the company when selecting suppliers, with Monnalisa expecting a minimum level of CSR performance from suppliers.

Monnalisa plans and conducts inspections at suppliers' sites both directly or through a third-party. External audits are scheduled on the basis of several factors: the type of production; the size of supplier company; the location of the company; and the result of previous inspections. Based on the result of the inspections, non-compliant suppliers start to conform to CSR requirements by using a tool similar to SA8000, named WRAP (Worldwide Responsible Apparel Production[49]). The firm would prefer to conduct direct inspections in order to be more aware of the possible problems that suppliers can experience as to CSR. However, managers are not able to conduct them very often, due to time constraints. Inspections at suppliers take place annually, on average, and generally last about an hour. This is clearly a point of weakness for the company when monitoring suppliers.

Working conditions at suppliers' sites are good in terms of health and safety issues, at least compared to local standards. Monnalisa acknowledges not knowing all the local regulations applied in countries where suppliers are located. The firm tries to stimulate suppliers' awareness of CSR, for example by inviting suppliers to Italy to observe the way Monnalisa operates. On such occasions several documents, such as the firm's social report, are given to them. Because of the existing cultural differences along the chain, Monnalisa had to modify the self-evaluation checklist prepared for Italian suppliers when monitoring Chinese partners. A few years ago the firm decided to break up the relationship with a supplier that showed critical non-compliances (i.e. use of child labour).

Monnalisa believes that current consumer choices are mainly driven by price. According to the company, as long as the consumer does not consider social and environmental principles, CSR can generate profits only for companies selling luxury products (e.g. on the basis of Italian design). This is why the company has not yet invested in promoting the CSR initiatives currently implemented. For example, the label on the items sold does not show that products are manufactured according to SA8000. When consumers are more aware, Monnalisa will create an ethical label to show the ethical traceability of its products. To this end, the company needs to make contact with local networks of supporting organizations, especially in China, to get additional information on regulation and cultural differences which are relevant in order to identify how CSR issues can be managed and implemented in different countries.

Table 11.1 summarizes the most relevant information on the company and its supply chain.

Table 11.1 Supply chain and CSR issues for case company Monnalisa

Supply chain / CSR issues	Information
Final customers	Parents buying on behalf of children
Order winner	Design
Mission	Design and production control of garment
First-tier suppliers	Medium-sized outsourcers of garment production abroad
Second-tier suppliers	No information
First-tier customers	Large retail chain and independent retailers (export)
Second-tier customers	Final customers
Initiative to adopt SA8000	Focal firm (intrinsically motivated)
CSR towards first-tier suppliers	Agreement to respect SA8000 principles Inspections Questionnaires
CSR towards second-tier suppliers	No information
CSR by first-tier customers	No
CSR by second-tier customers	No premium price for CSR

Discussion

The supply chain the case firm participates in is quite simple. Monnalisa focuses on design, and faces price competition because of the degree of exclusivity of the designs. The company's mission concentrates in essence on one process within the chain. The firm deals with products that are easily recognisable by its final customers. Its first-tier suppliers are from abroad, i.e. in developing countries. Monnalisa has only limited control over them, as its orders represent a limited part of suppliers' total production. The company does not have information on second-tier suppliers. The first-tier customers are a limited number of retailers in a specific market segment. The second-tier customers are the final customers.

The initiative to implement SA8000 in this supply chain stems from the owners of the firm, which seems to be intrinsically motivated to implement CSR in general and SA8000 in particular. Monnalisa can act as the chain director despite its size, because of its ability to design products that fit perfectly with the demands of the market niche served, thus constructing a buyer-driven chain. In its supply chain the firm acts as the principal. The other companies are the agents, who have to live up to the principals' requirements because of economic reasons.

As to Proposition 1, although all supply chain partners have as a common goal to increase the competitiveness of the chain, each also has, to a certain extent, a conflicting goal: to increase its own benefits from the chain. Reward structures are not sufficient to safeguard against this risk because of incompleteness and/or lack of contracts, as well as the intangibility of certain aspects of the relationships, e.g. the use of child labour. This requires additional actions on behalf of the principal to ensure that all agents live up to the norms to reduce information asymmetry. In the case analysed, such actions include the use of SA8000 by the principal and compliance with that code by all the agents in the supply chain. The intangible aspects of business materialized in the issues addressed by the SA8000 principles (e.g. child labour) and hence communication between direct partners is facilitated. In addition to this, the third party monitors all partners. As a consequence, the principal is able to have more credible information about the agents and information asymmetry between partners is reduced.

As to Proposition 2, since none of the suppliers was SA8000-certified before the contract was negotiated, the code did not help to reduce adverse selection in the search process. The principal, although it is an SME, is able to exert pressure on the agents to fulfil SA8000 requirements. During the initial selection of suppliers, however, the principal had to rely on other tools to reduce adverse selection. After that, the company had to convince their partners during the negotiation process that SA8000 would facilitate cooperation. The principal could only be sure that the agents agreed to put in writing the fulfilment of SA8000 principles. The agents, who are assumed to be risk-averse, would only agree to this if they intended to live up to the behaviour prescribed by SA8000. If they did not live up to these norms, this would be discovered during the monitoring sessions. Moreover, even if SA8000 did not solve the adverse selection problem in the process of seeking and identifying new suppliers, during the negotiation process the suppliers accepted the certification as well as the related procedures which would show non-compliance. Hence SA8000 can solve the problem of adverse selection when negotiating intangible issues in new contracts with current suppliers. The principal thus has a tool to be used in case the agents act opportunistically by providing false information about their intentions.

As to Proposition 3, moral hazard problems are reduced as the certifying agency audits all certified chain members on a regular basis, checking whether they still live up to the norms and act accordingly. Transaction costs are reduced because of simpler contracting, a lower risk of opportunism and related costs to prevent it and correct it if it occurs. All supply chain partners, including the principal, are monitored according to SA8000 procedures by a third party, which increases transparency for all chain partners. Third-party monitoring by local SA8000 auditors facilitates this for SMEs in particular, due to less expensive visits, familiarity with local circumstances, and greater perceived objectivity. On the other hand, such inspections have several limitations, since they are generally agreed in advance, have a limited frequency and duration. Monnalisa thinks that these limitations make it difficult to carefully check suppliers' respect for working conditions and human rights. In this case, in addition to the SA8000 procedures, the agents are invited to visit Italian plants so they can learn best CSR practices. Agents can thus have a better understanding of what their final customers expect from them and consequently information asymmetry can be reduced. In short, monitoring reduces the moral hazard problem faced by SMEs. Communication between parties in the chain, in particular on intangible aspects of the business, is also facilitated and risk-averse agents may fear that not living up to the norms will be detected and that the monitoring party would discover if they tried to hide any case of non-compliance. All parties involved, namely the certifying agent, the principal, the agent and the public, should be able to rely on this to make the standard effective. Hence these audits should solve the moral hazard problem by means of additional communication mechanisms provided by the code, for example third-party monitoring.

As to Proposition 4, agents could meet bonding costs to show that they are living up to expectations set out in the certification process by providing additional information to the principal. In addition to this, the certifying organization may require additional material (e.g. annual reports) from the agents to further reduce agency problems: risk-averse agents provide risk-neutral principals with information to show their performance. Suppliers of Monnalisa prepare self-evaluations to facilitate monitoring in a way that suits suppliers in various countries. In addition to the visits of the certifying agency, the suppliers provide evidence to the principal showing to what extent they live up to norms, in this way contributing to communications on intangible aspects of CSR. These bonding activities facilitate the work of the monitoring agencies and ensure even more security on whether the supply chain as a whole lives up to the promises made to the public about intangible aspects of the products, such as the use of child labour.

Conclusions

In this chapter we showed how codes of conduct like SA8000 enable the exchange of more relevant and focused information on intangible aspects in a supply chain between partners. Codes, as a hybrid coordination mechanism, introduce aspects of hierarchy in market relationships because third parties will monitor agents' behaviour. Principals will benefit from this, in particular when they are SMEs with limited resources. In addition, transparency is increased as norms are known in advance and all parties, the principal included, are monitored along the same lines.

In the case analysed, the agents were not yet certified when they were selected, but negotiations were facilitated as the suppliers agreed to live up to the SA8000 norms. Hence the adverse selection problem was reduced. Moral hazard problems were reduced in a similar way, as the certifying agency audits all certified chain members on a regular basis. However, these monitoring results provide only a snapshot that might not fully reflect required behaviour, although it should be in the common interest of all parties involved to show their commitment. Doubts may exist about whether the agents do respect the codes' requirements. They can reduce these doubts by meeting bonding costs to show the principal and the public that they do indeed live up to the requirements.

At the moment it is not certain that customers are willing to pay a premium for the application of CSR practices and codes such as SA8000. Consequently, the additional certification, monitoring and bonding costs are not covered by higher incomes for the chain as a whole. Further research could investigate how to raise awareness among customers and the broader public, make them willing to reward socially responsible companies, and identify instruments to redistribute supply chain profits among partners in line with their overall contribution.

The results suggest some recommendations for managers. One limitation of the implementation of codes like SA8000 along the supply chain is that the risk of opportunistic behaviour is not completely eliminated, as the chain director may not be able to identify all violations of the standard. To some extent, company managers need to rely on other parties, such as local NGOs, for additional safeguarding and interpretation of behaviour. This becomes even more important as the geographic, economic and cultural distance between partners increases.

For chain directors, SA8000 can facilitate direct and, in some cases, indirect coordination. For SMEs, which are often not chain directors, the advantage is a reduction in transaction costs: supplier selection, negotiation and monitoring all become simpler if such companies deal with certified partners. This could be an incentive for different kinds of firms to implement CSR by means of a certification like SA8000. As a consequence, managers and consultants need not pursue CSR only because they believe in it, but also because of the advantages they can gain. In other words, in addition to the ethical aspects, managerial and economic implications play a role as well.

Notes

1   Commission of the European Communities (2001), *Green Paper. Promoting a European Framework for Corporate Social Responsibility*, COM (2001) 366 final, Brussels.

2   OECD (2001), 'Making Codes of Corporate Conduct Work: Management Control Systems and Corporate Responsibility', *Working Papers On International Investment*, No. 2001/3.

3   Gereffi, G. (1999), 'International trade and industrial upgrading in the apparel commodity chain', *Journal of International Economics*, Vol. 48, No. 1, pp. 37–70.

4   Sarkis, J. & Talluri, S. (2004), 'Evaluating and selecting e-commerce software and communication systems for a supply chain', *European Journal of Operational Research*, Vol. 159, No. 2, pp. 318–329.

5   Choi, T.Y. & Krause, D.R. (2006), 'The supply base and its complexity: Implications for transaction costs, risks, responsiveness, and innovation', *Journal of Operations Management*, Vol. 24, No. 5, pp. 637–652.

6   Harrison, A. & New, C. (2002), 'The role of coherent supply chain strategy and performance measurement in achieving competitive advantage: An international survey', *Journal of the Operational Research Society*, Vol. 53, Vol. 3, pp. 263–271.

7   Fama, E.F. (1980), 'Agency problems and the theory of the firm', *Journal of Political Economy*, Vol. 88, No. 2, pp. 288–307.

8   Fama, *op. cit.*

9   Eisenhardt, K. (1989), 'Agency theory: An assessment and review', *Academy of Management Review*, Vol. 14, No. 1, pp. 57–74.

10   Halldorsson, A., Kotzab, H., Mikkola, J.H. & Skjoett-Larsen, T. (2007), 'Complementary theories to supply chain management', *Supply Chain Management: An International Journal*, Vol. 12, No. 4, pp. 284–296.

11   Eisenhardt, K. (1989), 'Building theories from case study research', *Academy of Management Review*, Vol. 14, No. 4, pp. 532–550.

12   www.iso.org/iso/iso_14000_essentials. Last access: March 28, 2012.

13   www.sa-intl.org. Last access: March 28, 2012.

14   www.bsigroup.com/en/Assessment-and-certification-services/management-systems/ Standards-and-Schemes/BSOHSAS-18001. Last access: March 28, 2012.

15   Emmelhainz, M.A. & Adams, R.J. (1999), 'The apparel industry response to "sweatshop" concerns: A review and analysis of codes of conduct', *Journal of Supply Chain Management*, Vol. 35, No. 3, pp. 51–57.

16   Roberts, S. (2003), 'Supply chain specific? Understanding the patchy success of ethical sourcing initiatives', *Journal of Business Ethics*, Vol. 44, No. 2/3, pp. 159–170.

17   Salomone, R. (2008), 'Integrated management systems: Experiences in Italian organizations', *Journal of Cleaner Production*, Vol. 16, No. 16, pp. 1786–1806.

18   Cramer, J.M. (2008), 'Organising corporate social responsibility in international product chains', *Journal of Cleaner Production*, Vol. 16, No. 3, pp. 395–400.

19   Dewally, M. & Ederington, L. (2006), 'Reputation, certification, warranties, and information as remedies for seller-buyer information asymmetries: Lessons from the online comic book market', *Journal of Business*, Vol. 79, No. 2, pp. 693–729; Terlaak, A. & King, A. (2006), 'The effect of certification with the ISO 9001 quality management standard: A signalling approach', *Journal of Economic Behaviour and Organization*, Vol. 60, No. 4, pp. 579–602.

20   Emmelhainz & Adams, *op. cit.*

21   Emmelhainz & Adams, *op. cit.*

22   Preuss, L. (2009), 'Ethical sourcing codes of large UK-based corporations: Prevalence, content, limitations', *Journal of Business Ethics*, Vol. 88, No. 4, pp. 735–747.

23   Hwang, I., Radhakrishnan, S. & Su, L. (2006), 'Vendor certification and appraisal: Implications for supplier quality', *Management Science*, Vol. 52, No. 10, pp. 1472–1482.

24   Leipziger, D. (2001), *SA8000: The Definitive Guide to the New Social Standard*, Financial Times–Prentice Hall, London.

25   www.saasaccreditation.org/certfacilitieslist.htm. Last update: March 31, 2011.

26   Leipziger, *op. cit.*

27   Rohitratana, K. (2002), 'SA 8000: A tool to improve quality of life', *Managerial Auditing Journal*, Vol. 17, No. 1/2, pp. 60–64.

28   Salomone, R. (2008), 'Integrated management systems: Experiences in Italian organizations', *Journal of Cleaner Production*, Vol. 16, No. 16, pp. 1786–1806.

29   Rohitratana, *op. cit.*

30   Henkle, D. (2005), 'Cap Inc. sees supplier ownership of compliance with workplace standards as an essential element of socially responsible sourcing', *Journal of Organizational Excellence*, Winter, pp. 17–25.

31   Ciliberti, F., de Groot, G., de Haan, J. & Pontrandolfo, P. (2009), 'Codes to coordinate supply chains: SMEs' experiences with SA8000', *Supply Chain Management: An International Journal*, Vol. 14, No. 2, pp. 117–127.

32   Miles, M.P. & Munilla, L.S. (2004), 'The potential impact of social accountability certification on marketing: A short note', *Journal of Business Ethics*, Vol. 50, No. 1, pp. 1–11.

33   Wolters, T. (2003), 'Transforming international product chains into channels of sustainable production. The imperative of sustainable chain management', *Greener Management International*, Vol. 43, pp. 6–13.

34   Ciliberti, F., Pontrandolfo, P. & Scozzi, B. (2008), 'Investigating corporate social responsibility in supply chains: A SME perspective', *Journal of Cleaner Production*, Vol. 16, No. 15, pp. 1579–1588.

35   Mueller, M., Gomes dos Santos, V. & Seuring, S. (2009), 'The contribution of environmental and social standards towards ensuring legitimacy in supply chain governance', *Journal of Business Ethics*, Vol. 89, No. 4, pp. 509–523.

36   Mueller, Gomes dos Santos & Seuring, *op. cit.*

37   Stigzelius, I. & Mark-Herbert, C. (2009), 'Tailoring corporate responsibility to suppliers: Managing SA8000 in Indian garment manufacturing', *Scandinavian Journal of Management*, Vol. 25, No. 1, pp. 46–56.

38   Stigzelius & Mark-Herbert, *op. cit.*

39   Jensen, M. & Meckling, W. (1976), 'Theory of the firm: Managerial behaviour, agency costs and owner structure', *Journal of Financial Economics*, Vol. 3, No. 4, pp. 305–360.

40   Pedersen, E.R. & Andersen, M. (2006), 'Safeguarding corporate social responsibility (CSR) in global supply chains: How codes of conduct are managed in buyer-supplier relationships', *Journal of Public Affairs*, Vol. 6, No. 3–4, pp. 228–240.

41   Easterwood, J.C. & Singer, R.F. (1981), 'Are the motivations for leveraged buyouts the same for large and small firms?', in: Yazdipour, R., (Ed.), *Advances in Small Business Finance*, Kluwer Academic Publishers, Boston, pp. 79–92.

42   Hand, J.H., Lloyd, W.P. & Rogow, R.B. (1982), 'Agency relationships in the close corporation', *Financial Management*, Vol. 11, No. 1, pp. 25–30.

43   Pettit, R.R. & Singer, R.F. (1985), 'Small business finance: A research agenda', *Financial Management*, Vol. 14, No. 3, pp. 47–60.

44   Lepoutre, J. & Heene, A. (2006), 'Investigating the impact of firm size on small business social responsibility: A critical review', *Journal of Business Ethics*, Vol. 67, No. 3, pp. 257–273.

45   Ang, J.S. (1991), 'Small business uniqueness and the theory of financial management', *Journal of Small Business Finance*, Vol. 1, No. 1, pp. 1–13.

46   Bremer, J. & Udovich, J. (2001), 'Alternative approaches to supply chain compliance monitoring', *Journal of Fashion Marketing Management*, Vol. 5, No. 4, pp. 333–352; Welford, R. & Frost, S. (2006), 'Corporate social responsibility in Asian supply chains', *Corporate Social Responsibility and Environmental Management*, Vol. 13, No. 3, pp. 166–176.

47   Jenkins, H. (2004), 'A critique of conventional CSR theory: An SME perspective', *Journal of General Management*, Vol. 29, No. 4, pp. 37–57.

48   Yin, R.K. (2003), *Case Study Research: Design and Methods*, Sage Publications, Newbury Park.

49   www.wrapcompliance.org/. Last access: October 1, 2011.

CHAPTER 12

Environmental Standards and Certifications in a Value Chain Perspective: NGOs' View on the Legitimacy of the Process

MARTIN MÜLLER,* STEFAN SEURING† AND
VIRGINIA GOMES DOS SANTOS‡

Keywords

Environmental standards, Forest Stewardship Council, Programme for the Endorsement of Forest Certification Schemes, Marine Stewardship Council, ISO 14011, NGO, legitimacy.

Introduction

In recent years, sourcing from and production in so-called low-wage countries have become increasingly important in many industries. Sometimes, this goes hand-in-hand with a lack of acceptable environmental protection and appropriate working conditions. Non-governmental organizations (NGOs) counter such grievances in the supply chain by making them public.[1] This can endanger the reputation of well-known brands and may cause competitive disadvantages,[2] as has happened in the past in cases such as Nike, Dole Food, and GM.[3] Most companies are aware of the need to react to such criticism, and a common modality for doing this is the implementation of social and environmental standards along their supply chain, including supplier control mechanisms.[4] Therefore, the importance of such standards has steadily increased over the past few years. Examples include the Forest Stewardship Council (FSC), the Programme for the Endorsement of Forest Certification Schemes (PEFC), the Marine Stewardship Council (MSC) or ISO

* Professor Dr. Martin Müller, Department of Sustainable Knowledge, Sustainable Education and Sustainable Economy, University of Ulm, Helmholtzstraße 20, 89081 Ulm, Germany. E-mail: Martin.mueller@uni-ulm.de. Telephone: +49 731 50 32350.

† Professor Dr. Stefan Seuring, Department of International Management, Faculty of Organic Agricultural Sciences, University of Kassel, 37213 Witzenhausen, Germany. E-mail: seuring@uni-kassel.de. Telephone: +49 5542 98 1206.

‡ Dr. Virginia Gomes dos Santos, AXA AG, Colonia-Allee 10-20, Cologne, Germany. E-mail: virginia.gonmesdos santos@axa.de. Telephone: +49 179 90 980 32.

14001. There are several studies that discuss the credibility of social and environmental standards.[5]

It is often argued that the implementation of environmental and social standards is caused by pressure campaigns by NGOs.[6] Nonetheless, it is the public, i.e. the customer, who ultimately deprives the companies of resource legitimacy – or not. The question of how customers respond remains open. If customers affirm the efforts and the standards of a company, the company maintains its legitimacy. Certainly, companies often remark that customers do not consider standards or labels when making their buying decision.[7] Furthermore, shock-triggered brand crises often have a limited time span. After eight to ten weeks, old buying habits return.[8] Nevertheless, implementing standards in the supply chain is an important element of risk management for the focal company.[9] Another important factor for the implementation of the standards is the relationship between the links in the chain. However, relationships between manufacturers, retailers and end users are not the main focus of this chapter.

The focus of this chapter is on environmental standards, in particular the relationships between NGOs and companies. NGOs support the development and implementation of environmental standards by companies. If the effectiveness of such standards is questionable, then the credibility of the NGOs is also at risk. NGOs hold a high level of credibility with the public. For example, a global opinion poll of 37,572 people in 32 countries, commissioned by the BBC World Service in January 2006, showed the level of approval for a variety of institutions to be highest for NGOs (60 per cent of respondents felt NGOs had a mainly positive influence, only 12 per cent thought they had a mainly negative influence). This placed NGOs higher in terms of public approval than both the United Nations and the World Bank. Europeans and North Americans are especially positive about NGOs – Britain has a 70 per cent approval rate, the USA 64 per cent and France 80 per cent, respectively.[10]

This credibility plays a key role in allowing NGOs to influence public opinion.[11] A loss of credibility would therefore have serious consequences for them.

This leads to the following research question: What type of standard can NGOs support if credibility is not to be lost? To answer this question, the concept of normative legitimacy, which is derived from political science, will provide the framework for the analysis. For this research, 22 members of NGOs were interviewed to form the observation base to answer the research question. We focused on welfare-oriented NGOs that attract attention by campaigning against ecological problems. It is important to say that it was a piece of qualitative research with a low number of interviewees, so the results must be interpreted carefully.

Literature Review

Various NGOs have identified and published unacceptable environmental and inappropriate working conditions in countries like China or India.[12] Such public announcements may cause dramatic consequences for companies, as in the case of Nike or Dole Food. Both companies experienced reputation losses following criticism of conditions at their suppliers.[13]

It is not only the focal company itself that is relevant, but its whole supply chain.[14] One way to tackle this is through the implementation of social and environmental standards, including supplier control mechanisms.[15] Standards have gained wider consideration since 1990[16] and the number of standards has increased continuously. However, this method of implementing standards in the supply chain is subject to much debate.

From a positive perspective, it is viewed as a constituent element of global corporate governance reaching beyond national regulation. Critics, however, question their legitimacy and credibility.[17] Comparisons with other types of standards, e.g. ISO 14000, raise the question whether environmental issues are the main drivers for the companies and whether a full implementation occurs.[18]

NGOs suspect the instrument of voluntary environmental and social standards to be used just as a marketing tool in order to conceal violations of social and environmental aspects and to strengthen the company's competitiveness on the global market.[19] To highlight this, some activist groups even award so-called "greenwash" awards – see for instance CorpWatch).

The two most common critiques of codes are the lack of accountability mechanisms such as monitoring provisions and sanctions, and the inability or unwillingness of corporations to effectively implement code commitments. [...] Many codes are written as vague and/or broad philosophical concepts with little to no information on specific actions to be taken or plans for implementation, and the meaning of commitments can vary depending on the perspective and intent of the reader (Bondy/Matten/Moon 2007).

Theoretical Background: Normative Legitimacy

To examine under which conditions NGOs can support environmental standards, the concept of normative legitimacy is helpful. The normative appreciation defines the conditions under which sound reasons exist to accept social terms and structures as justified. A rule is legitimate when the procedure of enforcing it follows certain normative requirements (see Dingwerth 2004, p. 8).[20]

In this context, input-legitimacy, throughput-legitimacy and output-legitimacy can be distinguished.[21]

- Input-legitimacy needs the approbation of all addressees. This can be done indirectly, for example by the election of a parliament, which then makes decisions.
- Throughput-legitimacy is achieved if decisions are made on the basis of a fair procedure.
- Output-legitimacy is established when a decision fulfils all the relevant requirements.

This idea forms a reference point for the subsequent analysis of the support of environmental standards by NGOs.[22] However, for this it is necessary to adapt this concept to the context of the development and use of environmental standards. We followed Dingwerth (2005) and Bouwen (2003) and use their concept.[23] Three requirements are put forward which a normative legitimacy concept has to fulfil: inclusivity (input-legitimacy), discursive quality (throughput-legitimacy) and control/transparency (output-legitimacy), which will briefly be introduced below. So inclusivity is a synonym for input-legitimacy, discursive quality for throughput-legitimacy and control/transparency for output-legitimacy.

In the case of the first principle of "inclusivity", it is preferable to include all NGOs concerned with the development process by means of a positive inclusion into the organizational decision-making processes.[24] The formal integration into international negotiating systems for standardization is consequently a constitutive element of a standard-developing process. When requirements from NGOs are clarified in a practical discourse and commonly accepted concepts of actions are found, standards can be considered as legitimate from an NGO's perspective. In this case, the question of the experience of the NGO members in the development of the standard is important. How extensively are NGOs integrated in the process of developing standards? How could such integration be realized? To what extent are NGOs involved in the process of extension of a standard?

The second aspect of normative legitimacy is "discursive quality". This is concerned with the possibility of considering all requirements from NGOs. This is not an easily discernable criterion, as NGO groups may differ in their agendas, or ignore discourses. Also, any questions arising, in the case of compromises and reasons for terminating a dialogue, are important.

Normative decisions have to be made regarding what degree of legitimacy social and environmental standards directly achieve. Legitimacy is not automatically guaranteed for the future, but has to be permanently renewed by NGOs. This is shown by the practical experience of applying the standard and has to be controlled in detail, e.g. whether ecological and social effects emerge. Certification and accreditation, and their effects, are the central points of "control/transparency". Which requirements on certification systems exist? What is the difference between the certification systems in different industries? Furthermore, transparency about the effects and results for the stakeholders, e.g. by reports, is a very important indicator for the quality of standards and their legitimacy. What kind of reporting is desired and how large should it be? Which standards have good practice?

This leads us to the identification of relevant criteria for legitimacy which is summarized in Table 12.1.

Furthermore, questions about actual experiences with environmental standards are discussed. The reason for this question was to judge the answers given by the interviewees.

Before the results of the interviews are discussed, the research methodology will be presented.

Table 12.1 Legitimacy questions

Criteria	Questions
Inclusivity	• How far are NGOs integrated? • How could such integration be realized? • To what extent are NGOs involved in the process of development or the extension of a standard?
Discourse quality	• Is it possible to consider all requirements from NGOs? • What are the reasons for terminating a dialogue concerning a standard?
Control/ transparency	• Which requirements for certification systems exist? • Is there a difference between certification systems? • Which transparency/reporting is desired and how extensive should it be?

Methodology

In this research project, a qualitative research design was chosen. The aim of the research was to obtain a picture of how feasible it is for NGOs to support environmental standards. This question could be better answered by qualitative interviews than by quantitative surveys. Moreover, call-backs are needed, and the field of environmental standards is so heterogeneous that standardized questions could not be used.

The research design shows the process of data collection, data analysis and performance criteria.

METHOD OF DATA COLLECTION

In the process of problem-oriented interviews, the researcher returns to the problem and his/her question guide. In this chapter, the interview guide is based on the normative theory of legitimacy. However, the interviewee should answer freely, and an open discussion must be possible.[25] Before the first interview, one pre-test was made and afterwards the interview guide was adapted (for the sequence of the questions see Table 12.1). After this, 22 interviews of approximately one hour were held (participating NGOs will not be named for confidentiality reasons). We only interviewed one person per NGO. The interview guide contains only the central aspects of the interview, and bullet points are often used. It is important for establishing the right atmosphere to have a good opening and closing question. All interviewees agreed to an audio tape recording. Afterwards, a comprehensive summary was made of each interview. Very important statements or examples were transcribed.

At the beginning of each interview, the goal and the background of the research project was elucidated. Further on, the anonymity of the answers was guaranteed. After questions about the financing of the project from the first interviewees, a statement on the financial background (self-financed by the university) was integrated. The last question was an open question about aspects which had not been discussed up to that point, but which were very important for the research project.

It was interesting to discover the experiences of the NGO members with environmental standards. Indeed, the interviewees were initially identified on the websites of the NGOs and through publications about the subject. However, although all interviewees were experts, individually they only had experience with one or two standards. Other standards were known, but not in detail. For example, the certification system of other standards was unknown.

DATA ANALYSIS

The interviews were reduced to the essential content, considering relevant connections. In the next step, the remaining content was structured. Unclear text passages were clarified with the interviewees, who read the interviews and gave their approval. Inconsistent results were identified, highlighted and a possible explanation was added. The interviews were transcribed, and interpretations were made and always justified, for example by citing the experts.

The summaries of the interviews were evaluated using the qualitative content analysis proposed by Mayring (2002).[26]

QUALITY OF THE RESEARCH PROCESS

The end of the research design was the discussion of the results by performance criteria. Mayring (2002) developed six performance criteria for qualitative research,[27] which could be used in this research project (Table 12.2).

Table 12.2 Quality of research

Criteria	Realization
Documentation of research process	The documentation of the research process is warranted because every step was documented in detail
Validation of interpretation	All interviews were done by two researchers, and the results were discussed with other researchers, so the interpretation of the results was validated
Research process followed rules	The research process followed clear rules. The literature was analysed, interview guides were developed, summaries of the interviews and an interpretation of the results were made
Nearness to research	The researcher has extensive experience in the field of environmental standards because of earlier research projects and publications
Communicative validation	The communicative validation means a proof of the results by the interviewee. First drafts were sent to all interviewees for their comments. No hermeneutic or psychological interpretation was needed, so mistakes in interpretation could be excluded
Triangulation of methods	Interviews and documents (literature, articles) were analysed. Observational research (process of certification for example) was not possible

Results of the Interviews

The objective of this chapter is to discuss the questions regarding the different aspects of legitimacy one by one and to apply them to the standards (FSC, PEFC, MSC and ISO 14001).

INCLUSIVITY

How extensively are NGOs integrated in the process of developing standards?

When developing a standard, the involvement of everyone concerned is very important for obtaining legitimacy, as was stated by all interviewees. The development of a standard should take place through a consensus of all persons concerned. Often addressed here are labour unions, NGOs and the companies in the supply chain. In addition, the sector determines which other important groups should participate. In the food sector, for example, this includes the local population, farmers, distributors and customers. The idea that all participants in the supply chain should be integrated was expressed by many of the interviewees.

How could such integration be realized?

A lot of interviewees (18) stressed the importance of a fair balance between environmental, social and economic stakeholders. This means that each group has an equal vote in the improvement of standards. A good example given by the interviewees is the system of the Forest Stewardship Council (FSC). The FSC is divided into three sections: economic, social and environmental. The NGOs have the same votes as other participating groups. If one section of the FSC objects to an idea, no change of the standard is possible.[28]

Twenty interviewees had suffered negative experiences. Often, the NGOs participated in the process, but did not ultimately assist in the final decision-making process. One interviewee reported an experience during the development of the Programme for the Endorsement of Forest Certification Schemes (PEFC), the standard of the FSC. The NGO was asked for its opinion of the standard, and it provided extensive criticism in a statement. However, none of these arguments were considered. Despite this, when the standard was published, it was stated that the important environmental NGOs had participated in its development.

One further example that was addressed is the development of the MSC, where only one company (Unilever) and one NGO (World Wildlife Fund) were involved. Furthermore, organizations for standardization (ISO 14001) are subject to harsh criticism. The integration of so-called interested parties – for example NGOs – with the aim of avoiding one-sided orientation in interests, is unrealized because of the "principle of territorial representation" in European and international standardization work. This principle implies that only consistent national positions can be placed; for example, that consumers and environmental councils are able to participate on European and international levels, but are not allowed to vote. Groups without the required financial and organizational background are not able to see their interests represented, as the cost of participation in international meetings of the standardization institutions cannot be met.[29]

To what extent are NGOs involved in the process of the development or the extension of a standard?

At the beginning of the FSC, the level of participation of a broad stakeholder basis (including NGOs) was insufficient, as participation was by invitation and therefore based on a professional network. The FSC worked on facilitating the NGO involvement, for example during the revision of the German FSC Standard 2008. In developing the PEFC, NGOs participated and were involved in negotiations about the standard, although they had no voting rights. Other interviewees reported that during the development of a standard in the banana producing sector, no NGO was involved.

The involvement of local NGOs was highlighted as a very important aspect. Often, in developing standards in the past, no local NGO was involved (ISO 14001), although the main field of application was in countries in the global south. A positive example is the MSC, where the NGO World Wildlife Fund (WWF) was involved by the development.

It was a result of our activities that the measures for the protection of the primeval forest in Russia intensified e.g. 150 companies have been certificated in the last five years (Interview 11).

DISCOURSE QUALITY

Is it possible to consider all requirements from NGOs?

In the context of discourse quality, roughly the same arguments as those found with inclusivity were seen. Positively highlighted was the FSC system, due to several advancements made. The balance between the three sectors was stressed in particular. The core problem with most standards is that NGOs and unions are not integrated in the discourse process, as stated by many of the interviewees, even though companies communicate that participation from NGOs and unions takes place. Members of unions reported that, especially in the certification of social aspects, NGOs and unions were not involved. The possibility of influencing the standard process is the most important requirement of NGOs. This does not mean making them the dominant group, but requires them to be on an equal footing with the economic oriented participants. The PEFC was named as a bad example in this respect – only two votes from NGOs are possibly given, against 16 votes from industry.

A problem with discourse quality is the integration of indigenous people. Many NGOs argue that without the integration of these people, no support of the standard is possible. Often such groups are not organized and so a discussion is difficult.

What are the reasons for terminating a dialogue about a standard?

The process of advancing standards will be complex if the number of participants increases. This was one reason for the MSC to abstain from certain procedures used in the FSC. The MSC does not attempt to be democratic in its governance and this accounts for some of the challenges to the MSC's credibility, particularly within the international development NGO community, which regards inclusive consultation and democratic decision-making processes as crucial for legitimacy and effectiveness.[30] The complex process of implementing and further developing standards increases with the number of stakeholders involved, and the process takes longer. It is complicated to involve all NGOs and the potential for conflict increases. Four interviewees highlighted situations which gave cause for leaving the process. For example, in the "Business Social Compliance Initiative", NGOs had no position on the steering committee. In other processes, suggestions by NGOs to implement a complaint mechanism or to train employees were not considered.

Some interviewees define minimum requirements for a dialogue. One NGO would not discuss gene technology. In such cases the reproach of "greenwashing" is made, which is a reason to terminate the dialogue.

On questioning, interviewees revealed that it sometimes happens that NGOs that work together on the development of a standard have different concepts (including minimum requirements or persons involved, expectations of possible achievements, etc.). For example, with one standard initiative, some NGOs leave the process, while other NGOs do not. It is difficult to find a consensus and so each side must make compromises.

CONTROL/TRANSPARENCY

Which requirements for certification systems exist?

The first aspect of normative legitimacy focuses on the monitoring of the requirements for the environmental standards. The quality of the audits is an important factor according to 21 interviewees. An often-mentioned point (8 interviewees) was that a credible certification system, in particular, needs the involvement of employees. Also important is that the local public are helped to comprehend, for example through information meetings.

Several NGOs (10 interviewees) reported that in their experience the certifier does not talk to employees in the companies, or talks to them only in the presence of their supervisors. The countries of the global south especially see the employees as being under great pressure because they live on the poverty line and are afraid of losing their job. So often the information collected in audits about working conditions does not reflect reality.

To remedy this, the interviewees suggested that supervisors should not be present during the audit. Consequently, the whole audit process must change. First, an awareness of the involvement of employees, local NGOs and unions should be created. Also important is that the audit is no longer seen as a compliance check. The audit should be more of a training programme and an educational workshop. Other interviewees mentioned that it is necessary to build trust between the employees and the certifier.

> *Important is that the certifier is not a foreigner who comes only for the audit from New York (Interview 8).*

The certifier should come from the same region as the certified company and should know the political background of the country. From the interviewees' point of view, the difficulties of audits should also be admitted. Some aspects are often difficult to monitor. Often a free decision by the people in southern countries is determined by poverty, dependency and fear. In other words, a clear interpretation of the situation is necessary. This shows how important cooperation with local NGO auditing is. A study by the University of Sussex of 280 companies and 430 locations shows that ISO 14001 certified companies differ marginally in their environmental behaviour compared to companies without an ISO certificate. Additionally, this study shows that although the employers' behaviour changed slightly after certification, in some areas no improvements were found.[31] Therefore, insufficient legitimacy can be analysed for the control of the contents of ISO 14001 (set by the companies).

Is there a difference between certification systems?

The literature[32] discusses how the legitimacy of any certification system depends on the selection of the certifier. If the company chooses the certifier, resulting in a direct business contact, then the independence of the certifier is compromised. The ISO system is often criticised in this respect. Within the FSC, the PEFC and the MSC the companies who apply for certification select their own certifier. Three interviewees supported a different procedure that they knew from other standards, whereby the standard setting company (like the FSC or MSC) selects a certifier for the company, i.e. the company does not know which certifier will come to perform the audit. No direct business contact exists and the independence of the certifier is guaranteed. A positive example of such a certification system is the Fair Labor Association (FLA). However, this is not seen as an important improvement which is useful for all standards alike. The problem with the procedure is that the companies want a relationship of trust with the certifier and the tendency to disclose their business secrets is low. This position is respected by the NGO agents. They argue that participation in the standards is voluntary and they are afraid that such procedures reduce the motivation of the companies to participate.

The independence of the certifier is important. Some interviewees considered that this is not a problem with the big certification companies like PWC, because they are not financed by one company only. This appraisal was not shared by all interviewees, however. Ten were of the opinion that the big certification companies do an unsatisfactory job because they are not aware of the problems of the employees in the southern countries. The main focus is to make money and for this a good relationship with companies' management is important.

Another crucial question is whether the standard certificate norm should use, for example, the ILO norms, or if it is better only to standardize the process of norm building. Most interviewees supported process standards. The reason for this is that the concretizing of the content of the standards would be developed together with local NGOs and against the background of cultural factors. These statements are interesting because the standard which has the strongest process orientation is ISO 14001, which is also the standard most criticized by the NGOs. However, cooperation with NGOs is not considered with ISO 14001.

What transparency/reporting is desired and how extensive should it be?

Along with the impact of certification, the transparency of the audit results is also important. Such transparency – for example, with a report available to the public and the NGOs – is one element for obtaining legitimacy. This normative requirement was tested by a question on the transparency of the audit results.

All interviewees believed that reporting the results of audits is an important part of the certification process. In this context, a complaint system is a basic instrument. Too often companies use the reports for a positive profiling of their activities. It is therefore necessary to have an instrument for filing a complaint against the profiling of the companies and for describing the real situation.

Eight interviewees complained that the certification reports are published in a condensed version. It is critical that mistakes are reported, as well as success stories. The internet is a useful instrument for publishing current information on the results of the audits. The FSC, which has the chain-of-custody number on the homepage, has a completely transparent chain. However, a lot of interviewees saw problems with reporting. There is a fine line between company secrets on the one hand and public reporting on the other. Most companies exercise caution when reporting information about environmental aspects.

There are companies like Nike or Puma which show that reporting about problems is possible (Interview 9).

Legitimacy corresponds with responsibility for business actions. One interviewee mentioned how, for some years, companies denied responsibility for their suppliers. This has now changed. Companies know that they are responsible for their supply chain, even though a lot of deficit exists. The internal structures show a reality different from that communicated to the public. For example, companies may state that they consider environmental aspects when purchasing.

> ...but what is the reality – they choose the cheapest (Interview 6).

The final question gave the interviewees the opportunity to discuss aspects which had not been mentioned up to that point. The NGO members repeated statements which were very important from their perspective. No new argument was made, so we can presume that the important factors which influence the decision to support or to criticize environmental standards are discussed.

Discussion

We used the framework of the normative legitimacy concept – inclusivity, discourse and control/transparency – to structure the interviews and to find out what kind of standards NGOs can support. This chapter looked at different standards and in each case some deficits can be identified. It may even discredit these instruments, leaving only the classical ones of supplier control (for example, audits through the company) and creating higher costs than more exigent standards. In the following sections, we discuss each of the requirements the interviewees mentioned.

INCLUSIVITY

One important point was the *participation of NGOs* in developing and implementing standards. Not only NGOs, but also agents from unions and local groups from southern countries are important. To preserve legitimacy, the participation must be institutionalized to guarantee equality and that the NGOs *have an influence with their votes*. The system of the FSC was mentioned as a good example of this. It is also important in this respect that *NGOs are integrated in the process*.

Another important point is that *local NGOs* should not only be invited, they should also be *supported with financial resources to participate* in the process of developing standards.

A problem here is *to involve all "relevant" NGOs*. What are the criteria to select NGOs in the development of standards? By increasing the number of NGOs that participate, the *potential for conflict increases*. Also, a civil society with a wide spectrum of NGOs is not common in countries in the global south.

It is questionable if this could be a critical factor for supporting a standard. Probably, a standard without NGO participation could achieve high ecological requirements.

On the other hand, it is essential that NGOs are involved in the development of a standard. However, this could not be an argument to not support a standard.

DISCOURSE QUALITY

Concerning discourse quality, nearly the same arguments as those found for inclusivity were seen.

The *participation in problem solving* and critical points is a requirement of NGOs. Some interviewees define minimum requirements for a dialogue, but *different NGOs have different requirements*. Three interviewees stated situations which gave cause for leaving the process. At the same time, other NGOs involved saw no reason to leave the dialogue. It is hard to find *common requirements for all NGOs* in terms of discourse quality.

A problem with discourse quality is also the *integration of indigenous people*. Without the integration of these people, support for standards is not possible, according to interviewees. Often such groups are not organized and so a structured discussion is difficult. However, this argument is not a factor in rejecting the support of ecological standards.

CONTROL/TRANSPARENCY

In the case of monitoring and control, an important change is stipulated. Instead of anonymous compliance, audits in the presence of management agents represent an *integrity method*.[33] The integrity method uses the common development of norms and the intrinsic motivation by employees, which is caused by this process. Trust will be developed and in a sense of a common development strategy, the situation of environmental problems will be enhanced. Such an integrity method would avoid a lot of problems in interpreting the norms. The question of changing the accreditation system (direct between certifier and company or indirect between certifier and an independent institution) and the announcement of the visit of the certifier before the audit, no longer play an important role. However, it should be stated that the integrity method *is more expensive* than the compliance method.

The *transparency of the method* is also an important element for the NGOs. In relation to this, traceability takes on a high significance. The FSC with its chain-of-custody number is a good example given by interviewees. An *institution of complaint*, where complaints about the difference between communicated and real actions take place, is an important instrument to give external stakeholders the possibility of participating.

As an important result of the research concerning control, we can assess that NGOs have significant doubts about the support of environmental standards. Factories are certified which do not conform to the requirements of the standards. Circumstances which are *not in accordance to reality* are communicated to the public. For their part, companies prefer standards with low-level norms compared to standards with high-level norms. They prefer standards without NGO participation.

According to the interviewees, companies focus only on the structure of being granted the certificate and communicating this to the public. The NGOs suspect that the real activities in the companies are not what is being communicated. This effect is known in theory (new sociological institutionalism) as the decoupling effect. Meyer/Rowan (1977) argue that there is an antagonism between the expectation of the organization and the expectation of the environment, resulting in the fact that the members of the organization are in conflict with each other.[34] In the context of environmental standards, the conflict could be concerning the cost pressure on the one side and the environmental requirements of the standards, which often need investment, on the other.

Four interviewees stated that the companies do not choose the supplier with the best environmental performance but rather the cheapest one. In choosing suppliers, environmental criteria play no role. This does not mean that only environmental aspects should be relevant for supplier selection. Environmental criteria, however, should be integrated in supplier selection process. A good example of key performance measures for the automobile green supply chain is shown by Olugu, Wong and Shaharoun (2011). The developed indicators (for example, the level of supplier environmental certification) can be integrated in supplier evaluation and are one aspect for supplier selection.[35]

To the certifier and the public, accordance with the norms signals one thing, while members of the organization actually act differently. So the theoretic and real structures are decoupled. This phenomenon is often described in empirical research.[36] Also, the fact that in some industries the companies prefer low-level standards supports this argument. If the decoupling between real and theoretic structure is consolidated, NGOs could not support standards without the danger of losing their credibility.

The decoupling thesis discussed above does not automatically cause a negative effect in the long term. Research by Walgenbach (1991) shows that decoupling was only done partially by the implementation of the ISO 9000 standard.[37] Only those elements which are meaningful for the company, and which are coherent with the rationale, would be implemented. The others would be decoupled. Boiral (2003) arrives at similar results. In this context, it can be argued that implemented structures – even if they are implemented only for greenwashing or window dressing – over a longer period result in *changes in behaviour*.[38] A reason for this is, for example, that people who are engaged in implementing the standards find rational arguments for the new processes and help to break up rationality conflicts. From here, we can deduce that an adoption of external requirements (here the requirements from NGO members) takes place in companies not abruptly and completely, but in the longer term, with both setbacks and success stories. For companies to accept structures as legitimate in the long term, other companies in the industry should follow them and implement the structures while they assimilate successful strategies. First evidence of this exists because in the textile industry (and other industries) they are interested in the development of environmental and social standards.[39] This means that in the long term, structures like those of the FSC could be a guide for all other standards.

Table 12.3 summarizes the findings of the discussion.

Table 12.3 Requirements and problems of supporting standards

	Requirements	Problems
Inclusivity	• participation of NGOs • local groups from southern countries must be integrated • NGOs have an influence with their votes • supported with financial resources to participate	• involve all "relevant" NGOs • criteria to select NGOs • potential of conflicts increases
Discourse quality	• participation of NGOs • minimum requirements for a dialogue • the integration of indigenous people	• NGOs have different requirements for dialogue • indigenous people often are not organized
Control/transparency	• integrity method of monitoring and control • transparency of the method • institution of complaint • circumstances which are not in accordance with the real situation are communicated to the public (decoupling effect)	• integrity method is more expensive • limits of certification • implemented structures over a longer period result in changes in behaviour

However, if the requirements of the NGOs which are mentioned here are considered during the further development of environmental standards, the chances that many NGOs will support them increase. This would be of advantage for companies in order to rebuild legitimacy in the framework of corporate social responsibility and along the supply chain among stakeholders. Environmental standards like the FSC already reconsider this, demanding that every part of the supply chain fulfil the requirements to guarantee sustainability along the whole chain. Barriers are high for the participating companies, from producers to retailers. Even though these efforts may be contradicted by easily achievable standards, NGO supported standards contain a certain guarantee. The risk of failing in public is too high to be taken, given the efficiency of the internet as a news spreading medium. Big companies like Nike have already experienced this and suffered high losses, not only in money, but also in reputation. Furthermore, the whole supply chain, including all the participating companies, will be the focus of examination and evaluation. Even though we saw many problems, it is not easy to define clear requirements for supporting standards by NGOs.

Limitations and Future Research

Also to be considered is that only a small number of NGOs was interviewed. This means the discussed perspective is limited. The process of developing a standard requires a lot of agents, which was not discussed during the interview. For example, the supplier was not considered here. An interesting question could be: Do the suppliers in the southern hemisphere support all these ideas from NGOs or do they prefer to temporarily be less "green" but more "wealthy"?

It is difficult to generalize the results because only 22 NGO members were interviewed, but the number of NGOs which support standards is limited. We identified and interviewed the biggest and most important NGOs. So although we cannot generalize our results, we can assert that we had a good impression of the NGOs' opinions.

However, the discussion here gives a good basis for further discussion. A great deal of standard initiatives exist, for example, in the biofuel sector. For these initiatives, the research can give helpful advice on further development.

The key role of the NGOs is based on a thesis that is questionable. Is the impact of campaigns so critical for companies? What can be said about companies which have no contact with the end customer, i.e. which have no brand, so that they are not afraid of reputation loss? Are all industries susceptible to campaigns from NGOs? Do specific environmental conditions exist in different industries? All these questions could not be answered in this discussion and are open for further research.

Notes

1   Argenti, P. A. (2004), "Collaborating with Activists: How Starbucks Works with NGOs", *California Management Review*, Vol. 47, No. 1, pp. 91–116; Green, K., Morten, B. & New, S. (1998), "Green Purchasing and Supply Policies: Do They Improve Companies' Environmental Performance?", *Supply Chain Management: An International Journal*, Vol. 3, No. 2, pp. 89–95.

2   DeSimone, L. D. & Popoff, F. (1997), *Eco-Efficiency: The Business Link to Sustainable Development*, MIT Press, Cambridge, MA; Simpson, D. F. & Power, D. J. (2005), "Use the Supply Relationship to Develop Lean and Green Suppliers", *Supply Chain Management: An International Journal*, Vol. 10, No. 1, pp. 60–68.

3   Lawrence, A. T. (2002), "The Drivers of Stakeholder Engagement. Reflections on the Case of Royal Dutch/Shell". In Andriof, J., Waddock, S., Husted, B. & Sutherland Rahman, S. (eds.), *Unfolding Stakeholder Thinking: Theory, Responsibility and Engagement*, Greenleaf Publishing, Sheffield, pp. 185–199; Winstanley, D., Clark, J. & Leeson, H. (2002), "Approaches to Child Labour in the Supply Chain", *Business Ethics: A European Review*, Vol. 11, No. 3, pp. 210–223.

4   Barrientos, S. (2002), "Mapping Codes through the Value Chain – from Researcher to Detective". In Jenkins, R., Pearson, R. & Seyfang, G. (eds.) *Corporate Responsibility and Labour Rights: Codes of Conduct in the Global Economy*, Earthscan, London, pp. 61–76.

5   Ebenshade, J. (2004), "Codes of Conduct: Challenges and Opportunities for Workers' Rights", *Social Justice*, Vol. 31. No. 3, pp. 40–59; O'Rourke, T. (2000), *Monitoring the Monitors. A critique of Price Waterhouse Coopers*, MIT.

6   Seuring, S. & Müller, M. (2008), "From a Literature Review to a Conceptual Framework for Sustainable Supply Chain Management", *Journal of Cleaner Production*, Vol. 16, No. 15, pp. 1699–1710.

7   Spiller, A. (1996), *Ecological Product Policy*, Metropolis, Marburg.

8   Tiemann, F. M. (2007), *Ereignisinduzierte Markenkrisen – Phänomen und Krisenmanagement in der Markenführung* (Event-triggered Brand Crisis), Peter Lang Verlag, Frankfurt am Main.

9   Seuring & Müller (2008), *op. cit.*

10 Globescan/PIPA (2006), "BBC World Service economic opinion survey", GlobeScan Incorporated and The Program on International Policy Attitudes joint survey, available at: www.globescan.com/news_archives/bbcpoll06–2.html#media.

11 Lawrence, A.-T. (2002), "The Drivers of Stakeholder Engagement. Reflections on the Case of Royal Dutch/Shell". In Andriof, J., Waddock, S., Husted, B. & Sutherland Rahman, S. (eds.), *Unfolding Stakeholder Thinking: Theory, Responsibility and Engagement*, Greenleaf Publishing Sheffield.

12 Argenti (2004), *op. cit.*; Green, et al. (1998), *op. cit.*

13 Lawrence (2002) *op. cit.*; Winstanley, et al. (2002), *op. cit.*

14 Seuring, S. (2004), "Integrated Chain Management and Supply Chain Management: Comparative Analysis and Illustrative Cases", *Journal of Cleaner Production*, Vol. 12, No. 8–10, pp. 1059–1071.

15 Barrientos, 2002; Jenkins, et al., 2002; Beschorner, T., Müller, M. (2007), "Social Standards: Functioning and Conditions Toward an Active Ethical Involvement of Businesses in Developing Countries", *Journal of Business Ethics*, Vol. 73, No. 1, pp. 11–20; Seuring & Müller (2008) *op. cit.*

16 Bass, S., Font, X. & Danielson, L. (2001), "Standards & Certification: A Leap Forward or a Step Back for Sustainable Development?" *The Future Is Now: Equity for a Small Planet*, Vol. 2, International Institute for Environment and Development, London, pp. 21–31; Roberts, S. (2003), "Supply Chain Specific? Understanding the Patchy Success of Ethical Sourcing Initiatives", *Journal of Business Ethics*, Vol. 44, No. 2–3, pp. 159–170.

17 Bondy, K., Matten, D. & Moon, J. (2007), "Codes of Conduct as a Tool for Sustainable Governance in MNCs". In Benn, S. & Dunphy, D. *Corporate Governance and Sustainability – Challenges for Theory and Practice*, Routledge, London, pp. 165–186; Kolk, A. & van Tulder, R. (2006), "International Responsibility Codes". In Epstein, M.J. & Hanson, K.O. (eds.) *The Accountable Corporation: Corporate Social Responsibility*, Vol. 3, Praeger Publishers, Westport, CT, pp. 147–173; Müller, M. & Nofz, K. (2008), "Umwelt – und Sozialstandards am Scheideweg – eine empirische Untersuchung bei NGOs", *Zeitschrift für Umweltpolitik und Umweltrecht*, Vol. 31, No. 2, pp. 245–271; O'Rourke, D. (2000), *Monitoring the Monitors: A Critique of PricewaterhouseCoopers Labor Monitoring*, MIT, Boston, MA.

18 See for example Chin, K.-S. (1999), "Factors Influencing ISO 14000 Implementation in Printed Circuit Board Manufacturing Industry in Hong Kong", *Journal of Environmental Planning and Management*, Vol. 42, No. 1, pp. 123–134; Corbett, C.J. & Kirsch, D.A. (2001), "International Diffusion of ISO 14000 Certification", *Production and Operations Management*, Vol. 10, No. 3, pp. 327–342; Quazi, H.A., Khoo, Y.-K., Tan, C-M. & Wong, P.-S. (2001), "Motivation for ISO 14000 Certification: Development of a Predictive Model, *Omega*, Vol. 29, No. 6, pp. 525–542; Walgenbach, P. (2000), *Die normgerechte Organisation. Eine Studie über die Entstehung, Verbreitung und Nutzung der DIN EN ISO 9000er Normenreihe*. Schäffer-Poeschel, Stuttgart.

19 Jenkins, R., Pearson, R. & Seyfang, G: (2002), *Corporate Responsibility and Labour Rights: Codes of Conduct in the Global Economy*, Earthscan, London; for further information see Howard, J., Nash, J. & Ehrenfeld, J. (1999), "Industry Codes as Agents of Change: Responsible Care Adoption by US Chemical Companies", *Business Strategy and the Environment*, Vol. 8, No. 5, pp. 281–295.

20 See Dingwerth (2004), *op. cit.* p. 8.

21 Bouwen, P. (2003), *The Democratic Legitimacy of Business Interest Representation in the European Union: Normative Implications of the Logic of Access*, Bonn, www.coll.mpg.de/

pdf_dat/2003_8online.pdf, 26.07.2007; Dingwerth, K. (2005), *The Democratic Legitimacy of Transnational Rule-making: Normative Theory and Empirical Practice*, Berlin.

22 Mitchell, R. K., Agle, B. R. & Wood, D. J. (1997), "Towards a Theory of Stakeholder Identification and Salience: Defining the Principle of Who and What Really Counts", *Academy of Management Review*, Vol. 22, No. 4, pp. 853–886; Phillips, R. (2003), "Stakeholder Legitimacy", *Business Ethics Quarterly*, Vol. 13, No. 1, pp. 25–41.

23 Dingwerth (2004) *op. cit.*; Bouwen (2003) *op. cit.*

24 Henry, S. (1983), *Private Justice: Towards Integrated Theorising in the Sociology of Law*, Routledge and Kegan Paul, London.

25 Mayring, P. (2002), *Introduction to Qualitative Research*, Beltz Verlag, Weinheim & Basel.

26 Mayring (2002), *op. cit.*

27 Based on Kirk, J. & Miller, M. L. (1986), *Reliability and Validity in Qualitative Research*, Sage, Beverly Hills, CA.

28 See for FSC Müller, M. & Seuring, S. (2007), "Legitimacy about Environmental and Social Standards against Stakeholders", *ZfU*, Vol. 3, pp. 257–285.

29 Mitchell, Agle & Wood, (1997), *op. cit.*

30 Fowler, P. & Heap, S. (2000), "Bridging Troubled Waters. The Marine Stewardship Council". In Bendell, J., *Terms of Endearment. Business, NGOs and Sustainable Development*, UK, pp. 135–148.

31 Berkhout, F., Hertin, J., Wagner, M. & Tyteca, D. (2008), "Are EMS Environmentally Effective? The Link between Environmental Management Systems and Environmental Performance in European Companies", *Journal of Environmental Planning and Management*, Vol. 51, No. 2, pp. 259–283.

32 Müller & Seuring (2007), *op. cit.*

33 See Paine, L. S. (1994), "Managing for Organizational Integrity", *Harvard Business Review*, Vol. 72, No. 2, pp. 106–117.

34 Meyer, J. & Rowan, B. (1977), "Institutionalized Organizations: Formal Structure as Myth and Ceremony", *American Journal of Sociology*, Vol. 83, No.2, pp. 340–363.

35 Olugu, E. U., Wong, K. Y. & Shaharoun, A. M (2011), "Development of Key Performance Measures for Automobile Green Supply Chain", *Recources, Conservation and Recycling*, Vol. 55, pp. 567–579.

36 Lee, B. H. & Lounsbury, M. (2005), "Decoupling and the Cultures of Global Finance", *International Studies of Management and Organization*, Vol. 34, pp. 116–134; Walgenbach, P. (2001), "The Production of Distrust by Means of Producting Trust", *Organization Studies*, Vol. 22, pp. 693–714; Westphal, J. D. & Zajac, E. J. (2001), "Decoupling Policy from Practice: The Case of Stock Repurchase Programs", *Administrative Science Quarterly*, Vol. 46, pp. 202–228.

37 Walgenbach, P. (2001), "The Production of Distrust by Means of Producing Trust", *Organization Studies*, Vol. 22, 693–714.

38 Boiral, O. (2003), "ISO 9000: Outside the Iron Cage", *Organization Science*, Vol. 14, No. 6, pp. 720–737.

39 Koplin, J. (2006), *Sustainable Development in Supply Chain Management. A Concept to Integrate Environmental and Social Standards*, DUV, Wiesbaden.

13 *Applying Economic Non-Market Valuation for Sustainable Supply Chain Performance Measurement and Evaluation*

JOSEPH SARKIS,* AREF AGHAEI HERVANI,† AND
MARILYN HELMS‡

Keywords

Non-market valuation, sustainable supply chain, performance measurement, performance evaluation.

Introduction

This chapter compiles and discusses a list of non-market valuation tools for sustainable supply chain performance measurement. The aim is to provide researchers and practitioners with a toolbox from which they can select the appropriate measurement tool for the respective stakeholder.

This chapter is organized into two parts. In the first part, the state of the art in measuring the sustainability of global supply chains is reviewed. While sustainability is an issue of growing concern for the long-term existence and advancement of companies in competitive global markets, little knowledge exists on how to assess, control, and manage the greening of global supply chains. Next, a framework delineating the structure of green supply chain management is presented along with a suggestion that sustainable performance measurement should follow the Plan-Do-Check-Act (PCDA) paradigm.

*   Professor Joseph Sarkis, Professor of Operations and Environmental Management, Clark University, Graduate School of Management, 9950 Main Street, Worcester, MA 01610. E-mail: jsarkis@clarku.edu Telephone: (508) 793-7659.

†   Professor Aref Hervani, Associate Professor of Economics, Chicago State University, 9501 South King Drive, Chicago, IL 60628-1598. E-mail: ahervani@csu.edu Telephone: 773-995-3827.

‡   Professor Marilyn M. Helms, Sesquicentennial Chair and Professor of Management, School of Business, Dalton State College, 650 College Drive, Dalton, GA 30736. E-mail: mhelms@daltonstate.edu. Telephone: 706-272-2600.

In the second part of the chapter, market and non-market methods of valuation are presented. Focusing on non-market approaches, an extensive list of value concepts that can be used for environmental benefit measurement is presented. Value concepts are explained in more detail and illustrated with the help of company examples from various industries.

Performance measurement and assessment of results takes on new importance when applied to measuring innovative practices such as the greening of supply chains and the reverse logistics (product recovery) operations of manufacturers. Recent works emphasize how performance measurement within green supply chain management is critical as new insights from frameworks and methodologies continue to develop.[1] Managerially, internal and external pressures have caused organizations to explicitly consider the environment in their strategic and operational planning and response to these pressures has extended across the supply chain. Global supply chain management (GSCM) strategies have become more complex and need greater levels of investment and involvement in relationships to tap into the potential for enhancing competitive advantage.[2] To aid GSCM implementation and introduction, there is a need to at least plan for and conceptualize performance measurement systems and their requirements.

Performance measurement systems (PMS) frameworks have recently been proposed for green supply chain management and for developing a methodology to implement a global supply chain management.[3] These frameworks and methodologies have introduced flows and pressures as well as listing various environmental measures for manufacturers to consider in their design, operations, and reverse reclamation processes.

There are numerous issues and concerns about GSCM/PMS, ranging from the variety of internal/external pressures, the types of metrics to be developed, potential designs of GSCM/PMS, and tools and results analysis of a GSCM/PMS. These systems have yet to fully exist and operate within many organizations, yet their development and introduction seem inevitable as further integration and pressures cause organizations to seriously consider them for their long-term survival.

Performance measurement in supply chains is difficult, however, especially when investigating numerous supply chain tiers. GSCM/PMS has been, and still is, virtually non-existent in terms of investigation. The basic purposes of GSCM/PMS may include: external reporting, internal control (managing the business better), and internal analysis (understanding the business better and continuous improvement). These are the fundamental issues that drive the development of frameworks for business performance measurement. GSCM/PMS development and investigations requires evaluation and consideration of general supply chain management and performance measurement principles plus inter-organizational dimensions, including shared environmental management systems, proprietary data sharing, life cycle analysis, and supply chain responses to regulatory policy. Environmental performance measures continue to grow in importance due to internal corporate pressures as well as external competitive and environmental issues.

The successful management of a supply chain is also influenced by customer expectations, globalization, information technology, government regulation, competition, and the environment. Corporate performance measurement and its application continue to grow and encompass both quantitative and qualitative measurements and approaches. The variety and level of performance measures depends greatly on the goal of the organization or the characteristics of the individual strategic business unit. For example, when measuring performance, companies must consider existing financial measures such as return on investment, profitability, market share, and revenue growth at a more competitive and strategic level. Other measures such as customer service and inventory performance (supply, turnover) are more operationally focused, but may necessarily be linked to strategic level measures and issues. Valuation issues are central to performance measurement, whether the valuation is economic or otherwise.

One fertile area of valuation approaches, especially ecological valuation, which seems to have remained untapped, is that of economic valuation approaches. The integration of economic valuation method into firms' analysis would allow firms to measure the direct value added and indirect value added from GSCM and reverse logistics activities. For example, social aspects of reverse logistics can be measured through the use of non-market valuation methods. The non-market valuation methods can measure proxy values for people's willingness to pay in order to preserve the environment, especially the environment that is utilized by manufacturing activities of the firm's operation.

These approaches include market and non-market valuations. Some of them are quite capable of developing non-tangible as well as tangible valuations for environmental benefits. Even though most economic non-market valuation approaches, which is the primary focus of this chapter, have been used on individual or policy level analyses, organizational and supply chain level analyses and investigation can benefit from these techniques. This work is underrepresented in the core supply chain and organizational management literature and can provide significant development as these techniques are adjusted for a different level of analysis. That is, instead of macro-economic and policy level analysis, we focus on supply chain and organizational level valuation analysis.

The rest of this chapter will include foundational and developmental insights that can help guide this field of study. The next section will focus on general performance measurement systems and a discussion of the supply chain background. We then narrow the discussion to focus on performance evaluation within green supply chains. We then give an overview of various valuation techniques from the general economics literature. The relevance and application of these tools to various stakeholders and elements within green supply chains are then introduced. Conclusions and future developmental directions appear in the final section of this chapter.

Performance Measurement Systems in the Supply Chain

PMSs are unique to each organization but share common measures and traits. We overview some of these traits. PMSs may have both tangible and intangible measures, with a balance of both types used to accurately measure performance. Measures should be dynamic and present at multiple levels of the organization and the supply chain. Both products and processes need to be included in the measurement systems and such systems and measures are best developed through a team approach with derivation from and links to the overall corporate strategy. Systems must have effective internal and external communications among the partners. Responsibility and accountability for results must be clearly assigned and be thoroughly understood. Systems must provide intelligence for decision makers and not just compile data. Finally, the system should be capable of linking compensation, rewards, and recognition to performance measurement.

Even though significant work has been completed on performance measurement and management on internal organizational operations, the emphasis on supply chain performance measurement (especially with an inter-organizational focus), in either the practitioner or research community, has been relatively limited.[4] Difficulties arise in finding acceptable measures when organizations in a supply chain may have differing competitive and strategic priorities. Meshing these measures to overall supply chain goals becomes a complex exercise. In addition, the identification and application of appropriate measures and who manages them is a concern, as power dynamics come into play. Satisfying the ultimate customer must be considered, but identification of the ultimate customer or stakeholder becomes a difficult exercise.

To summarize, some logistics and supply chain performance measurement systems research showed that internal PMSs were related to advantages connected with convenience and the avoidance of implementation problems, while power, purpose, and implementation were found to be important design factors.[5] Challenges for performance measurement within a holistic systems-based framework (e.g. supply chain frameworks) are both integrated and concurrent.[6] Awareness about performance requirements and top management commitment are enablers for PMS development.[7] All these characteristics need to be considered when designing PMSs in supply chains.

Recent advances in supply chain performance measurement have considered the various dimensions of recent supply chain practices, including lean, agile, resilient and green (LARG) supply chains.[8] Performance measures in these systems require an organization's operational, economic, and environmental performance as well as improved competitiveness to be considered. One important aspect of appropriate measure is that context is always a concern when considering supply chain performance.[9] Whether it is some LARG practice or industry characteristic, performance systems need to be carefully developed. Also, country-based analyses show variations in performance contexts.[10]

PERFORMANCE MEASUREMENT AND GSCM

Figure 13.1 describes[11] GSCM graphically, where reverse logistics "closes the loop" of a typical forward supply chain and includes reuse, remanufacturing, and/or recycling of materials into new materials or other products with value in the marketplace. The idea is to eliminate or minimize waste (energy, emissions, chemical/hazardous, solid wastes). This figure is representative of a single organization's internal supply chain, its major operational elements and the linkage to external organizations. A number of environmentally conscious practices are evident throughout the supply chain. GSCM is concerned with inter-organizationally sharing responsibility for environmental performance. For example, just shifting the burden to another stage or partner in the supply chain may actually cause greater environmental harm. Having broad-based supply chain and inter-organizational environmental measures may effectively capture the overall supply chain environmental burdens. GSCM should promote the sharing of environmental responsibility and lend itself to achieving a reduced environmental burden.

The traditional performance measurement structure of the supply chain must be extended and include mechanisms for product recovery (reverse logistics) and the establishment and implementation of new performance measurement systems.[12] Environmental performance measurement and supporting systems across supply chains

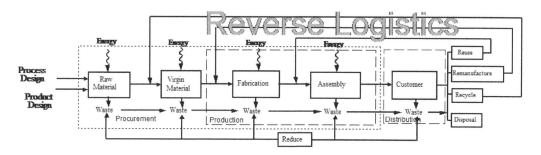

Figure 13.1 The green supply chain management system

has not been as extensively studied.[13] The broad-based supply chain (global) rather than individual (local) organization focus can lead to global optimization of environmental performance. For example, just shifting greenhouse gas emissions from one company to another through outsourcing activities within the supply chain may not truly decrease a product's carbon footprint. Integrating a broader life cycle or environmental economic analysis would be more effective. A broadening of environmental performance measures perspectives is needed to fully appreciate the true environmental performance of supply chain processes and product material flows.

These GSCM/PMS systems are valuable for integrated supplier evaluation models, which consider a supplier's environmental performance together with price, production capability, reliability, and service to improve GSCM.[14] More broadly, managing strategic supply chain partnerships for environmental supply chain management has also been a goal.[15] A holistic approach, similar to basic SCM, has been mentioned as an effective approach for GSCM (closed loop) performance measurement.[16]

The design of a GSCM/PMS should begin by defining the overall goal(s) of the system. The design should also fit the environmental management systems of organizations. These environmental management approaches range from ISO 14000 to total quality management programs, many of which are focused on continuous improvement loops.[17]

Monitoring supply chain environmental performance may give a competitive advantage to organizations seeking to show final customers and other stakeholders how well they are performing, the continuous improvement of performance, and their long-term goals to reduce risk of closure due to environmental penalties.

Selected measures and metrics, as shown in Figure 13.2, must be implemented within a framework much like the strategic planning model, beginning with an organization's mission and vision as the starting point for developing appropriate measures.[18] Using the supply chain operations reference (SCOR) model has also been a useful benchmark of performance measures to be utilized in GSCM.[19] Extending to more holistic measures, such as lean and green approaches for performance, has also been recommended in the holistic literature.[20]

Overall, there is no one perfect tool for a GSCM/PMS (which in itself is a tool), but any tools used for planning, assessment, and management is heavily dependent on agreement across organizations and the ease and accessibility of data and knowledge to apply these tools. Yet, these organizational tools can be further enhanced by investigating the applicability of broader economic tools.

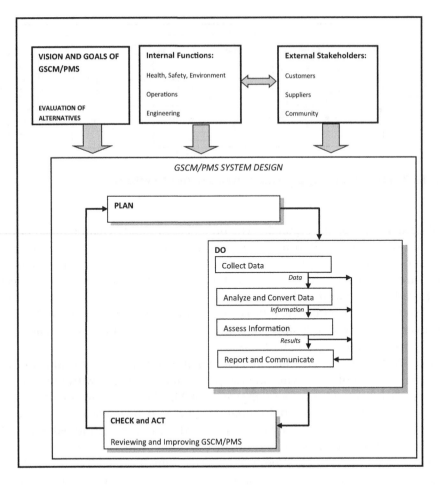

Figure 13.2 Design of a performance measurement system utilizing the continuous improvement Plan-Do-Check-Act process from ISO 14031 guidelines

While the existing performance measurement toolset for environmental operations is growing, it may not yet be adequate to fully assess GSCM. Multiple researchers have illustrated the use of the analytical hierarchy process as a decision support model to help managers understand the trade-offs between environmental dimensions.[21] The "balanced scorecard" is another popular tool within the corporate performance management literature.[22] Advanced techniques such as probabilistic neural network models,[23] rough set approaches,[24] fuzzy rule techniques,[25] and case-based reasoning[26] have been applied in performance evaluation for GSCM practices.

Given the overview of GSCM/PMS practice and requirements, we now turn our attention to a review of economic environmental evaluation methods, which can help set the stage for integration of new techniques and valuations for GSCM/PMS.

ECONOMIC ENVIRONMENTAL VALUATION METHODS

There are two major approaches in general economic literature to measuring environmental benefits: (1) market valuation techniques and (2) non-market valuation techniques. Market valuation techniques include physical linkages, and non-market valuation techniques tend to include behavioral linkages. Economists typically rely on direct observable market interactions to place monetary values on goods and services. Markets enable economists to measure an individual's willingness to pay to preserve environmental services. Consumers reveal their preferences through the choices they make in allocating scarce resources among competing alternatives. There are a number of market-based methods of environmental valuation such as: factor of production approach; change in producer/consumer surplus; and examination of defensive expenditures.

The various techniques may take a costs or benefits perspective. For example, market-based methods encompass the physical linkage approach which utilizes dose-response functions such as: changes in outputs (productivity); changes in inputs (resource costs); cost-of-illness; and replacement cost. The physical linkages approach includes damage function methods and models the relationship between a contaminant and its observed effects as a way to estimate damage reductions arising from policy. The damage function method estimates only one aspect of incremental benefits and is not capable of simultaneously monetizing the benefits it quantifies. We will provide more detail on the non-market valuation techniques.

Non-market valuation techniques can be classified into: (1) market-based techniques such as productivity changes method, defensive expenditures, replacement costs, shadow price, and opportunity cost method; (2) proxy or surrogate market techniques such as the wage differential method, property value approach or hedonic pricing models, and travel cost methods; and (3) hypothetical market or survey techniques such as contingent valuation method, contingent ranking, and choice modeling. The benefit transfer technique is also sometimes used to value non-market changes in welfare. The technique borrows values from other studies and applies these values to the study site in question. James and Gillespie[27] provide a description and comparison of each of these non-market valuation techniques.

Total economic value includes both "use value" and "non-use value." Use value includes "direct use" and "indirect use," and non-use value includes option values, bequest values, and existence values. Economic benefits accrue whenever economic goods are produced and consumed. An economic good contributes to one or more person's well-being. Use value is obtained when someone gets enjoyment from some form of direct interaction with the resource. This type of value may also be obtained from scenic views or by benefiting from enhanced water purity. The vast majority of empirical studies on the economic value of forest preservation have focused on recreational benefits.[28]

Many people derive satisfaction in a passive manner. Passive-use value or non-use values can take three distinct forms: existence value, option value, and bequest value. In the case of existence value, a person derives satisfaction simply from knowing that a resource (such as a species or pristine wilderness area) exists. There are several possible motives underlying existence value. These may include altruism, the desire to leave a bequest to future generations, or perhaps the capacity of people to derive satisfaction directly from the knowledge of the existence of certain species or wild areas.

The literature on the factors that underlie non-use value is extensive.[29] The concept of non-use value originated from Weisbrod[30] and Krutilla.[31] Bishop and Heberlein[32] conclude that non-use value could be motivated by sympathy for and empathy with people and animals, environmental linkages, feelings of environmental responsibility, and bequest goals. Existence value is the benefit generated today by knowing that a resource exists, even if no onsite use is anticipated.

A second type of passive-use value is bequest value. Bequest value arises because there is uncertainty about the future value of many natural resources. Bequest value is the value individuals gain from the preservation of the resource for use by their heirs. The distinction between existence and bequest value still persists in parts of the literature.[33]

A third concept often associated with non-use value is option value. Option value, by this definition, represents a willingness to pay for resource preservation over and above any expected consumer benefit that the person would receive from future use of the resource.

Table 13.1 provides a summary of information on non-market valuation methods, including the type of general approach (behavioral or physical), a definition of the specific technique, the type of value (use or non-use) measured, and exemplary research on the topic.

VALUATIONS ALONG THE SUPPLY CHAIN

We now provide a brief overview of how some of these techniques can be used to evaluate corporate greening or environmental efforts across the supply chain. The supply chain "stakeholders" can be suppliers, the organization itself (focal organization), customers, and reverse logistics providers that close the loop. Arguably, each of these various supply chain members can use and be evaluated on performance with various valuation techniques identified using market and non-market valuation techniques. In this section we briefly outline how some techniques can be used throughout the supply chain for these purposes. Also, as a summary, Table 13.2 is provided for use by researchers and managers in identifying and applying techniques that may prove valuable for various members of the supply chain. It can be a useful worksheet to identify the relevance to the organization as well as downstream, upstream, and reverse logistics goals, and includes space to evaluate behavioral and physical linkage estimation methods.

The next four sections briefly review examples of how various techniques may be applied to each of the supply chain locations: downstream (customers), focal company, upstream (suppliers), and closing the loop (reverse logistics).

Table 13.1 Non-market valuation methods (direct and indirect estimation methods) for environmental benefit measurement

I. Behavioral Linkage Approach: Indirect Estimation Methods	Non-Market Valuation Methods		
	Definition	Type of values	Existing Research
I.1. Non-Use or Passive-Use Values	In contrast to the direct values people derive from using or experiencing environmental resources, non-use or passive-use values are indirect values that can be broken into three categories: existence value, bequest value, and option value.	Use values Non-use values	Meyer (1974)[34] Randall & Stoll (1983)[35] Sanders, Walsh & Loomis (1990)[36] Boyle et al. (1998)[37]
I.1.a. Existence value	This refers to the value that people get from simply knowing that an environmental resource is conserved.	Non-use values	Edwards (1986)[38] Bishop & Welsh (1992)[39] Johnston et al. (2002)[40]
I.1.b. Bequest value	This refers to the value that individuals gain from being able to pass a resource on to future generations even if they may not ever directly use or experience the resource themselves.	Non-use values	Whitehead & Thompson (1993)[41] Walsh, Loomis & Gillman (1984)[42] James & Gillespie (1997)[43]
1.1.c. Option value	This refers to the value individuals receive from reserving the option of utilizing a resource in the future.	Use values	Brookshire, Eubanks & Randall (1983)[44] Barrick & Beazley (1990)[45] De Groot (1992)[46]
I.2. Revealed Preference Methods	An approach that is used to identify the underlying preferences, and thus demands of individuals, based upon the choices each reveals in their consumption.	Use values Non-use values	Bell & Leeworthy (1990)[47] Benson, Hansen et al. (1998)[48] Bergstrom, Dorfman et al. (2004)[49]
1.2.a. Hedonic pricing	This method assesses the value of an environmental feature (clean air, clean water, serenity, view) by examining actual markets where the feature contributes to the price of a marketed good.	Use values Non-use values	Anderson & Crocker (1971)[50] Freeman (1979b)[51] Bartik (1988)[52] Taylor (2003)[53]
1.2.b. Travel costs	This method (TCM) estimates economic values associated with ecosystems or sites that are used for recreation. It assumes that the value of a site can be deduced from how much people are willing to pay to travel to visit the site.	Use values	Loomis (1989)[54] Bennett & Carter (1993)[55] Bergstrom, Dorffman, & Loomis (2004)[56]
1.2.c. Averting expenditures	This method can be used to measure actions and expenditures incurred to reduce risks. In some cases, it is possible to engage in actions that reduce risks (e.g. staying indoors on days with high air pollution) but it is not easy to place a monetary value on these actions.	Use values	Harrington, et al. (1987)[57] Whitehead et al., (1998)[58] Abrahms, et al. (2000)[59]
1.2.d. Random utility model	This model (RUM) is a model of consumer choice in which the consumer is assumed to have perfect discrimination capability between goods or activities in order to maximize their "utility" (relative attractiveness of competing alternatives).	Use values	Hanemann (1984)[60] Kaoru, Smith, & Long (1995)[61] Bhat (2008)[62]
1.2.e. Benefit transfer method	This method "estimates economic values by transferring existing benefit estimates from studies already completed for another location or issue."	Use values	Downing & Ozuna (1996)[63] Brouwer (2000)[64] Loomis & Rosenberger (2006)[65]

Table 13.1 Continued

Non-Market Valuation Methods			
I. Behavioral Linkage Approach: Indirect Estimation Methods (Cont.)	**Definition**	**Type of values**	**Existing Research**
I.3. Stated Preference Methods	Utilized when the researcher does not have actual data on behavior with regards to a certain environmental good or service. The individuals are provided with hypothetical scenarios, based on plausible outcomes and options, and their choices are used to determine the value of the environmental good or service.	Use values Non-use values	Bell & Leeworthy (1990)[66] Adamowicz, et al. (1998)[67] Arin & Kramer (2000)[68]
I.3.a Contingent valuation	The CVM or CV usually takes the form of a survey questionnaire, which elicits values for environmental goods and services based upon hypothetical situations.	Use values Non-use values	Smith, William, & Freeman III (1985)[69] Willis (1993)[70] Johnston et al. (2002)[71]
I.3.b. Contingent choice method	This method can be used to estimate economic values for virtually any ecosystem or environmental service, and can be used to estimate non-use as well as use values.	Use values Non-use values	Hanemann 1984[72] Mazotta & Opaluch (1995)[73] Louviere et al. (2000)[74]
I.3.c. Discrete Choice	This method uses models of consumer choice in which the good or alternative chosen by the consumer is available only in discrete (integer) units.	Use values	Tversky (1972)[75] Ben-Akiva, et al. (1995)[76] Haab & McConnell (2002)[77]
I.3.d. Paired ranking	The method of paired comparisons is used to measure individuals' preference orderings of items presented to them as discrete binary choices.	Use values Non-use values	Desvousges, et al. (1993)[78] Champ & Loomis (1998)[79] Thomas, et al. (2008)[80]
I.3.e. Referendum method	This is a survey method in which the respondent is asked to respond "yes" or "no" to a hypothetical tradeoff between some amount of environmental good or service and something else of value (typically money).	Non-use values	Cameron (1988)[81] Diamon & Hausman (1994)[82] Nunes & Schokkaert (2003)[83]
I.3.f. Calibrated and conjoint analysis	Statistical technique used to determine how people value different features that make up an individual good or service; it can be used to determine the values attributed to different dimensions of an environmental resource.	Use values	Chapman & Staelin (1982)[84] Cameron & Quiggin (1994)[85] Foster & Mourato (2002)[86]
I.3.g. Choice experiments	This method estimates economic values for virtually any ecosystem or environmental service by asking people to make tradeoffs among sets of ecosystem or environmental services or characteristics. Choice experiments do not directly ask for willingness to pay; this is inferred from tradeoffs that include cost as an attribute.	Use values	Chu & Chu (1990)[87] Adamowicz, Boxall, & Louviere (1998a)[88] Braga & Starmer (2005)[89]

Table 13.1 *Concluded*

Non-Market Valuation Method			
II. Physical Linkages Approach: Direct Estimation Methods	**Definition**	**Type of values**	**Existing Research**
II.1. Cost-Based Method or Expenditure Analysis	Expenditure analysis examines indirect expenditures that are tied to environmental resources, which are often left out of many traditional analyses.	Use values	
II.1.a. Productivity method	The productivity method is used to estimate the economic value of ecosystem products or services that contribute to the production of commercially marketed goods.	Use values	Anderson (1989)[90] Loomis & Larson (1994)[91] Bell (1997)[92]
II.1.b. Cost of illness	Can be utilized to measure human health effects. It is relatively easy to perform, but fails to capture the value of the discomfort of being sick.	Use values	Cropper (1981)[93] Harrington & Portney (1987)[94] Usha Gupta, 2008[95]
II.1.c. Avoided cost method	This method calculates the economic value of benefits that an ecosystem provides that would not exist without the ecosystem in place, and therefore, would represent an added cost to society if this environmental service no longer existed.	Use values	Costanza, & Maxwell (1989)[96] Bockstael, Freeman, Kopp, Portney & Smith, (2000)[97] Randall (2002)[98]
II.1.d. Damage assessment model	This model is much like the avoided cost method. It uses a damage function to calculate the environmental and social costs of alterations to the natural environment.	Use values	Castle, Berrens & Adams, (1994)[99] Randall (1997)[100] MacDonald, Boyce, et al. (2002)[101]

Table 13.2 Non-market valuation method: appropriateness for various supply chain stakeholders

	Non-Market Valuation Methods			
	Relevance to Customers (Downstream)	Relevance to Focal Organizations	Relevance to Suppliers (Upstream)	Relevance to "Reverse Logistics"
I. Behavioral Linkage Approach: Indirect Estimation Methods				
I.1. Non-Use or Passive-Use Values				
I.1.a. Existence Value				
I.1.b. Bequest Value				
I.1.c. Option Value				
I.2. Revealed Preference Methods				
I.2.a. Hedonic Pricing				
I.2.b. Travel Costs				
I.2.c. Averting Expenditures				
I.2.d. Random Utility Model				
I.2.e. Benefit Transfer Method				
I.3. Stated Preference Methods				
I.3.a. Contingent Valuation				
I.3.b. Contingent Choice Method				
I.3.c. Discrete Choice				
I.3.d. Paired Ranking				
I.3.e. Referendum Method				
I.3.f. Calibrated and Conjoint Analysis				
I.3. g. Choice Experiments				
II. Physical Linkages Approach: Direct Estimation Methods – (Cost-Based Method or Expenditure Analysis)				
II.1.a. Productivity Method				
II.1.b. Cost of Illness				
II.1.c. Avoided Cost Method				
II.1.d. Damage Assessment Model				

RELEVANCE TO CUSTOMERS

The customers in the supply chain may be industrial or end-user consumers. Thus, the application of various valuation techniques may require some flexibility depending on whether the analysis will be based on individual consumers or corporations and their representatives.

Market valuations would be appropriate in most circumstances since customers are very market and marketing oriented. From a non-use or passive use value, each approach can prove useful. As an example, consider the existence value of having the flexibility or option to have a certain resource available. An example of this type of valuation would be to make sure that a customer has a supply of a particular resource available in the future. One very specific example is the seafood supply chain. Overfishing has caused many seafood retailers (e.g. Wal-Mart or McDonalds) to have a limited supply of certain types of seafood. Having a sustainable supply chain (existence) for fish can be of significant value to these organizations. In this situation having a supply of a resource or material that others do not have will give an organization a competitive advantage, provide consistent sales, and allow for a premium price to be charged for that product or material. The value for these items can be considered as the marginal increase in price or potential new revenue or market share from the existence of this resource. A similar analysis can be completed from having the option to acquire certain resources by the customers.

These non-valuation techniques can also be applied across the remaining supply chain participants and thus we will focus on some other non-use valuation examples for other members of the supply chain.

RELEVANCE TO FOCAL ORGANIZATIONS

From a focal organizational level of analysis, non-use valuations can be derived from both internal and external stakeholders. Internal stakeholders may be employees or managers within an organization. Within organizations valuation can be completed using an existence value by asking workers how much they value the savings completed through recycling or energy savings. Organizations can easily assign values by evaluating programmatic aspects such as their waste disposal or energy savings. But, workers, especially those that may be intrinsically motivated, may get internal satisfaction from these environmental savings. This internal motivational value would need to be enumerated using specific utility determination approaches.

As an example, averting expenditures is a benefit of recycling. As landfill space becomes more limited and tipping fees increase along with fuel costs and other transportation charges to dispose of waste, finding creative ways to reuse waste products can save money lost to the logistics of disposal. These costs of disposal also include special trash receptacles, vehicles for waste disposal, and personnel, including drivers to transport the waste. Considering all the costs involved, finding new uses for waste can save money and even make money for an organization. Recycling cell phones and accessories can provide needed phones to charities, or phones can be refurbished and sold at a discount to those in need. In addition usable materials including metals, copper, and plastics are kept out of the landfill. Drop-off and mail-in programs are in place to recycle a variety of phones, batteries, chargers, and other accessories. But, the costs and values associated with these items may need to incorporate the benefits of "doing good" to the stakeholders.

RELEVANCE TO SUPPLIERS

Supplier relevance of the non-market valuation approaches can consider the supplier's situation with a specific customer or industry. A focal organization would primarily be concerned with internal values, while a supplier would be concerned about implications across organizational boundaries and as a supplier in a supply chain.

One example is packaging reduction and its valuation from a non-use non-market perspective. Working to reduce packaging is of benefit to suppliers, but suppliers must choose between the costs they would be willing to encounter to reduce packaging. Also they must be willing to pay for the new packaging, thus the program is contingent on a cost-benefit analysis.

In some cases, new formulations must be developed and new packaging options created, which means new manufacturing of filling equipment and redesigned transportation containers. However, the results may be extremely profitable for all concerned. Many cleaning products for home and industrial use are now highly concentrated. This means they use fewer chemicals, less packaging, and decreased amounts of fuel to transport. Thus the overall carbon footprint is lower. Packaging and instructions typically have to be redesigned to explain the dilution ratios to customers. In the revealed preference method, suppliers collaborating with a focal organization/customer may value the various packaging reduction and redesign alternatives using a benefit transfer method, or a choice experiment. The choice experiment could jointly be considered by various suppliers (who join a packaging reduction program) to ask about tradeoffs between various influences (e.g. carbon footprint, fewer chemicals, and extra costs associated with finding alternatives).

RELEVANCE TO REVERSE LOGISTICS PROVIDERS

Of particular relevance to reverse logistics providers is the value of extending a product's life, an example of the "physical linkage" approach. The avoided cost argument is valid in this circumstance and the supply chain itself can benefit from the avoided environmental costs. In addition, there the damage assessment model is applicable since the product life extension can lessen its environmental effects.

An overarching example for having a reverse logistics function could be through an avoided costs method. We would calculate the economic and environmental value that a reverse logistics provider (or a reverse logistics system) provides that would not exist without the reverse logistics system in place. What would be the added cost to society if this service were not provided? This approach fits in with recent efforts to assign not only environmental value and costs but also social sustainability values and costs to reverse logistics.[102]

This brief overview provides examples of how the various valuation approaches can be utilized by different players within the supply chain, separately, or concurrently. Some of these techniques can be integrated with the application of other tools. We give one example of a performance measurement tool to statistically or empirically evaluate in the next section.

Additional Integration and Linkage of Valuation Techniques

Given the disparate techniques briefly introduced above, developing a single valuation score across the supply chain is a valuable managerial result. One such tool used for performance measurement and benchmarking is data envelopment analysis (DEA). DEA could be a particularly suitable tool for benchmarking the efficiency of multiple supply chains along various value dimensions. Without such an integrative technique, internal and external stakeholders may be overwhelmed by the richness of valuation methods and their outcomes.

To make supply chains accountable from a sustainability point of view, it is fundamental to condense rich information into a format that can be easily communicated to a broader audience for review and comparison. For example, the success of the net-promoter score (NPS) as a marketing metric can largely be attributed to its ease of communication (it is just a single number) and the possibility to benchmark various companies on their NPS score. A similar approach in the supply chain context could help to promote the sustainability idea and make it more visible among the different stakeholders.

Other aggregation techniques, whether as complex as DEA or just simple weighted scoring, can be used. These techniques will need to be tested and evaluated to determine whether they are feasible and practically valuable to supply chain managers. Given that supply chain management and green supply chain management performance measurement are still in their infancy, economic valuation approaches could provide additional utility to these systems. Integrative tools will eventually be necessary as well.

Conclusions

This chapter provided an overview of performance measurement within sustainable (green) supply chains. As part of a performance measurement and evaluation system of a supply chain, valuation approaches may be necessary to help develop a "business case" for various activities and from various stakeholder perspectives. One area with an ample set of resources that can be used by organizations for sustainability valuation is through the application of economic non-market valuation models to relevant stakeholders, including customers, suppliers, employees, and reverse logistics.

IMPLICATIONS FOR MANAGERIAL PRACTICE

The contribution of this chapter, however, is in highlighting the linkages between the direct and indirect estimation methods for non-market valuation and exploring how organizations can use the measurement methods in general PMS in planning. In planning, organizations should select the appropriate environmental performance index and link to both internal and external stakeholders. Using the framework introduced in this chapter can help businesses identify tools to use in PMS from the green supply chain perspective, whether this perspective is analysis at the level of an individual entity (e.g. supplier, customer) or more holistic analysis (e.g. reverse logistics overall as part of a supply chain).

These tools are applicable to most dimensions of the logistics and supply chain elements, including upstream and downstream, as well as closing the loop with reverse logistics for recycling, reuse, and reclamation. The framework provides a structure for organizations to consider as an initial starting point in implementing non-market valuation models. A general framework (Table 13.2) operationalized as a planning guide may help identify appropriate non-market valuation techniques for the organization's location within the supply chain. Not all techniques are equally effectively for each supply chain organization or entity, so a more rigorous evaluation approach is possible using this table.

Integrative aspects may also be needed for managers whose focus is beyond the single or dyadic relationship within the supply chain, for example multiple tiers up and down the supply chain. These economic tools are useful for making the business case for practitioners where a more complete evaluation will help managers implement GSCM practices that may not have been justified using traditional evaluation techniques such as return on investment or simple financial appraisal approaches.

Practically, it may require significant education and insight to apply these tools directly without additional development. Whether practitioners have the capabilities to easily implement and understand these tools is still open to question. This is why additional research is needed to further identify how the tools may be used, how to simplify these evaluation tools, and how make them more effectively applicable to a variety of settings.

Implications for Future Research

The next steps are for organizations to determine which measures are best or most appropriate for their company and industry and then assign weightings or rankings to the measures in order of importance. This then becomes an internal model of how organizations can conduct performance measurement systems and provides a set of tools. The toolset, as summarized in Table 13.2, is very large and the model has not been populated with data. Although they are beyond the scope of this introductory chapter, the next step for continuing research and model development is to apply the tools in various industries and organizations for validation and further theory building from testing of the most appropriate tools.

Even though examples of non-market valuation approaches as applied to various entities within the supply chain were provided in this chapter, additional investigation is warranted. This investigation could be completed in two ways – by asking and providing additional examples to practitioners, or by addressing approaches from a research perspective. That is, additional research to further develop these tools for organizational, rather than economic, level analysis is needed. Examples do exist in the literature (e.g. conjoint or paired ranking analysis) for sustainability and economic valuation, while others are less developed, e.g. bequest valuations. A more thorough review is needed to go beyond the introductory development in this chapter.

Whether models need to undergo revision and adjustment also needs to be investigated. Our initial goal, however, is to raise awareness of these economic and non-economic valuation tools that can be applied at the lower level of analysis within and between supply chain members and partners. Broad economic tools have a place in organizational and supply chain research for valuation purposes. We believe this chapter can provide a solid foundation for researchers to further investigate these existing resources for a rigorous evaluation of green supply chain performance evaluation.

Notes

1   Cuganesan, S. and Donovan, J. (2011). "Investigating the Links Between Management Control Approaches and Performance Measurement Systems," in Marc J. Epstein and John U. Lee (ed.) *Advances in Management Accounting*, Volume 19, Emerald Group Publishing Limited, 173–204.

2   Anil, B. and Nidhi, M. B. (2011). "Green Supply Chain Management: A Conceptual Framework," Institutional Repository of the College of Engineering Knowledge Base, Trivandrum. http://117.211.100.42:8180/jspui/handle/123456789/1269.

3   Hervani, A., Helms, M. and Sarkis (2005). "Performance Measurement for Green Supply Chain Management," *Benchmarking: An International Journal*, Vol. 12, No. 4, pp. 330–353.

4   Gunasekaran, A., Patel, C. and McGaughey, R. E. (2004). "A Framework for supply Chain Performance Measurement," *International Journal of Production Economics*, Vol. 87, No. 3, pp. 333–347.

5   Forslund, H. (2011). "The Size of a Logistics Performance Measurement System," *Facilities*, Vol. 29, No's 3/4, pp. 133–148.

6   Bititci, U., Garengo, P., Dörfler, V. and Nudurupati, S. (2011). *Performance Measurement: Challenges for Tomorrow*, Wiley Publishing; Olugu, E. U., Wong, K. Y. and Shaharoun, A. M. (2010). "A Comprehensive Approach in Assessing the Performance of an Automobile Closed-Loop Supply Chain," *Sustainability*, Vol. 2, No. 4, pp. 871–889; Shaw, S., Grant, D. B. and Mangan, J. (2010). "Developing Environmental Supply Chain Performance Measures," *Benchmarking: An International Journal*, Vol. 17, No. 3, pp. 320–339.

7   Charan, P., Shankar, R. and Baisya, R. K. (2008). "Analysis of Interactions Among the Variables of Supply Chain Performance Measurement System Implementation," *Business Process Management Journal*, Vol. 14, No. 4, pp. 512–529.

8   Azevedo, S. G., Carvalho, H. and Cruz-Machado, V. (2011). "A Proposal of LARG Supply Chain Management Practices and a Performance Measurement System," *International Journal of e-Education, e-Business, e-Management, and e-Learning*, Vol. 1, No. 1: April, pp. 7–14.

9   Cuthbertson, R. and Piotrowicz, W. (2011). "Performance Measurement Systems in Supply Chains: A Framework for Contextual Analysis," *International Journal of Productivity and Performance Measurement*, Vol. 60, No. 6, pp. 583–602.

10   Hong, P. and Hwang, W. (2011). "Operational Capabilities and Performance Toward Global Supply Chain: An Overview of Korean Manufacturing and Service Firms," *International Journal of Logistics Systems and Management*, Vol. 8, No. 2, pp. 183–197; Singh, R. K. (2011). "Developing the Framework for Coordination in Supply Chain of SMEs," *Business Process Management Journal*, Vol. 17, No. 4, pp. 619–638.

11   Hervani, A., Helms, M. and Sarkis (2005). "Performance Measurement for Green Supply Chain Management," *Benchmarking: An International Journal*, Vol. 12, No. 4, pp. 330–353.

12   Beamon, B. M. (1999). Measuring supply chain performance. *International Journal of Operations and Production Management*, Vol. 19, No. 3, pp. 275–292.

13   Hervani, A., Helms, M. and Sarkis (2005). "Performance Measurement for Green Supply Chain Management," *Benchmarking: An International Journal*, Vol. 12, No. 4, pp. 330–353.

14   Sun, M. and Ye, D. (2009). "Integrating Environmental Performance into Supplier Evaluation: A GRA-Based Method," *Industrial Engineering and Engineering Management, 16ᵗʰ International Conference*, October 21–23, 2009: 162–166.

15   Youn, S., Yang, M. G. (Mark), Hong, P. and Park, K. (2011). "Strategic Supply Chain Partnership, Environmental Supply Chain Management Practices, and Performance Outcomes: An Empirical Study," *Journal of Cleaner Production*, Vol. 9, No. 5, pp. 414–432.

16   Olugu, E. U. and Wong, K. Y. (2012). "An Expert Fuzzy Rule-Based System for Closed Loop Supply Chain Performance Assessment in the Automotive Industry," *Expert Systems with Applications*, Vol. 39, No. 1: January, pp. 375–384.

17   Hwang, Y.-D., Wen, Y.-F. and Chen, M.-Ch. (2010). "A Study on the Relationship Between the PDSA Cycle of Green Purchasing and the Performance of the SCOR Model," *Total Quality Management and Business Excellence*, Vol. 21, No. 12, pp. 1261–1278.

18   Hervani, A., Helms, M. and Sarkis (2005). "Performance Measurement for Green Supply Chain Management," *Benchmarking: An International Journal*, Vol. 12, No. 4, pp. 330–353.

19   Hwang, Y.-D., Wen, Y.-F. and Chen, M.-Ch. (2010). "A Study on the Relationship Between the PDSA Cycle of Green Purchasing and the Performance of the SCOR Model," *Total Quality Management and Business Excellence*, Vol. 21, No. 12, pp. 1261–1278; Bai, C., Sarkis, J., Wei, X. and Koh, L. (2012). "Evaluating Ecological Sustainable Performance Measures for Supply Chain Management," *Supply Chain Management: An International Journal*, Vol. 17, No. 1, pp. 78–92.

20   Azevedo, S. G., Carvalho, H. and Cruz-Machado, V. (2011). "A Proposal of LARG Supply Chain Management Practices and a Performance Measurement System," *International Journal of e-Education, e-Business, e-Management, and e-Learning*, Vol. 1, No. 1: April, pp. 7–14; Soni, G. and Kodali, R. (2009). "Performance Value Analysis for the Justification of the Leagile Supply Chain," *International Journal of Business Performance Management*, Vol. 11, No. 1–2: pp. 96–133.

21   Handfield, R., Walton, S. V., Sroufe, R. and Melnyk, S. A. (2002). "Applying Environmental Criteria to Supplier Assessment: A Study in the Application of the Analytical Hierarchy Process," *European Journal of Operational Research*, Vol. 141, pp. 70–87; Sarkis, J., (1998). "Evaluating Environmentally Conscious Business Practices," *European Journal of Operational Research*, Vol. 107, No. 1, pp. 159–174; Sarkis, J., (2003). "A Strategic Decision Making Framework for Green Supply Chain Management," *Journal of Cleaner Production*, Vol. 11, No. 4, pp. 397–409.

22   Wittstruck, D. and Teuteberg, F. (2011). "Development and Simulation of a Balanced Scorecard for Sustainable Supply Chain Management: A System Dynamics Approach," *Wirtschaftinformatik Proceedings 2011*, Paper 86. http://aisel.aisnet.org/wi2011/86.

23   Kailun, H., Huijun, X. and Maohua, X. (2010). "The Application of Probabilistic Neural Network Model in the Green Chain Performance Evaluation for Pig Industry," 2010 *International Conference on E-Business and E-Government*, Guangzhou, China, May 7–9.

24   Bai, C., Sarkis, J., Wei, X. and Koh, L., (2012). "Evaluating Ecological Sustainable Performance Measures for Supply Chain Management," *Supply Chain Management: An International Journal*, Vol. 17, No. 1: forthcoming.

25   Olugu, E. U, and Wong, K. Y. (2012). "An Expert Fuzzy Rule-Based System for Closed Loop Supply Chain Performance Assessment in the Automotive Industry," *Expert Systems with Applications*, Vol. 39, No. 1: January, 375–384.

26   Wang, C., Vaughan, J., Mercer, J. and Zaho, Y. (2011). "A Case-Based Model Facilitating Retailing Operations Going "Green": A Proposed Research Agenda With a Consideration of Recession," *Business Innovation and Technology Management*, 2011 *IEEE International Summer Conference of Asia Pacific*, July 10–12, 2011: 1–4.

27   James, D. and Gillespie, R. (1997). *Draft EIS Manual: Economic Effects and Evaluation in Environmental Impact Assessment*, prepared for the NSW Department of Urban Affairs and Planning.

28   Walsh, R. G., Johnson, D. M. and McKean, J. R. (1989). "Issues in Nonmarket Valuation and Policy Application: A Retrospective Glance," *Western Journal of Agricultural Economics*, Vol. 14, No. l: July, pp. 178–88.

29   McConnell, K. E. (1983). "Existence and Bequest Value," in R. D. Rowe and L. G. Chestnut (eds.) *Managing Air Quality and Scenic Resources at National Parks and Wilderness Areas*, Westview Press; Randall, A. and J. R. Stoll. (1983). "Existence Value in a Total Valuation Framework," in R. D. Rowe and L. G. Chestnut (eds.) *Managing Air Quality and Scenic Resources at National Parks and Wilderness Areas*, Westview Press; Brookshire, D. S., Eubanks, L. S. and Sorg, C. F. (1986). "Existence Values and Normative Economics: Implications for Valuing Water Resources," *Water Resources Research*, Vol. 22, No. 11, pp. 1509–1518; Edwards, S. F. (1986). "Ethical Preferences and the Assessment of Existence Values: Does the Neoclassical Model Fit?" *Northeastern Journal of Agricultural and Resource Economics*, Vol. 15, No. 2, pp. 145–150; Edwards, S. F. (1986). "Ethical Preferences and the Assessment of Existence Values: Does the Neoclassical Model Fit?" *Northeastern Journal of Agricultural and Resource Economics*, Vol. 15, No. 2, pp. 145–150; Boyle, K. J. and R. C Bishop (1987). "Valuing Wildlife in Benefit-Cost Analysis: A Case Study Involving Endangered Species," *Water Resources Research*, Vol. 23, No. 5, pp. 943–950; Loomis, J. B. (1988). "Broadening the Concept and Measurement of Existence Values," *Northeast Journal of Agricultural and Resource Economics*, Vol. 17, pp. 23–29; Stevens, T. H., Echeverria, J., Glass, R. J., Hager, T. and More, T. A. (1991). "Existence Value of Wildlife," *Land Economics*, Vol. 67, No. 4, pp. 390–400; Bishop, R. C. and Welsh, M. P. (1992). "Existence Values in Benefit Cost Analysis and Damage Assessment," *Land Economics*, Vol. 68, No. 4, pp. 405–417; Silberman, J., Gerlowski, D. A. and Williams, N. A. (1992). "Estimating Existence Value for Users and Non-Users of New Jersey Beaches," *Land Economics*, Vol. 68, No. 2, pp. 225–236; Kopp, Raymond J. (1992). "Why Existence Value *Should* be Used in Cost-Benefit Analysis," *Journal of Policy Analysis and Management*, Vol. 11, pp. 123–130; Larson, D. M. (1993). "On Measuring Existence Value," *Land Economics*, Vol. 69, No. 4, pp. 377–388; Freeman A. (1993). *The Measurement of Environmental and Resource Values*, Resources for the Future, Washington; McConnell, K. E. (1995). "Consumer Surplus from Discrete Choice Models," *Journal of Environmental Economics and Management*, Vol. 29, No. 3: Part 1 November, pp. 263–70; Kramer, R. A. and Mercer, D. E. (1997). "Valuing a Global Environmental Good: U. S. Residents' Willingness to Pay to Protect Tropical Rain Forests," *Land Economics*, May 1997; Johnston, R. J., Grigalunas, T. A., Opaluch, J. J., Mazzotta, M. and Diamantedes, J. (2002). "Valuing Estuarine Resource Services Using Economic and Ecological Models: The Peconic Estuary System Study," *Coastal Management*, Vol. 30, No. 1, p. 47.

30   Weisbrod, B. A. (1964). "Collective-Consumption Services of Individual-Consumption Goods," *Quarterly Journal of Economics*, Vol. 78: August, pp. 471–477.

31   Krutilla, J. V. (1967). "Conservation Reconsidered," *The American Economic Review*, Vol. 57, pp. 777–786.

32   Bishop, R. C. and Heberlein, T. A. (1984). *Contingent Valuation Methods and Ecosystem Damages From Acid Rain*. Staff Paper No. 217. Madison, Wisconsin: Department of Agricultural Economics, University of Wisconsin.

33   McConnell, K. E. (1983). "Existence and Bequest Value," in R. D. Rowe and L. G. Chestnut (eds.) *Managing Air Quality and Scenic Resources at National Parks and Wilderness Areas*, Westview Press; Walsh, R. G., Loomis, J. B. and Gillman, R. A. (1984). "Valuing Option, Existence and

Bequest Demands for Wilderness," *Land Economics*, Vol. 60, No. 1, pp. 14–29; Loomis, J. B. (1989). "Bioeconomic Approach to Estimating the Economic Effects of Watershed Disturbance on Recreational and Commercial Fisheries," *Journal of Soil and Water Conservation*, Vol. 44, No. 1, p. 83; Whitehead, J. C. and Thompson, C. Y. (1993). "Environmental Preservation Demand: Altruistic, Bequest, and Intrinsic Motives," *American Journal of Economics and Sociology*, Vol. 52, No. l, pp. 19–30; James, D. and Gillespie, R. (1997). *Draft EIS Manual: Economic Effects and Evaluation in Environmental Impact Assessment*, prepared for the NSW Department of Urban Affairs and Planning.

34   Meyer, P. (1974). *Recreation and Preservation Values Associated With Salmon of the Frasier River*. Environment Canada. PAC/IN-74–1, Vancouver, Canada.

35   Randall, A. and Stoll, J. R. (1983). "Existence Value in a Total Valuation Framework," in R. D. Rowe and L. G. Chestnut (eds.), Westview Press.

36   Sanders, L. D., Walsh, R. D. and Loomis, J. B. (1990). "Toward Empirical Estimation of the Total Value of Protecting Rivers," *Water Resources Research*, Vol. 26, No. 7, pp. 1345–1357.

37   Boyle, K. J., MacDonald, H. F., Cheng H.-T. and McCollum, D. W. (1998). "Bid Design and Yea Saying in Single-Bounded, Dichotomous-Choice Questions," *Land Economics*, Vol. 74, No. 1, pp. 49–64.

38   Edwards, S. F. (1986). "Ethical Preferences and the Assessment of Existence Values: Does the Neoclassical Model Fit?" *Northeastern Journal of Agricultural and Resource Economics*, Vol. 15, No. 2, pp. 145–150.

39   Bishop, R. C. and Welsh, M. P. (1992). "Existence Values in Benefit Cost Analysis and Damage Assessment," *Land Economics*, Vol. 68, No. 4, pp. 405–417.

40   Johnston, R. J., Grigalunas, T. A., Opaluch, J. J., Mazzotta, M. and Diamantedes, J. (2002). "Valuing Estuarine Resource Services Using Economic and Ecological Models: The Peconic Estuary System Study," *Coastal Management*, Vol. 30, No. 1, p. 47.

41   Whitehead, J. C. and Thompson, C. Y. (1993). "Environmental Preservation Demand: Altruistic, Bequest, and Intrinsic Motives," *American Journal of Economics and Sociology*, Vol. 52, No. l, pp. 19–30.

42   Walsh, R. G., Loomis, J. B. and Gillman, R. A. (1984). "Valuing Option, Existence and Bequest Demands for Wilderness," *Land Economics*, Vol. 60, No. 1, pp. 14–29.

43   James, D. and Gillespie, R. (1997). *Draft EIS Manual: Economic Effects and Evaluation in Environmental Impact Assessment*, prepared for the NSW Department of Urban Affairs and Planning.

44   Brookshire, D. S., Eubanks, L. S. and Randall, A. (1983). "Estimating Option Prices and Existence Values for Wildlife Resources," *Land Economics*, Vol, 59. p. 1.

45   Barrick, K. A. and Beazley, R. I. (1990). "Magnitude and Distribution of Option Value for the Washakie Wilderness, Northwest Wyoming, USA," *Environmental Management*, Vol. 14, No. 3, pp. 367–380.

46   De Groot, R. S. (1992). *Functions of Nature: Evaluation of Nature in Environmental Planning, Management and Decision Making*, Wolters-Noordhoff.

47   Bell, F. W. and Leeworthy, V. R. (1990). "Recreational Demand by Tourists for Saltwater Beach Days," *Journal of Environmental Economics and Management*, Vol. 18, No. 3: May, pp. 189–205.

48   Benson, E. D., Hansen, J. L., et al. (1998). "Pricing Residential Amenities: The Value of a View," *The Journal of Real Estate Finance and Economics*, Vol. 16, No. 1, p. 55.

49   Bergstrom, J. C., Dorfman, J. H. and Loomis, J. B. (2004). "Estuary Management and Recreational Fishing Benefits," *Coastal Management*, Vol. 32, No. 4, p. 417.

50   Anderson, R. J. and Crocker, T. (1971). "Air Pollution and Residential Property Values," *Urban Studies*, Vol. 8, pp. 171–190.

51   Freeman, A. M. III (1979). "Hedonic Prices, Property Values and Measuring Environmental Benefits: A Survey of the Issues," *Scandinavian Journal of Economics*, Vol. 81, pp. 154–173.

52   Bartik, T. J. (1988). "Measuring the Benefits of Amenity Improvements in Hedonic Price Models," *Land Economics*, Vol. 64, No. 2, pp. 172–183.

53   Taylor, L. O. (2003). "The Hedonic Method," in P. A. Champ, K. J. Boyle and T. C. Brown (eds.) *A Primer on Non-market Valuation*, Kluwer Academic Publishers, 331–394.

54   Loomis, J. B. (1989). "Bioeconomic Approach to Estimating the Economic Effects of Watershed Disturbance on Recreational and Commercial Fisheries," *Journal of Soil and Water Conservation*, Vol. 44, No. 1, p. 83.

55   Bennett, J. W. and Carter, M. (1993). "Prospects for Contingent Valuation: Lessons from the South-East Forests," *Australian Journal of Agricultural Economics*, Vol. 37, No. 2: August, pp. 79–93.

56   Bergstrom, J. C., Dorfman, J. H. and Loomis, J. B. (2004). "Estuary Management and Recreational Fishing Benefits," *Coastal Management*, Vol. 32, No. 4, p. 417.

57   Harrington, W. and Portney, P. (1987). "Valuing the Benefits of Health and Safety Regulation," *Journal of Urban Economics*, 22: 101–112.

58   Whitehead, J. C., Haab, T. C. and Huang, J.-Ch. (1998). "Part-Whole Bias in Contingent Valuation: Will Scope Effects Be Detected with Inexpensive Survey Methods?" *Southern Economic Journal*, Vol. 65, pp. 160–168.

59   Abrahams, N. A, Hubbell, B. J. and Jordan, J. L. (2000). "Joint Production and Averting Expenditure Measures of Willingness to Pay: Do Water Expenditures Really Measure Avoidance Costs?" *American Journal of Agricultural Economics*, Vol. 82: May, pp. 427–37.

60   Hanemann, W. M. (1984). "The Discrete/Continuous Model of Consumer Demand," *Econometrica*, Vol. 52, pp. 541–561.

61   Kaoru, Y., Smith, V. K and Liu, J.-L. (1995). "Using Random Utility Models to Estimate the Recreational Value of Estuarine Resources," *American Journal of Agricultural Economics*, Vol. 77, No. 1: February, pp. 141–51.

62   Bhat, C. R. (2008). "The Multiple Discrete-Continuous Extreme Value (MDCEV) Model: Role of Utility Function Parameters, Identification Considerations, and Model Extensions," *Transportation Research Part B*, Vol. 42, No. 3, pp. 274–303.

63   Downing, M., Ozuna, T., Jr. (1996). "Testing the Reliability of the Benefit Function Transfer Approach," *Journal of Environmental Economics and Management*, Vol. 30, No. 3: May, pp. 316–22.

64   Brouwer, R. (2000). "Environmental Value Transfer: State of the Art and Future Prospects," *Ecological Economics*, Vol. 32, No. 1, p. 137.

65   Loomis, J. B. and Rosenberger, R. S. (2006). "Reducing Barriers in Future Benefit Transfers: Needed Improvements in Primary Study Design and Reporting," *Ecological Economics*, Vol. 60, No. 2, p. 343.

66   Bell, F. W. and Leeworthy, V. R. (1990). "Recreational Demand by Tourists for Saltwater Beach Days," *Journal of Environmental Economics and Management*, Vol. 18, No. 3: May, pp. 189–205.

67   Adamowicz, W., et al. (1998). "Stated Preference Approaches for Measuring Passive Use Values: Choice Experiments and Contingent Valuation," *American Journal of Agricultural Economics*, Vol. 80, No. 1, pp. 64–75.

68   Arin, T. and Kramer, R. A. (2002). "Divers' Willingness to Pay to Visit Marine Sanctuaries: An Exploratory Study," *Ocean & Coastal Management*, Vol: 45, No. 2–3, p. 171.

69   Smith, V. K., Desvousges, W. H., Freeman, A. M. III. (1985). "Valuing Changes in Hazardous Waste Risks: A Contingent Valuation Analysis," Economic Analysis Division, U.S. Environmental Protection Agency. February 1985. Report Number: Research Triangle Institute Project No. 41U-2699.

70   Willis, K. G. and Garrod, G. D. (1993). "Valuing Landscape: A Contingent Valuation Approach," *Journal of Environmental Management*, Vol. 37, No. 1, pp. 1–22.

71   Johnston, R. J., Grigalunas, T. A., Opaluch, J. J., Mazzotta, M. and Diamantedes, J. (2002). "Valuing Estuarine Resource Services Using Economic and Ecological Models: The Peconic Estuary System Study," *Coastal Management*, Vol. 30, No. 1, p. 47.

72   Hanemann, W. M. (1984). "The Discrete/Continuous Model of Consumer Demand," *Econometrica*, Vol. 52, pp. 541–561.

73   Mazzotta, J. J., Opaluch, J. J. and Grigalunas, T. A. (1994). "Natural Resource Damage Assessment: The Role of Resource Restoration," *Natural Resources Journal*, Vol. 34, pp. 153–78.

74   Louviere, J. J., Hensher D. A. and Swait J. D. (2000). *Stated Choice Methods. Analysis and Application*. Cambridge University Press.

75   Tversky, A. (1972). "Elimination by Aspects: A Theory of Choice," *Psychological Review*, Vol. 79, pp. 281–299.

76   Ben-Akiva, M. E. and Boccara, B. (1995). "Discrete Choice Models with Latent Choice Sets," *International Journal of Research in Marketing*, Vol. 12, pp. 9–24.

77   Haab, T. C. and K. E. McConnell (2002). *Valuing Environmental and Natural Resources: The Econometrics of Nonmarket Valuation*. Edward Elgar.

78   Desvousges, W. H., Gable, A. R., Dunford, R. W. and Hudson, S. P. (1993). "Contingent Valuation: The Wrong Tool for Damage Assessment," *Choices*, Vol. 8, No. 2, pp. 9–11.

79   Champ, P. A. and Loomis, J. B. (1998). "WTA Estimates Using the Method of Paired Comparison: Tests of Robustness," *Environmental and Resource Economics*, Vol. 12, pp. 375–386.

80   Brown, T. C., Kingsley, D., Peterson, G. L., Flores, N., Clarke, A. and Birjulin, A. (2008). "Reliability of Individual Valuations of Public Goods and Private Goods: Choice Consistency, Response Time, and Preference Refinement," *Journal of Public Economics*, Vol. 92, pp. 1595–1606.

81   Cameron, T. A. (1988). "A New Paradigm for Valuing Non-Market Goods Using Referendum Data: Maximum Likelihood Estimation by Censored Logistic Regression. *Journal of Environmental Economics and Management*, Vol. 15, pp. 355–379.

82   Diamon, P. A. and Hausman, J. A. (1994). "Contingent Valuation: Is Some Number better than No Number?" *The Journal of Economic Perspectives*, Vol. 8, No. 4: Autumn, pp. 45–64.

83   Nunes, P. A. L. D. and Schokkaert, E. (2003). "Identifying the Warm Glow Effect in Contingent Valuation," *Journal of Environmental Economics and Management*, Vol. 45, pp. 231–245.

84   Chapman, R. G. and Staelin, R. (1982). "Exploiting Rank Ordered Choice Set Data within the Stochastic Utility Model," *Journal of Marketing Research*, Vol. 19, pp. 288–301.

85   Cameron, T. A. and Quiggin J. (1994). "Estimation Using Contingent Valuation Data from a 'Dichotomous Choice with Follow-Up' Questionnaire," *Journal of Environmental Economic Management*, Vol. 27, pp. 218–234.

86   Foster, V. and Mourato, S. (2002). "Testing for Consistency in Contingent Ranking Experiments," *Journal of Environmental Economics and Management*, Vol. 44, pp. 309–328.

87   Chu, Y. P, and Chu, R. L. (1990). "The Subsidence of Preference Reversals in Simplified and Marketlike Experimental Settings," *American Economic Review*, Vol. 80, pp. 902–911.

88 Adamowicz, W., Boxall, P., Williams, M. and Louviere, J. (1998). "Stated Preferences Approaches to Measuring Passive Use Values," *American Journal of Agricultural Economics*, Vol. 80, pp. 64–75.

89 Braga, J. and Starmer, C. (2005). "Preference Anomalies, Preference Elicitation and the Discovered Preference Hypothesis," *Environmental and Resource Economics,* Vol. 32, pp. 55–89.

90 Anderson, E. E. (1989). "Economic Benefits of Habitat Restoration: Seagrass and the Virginia Hard-Shell Bluecrab Fishery," *North American Journal of Fisheries Management*, Vol. 9, No. 2, p. 140.

91 Loomis, J. B. and Larson, D. M. (1994). "Total Economic Values of increasing Gray Whale Populations: Results from a Contingent Valuation Survey of Visitors and Households," *Marine Resource Economics*, Vol. 9, No. 3, p. 275.

92 Bell, F. W. (1997). "The Economic Valuation of Saltwater Marsh Supporting Marine Recreational Fishing in the Southeastern United States," *Ecological Economics*, Vol. 21, No. 3, p. 243.

93 Cropper, M. L. (1981). "Measuring the Benefits from Reduced Morbidity," *American Economic Review*, Vol. 71, No. 2: May, pp. 235–240.

94 Harrington, W. and Portney, P. (1987). "Valuing the Benefits of Health and Safety Regulation," *Journal of Urban Economics*, Vol. 22, pp. 101–112.

95 Gupta U. (2008). "Valuation of Urban Air Pollution: A Case Study of Kanpur City in India," *Environmental & Resource Economics*, European Association of Environmental and Resource Economists, Vol. 41, No. 3: November, pp. 315–326.

96 Costanza, R., Farber, S. C. and Maxwell, J. (1989). "Valuation and Management of Wetland Ecosystems," *Ecological Economics*, Vol. 1, No. 1, pp. 335–61.

97 Bockstael, N., Freeman, A., Kopp, R., Portney, P. and Smith, V. (2000). "On Measuring Economic Values for Nature," *Environmental Science and Technology*, Vol. 34, No. 8, pp. 1384–1389.

98 Randall, A. (2002). "Valuing the Outputs of Multifunctional Agriculture," *European Review of Agricultural Economics*, Vol. 29, No. 3, pp. 289–307.

99 Castle, E. N., Berrens, R. P. and Adams, R. M. (1994). "Natural-Resource Damage Assessment: Speculations About a Missing Perspective," *Land Economics*, Vol. 70, No. 3, pp. 378–385.

100 Randall, A. (2002). "Valuing the Outputs of Multifunctional Agriculture," *European Review of Agricultural Economics*, Vol. 29, No. 3, pp. 289–307.

101 MacDonald, K., Boyce, D., et al. (2002). "Application of Environmental Damage Assessment and Resource Valuation Processes in Atlantic Canada," Study prepared for the *OECD (2002) Handbook of Biodiversity Valuation*. OECD.

102 Sarkis, J., Helms, M. M. and Hervani, A. (2010). "Reverse Logistics and Social Sustainability," *Corporate Social Responsibility and Environmental Management*, Vol. 17, No. 6, pp. 337–354.

Sustainable Value Chains: Managing Networks and Collaboration

CHAPTER 1

14 *Green Offerings and Buyer–Supplier Collaboration in Value Chains*

P. MATTHYSSENS* AND W. FAES†

Keywords

Green supply chain, sustainable purchasing, supplier development, B2B marketing, sustainable networks, co-evolution in business markets.

Introduction

Corporate social responsibility (CSR) stands high on the agendas of managers and researchers. According to Lindgreen, Maon and Swaen[1] CSR has moved 'from ideology to reality.' Especially in the field of supply chain management and purchasing, (large) multinational companies are increasingly undertaking CSR initiatives, often under pressure from different stakeholders.[2] As a result, most of them have defined codes of conduct for their supply chain partners. Nevertheless, authors stress that only few of them have actually been able to put these ethical standards fully into practice.[3]

Several authors indicate that adapting the supply chain to 'greener' standards is not only an ethical thing to do for companies, but contributes substantially to the innovative content of the supply chain.[4] There are numerous pleas for more integrated supplier–customer relationships intended to create green products jointly.[5] This allows the buying company to (1) reduce the quantity of supplied components (and hence reduce the complexity to recycle), (2) control the cost of their green products, (3) reduce the company's time-to-market for green products, and (4) avoid problems associated with the green image. The need for collaboration between customers and suppliers in the frame of the global supply chain (GSC) concept as practiced by companies such as Xerox and Sony, is highlighted by Lu, Wu and Kuo and others.[6] GSC management implies 'a variety of approaches through which companies work with their suppliers to improve

* Prof. Paul Matthyssens, Chairman and Professor Department of Management, University of Antwerp, and Professor at Antwerp Management School. E-mail: paul.matthyssens@ua.ac.be. Telephone: +32 3 265 50 63.

† Wouter Faes, Researcher, Faculty of Business Management and Sciences, Department of Marketing, Hasselt University. E-mail: wouter.faes@uhasselt.be. Telephone: +32 11 26 86 47.

the environmental performance of the products or manufacturing processes of suppliers and customers.'[7] As such it requires collaboration and integration among multiple levels of the supply chain.

There is a growing need for sustainable and CSR-proof supply chains, not only in large-scale enterprises but also in SMEs, and additional research on 'the management of supply chain CSR relationships,' specifically with regard to the development of new and innovative products and supply chains, remains one of the key gaps to be addressed[8]. This chapter will contribute to filling this gap by confronting suppliers' efforts to augment their offerings in a 'green way' with buyers' reactive and/or proactive sustainability strategies. We intend to investigate some of the forces shaping and influencing 'green' collaboration between the partners in the supply chain. We intend to contribute to answering a number of important questions: Can green value really be captured by supply chain partners? What are the key processes leading to successful green supply chain initiatives? Which strategic paths can be followed in order to stimulate collaboration related to sustainability in supply chains by 'vertical' partners? Which problems have to be surmounted in doing so?

We will study how B2B supply chains collaborate in order to realize ground-breaking sustainable product initiatives and we will try to uncover patterns in such value chain initiatives. Which determinants influence green supply chain collaboration? We performed case-based research on two focal companies which dealt with two suppliers on diverse initiatives. This chapter is structured as follows. First, the literature review section introduces key concepts and key perspectives such as cradle to cradle. It provides a brief status report of both the purchasing and marketing sides of green collaboration. Next a short section introduces the methodology that is used in this study. Then a rich case description is presented describing different types of green collaboration. The findings from the cases are next interpreted, leading to a model and preconditions for value creation with green innovations. The chapter closes with conclusions and limitations/suggestions for future studies.

Literature Review

This chapter builds on a short literature review of the greening of the supply chain, the collaboration between different partners in the supply chain to develop new and innovative products, and the evolutionary path towards purchasing maturity and ecological adulthood in supply chains, looking simultaneously at the supply side and the (B2B) demand side.

TOWARDS GREEN PURCHASING AND GREEN SUPPLY CHAINS

The interest in green supply chain has been increasing over recent years. The literature is now extensive[9] and covers a large number of different issues. It would be impossible within the framework of this chapter to enumerate all topics in great detail. Specifically research has focused on themes such as drivers and inhibitors for companies to develop green supply chains,[10] the improvement of results on a financial, ecological and marketing level that can be expected when introducing a greener supply chain[11] and the role of the employees in capturing this value,[12] the advantage of using general standards to apply such as ISO 14001;[13] the development of managerial practices involving amongst other things a different interpretation of the categorizations of purchasing items in the purchasing matrix,[14] the use of adapted supplier performance measurements tools[15] and the use of life cycle management.[16] Finally, attention has been paid to the necessity to integrate both upstream and downstream activities to be successful in developing a greener image.[17]

This evolution is close to the observation that on the side of the *suppliers*, the so-called 'servitization concept'[18] within the broader literature on 'product-service systems' (PSS) focuses on the potential environmental, rather than commercial benefits of offering service dominated bundles.[19] The servitization literature was triggered by a number of policy reports recommending service as a means of reducing consumption. As such, PSS has tended to be focused on social and environmental issues. What is more, in an effort to fight commoditization, many suppliers seek a service addition pathway to enrich and differentiate their value offerings.[20] B2B suppliers build service packs and integrated solutions, thereby often taking end-to-end responsibilities and providing performance guarantees to their customers. This approach can be easily extended to environmental initiatives. Moreover, Sharma, Iyer, Mehrotra and Krishnan[21] highlight marketing's role in creating green supply chains. They describe how such a strategy is essential for achieving superior competitive advantage and offer two roads to reach this position: 1) reduction of surplus supply and 2) reduction of reverse supply. Marketing needs an expanded focus, they claim, balancing demand and supply management while combining practices such as targeting green customers, stimulating the demand for recycled, remanufactured, environmentally friendly, and/or build-to-order products, designing for modularity and disassembly, etc.

At the same time, we observe that on the side of the *customers*, the number of original equipment manufacturers (OEM's) which are developing green supply chains and setting up key performance indicators for monitoring green performance is increasing.[22] Many facilities worldwide have adopted 'environmental management systems' and such systems may stimulate companies to expand their environmental concerns beyond their internal boundaries to their suppliers and customers.[23] Green purchasing is increasingly being adopted and incorporated into the framework of ISO 14000.[24] Thus a large number of companies that are adopting environmental management systems, such as ISO 14001, environmental audits or environmental performance indicators, also adopt green supply chain management initiatives to a large extent. Such initiatives refer to assessments of the environmental performance of suppliers, imposing requirements on suppliers to undertake environmental measures, and informing suppliers on how to improve their green performance.

Green purchasing, also called 'environmentally preferable procurement,' indicates that the buying company tries to buy goods and services that are less harmful, thereby also reducing the consumption of resources and the production of waste, minimizing potentially adverse health side-effects and reducing costs.[25] Turner and Houston[26] state that green sourcing adds the notion of environmental impact (transportation, materials, energy usage, packaging) on the ecological footprint. Nidumolu, Ram, Prahalad and Rangaswami[27] argue that there is no alternative to sustainable development for companies and show how Western companies create sustainable supply chains. Wal-Mart is a case in point:

... in October 2008 Lee Scott, then Wal-Mart's CEO, gave more than 1,000 suppliers in China a directive: Reduce waste and emissions; cut packaging costs by 5% by 2013; and increase the energy efficiency of products supplied to Wal-Mart stores by 25% in three years' time. In like vein, Unilever has declared that by 2015 it will be purchasing palm oil and tea only from sustainable sources, and Staples intends that most of its paper-based products will come from sustainable-yield forests by 2010.[28]

Ever more buyers are investing in integrated relations with their suppliers to design green products. In fact, not only Wal-Mart but also companies as diverse as Cargill, Ikea and Dow Chemical evaluate suppliers' environmental performance and guide them in taking green initiatives. It is evident that SMEs have more difficulties in adopting green initiatives due to limited resources. Nevertheless, Noci and Verganti[29] suggest that 'green' product innovation eventually will also occur in smaller firms. Based on case studies, they propose three strategies along which this development might occur: 1) a reactive approach triggered by external stimuli, 2) an anticipatory strategy in which via 'pacing' a (temporary) competitive advantage is sought, and 3) an innovation-based strategy where sustainability is considered a strategic priority and innovative solutions are actively pursued. In the latter strategy, 'network infrastructure' plays a key role, i.e., suppliers get a key role in order to provide necessary knowledge and logistics competencies.

Models have also been proposed to *select* the most effective *suppliers* from an environmental strategy perspective.[30] The system proposed by Noci[31] distinguishes supplier selection procedures according to the environmental strategy of the buying company. On the one hand, a more compliance-oriented (i.e., reactive) company will assess its suppliers on the consistency of its environmental performance on well-defined explicit standards, such as environmental efficiency (waste water, emissions, solid wastes, energy consumption) as well as on life cycle costs. On the other, an OEM with a proactive green strategy will use on top of these criteria also the 'green potential' of a supplier, referring to categories such as the suppliers' green competencies (availability of clean technologies, green material usage) and the suppliers' green image. Lu et al.[32] suggest a set of evaluation criteria that can be grouped in the following categories: (a) pre-manufacturing, (b) manufacturing, (c) packaging and distribution, (d) use and maintenance, (e) end of life. Ecovadis[33] is a commercial platform that offers a database on suppliers' social and environmental risks. According to their electronic leaflet, they evaluate each supplier on a set of criteria that can be grouped in four categories: environment, social, ethics and supply chain. According to the same source, companies such as Alcatel-Lucent, Atos Origin, Alcan and Bouygues have used this method to evaluate their suppliers.

LIFE CYCLE MANAGEMENT

The greening of the supply chain often involves life cycle management strategies. Life cycle management is defined as a way to improve environmental performance by managing the design of the product well, while considering its total environmental impact over the usage cycle. It is more a form of accounting than an empirical, observational science. Thus, the life cycle approach implies a kind of 'social planner's view' on environmental issues, rather than the minimization of a company's direct environmental liabilities.[34] It requires a dedicated effort of the whole management team and the different functions in the company in close cooperation with the suppliers' team.[35]

Two characteristics of life cycle management are mentioned in literature: design for the environment and the 'cradle-to-cradle' principle.[36] Design for the environment (DfE) contains a number of activities or components, executed by a value chain which is as integrated as possible. It contains the following aspects:[37]

- Design for compliance, i.e., ensuring that products meet new regulatory requirements for energy usage, material safety, etc.;
- Design for end-of-life management, which is designing a product in such a way that it is easy to refurbish and reuse or disassemble and recycle;
- Life cycle assessment[38] and carbon footprint reduction referring to the environmental impact of producing the product, shipping it, usage by the consumer, and reclamation and recycling, by evaluating carbon trade-offs through the manufacturing, distribution and transportation processes;
- Material selection, i.e., choosing materials that are renewable, recyclable and non-toxic;
- Packaging design: designing packaging to minimize waste and to make it lighter, easier and less energy costly to transport, and easier to recycle.

The 'cradle-to-cradle' principle implies that all materials used in industrial or commercial processes, such as metals, fibers and dyes, fall into one of two categories: 'technical' or 'biological' nutrients. Technical nutrients are strictly limited to non-toxic, non-harmful synthetic materials that have no negative effects on the natural environment; they can be used in continuous cycles as the same products without losing their integrity or quality. In this manner these materials can be used over and over again instead of being 'downcycled' into lesser products, ultimately becoming waste.[39] The technical 'metabolism' thus consists of artificially created and actively managed material flows. The idea is that industrial mass is allowed to circulate in 'closed systems' whilst maintaining a constant quality level. The fact that the system is a closed one is a prerequisite for the possible use of toxic substances. Figure 14.1 depicts this closed loop effort, based on life cycle analysis. Products and materials in this cycle are often called products for service (the name is derived from the concept of a service product). Washing machines, for example, are no longer bought but rather their service is used at a charge. As such, this 'leasing' principle means that the material remains in the ownership of the manufacturer and is returned to them after a certain defined period of usage. One advantage of this system is that the manufacturer can use materials of a higher standard and quality.

The cradle-to-cradle framework addresses energy, water and social responsibility through the following principles:

- **Eliminate the concept of waste: 'Waste equals food.'** Design products and materials with life cycles that are safe for human health and the environment and which can be reused perpetually through biological and technical metabolisms. Create and participate in systems to collect and recover the value of these materials following their use.
- **Power with renewable energy: 'Use current solar income.'** Maximize the use of renewable energy.
- **Respect human and natural systems: 'Celebrate diversity.'** Manage water use to maximize quality, promote healthy ecosystems and respect local impacts. Guide operations and manage stakeholder relationships using social responsibility.[40]

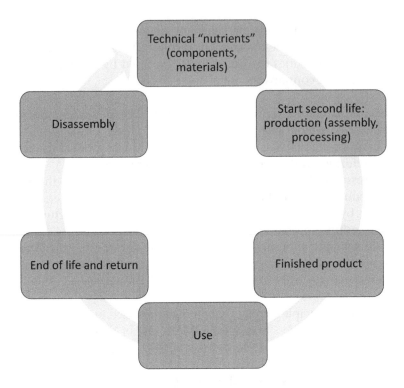

Figure 14.1 Closed loop of technical nutrients in the cradle-to-cradle system

These characteristics, just like the life cycle management system to which they belong, necessitate the building and exploiting of good relationships between all partners in the supply chain.[41] The development of more cooperative supplier relationships itself is a research study topic in both the business marketing and purchasing literature. Both indicate a growing need for collaboration between all partners in the supply chain.

COLLABORATION IN (GREEN) SUPPLY CHAINS

The *customer* and its needs are the focus of the supply chain systems approach. The objective is to develop a customer-centered chain that uses every opportunity to delight customers, foster their loyalty and build long-term mutually beneficial relationships. Introducing supply chain systems ensures rapid response to customer requirements, achieves the goal of better servicing customers at a lower cost and in less lead time. It is not only based on technology. It also involves the development of personal and organizational relationships.[42] Most buyers and sellers recognize the need for collaboration as the best way to improve costs, quality, delivery, time and other measures of performance. The relationship is bilateral, which means that both parties have the power to shape its nature and future direction. Mutual commitment and balanced power are key features. Commitment enables both parties to keep the relationship working over time, and keep it in balance, to ensure mutual benefits.[43]

Liker and Choi[44] also contend that businesses are largely relying on their suppliers to reduce costs, enhance quality and develop innovations faster than their competitors' suppliers can. One way of achieving this is to build networks of suppliers that learn, improve and grow.[45] The consequence is that supplier relationships have evolved from being transactional to being alliance-based networks. The key to success is to develop 'an appropriate' relationship, which is not always of a win-win type, but certainly in accordance with strategic sourcing principles.[46] The more innovative products become, the more the transactional nature of the interface between buyers and sellers gives way to more collaborative relationships and sometimes even closer alliances.[47] Along the same lines, Matthyssens, Vandenbempt and Weyns[48] describe how both partners involved in a co-development effort have to be situated on the same level of competence, knowledge and technical expertise to create value in a competitive way. If one of both partners is situated at a lower level, the 'higher partner' has to try to increase the expertise and experience of the 'lower one' to increase the likelihood of success.

The business-to-business *marketing* literature further indicates that manufacturers increasingly seek new ways to differentiate in buyer–seller relations.[49] Yet, suppliers and customers seem to have different views on what is a customer solution. Customers view solutions as being predominantly a marketing gimmick, whereas suppliers tend to have a more product-centric view of these solutions.[50] This research demonstrates that solution effectiveness depends on both supplier and customer behavior. Mutual adaptations and close interactions are a precondition for a solution oriented transition to a new 'value-added' market approach. This approach seems to have some important characteristics, such as (1) the need to adapt the firm's activities and to realize organizational changes, (2) behavioral adaptations such as the willingness to accept higher levels of risk, increased empowerment and a more professional service approach, and (3) the acknowledgement that the extent and content of a company's offering must shift from a commodity-based business model toward a new value-added and service-based business model.[51] These processes must also be managed to become successful: efficiency and effectiveness have to be introduced into the entire supply network using mutual learning as a modus operandi.[52]

In fact, the importance of collaborative relationships between the different layers of the supply chain can not be underrated.[53] They are a key contributor to better economic and ecological results for the partners in the supply chain.[54] These positive results relate to shorter development times, lower costs and better quality, as well as to a lower carbon footprint and less waste. In general, collaboration with suppliers yields better results than collaboration with customers, although customer pressure was recognized as an important factor inciting supply chains to go 'greener,' certainly when suppliers are only medium-sized or small.[55]

This process of collaboration is very much also a characteristic of *purchasing maturity*. This notion is similar to concepts such as 'levels of strategic purchasing' developed by several authors.[56] In fact, in the conceptualization of the model by Telgen and Pop Sitar,[57] a company needs to 'step up' in purchasing maturity towards supply chain and value chain orientations in order to succeed in innovation. These stages of development involve among other things (1) the comparison of offers on total cost of ownership criteria, (2) the development of closer cooperation on logistic and quality levels and a more strategic approach to sourcing in general, (3) a more cooperative relation with suppliers and early involvement in new product development and (4) extensive use of cross-functional supplier development teams, an upgrading of supplier capabilities and collaboration on advanced technology with suppliers, as well as continuous improvement measures of supplier performance and an eye on the satisfaction of the end customer. We believe 'green innovations' require a similar up-scaling in purchasing maturity.

A greening of the supply management of a company seems to imply a parallel evolution from transactional to collaborative activities and from basic green activities to the full development of next generation technology-based green value chains, as depicted by a number of evolutionary models that have been developed. Appendix 1 compares those models with one another and indicates their salient characteristics.[58]

Research on how this collaborative process evolves over time in ecological innovative supply chains is relatively scarce. So far, we can only rely on relatively general literature on buyer–supplier relations.[59] Formal models on how to be effective in developing green supply chains and motivating supply partners do not yet exist. For the sake of all stakeholders involved in or directly impacted by greening of supply chains, it is extremely important to know how such a collaboration can be unleashed and facilitated. We must learn from best practices and infer implications. Theoretical generalizations on how green collaboration can be triggered still need further development.

Research Methodology

We decided to look into this matter using qualitative research in our field study. This choice can be defended as follows. A qualitative research approach in general and case study in particular are deemed useful to address 'how' and 'why' questions in underexplored research areas.[60] Rich qualitative 'inductive' evidence, coupled to interpretive techniques and analytical initial frames, can unleash a process of deductive theory development and testing. Qualitative case research is also deemed useful to look deeper into the strategy context, to study multilevel phenomena (such as supply chains) and to look into managerial cognitions.

Two case studies describing experiences of suppliers and buyers in innovative green projects based on a minimum of two interviews (a two-sided view) were developed. The interviewees were the key people involved in the decision making unit of the different partners in both supply chains and they were knowledgeable about the commercial, technical and ecological aspects of each project. We also selected them on the basis of their involvement in the project from the first. The list of interviewees for both cases, which are described below, can be found in Appendix 2. The interviews were tape recorded, typed out, sent to our interviewees and in a second round of talks they were re-discussed with the key informants so as to make sure that our interpretation of the collected data was correct and citations reflected the real meaning our contact partners wanted to convey. The first interviews lasted between one and one and a half hours, the interviews in the second round were somewhat shorter. After each interview, both authors discussed the content of the case under study and compared the phenomena observed with extant theoretical frames. Some intermediary matrices and tables were developed in order to distinguish the cases and interpret these (this type of 'loop' between data and theory is known as 'iterative grounded theory'). Attention was thus paid to methodological rigor and the robustness of the multiple case study methodology using the methodological prescriptions of the best authors in the field.

The selection of the two case companies was based on their involvement with one of the two main strategies mentioned in our literature review to develop innovative green products, namely 'design for the environment' and the 'cradle-to-cradle' concept, which are both intricately linked to life cycle studies indicating whether products throughout their full life cycle have the least possible impact on the environment at large. This way we were deliberately seeking diverse cases, through theoretical sampling, in order to maximize insight.

Two Buying Companies in a Green Collaboration with Suppliers ... and Customers

COMPANY X AND GREEN SUPPLY MANAGEMENT

The mission statement of COMPANY X contains a clear strategy on environmental issues. At best, three basic goals (People, Planet and Profit) have to be served simultaneously. This company has a 'long tradition' in trying to be as environmentally friendly as possible in all stages of the product life cycle of its products. COMPANY X is aiming to reduce its environmental footprint. Its 'cradle-to-grave' mentality was transformed into a 'cradle-to-cradle' perspective, thus indicating the willingness of the company to be among the leading companies in the world in this respect. This means that COMPANY X tries to create competitive advantage both by reducing surplus supply and reverse supply.[61] The company is among the world class leaders in terms of excellence on sustainability because it actively tries to design sustainable products and services. It does so, amongst other means, by developing a new 'green' business model in which all of its supply chain partners have to be actively involved or are encouraged to be. They actively follow the principles of design for the environment, as depicted in the literature section.

As a customer, COMPANY X selects suppliers which are capable of collaborating in this effort. Not only do these suppliers have to be ISO 14000-certified, but they have to be audited separately by COMPANY X auditors on a number of criteria. These criteria are described in the 'Supplier Code of Conduct,' and relate to four fields of interest, namely business commitment, security of supply, sustainability and quality assurance. Sustainability is rated on an equal footing with the other, more traditional selection criteria for supply partners. Suppliers are rated on diverse aspects such as (1) the sustainability of their products and processes (in terms of raw materials used, production processes and uses of materials in them), (2) on their efforts to decrease their ecological footprint in terms of water consumption, air pollution, fuel consumption, carbon dioxide exhaust, (3) their waste management and (4) on the records they keep to track and manage ecological improvements. The performance of suppliers on those criteria is regularly audited by COMPANY X itself, sometimes and for some items with the help of third party auditors. Suppliers that do not meet expectations are urged to (re-)adapt to the standards, otherwise they might be dropped as suppliers. But COMPANY X offers help as well, if these suppliers meet too large difficulties in adhering to the standards set. This is part of COMPANY X's 'supplier development program,' which wants to help suppliers in contributing as much as all other parties in the supply chain to the development of more environmentally friendly products and processes.

With regard to its own environmental performance, COMPANY X tries to limit its own ecological footprint to the minimum. Thus a review of all products offered to customers has been ongoing since 2008. Its purpose is to use DfE to improve the life cycle of the products at all stages, from 'cradle to cradle.'

In this case study we describe the development of three new more environmentally friendly end products by COMPANY X and its supply chain, and try to indicate who took the initiative (COMPANY X or the supplier), which arguments were used to convince the other parties in the supply chain to join and how the activities were structured. The three products were developed in close cooperation with two suppliers only. For reasons of confidentiality, their names must be omitted and replaced by A and B in this case study.

TWO PRODUCTS DEVELOPED WITH SUPPLIER A (BIODEGRADABLE PACKAGING AND BIODEGRADABLE RESIN FOR COATING PURPOSES)

Supplier A is a relatively small company that is very active in the development of application products in which the content of petroleum-based derivatives is limited or replaced by biological alternatives. Since start-up of this supplier, COMPANY X was very interested in the activities put forward in its mission statement. As a result, COMPANY X even participated as a minority shareholder in 2007. The R&D is done by Supplier A in its own laboratories and they are very independent in proposing environmentally friendly products to the market, not only to shareholder companies that might be customers as well (such as COMPANY X).

Supplier A and COMPANY X have developed a biodegradable polymer, mainly used for packaging purposes, which contains biologically degradable oils and fatty acids instead of petroleum derivatives: 70% of the derivatives stem from vegetable oil, extracted from beans. Moreover, 98% of the vegetable oil content contained in used end products produced with this polymer can be extracted and recycled. Supplier A was able to develop this product because it has a large network of researchers in bio-agriculture and partners in the development of value-added products out of simple agricultural crops, and it could also count on the active support of COMPANY X itself. For both companies, the product lies at the heart of their marketing efforts.

The marketing manager of Supplier A put it this way:

> It is our mission to bring economic viability to value-added products from agricultural origin … Our customers are very interested in biodegradability of our products and consequently of their products as well. They are then able to project a better and more socially acceptable image to the world, their shareholders and their customers.

From the point of view of COMPANY X the chief buying officer and the marketing officer both stated:

> Suppliers have often a more extensive knowledge of new materials and technologies than we do. We might be more intelligible than most of our suppliers, however, for the application technology and whether a product is viable, on which markets and with which mark-ups … Our market research is more effective than theirs.

Both concluded that 'a close cooperation can only benefit both of us.'

The development process started with Supplier A's idea being proposed to COMPANY X's marketing division and they agreed on the testing of the idea. Perhaps not surprisingly,

Supplier A and COMPANY X have a different perspective on who took the lead for the development. As far as Supplier A is concerned, their development and marketing department clearly took the initiative:

COMPANY X was in our eyes an ideally suited customer, interested in offering a 'green' value-added product to the market. But we had to convince them to look at the benefits on their market of offering a new recyclable product.

COMPANY X's marketing states that:

... without our knowledge of the potential of green packaging materials and our experience in developing them, there wouldn't be a product ... We had to tell A that vegetable extracted oils were a viable alternative to petroleum based alternatives hitherto used.

Anyway, close collaboration by the development and sales/marketing department of both companies was present in the initial stages of the product design. In that sense, we can speak of *a push-version of 'green development'* as the 'upstream' stages in the value chain (producers of raw materials and original end product) are at the origin of the new application and the marketability is then proven to their customers further down the value chain ('midstream' and 'downstream').

A lot of laboratory production trials by Supplier A, with some help and suggestions by COMPANY X, followed. In this stage, the role of marketing was less visible and probably also less present. The development departments of both Supplier A and COMPANY X stress this fact. In the words of COMPANY X's development officer, 'Going through the numerous test runs was a time consuming activity, but we believed that it was feasible based on our knowledge of organic chemistry.' Supplier A's laboratory manager adds to this, 'COMPANY X's ideas were helpful and to-the-point. We couldn't have done it alone, but our experience with vegetable extracts added a lot to the success as well.'

When finally Supplier A seemed to be capable of producing the product, it was tested in the production facilities of COMPANY X, where small-scale production and simulation of the recycling process took place. After a few test runs and mutually agreed upon improvements, the product was ready. Launch and final production were executed by COMPANY X in two stages: a couple of pilot customers were first convinced to try the product, then full marketing could start. According to a manager of Supplier A, the main argument is that the material offers customers the potential to crucially limit their ecological footprint:

We try to convince our customers by showing them the results of the life cycle analysis we perform on the product. We explain that in every stage of the 'cradle to cradle cycle' ecological benefits may accrue and that being part of such a value chain ... will become a more important buying criterion of their own B2B-customers.

The whole process took about 17 months to complete. It was a success. Therefore, COMPANY X and Supplier A also developed a biodegradable resin for coating purposes together. The process that was used to do this was very similar, but some significant differences with regard to the partner taking the initiative were mentioned during our interviews. In this case, the market knowledge of COMPANY X was undeniably more important than in the former case. The marketing manager of Supplier A agrees with this:

The resin market is little known to us. We do not have a lot of experience in producing the raw materials and adapting them to specific target applications. COMPANY X offered us the opportunity to be part of such a venture. From a marketing point of view, we saw this as a way of diversifying into value-added applications for vegetable extracts and recycling agricultural waste. Moreover, we acquired more expertise and knowledge.

COMPANY X indicates the same thing, but stresses the importance of the final customers also in realizing the project. Their chief marketing officer expressed this thus:

Clearly A did not think of resins as a field of application in recycling agricultural waste. We believed in it, but we had to find the right application. Biodegradability is one advantage of 'greener' resins customers crave for. But since coatings have a negative environmental image, the longevity of the final product, reduced use of toxic substances and reducing the volume of product needed to coat a certain surface are the main 'green' targets our customers are pushing us towards. We are one of the world leaders in developing the main components of coatings, the resins, but we have less knowledge about coatings and their impact on the environment than our customers. And they really want their image to improve.

Although the process used to develop the resin was fairly similar to the one used in developing the packaging material, differences became clear as well, supporting our previous thoughts. COMPANY X's development manager stated:

We had to manage the process actively. Our suggestions seemed to be the starting point of any test run. The experience of [Supplier] A lay clearly in looking at the biodegradability characteristics of different agricultural waste extracts and their suitability for usage. We were in the driver's seat but had to consult our customers, specifically when it came to using the resin in the coating.

Supplier A agrees:

We couldn't have started this development on our own. The probability of success was greatly improved thanks to the experience of COMPANY X in coating applications. Their belief in the viability of the project was inspiring. Their size also allows them to be more active in various fields of applications than ours.

Contrary to the development of the biodegradable packaging material, this looks more like a *pull-version of the development of a 'greener supply chain.'* The final customers incite upstream partners to think of greener alternatives to the products they buy from them, up to the second and third tier of suppliers of raw materials.

The difference from the previous model of product innovation can be explained by two main factors. The most important one is which partner in the value chain possesses the knowledge and expertise most crucial to limit the environmental impact of the final application. Supplier A and COMPANY X were clearly more equal partners for the biodegradable packaging material, with a slight 'upstream' competence advantage. In the second case (the biodegradable resin), COMPANY X and its customers were more knowledgeable. The second factor is the type of application by which the environmental advantage is acquired: this is mainly the application of the product itself for the resin, which means that the customer can market the product advantage more directly and actively, whereas the recycling process is more important for the packaging material, which means that not the use, but the total life cycle costs on environmental level have to be sold to final customers.

One last remark must be made when looking at both product cases where Supplier A was the supply partner. In the long run COMPANY X and Supplier A are talking about a long-term relationship, irrespective of who is considered to be the lead partner in the mutual collaboration needed in developing environmentally friendly products. COMPANY X's marketing people state:

One cannot look at the development of both products separately. Without our help [Supplier] A couldn't have developed the resin, but without their knowledge [in] the process of developing the packaging material, it would have taken us years more to do so. So we are talking about mutual help and development, based on previously established mutual trust. You have to be willing to engage in long term team work and intense collaboration in different fields (chemical development, testing and so on) … Competitiveness is measured on the level of the full supply or value chain …

The CEO of Supplier A concluded with a hope for the future:

We hope that COMPANY X and our firm can be effective in the long run together. It is in both our mission statements explicitly stated that we want to offer value added green products …

THIRD PRODUCT, DEVELOPED WITH SUPPLIER B

Supplier B is somewhat larger than Supplier A and is active in the chemical industry, just like COMPANY X. Supplier B's main goal is to develop 'greener' chemical products by pooling technology and development, but also pooling marketing resources at best. The major target is to look at the energy, water and land consumption of raw materials during the production, usage and recycling processes of chemicals. Supplier B is an expert in this field, as well as in the field of biodiversity, much more so than COMPANY X is, but it is too small to actively market viable products globally and to develop the applications for the intended market segments.

Supplier B and COMPANY X closely cooperated to develop a wine stabilizer that diminished the water consumption in the wine industry by as much as 25–30%, mainly in the cooling and transportation stages of the chain which brings the wine to consumers. In this case Supplier B was expert in developing the substance, COMPANY X in looking at its compatibility with wine as a substance without impairing the intrinsic quality of the product. Thus the expertise of both companies was complementary. But the marketing knowledge of COMPANY X was predominant in looking at the wine industry as an application and in finding out whether the interest of wine growers and other partners in this chain would be great enough to support the development of the product.

Supplier B's research and development manager expresses this feeling:

COMPANY X did most of the market analysis and supported us in looking at the right application compatible with wine. We knew what was needed to limit water consumption in a cooling process on a more environmentally friendly basis as before. Thus pooling our resources was the obvious thing to do.

On the other hand, COMPANY X's marketing manager said:

[Supplier] B is excellent at developing any product limiting water consumption. But looking at stabilizers for the wine growing and producing industry and knowing how to keep quality up while still improving the environmental characteristics of the wine is more our thing.

The customers (the wine growing industry) had to be convinced actively by COMPANY X of the need to use the product. In this case the market clearly was lagging behind the industry in asking for more environmentally friendly products, although EU-regulations set targets for water consumption in agriculture, and specifically in viticulture. However, the fear of a negative effect on the quality of the product by an additive was very great, both at the growing stage of the value chain and at the distribution level. The distribution level of the supply chain was more interested in the notion because quality is just one element of consideration in their business model alongside profit per cubic centimeter of space occupied. Limiting the consumption of water and energy due to the cooling process is one way to reduce costs per cubic centimeter and thus they were more interested in listening to COMPANY X. COMPANY X's marketing people talked about it thus:

We increased pressure on the wine growers, who initially were not interested at all, by first selling the idea to their distribution channel. The sales argument to the distribution level was cost-effectiveness, whereas the wine growers were convinced by arguments about keeping the quality of the product up for a longer period of time. We did the marketing because we knew the application well and had the data and figures on water consumption. We had to wait for several wine growers in one region to be convinced. They usually do not take any risk. We always used test results by [Supplier] B with wine growers we had convinced to sell the idea to other growers, until we achieved a critical mass of potential customers. Without [Supplier] B we could not have started the project as they know much more about the stabilizer.

The product eventually became a success when the test cases were accepted by groups of wine growers in their own, often very regionally oriented, a kind of collective decision making club. Each wine grower individually perceived the risk of switching too high as long as some of his competitors were not prepared to join the effort. This makes the case even more complicated in terms of who is involved at the different levels of the complete supply or value chain. But it is also a case of *pushing the idea* through the chain by COMPANY X on the basis of data provided by Supplier B. It was a *joint effort* in offering environmental value to a customer base.

The case indicates further that green collaboration can also stem from a dyadic relationship between seller and customer, specifically when their capacities are complementary. The case proves also that the co-development of commercially viable green products sometimes requires *the convincing of every partner in the B2B value chain at different levels*. Not only 'green advantages' have to be taken into account. The basic quality of an application product is a major concern of the customers as well. A green alternative is only viable if and when these concerns can be alleviated and when the same quality as today can be guaranteed, while at the same time offering an environmental advantage.

COMPANY Y AND A GREEN PROCUREMENT CHAIN

Company Y as a company is active in developing, producing and selling conveyer belts and warehouse management systems. It employs over 1200 people, mainly in the Netherlands, and has recently begun to look at the environment as an important factor in its activities. Thus it is now trying to systematically develop its newer products along the 'cradle to cradle' principle depicted in the literature section. Company Y tries to follow these principles as best it can, but has no intention of getting into the 'leasing' principle. In other words, the company does not want to be certified according to these rules.

The first product of the company is the environment-friendly 'BLUEVEYOR' conveyor system shown for the first time at the Airport Expo 2011 in Dubai in May–June 2011. This conveyor system takes a significant step forward in increasing the sustainability of airport baggage handling operations and is a fundamental phase in the company's evolution of rethinking design, assembly, installation and maintenance across its full range of material handling systems. The company is also realizing improvement opportunities in both project execution and its own operational processes. The system tries to minimize energy consumption, use of natural resources and environmental impact. Thus the total cost of ownership is influenced positively by the energy savings, lower maintenance requirements and high rest value. As well as offering direct savings in operating costs to customers, the system also helps customers (airports) to meet their own sustainability targets. Its main features are:

1. **The conveyer system is completely PVC-free**
   'BLUEVEYOR' reduces the weight of the total conveyor system by about 50%, and is made almost completely of non-toxic, recyclable materials that can easily be separated. PVC is replaced by recyclable polyester, thereby eliminating one of the main environmental threats posed by conventional systems of this kind. As a consequence, each drive in the conveyor system uses 100 kg less natural resources than conventional systems. The use of homogeneous materials allows all constituents to be returned to technical closed loop cycles at end-of-life, in accordance with cradle-to-cradle principles.
2. **Energy savings of up to 80%**
   Energy savings of up to 80% compared with conventional conveyors are achieved by a redesign of the drive system. Key factors in these energy savings are the elimination of the usual complex belt routing through the drive system, and a new 'lean' design that reduces both mass (amongst others by using no PVC) and the number of moving parts.
3. **Reduced maintenance cost and time**
   A further advantage is the savings in maintenance time and cost, thanks to the modular concept that allows easy dismantling and replacement of key components. The simplified belt routing means no adjustment and tensioning are required, further saving maintenance time. And the 'lean' concept means fewer spare parts are required.

The case deals with the use of PVC-free components in the conveyer belt system. To safely and effectively manage the flows of polymers, rare metals and high tech materials for industry, Company Y has developed a management system for the technical metabolism, which is similar to the cradle-to-cradle intelligent materials pooling (IMP) concept. IMP is a collaborative approach to material flows management involving multiple companies working together to entirely eliminate hazardous materials.[62] Partners in an IMP form a supportive business community, pooling information and purchasing power. The concept was not fully applied in this case, but a joint effort was needed to realize the end result. Partners in the development process were important key customers, the polyester producer and the components manufacturers who use the chemical in their production:

We had to look differently at the development of new modular components in different materials. Suppliers of both the first and second tier had to be involved. The development of the modular components in the PVC free polyester had to be co-engineered by us, the supplier of the new plastic (2nd tier supplier) and the component manufacturer (1st tier supplier). The modularity was developed by our engineers together with the 1st tier component supplier ... The whole supply chain was involved. (Purchasing Manager, Company Y)

The role of the customer in this development is important, but not essential. The company itself is the driver of the development, due to market circumstances. Company Y's sales manager indicates this by saying:

We develop and sell products in a highly competitive market where most suppliers are capable of delivering equivalent products to the customer (companies exploiting airports). Anything which adds value to the final product is an extra stimulus for them to prefer you over your competitors. This goes from a better tracking system of luggage units in order to bring the loss rate down to savings in maintenance costs of belt units. Green arguments become more important for them as they are forced to lower their carbon footprint and want to act as responsible citizens. Thus the idea of saving wear-out costs and energy is appreciated by them ... That is why we developed this new belt. (Sales Manager, Company Y)

This case is more a case illustration of *a full supply chain involved* in green development, where the main aspect is not the power structure of the value chain and the push or pull effect. In fact, the final customer (the airports) did not play a big part in it. This case tries to uncover who took the lead *in the pyramidal tier structure* used in producing some components of the final conveyer belt and the importance of the pyramid cooperating fully. The different tiers of suppliers indeed played a much more important role than the customer:

The team which developed the belt believed that sustainability is more than fulfilling the strictly needed legal requirements (compliance). It can actually be a driver for innovation ... So our creative list of sustainability ideas was weeded out with the help of our suppliers. In fact, it was a cross-company effort. (Purchasing Manager Company Y)

In what follows, the polyester producer is called Supplier C and the components manufacturer is called Supplier D. Supplier C's role was quite simple. The polyester used in the belt existed already, as a number of suitable alternatives. C had to propose the best alternative to Supplier D and Company Y based its decision on the following criteria:

it had to be lightweight, hard enough to resist long use, but at the same time create no friction with non-coated aluminum (the material out of which the belt substructure is made) and recyclable in the factory (criteria mentioned by the R&D manager of Company Y). Supplier C was in competition with one other supplier, but could prove that the polyester proposed promised better results on the technical level (both the R&D and purchasing manager of Company Y stressed this).

> *The final offer was based on the criteria which Company Y and Supplier D had given to us. We did not develop anything new, but the results are interesting for future projects ... This time we were played into a more passive role, probably due to the second tier position we were in. Next time we will actively look for lead customers who can benefit from this expertise and 'sell' them the 'cradle-to-cradle principles' idea ... (Sales Manager, Supplier C)*

Supplier D was an active partner in the green development, both in specifying for and designing with the preferred polyester. For them it involved working with an innovative new technology and designing in a modular way so as to avoid waste, which constituted their commercial benefit in the short run.

> *Our largest contribution was in the modular design of our components together with the engineers of Company Y and this in such a way that they could be produced with simple tools. We also tested the results on the energy consumption and the longevity of the components. A shorter life span than the one of existing alternatives would have been unacceptable ... Let us say that our design knowledge was very important to realise the project and that environmentally friendlier alternatives are a market to conquer. (Sales Manager, Supplier D)*

In the long run Supplier D's benefit thus lies in having several pilot projects that will help the company use the environment as an active value-added argument for sales. At the moment it is still taking a more opportunistic and laid-back attitude, in the words of the sales manager:

> *It is our business to produce 'maintenance poor' components. We want to expand by value-added products, but we must be sure there will be a future market for it among the different sectors we serve. Green is the future, but we will not take risks alone.*

The purchasing manager of Company Y agrees, 'We had to "sell" the pilot project to them [the suppliers].' And according to the sales manager of Supplier D, 'Company Y is an ideally suited customer, interested in offering a "green" alternative system to their market ... We did not have to convince them of the benefits, but as a "smaller" component manufacturer in the value chain we would not be taking the risk alone.'

Still Company Y points out that the perseverance of Supplier D was an important factor in going for the result with them:

> *Their know-how became more important and at the end of the road we are convinced that they were as creative as we were. They regularly pointed out opportunities to our engineers. The idea of having to look at the routing of the belt system was theirs ... This is also proof of the fact that you cannot look at the components ... only when designing a 'green' system. You have to manage the different supply chain levels simultaneously. (R&D manager, Company Y)*

Henceforth, concurrent engineering in the so-called IMP is needed or that in ideal circumstances an IMP is actually set up. The case also illustrates the fact that several 'pyramids' will have to work with one another over time to finally realize the full potential of the idea.

Supplier D also set up reverse logistics programs for used components with Supplier C, which illustrates the work on the other part of the pyramid we observed.

Interpretation

The cases above all depict the dynamics of the supply chain network when developing new and more sustainable solutions. In this section we try to interpret these cases by formulating answers to a number of important questions on the co-development of these green supply offerings. These questions deal with the composition of the sustainable supply chain network and the partner taking the lead, the development stage the network is situated in, the way in which the involved partners dynamically 'co-develop' the greener supply solutions and the co-development mechanisms used.

First, it is clear from all cases that a sustainable supply chain involves a larger number of partners than just the supplier–buyer dyad. In the three chemical cases a network that also involves distributors and final customers is active, whereas the conveyer belt case proves that the whole supply pyramid (in this case the first and the second tier supplier mainly) has to be effectively involved to be successful.

Moreover, the partner playing the most important part in the network and leading the development effort is not always the purchasing company. In fact, all partners, whether they are situated upstream or downstream, play a certain role to achieve success. In the case of the biodegradable polymer for packaging purposes, the customers are clearly the most interested parties and play first fiddle, together with the chemical company buying the ingredient. They had to convince the upstream partners to be involved in the innovation. In the biodegradable resin case, the chemical company buying the product is the most important player, as is also the case with the wine stabilizer. But in both of those cases the downstream partners still play a certain role as well, namely to convince the final customer of the advantages of using the more environmentally friendly product. In the conveyer belt case, the first tier supplier is the leading partner of the network. Thus the leading partner may be situated on both the *horizontal level* of the supply chain network (the chain from the supplier to the final customer) and *the vertical level* (the supply pyramid delivering to the industrial buyer, which is not the final customer).

On horizontal level, we can thus make a distinction between *pull situations* in which the interest of the customers in sustainability is extremely high and the main reason for the development of the new solution or new products by upstream partners, and *push situations* in which the supply market has to convince the downstream partners of the advantages of the newly developed more sustainable solution. The forces shaping the sustainable value creation process on this level are the recognition of market opportunities and the recognition and capturing of the technology and process opportunities. In pull situations partners closer to the market or customers (the packaging for example) will most probably take the lead; in push situations the suppliers will possess more expertise in developing and benefiting from the technological opportunities and realize the importance of the market value first (the conveyer belt for example).

On vertical level, the depth of the co-development effort may vary, depending on the number of supply tiers involved. If the pyramidal supply chain structure has to be involved in full (as in the conveyer belt case), the solution can be called rather deep compared to the other cases. On this vertical level the forces shaping the sustainable value creation process are quite different from the ones mentioned on the horizontal level. On the one hand the expertise and know-how in process technology, leading to a better understanding of the opportunities of the technology as such, is important for the first tier of the supplier pyramid, whereas the know-how and expertise in developing components and products is important for upstream tiers. Thus, deep solutions exist when both product and process technology have to be harmonized in order to create the sustainable solution and capture its value, whereas 'limited depth' solutions exist when mainly process changes create the opportunities for more sustainable alternatives.

Thus a typology of four types of situations can be developed, based on the opposing forces depicted in Figure 14.2 At the same time, we have situated our four cases on this grid.

Unfortunately, only three of the four potential situations are present in our four case examples. What is important, however, is that although one partner will take the lead in green development, all other partners of the supply chain involved have to cooperate to make the whole supply system work towards one goal, no matter whether we observe push or pull situations. For example, in push situations, although the suppliers take the lead, partners close to the market have to convince final customers that they will benefit from the greener product. Further research will moreover have to investigate how far these different forces really co-exist and shape the structure and working of the

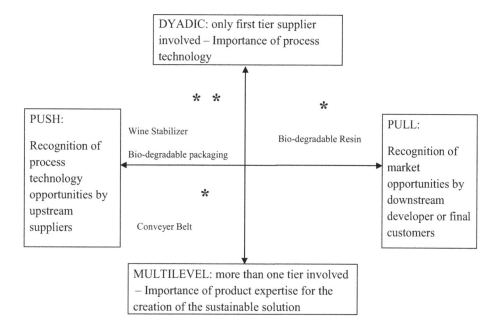

Figure 14.2 Forces shaping the value creation process in the sustainable supply network

sustainable supply chain network and in which sectors of industry or with which profiles of companies they are more or less common.

Second, it is important to situate our case examples on the aforementioned stage models[63] towards *innovation excellence in sustainability*, particularly on the Nidumolu model. The model describes how companies' first sustainability challenge is to view compliance 'as an opportunity to experiment with sustainable technologies, materials and processes' (see Appendix 2). The Nidumolu model, however, only depicts where Suppliers A and B are situated on an evolutionary scale in sustainability. It does not clarify how much the whole supply chain really contributes to this aim. In other words, the model is very nice, but we still have to wonder whether key suppliers and buyers co-evolve along this model and how they will influence each other, nor does it indicate whether the partners in the chain are synchronously 'stepping up' from one stage to the next.

In all of our examples, the depicted supply chains cannot be considered to be nucleuses of new greener business models or green practice platforms, situated at the top of the evolutionary scale towards sustainability.[64] At best our cases are situated in the third stage of the model. The companies involved have indeed all redesigned existing product offerings to become more eco-friendly and did so by pooling acquired skills and know-how in scaling and manufacturing these products, using an excellent life cycle analysis. Moreover they are well aware of the fact that their solutions will not create a *'greenwash* effect,' but will effectively be considered by the market as more sustainable alternatives to current business practices. The 'design for the environment' and 'cradle-to-cradle' principles are a guarantee of that. We believe that in this stage of the evolution, real characteristics of co-development show up. Close cooperation between all partners in the value chain, mutual help and exchange of knowledge on different levels are described by the interviewees in each of the four cases. These are all characteristics of joint development of products and services, in both the cited marketing and purchasing literature. This confirms the scientific assessment that creating and manufacturing value-added products in B2B markets is only possible when new and more challenging methods to improve the supply chain are experimented with. Developing sustainable alternatives is not different with regard to these general product development characteristics. A full network involvement is necessary for successful cooperation efforts, as is the case in all of our examples.

Matthyssens, Vandenbempt and Weyns[65] have indicated that, as previously stated, suppliers and buyers have to co-evolve simultaneously along the co-evolution ladder in order to optimize value creation. Is this also the case in the co-development of sustainable supply chain solutions? In Figure 14.3 we have depicted this process, combining the Matthyssens model with the stages in the Nidumolu model.[66]

One can see that buyers might be at higher levels, or alternatively the supplier might be at a higher level of 'greening' respective the other partner in the chain. What happens then?

As the preparatory stages of the development efforts were not treated in our interviews, we can only draw conclusions to later stages of the sustainable development effort. What is clear is that all parties involved were not situated at the same level (or step) of the 'value creation ladder' in terms of having acquired the technology to develop sustainable alternatives in our cases. Thus we observed several 'misfits' in sustainability level between suppliers and buyers. This was certainly the case between the first and second tier supplier

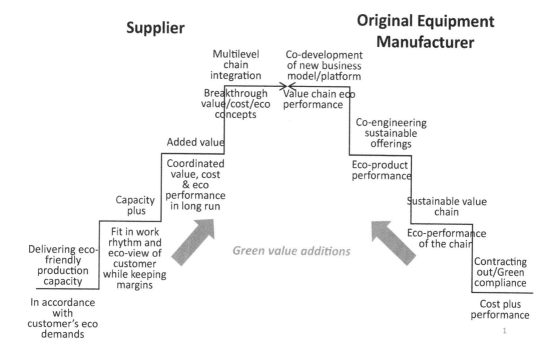

Figure 14.3 The green staircase. Based on explorative study and inspired by Matthyssens, Vandenbempt & Weyns (2008, 2009) and Nidumolu, Prahalad & Rangaswami (2009)

in the conveyer belt case, but might also be valid when looking at the relationship between the chemical buying company and Supplier A (for both the biodegradable product cases we described). The interviews indicate that the partner in the value chain with the most expertise in either process or product technology (in push cases) and/or experience with customer demand (in pull cases) took the lead in the development process and tried to bring the other members of the supply chain up to a same level of understanding and expertise through the active exchange of ideas and technology. This requires considerable mutual trust.

In Figure 14.4 one can see a potential 'misfit' between an OEM-customer being situated higher up the eco ladder and its supplier. That said, the reverse might be true, as was observed in some of the cases, such as the resin case. In any case, only if co-evolution really materializes can the greening of a supply chain be realized. But co-evolution must actively be managed, and not solely from a dyadic supplier–buyer perspective (either the supplier 'helping' the customer to climb the green staircase towards his level, or vice versa). Also from a value chain logic the staircase must be managed whereby sometimes 'upstream' higher tier suppliers or 'downstream' customers need to be mobilized and incited to climb the staircase. This way, partners must be stimulated and empowered to outgrow their traditional buyer–supplier relations.

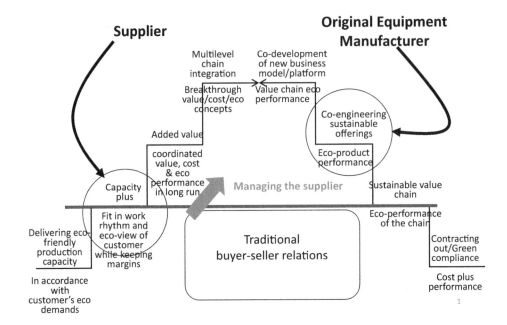

Figure 14.4 The green staircase: misfit. Based on explorative study and inspired by Matthyssens, Vandenbempt & Weyns (2008, 2009) and Nidumolu, Prahalad & Rangaswami (2009)

In fact, in the first case both the technical expertise and the relationship with the final customer of the first tier supplier made them incite the second tier supplier to follow suit, thus serving the interest of the whole supply chain. In doing so the first tier supplier clearly had to actively help the second tier supplier and bring it up to the required level in terms of functionality and value/cost equilibrium. As far as the relationship between the chemical buying company and Supplier A is concerned, for the mutually developed biodegradable resin the expertise and market interest of Supplier A was much lower than for the biodegradable packaging material. For the first product the buyer had to prove the added value of the product to Supplier A, whereas for the second product Supplier A was fully convinced of the breakthrough advantages it could achieve together with the chemical company on the market. The case with Supplier B is an exception in our data set because both buyer and supplier were situated on nearly the same level of expertise and had to push the product to the market in a mutual effort.

Thus, in co-developing sustainable alternatives, the initial position on the value ladder of both partners apparently does not need to be equally high, but the willingness of the partner highest up on the ladder to help the other in climbing up to its own level is a crucial factor indeed. Co-evolution based on mutual help is thus part of the dynamics which we observed in our cases. We did not encounter any example in which too large a distance between the partners on the value ladder existed and we believe that such a situation would have made things more complicated or impossible. In all of our cases the interviewees stressed the importance of a *joint marketing effort* towards the customer base. It might well be that the higher rungs of the eco value ladder in Figure 14.4 require multilevel 'co-marketing' of the sustainable solution in the value chain, and not just co-engineering or joint development.

Moreover, as we are talking about a full sustainable value chain comprising more than two partners, the situation is actually even more complex. There is not just one 'green staircase' in which efforts are made to bring both partners up to the same level, but several interconnected ones, namely between each of the supplier–buyer dyads in the chain. And all should be helped to acquire the same level of expertise and knowledge to work closely and effectively together. We should actually be talking about a 'multiple staircase' model.

Third, it is important to notice that in those cases were the customer was higher up on the co-evolutionary value ladder and pulled the supplier up to an equivalent level, extensive exchanges of information and laboratory tests were used to gradually improve the effectiveness of the intended solution. Multifunctional teams of the partners involved were active in realizing this goal. This is in line with the literature on *buyer–supplier collaboration* in the field of innovations. Industrial marketing and purchasing (IMP) group scholars have amply demonstrated how interaction within a network perspective can stimulate innovation.[67] They suggest that innovation is the result of interactions between buyer and supplier and that the management of relationships between organizations has become a cornerstone of more advanced approaches to the extended supply chain, requiring the developments of specific relational capabilities not only at the manufacturer level but also at the supplier level. Existing research efforts did not exactly specify how buyer–supplier relationships impact on a supplier firm's innovativeness, especially regarding innovative green product service systems.

The cases we observed suggest that green innovations largely follow this general picture. The importance of the fact that at least one partner in the innovative network understands the benefits of the innovation for final customers or is helped in understanding it by the customers themselves (in pull cases) is apparent in all our cases. It may well be that although the capturing of the market value of the newly developed sustainable solutions is obvious to the partners in the supply chain, the benefits might have to be extensively explained to the customers anyway. The wine stabilizer case is a good example of this.

Finally, we can link green purchasing to the concept of *purchasing maturity*,[68] which is similar to notions such as 'levels of strategic purchasing' developed by several authors.[69] In the conceptualization of the model by Telgen and Pop Sitar,[70] a company needs to 'step up' in purchasing maturity towards supply chain and value chain orientations in order to succeed in green initiatives. These stages of development involve, as indicated, (1) closer and more cooperative relations with suppliers and early involvement in new product development and (2) extensive use of cross-functional supplier development teams, (3) a more cooperative relationship with suppliers and early involvement in new product development and (4) extensive use of cross-functional supplier development teams. This upgrading of supplier capabilities and collaboration on advanced green technology with suppliers, as well as the use of continuous improvement measures, were observed in our cases.

Conclusion and Limitations of the Study

We can conclude that managing green offerings in business markets necessitates a dynamic and dyadic approach, sometimes expanded to a whole multilevel value chain network. The experiences of our case companies clearly indicate that only through buyer–supplier and value chain integration can sustainable products and services be co-created. Co-evolution seems to be a precondition. The dynamism involved relates to the understanding of the market advantages as well as to the technical skills and expertise needed to co-develop a viable and more sustainable alternative to existing products. Our research thus suggests that buyer–supplier and network interactions on multiple levels must be stimulated in the area of sustainable supply initiatives.

To purchasing and marketing scholars this insight contributes by highlighting how 'green capabilities' evolve and co-evolve within supply chains. Moreover, it incites them to combine knowledge from several research streams (i.e., purchasing, B2B marketing, co-development and evolutionary models) when trying to understand complex co-development processes in practice. The paper contributes to the literature on green supply management by providing rich insight into the dynamics present in green supply chain initiatives. Processes of co-evolution and co-marketing have so far been neglected in this context. This study uncovers some of the processes enabling green supply initiatives. As such it suggests that a purely ethical (CSR based) or technical (operational) green capabilities approach needs to be complemented with a (multilevel) relational and co-marketing capabilities approach.

To managers, our results show that green development needs to be supported actively all the way through, and involving all members of, the supply chain. To avoid being suspected of only wanting to 'greenwash' the company's image, both customer ideas and supplier capabilities have to be taken into account, and managed actively. This requires a long and tedious process of exchange of information and sharing of research and development efforts with these partners in the supply chain. Purchasing and marketing managers should work closely together and jointly take the lead in the company, stimulating all other departments needed. Patience and perseverance are important factors since markets might pressure for quick results.

Our research comprised a limited number of cases and interviews and hence cannot claim to do more than give scholars and managers a first glance into the co-development process of green market initiatives. Indeed, it is probably only the start of a research venture to uncover green collaboration. Any further research should, we believe, try to find cases more regularly spread over the different segments of Figure 14.2.

Given the increasing importance of gaining access to suppliers' capabilities through global supply relationships,[71] it is moreover paramount to understand how and which factors impact on suppliers' green innovativeness. Some of these factors have been enumerated in this study, such as the depth of the supply chain involved, the partner taking the initiative and the importance of customer interest. The present cases do not allow us to assess other factors influencing this process. For instance, the management of risks when developing green products along a supply chain (especially when supply chain partners are small or medium-sized, as in the case of supplier D) was not taken into account. This might to be a very relevant driver for supply chain collaboration focused on green products. More research is clearly needed in this field, linking the existing literature on drivers and inhibitors of green purchasing to specific profiles of companies and/or sectors of industry. Future research should also focus on the co-existence of these forces in different situations.

More in-depth research on the different methods and techniques relevant to making this co-development process work is also needed. Thus longitudinal studies of a larger number of cases are necessary to validate the findings and at the same time gain more insight in the processes really at work. A team of experts in different fields (marketing, purchasing, innovation, human resources and engineering) should be composed to do so.

Appendix 1

Comparison of Several Evolutionary Models in Green Purchasing

Evolutionary steps	Model of Bruet, Menuet & Thaker (2009)		Model of Bobis & Staniszewski (IBM) (2009)		UNEP Model (2008)		Model of Nidumolu, Prahalad & Rangaswami (2009)	
	Focus	Methods, means and people	Internal evaluation basis	Green 'results'	Motives	Characteristics	Competencies	Innovation opportunity
Incremental/ Innocence	Transactional; Passive buying	Green purchasing unknown or little known	Costs	None	Short-term durability and quality of products; Safety of products; Compliance to standards; Support image	Standards imposed on suppliers; Auditing = policing; Cost improvement measured; No knowledge about green quality of suppliers	Anticipate and shape regulations; Skill to work with other companies, including rivals	Using compliance to induce the company and its partners to experiment with sustainable technologies, materials, and processes
Incremental/ Awareness; Viewing compliance as opportunity	Internal improvement; Risk mineralization; Cooperation with suppliers	Portfolio management; Process and specs improvements; Ask suppliers to comply to standards; First steps towards common improvement; Supplier rating models	Cost improvements	Compliance to standards and regulations				
Strategic/ Understanding; Make value chain more sustainable	Training of buyers is intensified	Training of buyers is intensified	Cost improvements	Tactical saving of energy costs; No measurement of results	Lower energy usage; Productivity improvement; Customers' pressure; Brand recognition and building	Training and support of suppliers; Category management; Suppliers involved in sustainability development	Expertise in techniques (LCA); The ability to redesign operations; The capacity to ensure that suppliers and retailers make their operations eco-friendly	Developing sustainable sources; Increasing the use of clean energy; Finding innovative uses for returned products
Strategic/ Competence; Design sustainable products and services	External optimization; Lower total cost of ownership; Innovation stimulated through value analysis/value engineering	All risks known and evaluated; Preventive actions undertaken; Eco-design and innovation; In-depth cooperation with suppliers; Buyers also evaluated on green results; Intensive mutual communication with suppliers; Supplier satisfaction	Total cost of ownership	Intelligent design; Recycling and by-product valuation; Image improvement; Product- and process quality improvement; Quality improvement		Adaptive behavior is supported; Continuous improvement; Active marketing of sustainable products; Green image promoted	Skills to determine whether products are eco-friendly; Getting a positive green image; Create measurement for supplier capabilities towards the environment	Applying advanced techniques such as biomimicry; Eco-friendly packaging alternatives developed

Comparison of Several Evolutionary Models in Green Purchasing (cont...)

Transformational/ Excellence/ Leadership	Purchasing is strategic element in sustainability	Total cost of ownership	Design for the environment	Creation of markets	Re-engineering of supply chain	Understand what customers want	New delivery models
External optimization Globalization Develop new business models	All processes are optimally designed to allow greener purchasing Characteristics of previous stage are supported further		Product and process innovation LCA Measurement on value chain or organizational level	Long term supply Quality is paramount Innovation of products and processes Influencing green customer demand	Innovation All stakeholders involved Global standards Costs become less important	Understand how partners create and enhance value	Services are also involved Develop models that enhance physical and digital infrastructure of supply chain
Create next practice platforms						Knowledge of complete ecosystems Expertise to synthesize business models/technologies	Build new value for customers Reduce use of energy and water Cradle-to-cradle technology

Appendix 2

Interviews for Case Company X

	Interviews with:
COMPANY X	Marketing manager and 2 assistants R&D manager Purchasing manager
Supplier A	Marketing manager R&D officer and assistant Company CEO
Supplier B	R&D officer Plant manager

Interviews for Case Company Y

	Interviews with:
Company Y	Sales manager R&D manager Purchasing manager
Supplier A	Sales manager
Supplier B	Sales manager

Notes

1   Lindgreen, A., F. Maon & V. Swaen (2009), 'Guest editorial', *Supply Chain Management: An International Journal*, Vol. 14, No. 2.

2   Lindgreen, A. et al. (2009), *op. cit.*; Andersen, M. & T. Skjoett-Larsen (2009), 'Corporate social responsibility in global supply chains', *Supply Chain Management: An International Journal*, Vol. 14, No. 2, pp. 75–86.

3   Roberts, S. (2003), 'Supply chain specific? Understanding the patchy success of ethical sourcing initiatives', *Journal of Business Ethics*, Vol. 44, No. 2/3, pp. 159–170; Andersen, M. & T. Skjoett-Larsen (2009), *op. cit.*, p. 77.

4   Correia de Sousa, M. (2005), 'The sustainable Innovation Engine', *The Journal of Information and Knowledge Management Systems*, Vol. 34, No. 6, pp. 398–405; Chung T.C. & C.H. Tsai (2007), 'The effect of green design activities on new product strategies and performance *International Journal of Management*, Vol. 24, No. 2, pp. 276–289; Srivastava, S.K. (2007), 'Green supply chain management: a state-of-the-art literature review', *International Journal of Management Reviews*, Vol. 9, No. 1, pp. 53–80; Preuss, L. (2007), 'Contribution of purchasing and supply management to ecological innovation', *International Journal of Innovation Management*, Vol. 11, No. 4, pp. 515–537.

5   Noci, G. (1997), 'Designing "green" vendor rating systems for the assessment of a supplier's environmental performance', *European Journal of Purchasing & Supply Management*, Vol. 3 No. 2, pp. 103–114; Linton, J.D., R. Klassen & V. Jayaraman (2007), 'Sustainable supply chains: an introduction', *Journal of Operations Management*, Vol. 25, pp. 1075–1082; Gonzalez-Padron, T., T.M. Hult & R. Calantone (2007), 'Exploiting innovative opportunities in global purchasing: an assessment of ethical climate and relationship performance', *Industrial Marketing Management*, Vol. 37, No. 2, pp. 69–82.; Preuss, L. (2007), *op. cit.*.; Vachon, S. & R. Klassen (2008), 'Environmental management and manufacturing performance: the role of collaboration in the supply chain', *International Journal of Production Economics*, Vol. 111, pp. 299–315.

6   Lu, L., C.H. Wu & T.-C. Kuo (2007), 'Environmental principles applicable to green supplier evaluation by using multi-objective decision analysis', *International Journal of Production Research*, Vol. 45, No. 18–19, pp. 4317–4321; Gonzalez-Padron, T. et al. (2007), *op. cit.*; Vachon, S. & R. Klassen (2008), *op. cit.*, pp. 303–304.

7   Lu, L. et al. (2007), *op. cit.*, p. 4318.

8   Lindgreen, A. et al. (2009), *op. cit.*; Srivastava, S.K. (2007), *op. cit.*, p. 72 ; Walker, H. & W. Phillips (2009), 'Sustainable procurement: emerging issues', *International Public Procurement Conference Issues,* 21–23 September 2006, pp. 559–586.

9   Srivastava, S.K. (2007), *op. cit.*

10 Carter, C.R. & M. Dresner (2001), 'Purchasing's role in environmental management: cross-functional development of grounded theory', *Supply Chain Management*, Vol. 37, No. 3, pp. 12–26; Krause, D.R., S. Vachon & R.D. Klassen (2009), 'Special topic forum on sustainable supply chain management: introduction and reflections on the role of purchasing management', *Journal of Supply Chain Management*, Vol. 45, No. 4, pp. 18–25; Min, H. & W.P. Galle (2001), 'Green purchasing practices of US firms', *International Journal of Operations and Production Management*, Vol. 21, No. 9, pp. 1222–1238; Walker, H., L. Di Sisto & D. McBain (2008), 'Drivers and barriers to environmental supply chain management: lessons from public and private sectors', *Journal of Purchasing and Supply Management*, Vol. 14, No. 1, pp. 69–85; Zhu, Q. & J. Sarkis (2006), 'An inter-sectoral comparison of green supply chain management in China: drivers and practices', *Journal of Cleaner Production*, Vol. 14, No. 5, pp. 472–486.

11 Hervani, A. & M. Helms (2005), 'Performance measurement for green supply chain management. Benchmarking', *Supply Management: An International Journal*, Vol. 12, No. 4, pp. 330–353; Orsato, R. (2006), 'Competitive environmental strategies: when does it pay to be green?' *California Management Review*, Vol. 48, No. 2, pp. 127–143; Piercy, N.F. (2009), 'Strategic relationships between boundary-spanning functions: aligning customer relationship management with supplier relationship management', *Industrial Marketing Management*, Vol. 38, No. 6, pp. 857–864; Porter, M.E. & C. Van der Linde (1995), 'Green and competitive', *Harvard Business Review*, September–October, pp. 120–134; Preuss, L. (2007), *op. cit.*; Rao, P. & D. Holt (2005), 'Do green supply chains lead to competitiveness and economic performance?', *International Journal of Operations and Production Management*, Vol. 25, No. 9–10, pp. 898–916; Turner, M. & P. Houston (2009), 'Going Green? Start with sourcing', *Supply Chain Management Review*, Vol. 13, No. 2, pp. 14–21.

12 Hanna, M.D., W.R. Newman & P. Johnson (2000), 'Linking operational and environmental improvement through employee involvement', *International Journal of Operations and Production Management*, Vol. 20, No. 2, pp. 148–165; Henriques, I. & P. Sadorsky (1999), 'The relationship between environmental commitment and managerial perceptions of stakeholder importance', *Academy of Management Journal*, Vol. 42, No. 1, pp. 87–99.

13   Chung-Chiang, C. (2005), 'Incorporating green purchasing into the frame of ISO 14000', *Journal of Cleaner Production*, Vol. 13, pp. 927–933; Montabon, F., S.A. Melnyk, R. Sroufe & R.J. Calantone (2000), 'ISO 14000: assessing its perceived impact on corporate performance', *The Journal of Supply Chain Management*, Vol. 4, No. 3, pp. 4–16.

14   Pagell, M., Z. Wu & M. Wasserman (2010), 'Thinking differently about purchasing portfolios: an assessment of sustainable sourcing', *Journal of Supply Chain Management*, Vol. 46, No. 1, pp. 57–73.

15   Chen, C.-C., C.-W. Hsu, K.-S. Wu & H.-J. Shyur (2010), 'Using ANP for the selection of green supply chain management strategies', *Journal of Supply Chain Management*, Vol. 46, No. 4, pp. 213–224; Hamner, B. (2006), 'Effects of green purchasing strategies on supplier behavior', in Sarkis, J. (2006). *Greening the Supply Chain*. London: Springer, pp. 31–34; Noci, G. (1997), *op. cit.*; Stokes S. & N. Tohamy (2009), '7 traits of a green supply chain', *Supply Chain Management Review*, October 2009, Vol. 13, No. 7, pp. 8–9.

16   Heiskanen, E. (2002), 'The institutional logic of life cycle thinking', *Journal of Cleaner Production*, Vol. 10, No. 5, pp. 427–437; Overby, C. (1990), 'Design for the entire life cycle: a new paradigm', *American Society of Engineering Education Annual Conference*, pp. 552–563; Seuring, S. (2004), 'Industrial ecology, life cycles, supply chains: differences and interrelations', *Business Strategy and the Environment*, Vol. 13, No. 4, pp. 306–319.

17   Van Hoek, R.I. (1999), 'From reversed logistics to green supply chain', *Supply Chain Management*, Vol. 4, pp. 129–135; Vachon, S. & R.D. Klassen (2006), 'Extending green practices across the supply chain: the impact of upstream and downstream integration', *International Journal of Operations and Production Management*, Vol. 26, No. 7, pp. 795–821; Walton, S.V., R.B. Handfield & S.A. Melnyk (1998), 'The green supply chain: integrating suppliers into environmental management processes', *International Journal of Purchasing and Materials Management*, Spring, pp. 2–11.

18   Vandermerwe, S. & J. Rada (1988), 'Servitization of business: adding value by adding Services', *European Management Journal*, Vol. 6, No. 4, pp. 314–324.

19   Pawar, K.S., A. Beltagui & J.C.K.H. Riedel (2009)', The PSO triangle: designing product, service and organization to create value', *International Journal of Operations and Production Management*, Vol. 29, No. 5, pp. 468–493.

20   Matthyssens, P. & K. Vandenbempt (2010), 'Service addition as business market strategy: identification of transition trajectories', *Journal of Service Management*, Vol. 21, No. 5, pp. 693–714.

21   Sharma, A., G.R. Iyer, A. Mehrotra & R. Krishnan (2010), 'Sustainability and business-to-business marketing: a framework and implications' *Industrial Marketing Management*, Vol. 39, No. 2, pp. 330–341.

22   Svensson, G. (2007), 'Aspects of sustainable supply chain management: conceptual framework and empirical example', *Supply Chain Management: An International Journal*, Vol. 12, No. 4, pp. 262–266; Olugu, E.V., K.Y. Wong & A.M. Shaharoun (2011), 'Development of key performance measures for the automobile green supply chain', *Resources, Conservation and Recycling*, Vol. 55, No. 6, pp. 567–579.

23   Darnall, N., G.J. Jolley & R. Handfield (2008), 'Environmental management systems and green supply chain management: complements for sustainability?' *Business Strategy and the Environment*, Vol. 18, 30–45.

24   Chen, C.-C. (2005), 'Incorporating green purchasing into the frame of ISO 14000', *Journal of Cleaner Production*, Vol. 13, pp. 927–933; Montabon, F., S.A. Melnyk, R. Sroufe & Calantone R.J.

(2000), 'ISO 14000: assessing its perceived impact on corporate performance', *Journal of Supply Chain Management*, Spring, pp. 4–16.

25 Fischer, P., L. Nielsen & C. Wolnik (2008), *At the Source. Green Procurement Edition*. Spring 2008, Canadian Centre for Pollution Prevention.

26 Turner, M. & P. Houston (2009), 'Going Green? Start with sourcing', *Supply Chain Management Review*, Vol. 13, No. 2, pp. 14–21.

27 Nidumolu, R., C.K. Prahalad & M.R. Rangaswami (2009), 'Why sustainability is now the key driver of innovation', *Harvard Business Review*, Vol. 87, No. 9, pp. 56–64.

28 Nidumolu, R. et al. (2009), *op. cit.*, p. 56.

29 Noci, G. & R. Verganti (1999), 'Managing "green" product innovation in small firms', *R&D Management*, Vol. 29, No. 1, pp. 3–15.

30 Noci, G. & R. Verganti (1999), *op. cit.*; Lu, L. et al. (2007), *op. cit.*

31 Noci, G. (1997), *op. cit.*

32 Lu, L. et al. (2007), *op. cit.*

33 Ecovadis (2011), *Sustainable Supply Management*, Company leaflet (electronic).

34 Heiskanen, E. (2002), *op. cit.*, pp. 428–430; Hamner, B. (2006), *op. cit.*, p. 31; Stokes, S. & N. Tohamy (2009), *op. cit.*, p. 9.

35 Turner, M. & P. Houston (2009), *op. cit.*, pp. 19–20; Chen, C.-C., C.-W. Hsu, K.-S. Wu & H.-J. Shyur (2010), *op. cit.*; pp. 218–219.

36 Sharma, A., G.R. Iyer, A. Mehrotra & R. Krishnan (2010), 'Sustainability and business-to-business marketing: a framework and implications', *Industrial Marketing Management*, Vol. 39, No. 2, pp. 330–341; McDonough, W. (2003), 'Towards a sustaining architecture for the 21st century', *Industry and Environment*, Vol. 26, No. 2–3, pp. 3–10.

37 Bruel, O., O. Menuet & P.F. Thaler (2009), *Sustainable Procurement: A Crucial Lever to end the Crisis?* White paper based on the HEC 2009 Sustainable Procurement Benchmark and 21 interviews with Procurement Directors. HEC Paris, SNCF, EcoVadis, Ariba; Bobis, V. & J. Staniszewski (2009), *Making the Case for Sustainable 'Green' Procurement*. IBM.

38 Heiskanen, E. (2002), *op. cit.*, pp. 425; Turner, M. & P. Houston (2009), *op. cit.*, p. 19.

39 McDonough, W. (2003), *op. cit.*, pp. 4–5.

40 *Ibidem*, pp. 6–8.

41 Hamner, B. (2006), *op. cit.*, pp. 29–30; Preuss, L. (2007), *op. cit.*, pp. 529–530.

42 Fawcett, S.E., L.M. Ellram & J. Ogden (2007), *Supply Chain Management: From Vision to Implementation*. Upper Saddle River, NJ: Pearson Prentice-Hall, pp. 341–343; Swink M., S.A. Melnyk, M.B. Cooper & J.L. Hartley (2011), *Managing Operations Across the Supply Chain*. New York: McGraw-Hill, p. 274.

43 Burt, D.N., S Petcavage & R. Pinkerton (2010), *Supply Management*. 8th edn. Boston: Irwin McGraw-Hill, pp. 61–63; Liker, J.K. & T.Y. Choi (2006), 'Building deep supplier relationships', *Harvard Business Review on Supply Chain Management*. Boston: Harvard Business School Press, pp. 20–21; Monczka, R.M., R.B. Handfield, L.C. Giunipero, J.L. Patterson & D. Waters (2010), *Purchasing and Supply Chain Management*. Hampshire, UK: South-Western Cengage Learning, pp. 107–109.

44 Liker, J.K. & T.Y. Choi, (2006), *op. cit.*, p. 23.

45 Lysons, K. & M. Gillingham (2003), *Purchasing and Supply Chain Management*. 6th edn. Harlow: Prentice Hall Financial Times, pp. 372–374; Burt, D.N. et al. (2010), *op. cit.*, p. 65.

46 Fawcett, S.E. et al. (2007), *op. cit.*, pp. 347–349 ; Swink, M. et al. (2011), *op. cit.*, pp. 294–295; Van Weele A.J. & C. Gelderman (2003), 'Handling measurement issues and strategic directions in Kraljic's portfolio model', *Journal of Purchasing and Supply management*, Vol. 9, pp. 207–216;

Matthyssens, P. & W. Faes (2009), Insights into the process of changing sources, *Journal of Business and Industrial marketing*, Vol. 24, No. 3–4, pp. 245–255.

47   Gullett, J., L. Do, M. Canuto-Carranco, M. Brister, S. Turner & C. Caldwell (2010), 'The buyer-supplier relationship: an integrative model of ethics and trust', *Journal of Business Ethics*, Vol. 90, pp. 329–341; Liker, J.K. & T.Y. Choi (2006), *op. cit.*, pp. 23–24; Lysons, K. & M. Gillingham (2003), *op. cit.*, pp. 378–379.

48   Matthyssens, P., K. Vandenbempt & S. Weyns (2008), 'Value creation options for contract manufacturers: market strategy transition and co-evolution in networks', *Advances in Business Marketing & Purchasing*, Vol. 14, pp. 449–477; Matthyssens, P., K. Vandenbempt & S. Weyns (2009), 'Transitioning and co-evolving to upgrade value offerings: a competence-based marketing view', *Industrial Marketing Management*, Vol. 38, No. 5, pp. 504–512.

49   Ulaga, W. & A. Eggert (2006), 'Value-based differentiation in business relationships: gaining and sustaining key supplier status', *Journal of Marketing*, Vol. 70 (January), pp. 119–136.

50   Tuli, K.R., A.K. Kohli & S.G. Bharadwaj, (2007), 'Rethinking customer solutions: from product bundles to relational processes', *Journal of Marketing*, Vol. 71 (July), pp. 1–17.

51   Oliva, R., & R. Kallenberg (2003), 'Managing the transition from products to services', *International Journal of Service Industry Management*, Vol. 14, No. 2, pp. 160–172; Gebauer, H. & T. Friedli (2005), 'Behavioral implications of the transition process from products to services', *Journal of Business and Industrial Marketing*, Vol. 20, No. 2, pp. 70–78; Ford, D., L.-E. Gadde, H. Hakansson & I. Snehota (2003), *Managing Business Relationships*. 2nd edn. Chichester: John Wiley & Sons, pp. 88–93.

52   Möller, K., & P. Törrönen (2003), 'Business Suppliers' value creation potential. A capacity-based analysis', *Industrial Marketing Management*, Vol. 32, No. 2, pp. 109–118.

53   Correia de Sousa, M. (2005), *op. cit.*; Chung T.C. & C.H. Tsai (2007), *op. cit.*; Srivastava, S.K. (2007), *op. cit.* p. 55–56; Preuss, L. (2007), *op. cit.*

54   Linton, J.D. et al. (2007), *op. cit.*; Gonzalez-Padron, T. et al. (2007), *op. cit.*

55   Vachon, S. & R. Klassen (2008), *op. cit.*; Lee, S.-Y. (2008), 'Drivers for the participation of small and medium-sized suppliers in green supply chain initiatives', *Supply Chain Management: An International Journal,* Vol. 13, No. 3, pp. 185–198.

56   Paulraj, A., I.J. Chen & J. Flynn (2006), 'Levels of strategic purchasing: impact on supply integration and performance', *Journal of Purchasing & Supply Management*, Vol. 12, No. 3, pp. 107–122; Telgen, J. & C. Pop Sitar (2001), 'Possible kinds of values added by the purchasing department', *Proceedings of the 10th Annual IPSERA Conference*, pp. 803–813; Van Weele, A.J., F.A. Rozemeijer & G. Rietveld (1998), 'Professionalizing purchasing organizations: towards a purchasing development model', in *Conference Proceedings of Seventh International Annual IPSERA Conference*, London, pp. 515–523.

57   Telgen, J. & C. Pop Sitar (2001), *op. cit.*, p. 518.

58   Bruel, O. et al. (2008), *op. cit.* ; Bobis V. & J. Staniszewski (2009), *op. cit.;* UNEP, United Nations Environment Programme. (2008), *Innovative Approaches to Sustainable Supply. Unchaining Value.* SustainAbility, UNEP and UNGC; Nidumolu, R. et al. (2009), *op. cit.*

59   Srivastava, S.K. (2007), *op. cit.*, p. 72; Walker, H. & W. Phillips (2009), *op. cit.*, pp. 570–574; Bai C. & J. Sarkis (2010), 'Green supplier development: analytical evaluation using rough set theory', *Journal of Cleaner Production,* Vol. 18, pp. 1200–1210.

60   Eisenhardt, K.M., (1989), 'Building theories from case study research', *Academy of Management Review,* Vol. 14, No. 4, pp. 532–550; Miles, M.B. & A.M. Huberman (1994), *Qualitative Data Analysis.* Thousand Oaks: Sage Publications; Yeung, H.W.-C. (1995), 'Qualitative personal interviews in international business research: some lessons from a study of Hong Kong

transnational corporations', *International Business Review*, Vol. 4, No. 3, pp. 313–339; Yin, R.K. (1994), *Case Study Research: Designs and Methods*, Thousand Oaks: Sage Publications; Woodside, A.G. & E. Wilson (2003), 'Case study research method for theory building', *Journal of Business & Industrial Marketing*, Vol. 18, No. 6/7, pp. 482–493. Matthyssens, P. & K. Vandenbempt (2003), 'Cognition-in-context: reorienting research in business market strategy', *Journal of Business & Industrial Marketing*, Vol. 18, No. 6/7, pp. 595–606.

61   Sharma, A. et al. (2010), *op. cit.*

62   McDonough, W. (2003), *op. cit.*

63   Nidumolu, R. et al. (2009), *op. cit.*, p. 60.

64   *Ibidem*, p. 61

65   Matthyssens, P. et al. (2008), *op. cit.*, pp. 471; Matthyssens, P. et al. (2009), *op. cit.*, pp. 508.

66   Nidumolu, R. et al. (2009), *op. cit.*; Matthyssens, P. et al. (2009), *op. cit.*, p. 509.

67   Roy, S., K. Sivakumar & I.F. Wilkinson (2004), 'Innovation generation in supply chain relationships: a conceptual model and research propositions', *Journal of Academy of Marketing Science,* Vol. 32, No. 1, pp. 61–79; Johnsen, R.E. & D. Ford (2006), 'Interaction capability development of smaller suppliers in relationships with larger customers', *Industrial Marketing Management*, Vol. 35, pp. 1002–1015; Sobrero, M. & E.B. Roberts (2002), 'Strategic management of supplier–manufacturer relations in new product development', *Research Policy*, Vol. 31, No. 1, pp. 159–182.

68   Schiele, H. (2007), 'Supply management maturity, cost savings and purchasing absorptive capacity: testing the procurement-performance link', *Journal of Purchasing & Supply Management,* Vol. 13, No. 4, pp. 274–293.

69   Paulraj, A. et al. (2006), *op. cit.*, pp. 107–122; Telgen, J. & C. Pop Sitar (2001), *op. cit.,* pp. 803–813; Van Weele, A.J., F.A. Rozemeijer & G. Rietveld (1998), *op. cit.*, pp. 515–523.

70   Telgen, J. & C. Pop Sitar (2001), *op. cit.*

71   Kotabe, M. & R. Mudambi (2009), 'Global sourcing and value creation: opportunities and challenges', *Journal of International Management*, Vol. 15, No. 2, pp. 121–125.

15 Multi-Stakeholder Initiatives in Cotton Value Chains: Towards a Theoretical Framework and a Methodology

PETER LUND-THOMSEN[*]

Keywords

Multi-stakeholder initiatives, global value chains, cotton, West Africa, South Asia.

Introduction

The last decade has seen a proliferation of multi-stakeholder initiatives (MSI) aimed at improving working conditions and reducing environmental pollution in export-oriented industries in developing countries.[1] This proliferation of MSIs is taking place in a context dominated by the liberalization of international trade, privatization of state enterprises, deregulation of developing country economies, and the rise of global supply chains.[2] In this context, MSIs – as a form of co-regulation – are seen as an important alternative to corporate self-regulation through the implementation of codes of conduct in global supply chains. Company codes of conduct are voluntary social and environmental guidelines adopted by developed country firms that they require their developing country suppliers to abide by. These codes have thus been criticized for (i) mainly reflecting the interests of developed country consumers/interest organizations, (ii) not giving local producers and workers any say in their formulation, (iii) only bringing about limited improvements in the work and environmental conditions of local producers and workers, and (iv) excluding small-scale producers from the supply chain as they might not have technical capacity or resources to comply with such codes.[3] As social and environmental standard-setting bodies, MSIs are thought to be more inclusive in terms of stakeholder participation. They are often portrayed as more legitimate, as they include civil society participation. They are considered to have the potential to ratchet up standards, as they are jointly implemented by public and private actors. Finally, they are perceived as

* Associate Professor Peter Lund-Thomsen, Center for Corporate Social Responsibility, Copenhagen Business School, Porcelænshaven 18A, 2000 Frederiksberg. Email: plt.ikl@cbs.dk. Telephone: 00 45 38 15 31 92.

promoting innovative solutions to complex challenges arising from the economic, social, and environmental externalities related to industrial production in global value chains.[4] Yet, more critical recent work suggests that MSIs may not live up to their promises, because independent civil society monitoring of standards implementation is often limited, all relevant stakeholders may still not be represented at the negotiating table (e.g., small farmers from developing countries), or may be incorporated in a way that delegitimizes their interests.[5] At present, however, we still lack more detailed studies of (i) whether MSIs are indeed able to live up to their promise of being a more democratic, participatory, and legitimate form of social and environmental standard setting, and (ii) whether the political processes through which MSIs shape standard setting, implementation, and monitoring affect the income, work, and environmental conditions of local producers and workers in developing countries in any way.

In this chapter, I make a contribution towards filling this gap in the literature on MSIs. I argue that it is necessary to connect two different strands in the literature on MSIs that have so far not been explicitly linked. One strand relates to the *political processes* through which MSIs are formulated, implemented, and monitored, and the other to the *effects* that voluntary social and environmental standards have on the income, work, and environmental conditions of local producers and workers in developing countries. I do this by creating an integrated analytical framework that combines insights from these two different literatures and then demonstrate how this framework might be applied to analysing a particular value chain, the cotton value chain, in two different regional contexts: West Africa and South Asia. This is done by outlining a detailed methodology that might be used in an empirical investigation of two key research questions that are based on the main concerns identified in the above literatures: (i) how are the production criteria of sustainable cotton MSIs formulated, implemented, monitored, and their impact assessed in different regional contexts (in this case, West Africa and South Asia)? and (ii) what difference, if any, does MSI implementation make for the income, work, and environmental conditions of cotton farmers and on-farm workers in these regional contexts?

The chapter is structured as follows. The first section introduces the integrated theoretical framework on MSIs. The next session discusses why this framework should be applied in the regional contexts of West Africa and South Asia. Third, the chapter outlines a suggested methodology for combining the analysis of the political evolution and effects of MSIs in these contexts before analysing the practical feasibility and ethical implications of undertaking such an analysis. Finally, the conclusion summarizes the main findings of the chapter.

Towards an Integrated Theoretical Framework

According to Tallontire and Tallontire et al., it is possible to analyse whether MSIs are fulfilling their potential for enabling a more participatory, transparent, and legitimate approach to standard/setting by analysing the legislative function of MSIs (how are they formulated?), the executive function of MSIs (how are they implemented?), and the judicial function of MSIs (how is compliance monitored and impact assessed?).[6] This analysis has been extended by Nelson et al. (forthcoming) who argue that the legislative, executive, and judicial processes of MSIs take place in (a) different spaces (i.e., decision-making fora), in different geographical places (e.g., in both the developed and the developing world); (c) are mediated by different power relations (in terms of the inclusion/exclusion of particular issues and actors from these processes); and take on different pathways (i.e., change over time). Combining the work of Tallontire and Nelson et al. we can thus identify a series of questions through which it is possible to analyse how the legislative, executive, and judicial functions of MSIs evolve in different spaces, across different geographical contexts, and take on different pathways.[7]

We can link the above framework on the political evolution of MSIs to an understanding of whether MSIs actually make any difference to the income, work, and environmental conditions of workers in developing countries. This can be done with reference to the literatures on global value chains, industrial upgrading strategies, local institutional contexts, and the agency of workers in developing countries. The global value chain literature has been particularly useful in highlighting how power is exercised in global production networks linking dispersed consumers and international buyers in developed countries with local producers and workers in the developing world. Power is here understood as the ability of internationally branded lead firms to coordinate such networks, determining what is to be produced, where, when, how, by whom, in which quantity, and at what price.[8] The introduction of MSIs can thus been seen as part of the broader international context that affects power relations in global value chains. At one extreme, MSIs could promote fair trade based on a vision of empowering small-scale agricultural producers in developing countries through long-term trading relationships, stability of demand, and a minimum price provided to local producers. This value chain would be dominated by social economy actors such as cooperatives in developing countries and alternative trade organizations/NGOs/small fair trade shops in the developed world. At the other extreme, MSIs could aim to promote a vision of ethical trade where global value chains might be dominated by corporate actors such as internationally branded buyers. These buyers will typically require their large-scale suppliers, e.g., plantations, to

Table 15.1 An analytical framework for understanding the evolution of MSIs

	Legislative	Executive	Judicial
Spaces	In which spaces are MSI standards formulated?	In which spaces are MSIs implemented?	In which spaces are MSI monitored/their impact assessed?
Places	In which places are MSI standards formulated?	In which places are MSIs implemented?	In which places are MSIs monitored/their impact assessed?
Power relations	Who/which issues are included in/excluded from the process of MSI formulation?	Who/which issues are included in/excluded from the process of MSI implementation?	Who/which issues are included in/ excluded from the process of monitoring/impact assessment?
Pathways	When was/is the MSI standard formulated?	When was/is the MSI implemented?	When was/is the MSI monitored/its impact assessed?

abide by their social and environmental guidelines. In such chains, production is for the mass market, demand changes, and prices fluctuate.[9]

Participation in MSIs could also be seen as a form of industrial upgrading. According to Humphrey and Schmitz, industrial upgrading refers to local producers making better products, more efficiently, moving into higher aspects of the global value chain such as design and marketing of products, or using skills gained in sector in order to move into another sector.[10] Participation in MSIs might allow local producers to improve the quality of their products, raise their productivity levels, and reduce environmental risks and labour rights violations related to production. However, MSIs could also exclude small-scale producers from chain participation as they might not have the financial or organizational capacity to meet the criteria for sustainable production laid down in MSIs. As a result, farmers might be forced to 'downgrade'. Downgrading here refers to improving producer competitiveness by lowering product quality, selling to less demanding international buyers, squeezing workers wages, and letting them to work under hazardous environmental conditions.[11]

The institutional contexts in which MSIs become embedded may also play an important role in co-determining the income, work, and environmental conditions of small-scale producers and workers in developing countries. By institutions we here mean the formal and informal rules of the game that govern production at the international, national, and local levels.[12] At the international level, subsidies provided to developed country producers might deflate the prices that developing country producers receive for their products.[13] At the national level, governments in the developing world might tightly control the cotton production chain, which could limit the ability of MSIs to establish alternative ways of producing sustainable cotton. They might also favour a more market-based environment where MSIs would have greater influence in terms of their ability to establish alternative sustainable cotton supply chains.[14] Finally, at the local level, small-scale producers and workers might co-determine their income, work, and environmental conditions.[15] Drawing on the work of Riisgaard et al. and Bolwig et al., we can say that they may choose to engage in either conventional cotton supply chains or those created by sustainable cotton MSIs.[16] Second, they may choose to sell the sustainable cotton they produce in the open market or to the MSI-created supply chain. Finally, cotton farmers and on-farm workers may opt in or out of cotton production altogether based on the financial (unviability) of producing this crop.

MSIs in the Cotton Value Chain of West Africa and South Asia

In the previous section, an analytical framework was outlined that combined a consideration of the evolution of political processes within MSIs and their effects on farmers and on-farm workers in developing countries. The next section explains why West Africa and South Asia as regional contexts are particularly important for the study of the political evolution and effects of sustainable cotton value chain MSIs. The fact that the cotton value chains in West Africa and South Asia are used as examples here does not necessarily mean that the theoretical framework outlined above cannot be applied to other agro-industrial value chains and institutional contexts. In fact, it would be interesting to test its applicability to other chains and contexts. Reference to the West African and South Asian contexts is only intended to illustrate why a comparative analysis of the political evolution and the effects of MSIs might be particularly relevant in these regions.

From a societal perspective, cotton production in West Africa and South Asia is important, because the livelihoods of millions of poor farmers depend upon it, because cotton production is a vital source of foreign currency earnings for these countries, and since cotton farmers and on-farm workers risk their lives producing cotton under hazardous social and environmental conditions.[17] The emergence of MSIs in the cotton industry only dates back to 2005 when the Better Cotton Initiative (BCI) was formed and the Fairtrade Labelling Organization[†] (FLO) launched the first standard for fair trade cotton. Both MSIs have recently completed their first "sustainable cotton harvest" which makes it possible to make an in-depth investigation of both their institutional evolution and their effects in West Africa and South Asia.

West Africa and South Asia are also the main regions where the Better Cotton Initiative is under implementation. Both regions are highly dependent on cotton production for foreign currency earnings and employment. They are susceptible to the adverse effects of depressed prices due to EU/US subsidies on cotton production. Finally, the labour-intensive, handpicking of cotton is used during the harvesting season, significantly increasing the risk of pesticide poisoning as small-scale farmers and farmworkers generally do not wear protective equipment.[18] Hence, if MSIs do have a significant impact on the health and well-being of these lower-level actors in the cotton value chain, we should be able to observe it in both the South Asian and West African contexts.

However, there are also significant differences *between* West Africa and South Asia and *within* both regions that pose particular challenges for the implementation of MSIs. First, while the cotton supply chain in West Africa is heavily dominated by national or semi-privatized cotton companies, the cotton produced is not used domestically but instead exported via international agricultural commodity trading companies to textile producers around the world.[19] By contrast, in South Asia, domestically produced cotton mostly feeds into national-level textile chains where many large-scale, sometimes vertically integrated textile/garment companies supply directly to internationally leading branded companies.[20] This difference means that the successful implementation of MSIs in West Africa require close cooperation with government agencies, whereas MSIs need to interface to a greater extent with the private sector actors in South Asia. Within West Africa and South Asia, it might be useful to focus on Mali, Benin, Pakistan, and India as these countries may be considered critical cases to the study of MSIs in the cotton value chains of these two regions. In other words, due to their different characteristics, it becomes possible to make wider claims about the significance of MSIs in South Asia and West Africa. In Pakistan, MSIs have to de-facto establish minimum social and environmental standards, as agricultural workers are not protected by any labour laws. By contrast, in India, MSIs face the challenge of either enhancing or undermining existing efforts of the Indian national government to improve the social and environmental conditions of farmers and on-farm workers. In Mali, MSIs have no option but to work in collaboration with the country's recently privatized, monopoly cotton company whereas its counterpart in Benin has been privatized for a longer time, leaving it more susceptible to CSR pressures of its international investors.

---

†   The FLO has 25 member organizations and formulates international fair trade standards and provide assistance to fair trade producers (www.fairtrade.net/about_us.html, accessed 21 January 2012).

A Methodology for Studying the Evolution and Effects of MSIs

The previous section tried to illustrate why it is important to consider the similarities and the differences in the institutional contexts within which MSIs are implemented, as these might significantly influence the political evolution and the effects of MSIs within these contexts. This section sets out a methodology that could be used to empirically investigate both the political processes and the effects of sustainable cotton value chain MSIs in West Africa and South Asia.

In applying the integrated theoretical framework to study the cotton value chains of West Africa and South Asia, employing a comparative, multiple case study design might be helpful.[21] It would be useful in establishing the common and differential factors that are likely to affect the (un)successful implementation of MSIs in both regions. Using a largely similar data generation method in both locations, the comparative, multiple case study design allows for an identification of the particular conditions under which MSIs improve or worsen the income, work, and environmental conditions of cotton farmers and on-farm workers. In this way, it becomes possible to acquire a deeper appreciation of how different national contexts facilitate or constrain MSI implementation. Within this broader research design, it is possible to develop a methodology for studying the evolution of the political processes within MSIs and their external effects on West African and South Asian farm and on-farm workers through four consecutive steps. These include the analysis of (i) legislative governance, (ii) executive governance, (iii) judicial governance, and (iv) a preliminary assessment of MSI effects.

STEP 1: "LEGISLATIVE GOVERNANCE" – HOW ARE THE BETTER COTTON INITIATIVE'S/THE FAIRTRADE LABELLING ORGANIZATION'S CRITERIA FOR SUSTAINABLE COTTON PRODUCTION FORMULATED?

Regarding *legislative governance*, the suggested methodology would start with a mapping of the spaces, geographical places, and particular times at which the BCI's/FLO's criteria for sustainable cotton production were formulated as well as the power relations involved in this exercise. Initially, this could happen through interviews in *Europe/North America*. Interviews could be undertaken with the BCI/FLO secretariats about the main factors leading to the formulation of sustainable cotton initiatives, how these initiatives were established in practice, what their main decision-making bodies are, how decisions are made in these fora, how their sustainable cotton criteria were developed, and what the main challenges in formulating these criteria were. In addition, it would be important to talk to a mixture of the private sector, intergovernmental, and civil society stakeholders involved in the formulation of these sustainable cotton initiatives, asking them how and why they became involved in the process, what their main interests were in the BCI's/FLO's work, how they participated in the formulation of criteria for sustainable cotton production, what the main challenges were in this process, and whether they felt that their concerns were taken into account. Next the methodology would involve interviews *in Mali, Benin, Pakistan, and India*, including private sector, government, and civil society stakeholders that took part in regional working groups or provided input to the process of formulated the BCI's/FLO's criteria for sustainable cotton production. Key themes to explore in these interviews would be how they came to be involved in these processes, why they took part, which voices were heard and what issues discussed, and whether the final BCI/FLO criteria reflected the key priorities that they believed were important in their particular contexts. A final part of the methodology related to investigating legislative governance would be to undertake a *review of policy documents*. This would include a review of the websites and publicly available information that documents the evolution of the FLO/BCI's sustainable production criteria, including the reports of the BCI's regional working groups in West Africa and South Asia, the external evaluation of the BCI's work between 2007 and 2009, and the recent impact assessment of FLO's sustainable cotton projects in West Africa and India.

STEP 2: "EXECUTIVE GOVERNANCE" – HOW ARE THE BETTER COTTON INITIATIVE'S/THE FAIRTRADE LABELLING ORGANIZATION'S SUSTAINABLE COTTON PROJECTS IMPLEMENTED IN MALI AND INDIA?

Here the methodology would focus on Mali and India as the two sites for investigating how the BCI's and FLO's sustainable cotton projects have been institutionalized, as these are the only countries in the world where both the BCI's and the FLO's projects have so far been *simultaneously* implemented. In India, the state of Andra Pradesh would be chosen, as this is where the greatest diversity of FLO/BCI supported projects exists. It would here be possible to map the supply chains, the industrial upgrading strategies used by the BCI/FLO supported projects, and the inclusion/exclusion of particular actors from these chains due to MSI implementation. It would thus be possible to map the *chains* that FLO-certified and BCI-sponsored initiatives are trying to develop. In India and Mali, this could involve tracing how cotton is transported from the farm level to the ginning mills, marketed, and subsequently sold in domestic and international markets. In Mali, it would be important to interview the former cotton monopoly company, CMDT, asking how it structures a conventional cotton supply chain by supplying inputs and credits to farmers and arranging for the transportation of the picked cotton from farm-level to local ginners, and subsequently markets and sells the cotton abroad. In addition, questions could be asked about how the CMDT helps the FLO/BCI establish alternative supply chains for sustainable cotton, how CMDT works together with the FLO/BCI, and what the CMDT views as the strengths and weaknesses of the BCI/FLO-supported initiatives versus conventional cotton production in Mali. In addition, it would be important to talk to local cooperatives about how they produce sustainable cotton, the challenges they face in this work, their relationship with Solidaridad (the NGO implementing both BCI/FLO-sponsored initiatives), and how they work together with village-based CMDT representatives. In India, it would be necessary to speak intermediary organizations such as Zameen Organics, Chetna Organic Farmers Cooperative, and Agrocel about how they structure the chain upstream vis-à-vis local farmers, and market and sell this cotton downstream to local textile manufacturers such as Rajlakshmi Mills and Super Spinning Mills. In particular, it would be important to clarify how this differs from a conventional supply chain for cotton as it moves from the farm-level to local ginning factories. In terms of *producer upgrading*, village-based cooperatives in Mali and the BCI/FLO-sponsored support organization, Solidaridad, as well as the intermediary organizations in Andra Pradesh, India, could be interviewed about how they organize farmers, attempt to improve their organizational capacity, raise awareness of their position in the supply chain, lower their input costs, and reduce the exposure of farmers/workers to hazardous substances.

Regarding the question of how *international and national-level contextual factors* affect the implementation of MSIs in West Africa and South Asia, a review could be conducted of publicly available reports, journal articles, and books. The review could focus on how the World Trade Organization's liberalization policies and the subsidies provided to US and European producers affect cotton and textile exports from West Africa and South Asia. It might also touch upon the national cotton policy documents of the Mali and Indian governments. Interviews could be undertaken with national-level cotton policymakers in the agricultural ministries, labour, and environmental ministries as well as NGOs (e.g., micro-credit and child labour), trade unions, and farmers' organizations in Mali and India. These interviews could focus on issues such as the national policy for the promotion of growth in the cotton sector, labour (e.g., bonded and child labour) and environmental laws (e.g., regarding the use of genetically modified organisms). They might also cover topics such as land ownership patterns, issues of ethnicity and caste in cotton production, farmers' access to credit, levels of debt, and inputs of fertilizers and pesticides.

STEP 3: "JUDICIAL GOVERNANCE" – HOW ARE THE BETTER COTTON INITIATIVE'S/THE FAIRTRADE LABELLING ORGANIZATION'S SUSTAINABLE COTTON PROJECTS MONITORED AND THEIR IMPACTS ASSESSED IN MALI AND INDIA?

Under judicial governance, an analysis could be made of how the FLO and BCI monitor conformity with their sustainable cotton production principles, and what sanctions (if any) exist in the case of non-compliance with their criteria for sustainable production. In relation to the FLO, this analysis could concentrate on understanding how the FLO-Cert – the independent auditing wing of the FLO – conducts initial audits to verify compliance with the fair trade cotton standard, how it issues fair trade certificates, and how it deals with complaints against its work, and continue supervision of the production through a series of surveillance activities. It would also be possible to map how BCI-supported projects conduct their own regular monitoring by letting local farmers gather data on a range of indicators with the aim of learning from each other and collaborating in finding new ways of improving their cotton growing methods. These data are then gathered by the local implementing partner (WWF Pakistan/Solidaridad), the regional coordinator, and presented in the BCI's annual report. In relation to impact assessment this is an area which is under development in both the FLO and the BCI. It would be important to look at how the FLO and BCI are attempting to bring their impact assessment into conformity with the draft impact assessment code of ISEAL. The ISEAL Alliance is a global association that develops guidance and helps strengthen the impact of voluntary social and environmental standards implemented in the agricultural sectors of developing countries.

STEP 4: DO THE BETTER COTTON INITIATIVE'S/THE FAIRTRADE LABELLING ORGANIZATION'S PROJECTS FOR SUSTAINABLE COTTON PRODUCTION MAKE ANY DIFFERENCE TO THE INCOME, WORK, AND ENVIRONMENTAL CONDITIONS OF FARMERS AND ON-FARM WORKERS IN MALI AND INDIA?

In Mali and India, a preliminary assessment could be made of effects of the sustainable cotton MSI projects on the income, work and environmental conditions of farmers and on-farm workers. These are implemented by the local-level partners of the BCI and the FLO. In terms of research strategy, a maximum variation case study sampling strategy could be employed in choosing these initiatives. Together with a control group of farmers/workers engaged in conventional cotton production these could be purposefully selected to give a sense of the likely range of incomes, work, and environmental conditions of local cotton farmers or workers in Mali and India. For example, this might involve a combination of 30 individual farmer interviews and/or on-farm worker interviews for each initiative/the control group (ensuring a balance in terms of gender, age, etc.), and four focus interviews with farmers/workers in each initiative asking about their views of the BCI and FLO-supported initiatives.

In individual interviews, local farmers and on-farm workers could be asked whether and if so why they choose to sell their cotton in the FLO/BCI-sponsored chain, or why they choose to opt in or out of the BCI/FLO initiatives. Farmers/workers in these initiatives and the control group could also be interviewed about possible changes on a variety of indicators after the introduction of the same local-level MSI projects referred to above. This could include the cotton rates received, personal monthly income, monthly expenditures, costs associated with purchase of seeds/fertilizers/chemicals, access to credits, possible savings, debts accruing from the purchase of these inputs, and other assets in the form of land, housing, animals, etc. In terms of labour conditions, questions could be asked about changes observed after the introduction of local-level MSI projects. In particular, local farmers and on-farm workers could be interviewed about their daily working hours, the number of days worked in a week, occupational health and safety risks associated with cotton spraying, and access to medical facilities. It would also be useful if these interviews addressed topics such as support for children's schooling, the presence/absence of forced labour/child labour in the cotton fields, and possibilities for collectively organizing farmer organizations or trade unions. In environmental terms, the questionnaire should cover questions related to possible water savings, changes in the amount of pesticides/fertilizers used, storage of rainwater, etc.

In focus group interviews, it would be important to probe farmers'/farmworkers' collective perceptions of whether the initiatives have increased their ability to collectively organize with the aim of strengthening their bargaining position, reducing input prices, obtaining better sales prices, achieving economies of scale, developing their communities via joint infrastructure projects, etc. Their views should be sought on the decision-making processes related to sustainable cotton projects whether in relation to their support agencies, traders, or internally within the "democratic" farmer cooperatives, inquiring about their perception of the advantages and disadvantages of taking part in such alternative production schemes vs. participation in conventional cotton production.

The Methodology's Practical Feasibility and Ethical Considerations

In the previous section, I pointed towards a four-step methodology that might make it possible to undertake a combined analysis of the evolution of political processes within MSIs and their effects on farmers and on-farm workers in two specific institutional contexts. In doing so, I suggested that a comparative approach to studying both the institutionalization of MSIs and their effects within different regional contexts might be particularly helpful in improving our understanding of the potential and limits of MSIs as a policy instrument aimed at improving sustainable value chain management. In this section, I discuss whether it is at all feasible to employ such a methodology. All too often using a particular methodology in undertaking fieldwork in developing country contexts might seem desirable. However, there are very "real-life" questions of how to access different stakeholders involved in global manufacturing chains and ethical issues that need to be addressed if the proposed research is not to cause more harm than good through its implementation. I will start here with the practical feasibility of undertaking such a study and then turn to the ethical questions that arise during this kind of research.

ACCESS TO STAKEHOLDERS ALONG THE VALUE CHAIN

Regarding access to stakeholders along the (in this example, cotton) value chain, it would be important to seek and obtain the support of the MSIs themselves (here, the FLO and BCI) in relation to undertaking the study and the proposed fieldwork. Without support from the MSIs, it would be close to impossible to undertake such a study, because access to their staff, member firms, and farmer/on-farm beneficiaries is largely dependent upon the consent of the MSI. Accessing MSIs could either be done through personal connections – for example, a member of the research team having had previous contact with MSI staff. Or it can be done by writing an e-mail or official communication to the MSI secretariat, followed up by phone calls, explaining the intended purpose of undertaking the study, how the study might benefit the MSI, the level of expected involvement of the MSI, and how the results might be fed back to the MSI and its members. In this connection, it is sometimes a good idea to initially approach the MSI, asking for their input to the design of the study so that it may be of use from both an academic and an MSI-policy perspective. Project findings could also communicated to the MSIs through briefing papers and through mid-term and end-of-project workshops. In all instances, time is often a "scarce" resource for underfunded and overworked MSI staff. Hence, it is important from the beginning to consider how to minimize interruptions to the daily work routines of MSI staff and also consider applying for funds that could cover the time MSI staff spend on assisting research teams in the field, as MSIs might not themselves be able to cover these expenditures through their own budgets.

Regarding access to stakeholders at the developing country end of the value chain, this often turns out to be a particularly challenging task when studying MSI initiatives. Once permission has been obtained from the MSI headquarters, it is often possible to get an introduction to field-level staff with whom most of the subsequent interaction takes place during the study. However, interviewing member firms or local industry associations that also form part of MSIs can sometimes be tricky. For many developing country firms supplying international markets in Western Europe or the United States, there is a very real concern about how the information they provide will be used. Often international NGOs publish reports of poor work conditions in developing country supply chains, and this may have the consequence of straining or directly putting an end to supplier–buyer relations depending upon how international buyers react to the publication of such reports. For developing country suppliers, it may thus be hard to distinguish between researchers from NGOs who aim to use the information obtained to apply pressure on local manufacturers to improve work conditions through naming and shaming techniques, and academics who are more interested in using the information for publication and/ or teaching purposes. Thus, for suppliers to let themselves be interviewed, there often has to be a direct business incentive to do so. Hence, it is often a good idea to first enter into contact with the international buyers of these local suppliers, introduce the purpose of the research, and ask for their help in accessing their developing country suppliers. If such an introduction is given, developing country suppliers will rarely refuse to give an interview, although it may sometimes be difficult for them to do so at the particular time requested given the many, simultaneous commitments that they are trying to address – e.g., buyer visits, relations with their own suppliers, overseas travels to trade fairs, etc.

Accessing workers can also be a very challenging task when studying MSIs in developing country settings. Local manufacturers and contractors/subcontractors are unlikely to welcome their workers being interviewed by outsiders. Hence, it is usually a good idea to enter into alliances with local research institutes, NGOs, or trade unions that are well connected in the communities in which the workers live with their families. They will often have a very good idea about how to access farmers and on-farm workers in such a way that these stakeholders will be able to speak their mind freely. In this connection, it is crucial that workers are not interviewed in the presence of their employers, contractors or others that might affect their responses. Worker interviews should preferably take place away from the work premises – for example, in the farmers'/on-farm workers' own homes, in public lunch places or other locations where these stakeholders will be able to speak freely to the interviewers. Otherwise the information obtained may not accurately reflect their views.

ETHICAL CONSIDERATIONS

When planning interviews (with brands, suppliers, contractors, MSI staff, farmers, on-farm workers or other stakeholders) as suggested in the above methodology, ethical considerations should be taken into account. In general, it is recommended that MSI researchers should follow the informed consent and no harm clauses – i.e., that the interviewees will be informed of the purpose of the research, that their identities will remain anonymous, that they have the right to refuse participation (or recording of the interview), stop the interview (including the recording) at any time, and that the information will stored in a safe way. However, since many of the farmers and on-farm workers may be illiterate, it will be necessary to orally explain the above issues and secure their consent in their own local languages through resource counterparts – i.e., local coordinators and field assistants.

A particular concern is interviews with farmers and workers participating in the various sustainable cotton initiatives, as they might be pressurized by project staff and/or contractors in the cotton chain not to convey particular types of information that could cast the initiatives in a negative light. This issue can be addressed by interviewing farmers and workers in their own homes without the presence of project staff or contractors to ensure that interviewees feel at ease. In this connection, it is also important to spend a lot of time training interviewers and conducting test interviews in cooperation with partner organizations in developing countries.

An additional benefit of carrying out interviews with farmers and on-farm workers in their own communities is that transportation costs associated with their travel can be reduced. It might also be a good idea to limit the length of individual and focus group interviews to a maximum of 1 hour, in order to keep any disruption to interviewees' daily work, routines, and family life to an absolute minimum. An additional consideration is whether to compensate farmers and on-farm workers for their time spent in interviews. On the one hand, compensating them for their time may be ethical from the viewpoint of making up for any loss of income they may suffer as a consequence of taking part in the interview. However, on the other hand, farmers and on-farm workers may come to expect being compensated for their time. This could have the unintended consequence that local NGOs and research institutes may not be able to conduct studies in these communities in the future as they may not possess the resources required to compensate farmers and on-farm workers for their time. Hence, the recommendation here is that no remuneration should be given to farmers and/or on-farm workers, but that the research team instead should seek to provide feedback from their findings to relevant stakeholders, providing specific recommendations on how the situation of farmers and on-farm workers can be improved as part of ongoing MSI interventions.

In the case of cotton and other forms of agro-industrial production, there is also a risk that a research team may come across instances of bonded child workers taking part in cotton-picking. In such instances, it is recommended that permission is sought from the child's parent to interview them in the parent's presence so that the children may not feel under undue pressure from the research team. However, it may not always be desirable to inform the sustainable cotton initiatives of the presence of bonded child workers on their cotton farms as this could have negative repercussions for children identified since the initiatives are unlikely to welcome research findings that display serious violations of their criteria for sustainable cotton production. If such instances are indeed discovered, a feasible alternative may be to inform other local-level support organizations that can help these children (e.g., Save the Children).

Finally, as investigating the effects of MSIs on local farmers and on-farm workers is likely to be fraught with ethical dilemmas, it might be a good idea to establish an ethical review committee which can be used to give input into the suggested methodology and also to provide assistance in case of "ethical emergencies," such as the research team identifying bonded child labourers during their study. At present, this is a standard requirement in the UK and at EU level, but it is still not a widespread practice in all countries.

Conclusion

In this chapter, it was argued that two different lines of research have so far dominated academic and policy-level thinking about MSIs aimed at improving sustainable value chain management. The first relates to the political level processes through which MSIs are formulated, implemented, and monitored. The second has to do with the literature that tries to assess the impacts MSIs have on local firms, farmers, and workers in developing country settings. In this chapter, a preliminary theoretical framework was outlined for combining these types of analysis: horizontal analysis of the spaces, places, pathways, and power relations in legislative, judicial, and executive governance of MSIs, and vertical analysis of the power relations, upgrading, and standard-setting functions in global value chains. In addition, a detailed methodology was outlined for how this framework might be employed to empirically investigate how MSIs are institutionalized within a given value chain (the cotton value chain) and different regional contexts of production (South Asia and West Africa). Finally, it was argued that consideration must be paid to both the practical feasibility of undertaking such research projects and to the many ethical dilemmas that are likely to arise during a combined study of the political evolution of MSIs and their effects on local firms, farmers, and workers in developing country contexts. It is hoped that the theoretical framework, institutional context descriptions, methodology and practical-ethical challenges outlined in this chapter may be of use to academics, practitioners, Ph.D. and other types of students interested in pursuing further research in the political processes surrounding the evolution and effects of sustainable value chain MSIs in developing country contexts.

Notes

1   Martens, J. (2007), *Multi-Stakeholder Partnerships – Future Models of Multilateralism?* Dialogue on Globalization, Occasional Papers, no. 29, Friedrich Ebert Stiftung, Berlin.

2   Utting, P. and Zammit, A. (2009), "United Nations business partnerships: good intentions and contradictory agendas", *Journal of Business Ethics*, Vol. 90, Supp. 1, pp. 39–56.

3   Ethical Trading Initiative (2006), *ETI Code of Labor Practice – Do Workers Really Benefit?*, Institute of Development Studies, Sussex; Barrientos, S. and Smith, S. (2007), "Do workers benefit from ethical trade? Assessing codes of labour practice in global production systems", *Third World Quarterly*, Vol. 28, No. 4, pp. 713–729; Nelson, V. et al. (2007), "The impacts of codes of practice on worker /livelihoods: empirical evidence from the South African wine and Kenyan cut flower industries", *Journal of Corporate Citizenship*, Vol. 28, No. 4, pp. 61–72; Lund-Thomsen, P. (2008), "The global sourcing and codes of conduct debate: five myths and five recommendations", *Development and Change*, Vol. 39, No. 6, pp. 1005–1018; Lund-Thomsen, P. (2009), "Assessing the impact of public-private partnerships in the global South: the case of the Kasur tanneries pollution control project", *Journal of Business Ethics*, Vol. 90, Supp. 1, pp. 57–78.

4   Dolan C.S. and Opondo, M. (2005), "Seeking common ground: multi-stakeholder processes in Kenya's cut flower industry", *Journal of Corporate Citizenship*, Vol. 18, pp. 87–98; Lund-Thomsen, P. and Nadvi, K. (2010), "Clusters, chains and compliance: governance and corporate social responsibility in the South Asian football manufacturing industry", *Journal of Business Ethics*, Vol. 93, Supp. 2, pp. 201–222; Nelson, V. et al. (forthcoming), "Pathways of transformation or transgression? Power relations, ethical space and labour rights in Kenyan cut flower value chains", in M. Goodman and C. Sage (eds.) *Food Transgressions: Making Sense of Contemporary Food Politics*, Ashgate, Aldershot.

5   Cheyns, E. (2011), "Multi-stakeholder initiatives for sustainable agriculture: the limits of the 'Inclusiveness Paradigm'", in S. Ponte et al. (eds.), *Governing through Standards – Origins, Drivers and Limitations*, Palgrave Macmillan, London, pp. 210–235; Fuchs, D. et al. (2011), "Actors in

private food governance: the legitimacy of retail standards and multistakeholder initiatives with civil society participation", *Agriculture and Human Values*, Vol. 28, No. 1, pp. 353–367.

6   Tallontire, A. (2007), "CSR and regulation: towards a framework for understanding private standards initiatives in the agri-food chain", *Third World Quarterly*, Vol. 28, No. 4, pp. 775–791; Tallontire, A. et al. (2011), "Beyond the vertical? Using value chains and governance as a framework to analyse private standard initiatives in agri-food chains", *Agriculture and Human Values*, Vol. 28, No. 3, pp. 427–411.

7   Tallontire, *op. cit.* Nelson et al., forthcoming, *op. cit.*

8   Schmitz, H. (2004), *Local Enterprises in the Global Economy: Issues of Governance and Upgrading*, Edward Elgar, Cheltenham; Nadvi, K. (2008), "Global standards, global governance and the organisation of global value chains", *Journal of Economic Geography*, Vol. 8, No. 3, pp. 323–343.

9   Reed, D. (2009), "What do corporations have to do with fair trade? Positive and normative analysis from a value chain perspective", *Journal of Business Ethics*, Vol. 86, Supp. 1, pp. 3–26.

10   Humphrey, J. and Schmitz, H. (2002), "How does insertion in global value chains affect upgrading in industrial clusters?", *Regional Studies*, Vol. 36, No. 9, pp. 1017–1027.

11   Gibbon, P. and Ponte, S. (2005), *Trading Down: Africa, Value Chains and the Global Economy*, Temple University Press, Philadelphia.

12   Neilson, J. and Pritchard, B. (2009), *Value Chain Struggles: Institutions and Governance in the Plantations of South India*, Wiley-Blackwell, London.

13   Basset, T.J. (2010), "Slim pickings: fair trade cotton in West Africa", *Geoforum*, Vol. 41, No. 1, pp. 44–55.

14   Bitzer, V. and Glasbergen, P. (2010), "Partnerships for sustainable change in cotton: an institutional analysis of African cases", *Journal of Business Ethics*, Vol. 93, Supp. 2, pp. 223–240.

15   Lund-Thomsen, P. et al. (2011), *Labor in Global Production Networks: A Comparative Study of Workers Conditions in Football Manufacturing in China, India, and Pakistan*, Center for Corporate Social Responsibility/Center for Business and Development Studies, Working Paper no. 01–2011, Copenhagen Business School, Copenhagen.

16   Riisgaard, L. et al. (2010), "Integrating poverty and environmental concerns into value chain analysis: a strategic guide and practical framework", *Development Policy Review*, Vol. 28, No. 2, pp. 195–216; Bolwig, S. et al. (2010), "Integrating poverty and environmental concerns into value-chain analysis: a conceptual framework", *Development Policy Review*, Vol. 28, No. 2, pp. 173–194.

17   Larsen, M. (2008), "The global cotton market and cotton sector reforms in Sub-Saharan Africa", in N. Fold and M. Larsen, *Globalization and Restructuring of African Commodity Flows*, Nordiska Afrika Institutet, Uppsala, pp. 156–183; Worldwide Fund for Nature (WWF) (2009), *Cleaner, Greener Cotton – Impact and Better Management Practices*, WWF, Zeist.

18   Better Cotton Initiative (2006), *BCI Scoping Research on Labor and Social Issues in Global Cotton Cultivation – Final Report to BCI Steering Committee*, Ergon, London.

19   Bitzer and Glasbergen, *op. cit.*

20   Banuri, T. (1998), *Cotton and Textiles in Pakistan*, Report prepared for the United Nations Environment Programme, UNEP, Nairobi.

21   Bryman, A. (2008), *Social Research Methods*, 3rd edn., Oxford University Press, Oxford.

16 Barriers and Facilitators to Developing Sustainable Networks: UK Local and Regional Food*

MARTIN HINGLEY† AND ADAM LINDGREEN‡

Keywords

Sustainable, food, barriers, facilitators, local, regional, UK.

Introduction

This chapter focuses on the role of local and regional food businesses within networks to present a sustainable food market. Interest in and demand for local and regional food is well documented, and the argument for (socially and environmentally) sustainable food has been well made. What remains unclear is how to create an environment that encourages the success of local and regional food. Is stimulation and support from local and regional authorities and support organisations necessary, or is their effect minimal and overly bureaucratic? Furthermore, what roles do businesses themselves play in their success; what factors support or hinder development? These issues are crucial, considering the extensive assistance granted to small rural food enterprises, at local, regional, national and European levels. If this assistance is not effective, it may be time to consider other means to support food chain sustainability and thus relieve some of the burden on resource-strapped public sector support agencies.

We begin with consumer and market rationales for the development of local and regional foods. Then we outline issues of business development from a corporate and network approach, consider the importance of the interplay of channel organisations

*   Parts of this chapter have appeared in Hingley, M. (2010), Networks in socially embedded local food supply: The case of retailer co-operatives, *Journal of Business Market Management*, 4 (3), 111–128; Hingley, M., Boone, J. and Lindgreen, A. (2010), Development of local and regional food networks: Cases from the UK, *Proceedings of the 26th Annual Conference of the Industrial Marketing and Purchasing Group*, Corvinus University of Budapest, 2–4 September, 2010; Hingley, M.K., Lindgreen, A. and Beverland, M.B. (2010), Barriers to network innovation in U.K. ethnic fresh produce supply, *Entrepreneurship and Regional Development*, 22 (1), 77–96.

†   Professor Martin Hingley, Lincoln Business School, University of Lincoln, Brayford Pool, Lincoln LN6 7TS, UK. E-mail: mhingley@lincoln.ac.uk. Telephone: +44 (0) 1522 835683.

‡   Professor Adam Lindgreen, Cardiff Business School, Cardiff University, Aberconway Building, Colum Drive, Cardiff, CF10 3EU, UK. E-mail: LindgreenA@cardiff.ac.uk. Telephone: + 44 (0) 29 2087 6668.

and note their relative positioning, as influenced by channel and market power. We also review the changing business and support environment surrounding local and regional food network developments. In our methodological approach, we aim to consider both barriers to and facilitators of food network development, so we evaluate the contributions of various governmental, commercial and voluntary support agencies. Our empirical analysis draws on three representative local and regional food network cases in the UK. With a complementary mix of qualitative and quantitative methods, we gather data about these cases, then use market mapping to illustrate the roles of organisations in each case, along with their networks, core supply chain structures, the enabling environment and institutional roles for market development. In analysing each case and the cross-case findings, we lead into a discussion of barriers to and facilitators of development in local and regional food businesses in a network context. In the conclusion, we make several recommendations and pose managerial implications regarding the future development of local and regional food organisations and networks.

Consumer Interest in Local and Regional Food and Sustainable Consumption

Starting in the 1980s, chain retailers' national buying policies and centralised efficiency drives made localism and community-based businesses relatively unfashionable in the UK,[1] coinciding with the 'golden age' of supermarket growth.[2] This age has come to an end; the local food sector today is praised for offering a more environmentally and socially sustainable alternative to conventional food supply chains built around national sourcing.[3] Despite the recent economic downturn, UK consumers continue to express increasing interest in reconnecting with their food and the people, places and processes involved in local production and supply. Surveys of buyer attitudes suggest that local foods are perceived as offering higher quality than alternatives, and consumers appear to support local farmers.[4]

Food scares have also prompted consumer interest in the ability to trace food back to its individual source.[5] Demands for food of known provenance offer key market opportunities for small local food businesses that can communicate clear messages about their production origins and supply chain traceability. In turn, localised food networks have developed, and supermarkets have responded with policies to stock products sourced from a specified radius (e.g., 30, 50, 60 miles), county or region.[6] Then increased visibility and availability of local food has further fuelled demand. Even indications of support for the local economy have increased.[7]

Power and Network Relationships

Creating distribution networks that offer an alternative to national and international food retailing chains, as well as establishing some degree of (perhaps countervailing) market power, remain major challenges for small producers and their local/regional support organisations. However, it is important to understand the potential benefits of these efforts in a business network context, to fully appreciate the impact of power relationships and the role of lead organisations within networks.

Business relationships take place within a network context,[8] as aptly demonstrated by authors who contend that individual organisations and dyadic relationships are both part of networks of inter-relationships.[9] A network approach to supply chain relationships is borne out in practice in the agri-food industry, in which economic and trading circumstances have resulted in changes to organisational structures. Competition in the UK agri-food industry, for example, occurs between the supply networks led by national and multinational food retailers such as Tesco, J. Sainsbury and Asda. Each employs a supply hub, centred on its own middlemen.[10] These hubs enable regional distributions of national, international and regional suppliers' products, in conjunction with the retailers' regional distribution network.

Important to the discussion of food industry network relationships is the issue of power and where it lies. Power may have a negative influence, in that stronger network members benefit more than dependents, which can lead to breakdowns of network co-operation, trust and ultimately relationships.[11] Some food industry suppliers worry about the expression of retailer power allowed by the imbalance, as well as the potential for abuses of power.[12] However, others consider power imbalance to be a normal phenomenon,[13] so it appears more important to focus on managing that imbalance and ensuring that power is fluid and changeable among network members, who accordingly should adapt to changes in circumstance.[14] Weaker parties, such as small-scale suppliers, in relationships with more powerful channel buyers may have to accept an imbalance in decision-making power and rewards, but they also gain market stability and reduced transaction costs through their association with networks led by a powerful channel leader.[15] Success then depends on the intent of the powerful channel leader, whether benign, constructive and helpful; based on confrontation;[16] or actually destructive.[17] For reasons of self-interest, powerful or leading network members may act as 'blockers' or 'gatekeepers' and thus prevent co-operation and cohesion in the network.[18] In the UK food market, the main channel to consumers is large food retailing chains,[19] which act as gatekeepers between producers and consumers and thereby wield considerable power. In analysing the cases for this study, we identify principal stakeholders within networks related to local and regional food supply and their role in facilitating or hindering development.

Support for Local and Regional Food

The UK public authorities regard assistance to quality food producers as an important regional and local development issue. The recently published 'Food 2030 Strategy' features a recognition of the need to continue promoting traditional, local, regional and speciality foods, by encouraging greater uptake of the EU Protected Food Name Scheme and development of farmers' markets and other direct sales outlets.[20] There is general agreement that such support provides farmers and producers with a way to add value and find alternative routes to market, while effectively meeting consumer demand. Many local food proponents, including regional developers, pressure groups and promotional websites, argue that local food purchases are better for the rural economy than supermarket shopping. One frequently cited survey asserts that money spent with a local food initiative generates almost twice as much income for the local area as the same amount spent in a supermarket, because the money stays in the vicinity, where its value is increased by a multiplier effect.[21]

Micro- and macro-factors within a regional business environment also mean that the development and growth of the resurgent local food sector depend on commercial and institutional support networks, as well as the influence of supply channel gatekeepers.[22] As small-scale agricultural producers move away from traditional skill-sets, they also must adapt to different market conditions by acquiring new skills, such as in marketing and building links with retailers, as well as in investing in new capital equipment or technologies.[23] The lack of such skills creates a significant barrier to entry, especially against the background of globalisation and the predominance of trans-national food brands in the modern marketplace. The EU, the UK Department for Food and Rural Affairs (Defra), and regional, county and local agencies all have recognised the need to fund and support business restructuring, skills development, set-up costs and network management. These entities made extensive resources available to regional food networks, but funding was reduced or withdrawn during UK budgetary restructuring after the global economic crisis and with change of government in 2010. The central tier responsible for regional development, Regional Development Agencies (RDAs), was abolished by the incoming Conservative–Liberal Democrat coalition government. Some of its responsibilities were taken over by a network of Local Enterprise Partnerships (LEPs), which can bid for funding from regional growth funds. However, LEPs do not cover all areas yet.[24]

In the past, support services and funding for the local and regional food sector came through a lengthy, complex supply network that evolved over time. Multiple regional food marketing groups were established by the late 1990s, with encouragement from Defra and local authorities. By 2002, Food from Britain (FFB) took on a national promotional role for the regional food sector and was working with 17 representative organisations,[25] including co-ordinating seven regional groups. However, a report in that year also highlighted concerns about the duplication of roles and message fragmentation.[26] In response, Defra investigated ways to co-ordinate regional and local food groups. As a short-term measure, during 2004–2008, the government provided FFB with £5 million to support quality regional food initiatives, within a revised structure set out in the UK government's *Sustainable Strategy for Farming and Food* and its *Regional Food Strategy*.[27]

In England, funding became available 'for activities linked to the promotion of quality regional and local food culture'.[28] The European Commission approved a *Rural Development Programme for England* (RDPE), which provides support for improving the competitiveness of rural businesses, including food businesses. Both sources of funding were channelled through the nine former RDAs, to corresponding Regional Food Groups (RFGs), then on to county marketing groups and perhaps smaller local organisations. However, now that the RDA structure is being dismantled, the UK government is considering how to administer funding from the EU through the RDPE.[29] Prior to the most recent regional funding shake-up, the Regional Food Group Alliance provided umbrella group support for eight English RFGs, representing small and medium-sized food and drink producers within their region. However, the future of such support remains uncertain too.

In addition to the hierarchical public sector structure, a plethora of non-governmental organisations (NGOs) and pressure groups have taken an interest in local food. Although 'no one knows the exact figure ... there are scores of local and regional groups providing marketing support, showcasing products, advising and training'.[30] As with government support agencies, these organisations have started to coalesce into alliances, particularly to obtain funding. A review of their partnership details and links provided on their websites reveals a complex web. The Local Action on Food group contains national organisations that support local and regional promotion of healthy and sustainable food through projects, events, good practices and other support services; it was established in 2008 and is co-ordinated by Sustain. It builds on the work of two former groups: Food Links UK and Sustain's Food Access Network. Local Action on Food also is a consortium partner in the national Making Local Food Work programme, which is funded by the Big Lottery Fund and co-ordinated by the Plunkett Foundation. This alliance also includes the Campaign to Protect Rural England, Co-operatives UK, The National Farmers' Retail & Markets Association and the Soil Association.

This complex support structure for local and regional food leaves small suppliers easily confused and overwhelmed by all the changes in names and connections among different organisations, initiatives and funding sources, which often offer overlapping training, advice or grants. Funding usually has been short-term, and agreements for projects have been delayed by complicated application and approval procedures. Recipients often must rush to spend grants by the end of the financial year in March, a very busy time for small farm businesses. Those businesses frequently complain that the financial support they need to develop their businesses is going instead to researchers, consultants, advisors and trainers.

Method

This case analysis includes three local or regional food supply and marketing networks in different areas of the UK. A case study design was chosen because there is a distinct lack of research on how organisations (particularly small ones) act and react to their network environment. Therefore, an exploratory, theory-building approach is appropriate.

Our aim is to identify commonalities and disparities in the development of networks and to examine how food businesses fit into the environment of local and regional marketing. We thus identify both barriers to and facilitators of sustainable development and evaluate the role of support and advisory bodies. In addition, each case highlights a distinct facet of network arrangements (e.g., ethical and social impacts of sourcing, distribution and consumption of local products, cultural disconnection among network members, cohesive identities and entrepreneurship).

We present an outline of each network using a modified 'market map'.[31] This tool was designed for use in less developed countries; it is useful here as a simple descriptive framework for a market system that goes beyond traditional marketing channels or supply chain diagrams. The map identifies not only small-scale producers and other value chain actors but also support services and the commercial and institutional environment that affects the chain.

Cases

CASE 1: MADE IN LANCASHIRE: THE LOCAL FOOD MARKETING GROUP

Made in Lancashire (Figure 16.1) is a local food marketing group, whose membership consists of specialist food and drink producers and retailers in the county of Lancashire. It was established in 2002, after an outbreak of foot and mouth disease, to help the farming community diversify and create additional outlets. The members are generally micro or small businesses with a craft or artisanal focus. This brand identity supports members' access both to local outlets and national/international retailers. Made in Lancashire and its neighbouring county food groups, Made in Cheshire and Made in Cumbria, are partners in the Food Northwest RFG, which has obtained funding from the Northwest Regional Development Agency.

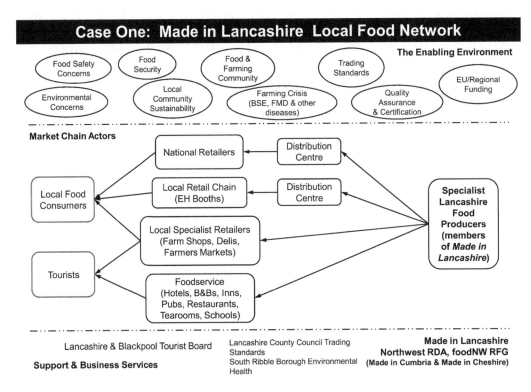

Figure 16.1 Market map for Case 1

CASE 2: THE LINCOLNSHIRE CO-OPERATIVE SOCIETY: SOCIALLY EMBEDDED LOCAL SOURCING

The Lincolnshire Co-operative Society (LCS; Figure 16.2) is a regional consumer co-operative, operating predominantly within the county of Lincolnshire in the East Midlands region. It is one of 20 regional retail societies that make up the Co-operative Group (the fifth largest grocery retailer in the UK). The case study focuses on the development of local sourcing for livestock and meat in the county by an ethically driven retailer, which helped build a community-centred network infrastructure around the supply chain (incorporating farmers, processors, retailers and local consumers) specifically to enhance sustainable social and environmental benefits, derived from the local food supply.

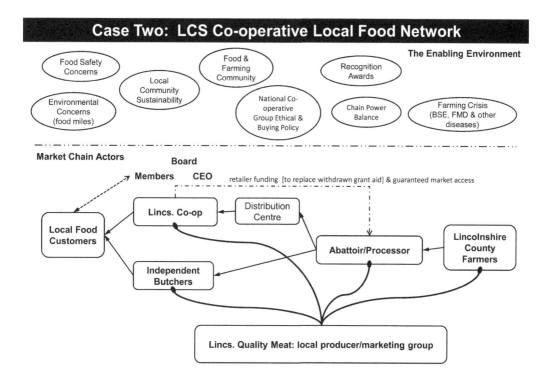

Figure 16.2 Market map for Case 2

CASE 3: THE WEST MIDLANDS ETHNIC PRODUCE NETWORK

The third case (Figure 16.3) involved a regional developmental initiative to integrate supply chain members (fresh produce growers, distributors, wholesalers, retailers/ foodservice) to exploit an ethnic market opportunity. The West Midlands Ethnic Produce Network was designed to bring together rural fresh produce growers to supply specialist produce to predominantly urban consumers of Asian heritage and wider ethnic groups in the West Midlands area. As a further ethical agenda, it aimed to substitute imported produce with locally sourced alternatives. The initiative had widespread support from the regional government, a regional university, the farming lobby and an agency representing Asian business interests.

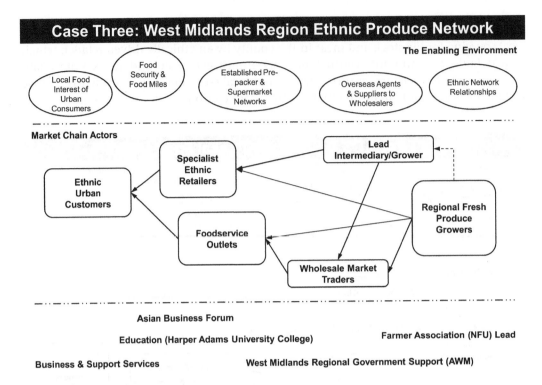

Case Three: West Midlands Region Ethnic Produce Network

The Enabling Environment

- Local Food Interest of Urban Consumers
- Food Security & Food Miles
- Established Pre-packer & Supermarket Networks
- Overseas Agents & Suppliers to Wholesalers
- Ethnic Network Relationships

Market Chain Actors

- Specialist Ethnic Retailers
- Lead Intermediary/Grower
- Ethnic Urban Customers
- Regional Fresh Produce Growers
- Foodservice Outlets
- Wholesale Market Traders

Asian Business Forum

Education (Harper Adams University College)

Farmer Association (NFU) Lead

Business & Support Services

West Midlands Regional Government Support (AWM)

Figure 16.3 Market map for Case 3

Research Protocol

In our primary investigation, we used semi-structured depth interviews and questionnaire surveys, involving both business participants and support staff. We also conducted focus group discussions and dissemination fora. We summarise the methods for each case in Table 16.1.

Table 16.1 Research methods employed

	Case 1. Made in Lancashire: The local food marketing group	Case 2. The Lincolnshire Co-operative Society: Socially embedded local sourcing	Case 3: The West Midlands Ethnic Produce Network
Depth interviews	4 producer members 2 industry experts	Chief executive officer 2 livestock producers A processor/marketing group Feedback to respondents & repeat longitudinal interviews	29 wholesale traders 20 retailer & foodservice businesses 1 wholesale/retail trade association 1 lead intermediary 1 regional co-operative retailer
Group discussion/ dissemination		2 business/ other stakeholder conference dissemination sessions	3 group discussions with producers, a product packer-distributor & advisory/support bodies 2 open forum dissemination session in the West Midlands region
Postal questionnaires	108, including all 80 producer members (29% response rate)		460 growers in the West Midlands region (14% response rate)

Findings

CASE 1

The Made in Lancashire producer members supply directly (without intermediary distribution or wholesaling) to specialist retailer outlets, including retailer members and national supermarket and local chain retailers. Most respondents in this case considered a local marketing strategy beneficial for small food businesses and a source of competitive advantage, in the belief that supporting the local economy was appealing to consumers. The concepts of freshness and origin of food were important, and more than 90% of the businesses surveyed agreed that correct target marketing of such attributes improved product performance. A shortcoming identified in the case, however (corresponding to prior literature), was the lack of agreement on the definition of the term 'local food'.

Respondents concurred that it encompassed the county boundary and the community area, with local practices and origins integral to the perception. Most survey respondents asserted that the definition should include the distance travelled by products, from source to consumer, and 'less than 30 miles' was a typical limit. Thus localness appeared bound by county and sub-county distances. The Lancashire regional supermarket chain, EH Booths, was frequently cited as a retailer that occupied a middle ground between farm shops and national or international supermarkets. Its regional distribution of only 30 miles was a prime factor in the chain's appeal, offering it an advantage over larger national retailers that operated national buying and centralised distribution systems. This impression corresponds with an existing research view that notes the supply chain difficulties of national food retail chains that cannot claim 'localness'.[32] Made in Lancashire's consumers also indicated increasing price and value consciousness, which made it harder for small food businesses to compete with the economies of scale realised by larger retailers, with their national/global product sourcing. However, respondents believed that local/regional food could succeed, because of the close relationship that members have with local consumers and their interest in reconnecting with food. The challenge would be to influence consumer behaviour through marketing and education.

Respondents also claimed that the cheap food policy of the UK indicated the government's failure to manage the industry, leading to more imports and an abdication of control over food safety or security to the large food corporations. The major retailers were regarded as the new gatekeepers of consumer satisfaction and protection.[33] Over-restrictive business and food sector regulations, as well as excessive business rates and bureaucratic hurdles, also were mentioned as disproportionately greater barriers for small and micro-businesses. Access to finance (to a certain degree) and insufficient business knowledge were cited as additional issues. Some respondents also noted a lack of industry organisation support. For members, the burden of legislation in the food market appeared onerous and even excessive, considering the small size, scope and turnover of their businesses.

CASE 2

According to the CEO of LCS, the most fundamental difference offered by a local co-operative food retailer chain, compared with a public limited company that functions through national and international retailers, is that the supply network, customers, membership and community are inter-related and inter-dependent. As a local retail co-operative, they are there to serve the people in the local area, and this association with the county and local communities distinguishes what they do from the practices of other food retail chains.

The LCS takes a dual approach to supplying food to its stores. It accesses the Co-operative Group national buying facility for mainstream national and international products (and therefore is part of the marketing and distributive processes that serve all Co-operative Group stores), but also maintains a strong local sourcing agenda. The strategy to develop ranges of locally sourced product has resonance in the wider community, given the rural and agricultural nature of the region. A further motivation thus was to support the economy of the county, even against the backdrop of rural decline.

Accordingly, the LCS was instrumental in ensuring the continuation of a local, farmer-controlled meat supply group, Lincolnshire Quality Beef, Lamb and Pork. As the chair of this group explained, when its grant aid ran out in 2002, it 'couldn't have survived' without the support of LCS. Had it not provided funding and become a major customer, offering guaranteed market access, the Lincolnshire Quality meat group would not have gained a sufficient volume of consistent sales. Furthermore, the LCS sat on the steering board of this organisation, alongside farmer and processor representatives, and invested in the principal abattoir that processed the meat. The Lincolnshire Quality livestock and meat chain offered a localised 'closed loop' (county farmers, processors, stores, co-operative members and customers), an ethical trading organisation and an origin-traceable sourcing venture. Its products feature, on both the packaging and in stores, the Lincolnshire Farm Assured and Quality Lincolnshire rosette logo. Furthermore, the supply chain works to minimise its environmental impact by achieving minimal 'food miles'. The LCS even promises, in point-of-sale and promotional literature, that the meat may have travelled as little as 60 miles from farm to abattoir to store. The co-op uses these methods to underpin its commitment to both local economy and community.

The Lincolnshire Quality scheme also was recognised with a 2008 national UK Rural Action award, won through the Business in the Community scheme. The award went to the LCS, farmers, the abattoir and the independent butchers that participated in the Lincolnshire Quality scheme. The success of local food marketing, based on sustainable, community-centred, ethical trading with local suppliers, represented an outcome of the co-operative approach to sourcing, which might not have worked within centralised private sector structures or traditional retailers that would probably have expected a national roll-out. Even within the LCS, it was not easy initially to match the expectations of the national Co-operative Group's buying policy; some initial resistance at the national level contested the LCS's plan to buy meat from local sources instead of nationally.

CASE 3

Few of the grower respondents from the West Midlands region sold directly to supermarkets. Instead, wholesalers provided them with easy, regular routes to market, provided regular payments and seemed less exacting than produce pre-packers and supermarkets. However, using wholesale channels raised issues with seasonal trading variations and price instability.

At the time of this research, few growers produced crops specifically targeted at the ethnic minority consumer market. They identified specialist crops they might consider growing and assumed that any market gaps could be filled, efficiently and cheaply, by imports. For West Midlands growers, the most important issues in marketing their local produce involved market knowledge (e.g., access to relevant consumer sales data) and advice about how new specialist crops might fit into the existing seasonal cycle. Not surprisingly, other important issues for growers included production (agronomic and technical advice), product quality (e.g., how to grow high-quality specialist crops), price and supply continuity. Finally, they noted the possible need for specialist machinery to produce and harvest new types of crops.

The growers appeared divided with regard to whether consumers were interested in buying local or regional produce. Qualitative comments revealed that the value competitiveness of national/international supermarkets continued to threaten local product marketing. However, the popular impact of emerging environmental, sustainability and social issues, such as 'food miles', appeared to reflect a consumer influence too.

Because urban consumer awareness of local production was low, wholesalers relied on promotional materials from their overseas agencies, which meant few promotions about local sourcing actually reached consumers.

Growers clearly understood the market opportunities offered by reconnection with the regional urban population and ethnic markets, but the focus groups confirmed their generally negative view of pursuing such opportunities. This negativity derived from a general risk aversion among growers. Growers worried about the channel power of retailer and wholesaler customers and questioned the level of customer interest in and loyalty towards buying local and regional produce, especially for customers with easy access to cheap overseas produce. The cultural issues also highlighted disconnections in the supply chain; the predominantly white, rural growers did not understand urban ethnic minority business customers and end-consumers, and the channels were fragmented by language and culture.

All of the wholesaler respondents sold some UK produce but also found it easier to source produce from abroad, because they believed that UK growers could not supply them with sufficient and continuous quantities. Most wholesalers claimed that West Midlands produce was uneconomical (outside the peak UK summer season) and not viable. They also questioned the producers' ability to 'sell themselves'. On the other side, the wholesalers already had developed long-term relationships with foreign suppliers, including family connections (typically in Pakistan or India) or subsidiary relationships with international trading companies. The wholesalers were simply not motivated to seek local produce alternatives to imported produce, because they preferred the simple (one-stop) business transactions they already used. In their past experiences, local growers could not offer such convenience. Moreover, the wholesalers claimed to prefer the appearance and taste of imported products, though none of them mentioned freshness. Their overall indication was that local food was no more profitable to sell than imported produce but was more problematic to source. Seasonality issues seemed critical; by sourcing abroad, wholesalers could guarantee year-round supply. Changing suppliers by season was regarded as complicated, so they expressed no desire to start dealing with a vast number of local and regional growers. Finally, nearly all the wholesalers believed that local sourcing was not important to their customers; customers neither asked about nor cared where the produce came from, as long as it was of adequate quality and sold at a reasonable price.

The retailer and foodservice respondents mostly obtained fresh produce by visiting wholesale markets, although they also received deliveries from wholesalers. Other respondents from this group sourced fresh produce directly from farms, and one restaurateur grew his own garden herbs. When asked to identify preferred supply routes for fresh produce, these respondents mostly indicated they would continue to collect from wholesale markets, which offer classic one-stop opportunities. However, these businesses also noted opportunities for 'import substitution' of speciality crops that they bought from wholesalers that relied on imported sources. Herbs were a typical case. In contrast with the wholesale suppliers, retailers and foodservice operators expressed interest in buying local or regional fresh produce, citing freshness and support for local supply networks as reasons. However, they also voiced the typical concerns related to seasonality and availability. For them, the decision to use local or regional produce currently and in the future would depend on two key issues, quality and price. But they also noted influential factors such as availability, reliability and delivery issues, which reflect the common issues with respect to developing consumer markets for local foods.[34]

Ethnic produce offers considerable untapped potential for growers. The lead intermediary of the West Midlands-based organisation JK Fresh Produce offered a model for reconnecting the regional fresh produce supply chain. The company was established by an Asian grower, who now farms 1,200 acres but also buys specialist fresh produce and pre-packs and distributes it to the wholesale markets. Asian entrepreneurs might offer a distinct advantage to some customers; just as wholesalers develop overseas affinities based on ethnicity, UK supply channels involving Asian growers might offer similar advantages. The cultural disconnection problem thus could be solved by this grower, who offers a bridge to the Asian, culturally bound predominance of the fresh produce wholesale markets. Furthermore, the grower offers wholesale access to other local growers of other specialist crops destined for Asian end-users by acting as a packing and marketing hub.

This case identifies several opportunities, due to increased demand among growing ethnic minority populations for specialist produce grown in the West Midlands. However, the opportunities may be tempered by supply channel disconnection and the strength of the existing importer and wholesale channel, which prefers to import. The access to and availability of local produce thus depends on the strength of the intermediary wholesale channel, which displays no loyalty to local sourcing.

Discussion

A common link between Cases 1 and 2 is the involvement of facilitating, 'benign' local retail chains. Such local distributive networks offer marketable advantages with regard to localness and a positive contribution to the 'food miles' debate. The West Midlands Ethnic Produce Network in Case 3 seemingly offers similar potential for similar supportive distributive networks (through its lead intermediary, JK Fresh Produce) and the West Midlands regional retail co-operative society, which also offers a potential outlet for specialist fresh produce. However, risk aversion among local growers and a lack of network integration effectively has stalled such equivalent facilitation in this case.

Previous literature has suggested that in the food sector, gatekeeper-controlled market concentration can lead to inequalities and negative social and environmental effects.[35] All three cases provide opportunities for local food marketing by taking advantage of underlying consumer demand for reconnection with local food. Each case also features similar and unique angles for exploiting local food markets. Yet a counter-theme also emerged – namely, that consumers' demand for value (especially in uncertain economic times) and the attractive value-based offer of national or international food businesses meant that local food marketing would require additional (realistically, niche) advantages to counter the general demand for price-based value in a harsh economic climate. The strong identities provided through umbrella marketing by Made in Lancashire and the LCS enabled effective marketing communication regarding the positive societal benefits of local food. In contrast, the apparent lack of identity for the fresh produce of the West Midlands region meant that retailers and end-users, although aware of an opportunity offered by reconnection, import substitution and food miles, could not express these messages because they lacked a joint communication network.

Local businesses, at the heart of local sourcing networks, are innovative and different from the norm.[36] Both Cases 1 and 2 concur with this view; Case 2 in particular demonstrates the importance of the bond between network businesses and the consumer in the heart of local community. In the first two cases, local food and engagement with local communities represented part of an important ethical and social sustainability agenda, as much as an environmental agenda based on low food miles. In contrast, in Case 3, any support for local and regional food was limited by wholesaler self-interest, despite some appeals from retailer and foodservice businesses to obtain regional produce 'to support the regional economy'. There was clearly a sense of community and network integration in the urban West Midlands, exemplified in the strong ethnic and cultural ties with overseas fresh produce suppliers, wholesalers, retailers, foodservice operators and consumers (particularly those of Asian origin). However, these ties were not connected to regional fresh produce production. In the rural counties of the West Midlands, white growers sensed little connection with the urban, ethnic minority-based food network. Case 3 offered some hope of rural-urban reconnection through the development of a networking hub, based in one of the rural counties, and through the proposition of a cultural and physical bridge. With a collaborative approach, growers could actively court interactions with wholesalers, retailers and foodservice customers. But growers, wholesalers, retailers and caterers also would need to undergo considerable education to overcome their supply issues and preconceptions.

The enthusiasm for market making and market satisfaction in terms of local food makes it easy to ignore issues of market power and the role of channel leaders or gatekeepers, despite research confirming their significance and impact.[37] These considerations can confound new market channels or enforce the *status quo*. Wholesalers act as gatekeepers for the fresh produce industry in the West Midlands; although their desire for 'an easy life' through existing connections with imported produce suppliers is understandable, their lack of understanding or flexibility in their attitudes toward home-grown production and producers represented a major barrier to local and specialist fresh produce. Thus from all three cases, we can conclude that support from a benign power authority directs the local network and gives it cohesive direction and purpose, whereas indifferent or hostile parties with channel power confound its development. Local food network members consider the market power of channel leaders outside their local sphere (e.g., national retail chains) as the greatest danger they face.

Despite the obvious advantages of big business (in the modern business climate, the imbalance of opportunity clearly favours larger retailers, through lower transaction costs, greater economies of scale, spread costs of quality control and so forth), small businesses should regard economies of scale as an opportunity to create a profitable, niche-based differential. Small businesses are run by individuals who by definition tend to be individualistic. This approach can be an advantage, in the form of a creative, entrepreneurial spirit (e.g., many of the members of Made in Lancashire), or it can create a disadvantage for network co-ordination, if small businesses lack any common direction. This latter effect appears among many of the growers in the rural West Midlands, as well as in the more individualist 'lifestyle' businesses in the Made in Lancashire group.

Finally, the local food sector remains relatively small within the food industry; if targeted changes were implemented in its pricing, accessibility and awareness, consumer interest should lead to increased spending. Available government and industry sector support (e.g., regional aid, small business emphasis) is important for the development of the local food economy, but it cannot force the successful development of a network. All three cases in this study featured extensive network support from governments and NGOs that was useful and effective (e.g., creating an umbrella image of Made in Lancashire). However, network support cannot replace the will of small businesses to succeed (e.g., the enthusiasm and creativity of the Made in Lancashire members and farmer supplier/processors in the LCS versus the reserved, risk-averse nature of the West Midlands growers). Support agencies might create the right atmosphere for success, but they can only facilitate. The directional lead comes from the vested interest of a (benign) power. A further issue entails the confusing layers of diverse governmental, regional, local and NGO support agencies, which often overlap in their responsibilities and activities. It thus is easy for small businesses to confuse the roles and relative importance of different support agencies. Such confusion is compounded by the uncertainty derived from the abolition of RDAs and questions about what will replace them; the answers to these questions have notable implications for the future of RFGs. These conditions make for an uncertain future for local and regional food in England. Table 16.2 summarises key issues arising from the three cases, demonstrating some common issues related to barriers to and facilitators for growth and network development.

Table 16.2 UK regional food networks: cross-case analysis

	Case 1: Made in Lancashire	Case 2: Lincolnshire Co-operative	Case 3: Regional Ethnic Food Supply
	SUCCESSFUL	SUCCESSFUL	FAILURE (on hold)
Barriers * Local food: issues of 'access' + Issues of 'agency overlap/ conflict'	• Overlap between local and regional bodies+ • Overlap between voluntary & public sector support+ • Confusion/replication – too many agencies+ • Diverse nature of business objective, for example, lifestyle versus professional food marketing make it hard to create a cohesive food policy • Burden of taxation and bureaucracy on small business	• Conflict between national and local decision making – centralised vs. decentralised buying – dichotomous conflict*	• Lack of cohesion – not a joined up supply channel • Channel gatekeeper roles inhibit innovation** • Risk aversion • Top down (artificial) initiative – lack ownership • Urban consumers lack interest in local produce* • Cultural and language disconnection (lack of trust) v. established importing relationships* • Regional – not contributing to local sustainability* • Poor channel member/ network marketing and product identity

Table 16.2 *Concluded*

	Case 1: Made in Lancashire	Case 2: Lincolnshire Co-operative	Case 3: Regional Ethnic Food Supply
	SUCCESSFUL	SUCCESSFUL	FAILURE (on hold)
Local impact ++ Importance of 'local food'	• Cohesive identity for local products*++ • Local food in local stores*++ • Local decision making++	• Ethical issues – food miles multiplier effect –stakeholder engagement++ • County-based local buying policy of • Co-op++	• Regional disconnection not linking local initiatives++
Network ties **Network 'gatekeepers' *** Issues of 'benign' and 'hostile' power	• Individualistic – entrepreneurial mentality • Networking synergy • Importance of supportive local retail chain**^	• Strong supportive local retail chain* *** ^ • Strong – co-op integrated – involved in production, retail infrastructure, joined up promotional campaigns and good marketing image^ • 'Closed loop' of integration for local food between suppliers, processors, retailer and community retail facilitation using (benign) power/ commitment** ++ ***	• Weak ties – disconnected* ** • Network support exists but can't force cohesion despite market potential* • Status quo – no incentive to change • Wholesalers block integration (hostile) gatekeeper power** *** • Lead local intermediary and regional co-op retailer would support but network wide integration lacking**

Conclusions and Managerial Implications

Despite a lack of specific definition, local food marketing has demonstrated its potential to exploit niches to provide business alternatives to national/international food marketing organisations and structures, as well as champion environmental and social sustainability. The results and common conclusions from the three cases emphasise the importance of stakeholder engagement and network collaboration as necessary to achieve local food marketing success. This analysis also demonstrates the contribution of common, accepted network directions and strategies for local food businesses and groupings, supported by strong and clear marketing. The role of support organisations is critical to the development of network cohesion. However, they also cause some confusion, due to their multi-agency and multi-layered nature, which has developed over time and circumstances, even as the future of regional support bodies is less than certain. The role of supply channels, network gatekeepers and benign self-interested powers have been less considered in terms of their impact on business organisations, yet we show that they can have either restrictive or facilitating roles, and perhaps a more direct impact than that of support bodies, which influence but do not necessarily direct successful local and regional food network development.

Limitations and Recommendations for Further Research

These cases are typical of those encountered in the local and regional development of the food industry, but we recommend widening this study to include other country and sector contexts and thus explore the key contributions of various local and regional marketing networks. For example, researchers should consider collaborative stakeholder engagement, cohesive marketing, the value of support agencies and infrastructure, the local economic and community benefit and the role of benign versus unbalanced, indifferent or negative network powers.

Notes

1   Sodano, V. and Hingley, M. (2009), Innovation in food networks and organizational diversity: A case study from the UK retail cooperative sector, in: *Proceedings of 3rd International European Forum on Innovation and System Dynamics in Food Networks* in Innsbruck-Igls, Austria, 16–20 February 2009.

2   Hallsworth, A. and Bell, J. (2003), Retail change and the UK co-operative movement: New opportunity beckoning? *International Review of Retail, Distribution and Consumer Research*, Vol. 13, No. 3, 301–315.

3   Ilbery, B., Watts, D., Simpson, S., Gilg, A. and Little, J. (2006), Mapping local foods: Evidence from two English regions, *British Food Journal*, Vol. 108, No. 3, 213–225; Jones, P., Comfort, D. and Hillier, D. (2004), A case study of local food and its routes to market in the UK, *British Food Journal*, Vol. 106, No. 4, 328–335; Watkins, J. (2008), Regional groups instrumental in encouraging local markets, *Farm Business*, 16 May 2008, 28.

4   Chambers, S., Lobb, A., Butler, L., Harvey, K. and Traill, B.W. (2007), Local, national and imported foods: A qualitative study, *Appetite*, Vol. 49, No. 1, 208–213; Mintel (2010), *op. cit.*

5   Knight, J., Holdsworth, D. and Mather, D. (2007), Determinants of trust in imported food products: Perspectives of European gatekeepers, *British Food Journal*, Vol. 109, No. 10, 792–804.

6   Mintel (2008), *Locally Sourced Foods, UK*. London: Mintel.

7   IGD, *op. cit.*

8   Gummesson, E. (1996), Relationship marketing and the imaginary organisation: A synthesis, *European Journal of Marketing*, Vol. 30, No. 2, 31–44; Healy, M., Hastings, K., Brown, L. and Gardiner, M. (2001), The old, the new and the complicated: A trilogy of marketing relationships, *European Journal of Marketing*, Vol. 35, No. 1, 182–193.

9   Anderson, J.C., Håkansson, H. and Johansson, J. (1994), Dyadic business relationships within a business network context, *Journal of Marketing*, Vol. 58, No. 4, 1–15; Håkansson, H. and Snehota, I. (1990), No business is an island: The network concept of business strategy, in: Ford, D. (ed.), *Understanding Business Markets: Interactions, Relationships and Networks*. San Diego: Academic Press; Johnsen, R.E. and Ford, D. (2002), Developing the concept of asymmetrical and symmetrical relationships: Linking relationship characteristics and firms' capabilities and strategies, in: Spencer, R., Pons J-F. and Gasiglia H. (eds.), *Proceedings of 18th Annual Conference of the Industrial Marketing and Purchasing Group*, Graduate School of Business and Management, Dijon, France, 5–7 September, 2002.

10 Hingley, M. (2005), Power to all our friends? Learning to live with imbalance in UK supplier-retailer relationships, *Industrial Marketing Management*, Vol. 34, No. 8, 848–858.

11 Doney, P.M. and Cannon, J.P. (1997), An examination of the nature of trust in buyer-seller relationships, *Journal of Marketing*, Vol. 61, No. 2, 35–51.

12 Duffy, R., Fearne, A. and Hornibrook, S. (2003), Measuring distributive justice and procedural justice: An exploratory investigation of the fairness of retailer-supplier relationships in the UK food industry, *British Food Journal*, Vol. 105, No. 10, 682–694.

13 Batt, P.J. (2004), Power-dependence in agricultural supply chains: Fact or fallacy?, in: *Proceedings of 20th Annual Conference of the Industrial Marketing and Purchasing Group,* Copenhagen, 2–4 September 2004.

14 Cox, A. (2004), The art of the possible: Relationship management in power regimes and supply chains, *Supply Chain Management*, Vol. 9, No. 5, 346–356; Hingley, *op. cit.*

15 Hingley, *op. cit.*

16 Kumar, N. (2005), The power of power in supplier–retailer relationships, *Industrial Marketing Management*, Vol. 34, No. 8, 863–66; Kumar, N., Scheer, L.K. and Steenkamp, J-B.E.M. (1998), Interdependence, punitive capability, and the reciprocation of punitive actions in channel relationships, *Journal of Marketing Research*, Vol. 35 (May), 225–235.

17 Duffy et al., *op. cit.*

18 Hingley, M., Lindgreen, A. and Beverland, M. (2010), Barriers to network innovation in UK ethnic fresh produce supply, *Entrepreneurship and Regional Development*, Vol. 22, No. 1, 77–96.

19 Lang, T. (2003), Food industrialization and food power: Implications for food governance, *Development Policy Review*, Vol. 21, No. 5–6, 555–568.

20 Defra (Department for Food and Rural Affairs) (2010), *Food 2030 Strategy*. Available from Defra: www.defra.gov.uk/foodfarm/food/strategy/index.htm [Accessed 1 March 2011].

21 New Economics Foundation (2001), Press Release: *Local food better for rural economy than supermarket shopping*. London.

22 Hingley et al., *op. cit.*

23 Beer, S., Hingley, M. and Lindgreen, A. (2009), Ethnic opportunities: The emergence of new supply chains that stimulate and respond to the need for 'new' ingredients, in: Lindgreen A. and Hingley, M. *The New Cultures of Food: Marketing Opportunities from Ethnic, Religious and Cultural Diversity*. Aldershot: Gower, 57–72.

24 U.K. Parliament Briefing Paper (2011), Local enterprise partnerships, House of commons library, briefing paper, SN/EP/5651. Available from: www.parliament.uk/briefingpapers/commons/lib/research/briefings/SNEP-05651.pdf [accessed 1 March 2011].

25 Rod, A. (2002), Giving local directions: Local food groups' funding is short-term, their services overlap and definitions confuse, *The Grocer*, 13 July 2002.

26 Policy Commission on Farming and Food (2002), *Farming and Food: A Sustainable Future*, HMSO: Report of the Policy Commission on the Future of Farming and Food, January.

27 Defra (Department for Food and Rural Affairs) (2009), *Regional and Local Food*. Available from Defra: www.defra.gov.uk/foodfarm/food/industry/regional/index.htm [Accessed 1 March 2011].

28 *Ibid.*

29 UK Parliament, *op. cit.*

30 Rod, *op. cit.*

31 Albu, M. and Griffith, A. (2006), Mapping the market: Participatory market-chain development in practice, *Small Enterprise Development*, Vol. 17, No. 2, 12–22.

32 Sodano and Hingley, *op. cit.*

33 Lang, *op. cit.* similarly notes the increasing power of food retailers

34 Chambers et al., *op. cit.*

35   Lang, *op. cit.*; Sodano and Hingley, *op. cit.*
36   Sodano and Hingley, *op. cit.*
37   Hingley et al., *op. cit.*

17 Incorporating Impoverished Communities in Sustainable Supply Chains

JEREMY HALL[*] AND STELVIA MATOS[†]

Keywords

Base of the Pyramid, Brazilian biofuels, sustainable supply chains, social exclusion, transaction cost economics.

Introduction

Biofuels have been recognized as a more sustainable energy source than fossil carbon sources such as oil, coal and natural gas due to their potential to be renewable and reduce environmental impacts such as CO_2 emissions.[1] However, they have also been criticized for creating the so-called "food for fuel crisis," where the demand for biofuels may have increased prices for commodities such as corn and soybeans, with harsh impacts on impoverished communities,[2] or exacerbated social exclusion by concentrating agricultural production at the expense of small-scale farmers.[3] Paradoxically, biofuels have also been identified as a potential source of employment for subsistence farmers in, for example, Brazil, one of the world's leading agricultural producers and a technology leader in biofuels.[4] Recent Brazilian policies have encouraged refiners and distributors to source from small-scale farmers who have previously been excluded from participating in Brazil's growing agricultural sector; yet there remain major problems with these wider participatory schemes.

Drawing on our previously published studies,[5] we discuss recent Brazilian policies designed to encourage impoverished farmers to participate in the biofuels supply chain, and the problems that have emerged due to a lack of understanding and trust among supply

[*] Professor Jeremy Hall, Beedie School of Business, Simon Fraser University, 8888 University Drive, Burnaby, BC, Canada, V5A 1S6. E-mail: jkh5@sfu.ca; Telephone: 778-782-5891.

[†] Dr. Stelvia Matos, Beedie School of Business, Simon Fraser University, 8888 University Drive, Burnaby, BC, Canada, V5A 1S6. E-mail: smatos@sfu.ca; Telephone: 778-782-5891.

chain members. We frame the research within the discourse concerned with sustainable supply chains[6] and transaction cost economics, specifically economizing pressures that may discourage the inclusion of social parameters in supply chain management. We use Seuring el al.'s (2008) definition of sustainable supply chain management as *"the management of material and information flows as well as cooperation among companies along the supply chain while taking goals from all three dimensions of sustainable development, i.e. economic, environmental and social, and stakeholder requirements into account."*[7]

This chapter focuses on the relationship between relatively modern organizations employing educated personnel and their supply chain relationships with poor, often illiterate farmers at the "Base of the Pyramid" (BOP), where some 4 billion people in impoverished regions earn less than $2,000 per year.[8] Such approaches that recognize the importance of poverty reduction align with the holistic approach to sustainable development, where interdependence among social, economic and environmental parameters from an intergenerational perspective is recognized.[9] However, most studies on sustainable supply chains are focused on environmental concerns, whereas contributions to social issues are only beginning to be investigated.[10] Furthermore, until recently, few studies had explored the integration of illiterate BOP populations within the supply chain (although Majumdar and Nishant[11] have acknowledged this as an important issue), yet such segments of society are particularly vulnerable and may hinder wider environmental and social improvement out of desperation.

Social Inclusion versus Economizing in Supply Chains

According to Seuring and Muller,[12] over 190 papers have been published on sustainable supply chains. Common themes within this literature are that systemic approaches to sustainability concerns are necessary – i.e. pollution does not necessarily respect firm boundaries – and that knowledge transfer between supply chain members is necessary for successful sustainable supply chains, and that that sustainable supply chains need to go beyond purely environmental impacts and look at the more complex relationships among economic, social and environmental parameters.[13] In this section, we discuss two broad areas within the literature: pressures to economize and the often contradictory pressure to include the poor within value chains.

ECONOMIZING PRESSURES WITHIN THE SUPPLY CHAIN

Given that there have been numerous studies on sustainable supply chains, it can be expected that a number of theoretical lenses have been applied. One of the more common is transaction cost economics,[14] which has been applied to sustainable supply chains by, for example, Tate et al.,[15] Carter and Rogers,[16] Connelly et al.[17] and Hall.[18] Williamson[19] argues that the primary objective of the "make or buy" decision is to minimize production and transaction costs, which in turn are shaped by asset specificity, purchasing frequency and uncertainty in the form of shirking.[20] According to Connelly et al.,[21] transaction cost economics suggests that firms base their decisions about sustainability practices primarily on the economic merits of the market versus hierarchy costs associated with those practices; firms will likely engage in more sustainable products or services when there is a clear economic rationale. For example, Delmas and Montiel[22] predict that firms are more likely to adopt ISO 14001 environmental standards when transactions involve high specific investments, and therefore greater dependency on their current customers, than firms with lower asset specificity. Tate el al.[23] found that suppliers are more likely to adopt environmental practices if information seeking, bargaining and enforcement costs are minimized, especially if they believe the buyer–supplier relationship is on-going. However, the benefits from adoption must outweigh the costs associated with these practices, including the potential cost of lost business.

According to Connelly et al.,[24] while transaction cost economics may provide insights about how economic decision making is formulated, it underemphasizes environmental and social issues. Hall[25] argues that, while transaction cost economics is a useful theoretical starting point, it does not fully describe environmental innovation dynamics within the supply chain, but rather focuses on cost reduction in relatively stable supplier relationships. While transaction costs have been widely used within the sustainable supply chain discourse, it does not adequately address environmental and social concerns, and as a result most studies combine it with other theories. For example, Carter and Rogers[26] combine it with resource dependence theory, population ecology and the resource-based view of the firm, Delmas and Montiel[27] combine it with information economics, and Tate et al.[28] with institutional theory. Here, we suggest that recent BOP discourse may provide complementary insights in understanding the trade-off between economizing pressures of managing transaction costs and the inclusion of social parameters in supply chain management.

INTEGRATING THE BASE OF THE PYRAMID WITHIN SUSTAINABLE SUPPLY CHAINS

As discussed previously, few sustainable supply chain studies have explored the integration of illiterate populations within the supply chain,[29] yet such segments of society are particularly vulnerable and may hinder wider environmental and social improvement out of desperation due to extreme poverty and/or poor governance structures.[30] Excluding such populations from economic integration causes wider social and economic problems, and these costs may not be adequately reflected in market prices.[31] According to Ocampa,[32] Latin America is one such example where a failure to integrate poorer segments of society led to an increase in the informal and often illegal economy. In Brazil, Hall et al.[33] argue that social exclusion, "the denial of equal access to opportunities imposed by certain groups of society[34]" led to wider problems such as crime and corruption.

A number of scholars have attempted to address poverty reduction in the BOP by illustrating business opportunities within poor communities. For example, Hart,[35] London and Hart[36] and Prahalad[37] argue that mature markets in industrialized nations are becoming increasingly saturated, whereas BOP markets remain untapped, because individual income levels are too low, but as a whole may be very large. Most of the BOP research to date has been focused on the multinational corporation (MNC) perspective,[38] and specifically how MNCs can turn BOP populations into lucrative markets. Prahalad,[39] however, has emphasized the role of local entrepreneurship as a mechanism for long-term poverty reduction, while Karnani[40] argues that the BOP is a source of self-reliant producers and consumers who can design and make products suitable for sale in both BOP and mature markets, thus providing greater economic stability through integration into the global economy. BOP research should therefore include studies on producers and entrepreneurs rather than only customers.[41]

While the BOP discourse has recognized the importance of including poor populations within supply chains, it is a relatively new area of research, and as a result most studies call for further research. Kandachar and Halme,[42] for example, suggest that research addressing unintended social and ecological impacts from BOP initiatives needs detailed exploration, particularly regarding policy and institutional design for improved innovation. Hall et al.[43] found that entrepreneurial dynamics within the BOP differ from developed economies, due to weaker institutions and negative learning references (e.g. corrupt government officials, criminals, etc.) that may direct entrepreneurs towards destructive activities. Thus, while we respond to calls for further BOP research on the poor as producers, and specifically how they can be included within supply chains, we will show that there are often unanticipated detrimental outcomes, and that economizing pressures may work against the inclusion of BOP suppliers.

Methodology

Drawing on Yin[44] and Siggelkow,[45] we used a case study methodology to sharpen the existing sustainable supply chain discourse, specifically by pointing to gaps regarding the integration of impoverished communities in the supply chain and filling them in. Our objective is to investigate the difficulties of incorporating impoverished communities within the supply chain, as part of policy and industry attempts to improve their overall sustainability. We chose Brazil for two reasons. First, the country is a large emerging economy driven by a number of world-class industries, including an energy sector that has made the country energy self-sufficient, in part due to its leadership in biofuels production.[46] Second, the country also has major problems with poverty and social exclusion, and is now attempting to use biofuels as a means of reducing these social ailments while improving the sustainability of the energy matrix.[47]

We selected two cases from our previous research,[48] based on theoretical sampling:[49] the Brazilian Ethanol Program (ProAlcool) and the Biodiesel Program. In these two cases, the challenges of incorporating impoverished communities in the supply chain are "transparently observable"[50] allowing us to examine how entrepreneurs from the BOP can participate as productive supply chain members.

The Ethanol Program was developed as a response to the oil crises in the 1970s and to revive the sugarcane industry, as sugar prices were on a path of steady decline. At the beginning, advocates of the ProAlcool suggested involving impoverished communities in the program by including less concentrated production of sweet-potato and cassava, a starchy-root plant cultivated in the north and northeast of the country.[51] However, these crops were not competitive and were soon discarded. As a response to criticism from national and international media, the industry is now trying to become more socially inclusive by adopting corporate social responsibility principals in its operations. In contrast, the Biodiesel Program was developed to address increasing interest in the biofuels market, and to promote social inclusion and regional development. However, some of the challenges of its implementation involve the increasing pressure to compete with more efficient and well-established large-scale soybean biodiesel production. Additional challenges emerged when dealing with farmers with low levels of education.

Qualitative data was drawn from policy and technical documents, semi-structured interviews with 128 stakeholders and four focus groups with small-scale farmers between 2006 and 2009 (Table 17.1), conducted in a variety of Brazilian cities. Each interview lasted for approximately one and a half hours. A variety of stakeholders were interviewed in an attempt to provide insights from various perspectives of the supply chain, as suggested by Hall[52] (Table 17.1).

We recognized that, given the controversial nature of the research, there was a risk of social desirability bias, whereby research participants might express viewpoints that they think the interviewer wants to hear or are politically appropriate rather than what the participants truly believe.[53] To reduce this risk, we informed interview subjects that we would keep their names and participation confidential and would only use direct quotations with their permission, as suggested by Singer et al.;[54] that we would not use information that could place the interviewee in any form of jeopardy, and that we would check our data against that observed by other supply chain members interviewed in this research, as suggested by Hall.[55]

Our analysis started by identifying three common factors within the cases: a) policies towards social inclusion during the development phase, b) internal and external factors that helped shape the development and implementation of social inclusive policy and c) their strategies regarding social inclusion (corporate social responsibility programs or inclusive entrepreneurship). We used these three factors as the basis for conducting a systematic cross-case analysis, looking for differences and similarities in their approaches and outcomes, always interacting with the BOP and supply chain literatures.[56]

Table 17.1   Interview subjects by stakeholder category (number of subjects)

Energy sector: senior executives, middle managers, trade association officials	30
Agriculture sector: senior executives, middle managers, farmer association representatives, farmers (9 individual interviews, excluding 4 focus groups totaling 48 participants)	41
Chemical sector: senior executives, middle managers	7
Government officials: Brazilian senior officials	12
United Nations (UN) officials: Food & Agricultural Organization (FAO), UN Environmental Program, UN Division for Sustainable Development, Economic Commission for Latin America & Caribbean, UN Development Program	10
NGOs: Greenpeace Brazil, Greenpeace Canada, Greenpeace China, Greenpeace International, Sierra Club, Brazilian Institute for Consumer Defense, Project Tamar, Council for Canadians, Pembina Institute for Appropriate Development; Polo Sindical da Borborema (Borborema Farmers Union), Esperanca and Lagoa Seca divisions.	11
Community representatives	3
Academics	12
Total	126

Major Challenge in the Evolution of Brazilian Biofuels Sector

Previous generations of agricultural modernization, such as capital and chemical intensive "Green Revolution" techniques, the introduction of foreign crops such as coffee and soybeans, and most recently agricultural biotechnology, have increased economic efficiencies and exports, but have also been scrutinized for excluding small farmers from participation.[57] According to Hall et al.,[58] Brazilian policy-makers have recognized that these disruptions on small-scale farmers have contributed towards economic disparity and poverty and represent a major challenge in the evolution of the biofuels sector. Such concerns have been termed "social exclusion," and have been the topic of much discussion in Latin America[59] and emerged as an official policy mandate of Brazilian President Luiz Inácio "Lula" da Silva. According to Ocampa,[60] a paradox of emerging economies during the 1990s was their ability to produce companies capable of integrating into the global economy, but also a growth in the informal (often illegal) economy – the latter being mostly low-end entrepreneurial ventures and subsistence jobs that Mazza[61] calls "poverty" employment. According to government officials in the Ministry of Agriculture Development (a ministry established specifically for small-scale farming) and the Ministry of Social Development & Fight Against Hunger (established under President Lula to resolve social exclusion), there was a belief within policy circles that Green Revolution technologies, while vastly improving agricultural output, also led to millions of small farmers being dislocated. Many migrated to urban centers seeking other opportunities, but often ended up destitute and living in *favelas*, or shantytowns[62] known for high crime rates and other social problems.

THE BRAZILIAN ETHANOL PROGRAM

The development of ethanol as an automotive fuel is an example of this paradox. Fuel ethanol production in Brazil emerged with the Federal Government's ProAlcool Program, which was a response to the oil crises in the1970s, and to save sugarcane producers from bankruptcy after major modernization investments were followed by a significant drop in sugar prices.[63] Proponents of the ProAlcool Program suggested that it would reduce rural to urban migration by including less concentrated production of sweet-potato and cassava.[64] However, these crops were not as cost-effective as sugarcane and were soon discarded. The ProAlcool Program involved government agencies, the military, the ethanol industry, researchers, the media and established sugarcane producers controlled by wealthy families, all of whom engaged to create a market and stimulate the use of ethanol as an automobile fuel.[65] At the time, the national oil company Petrobras was opposed to the program. According to a senior Petrobras manager, oil and gas companies did not believe that ethanol was a viable energy source, and would only result in unfair competition due to the heavy subsidies that supported the ProAlcool Program. However, technological innovation, supply chain improvements and increases in petroleum prices made it a viable fuel, and it is no longer subsidized.

Sugarcane, a crop well suited for Brazil's climate, is currently the most efficient crop for ethanol production. For example, while Brazil produces an average of 7,000 liters of ethanol per hectare of sugarcane, the US produces 3,800 liters per hectare from corn and the EU 5,400 liters per hectare from sugar beet.[66] Today, Brazil is the world's largest producer of fuel ethanol, with a widely available distribution infrastructure and an automotive sector manufacturing a variety of "flex fuel" cars that can be powered by any mix of ethanol and gasoline.[67] Brazilian ethanol production is currently concentrated, capital-intensive and highly mechanized, although the harvest is still carried out manually, creating a strong demand for temporary low-skilled labor that has been heavily scrutinized for poor working conditions.[68]

Under the ProAlcool Program, government subsidies and credit programs favored large-scale farmers and sugar mill owners concentrated in the wealthier and more developed southeast and central regions of Sao Paulo and Mato Grosso, the location of the incumbent sugarcane producers, as opposed to poor northeast and north regions.[69] Many workers are illiterate and receive below minimum wage, and few independent small-scale farmers participate in this sector. Brazilian policy-makers have since recognized that such regional inequality had negative effects on employment and migration, exacerbating social exclusion. Thus, although considered a technical and economic success, the sector has also been under scrutiny for poor environmental performance and working conditions and not providing opportunities for small farmers.[70]

In response to environmental and social concerns, in 2007 the State Secretary of Environment and the association of sugarcane producers of Sao Paulo developed a protocol of economic, environmental and social practices to promote sustainable development in ethanol production. Its purpose was to encourage better practices in resource conservation, watershed recuperation and proper use of agro-chemicals. Over 90% of Sao Paulo producers voluntarily signed the Protocol pledging to eliminate burning by 2017, when all harvesting will be mechanized.[71] In addition, Coopersucar,[72] a cooperative that coordinates most of the Brazilian cultivation, processing and distribution of sugar and ethanol, has committed its members to adopting corporate social responsibility programs. Such commitments have led to an overall environmental improvement over the years, such as lower water consumption, and current and future projections of ethanol plantation expansion do not include important biomes such as the *cerrado* (savannah) and the Amazon Rainforest.[73] However, criticism over poor wages and working conditions continues. Wages of sugarcane cutters in Sao Paulo State are still low, industry investments in health and education remain modest and accusations of child labor also continue, and although Brazilian child labor laws follow international standards, enforcement is weak and inspections are done only in response to protests from NGOs, workers, media and trade unions.[74]

THE BRAZILIAN BIODIESEL PROGRAM

In response to the problems of social exclusion in ethanol and other agricultural sectors, the Federal Government of Brazil initiated an executive inter-ministerial commission for biodiesel production in 2003. It was composed of the Ministry of Mines and Energy, Petrobras, the Brazilian Agricultural Research Corporation (Empresa Brasileira de Pesquisa Agropecuária: EMBRAPA), a government-owned organization that played a major role in developing the biofuel sector and small farmers' capability development, the National Agency of Petroleum, and the Brazilian Development Bank among other institutions. The National Program of Production and Use of Biodiesel (Programa Nacional de Producao e uso de Biodiesel: PNPB) was launched in December 2004, with the explicit goals of stimulating the biodiesel market, promoting social inclusion and regional development in poor regions, and encouraging technology research.[75] The Program included mandates to stimulate market demand for biodiesel in the Brazilian energy matrix, requiring a minimum of 2% biodiesel in the national diesel supply between 2008 and 2013 and a minimum of 5% thereafter.[76] It also provides research incentives to promote technology development throughout the production chain, and encourages research networks from universities and other research institutions such as EMBRAPA.

A third pillar of the Program is an explicit policy to encourage small farmer participation in the supply chain through the "Social Fuel Stamp" (Selo Combustivel Social), through tax benefits and special credit to industries that encourage the participation of small producers from the poorer north and northeast regions, particularly for castor and palm seeds from small-scale producers. To receive the Social Fuel Stamp, biodiesel refiners and fuel distributors must purchase part of their feedstock from small farmers, sign commercial agreements with those farmers and provide them with technical assistance. The biodiesel producer can be awarded tax exemptions that range from R$.07 (approximately US$.03) to R$.218 (approximately US$.1) per liter, depending on the feedstock and the region were the industry is located, which represents about 4% to 12% of the retail price of diesel in Brazil. To receive the highest tax exemption, the industry must purchase castor or palm oil produced by small farmers in the north, northeast or semi-arid regions, crops which are more suitable for smaller-scale farming. The Government estimates that around 100,000 small-scale farming families have participated in the Program, based on contracts presented by biodiesel companies claiming the Social Fuel Stamp tax rebates.[77]

According to Hall et al.,[78] the results of the Program have been mixed. Many refiners and distributors were concerned whether farmers were able to produce what had been negotiated, and whether prices of, for example, soy, palm and castor for biodiesel would remain competitive with other markets. Soybeans, for example, are commodities with prices that fluctuate with global demand. Palm oil is valued for other industrial purposes, while castor oil's production costs are higher than for other oils and it is not currently suitable for mechanized production.[79] Furthermore, although the Social Fuel Stamp is relatively simple in theory, in practice there have been some problems between industry and farmers. One representative from a biodiesel refinery stated that some farmers fail to honor contracts and sell the seeds to other buyers, typically as a one-off, short-term sale at higher prices: "...sometimes it is hard to deal with these farmers. Because of their lack of education, they are not used to dealing with contracts and do not understand the advantages of a potential long term and stable business relationship against an unstable short opportunity." Our interview subjects stated that the level of education and experience in long-term planning played an important role in how small farmers responded to biodiesel business opportunities. Distrust between industry and farmers was common. Castor has many applications in the chemical industry, and can thus provide higher prices than other biodiesel feedstock such as soy and palm oil, albeit at much smaller volumes. However, farmers often expect similarly high prices, even though the volume needed for biofuels is much greater and thus may provide greater profitability through economies of scale.

Consistent with much of the sustainable supply chain literature, one of the requirements placed on industry to obtain the Social Fuel Stamp is providing technical assistance to small farmers. However, industry officials and EMBAPA officials stated that many farmers often did not follow advice. For example, since castor plants can be found almost anywhere (including empty lots and landfills), farmers unfamiliar with this crop assumed that specialized techniques were unnecessary, but without proper crop management, productivity is low and of poor quality.[80] Biodiesel refinery managers stated that the costs for the technical assistance were often higher than the Social Fuel Stamp tax exemptions, and that operational costs required to manage contracts with thousands of geographically dispersed small farmers also created difficulties. Most of these farmers had no experience with contracts, simple accounting principles or other basic management knowledge such as the benefits of scale economies. Many biodiesel refiners and distributors suggested that the costs of providing technical assistance, coupled with the transaction costs of dispersed suppliers outweighed the tax advantages. The president of a chemical company that refines castor oil and a senior manager of Petrobras stated that the social program for biodiesel will not work, and that it will follow a similar route as ethanol, with only large-scale producers, in spite of these tax incentives. They further suggested that soybeans would likely emerge as the dominant crop, which, in contrast to palm and caster, is highly suitable for mechanized, large-scale production and already had an established supply chain in Brazil (an attraction of castor and palm is that it is currently harvested most efficiently by non-mechanized techniques, making it suitable for small farmers).

Discussion and Conclusions

Within recent years the sustainability discourse, and more specifically the sustainable supply chain literature, has evolved from mostly an environmental focus towards the more holistic approach that considers the interactions among economic, environmental and social parameters. Another stream of sustainability research emphasizes the need to address the problems of impoverished BOP segments of society. This chapter discussed examples of where these two streams of research have met, specifically the challenges of incorporating impoverished, often illiterate farmers in the biofuels supply chain, an area underexplored empirically in the sustainable supply chain literature.

We used the cases of the ProAlcool and Biodiesel Programs in Brazil to explore the difficulties of incorporating impoverished communities in the supply chain. Table 17.2 summarizes the cross-case analysis factors, with examples of quotations from our interview subjects, as suggested by Eisendardt and Bourgeois.[81] These programs differ in terms of initial social inclusive policies, internal and external pressures, and strategies regarding social inclusion. Such differences helped to explain the process by which social inclusion policies evolved and what difficulties emerged. For example, we found that, although Brazilian policy-makers recognized the importance of providing opportunities for impoverished communities in the biofuels supply chain, there remains the considerable challenge of sourcing raw materials from often illiterate farmers who lack basic business knowledge, and often distrust industry and government policy. This distrust is perhaps understandable, given that previous attempts at agricultural reform led to social disruption. Regardless, such problems exacerbate transaction costs, making it more desirable to source from large-scale farmers rather than those within the BOP. Indeed, proponents of transaction cost economics would advise against social inclusion policies such as the Social Fuel Stamp, as they create inefficiencies in a business environment where trust is lacking, and ultimately work against the inclusion of impoverished suppliers.

Table 17.2 Cross-case analysis factors and examples of quotations‡

	ProAlcool Ethanol Program	**Biodiesel Program**
Policies towards social inclusion during development phase	Primarily focused on large-scale production with some initial social inclusive initiatives	Large-scale production with major social inclusion policies
Examples:	*Sugarcane producers have had historical contribution over the [Brazilian] economy, it was important to develop policies to sustain the industry* (farmer association representative)	*The Biodiesel Program has a strong social mandate to include the poor farmer and improve their standard of living* (federal gov't official; Ministry of Agricultural Development)
Internal and external factors that helped shape the development of social inclusion policies	Criticism/pressure from national and international media	Government response to social exclusion problems in previous economic development policies
Examples:	*... many organizations say bad things about sugarcane producers, but new management is being very proactive, trying to address problems with working conditions for example* (sugarcane industry association representative)	*The government is trying to avoid the same mistakes made with the ProAlcool ... Lula's mandate is to look after the excluded* (energy sector executive)
Strategies regarding social inclusion	Corporate social responsibility	Socially inclusive supply chain management
Examples:	*The new generation of sugarcane owners are different from the old school. Now there is an effort to implement corporal social responsibility, we invest in health, education for farmers' kids ... mechanization is going to improve working conditions by employing skilled people too* (energy sector executive)	*We want the farmers to participate as business partners so our objective is to enhance their capabilities as the provider of the oil and not just the seeds, which is a higher valued added product* (EMBRAPA instructor)

Government and industry could improve trust by engaging impoverished farmers in early stages of policy development. We further suggest that basic business education targeting impoverished farmers is needed. However, we also acknowledge that further research is needed to understand how such education can be provided to people who have never received formal training. More generally, we suggest that entrepreneurial dynamics within impoverished communities remains largely unexplored. For example, until recently the mainstream entrepreneurship journals such as the *Journal of Business Venturing, Entrepreneurship: Theory & Practice* and the *Journal of Small Business Management*

---

‡   Translated from the original Portuguese.

had published no substantial empirical studies on illiterate entrepreneurs,[82] whereas the empirically based sustainable supply chain literature has generally assumed relative homogenization of knowledge levels among supply chain members.

The recent BOP discourse is starting to explore entrepreneurial dynamics of illiterate entrepreneurs. An example within the Brazilian biodiesel supply chain and other agricultural sectors is the role played by cooperatives, and specifically the presidents of the cooperatives, who are often educated and competent entrepreneurs. Such actors are often capable of bridging the gap between impoverished farmers and the distributors and refiners, and could act as a conduit for the basic business education and the establishment of trust as discussed previously.

We contribute to the literature by suggesting that including socially disadvantageous segments of society within the supply chain exacerbates transaction costs due to their geographically dispersed, small-scale production, thus increasing purchasing frequency, an important issue that has not received adequate attention in the BOP or sustainable supply chain literature. However, we differ from much of the transaction cost economics discourse[83] and specifically those that have applied it within the context of sustainable supply chains by suggesting that, although the challenges of incorporating impoverished farmers within the biodiesel supply chain may seem inconsistent with the pragmatic approach of transaction cost economics, there are likely to be long-term benefits that may eventually make such efforts worthwhile.

The development of Brazilian ethanol involved a series of solutions to specific problems, which in turn created more problems that are now being addressed. Nelson and Winter[84] suggest that the emergence of such trade-offs can be expected with economic change, which resolves some problems but also creates negative externalities that must be addressed. During this process, Brazilian ethanol producers overcame significant challenges to become one the world's most efficient producers. Biodiesel refiners and distributors are now at a similarly challenging stage. Such dynamics would not emerge if supply chain policies were determined using Williamson's[85] arguments that minimizing transaction costs such as purchasing frequency and uncertainty determine, or Connelly et al.'s[86] argument that decisions about sustainability practices rest primarily on the economic merits of the market versus hierarchy costs. Nor is it consistent with Delmas and Montiel's[87] observation that firms encourage environmental standards within the supply chain primarily when transactions involve high specific investments, or Tate el al.'s[88] argument that environmental practices are more likely to be adopted if information seeking, bargaining and enforcement costs are minimized, and the buyer–supplier relationship is on-going. Indeed, Brazil's biofuels industry would likely remain underdeveloped if they followed the pragmatics of transaction cost economics (as is the case in much of the rest of the world). Thus, while the difficulties of engaging with subsistence farmers within the supply chain, stimulating basic business knowledge and establishing trust may appear daunting and counter to much of the sustainable supply chain literature, the potential payoff could open major sources of biofuel in other impoverished regions throughout the world, allowing the Brazilian biofuels industry to continue as one of the world's leading energy players.

Limitations and Implications for Further Research

Our findings are limited by the research design. Our empirical data does not go beyond what the interviewees were able to articulate and we were able to interpret, and these are not necessarily the only relevant perspectives on these issues. We tried to minimize these limitations by conducting interviews with a variety of stakeholders over a number of years, and triangulated with documentation and other interviewees.

Our cases were also limited to one country and one industry (albeit spanning agriculture and energy). Although Brazil has a large BOP population, it also has a relatively large industrial base, natural resources and infrastructure, and, like other emerging economies such as China and India, a growing middle class. Regional differences also played a major role in shaping Brazilian social inclusion policies, with parts of the country highly industrialized and others underdeveloped. It would thus be useful to study how social inclusion policies for supply chains in countries under different circumstances emerge.

Whereas the emerging sustainable supply chain literature has primarily focused on relatively wealthy and educated suppliers, a promising area of research involves the rich interactions among BOP and non-BOP entities, which we suggest differs substantially. This brings up two issues worthy of further research. The first is a more detailed exploration of how transaction costs are affected by potential suppliers from poor, illiterate communities, and how the trade-offs between pressures to economize versus social inclusiveness can be balanced. We also suggest that more research is needed to understand what can be done to improve trust.

Acknowledgements

The Social Sciences and Humanities Council of Canada (SSHRC) and Genome Canada supplied funding for this support. We would also like to acknowledge our colleagues, Drs. Bruno Silvestre, Mike Martin and Napoleao Beltrao, the five anonymous reviewers and book editors, as well as those that agreed to participate in our field studies.

Notes

1   Zarrilli, S. (2006). "The Emerging Biofuels Market: Regulatory, Trade and Development Implications." New York: United Nations Conference on Trade and Development. Available at: http://r0.unctad.org/ghg/events/biofuels/UNCTAD_DITC_TED_2006_4.Final.pdf. Accessed March 14, 2013.

2   Hoyos C. and Blas J. (2008). "Security fears over food and fuel crisis". *Financial Times*, June 20. Available at www.ft.com/cms/s/0/29cff8ec-3ef4–11dd-8fd9–0000779fd2ac.html?nclick_check=1. Accessed August 2, 2008; FAO: United Nations Food and Agriculture Organization (2008). "High-level conference on world food security: The challenges of climate change and bioenergy, food security and sustainability – Towards an international framework", Rome, 3–5 June 2008. Available at: ftp://ftp.fao.org/docrep/fao/ meeting/013/k2498e.pdf. Accessed May 24, 2008.

3   Hall, J., Matos, M., Severino, L. and Beltrao, N. (2009). "Brazilian Biofuels and Social Exclusion: Established and Concentrated Ethanol vs. Emerging and Dispersed Bio-diesel", *Journal of Cleaner Production*, Vol. 17, Supplement 1, pp. S77–S85.

4   Hall, Matos, Severino and Beltrao, *op. cit.*; Reid, M. (2007). *Forgotten Continent. The Battle for Latin America's Soul*. Yale University Press.

5   Hall, Matos, Severino and Beltrao, *op. cit.*; Hall, J. and Matos, S. (2010). "Incorporating Impoverished Communities in Sustainable Supply Chains", *International Journal of Physical Distribution & Logistics Management*, Vol. 40 No. 1–2, pp. 124–147; Hall, J., Matos, M. and Silvestre, B. (2012). "A Complexity Approach to the Triple Bottom Line in Sustainable Supply Chains", *International Journal of Production Research*, DOI:10.1080/00207543.2011.571930).

6   Green, K., Morton, B. and New, S. (1996). "Purchasing and Environmental Management: Interactions, Policies and Opportunities", *Business Strategy and the Environment*, Vol. 5: pp. 188–197; Hall, J. (2000). "Environmental Supply Chain Dynamics", *Journal of Cleaner Production*, Vol. 8, No. 6, pp. 455–471; Hall, J. (2001). "Environmental Supply Chain Innovation", *Greener Management International*, Vol. 35, pp. 121–135; Hill, K.E. (1997). "Supply-Chain Dynamics, Environmental Issues, and Manufacturing Firms", *Environment and Planning A*, Vol. 29, pp. 1257–1274; Lamming, R. and Hampson, J. (1996). "The Environment as a Supply Chain Management Issue", *British Journal of Management*, Vol. 7, pp. S45–S62; Linton, JD., Klassen, RB. and Jayaraman, V. (2007). "Sustainable Supply Chains: An Introduction". *Journal of Operations Management*, Vol. 25, No. 6, pp. 1075–1082; Sarkis, J. (2001). "Greening Supply-Chain Management: Introduction", *Greener Management International*, Vol. 35, pp. 21–25; Seuring, S., Sarkis, J., Müller, M. and Rao, P. (2008). "Sustainability and Supply Chain Management: An Introduction to the Special Issue", *Journal of Cleaner Production*, Vol. 16, No. 15, pp. 1545–1510; Srivastava, S.K. (2007). "Green Supply-Chain Management: A State-of the-Art Literature Review", *International Journal of Management Reviews*, Vol. 9, No. 1, pp. 53–80.

7   Seuring, Sarkis, Müller and Rao, *op. cit.*, see p. 1545.

8   Kandachar, P. and Halme, M. (2007). "An Exploratory Journey towards the Research and Practice of the 'Base of the Pyramid", *Greener Management International*, Vol. 51, pp. 3–17; London, T. and Hart, S.L. (2004). "Reinventing Strategies for Emerging Markets: Beyond the Transnational Model", *Journal of International Business Studies*, Vol. 35, No. 5, pp. 350–370; Prahalad, C. and Hammond, A. (2002). "Serving the World's Poor, Profitably", *Harvard Business Review*, Vol. 80, No. 9, pp. 48–58; Prahalad, C. (2007). *The Fortune at the Bottom of the Pyramid: Eradicating Poverty through Profits*. Upper Saddle River, NJ: Pearson Educational/ Wharton School Publishing.

9   Elkington, J. (1997). *Cannibals with Forks: The Triple Bottom Line of 21st Century*. Gabriola Island, British Columbia: New Society Publishers; WCED: World Commission on Environment and Development (1987). *Our Common Future*. New York: Oxford University Press; Matos, S. and Hall, J. (2007). "Integrating Sustainable Development in the Extended Value Chain: The Case of Life Cycle Assessment in the Oil and Gas and Agricultural Biotechnology Industries", *Journal of Operations Management*, Vol. 25, pp. 1083–1102.

10 Seuring, S. and Müller, M. (2008). "From a Literature Review to a Conceptual Framework for Sustainable Supply Chain Management", *Journal of Cleaner Production*, Vol. 16, No. 15, pp. 1699–1710.

11 Majumdar, S. and Nishant, R. (2008). *ICFAI Journal of Entrepreneurship Development*, Vol. 5, No.3, pp. 6–22.

12 Seuring and Muller, *op. cit.*

13 Linton, Klassen and Jayaraman, *op. cit.*; Matos and Hall, *op. cit.* Seuring and Muller, *op. cit.*

14 Coase, R. (1937). "The Nature of the Firm". Reprinted in: Williamson, O. and Winter, S. (eds.) (1993). *The Nature of the Firm, Origins, Evolution, and Development*. Oxford: Oxford University Press; Williamson, O.E. (1985). *Transaction Cost Economics: The Governance of Contractual Arrangements*. New York: Free Press; Williamson, O.E. (1975). *Markets and Hierarchies: Analysis and Antitrust Implications*. New York: Free Press.

15 Tate, W., Dooley, K. and Ellram, L. (2011). "Transaction Cost and Institutional Drivers of Supplier Adoption of Environmental Practices", *Journal of Business Logistics*, Vol. 32, No. 1, pp. 6–16.

16 Carter, C. and Rogers, D. (2008). "A Framework of Sustainable Supply Chain Management: Moving Toward New Theory", *International Journal of Physical Distribution & Logistics Management*, Vol. 38 No. 5, pp. 360–387.

17 Connelly, B., Ketchen, D. and Slater, S. (2011). "Toward a 'Theoretical Toolbox' for Sustainability Research in Marketing", *Journal of the Academy of Marketing Science*, Vol. 39, pp. 86–100.

18 Hall (2000), *op. cit.*

19 Williamson (1975), *op. cit.*

20 Williamson (1985), *op. cit.*

21 Connelly, Ketchen and Slater, *op. cit.*

22 Delmas, M. and Montiel, I. (2009). "Greening the Supply Chain: When Is Customer Pressure Effective?" *Journal of Economics & Management Strategy*, Vol. 18, No. 1, pp. 171–201.

23 Tate, Dooley and Ellram, *op. cit.*

24 Connelly, Ketchen and Slater, *op. cit.*

25 Hall (2000), *op. cit.*

26 Carter and Rogers, *op. cit.*

27 Delmas and Montiel, *op. cit.*

28 Tate, Dooley and Ellram, *op. cit.*

29 Majumdar and Nishant, *op. cit.*

30 Collier, P. (2007). *The Bottom Billion*. Oxford: Oxford University Press; Sachs, J. (2005). *The End of Poverty*. London: Allen Lane; Stiglitz, J. (2002). "Employment, Social Justice and Societal Well-Being", *International Labour Review*, Vol. 141, pp. 9–29.

31 Sen, A. (1997). *Social Exclusion. Concept, Application and Scrutiny*. Manila: Asian Development Bank, Social Development Papers No. 1.

32 Ocampa, J. (2004). "Economic Development and Social Inclusion", in Buvinic, M., Mazza, J. and Deutsch, R. (eds.) *Social Exclusion and Economic Development in Latin America*. Washington DC: Inter-American Development Bank & Johns Hopkins University Press, 33–41.

33 Hall, J., Matos, S. and Langford, C. (2008). "Social Exclusion and Transgenic Technology: The Case of Brazilian Agriculture", *Journal of Business Ethics*, Vol. 77, No. 1, pp. 45–63.

34 Behrman, J., Gaviria, A. and Szekely, M. (2003). *Who's In and Who's Out: Social Exclusion in Latin America*. Washington DC: Inter-American Development Bank.

35 Hart, S. (2007). *Capitalism at the Crossroads*. Upper Saddle River, NJ: Pearson Educational/Wharton School Publishing.

36 London, T. and Hart, S.L. (2004). "Reinventing Strategies for Emerging Markets: Beyond the Transnational Model, *Journal of International Business Studies*, Vol. 35, No. 5, pp. 350–370.

37 Prahalad, C. (2007). The *Fortune at the Bottom of the Pyramid: Eradicating Poverty through Profits*. Upper Saddle River, NJ: Pearson Educational/Wharton School Publishing.

38 Karnani, A. (2007). "Doing Well by Doing Good – Case Study: Fair & Lovely Whitening'. *Strategic Management Journal*, Vol. 28, pp. 1351–1357; London and Hart, *op. cit.*

39   Prahalad, *op. cit.*

40   Karnani, A. (2007). "Misfortune at the Bottom of the Pyramid", *Greener Management International*, Vol. 51, pp. 99–110.

41   Karnani, A. (2007). "The Mirage of Marketing to the Bottom of the Pyramid: How the Private Sector can help Alleviate Poverty', *California Management Review*, Vol. 49, pp. 90–111.

42   Kandachar, P. and Halme, M. (2007). "An Exploratory Journey towards the Research and Practice of the 'Base of the Pyramid', *Greener Management International*, Vol. 51, pp. 3–17.

43   Hall, J., Matos, S., Sheehan, L. and Silvestre, B. (2012). "Entrepreneurship and Innovation at the Base of the Pyramid: A Recipe for Inclusive Growth or Social Exclusion", *Journal of Management Studies*, DOI: 10.1111/j.1467–6486.2012.01044.x

44   Yin, R. (1984). *Case Study Research: Design and Methods*. Beverly Hills, CA: Sage.

45   Siggelkow, N. (2007). "Persuasion with Case Studies", *Academy of Management Journal*, Vol. 50, pp. 20–24.

46   Hall, J., Matos, S. Fergus, A. and Vredenburg, H. (2005). "Sua empresa é socialmente vulnerável?" (Are You Socially Vulnerable?), *Harvard Business Review* (Latin American edition), Vol. 83, No.8, pp. 26–33; Silvestre, B. and Dalcol, R. (2009). "Geographical Proximity and Innovation: Evidences from the Campos Basin Oil & Gas Industrial Agglomeration-Brazil, *Technovation*, Vol. 29, No. 8, pp. 546–561; Hall, J., Matos, M., Silvestre, B. and Martin, M. (2011). "Managing the Technological, Commercial, Organizational and Social Uncertainties of Industrial Evolution: The Case of Brazilian Energy and Agriculture", *Technological Forecasting and Social Change,* Vol. 78, pp. 1147–1157.

47   Hall, Matos, Severino and Beltrao, *op. cit.*

48   Hall, Matos, Severino and Beltrao, *op. cit.*; Hall and Matos (2010), *op cit.*; Hall, Matos and Silvestre (2012), *op. cit.*

49   Eisenhardt, K. (1989). "Building Theories from Case Study Research", *Academy of Management Review*, Vol. 14, pp. 532–550.

50   Pettigrew, A. (1990). "Longitudinal Field Research on Change: Theory and Practice", *Organization Science*, Vol. 1, No. 3, pp. 267–292 (see p. 275).

51   Oliveira, J. (2002). "The Policymaking Process for Creating Competitive Assets for the Use of Biomass Energy: The Brazilian Alcohol Programme", *Renewable Sustainable Energy Review*, Vol. 6, Nos. 1–2, pp. 129–140.

52   Hall (2000), *op cit.*

53   Fisher, R. (1993). "Social Desirability Bias and the Validity of Indirect Questioning", *Journal of Consumer Research*, Vol. 20, pp. 303–315.

54   Singer, E., Hippler, H. and Schwarz, N. (1992). "Confidentiality Assurances in Surveys: Reassurance or Threat", *International Journal of Public Opinion Research*, Vol. 4, pp. 256–268.

55   Hall (2000), *op cit.*

56   Eisenhardt, *op. cit.*

57   IFPRI: International Food Policy Research Institute (2002). Green Revolution: Curse or Blessing? Available at: www.ifpri.org/pubs/ib/ib11.pdf. Accessed August 2, 2008; Aerni, P. (2002). "Stakeholder Attitudes towards the Risks and Benefits of Agricultural Biotechnology in Developing Countries: A Comparison between Mexico and the Philippines", *Risk Analysis,* Vol. 26, No. 6, pp. 1123–1137.

58   Hall, Matos and Langford, *op. cit.*

59   Buvinic, M., Mazza, J. and Deutsch, R., eds. (2004). *Social Exclusion and Economic Development in Latin America*. Washington DC: Inter-American Development Bank and Johns Hopkins University Press.

60 Ocampa, *op. cit.*

61 Mazza, J. (2004). "Social Inclusion, Labor Markets and Human Capital in Latin America", in Buvinic, M., Mazza, J. and Deutsch, R. (eds.); Social *Exclusion and Economic Development in Latin America*. Washington DC: Inter-American Development Bank and Johns Hopkins University Press, pp. 179–200.

62 Ferraz, J. (1999). "A Insustentabilidade da Revolução Verde", *Informativo Meio Ambiente e Agricultura (EMBRAPA)*, Vol. 8, No. 28, pp. 25–28.

63 Rosillo-Calle, F. and Cortez, LA.B. (1998). "Towards ProAlcool II: A Review of the Brazilian Bioethanol Programme", *Biomass and Bioenergy*, Vol. 14, No. 2, pp. 115–124.

64 Oliveira, *op. cit.*

65 Oliveira, *op. cit.*

66 IAE: International Agency of Energy (2007). "Energy Technology Essentials – Biofuel Production 2007". Available at: www.iea.org/techno/essentials2.pdf. Accessed March 13, 2013.

67 Zarrilli, *op. cit.*

68 Hall, Matos, Severino and Beltrao, *op. cit.*; Saint, W. (1988). "Farming for Energy: Social Options under Brazil's National Alcohol Programme", *World Development*, Vol. 10, No. 3, pp. 223–238.

69 Martinelli, L.A. and Filoso, S. (2008). "Expansion of Sugarcane Ethanol Production in Brazil: Environmental and Social Challenges", *Ecological Applications*, Vol. 18, No. 4, pp. 885–898; Oliveira, *op. cit.*

70 Martinelli and Filoso, *op. cit.*; MST: *Movimento dos Sem Terra* (2007). Brazil stages raid against debt slavery at Amazon sugar cane-ethanol plantation, July 3. Available at: http://www.mstbrazil.org/?q=slavelaborandethanolinapreports. Accessed December 2, 2007.

71 UNICA: Uniao da Industria de Cana-de-acucar Website. Production Statistics Center-South Brazil. Available online at: www.unica.com.br/dadosCotacao/estatistica/.

72 Coopersucar (2012). Política de Sustentabilidade Coopersucar. Available online at: www.copersucar.com.br/sustentabilidade_politica.html.

73 Smeets, E., Junginger, M., Faaij, A., Walter, A., Dolzan, P. and Turkenburg, W. (2008). "The Sustainability of Brazilian Ethanol: An Assessment of the Possibilities of Certified Production", *Biomass Bioenergy*, Vol. 32, pp. 781–813.

74 Chagas, A.L.S., Toneto, R. and Azzoni, C.R. (2012). "A Spatial Propensity Score Matching Evaluation of the Social Impacts of Sugarcane Growing on Municipalities in Brazil". *International Regional Science Review*, Vol. 35, No. 1, pp. 48–69.

75 Governo Federal do Brazil (2008). Biodiesel – Programa Nacional de producao e uso de biodiesel. Historico do Programa. Available at: www.biodiesel.gov.br/. Accessed June 21, 2008.

76 Pousa, G., Santos, A. and Suarez, P. (2007). "History and Policy of Biodiesel in Brazil. *Energy Policy*, Vol. 35, No. 11, pp. 5393–539.

77 MDA. (2008). Ministério de Desenvolvimento Agrário. Portal SAF. Available at: www.mda.gov.br/saf. Accessed December 20, 2008

78 Hall, Matos, Severino and Beltrao, *op. cit.*

79 Garcia, J. (2007). *O Programa Nacional de Produção e Uso de Biodiesel Brasileiro e a Agricultura Familiar Na Região Nordeste*. Ph.D. Thesis, Federal University of Paraiba, Brazil.

80 Severino, L.S., Ferreira, G.B., Moraes, C.R.A., Gondim, T.M.S., Freire, W.S.A., Castro, D.A., Cardoso, G.D. and Beltrão, N.E.M. (2006). "Growth and Yield of Castor Bean Fertilized with Macronutrients and Minornutrients", *Pesquisa Agroepcuaria Brasileira*, Vol. 41, No. 4, pp. 563–568; Severino, L.S., Moraes, C.R.A., Gondim, T.M.S., Cardoso, G.D., Beltrão, N.E.M. (2006). "Yield of Castor Planted at Different Row Spacing", *Revista Ciência Agronômica*, Vol. 37, No. 1, pp. 50–54.

81   Eisenhardt, K.M. and Bourgeois, L.J., III (1988). "Politics of Strategic Decision Making in High-Velocity Environments: Toward a Midrange Theory", *Academy of Management Journal*, Vol. 31, No. 4, pp. 737–770.

82   Hall, J., Daneke, G. and Lenox, M. (2010). "Sustainable Development and Entrepreneurship: Past Contributions and Future Directions", *Journal of Business Venturing*, Vol. 25, pp. 439–448.

83   Williamson (1975), *op. cit.;* Williamson (1985), *op. cit.*

84   Nelson, R. and Winter, S. (1982). *An Evolutionary Theory of Economic Change*. Cambridge, MA: Harvard University Press.

85   Williamson (1985), *op. cit.*

86   Connelly, Ketchen and Slater, *op. cit.*

87   Delmas and Montiel, *op. cit.*

88   Tate, Dooley and Ellram, *op. cit.*

18 Learning to Improve or Deceive? Chinese Supplier Responses to MNC Codes of Conduct

NIKLAS EGELS-ZANDÉN[*]

Keywords

China, codes of conduct, decoupling, labor practices, learning, new institutional theory, private regulation, recoupling, supplier relationships, toy industry, workers' rights.

Introduction

Following the offshoring and outsourcing of production from Europe and the USA in the 1980s and early 1990s, workers' rights representatives criticized the poor working conditions at multinational corporations' (MNCs) suppliers.[1] In the aftermath of extensive media coverage of this "scandal," private sphere regulatory systems emerged to govern workers' rights in global value chains.[2]

These "private regulatory systems" are based on either corporate-driven codes of conduct or union-driven international framework agreements.[3] Since most Europe- and US-based MNCs have adopted codes of conduct, while only about 100 have signed international framework agreements as of 2012,[4] it is reasonable to focus on codes of conduct when studying the private regulation of workers' rights. The merits of codes of conduct in protecting workers' rights, however, are highly contested. While some claim that codes are likely to improve workers' rights,[5] others claim that such codes do little for workers.[6]

The conceptual debate regarding the merits of codes of conduct has suffered from a lack of empirical studies of the actual effects that codes of conduct have on the factory floor. Especially lacking are longitudinal studies that allow for discussion of the potential impacts of codes of conduct over time. Locke et al. examined 800 Nike suppliers in 51 countries between 1998 and 2005 in one of the few such longitudinal studies;[7] however, the authors relied on Nike's internal auditing protocols, which is problematic given that previous research has identified quality problems with corporate audits.[8]

* Associate Professor Niklas Egels-Zandén, School of Business, Economics and Law at University of Gothenburg, Box 100, 405 30 Gothenburg, Sweden. E-mail: niklas.zanden@handels.gu.se. Telephone: + 46 31 786 2729.

This chapter addresses this gap in previous research via a longitudinal study of four Chinese toy suppliers in the province of Guangdong. The suppliers were initially examined in 2004 via unannounced, unofficial interviews with employees outside supplier factories, and then reexamined in 2009 using a similar method. Analyzing the findings in light of the learning and new institutional literatures, this chapter considers whether codes of conduct actually improve workers' rights or simply improve suppliers' ability to deceive social auditors. The chapter demonstrates that while codes of conduct seem to initially generate symbolic actions (i.e., suppliers erect a façade intended to deceive auditors), over time codes can indeed generate substantive actions (i.e., actually improve workers' rights).

Previous Research into Codes of Conduct

GAPS IN GENERAL CODE OF CONDUCT RESEARCH

Codes of conduct are one of the most researched subjects in the area of corporate social responsibility. Related research themes include: i) degree of corporate adoption of codes,[9] ii) content of codes from a normative perspective,[10] iii) content of codes from a descriptive perspective,[11] iv) drivers of code adoption,[12] v) changes induced by codes,[13] and vi) code of conduct compliance.[14]

Despite this extensive research into codes of conduct, both Stevens' and Helin and Sandström's reviews of existing research identify a lack of research i) examining how receivers of such codes respond to them, ii) taking a process perspective on code of conduct implementation, and iii) formulating theoretical frameworks addressing these two research gaps.[15] This chapter addresses these gaps in previous research by analyzing what suppliers learn from being exposed to codes of conduct and how this changes over time, in light of the learning and new institutional literatures.

GAPS IN RESEARCH INTO CODE OF CONDUCT IMPLEMENTATION

Despite the extensive code of conduct research, little research has examined code of conduct implementation at supplier factories. What little such research there is paints a negative picture of the potential of codes of conduct. For example, Chan and Siu claim that "academic articles published on the impact of corporate social responsibility (CSR) initiatives are in basic agreement that the efforts to implement corporate codes of conduct are often ineffective."[16] Wells claims that "there has been little progress in improving labour standards through such [private] regulation,"[17] and Locke et al. argue that codes of conduct are "not producing the large and sustained improvements in workplace conditions that many had hoped [they] would."[18]

Empirically, Locke et al. found that approximately 80% of Nike's suppliers failed to improve over time and that more suppliers actually manifested worse rather than improved compliance.[19] Based on this, Locke et al. conclude that private regulation needs to move beyond policing and codes of conduct to more collaborative buyer–supplier relationships in order to improve workers' rights.[20] Other studies have found better working conditions at factories exposed to social labeling and codes of conduct,[21] that suppliers invest in working conditions in response to codes of conduct,[22] and that codes improve at least some forms of workers' rights.[23] The sparse previous research thus indicates that it is unclear whether suppliers learn to improve workers' rights after exposure to codes of conduct.

In addition to being sparse, previous research into how suppliers respond to codes of conduct suffers from certain methodological problems. Most empirical studies claiming to study whether codes of conduct make a difference rely on data collected at one time, i.e., they rely on retrospective interview accounts to create a reference point for comparisons.[24] Given the extensive turnover of workers in the studied industries (mainly the garment, footwear, and sportswear industries) and the unreliability of retrospective interview constructs of reference points, this research design is problematic.[25] One of the few studies to address this weakness is Locke et al.'s analysis of 800 Nike suppliers in 51 countries.[26] However, this study relies on Nike's internal auditing protocols, which is problematic given that previous research has identified quality problems with corporate audits.[27] By relying on data from four Chinese suppliers collected in 2004 and 2009 via unannounced, unofficial interviews with employees outside suppliers' factories, this chapter addresses these methodological problems in previous research.

Codes of Conduct: Learning to Improve or to Decouple?

SINGLE-LOOP LEARNING

A fundamental assumption in much previous research into codes of conduct, and into how they are applied in practice, is that such codes comprise learning systems that alter suppliers' operations so that they become increasingly compliant with MNC codes.[28] As Nijhof et al. note, the use of codes of conduct can be seen, from a process perspective, as enabling corporate responsibility learning processes.[29] Figure 18.1 outlines the logic of codes of conduct and auditing based on such a process perspective.

As shown in Figure 18.1, the code of conduct process starts with an MNC adopting a code, which is normally based on UN and ILO conventions. This code is then included in the purchasing contract that suppliers promise to fulfill. To ensure compliance, the

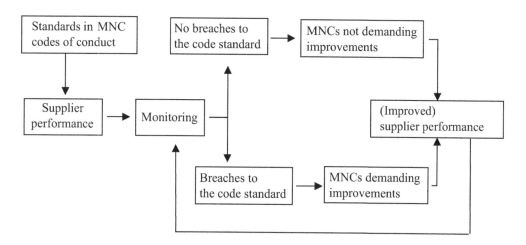

Figure 18.1 Codes of conduct as learning systems

MNC uses internal or external auditors who either find, or do not find, deviations from the terms of the code. If deviations are found, the MNC demands that suppliers take corrective actions and improve working conditions. Over time, with suppliers continuing to take corrective actions, supplier performance will increasingly become aligned with the standards defined in the code of conduct. To ensure improvements and compliance, the MNC conducts follow-up audits that restart the learning cycle. In instances when an MNC is not satisfied with a supplier's improvements, the MNC severs its working relationship with the supplier, ending its learning cycle.

The code of conduct process could—at least from the supplier perspective—be characterized as a single-loop learning system that aims at "general tightening and improvement in current procedures."[30] In other words, as a *single-loop* learning process, it comprises corrections without changes to the underlying assumptions, restricting itself to detecting and correcting errors within a given system of rules.[31] This is in contrast to a *double-loop* learning process, which comprises corrections made *after* questioning and changing the underlying assumptions and values.[32] In other words, double-loop learning resolves incompatible demands by setting new priorities, moving beyond a given system of rules.[33]

The same single-loop logic that characterizes codes of conduct also characterizes many other management systems, such as ISO certification and quality management systems. In the code of conduct case, suppliers are expected to alter their operations to become increasingly compliant with predefined code of conduct standards—no questions asked.[34] Suppliers are thus expected to correct their operations *without* challenging the underlying assumptions of the learning system. Suppliers' subordinate role in the code of conduct system is exemplified by the fact that code of conduct development rarely involves suppliers in any meaningful way.[35]

FORCED LEARNING

Beyond being considered simply a single-loop learning system, the code of conduct process can more accurately, and usefully, be described as a single-loop learning system based on negative feedback loops. It is deviations from code standards, not compliance with them, that are expected to trigger change (through MNC demands for change). In other words, supplier compliance is supposed to arise in response to non-compliance feedback, which in turn stems from MNC-commissioned audits.

A central condition for this system to work is an asymmetric power relationship between buyer and supplier,[36] since the underlying reason why MNCs adopt codes is that the MNCs are unsatisfied with, or suspicious of, how suppliers manage their operations. This suspicion is in turn related to the suspicions of NGOs, unions, and consumers regarding supplier operations and to the pressure these actors exert on the purchasing MNCs.[37] Hence, it is assumed that suppliers will not willingly alter their operations and that desired changes in working conditions must be forced on them. MNCs can exert such force because the power over production in industries with low-skilled employees and low investment thresholds (e.g., the toy, garment, and footwear industries) is possessed almost entirely by the buyers, i.e., the MNCs.[38] Suppliers operate under near-perfect competition, while the entry barriers are high on the buyer side of the value chain.[39] Hence, the bargaining power of suppliers is limited compared with that of buyers, making it necessary for suppliers to accept the conditions dictated by buyers in order to remain in business.[40]

We can conclude that codes of conduct are envisioned to comprise single-loop learning systems in which negative feedback triggers changes. The standards according to which suppliers are expected to alter their operations are determined by the buyers, which in turn are dependent on NGOs, unions, and consumers. Once a buyer has decided on the definition of "corporate responsibility" outlined in its code of conduct, the supplier is expected to implement this—no questions asked. This submissive role of suppliers is the consequence of the power balance in the buyer–supplier relationship. Whether or not suppliers want to alter their operations is considered beside the point: if they refuse to alter their operations, buyers will either force them to reconsider or force them out of business by severing business relationships with them.

LEARNING TO IMPROVE SYMBOLIC RATHER THAN SUBSTANTIVE ACTIONS

The underlying purpose of codes of conduct (and similar management systems) is to generate *substantive* change in the operational core of the organization. However, this idea is challenged by new institutional theory, which claims that codes are more likely to generate *symbolic* change and ceremonial compliance.[41] Symbolic change implies changes in symbolic actions such as policies, plans, programs, and formal strategies initiated mainly by top management or staff functions. Substantive change, on the other hand, implies changes in the actual day-to-day operational core of the organization. In the language of institutional theory, suppliers are likely to "decouple" their official formal policies/plans/programs/strategies (i.e., symbolic actions) from their actual day-to-day operational practices (i.e., substantive actions) in response to codes of conduct.[42] Decoupling implies that organizations "buffer their formal structures from the uncertainties of technical activities by becoming loosely coupled, building gaps between their formal structures [i.e., symbolic actions] and actual work activities [i.e., substantive actions]."[43]

Organizations decouple symbolic from substantive actions because this allows them to meet multiple external demands, albeit via different types of activities performed by different parts of the organization. In relation to codes of conduct, decoupling allows suppliers to create the appearance of improved workers' rights (e.g., salary increases, correct overtime compensation, and overtime limits) without bearing the costs and reduced ability to meet buyers' production deadlines associated with actual compliance. The possibility of conforming with inconsistent demands via decoupling is attractive, since suppliers generally perceive a clash between buyers' business demands (e.g., short lead times) and their code of conduct standards (e.g., limited overtime). As Jiang demonstrates, suppliers' "excessive overtime, low pay, and other poor working conditions are partly driven by unfair buying practice trends toward tough lead times and squeezing prices."[44] The new institutional literature expects suppliers to be more interested in obtaining the legitimacy and signaling the benefits accruing from *perceived* code of conduct compliance than in actually implementing the practices prescribed in buyers' codes of conduct.[45] The fact that supplier willingness to comply with code of conduct standards is due primarily to external institutional pressures from buyers bolsters this prediction that suppliers are likely to decouple symbolic from substantive actions.[46]

COMPETING PREDICTIONS

New institutional theory presents a competing prediction of what suppliers will learn from codes of conduct compared with the prediction embedded in the single-loop learning model of codes of conduct. Instead of expecting changes in substantive actions, i.e., actual improvements in workers' rights at supplier factories, as codes of conduct would imply, the new institutional literature would predict changes in symbolic actions, i.e., improved workers' rights policies, documents, and ceremonial actions of suppliers. These symbolic changes are in turn expected to work against substantive workers' rights improvements, since they alleviate the pressure for improvement by making it difficult for auditors to identify code of conduct violations. Hence, the code of conduct literature expects suppliers to behave according to the rules of the code of conduct process and does not challenge the underlying assumptions, i.e., engagement in single-loop learning and improvement of substantive (and potentially symbolic) actions. The new institutional literature, on the other hand, expects suppliers to move beyond the rules of the code of conduct process, to challenge the underlying assumptions and resolve incompatible code of conduct and purchasing demands, i.e., to engage in double-loop learning and achieve symbolic, but *not* substantive, improvements. These competing predictions are summarized in Figure 18.2.

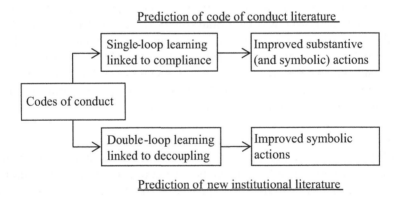

Figure 18.2 Predicted types of learning induced by codes of conduct

Method

To capture the type of supplier learning induced in practice by codes of conduct, we use the results of a study of four Chinese suppliers' compliance with Swedish toy retailers' codes of conduct conducted in 2004 and 2009 and interviews with purchasing managers, CSR managers, supplier managers, and NGOs active in codes of conduct and monitoring practices. Five years were allowed to elapse between the first and second examinations, mainly to allow time for changes to occur. By examining the same suppliers twice, in 2004 and 2009, rather than once and then relying on retrospective accounts, both reference points could be studied "with similar care and precision."[47] This is an important design difference from previous code of conduct studies that relied on workers' retrospective accounts,[48] which are problematic due both to high employee turnover in the studied industries and to the well-documented weaknesses of such a research design.[49] Both the 2004 and 2009 examinations of the suppliers were based on unannounced, unofficial interviews outside the supplier factories. This interview setting has previously been suggested to be the most reliable in terms of obtaining accurate information about working conditions and supplier practices in developing countries.[50]

In both the initial and follow-up studies, supplier compliance was examined based on eight criteria included in all the firms' codes of conduct and in Chinese labor law.[51] These eight criteria were selected because they comprise the core criteria of retailers' codes of conduct and are all highly relevant to workers in toy factories.

1. Working hours (a maximum of 40 hours base work per week, three hours overtime per day, and 36 hours overtime per month)
2. Working days per week (a maximum of six working days per week)
3. Guaranteed minimum wage
4. Overtime compensation (50% extra on weekdays and 100% extra on weekends)
5. Health and safety education
6. No child labor (minimum working age of 16)
7. Each employee has copy of employment contract
8. Accident and pension insurance

Material concerning supplier compliance was gathered mainly from interviews with workers. In total, over 100 workers were interviewed in both the initial and follow-up studies. A detailed discussion of the methods used, covering the selection of interviewees, formulation of interview questions, etc., is presented by Egels-Zandén's article.[52] The material was analyzed by first combining and comparing the workers' responses for each factory, which revealed little variance between employee answers at the same supplier. Suppliers were then categorized as non-compliant if at least two employees had identified non-compliance, and no other interviewed employee of the same supplier could provide evidence of compliance with the criterion in question. If only one department in a supplier's factory was non-compliant, the supplier was still categorized as non-compliant, since MNC codes of conduct specify the standards for all a supplier's employees and departments.

An important downside of this method, in which only approximately 5% of the workforce is interviewed per supplier, is that the results for each supplier are tentative and probably incomplete.[53] Therefore, meaningful comparisons between suppliers are impossible and findings can only be discussed in aggregate, meaning that no attempts can be made to distinguish between the learning patterns of the studied suppliers.

To provide a more holistic picture of the learning effects of codes of conduct, 15 additional semi-structured interviews were conducted with CSR and purchasing managers of Swedish toy and garment retailers. As discussed below, the toy and garment retailers that are proactive in terms of codes of conduct work similarly with codes and monitoring. Ten semi-structured interviews were also conducted with managers of Chinese toy suppliers in Guangdong Province, and announced factory visits were made to two of the four suppliers in 2009. In addition, five semi-structured interviews were conducted with representatives of Swedish and international NGOs active in workers' rights in China. Each interview lasted about one hour.

Brief Overview of the Toy Industry and Swedish Toy Retailers

The empirical setting for this chapter is four Chinese toy suppliers in Guangdong Province that make products for, among others, three of the most proactive Swedish toy retailers. The focus on Chinese toy suppliers is explained by the fact that 98% of the toy imports to the EU come from Asia and 91% of these come from China.[54] Globally, approximately 80% of the world's toys are produced in China, mostly in the southern province of Guangdong.[55] The Swedish toy market greatly resembles the European and global toy markets, with most imports coming from Guangdong. The Swedish toy market is dominated by Top Toy, with a market share of over 30%, followed by several companies with 5–7% market shares, such as Brio, Barnens Hus, Ica, Leklust, and Lekia, and a few companies with 2–3% market shares, such as Coop and Åhléns.

The discussion of workers' rights in the toy industry started on a large scale in the mid 1990s with two serious fires in Chinese and Thai factories. After an international campaign aimed at increasing the toy industry's responsibility for workers' rights at their suppliers, the International Council of Toy Industries (ICTI) adopted its first Code of Business Practice in 1995. ICTI is the main industry association for toy producers and includes toy association representatives from over 30 countries. However, reports and campaigns on substandard working conditions continued to highlight problems such as child labor, excessive overtime, and violations of trade union rights. These campaigns eventually led in 2004 to the establishment of an industry initiative to audit workers' rights at toy suppliers—ICTI CARE.

ICTI CARE is an independent organization that oversees and implements compliance with ICTI's code of conduct. Once suppliers are deemed to be in compliance according to ICTI-certified auditors, they are awarded a "Seal of Compliance." The audits conducted as part of the ICTI CARE process are announced and interviews with workers are conducted on factory premises. In China, about half of the existing 3500–4000 toy factories were part of the ICTI CARE program in 2009, i.e., the program has had a strong impact since it began in 2004. Many Swedish toy retailers, like many international toy retailers, are also part of ICTI's "Date Certain Program," meaning that they commit to buying only from factories that are part of the ICTI CARE process in the near future. In 2009, 77% of Top Toy's and 80% of Brio's suppliers were participating in the ICTI CARE process; all of the suppliers evaluated here were participating in the ICTI CARE process.

ICTI CARE operates in parallel with retailer audits, imposing another layer of code of conduct demands on suppliers. In other words, ICTI CARE demands are not, at least in the short term, harmonized with retailers' code of conduct demands, meaning that suppliers still have to comply with multiple buyers' potentially different codes of conduct. ICTI Care is also—like codes of conduct—based mainly on policing suppliers, i.e., auditing them regularly, and does not represent a shift toward a more collaborative approach to improving workers' rights. Still, ICTI CARE does offer some training for suppliers and workers, which certainly could facilitate supplier implementation of codes of conduct. In addition, ICTI CARE unifies the participating retailers and sends a strong signal to suppliers that code of conduct compliance is central to receiving orders. This signal improves the incentives for suppliers to comply with the codes, since they can no longer play buyers off against each other.

Parallel to the development of the ICTI code of conduct and ICTI CARE, the larger Swedish firms that directly import toys (in particular Top Toy, Brio, and Coop) adopted their own codes of conduct and auditing in the mid 1990s. The Swedish retailers' codes of conduct are similar to those of other international toy retailers and to those of Swedish and international retailers in other industries, such as the garment industry.[56] The similarities between the Swedish and international retailers' codes of conduct are particularly strong with reference to the eight criteria examined here, since all are based on Chinese labor law in addition to the retailer codes of conduct. After the initiation of ICTI CARE in 2004, the similarities between the Swedish and international toy retailers' codes of conduct and auditing practices increased further, with all Swedish retailers participating in ICTI CARE. In practice, this means that the Swedish retailers' suppliers are audited both by the Swedish retailers' own and hired auditors and by ICTI CARE-certified auditors. In addition, many of the suppliers are also audited by international retailers, such as Mattel, Walt Disney, and Wal-Mart, since they produce for these firms as well.

Initial Double-loop Learning: Decoupling

COLLAPSE OF THE ENVISIONED LEARNING SYSTEM

As discussed above, codes of conduct are based on the assumption of a forced single-loop learning system incorporating negative feedback loops. The 2004 examination of the four Chinese suppliers' compliance with the Swedish toy retailers' codes of conduct clearly indicates that this envisioned learning system had collapsed. As summarized in Table 18.1, in 2004, suppliers were complying with the retailer codes of conduct to only a limited extent.

Table 18.1 Suppliers' level of compliance with retailers' codes of conduct (2004)

Studied criteria	% of suppliers complying with the criteria (2004)
Working hours	0%
No. working days	0%
Minimum wage	25%
Overtime compensation	50%
Health and safety education	0%
Child labour	100%
Employee contract	75%
Pension and accident insurance	25%

As seen in Table 18.1, the results of the study are unambiguous: the examined suppliers did not comply with the retailer codes of conduct. The only notable exceptions to this non-compliance were that all suppliers complied with child labor regulations and that most complied with employee contract regulations. Despite being subject to the code of conduct learning system with extensive monitoring, little had changed in the suppliers' actual operations.[57] For example, several of the examined suppliers were audited several times a year by Swedish and international retailers, such as Mattel and Disney, but still violated most of the examined criteria.

UNDERSTANDING THE REASONS FOR THE COLLAPSE

To understand how this lack of compliance could occur, it is useful to revisit the code of conduct learning system outlined in Figure 18.1. There are two main points in this learning system at which it could collapse. First, the auditors could be incapable of detecting violations of the codes of conduct, despite their existence. This could in turn be related to: i) poor audit quality,[58] and/or ii) supplier deception of monitoring organizations.[59] If auditors do not detect violations, retailers will not demand, and suppliers will not undertake, corrective actions despite this being necessary to improve workers' rights. Second, when the auditors identify violations of the codes of conduct, the retailers might refrain from demanding alterations to suppliers' operations since this might negatively impact purchasing prices, delivery scheduling, and other purchasing criteria.

While the interviews with purchasing and CSR managers provided some limited support for the second explanation, such practices seem to have been fairly marginal. In general, purchasing managers did demand changes when breaches of the codes were detected. Furthermore, the companies' own results from auditing the four studied suppliers indicated that most of them had passed the audits with few areas of improvement identified. The toy retailers were also, or at least seemed to be, genuinely surprised by the lack of supplier compliance. Hence, the conducted interviews indicate that the first explanation—inability to detect breaches of codes—was the main explanation for the collapse of the envisioned learning system. The central question is then this: If suppliers do not learn how to improve working conditions and auditing does not identify code of conduct violations, what do suppliers learn from being exposed to codes of conduct?

DOUBLE-LOOP LEARNING: DECOUPLING

While the suppliers did not learn to improve workers' rights as envisioned by the code of conduct learning logic, the interviews with employees at the four suppliers indicated that suppliers in fact learned a great deal from being exposed to codes of conduct. In line with the expectations of the new institutional literature, the suppliers learned how to improve their symbolic (rather than substantive) actions and how to erect elaborate facades aimed at deceiving auditors.[60] This decoupling of policy and practice was materialized in numerous deception techniques such as i) instructing employees what to say on monitoring occasions, ii) providing financial compensation for "correct" answers on monitoring occasions, iii) punishing "wrong" answers given on monitoring occasions, iv) hiding part of the workforce on monitoring occasions, v) forging salary lists, vi) forging time cards, and vii) forging employee contracts.

Previous code of conduct research provides clear indications that these findings are not unique to the suppliers examined here. For example, Welford and Frost argue that the "proliferation of codes of conduct has probably simply resulted in a proliferation of record keeping."[61] Similarly, Sun and Ngai find that codes of conduct produce "the paradoxical result that more effort goes into paperwork than into actual advancement of labour rights protection."[62]

The supplier focus on falsified documentation and facades is related to the "ceremonial" nature of code of conduct audits.[63] Since code of conduct audits last only between one and two days, it is difficult for auditors to assess working conditions throughout the company. This forces auditors to rely on documentation when analyzing issues such as working hours, wages, overtime compensation, child labor, and insurance. Lack of structured documentation is another frequent auditor complaint.[64] As the new institutional literature would predict, in these circumstances, symbolic and substantive actions become decoupled and what suppliers learn is to create increasingly elaborate facades for social auditors to audit. Although not found at any of the examined factories, the interviews conducted for this study indicate that there are even consultants and courses to help factories improve their symbolic actions.[65] Furthermore, computerized salary and time systems are available in China that allow both correct (unofficial) and incorrect (official) numbers to be entered into the same computer system. However, since auditors have become suspicious of overly "correct" numbers, the computer systems add random errors to the incorrect (official) numbers to create the appearance of human error and provide auditors with minor non-compliance findings.

Suppliers learning to deceive auditors in increasingly sophisticated ways is best characterized as double-loop learning.[66] Hence, while the code of conduct learning system is intended to generate single-loop learning, it has in practice generated double-loop learning. Rather than accepting the underlying assumptions, i.e., that compliance with codes of conduct is necessary to retain buyer contracts, suppliers have figured out that *perceived*, rather than actual, compliance is sufficient. In line with the new institutional literature, suppliers have even figured out that compliance is detrimental to retaining buyers, since it increases costs and makes it difficult to comply with buyers' other purchasing criteria. In other words, decoupling is the rational response to codes of conduct, since it is the only way to comply with buyers' inconsistent business and codes of conduct demands.

This finding is interesting in relation to the learning literature, since much of this literature a priori equates learning (especially double-loop learning) with positive/desirable outcomes.[67] Double-loop learning is thus presented as strengthening managerial capacity to act humanely and effectively.[68] The present study demonstrates that this assumption is at best wishful thinking, and that double-loop learning could lead to the buffering of the technical core of the company, preserving inhumane modes of production.

Subsequent Single-Loop Learning: Recoupling

While the 2004 study demonstrated that suppliers had learned mainly to decouple symbolic from substantive actions after being exposed to codes of conduct, the 2009 follow-up study painted a different picture. As presented in Table 18.2, in 2009, the suppliers were complying with most of the code of conduct criteria. Furthermore, the incidence of elaborate forms of conscious deception had significantly decreased with, for example, only one supplier instructing workers how to respond when being questioned. On the other hand, one studied supplier that had used no deception techniques in 2004, had introduced forged time cards by 2009 to cover up excessive overtime, while another supplier, between 2004 and 2009, started allowing workers to take work home at night to complete at a piecework rate. Nevertheless, in 2009, no supplier was using deception techniques as systematically as in 2004. Something had occurred that shifted suppliers from double-loop learning linked to decoupling to single-loop learning linked to recoupling.[69] To clarify, this shift is itself considered single-loop learning, despite suppliers having consciously decided to change their practices, since, by 2009, suppliers had acted without challenging the underlying assumptions on which codes of conduct are based.

Table 18.2 Suppliers' level of compliance with retailers' codes of conduct (2009)

Studied criteria	% of suppliers complying with the criteria (2004)	% of suppliers complying with the criteria (2009)
Working hours	0%	0%
No. working days	0%	100%
Minimum wage	25%	100%
Overtime compensation	50%	100%
Health and safety education	0%	100%
Child labour	100%	100%
Employee contract	75%	100%
Pension and accident insurance	25%	50%

RECOUPLING OF SYMBOLIC AND SUBSTANTIVE ACTIONS

The identified recoupling of symbolic and substantive actions is surprising from a new institutional perspective, according to which decoupling is envisioned to persist over time.[70] Recent new institutional research, however, identifies two main reasons why companies might, over time, recouple symbolic and substantive actions: i) increased external demands,[71] and ii) change in the type of external demands to more outcome and transparency-oriented ones.[72] In addition, previous code of conduct research indicates that a move toward more collaborative buyer–supplier relationships could tighten couplings between symbolic and substantive actions.[73]

The empirical data provide clear indications with respect to these reasons. First, between 2004 and 2009, the Swedish toy retailers *increased* both their code of conduct demands and their auditing. Top Toy, for example, doubled the number of people working on supplier auditing, Brio initiated code of conduct training for factory managers, and Coop worked more systematically on internal and external, announced and unannounced audits. The interviewed factory managers also perceived that the codes of conduct demands had increased between 2004 and 2009, and that these increased demands had led to improved working conditions. Hence, in line with previous code of conduct research[74] and studies of recoupling,[75] increased auditing frequency and increased demands were found to push suppliers toward the originally envisioned single-loop learning linked to compliance.

Second, in 2004, ICTI CARE was initiated. This *increased* the code of conduct demands and audits, since ICTI CARE audits operate in parallel with retailer audits. In 2009, all the examined suppliers were ICTI CARE certified (versus none in 2004), meaning that they had been exposed to, and passed, ICTI CARE audits between 2004 and 2009. In addition to increasing the demands, the emergence of ICTI CARE also provided toy retailers with a united front vis-à-vis the suppliers, since most international retailers commit to purchasing only from suppliers participating in the ICTI CARE process. Given that Barrientos and Smith have found that codes of conduct have the greatest impact when suppliers see their various buyers making similar demands, the importance of presenting a united front should not be underestimated.[76] Some of the Swedish retailers also claimed that certain improvements, especially in health and safety measures and correct overtime compensation, were due largely to the emergence of ICTI CARE, and a China Labor Watch investigation concluded that suppliers with ICTI CARE certifications had higher compliance levels than did non-certified suppliers.[77]

Third, retailers, ICTI CARE, and social auditors *changed the type* of demands, including more transparency demands in 2009 than in 2004. As Welford and Frost noted, auditors "often say that their job is not to find out *whether* factories are cheating on the audit, but *how*."[78] This insight has led to an emphasis on transparency rather than initial compliance, i.e., suppliers are more severely punished for attempting to deceive auditors than for violating codes of conduct. This is in line with the finding that decoupling is more difficult to sustain when it is conscious and explicit than when it occurs in good faith.[79] Hence, while decoupling generates short-term legitimacy gains for suppliers, it simultaneously creates latent legitimacy threats.[80] When suppliers start to realize this (usually after having being caught attempting to deceive auditors), it becomes less rational to decouple.

Finally, although limited empirical material exists capturing how buyer–supplier relationships developed between 2004 and 2009 for the studied suppliers, the general development of toy manufacturers in China suggests that relationships became more collaborative. An ICTI CARE representative estimated that the number of Chinese toy factories declined from approximately 10,000 in 2004 to between 3500 and 4000 in 2009, due both to a poisonous lead paint scandal in 2007, which made Chinese authorities more restrictive in issuing export licenses, and to the global recession in 2008, which led to the closure of numerous toy factories. Furthermore, since most major toy retailers are now participating in ICTI CARE, most suppliers are likely have close relationships with at least some buyers that possess codes, making codes of conduct more embedded in collaborative relationships in 2009 than in 2004. It is reasonable to assume that the observed recoupling of policy and practice is at least somewhat due to changed buyer–ICTI–supplier relationships.

UNRELATED TRENDS CREATING RECOUPLING

While the above discussion indicates that, given time, codes of conduct were able to promote more than just symbolic compliance and thus improve workers' rights in practice, trends unrelated to codes of conduct should also be considered when seeking to explain the improvements in workers' rights. First, Chinese labor law changed between 2004 and 2009, making workers' rights regulations (especially governing employment contracts) more stringent. These legal changes have received extensive attention in China and are claimed to provide workers with a better means to enforce their rights through the formal legal system.[81] ICTI CARE representatives also recognize that the new labor law is an important reason for the improved situation in the toy industry.

Second, economic development in the province of Guangdong, where the examined suppliers are located, has been a driving force of the booming Chinese economy. The region has averaged 9.8% annual growth over the last 30 years, and even managed to grow by over 10% during the 2008 economic downturn.[82] The province's strong economic growth has given workers more employment choices in the region, in turn generating high employee turnover at the toy suppliers. For example, in one studied factory with 700 employees, workers claimed that about ten workers per day left the factory. In 2009, factory managers also claimed that there was a shortage of labor in Guangdong, which was not the case in 2004. In addition, the minimum wage in Guangdong has continued to rise, and manufacturing companies in the region expect it to continue to increase by an average of 20% per year up to 2015.[83] Guangdong authorities are increasing the minimum wage because they want to induce manufacturers to upgrade and shift into more value-added operations.[84] Furthermore, economic development in rural China has encouraged workers to remain in their home regions, leading to a shortage of migrant workers in Guangdong. Toy factories in Guangdong have apparently been forced to improve workers' rights due to a shortage of migrant workers and the need to offer better working conditions to retain existing workers.[85]

In sum, other factors unrelated to codes of conduct have likely contributed to improved working conditions at the examined suppliers. To understand the potential of codes of conduct, it is important to understand the legal and economic development in the region where the codes are supposed to make a difference. Still, there are enough indications in the empirical data to conclude that the improvements are not solely due to general economic and legal development in China, indicating that codes of conduct can indeed make a difference. The finding that the recoupling of symbolic and substantive actions is influenced by factors unrelated to the institutional pressure that led to the initial symbolic compliance is currently unrecognized in the new institutional literature, which focuses solely on increases or changes in the initial institutional pressures.

Code of Conduct Compliance: A Two-Step Learning Process

This chapter has demonstrated, based on an examination of four Chinese toy suppliers, that codes of conduct initially risk generating only symbolic compliance, i.e., suppliers decouple policy and practice. This is because suppliers are challenging the single-loop learning logic of codes of conduct, realizing that perceived, rather than actual, compliance is not only sufficient but usually preferable, since it allows them to comply with retailers' inconsistent purchasing criteria. In other words, as long as buyers (and ultimately consumers) are not prepared to pay a higher price and accept longer lead times, rational suppliers will attempt to deceive auditors rather than improve workers' rights. Codes of conduct can, at least initially, be expected to generate double-loop learning and elaborate facades intended to deceive auditors rather than improve workers' rights. Over time, symbolic and substantive actions may well be recoupled, however, leading to actual improvement in workers' rights through single-loop learning. This is particularly likely when buyers increase their code of conduct demands and auditing, coordinate their code of conduct activities throughout the industry, and value transparency more than actual initial compliance. If this coincides with economic and legal development in the relevant region, workers' rights in global supply chains could improve over time, thanks in part to retailers' codes of conduct.

As illustrated in Figure 18.3, these findings indicate that both the code of conduct and new institutional literatures must be consulted if we are to understand completely what suppliers learn from codes of conduct. When suppliers are initially exposed to codes of conduct (Phase I), the new institutional literature provides the most accurate description of their behavior. Over time (Phase II), however, the single-loop code of conduct literature helps us understand why suppliers, at least in the long term, might come to recouple symbolic and substantive actions and improve workers' rights.

This chapter contributes to the code of conduct literature in several important ways. It responds to calls for more research into how recipients of codes (in this case, suppliers) respond to codes of conduct, introduces a longitudinal process perspective into the literature, and outlines a useful theoretical framework for studying these two areas based on the learning and new institutional literatures. The chapter also contributes to the heated debate on the merits of codes of conduct by providing one of the first credible longitudinal studies of how codes affect workers' rights. The findings are interesting, since they—unlike those of most previous research—indicate that codes of conduct can have positive effects despite being based on policing rather than collaboration, providing the policing is sufficiently forceful and coordinated. Finally, the chapter contributes to the learning literature by emphasizing that double-loop learning could lead to the preservation of inhumane production methods, and contributes to the new institutional literature by demonstrating how the recoupling of policy and practice is influenced by factors unrelated to institutional pressure.

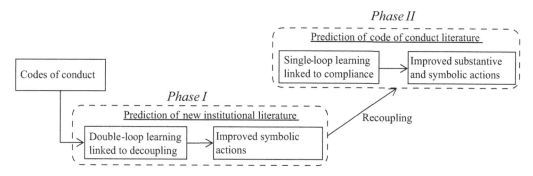

Figure 18.3 The two phases of code of conduct learning

Notes

1   van Tulder, R. & Kolk, A. (2001), "Multinationality and Corporate Ethics: Codes of Conduct in the Sporting Goods Industry", *Journal of International Business Studies*, Vol. 32, No. 2, pp. 267–283; Frenkel, S. & Kim, S. (2004), "Corporate Codes of Labour Practice and Employment Relations in Sports Shoe Contractor Factories in South Korea", *Asia Pacific Journal of Human Resources*, Vol. 42, No. 1, pp. 6–31.

2   Bartley, T. (2007), "Institutional Emergence in an Era of Globalization: The Rise of Transnational Private Regulation of Labor and Environmental Conditions", *American Journal of Sociology*, Vol. 113, No. 2, pp. 297–351; Locke, R. Kochan, T., Romis, M. & Qin, F. (2007), "Beyond Corporate Codes of Conduct: Work Organization and Labour Standards at Nike's Suppliers", *International Labour Review*, Vol. 146, No. 1–2, pp. 21–40.

3   Egels-Zandén, N. & Hyllman, P. (2007), "Evaluating Strategies for Negotiating Workers' Rights in Transnational Corporations: The Effects of Codes of Conduct and Global Agreements on Workplace Democracy", *Journal of Business Ethics*, Vol. 76, No. 2, pp. 207–223.

4   Cowton, C.J. & Thompson, P. (2000), "Do Codes Make a Difference? The Case of Bank Lending and the Environment", *Journal of Business Ethics*, Vol. 24, No. 2, pp. 165–178; Kaptein, M. (2004), "Business Codes of Multinational Firms: What Do They Say?", *Journal of Business Ethics*, Vol. 50, No. 1, pp. 13–31.

5   Pearson, R. & Seyfang, G. (2001), "New Hope or False Dawn?", *Global Social Policy*, Vol. 1, No. 1, pp. 49–78; Ruggie, J. (2004), "How to Marry Civic Politics and Global Governance". In A. Kuper (ed.), *The Impact of Corporations on Global Governance*, Carnegie Council on Ethics and International Affairs, New York, pp. 10–23; Zadek, S. (2004), "The Path to Corporate Social Responsibility", *Harvard Business Review*, Vol. 82, No. 12, pp. 125–32.

6   Frundt, H.J. (2004), "Unions Wrestle with Corporate Codes of Conduct", *Working USA*, Vol. 7, No. 4, pp. 36–69; Blowfield, M. & Dolan, C. (2008), "Stewards of Virtue? The Ethical Dilemma of CSR in African Horticulture", *Development and Change*, Vol. 39, No. 1, pp. 1–23.

7   Locke, R., Qin, F. & Brause, A. (2007), "Does Monitoring Improve Labor Standards? Lessons from Nike", *Industrial and Labor Relations Review*, Vol. 61, No. 1, pp. 3–31.

8   O'Rourke, D. (2002), "Monitoring the Monitors: A Critique of Third-Party Labor Monitoring". In R. Jenkins, R. Pearson & G. Seyfang (eds.), *Corporate Responsibility and Labour Rights: Codes of Conduct in the Global Economy*, Earthscan, London, pp. 196–208; Hemphill, T. (2004), "Monitoring Global Corporate Citizenship: Industry Self-regulation at a Crossroads", *Journal of Corporate Citizenship*, Vol. 14, pp. 81–95; Egels-Zandén, N. (2007), "Suppliers' Compliance with MNCs' Codes of Conduct: Behind the Scenes at Chinese Toy Suppliers", *Journal of Business Ethics*, Vol. 75, No. 1, pp. 45–62.

9   Nijhof, A., Cludts, S., Fisscher, O. & Laan, A. (2003), "Measuring the Implementation of Codes of Conduct: An Assessment Method Based on a Process Approach of the Responsible Organisation", *Journal of Business Ethics*, Vol. 45, No. 1, pp. 65–78.

10   Sethi, S.P. (2002), "Standards for Corporate Conduct in the International Arena: Challenges and Opportunities for Multinational Corporations", *Business and Society Review*, Vol. 107, No. 1, pp. 20–40.

11   van Tulder & Kolk, *op. cit.*; Kaptein, *op. cit.*

12   Weaver, G.R. (1993), "Corporate Codes of Ethics: Purpose, Process and Content Issues", *Business and Society*, Vol. 32, No. 1, pp. 44–58; van Tulder & Kolk, *op. cit.*

13   Cowton & Thompson, *op. cit.*

14   Frenkel, S. (2001), "Globalization, Athletic Footwear Commodity Chains and Employment Relations in China", *Organization Studies*, Vol. 22, No. 4, pp. 531–562; Barrientos, S. & Smith, S. (2007), "Do Workers Benefit from Ethical Trade? Assessing Codes of Labour Practice in Global Production Systems", *Third World Quarterly*, Vol. 28, No. 4, pp. 713–729; Locke, Qin & Brause, *op. cit.*

15   Stevens, B. (1994), "An Analysis of Corporate Ethical Code Studies: 'Where Do We Go from Here?'", *Journal of Business Ethics*, Vol. 13, No. 1, pp. 63–69; Helin, S. & Sandström, J. (2008), "Codes, Ethics and Cross-Cultural Differences: Stories from the Implementation of a Corporate Code of Ethics in a MNC Subsidiary", *Journal of Business Ethics*, Vol. 82, No. 2, pp. 281–291.

16   Chan, A. & Siu, K. (2010), "Analyzing Exploitation: The Mechanisms Underpinning Low Wages and Excessive Overtime in Chinese Export Factories", *Critical Asian Studies*, Vol. 42, No. 2, pp. 167–190, p. 167.

17   Wells, D. (2007), "Too Weak for the Job: Corporate Codes of Conduct, Non Governmental Organizations and the Regulation of International Labour Standards", *Global Social Policy*, Vol. 7, No. 1, pp. 51–74, p. 53.

18   Locke, Qin & Brause, *op. cit.*, p. 21.

19   Locke, Qin & Brause, *op. cit.*

20   Locke, Kochan, Romis & Qin, *op. cit.*; Locke, Qin & Brause, *op. cit.*; Locke, R., Amengual, M. & Mangla, A. (2009), "Virtue Out of Necessity? Compliance, Commitment and the Improvement of Labor Conditions in Global Supply Chains", *Politics & Society*, Vol. 37, No. 3, pp. 319–351.

21   Chakrabarty, S. & Grote, U. (2009), "Child Labor in Carpet Weaving: Impact of Social Labeling in India and Nepal", *World Development*, Vol. 37, No. 10, pp. 1683–1693.

22   Ngai, P. (2005), "Global Production, Company Codes of Conduct, and Labor Conditions in China: A Case Study of Two Factories", *The China Journal*, Vol. 54, pp. 101–113.

23   Barrientos & Smith, *op. cit.*

24   Barrientos & Smith, *op. cit.*; Chan & Siu, *op. cit.*

25   Boring, E.G. (1954), "The Nature and History of Experimental Control", *American Journal of Psychology*, Vol. 67, No. 4, pp. 573–589.

26   Locke, Qin & Brause, *op. cit.*

27   O'Rourke, *op. cit.*; Hemphill, *op. cit.*; Egels-Zandén, *op. cit.*

28   Doig, A. & Wilson, J. (1998), "The Effectiveness of Codes of Conduct", *Business Ethics: A European Review*, Vol. 7, No. 3, pp. 140–149; Nijhof, Cludts, Fisscher & Laan, *op. cit.*; Locke, Amengual & Mangla, *op. cit.*

29   Nijhof, Cludts, Fisscher & Laan, *op. cit.*

30   Swieringa and Wierdsma (1992), cited in Easterby-Smith, M. (1997), "Disciplines of Organizational Learning: Contributions and Critiques", *Human Relations*, Vol. 50, No. 9, pp. 1085–1113.

31   Argyris, C. & Schön, D.A. (1978), *Organizational Learning*, Addison Wesley, Reading, MA.

32   Argyris, C. (1976), "Single Loop and Double Loop Models in Research on Decision Making", *Administrative Science Quarterly*, Vol. 21, No. 3, pp. 363–375; Argyris, C. (1977), "Double loop learning in organizations", *Harvard Business Review*, Vol. 55, No. 5, pp. 115–125.

33   Argyris & Schön, *op. cit.*

34   Locke, Amengual & Mangla, *op. cit.*

35   Bartley, *op. cit.*; Ählström, J. & Egels-Zandén, N. (2008), "The Processes of Defining Corporate Responsibility: A Study of Swedish Garment Retailers' Responsibility", *Business Strategy and the Environment*, Vol. 17, No. 4, pp. 230–244.

36   Locke, Amengual & Mangla, *op. cit.*

37   van Tulder and Kolk, *op. cit.*; Locke, Amengual & Mangla, *op. cit.*

38   Gereffi, G. (1994), "The International Economy and Economic Development". In N. Smelser & R. Swedberg (eds.), *The Handbook of Economic Sociology*, Princeton University Press, Princeton, NJ, pp. 206–233; Traub-Werner, M. & Cravey, A.J. (2002), "Spatiality, Sweatshops and Solidarity in Guatemala", *Social and Cultural Geography*, Vol. 3, No. 4, pp. 383–401.

39   Traub-Werner & Cravey, *op. cit.*

40   For a competing view of buyer-supplier power see Locke, Amengual & Mangla, *op. cit.*

41   Meyer, J. & Rowan, B. (1977), "Institutionalized Organizations: Formal Structure as Myth and Ceremony", *American Journal of Sociology*, Vol. 83, No. 2, pp. 340–363; DiMaggio, P.J. & Powell, W. (1983), "The iron cage revisited", *American Sociological Review*, Vol. 48, No. 1, pp. 147–160; George, E., Chattopadhyay, P., Sitkin, S.B. & Barden, J. (2006), "Cognitive Underpinnings of Institutional Persistence and Change: A Framing Perspective", *Academy of Management Review*, Vol. 31, No. 2, pp. 347–365.

42   Meyer & Rowan, *op. cit.*

43   Meyer & Rowan, *op. cit.*, p. 341.

44   Jiang, B. (2009), "Implementing Supplier Codes of Conduct in Global Supply Chains: Process Explanations from Theoretic and Empirical Perspectives", *Journal of Business Ethics*, Vol. 85, No. 1, pp. 77–92, p. 88.

45   Meyer & Rowan, *op. cit.*; Tolbert, P.S. & Zucker, L.G. (1983), "Institutional Sources of Change in the Formal Structure of Organizations: The Diffusion of Civil Service Reform, 1880–1935", *Administrative Science Quarterly*, Vol. 28, No. 1, pp. 22–39.

46   Zucker, L.G. (1987), "Institutional Theories of Organizations", *Annual Review of Sociology*, Vol. 13, pp. 443–64.

47   Campbell, D.T. & Stanley, J.C. (1966), *Experimental and Quasi-Experimental Designs for Research*, Houghton Mifflin, Boston, MA, p. 6.

48   Barrientos & Smith, *op. cit.*

49   Stouffer, S.A. (1949), *The American Soldier*, Princeton University Press, Princeton; Boring, E.G. (1954), "The Nature and History of Experimental Control", *American Journal of Psychology*, Vol. 67, No. 4, pp. 573–589.

50   O'Rourke, *op. cit.*; Hemphill, *op. cit.*

51   Warner, M. (1996), "Economic Reforms, Industrial Relations and Human Resources in the People's Republic of China: An Overview", *Industrial Relations Journal*, Vol. 27, No. 3, pp. 195–210; Chan, A. (1998), "Labor Standards and Human Rights: The Case of Chinese Workers Under Market Socialism", *Human Rights Quarterly*, Vol. 20, No. 4, pp. 886–904; Ding, D.Z. & Warner, M. (1999), "'Re-inventing' China's Industrial Relations at Enterprise-Level: An Empirical Field Study in Four Major Cities", *Industrial Relations Journal*, Vol. 30, No. 3, pp. 243–260.

52   Egels-Zandén, *op. cit.*

53   Frenkel, *op. cit.*

54   Toy Industries of Europe (2008), "Facts and Figures", July 2008.

55   Australian Consumers Association, "Choice" July 2008, p. 27 and www.icti-care.org/foundation.html (accessed 27 August 2009).

56   Frenkel, *op. cit.*; van Tulder & Kolk, *op. cit.*; Sethi, *op. cit.*; Egels-Zandén, *op. cit.*; Ählström & Egels-Zandén, *op. cit.*

57   The empirical data for the 2004 study were collected on a single occasion, making discussion of precise changes in supplier operations uncertain. However, the employee interviews clearly indicated that workers had perceived little change since the introduction of codes of conduct,

and the extensive gap between code of conduct standards and supplier practices indicated that the system was malfunctioning in promoting improved working conditions.

58 O'Rourke, *et. cit.*; French, J.L. & Wokutch, R.E. (2005), "Child Workers, Globalization and International Business Ethics: A Case Study in Brazil's Export-oriented Shoe Industry", *Business Ethics Quarterly*, Vol. 15, No. 4, pp. 615–640.

59 Ngai, *op. cit.*; Blowfield & Dolan, *op. cit.*; Lund-Thomsen, P. (2008), "The Global Sourcing and Codes of Conduct Debate: Five Myths and Five Recommendations", *Development and Change*, Vol. 39, No. 6, pp. 1005–1018; Chan, A. (2009), "Challenges and Possibilities for Democratic Grassroots Union Elections in China: A Case Study of Two Factory-Level Elections and Their Aftermath", *Labor Studies Journal*, Vol. 34, No. 3, pp. 293–317; Jiang, *op. cit.*; Taylor, M. (2011), "Race you to the Bottom ... and Back Again? The Uneven Development of Labour Codes of Conduct", *New Political Economy*, Vol. 16, No. 4, pp. 445–462.

60 Meyer & Rowan, *op. cit.*

61 Welford, R. & Frost, S. (2006), "Corporate Social Responsibility in Asian Supply Chains", *Corporate Social Responsibility and Environmental Management*, Vol. 13, pp. 166–176, p. 169.

62 Sum, N-L. & Ngai, P. (2005), "Globalization and Paradoxes of Ethical Transnational Production: Code of Conduct in a Chinese Workplace", *Competition and Change*, Vol. 9, No. 2, pp. 181–200, p. 197.

63 Meyer & Rowan, *op. cit.*

64 Ngai, *op. cit.*

65 Roberts, D. & Engardio, P. (2006), "Secrets, Lies, and Sweatshops", *BusinessWeek*, 27 November.

66 Argyris 1976, *op. cit.*; Argyris 1977, *op. cit.*

67 Argyris, C. (1982), "The Executive Mind and Double-Loop Learning", *Organizational Dynamics*, Vol. 11, No. 2, pp. 5–22.

68 Ibid.

69 Espeland, W.N. (1998), *The Struggle for Water*, University of Chicago Press, Chicago, IL.

70 Meyer & Rowan, *op. cit.*

71 Kelly, E. & Dobbin, F. (1998), "How Affirmative Action Became Diversity Management", *American Behavioral Scientist*, Vol. 41, No. 7, pp. 960–984; Hallett, T. (2010), "The Myth Incarnate: Recoupling Processes, Turmoil, and Inhabited Institutions in an Urban Elementary School", *American Journal of Sociology*, Vol. 75, No. 1, pp. 52–74.

72 Johansson, S. (2003), "Independent Movement or Government Subcontractor? Strategic Responses of Voluntary Organizations to Institutional Processes", *Financial Accountability & Management*, Vol. 19, No. 3, pp. 209–224; Dobbin, F., Schrage, D. & Kalev, A. (2009), "Someone to Watch Over Me: Coupling, Decoupling, and Unintended Consequences in Corporate Equal Opportunity", Working Paper, Department of Sociology, Harvard University, Cambridge, MA; Sauder, M. & Espeland, W.N. (2009), "The Discipline of Rankings", *American Sociological Review*, Vol. 74, No. 1, pp. 63–82; Spillane, J.P., Parise, L.M. & Sherer, J.Z. (2011), "Organizational Routines as Coupling Mechanisms: Policy, School Administration, and the Technical Core", *American Educational Research Journal*, Vol. 48, No. 3, pp. 586–620.

73 Locke, Kochan, Romis & Qin, *op. cit.*

74 Esbenshade, J. (2004), *Monitoring Sweatshops: Workers, Consumers, and the Global Apparel Industry*, Temple University Press, Philadelphia.

75 Kelly & Dobbin, *op. cit.*; Hallett, *op. cit.*

76 Barrientos & Smith, *op. cit.*

77 China Labor Watch (2007), "Investigations of Toy Suppliers in China; Workers are still suffering", August.

78   Welford & Frost, *op. cit.*, p. 171.

79   Hernes, T. (2005), "Four Ideal-Type Organizational Responses to New Public Management Reforms and Some Consequences", *International Review of Administrative Sciences*, Vol. 71, No. 1, pp. 5–17.

80   MacLean, T.L. & Behnam, M. (2010), "The Dangers of Decoupling: The Relationship between Compliance Programs, Legitimacy Perceptions, and Institutionalized Misconduct", *Academy of Management Journal*, Vol. 53, No. 6, pp. 1499–1520.

81   *Newsweek* (2008), "Is China's Labor Law Working?" 14 February 2008, www.newsweek.

82   Swedish Consoul in Canton "Guangdongs ekonomi december 2008 – stark nog att rida ut den ekonomiska avmattningen?" 2 December 2008. Swedish Consoul in Canton "Guangdongs ekonomi inför Oxens år" 15 January 2009.

83   *South China Morning Post* (2011), "Factory bosses protest at pay rise", 9 November 2011.

84   Ibid.

85   Welford & Frost, *op. cit.*

CHAPTER 10

19 *Understanding Resilience of Complex Value-Chain Networks*

JERYANG PARK,* THOMAS P. SEAGER,† AND
P. SURESH C. RAO‡

Keywords

Resilience, adaptability, sustainable value chain, complex adaptive networks, $1/f^{\alpha}$ noise, inequality analysis.

Introduction

There are two strategies for incorporating sustainability into business management: (1) risk reduction, and (2) eco-efficient products or services.[1] Both start with the presumption that factors constraining or threatening the system performance are identifiable and predictable, and that optimization is possible for gaining maximum efficiency for desirable outcomes under a set of constraints. For example, a conventional risk-management approach starts with identifying risks (e.g., probabilistic estimates of harm) and designs a system which is able to tolerate predictable disturbances and avoids undesirable outcomes with safety margins set to maximize efficiency. Also, eco-efficiency tactics set multiple objective functions of the "triple bottom line" as the new risk factors, and design and manage a system for sustainable performance over the long term. For example, maximized efficiency is hypothetically expected by setting a strategy that maximizes economic returns (e.g., net profits while minimizing ecological impacts (e.g., waste disposal)).

In complex systems, however, unpredicted risks always exist and inevitably emerge, imposing significant threats on the maintenance of critical functions and structures throughout a system's life cycle.[2] As engineered systems and organizations increase in complexity, especially with regard to linkages with economic, social, and environmental domains, the concept of resilience has increasingly gained attention as being essential for sustainability, as it calls for strategies which respond to unknown hazards.[3] *Resilience* as

* School of Civil Engineering, Purdue University, 550 Stadium Mall Drive, West Lafayette, IN 47907-2051, USA. E-mail: jeryang@purdue.edu. Telephone: +1 765 404 9848.

† Associate Professor, School of Sustainable Engineering & the Built Environment, Arizona State University, Tempe, AZ 85287-9309, USA. E-mail: Thomas.Seager@asu.edu. Telephone: 480-967-0531.

‡ Lee A. Reith Distinguished Professor, School of Civil Engineering, Purdue University, 550 Stadium Mall Drive, West Lafayette, IN 47907-2051, USA. E-mail: pscr@purdue.edu. Telephone: +1 765-496-6554.

used here refers to the ability of a complex system to maintain its desired functionalities within some bounds by adapting its form to changed forcing. As modern value chains increase in spatial scale and enlarge to become globalized, the number of links between manufacturers and customers increases. This means the sustainability of value chain must be examined in the context of complex network systems.[4] When risks are managed and a complex system is optimized for short-term efficiency, improved diversity and adaptability, which are essential for resilience, are not likely to be the outcomes. An improved understanding of resilience is essential to sustainable value-chain management.

The following analysis is motivated by the need to understand efficiency and resilience as a basis for design and management of value chains. The following questions guided our analysis:

- Is efficiency-driven design and management inappropriate for complex value chains?
- What drives the resilience of complex value chain networks?
- What design features and operation strategies foster resilience of value-chain networks?

In this chapter, two different perspectives of design and management of value chains are discussed: (1) risk optimization for efficiency (the approach currently in vogue) and why it is not sufficient for designing and managing complex value-chain networks; and (2) a resilience-based approach as an alternative for sustainability. Next, the role of adaptability for the resilience of complex value-chain networks is explained. Finally, *complex adaptive networks* with several adaptive strategies are suggested as the design and management goal for resilient value chains. A diagnosis tool for identifying the adaptive state of a complex network is also presented.

RISK OPTIMIZATION FOR EFFICIENCY

From an efficiency-centered perspective, a system is typically designed by emphasizing safety margins, which are estimated by identification and prediction of risks, rather than the attributes critical to resilience (e.g., diversity, redundancy, substitutability, and flexibility). Nevertheless, recent catastrophes – such as the crisis at the Fukushima nuclear power plant, flooding caused by Hurricanes Katrina and Sandy, the Deep Water Horizon oil spill, and other examples – have renewed interest in the concept of resilience, especially as it relates the vulnerability of complex systems to unpredictable events with cascading failures.[5] Engineered systems like manufacturing production and distribution and urban infrastructures were designed to withstand potential hazards, as they are often equipped with appropriate safety measures (e.g., robustness, redundant systems or back-ups) based on conventional risk assessment. However, their failures, which were caused by low-probability shocks, suggest that engineered systems designed with a conventional risk-management approach alone are insufficient for achieving safety and reliability.[6] This is especially the case when the system failure is a catastrophe that results in devastating consequences, often at a spatial scale that is far beyond the boundary of the failed system. In a complex network perspective, such engineered systems exist as nodes in networks (e.g., a nuclear power plant is a hub node in a power grid network, meaning that the plant has numerous connections to other nodes). It is critical to ensure that the hub nodes are safe, because once they fail, the safety of a whole network is threatened. However, it is also important to consider that, when those nodes fail (as in the examples above), the design and operation of the network should be resilient for maintaining functionalities (e.g., maintaining power supply at some level despite the failures of the power plant). The importance of a hub node to resilience (or vulnerability) of a complex network will be discussed further in the section Value Chains as Complex Networks. The main problem is that probabilities of unexpected events, which would disrupt the hub nodes and eventually the whole network, were not considered in the system's design and operation.

A system that is designed to tolerate identified risks is regarded as successful only until catastrophic events call into question the suitability of the original design.[7] The problem is that when the robustness of a system is built upon resistance, which is a typical result of the efficient management of risks, the system tends to lose adaptability and will be locked in a rigidity trap.[8] Incorporation of new information and innovation is difficult under these conditions because additional resources may be required to change the rigid system beyond the investments already made. This explains, for example, why decision makers were reluctant to revisit the vulnerability of the Fukushima Daiichi nuclear power plant until the catastrophic earthquake and tsunami that devastated the plant in March 2011, in spite of the fact that the earthquake and tsunami in the region were accurately predicted a decade beforehand.[9] This implies that when an engineered system is designed only in pursuit of efficiency, it becomes rigid and is unable to cope not only with unknown hazards, but also with the hazards identified during post-disaster analyses.

Traditional risk management starts from the premise that the hazards are known, identifiable, and quantifiable.[10] External forcing of the system, from multiple sources, can be viewed as a composite of several stochastic processes, each with a characteristic range of amplitudes at various frequencies. These temporal variations in forcing may be statistically represented by probability density functions (*pdfs*), with specified moments (e.g., mean, variance, skewness). For systems with asymmetrical "long-tailed" *pdfs* (e.g., exponential or log-normal), characterizing the long tails is difficult because sufficient long-term data are unavailable for detecting few (low probability) high-magnitude events. Thus, available data represent a distally truncated *pdf*, leading to underestimation of unobserved low-probability but high-consequence risks. Such events may be characterized as "shocks" that can destabilize the complex system; examples include unexpected events such as the Fukushima tsunami and the subsequent power grid failure that disrupted supply chains at the global scale.

Such problems are exacerbated for systems characterized by *pdfs* with "heavy tails" (e.g., power law), which have indeterminate mean and variance of the *pdf*.[11] For example, the intensity of earthquakes and the size of power outages, and other catastrophic events, follow power law *pdfs*.[12] Systematic bias (e.g., focus on efficiency) leads to underestimation or ignorance of unknown risks. Generally, a cost-benefit analysis is used to determine the point of truncation on the heavy-tailed *pdf*. The truncated *pdf* can then be estimated using an exponential or log-normal or Pareto *pdf*, for which moments are known.[13] However, any such estimation is not representative of actual costs that will be incurred by the events beyond the truncation.

The unpredictable nature of the full spectrum of risks also applies to value-chain management, since the events that are characterized by heavy tails, such as the above examples, are not limited to a specific field. Supply-chain management through "just-in-time" delivery of components provides economic efficiency by reducing the need to maintain large inventories.[14] But, this strategy also leads to disruption of production schedules and financial losses when unexpected or uncontrolled cascading disruptions propagate through the supply chain. Therefore, efficiency-based approaches might be effective only under identified low-disturbance regimes.[15]

SUSTAINABILITY THROUGH RESILIENCE

Robustness can be achieved either by increasing resistance or resilience. The former approach is typical in an engineering system design and is achieved by increasing robustness, i.e. by improving resistance against predicted risks. In contrast, a complex adaptive system achieves robustness based on dynamic flexibility and diversity in its processes.[16] Static functionality may be possible under stationary forcing; that is, all potential perturbations are identifiable and the system is designed to be resistant enough to those perturbations. However, external forcing is often non-stationary, with perturbations that cannot be fully identified. Consistent with its original ecological applications, resilience refers to the capacity of a system to absorb disturbances without catastrophic loss of form or function.[17] During the disturbance-absorbing process (i.e., attenuation), adaptability of the complex system plays a key role. Thus, when a system loses its adaptability, the system's state is likely to cross a tipping point, leading to a regime shift; i.e., moving into an undesired and/or irrevocable regime in which the system fails to continue its desired functionality.

To enable resilience to be operationalized or quantifiable, engineering resilience has been defined in numerous, context-specific ways, which primarily emphasize the system's recovery performance for post-disturbance states.[18] Although the ability to recover to pre-disturbance state is important, current measures do not adequately capture performance in anticipating and preparing for unexpected forcing or in reducing the consequences of disturbances. Adaptability, as in the ecological context, should therefore occur continuously (pre-, during, and post-disturbance), since an important role of resilience is to prevent undesirable and unexpected regime shifts.

A resilient complex system has the capacity for accommodating inevitable changes and is able to recover to some desired state after undergoing an undesired change resulting from an unexpected shock.[19] Prompt accommodation to the changed conditions as new information is gained requires a continuous processes of sensing, anticipating, learning, and adapting (Figure 19.1),[20] as summarized below.

1. **Sensing** is the process by which new system stresses are monitored and incorporated into current understanding. Any rare signal that is out of the normal range should be considered as an early warning signal, and attention should be given to coping with the abnormality. Thus, the system needs to have *memory* and flexibility to adjust to both short-term and long-term stochasticity of the external drivers.

2. **Anticipation** is the process by which knowledge gained by *sensing* is used to anticipate possible crises and disasters. This also implies that memory of the temporal pattern (i.e., time series) of recent and distant past events is used to anticipate the near-term and long-term temporal patterns of future likely events. Such an approach can readily incorporate non-stationarity in forcing, either as a stochastic or a deterministic process. Anticipation permits the development of adaptation strategies and leads to further enhancement of sensing for the anticipated disturbance regimes.

3. **Adaptation** is the response taken after information from *sensing* and *anticipation* are carefully considered. In addition to the incremental change for solving the sensed and anticipated problems, innovative redesign, such as creative destruction, should be considered for a safe-fail mode.[21]
4. **Learning** is the process by which new knowledge is created and maintained as memory by observation of past actions, i.e., understanding of how various adaptive strategies have succeeded to buffer, delay or attenuate the variability arising from both internal and external factors. After adaptation, the level of appropriateness of adaptive actions can be assessed and future iterations can incorporate this knowledge.

Adaptation, as used here, includes the anticipation of risks, recovery after disturbances, and the flexibility in structure and management for dealing with unexpected disruptive events.[22] Thus, adaptation not only enables maintaining functionality within an acceptable range, but also plays an important role in recovery if the complex system transgresses thresholds. Because of the existence of human-system interfaces in engineered systems, even a highly engineered system can have adaptive responses to an unexpected non-stationary forcing.[23] That is, engineered systems must be designed with built-in adaptive features (e.g., diversity and flexibility) to allow the human operators to alter the system to cope with unexpected "outlier" disturbances.[24] A rigid design precludes appropriate human interference, and can cause an engineered system to fail, either temporarily or catastrophically.[25]

A complex engineered system should exert adaptive behavior to maintain its pre-determined desired *functionalities*. While natural complex systems adapt at a local level

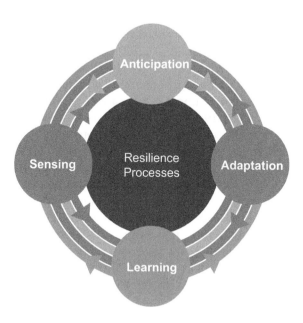

Figure 19.1 Schematic representation of the recursive process which leads to emergence of resilience in complex systems. The arrows in the figure do not necessarily mean a particular sequence between linked processes

without the consideration of consequences from self-organization at a system level, engineered systems must consider their global system-scale functionalities as an objective function for the adaptability. The difference of complex adaptive engineered systems from systems that are designed in conventional ways (e.g., efficiency-centered design) is that a static functionality is no longer an option. Static functionality may be possible if all potential perturbations are identifiable and the system is designed to be resistant enough to those perturbations; however, perturbations cannot be fully identified.

The foregoing discussion suggests that analyzing for and understanding *memory* of a system's past disturbances and performances is a key element of the recursive processes for increasing system resilience. From this perspective, resilience analysis can be understood as a differentiable and complementary process to risk analysis and is opposite to an optimization approach, with important implications for the adaptive management of complex, coupled ecological-engineering systems.

Value Chains as Complex Networks

NETWORK TOPOLOGY AND DISRUPTIONS

Modern value chains, at regional, national, and international scales, often take the form of complex, *dynamic*, and *directed* networks, which can be represented as several nodes (e.g., suppliers, assemblers, manufacturers, distributors, and retailers) connected by links (the connections between nodes).[26] Network structure (*topology*), indicated by the spatial structure of the network, the number of nodes, and connectivity, may be dynamic (expanding or shrinking), which further increases the complexity. The key performance indicator (*functionality*) for a value-chain network is the maintenance of flow of goods and services at the required levels.

The performance (e.g., resilience, efficiency) of a complex network strongly depends on its topology.[27] Topologies of complex networks (e.g., random, scale-free, hierarchical, and degree and locality-based attachment (DLA)) are determined by how the nodes are organized and connected (Table 19.1).[28] Node-degree of a random network is randomly distributed (e.g., normal or exponential *pdf*) by non-preferential attachment of a new node, while that of scale-free (or fractal) network is distributed preferentially, generating a power law *pdf* for node-degree distribution. Scale-free networks exhibit hub-and-node configurations, with a few, highly connected "hubs" and numerous "nodes" that have far fewer connections. Network size, characterized by the longest path through the network or the "diameter", can limit the largest number of links a node can have; thus, the power law *pdf*s in scale-free networks can be distally truncated (Pareto *pdf*). Hierarchical networks allow attachment only between different types of nodes (e.g., links between customers are not allowed), while DLA networks are configured by both preferential attachment and local distance. Network topologies evolve through attachment of new nodes and redirection of links.

Disruptions experienced by complex networks can be grouped into two broad categories: (1) *non-specific* (or random), where all nodes/links have equal probability of experiencing some level of disruption; and (2) *specific* (or targeted), where nodes with a high degree of connectivity are more likely to be disrupted.[29] Many disturbances can be viewed as a hybrid form of both characteristics.[30]

Table 19.1 **Topologies of complex networks. (a) Random network is generated by Erdös-Rényi model with 500 nodes and average node-degree of 2. (b) Scale-free network is generated by the model suggested in Pennock et al. (2002) with 500 nodes and same average node-degree as the random network. Pajek is used for both simulations**

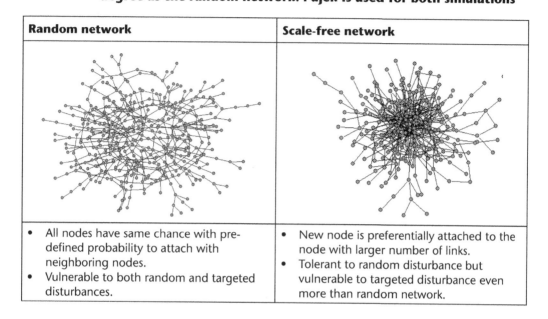

Random network	Scale-free network
• All nodes have same chance with pre-defined probability to attach with neighboring nodes. • Vulnerable to both random and targeted disturbances.	• New node is preferentially attached to the node with larger number of links. • Tolerant to random disturbance but vulnerable to targeted disturbance even more than random network.

EFFICIENCY VS. RESILIENCE APPROACHES

A value-chain network can be operated for either *efficiency* or *resilience* for optimal performance.[31] An efficiency-based approach might be effective under low-disturbance regimes, but a resilience-based approach generally is superior when continued functionality is required, especially when unexpected high-consequence "shocks" are likely. Redundancies can be built into the value-chain network (i.e., back-up capacity) to replace nodes that are out of service, or some or all of the nodes or links can be made more robust to survive "shocks". However, adding simple redundancy does not significantly reduce vulnerability when a system encounters unexpected disturbances (e.g. shocks, emergent risks), as the disturbances may have the same impact on the redundant components of the network (as was the case at Fukushima). These types of pre-emptive actions are not beneficial because they add rigidity to the complex network and also lead to a loss of economic efficiency.

An alternate resilience-based strategy is to invoke topological adaptations under stress. For example, the value-chain network can self-reorganize to transform its topology (e.g., add nodes, alter links) or temporarily alter its functions (operate at reduced serviceability) while experiencing external disruptions from upstream and downstream or internal changes within the network. Such changes come at an additional cost, and the cost-effectiveness of adaptive approaches should be evaluated. Thus, understanding the vulnerabilities of network topologies helps in choosing between efficiency or resilience strategies to survive expected disturbances and unexpected shocks.

PROPAGATION OF DISTURBANCES

If one of the nodes or links in the directed network fails, the impact of such failure may propagate along the network, often with the amplification of failure probabilities, to all connected nodes downstream.[32] For example, the shutdown of suppliers in the areas impacted by radiation leakage and tsunami flooding in the Sendai region of Japan created supply-chain logistical problems for major global automotive companies such as Volvo, Ford, and General Motors.[33] Even disruption at a small parts supply firm can stop the assembly lines at a global scale for manufacturing plants that depend on reliable part supplies.[34]

In a linear, directed serial chain that consists of n number of nodes (Figure 19.2a), the completion of a task at node i depends on the successful outcome of tasks at all upstream nodes ($i = 1, 2, \ldots, I - 1$) with a failure of any one being sufficient to cause failure of the final product. Given a chain of nodes, which represent upstream suppliers, let p_i be the probability to complete the task in the i-th step. Then, assuming that the probabilities of completion are independent of each other, the probability p that a focal node will complete its task in a given time is the product of the probabilities of all upstream nodes; such inter-dependence often generates an asymmetric (e.g., log-normal, Cauchy, or power law) pdf for the outcomes.[35] The case of a manufacturing a product with multiple components supplied in a parallel chain (Figure 19.2b) tends to a symmetric normal pdf as the number of suppliers increase. However, as supply chains are bounded to a finite number of suppliers, parallel chains are also likely to generate an asymmetric pdf.

A complex supply network can be thought of as a combination of multiple serial and parallel chains (Figure 19.3). With non-linear interactions along the links, a system response pattern will be different from a simple summation of individual chains. Instead, a node-degree pdf with strong asymmetry and heavy tails (e.g., a power law or Pareto pdf) is expected as the pattern. Simply put, as a supply chain becomes larger and as the number of branches increases, it is more likely to have unexpected events and outcomes. Even this simple logic calls into question the role of conventional risk-management practices that are ill-suited to deal with unpredicted risks. For complex networks, with increased uncertainty and vulnerability, resilience is necessary in addition to the approaches used for identified risks.

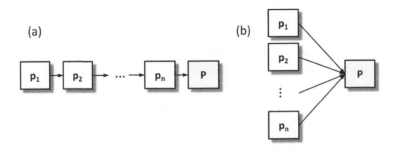

Figure 19.2 Simplified structure of a value chain, represented as (a) Serial supply chain, and (b) Parallel supply chain. Each structure can be part of a complex value-chain network

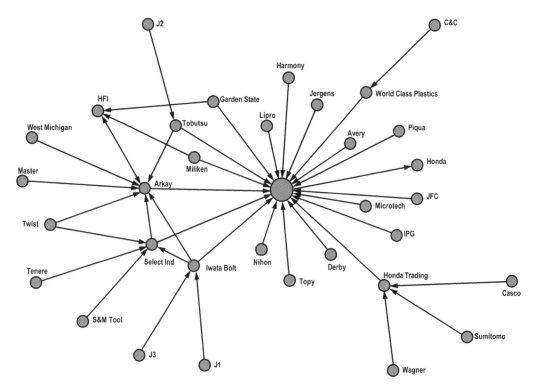

Figure 19.3 An example of a supply-chain network for the flow of materials in automobile manufacturing

Source: Reproduced from Kim et al. 2011, *Journal of Operations Management*: Structural investigation of supply networks: a social network analysis approach, Elsevier

METRICS FOR NETWORK PERFORMANCE

Certain topologies of a network are either vulnerable or tolerant depending on the perturbations (e.g., specific or non-specific failure). Zhao et al.[36] proposed several metrics to evaluate complex network responses when experiencing disturbances:

1. **Supply Availability Rate** is a measure of the aggregate performance of the complex network and is measured as the percentage of demand nodes that have access to supply nodes.
2. **Connectivity** as measured by the largest *functional* sub-network (LFSN) to consider the case of partitioning into several isolated sub-networks. The largest connected component (LCC) as a measure of network performance is suitable when all of the nodes are homogeneous.
3. **Average Supply-Path Length** is given by the average of the minimum supply-path lengths between all pairs of supply and demand nodes in the LFSN. This is a measure of the network accessibility, which can be used to examine cost and time efficiency. Higher accessibility means that supplies are closer to consumers, and they can receive them at lower cost or in lesser time.

4. **Maximum Supply-Path Length** is the longest supply-path length between any supply and demand pair and is used for examining the worst-case scenario of network accessibility.

These metrics can offer insight into the role of topological features for evaluating the network's robustness.

SPECTRAL ANALYSES OF NETWORK PERFORMANCE

In addition to these metrics, spectral analysis[37] can be used to examine the frequency-amplitude patterns and temporal correlations exhibited both in the perturbation and the response regimes (see Figure 19.4). Given a time-series data of disturbances or a system performance, two types of analysis are useful: (1) autocorrelation analysis, to reveal the temporal correlation within the data set, which explains the type of *memory* of the stochastic forcing;[38] and (2) spectral analysis reveals the periodicity of the forcing.[39] Spectral analysis in the frequency domain, which can be obtained by Fourier transform of the autocorrelation function, gives the amount of variance accounted for by each frequency (f) (or wave length, $1 = 1/f$) in the process;[40] that is, the relative power (P) of that frequency. The power spectral density (PSD), when plotted as log P vs. log f, will be a straight line with a constant slope if the time series data has similar degree of non-stationarity at all frequencies. However, if the PSD plot is a composite of two or more straight lines, the time-series data exhibits frequency-dependent non-stationarity. Thus, the disturbance and response regimes can be evaluated by examining the $1/f^{\alpha}$ noise, in which α is the slope of PSD plot, and serves as a convenient indicator of how the stochastic processes are influenced by past events (i.e., *memory*).[41]

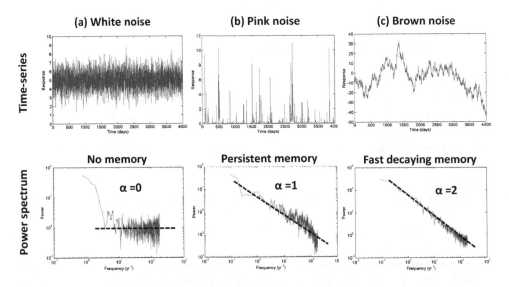

Figure 19.4 Examples of disturbance/response time-series patterns by the colors of noise and corresponding $1/f^{\alpha}$ power spectral density plots (log-log) in the frequency domain

Time-series analyses can be used as a proxy for sensing the current state of the system, to forecast possible future perturbations, and to analyze past performance. Thus, linking the network topology to types of external/internal disturbances helps understand the nature of the systems memory and its continued functionality (*serviceability*) of the value chain under stress. The manner in which the complex value chain responds to a time-series of disturbances therefore determines its resilience. In many complex systems (e.g., biological, ecological, psychological), the PSD tends to follow a power law [$p = \theta f^{-\alpha}$; θ and α are empirical constants]; the slope (α) of the log-log plot varies between 0 and 2 [$0 \leq \alpha \leq 2$].[42] "White noise," or a process with no memory, is represented by $\alpha = 0$; a Poisson process (e.g., rainfall) with short-term memory is one example (Figure 19.4a). "Pink noise" ($\alpha \approx 1$) is a process that depends on both recent and distant memory. As it combines the strong influence of all past events on the future, a process with $1/f$ noise is somewhat predictable,[43] but only if enough information on long temporal trends is available. Stream flow, resulting from filtering of memory-less rainfall patterns through the landscape, is one example of pink noise (Figure 19.4b).[44] In this case, the landscape retains "memory" of past rainfall events, indicated by the stochastic fluctuations in the amount of water stored in the landscape. When the influence of past decays linearly with time, "Brown noise" ($\alpha = 2$) is generated. Brownian motion, in which the present position of "particle" strongly depends on only its position at some prior time, is one example of such a stochastic process (Figure 19.4c).

NETWORK TOPOLOGY AND VULNERABILITY FROM DISRUPTIONS

Networks with different topologies respond differently depending on their ability to tolerate disturbances and how the disruptions are propagated. The robustness of complex networks is often evaluated by examining the loss of function after the removal of nodes. Zhao et al.[45] examined loss of functionality of complex networks with four types of topologies (random, hierarchical, scale-free, and DLA) when subjected to random or targeted disruptions. It is apparent that networks with different topologies have essentially similar trends in loss of function with "random" disruption: a linear loss of service availability rate with an increasing number of nodes removed. However, for "targeted" disruptions (removal of "hub" nodes with high node-degree) hierarchical and scale-free networks are the most vulnerable, while random networks are the least vulnerable. Networks with DLA topology were judged to have intermediate vulnerability, relative to other topologies, because the evolution of the network topology is based on balancing both efficiency and cost-effectiveness even under severe stress (loss of hub nodes).

Zhao et al.[46] analysis does not consider how resilience can be achieved through *adaptation*. Self-organization is a key feature of complex systems that results from the adaptation of entities (here, nodes and links). Nevertheless, most of the research regarding complex networks ignores adaptability by immediately deactivating nodes and/or links from the network as a result of disruption. In reality, even simple redundant strategies, such as inventory management or multi-contractors, allow for continued functionality at a node-scale. Therefore, *complex adaptive value-chain networks* need to be considered to appropriately account for adaptive strategies for resilience. For example, a temporary change in the network topology from an undesirable state to a desirable state may be considered.

As a way of evaluating the adaptability of complex value-chain networks, we suggest analysis of inequality in the loss of function with increasing node failure. Two types of response regimes can be identified (Figure 19.5): (1) less resilient, when the network is non-adaptive (rigid), but dependent on the network topology and the type of disturbance; and (2) more resilient, when the network includes some type of adaptive strategy. A simple empirical function that represents the possible range of network responses is given by Equation 1:

$$R = \frac{F}{F_{max}} = 1 - \left(\frac{n - n_{Th}}{N - n_{Th}}\right)^{\beta} \qquad \beta > 0 \qquad \text{(Eq. 1)}$$

where F is the network functionality with the subscript max denoting the maximum (desirable) functionality under no stress; n is the number of nodes that failed because of disruptions; n_{Th} is a threshold in terms of the number of nodes failure until which there is no functional loss; N is total number of nodes in the system; and β is an empirical coefficient ($\beta > 0$). Note that the results presented by Zhao et al.[47] and others are all below the 1:1 line of equality ($\beta = 1$) in the non-adaptive regime ($\beta < 1$); these curves are similar to complex network responses under targeted disruptions to nodes. The curves in the adaptive regime ($\beta > 1$) exist above the line of equality.

The parameter β implies that the distribution of node-degree is such that for $\beta \ll 1$ the topology becomes closer to a scale-free network. On the contrary, as β value approaches 1, the topology looks more similar to a random network. In contrast to the existing literature, the curve from the model can exist in the *adaptive regime* (beyond the equality line when $\beta > 1$), which means that the actual deterioration of function is less than the disruption originally imposed. This is possible when a high-degree node changes to a small-degree or is disconnected before a disruption; this strategy, in effect, can be implemented through sensing and anticipation.

A threshold value (n_{Th}) is also introduced in the model such that a network functions at full capacity even after some nodes fail because of redundant or alternate (equivalent) capacities. For example, loss of certain nodes may cause no significant loss of function, but if a specific or focused disruption occurs to a critical node (e.g., a node with the highest degree), system function may degrade following one of the curves in the non-adaptive regime ($\beta < 1$, Figure 19.5). If the intensity and location of the disruption are sensed, as it is likely to occur at a critical node, the consequences of the node failure can be anticipated. To avoid a large proportion of system's failure (e.g., curve of $\beta = 0.2$ in Figure 19.5), an adaptive strategy of changing the network topology can be exerted before the occurrence of the disruption. For example, an adaptive strategy would be to temporarily decrease the node-degree of the disrupted critical nodes. Moreover, with redundant capacity in other nodes, the system may function with the least amount of functional loss which pulls the curve beyond the equivalent (1:1) line ($\beta > 1$).

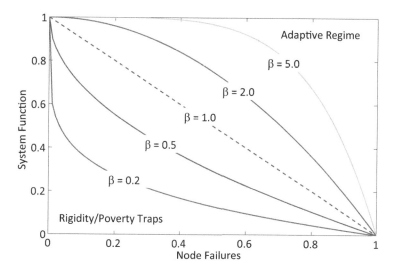

Figure 19.5 Inequality in the loss of the system functionality with increasing percentage of nodes failure; curves represent values for $n_{Th} = 0$, and β varies from 0.2 to 5. The diagonal blue dashed line ($\beta = 1$) represents the line of equality; i.e., linear loss in function with loss of nodes. The lines with $\beta > 1$ represent the likely responses in the adaptive regime, while curves with $\beta < 1$ are for response in the non-adaptive regime

STRATEGIES FOR COMPLEX ADAPTIVE NETWORKS

Carpenter and Brock[48] explored the adaptive capacity of complex social-ecological systems and how they can be locked into rigidity and poverty traps. Rigidity traps occur in a complex network when all nodes are fully connected in an inflexible and self-reinforcing way.[49] Rigidity generally emerges as a network grows by aiming for maximum efficiency (e.g., shortest paths between nodes for minimizing cost). On the other hand, poverty traps are the situations in which sufficient connectedness between nodes is not established because of a lack of resources such that the functionality of a system is not effective.[50] Adaptive or flexible capabilities of various nodes cannot be utilized collectively, thus precluding the emergence of beneficial outcomes at the system level. Both types of traps represent the cases when resilience is low or cannot be achieved. Complex networks in a non-adaptive regime (Figure 19.5) represent such traps, whereas those in the adaptive regime are resilient systems. The inequality analysis provides a means to diagnose whether a complex value-chain network is in traps or in an adaptive regime.

Resilience of a value chain is achieved by *self-reorganization* of the network topology as the primary adaptive strategy when encountering a threat that potentially disrupts the whole network function. Self-organization of a complex system emerges from the simultaneous and parallel adaptation of components at a local-level, such that their states are accommodated as a reaction to internal and external triggers for change.[51] Four groups of potential strategies for complex adaptive networks are suggested overleaf, by analogy to natural complex systems, to facilitate self-reorganization of a value-chain network enabling to continue critical functions.

Most value-chain networks are considered as scale-free networks, whose node-degree distribution closely follows a power law.[52] These networks are more vulnerable to disruptions to the "hubs" with high node-degree. Thus, the focus here is to ensure that scale-free value chains maintain the system-level functions from loss of "hubs". The relative merits of the suggested adaptive strategies must be evaluated based on their technical feasibility and cost-effectiveness.

DIVERSITY

A hallmark of resilient complex systems is diversity. Functional diversity or species diversity among functional groups in natural systems allows the continuity of the system (i.e., survival) even though one or more species are disrupted (e.g., extinction).[53] Because of heterogeneity within a functional group, each species has different sensitivity to a particular disruption. This feature allows substituting a disrupted species with a less disrupted one because of the already embedded capacity for taking on the role of disrupted function.

A prerequisite for applying this analogy as a design strategy is to allow for heterogeneity of nodes in a value-chain network. In a homogeneous network, node-degree is the only factor that determines the vulnerability to a specific disruption (e.g., same probability of failure is applied for the nodes with same node-degree). However, in a heterogeneous network, even if two nodes have the same node-degree but have different sensitivity to a given disruption, one node might be less disrupted while the other one loses its function. Heterogeneity represents an important feature in designing a resilient value-chain subject to unpredictable disruptions. On this basis, incorporating functional redundancy allows for the surviving nodes to substitute the role of the failed nodes. The operation strategy is to reconnect the links from the failed nodes to the surviving nodes that perform the same functions (Figure 19.6a).

Because of the modular design in modern manufacturing practices (e.g., cars, computer hardware), a plant can implement the capacity for producing diverse products. For example, in a chemical refinery, the use of different catalytic process allows the production of diverse chemicals. Although, it may seem cost-inefficient at the time of investment for implementing the functional diversity among nodes, it may outperform in the long-term, especially at the time of major disruptions.[54]

Links can also be diversified to activate new supplier nodes that have same function as the one that is already connected. This potential supplier may be in an inactive mode during normal operations, but becomes active to substitute the original supplier whose functions are disrupted (Figure 19.7b). Specifically, this strategy aims to enable a functional replacement by growth in a dynamic value chain. Complex networks are transient, meaning that nodes and links continuously "grow" and "die", either by external forcing or by a node's inherent characteristics, causing the longitudinal change in network traits (e.g., node-degree distribution and diameter). In a dynamic and competitive environment, diversified links will provide a benefit of a timely reconstruction of a lost link that will maintain the critical function of the whole network.

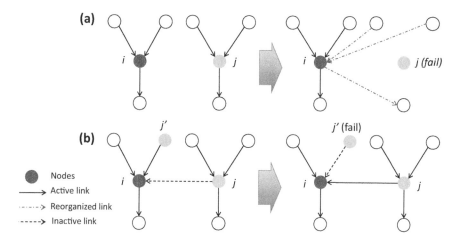

Figure 19.6 **Reorganization of topology through diversification. (a) Functional diversification at a node allows temporal reconnection of links of failed nodes to continue disrupted functions. Node-*i* performs different functions from the node-*j* during normal operation in a value chain. However, because of the functional diversity in the node-*i*, which has the capacity to do the function of the node-*j*, it may maintain both functions (with some loss of efficiency) to reduce the catastrophic loss due to the failure at node-*j*. (b) Diversification of links at a node. Node-*i* is supplied by the node-*j'* during normal operation, but because the failure of the node-*j'* is critical for network function, it established an inactive link with the node-*j* which will supply same function as the node-*j'*. Then the inactive link can be timely activated when the node-*j'* is disrupted**

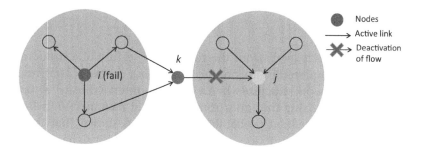

Figure 19.7 **Reorganization of topology through isolating the cluster in which an infected node is included. Node-*i* is failed by infection and the node-*k* is identified as the most effective point for isolating from the infected zone regarding direction of links and local clustering coefficient**

ISOLATION

The disrupted nodes can be a source of contagion, i.e., spreading direct or indirect negative impacts to other linked nodes. This is common for viruses (e.g., cholera, HIV, computer viruses) and food-supply chains. Isolation is a strategy that is frequently taken when it is difficult to identify the exact source of the infection, or when the time it takes to fix the node before it infects the neighboring nodes is relatively long. The infectious propagation of negative effects along a network can also be observed in a value chain that manufactures a product using numerous subcomponents and parts. The low quality of a final product can be the result of chronic dysfunctional components manufactured upstream. Temporary isolation (i.e., quarantine) for those components might be beneficial if the quality of the final product is critical for maintaining business reputation and customer trust.

A disrupted node with a few links (small node-degree) does not pose a significant threat because it is similar to a non-specific disruption. A considerable problem may arise when a hub or a node with a large node-degree is disrupted. In this case, disconnecting all the links from the disrupted node may require substantial efforts. Identifying the clusters in which the disrupted node is included may help an effective isolation strategy to be taken, since disconnecting only a few nodes will be necessary. Thus, knowledge of the clustering coefficient for the critical hub nodes will be an important network attribute for designing an isolation strategy.

Directed networks have very different network characteristics from undirected networks. Contagion spreads only through the links in the direction of flow. If the direction exists only from node i to j for all possible pathways, then the failure in node j will not pose any threat to node i. As most flow (e.g., material, cash) in a value chain is directed, the identification of points for isolating infected node or cluster will be node specific. Therefore, the most feasible disconnection point should be evaluated for each node or cluster and stored as knowledge for preparing for the disruption (Figure 19.7).

REWIRING

To reduce vulnerability that stems from the topological feature of a scale-free network, rewiring strategy has been studied to produce an ad-hoc network that resembles the topology of a random network structure when a hub encounters a threat.[55] This topological shift is based on disconnecting the links from a hub and reconnecting with randomly chosen nodes with a pre-defined probability. It has been shown that the robustness for continuing the network function (e.g., supply availability) has been improved considerably at the cost of efficiency for the rewired networks compared to the scale-free networks under both non-specific and specific disruptions.[56] These evaluations are for homogeneous and undirected networks, such that rewiring through random linking is an acceptable strategy. This is not the case for heterogeneous networks, and rewiring to transform the network topology requires additional knowledge about the functionalities of the disabled hubs, and others that can substitute the same functions. Rewiring is possible only to the hubs or nodes that share common functions; thus, the strategy of functional diversification of nodes and hubs will facilitate the rewiring strategy in real world. If the network is a directed network, changing the network topology through re-wiring must account for the specific directionality of the disabled nodes and their connectivity. Rewiring may temporarily decrease efficiency in maintaining material flows through the network, but increased resilience and maintaining supplies can compensate for loss of efficiency.

FLEXIBLE OUTPUTS

In the modern business world, most products and services require frequent alteration to meet rapidly changing consumer preferences and external constraints such as regulations and resource prices (e.g., material, energy, and labor costs). In order to maintain its role in a dynamic value-chain network, a node should have the capacity that enables timely adjustment for reallocating its products and services. Flexible manufacturing of vehicles in a manufacturing plant and poly-generation of a biorefinery (e.g., biofuels, electricity, heat) are good examples. While the strategy of functional diversity emphasizes the latent capacity that can be activated and beneficial at the time of disruption, the flexible output strategy emphasizes dynamic operation on already existing diversity at a node. A network node that adopts a flexible output strategy has diverse products and services. Such adaptive nodes would have a higher probability of forming inactive, but tighter, links with downstream nodes, such that these links can be activated when downstream nodes lose the existing links by disruption.

Summary

In this chapter, design and operation strategies that result in a resilient value chain are examined by considering a value chain as a complex network. As efficiency-driven strategies often degrade the features that are essential to resilience, a value chain should be designed and operated as a complex adaptive network which is able to cope with low-probability and high-consequence events. Resilience, in this context, is the emergent property of a complex system, and results from recursive processes involving sensing, anticipating, adapting, and learning. Integration of these processes in the operation of a complex value-chain network is important for continuing the services without losing its critical functions and structures.

Long-term monitoring (*sensing*) of the disturbance and response regimes, as well as the internal dynamics of the system, provides useful information on the patterns and relative importance of the underlying stochastic and non-stochastic processes. Spectral analysis of such time-series data also identifies the role of networks in reducing or adding "memory" as the external and internal disturbances propagate through the network. Such analyses enable *anticipation* of emergent risks based on the past, and evaluation of strategies that may have succeeded in the past. Systems with only short-term memory are ill prepared to deal with low-probability high-consequence shocks, but are well suited to deal with more "normal" (high probability) events. Systems with persistent memory (short- and long-term memory) are best at coping with all types of disturbances. That is, persistent memory improves the ability to *anticipate* extreme events, and enables *learning*.

A single network topology or a single adaptive strategy may not be optimal in coping with different types of forcing (random, targeted, emergent, etc.). A node that is optimally prepared for identified and expected forcing may fail when a different type of forcing occurs. Diversity and adaptability are among the most important features for ensuring resilience in complex systems. It is critical to design or manage complex networks such that they are not locked into a non-adaptive regime, and can move into an adaptive regime when faced with extreme disturbances. The methods that are proposed in this chapter provide new ways for viewing and diagnosing value chains as complex adaptive networks, thereby facilitating the emergence of resilience as a recursive process.

Complex network theory has gained increasing interest since the pioneering work by Barabasi and collaborators on scale-free networks.[57] Various types of real-world networks have been investigated using complex network theory, and supply-chain research has been one of the major fields that required a view of complex networks.[58] Investigating supply chains as complex networks has the advantage of diagnosing the vulnerability of a network in a systematic way by identifying the network topology and anticipated disruptions on hubs or randomly selected nodes. This will allow managers of an organization to set adaptive strategies, such as those suggested in this chapter, to enhance the resilience of complex value-chain networks under external stochastic forcing and unexpected shocks.

Acknowledgements

J. Park and P.S.C. Rao were supported, in part, by the Lee A. Reith Endowment in the School of Civil Engineering at Purdue University, while T.P. Seager was supported by the Arizona State University. Discussions with Dr. Heather Gall (Purdue University) related to networks and suggestions for improvement are much appreciated. Constructive comments from two anonymous reviewers also helped in improving this manuscript.

Appendix: Glossary (in alphabetical order)

Adaptability (Adaptive capacity): This is the ability of a system to adjust to changing internal demands and external circumstances, and is a central feature of resilience.[59] Walker et al.[60] defined adaptability as the collective capacity of actors in a system to intentionally manage resilience, which determines whether a system can successfully avoid crossing into an undesirable regime, or succeed in returning to the desirable one.

Complex network: A general terminology used in the field of network theory to represent a network with non-trivial topological features, such as scale-free and small-world phenomena, that do not occur in regular or random networks.

Complex system: Systems that exhibit following characteristics:[61] (1) composed of many autonomous and heterogeneous components; (2) self-organization (3) display emergent macro-level behavior from the actions and interactions of components that cannot be deduced from the behavior of parts; (4) adapt to their environment as they evolve.

Complex adaptive network: A complex network into which adaptability is intentionally built such that it can self-organize and be resilient to specific and non-specific disruptions.

Diversity: Diversity refers to the existence of various options or algorithms for achieving the same function. It is more than redundancy which is about preparing a larger number of same options/algorithms. While increasing inventory (one form of redundancy) of a product cannot cope with the shift of consumer preferences, diversity offers higher capacity to flexibly respond to a changing environment.

Disturbance regime: The concept originates from natural science, and describes the pattern of disturbances that shape a system over a long time scale. It describes a spatial disturbance pattern, a frequency and intensity of disturbances, and a resulting response pattern of a system over space and time. It is distinguished from a single event.

Low-probability shocks: Intense events with severe consequences that are typically ignored in probabilistic risk management because of the statistical rareness of their occurrence.[62] In general, the ignorance of extreme events results in underestimation of likely disruptions and associated costs.

Memory: In time-domain analysis, autocorrelation function of the stochastic or "noise" process gives the correlation between variables of the process at two different times. In this case, the stochastic memory of the process is defined as the speed of the decay of the autocorrelation function.[63] Long-term memory means a current variable depends on long, distant events, while short-term memory only depends on more recent events, and are independent of long-distant events.

Node-degree: The number of links attached to a node. In a directed network, in-degree and out-degree are distinguished by the direction of links. The distribution of node-degree characterizes the topology of a complex network.

Resilience: The ability of a complex system to maintain its desired functionalities within some acceptable bounds by adapting its form (or structure) in response to external forcing. This ability emerges from the recursive efforts of sensing, anticipating, adapting, and learning during the operation of a complex engineered system.

Resistance: Generally, this refers to the opposing force to or ability to withstand disruptions. It is one of measures of a system's robustness achieved by strengthening the structure. Compared to resilient systems, resistant systems tend to become rigid and brittle because of the loss of flexibility.

Robustness: This refers how much a system can produce desired function in spite of variability in the internal process and external forcing. Robustness and resilience are often used without clear discrimination. A system's robustness is characterized by variability in outcome while resilience is characterized by the process; that is, how the variability is controlled or absorbed. As argued in this chapter, an efficiency-driven system may also achieve robustness as far as all sources that cause variability can be fully identified.

Notes

1 Seuring, S. and Müller, M. (2008) "From a literature review to a conceptual framework for sustainable supply chain management," *Journal of Cleaner Production*, Vol. 16, No. 15, pp. 1699–1710.

2 Funtowicz, S. and Ravetz, J.R. (1994) "Emergent complex systems," *Futures*, Vol. 26, No. 6, pp. 568–582.

3 Berkes, F. (2007) "Understanding uncertainty and reducing vulnerability: lessons from resilience thinking," *Natural Hazards*, Vol. 41, No. 2, pp. 283–295; Fiksel, J. (2003) "Designing resilient, sustainable systems," *Environmental Science & Technology*, Vol. 37, No. 23, pp. 5330–5339; Korhonen, J. and Seager, T.P. (2008) "Beyond eco-efficiency: a resilience perspective," *Business Strategy and the Environment*, Vol. 17, No. 7, pp. 411–419.

4   Pathak, S.D., Day, J.M., Nair, A., Sawaya, W.J., and Kristal, M.M. (2007) "Complexity and adaptivity in supply networks: building supply network theory using a complex adaptive systems perspective," *Decision Sciences*, Vol. 38, No. 4, pp. 547–580.

5   Park, J., Seager, T.P., and Rao, P.S.C. (2011) "Lessons in risk- vs. resilience-based design and management," *Integrated Environmental Assessment and Management*, Vol. 7, No. 3, pp. 396–399.

6   *Ibid.*

7   Park, J., Seager, T., Rao, P.S.C.,Convertino, M., and Linkov, I. (2011) "Integrating risk and resilience approaches to catastrophe management in engineering systems," *Risk Analysis*, Vol. 33, No. 3, pp. 356–367.

8   Carpenter, S.R. and Brock, W.A. (2008) "Adaptive capacity and traps," *Ecology and Society*, Vol. 13, No. 2, pp. 40.

9   Normile, D. (2011) "Scientific consensus on Great Quake came too late," *Science*, Vol. 332, No. 6025, p. 22; Minoura, K., Imamura, F., Sugawara, D., Kono, Y., and Iwashita, T. (2001) "The 869 Jogan tsunami deposit and recurrence interval of large-scale tsunami on the Pacific coast of northeast Japan," *Journal of Natural Disaster Science*, Vol. 23, No. 2, pp. 83–88.

10   Korhonen and Seager, *op. cit.*

11   Pisarenko, V. and Rodkin, M. (2010) *Distributions of Characteristics of Natural Disasters: Data and Classification in Heavy-Tailed Distributions in Disaster Analysis*, Springer, Netherlands.

12   Pisarenko and Rodkin, *op. cit.*; Christensen, K., Danon, L., Scanlon, T., and Bak, P. (2002) "Unified scaling law for earthquakes," *Proceedings of the National Academy of Sciences of the United States of America*, Vol. 99, Suppl. 1, pp. 2509–2513; Clauset, A., Shalizi, C.R., and Newman, M.E.J. (2009) "Power-law distributions in empirical data," *arXiv:0706.1062*.

13   Aban, I.B., Meerschaert, M.M., and Panorska, A.K. (2006) "Parameter estimation for the truncated Pareto distribution," *Journal of the American Statistical Association*, Vol. 101, No. 473, pp. 270–277.

14   Pettit, T.J., Fiksel, J., and Croxton, K.L. (2010) "Ensuring supply chain resilience: development of a conceptual framework," *Journal of Business Logistics*, Vol. 31, No. 1, pp. 1–21.

15   Walker, B.H. and Salt, D.A. (2006) *Resilience Thinking: Sustaining Ecosystems and People in a Changing World*, Island Press, Washington, DC.

16   Page, S.E. (2010) *Diversity and Complexity*, Princeton University Press, Princeton, NJ.

17   Walker, B., Holling, C.S., Carpenter, S.R., and Kinzig, A. (2004) "Resilience, adaptability and transformability in social-ecological systems," *Ecology and Society*, Vol. 9, No. 2, pp. 5.

18   Hashimoto, T., Stedinger, J.R., and Loucks, D.P. (1982) "Reliability, resiliency, and vulnerability criteria for water-resource system performance evaluation," *Water Resources Research*, Vol. 18, No. 1, pp. 14–20; Mu, D., Seager, T.P., Rao, P.S.C., Park, J., and Zhao, F. (2011) "A resilience perspective on biofuel production," *Integrated Environmental Assessment and Management*, Vol. 7, No. 3, pp. 348–359; Moy, W.S., Cohon, J.L., and ReVelle, C.S. (1986) "A programming model for analysis of the reliability, resilience, and vulnerability of a water supply reservoir," *Water Resources Research*, Vol. 22, No. 4, pp. 489–498.

19   Madni, A.M. and Jackson, S. (2009) "Towards a conceptual framework for resilience engineering," *IEEE Systems Journal*, Vol. 3, No. 2, pp. 181–191.

20   Park, Seager, Rao, Convertino, and Linkov, *op. cit.*

21   Stanley, C.B.J. (2011) *The Ecological Economics of Resilience: Designing a Safe-Fail Civilization*, Master's thesis, University of Waterloo. Retrieved from https://uwspace.uwaterloo.ca/handle/10012/5896.

22 Shirali, G.A., Motamedzade, M., Mohammadfam, I., Ebrahimipour, V., and Moghimbeigi, A. (2012) "Challenges in building Resilience Engineering (RE) and adaptive capacity: a field study in a chemical plant," *Process Safety and Environmental Protection*, Vol. 90, No. 2, pp. 83–90.

23 Hollnagel, E., Woods, D.D., and Leveson, N. (2006) *Resilience Engineering: Concepts and Precepts*, Ashgate, Aldershot.

24 *Ibid.*

25 *Ibid.*

26 Pathak, Day, Nair, Sawaya, and Kristal, *op. cit.*; Zhao, K., Kumar, A., Harrison, T.P., and Yen, J. (2011) "Analyzing the resilience of complex supply network topologies against random and targeted disruptions," *IEEE Systems Journal*, Vol. 5, No. 1, pp. 28–39.

27 Zhao, Kumar, Harrison, and Yen, *op. cit.*; Kim, Y., Choi, T.Y., Yan, T.T., and Dooley, K. (2011) "Structural investigation of supply networks: a social network analysis approach," *Journal of Operations Management*, Vol. 29, No. 3, pp. 194–211.

28 Zhao, Kumar, Harrison, and Yen, *op. cit.*

29 Albert, R., Jeong, H., and Barabasi, A.L. (2000) "Error and attack tolerance of complex networks," *Nature*, Vol. 406, No. 6794, pp. 378–382.

30 Tanizawa, T., Paul, G., Cohen, R., Havlin, S., and Stanley, H.E. (2005) "Optimization of network robustness to waves of targeted and random attacks," *Physical Review E*, Vol. 71, No. 4, Article ID 047101.

31 Brede, M. and de Vries, B.J.M. (2009) "Networks that optimize a trade-off between efficiency and dynamical resilience," *Physics Letters A*, Vol. 373, No. 43, pp. 3910–3914.

32 Lee, H.L., Padmanabhan, V., and Whang, S. (1997) "The bullwhip effect in supply chains," *Sloan Management Review*, Vol. 38, No. 3, pp. 93–102.

33 Lohr, S. (2011) "Stress test for the global supply chain," *The New York Times* (March 19).

34 James, T. (2011) "Globalised," *Engineering & Technology*, Vol. 6, No. 4, pp. 60–62.

35 Montroll, E.W. and Shlesinger, M.F. (1982) "On 1/f noise and other distributions with long tails (log-normal distribution/levy distribution/Pareto distribution/scale-invariant process)," *Proceedings of the National Academy of Sciences of the United States of America-Physical Sciences*, Vol. 79, No. 10, pp. 3380–3383.

36 Zhao, Kumar, Harrison, and Yen, *op. cit.*

37 Jenkins, G. and Watts, D. (1969) *Spectral Analysis and its Applications*, Holden-Day, San Francisco.

38 Keshner, M.S. (1982) "1/f noise," *Proceedings of the IEEE*, Vol. 70, No. 3, pp. 212–218.

39 Jenkins and Watts, *op. cit.*

40 *Ibid*; Ochi, M. (1990) *Applied Probability and Stochastic Processes in Engineering and Physical Sciences*, John Wiley & Sons, New York; Diniz, A., Wijnants, M.L., Torre, K., Barreiros, J., Crato, N., Bosman, A.M.T., Hasselman, F., Cox, R.F.A., Van Orden, G.C., and Delignières, D. (2011) "Contemporary theories of 1/f noise in motor control," *Human Movement Science*, Vol. 30, No. 5, pp. 889–905.

41 Keshner, *op. cit.*; Diniz, Wijnants, Torre, Barreiros, Crato, Bosman, Hasselman, Cox, Van Orden, and Delignières, *op. cit.*

42 Diniz, Wijnants, Torre, Barreiros, Crato, Bosman, Hasselman, Cox, Van Orden, and Delignières, *op. cit.*; Kirchner, J., Feng, X., and Neal, C. (2000) "Fractal stream chemistry and its implications for contaminant transport in catchments," *Nature*, Vol. 403, No. 6769, pp. 524–527; Halley, J.M. and Inchausti, P. (2004) "The increasing importance of 1/f-noises as models of ecological variability," *Fluctuation and Noise Letters*, Vol. 4, No. 2, pp. R1–R26.

43 Keshner, *op. cit.*

44   Kirchner, Feng, and Neal, *op. cit.*

45   Zhao, Kumar, Harrison, and Yen, *op. cit.*

46   *Ibid.*

47   *Ibid.*

48   Carpenter and Brock, *op. cit.*

49   Gunderson, L.H. and Holling, C.S. (2002) *Panarchy: Understanding Transformations in Human and Natural Systems*, Island Press, Washington, DC.

50   Gunderson and Holling, *op. cit.*

51   Choi, T.Y., Dooley, K.J., and Rungtusanatham, M. (2001) "Supply networks and complex adaptive systems: control versus emergence," *Journal of Operations Management*, Vol. 19, No. 3, pp. 351–366; Prehofer, C. and Bettstetter, C. (2005) "Self-organization in communication networks: principles and design paradigms," *Communications Magazine, IEEE*, Vol. 43, No. 7, pp. 78–85.

52   Pathak, Day, Nair, Sawaya, and Kristal, *op. cit.*; Kim, Choi, Yan, and Dooley, *op. cit.*

53   Tilman, D., Knops, J., Wedin, D., Reich, P., Ritchie, M., and Siemann, E. (1997) "The influence of functional diversity and composition on ecosystem processes," *Science*, Vol. 277, No. 5330, p. 1300.

54   Narasimhan, R. and Kim, S.W. (2002) "Effect of supply chain integration on the relationship between diversification and performance: evidence from Japanese and Korean firms," *Journal of Operations Management*, Vol. 20, No. 3, pp. 303–323.

55   Zhao, K., Kumar, A., and Yen, J. (2011) "Achieving high robustness in supply distribution networks by rewiring," *IEEE Transactions on Engineering Management*, Vol. 58, No. 2, pp. 347–362; Sekiyama, K. and Araki, H. (2007) "Network topology reconfiguration against targeted and random attack," *Self-Organizing Systems*, Vol. 4725, pp. 119–130.

56   Zhao, Kumar, and Yen, *op. cit.*

57   Barabasi, A.L. and Albert, R. (1999) "Emergence of scaling in random networks," *Science*, Vol. 286, No. 5439, p. 509.

58   Pathak, Day, Nair, Sawaya, and Kristal, *op. cit.*; Kim, Choi, Yan, and Dooley, *op. cit.*; North, M.J. and Macal, C.M. (2007), *Managing Business Complexity: Discovering Strategic Solutions with Agent-Based Modeling and Simulation*, Oxford University Press, USA; Borgatti, S.P. and Li, X. (2009) "On social network analysis in a supply chain context," *Journal of Supply Chain Management*, Vol. 45, No. 2, pp. 5–22; Carter, C.R., Ellram, L.M., and Tate, W. (2007) "The use of social network analysis in logistics research," *Journal of Business Logistics*, Vol. 28, No. 1, pp. 137–168; Autry, C.W. and Griffis, S.E. (2008) "Supply chain capital: the impact of structural and relational linkages on firm execution and innovation," *Journal of Business Logistics*, Vol. 29, No. 1, pp. 157–173.

59   Carpenter and Brock, *op. cit.*

60   Walker and Salt, *op. cit.*

61   Sheard, S.A. and Mostashari, A. (2009) "Principles of complex systems for systems engineering," *Systems Engineering*, Vol. 12, No. 4, pp. 295–311.

62   Beniston, M., Stephenson, D.B., Christensen, O.B., Ferro, C.A.T., Frei, C., Goyette, S., Halsnaes, K., Holt, T., Jylha, K., and Koffi, B. (2007) "Future extreme events in European climate: an exploration of regional climate model projections," *Climatic Change*, Vol. 81, pp. 71–95.

63   Diniz, Wijnants, Torre, Barreiros, Crato, Bosman, Hasselman, Cox, Van Orden, and Delignières, *op. cit.*

Sustainable Value Chains:
Integrative Perspectives

20 Ever Expanding Responsibilities: Upstream and Downstream Corporate Social Responsibility

JUDITH SCHREMPF-STIRLING,* GUIDO PALAZZO,† AND
ROBERT A. PHILLIPS‡

Keywords

Corporate social responsibility, worker rights, human rights, value chain.

The Changing Nature of Corporate Social Responsibility

The debate on corporate social responsibility (CSR) has been on the public and academic agenda for several decades.[1] In general, CSR issues can be divided into production-related issues (along the supply chain – or how things are *made*) and consumption-related issues (towards the consumer and society at large – or how things are *used*). Following the terminology of Phillips and Caldwell,[2] upstream CSR refers to the CSR debate along the supply chain, and downstream CSR refers to corporate responsibility towards consumers and society at large. The chapter examines current CSR issues, and proposes a social connection model to understand the most recent CSR demands up and down the corporate value chain.

In the sweatshop debate of the 1990s,[3] corporations were criticized for the social and environmental harm created by themselves and their *direct* suppliers during the product finishing process.[4] The debates surrounding Nike or The Gap of the 1990s[5] were limited to the practices of the first-tier suppliers. Nike, The Gap and other corporations were criticized for outsourcing their production process to offshore factories in which workers

*   Assistant Professor Judith Schrempf, Robins School of Business, University of Richmond, 23173 VA. E-mail: jschremp@richmond.edu. Telephone: +1 8042876309.

†   Professor Guido Palazzo, University of Lausanne, HEC, 1015 Lausanne Dorigny, Switzerland. E-mail: guido. palazzo@unil.ch. Telephone: + 41216923373.

‡   Associate Professor Robert A. Phillips, Robins School of Business, University of Richmond, 23173 VA. E-mail: rphilli3@richmond.edu. Telephone: +1 8042898623.

worked under bad conditions such as below minimum wages, low or no health and safety standards, and uncompensated overtime hours.

Today, CSR demands go beyond contractors. As illustrated by the following examples, the current debate envelops the *whole value chain*, and includes challenges involving the geopolitical contexts in which the various steps of value creation occur. Also, CSR issues are increasingly related to product consumption.

In summer 2010, the UK based non-governmental organization (NGO) Global Witness[6] published a report illustrating how mineral and metal trading in the Democratic Republic of Congo fuels civil war, armed conflicts and violence. Minerals and metals are used in various electronic consumer products such as cellphones and computers. In the report, Global Witness[7] demands that electronics brands such as Hewlett-Packard and Motorola engage in greater oversight and exclude those conflict metals from their supply chain. In a similar fashion, other NGOs criticize various industries for financing civil war and violence through their material sourcing in conflict zones.[8] Multinational corporations (MNCs) are increasingly expected to support activities for generating and maintaining peace[9] or for fighting corruption and bribery[10] in those regions to which they are connected through their globally stretched production activities. These activities are referred to as *upstream corporate social responsibility*.

In addition to the expanded CSR demands for production-related (upstream) issues, extended CSR claims relating to *consumption* issues can be observed. That is, corporations are increasingly held responsible for how their products' use affects consumers and society at large – in cases of both intended and unintended uses.[11] This kind of corporate responsibility is referred to as *downstream corporate social responsibility*. One illustration of downstream CSR is the debate about the responsibility of fast-food corporations for the rising levels of obesity.[12] Critics charge that fast-food companies employ marketing communications that target vulnerable consumers (children), and mislead other consumers by using unbalanced information about the nutritional value of their products.[13] Even though obesity is the result of genetic and non-genetic factors, such as sedentary lifestyle or food choice,[14] fast-food chains have increasingly been criticized for their contribution to obesity.[15] Fast-food corporations are alleged to be responsible for products that are high in fat and sugar and contribute to the obesity epidemic in developed and developing countries.

The examples above illustrate the trend of ever expanding corporate responsibilities up and down the value chain. CSR has been on the academic and public agenda since the 1950s.[16] These latest CSR demands, however, are different. The traditional sweatshop debate has created an awareness of the social and environmental externalities in global production. The traditional CSR debate considers the alleviation of harm as a responsibility of (mainly multinational) corporations. In the sweatshop debate corporations were asked to use their business contracts with direct suppliers as a means to enforce decent working conditions. In contrast, the more recent claims refer to suppliers with whom MNCs normally do not have direct contractual links or even direct contact. The link between corporations and harm becomes increasingly stretched and tenuous the further one goes from the focal corporation. Invoking the idea of tensile strength of wires or cables, Phillips[17] refers to the effects of this stretching as "value chain tensility." Corporations are held responsible for things that they have not done themselves, but to which they are *connected* through global production networks – often several steps up and down the value chain.

These most recent discussions[18] on value chain responsibilities are important for how scholars in the business and society field conceptualize the scope and the limits of corporate responsibility. This chapter proposes to analyze value chain issues based on the *social connection logic* advanced by Young.[19] In this chapter, Young's work is used to inform our understanding of responsibility in non-proximate transactions.

The chapter is organized as follows. First, the current debate on expanding responsibilities up and down the corporate supply chains is examined, carving out the differences between this and the traditional sweatshop debate. Then, the social connection model is discussed, followed by an examination of its implications for the CSR debate. Finally, the challenges to an expanded concept of CSR are presented, before some tentative and preliminary conclusions are drawn.

New Corporate Responsibility: Upstreaming the Supply Chain

The discussion of CSR started upstreaming the supply chain as the sweatshop debate focused on the issue of production outsourcing and worker rights.[20] Since the 1970s and 1980s, corporations have established worldwide supply chain networks, especially in developing countries where production costs and working standards were often low.[21] Since the early 1990s, there has been an explosion of news stories regarding sweatshop conditions, highlighting concerns such as low security and safety standards, health concerns, unpaid overtime hours, low wages and child labor.[22]

NGOs started pressuring MNCs to improve those working conditions at their direct contractors.[23] At first, corporations were defensive and reluctant to act.[24] Phillips[25] isolates three forms that denials of responsibility took: control, connection and knowledge. MNCs claimed, in the first place, that their suppliers were independent corporations. The connection between the object firm and its suppliers was one of an arm's length transaction – all that mattered to the relationship inhered in the product and its delivery. Moreover, these firms claimed that they did not (and possibly could not) control the actions of other firms.[26] Finally, in many cases, the object firms claimed that they simply did not know what went on in these factories owned and operated by others.

As the anti-sweatshop campaigning continued, corporations realized that it exposed them to financial risks[27] and some responded by establishing supply chain management programs.[28] Nike, Wal-Mart and others introduced codes of conduct[29] and included code compliance as a requirement in their contracts with suppliers. While corporations in various industries have started to implement codes and audit systems for controlling the working conditions at their suppliers, criticism has not waned. It has, in fact, intensified as the engagement of MNCs is perceived as insufficient for improving working conditions at direct suppliers.[30] In summer 2010, for example, several suicides by factory workers of Foxconn, which supplies Apple, Hewlett-Packard and other electronics corporations, gained public attention.[31] Newspapers reported bad working conditions at Foxconn's factory such as 100 hours overtime without any time for recreation. Despite Apple's and Hewlett-Packard's supplier codes of conduct, the working conditions in the Foxconn factory were described as devastating.

UPSTREAM CSR: BEYOND DIRECT SUPPLIERS AND WORKER RIGHTS

However, beyond the immediate problems at their direct suppliers, corporations are expected to solve social and environmental concerns within their geopolitical sphere of influence irrespective of where issues occur in the corporate value chain. For example, Robin Wood, a German environmental organization, criticized Procter & Gamble (P&G) for its *indirect* participation in forced and violent relocation of Indian tribes in Brazil.[32] P&G's supplier, Aracruz, initiated the relocation to ensure cellulose sourcing from eucalyptus plantations.[33] Similarly, some NGOs criticize clothes retailers such as H&M and Wal-Mart for sourcing their cotton from Uzbekistan, where children are forced to harvest the raw product under severe conditions such as low pay and low health and safety standards.[34]

Still deeper into the supply chain, the Dutch NGO SOMO demanded that car manufacturers take "full supply chain responsibility that includes the use of metals."[35] As with many electronics, a portion of the minerals and metals used in automobile manufacturing are sourced in the eastern part of the Democratic Republic of Congo. The profits generated from the mining operations are reported to be used to finance civil war in the country and violence against the local population.[36] NGOs expect MNCs to take responsibility and ensure that the metals used in their consumer products do not contain any "blood minerals."[37] H&M has no direct contract with cotton farms in Uzbekistan, nor do car or electronics manufacturers have direct contracts with the mines in the Democratic Republic of Congo. In these and other examples, upstream CSR demands go beyond the direct suppliers to include the complete production process from resource extraction to product assembly.

In addition to addressing issues further up the value chain, upstream CSR demands also go beyond the harm occurring at the various steps of the globally stretched value chain. Upstream CSR demands go beyond worker rights, and include human rights violations in general. They increasingly include problems that occur in the social and political environment of the production activities themselves. As early as 1998, the diamond industry was accused of financing civil war through its diamond sourcing.[38] More recently, manufacturers of cellphones,[39] computers[40] and cars[41] are alleged to be financing civil war and armed conflicts through their material sourcing in conflict zones.

Corporations are increasingly considered to be political actors[42] in a double sense. On the one hand, they are expected to step in where governments are no longer able or willing to play their presumed regulatory roles.[43] On the other hand, they are expected to avoid situations where they could become accomplices of human rights violations in repressive political contexts. John Ruggie, the former Special Representative of the UN Secretary-General for Business and Human Rights, has defined corporate complicity as "knowingly providing practical assistance, encouragement or moral support that has a substantial effect on the commission of a crime."[44]

There have been numerous complicity accusations against corporations during the last decade, such as those against Talisman in Sudan[45] or Shell in Nigeria.[46] As reported by Amnesty International,[47] Talisman was complicit in human rights violations in Sudan. The NGO reported that civilians who lived close to the company's oil fields were forced to leave the area, or were killed by paramilitary groups. Shell faced similar problems with the local Ogoni people in Nigeria. The Ogoni people fought for greater control over the natural resources on their lands, leading to violent conflicts with national armed security forces.[48] As Shell was operating in Nigeria at that time, it found itself confronted with demands to investigate its involvement and contribution to the human rights violations in the Delta region.

As these examples illustrate, corporations are exposed to wider and more complex issues in and around their supply chains. The more their supply chains expand into weak or repressive geopolitical contexts, the more of these issues emerge on the corporate agenda. Hence, upstream CSR demands do not only cover worker rights issues, but have expanded to include human rights issues in general. Overall, MNCs are expected to manage their sphere of influence along and around the various supply chain operations to which they are connected.

New Corporate Responsibility: Downstreaming the Supply Chain

A similar development – from a more direct to a more indirect connection – can be observed in the downstreaming of the value chain towards the consumer. Obviously, corporations are liable for any harm caused by malfunctioning of their products. In classic product liability cases, it is somewhat easier to identify a causal link between the product and harm.[49] For example, in the 1970s car manufacturer Ford faced allegations that flaws in gas tank design led to severe safety risks in its Pinto car, resulting in deadly accidents.[50]

More recent consumption-related issues involve the misuse of otherwise legitimate products. In the US, new regulations have been put in place to curb the use of allergy medication in the production of methamphetamine. A Danish company, Lundbeck, has restricted the distribution of a drug used to treat epilepsy because some US states have adopted it for use in executing death row inmates by lethal injection. This followed on the heels of the American pharmaceutical firm Hospira's decision to stop selling an anesthetic after objections from the Italian government over its use in lethal injections.[51]

More broadly, accusations of corporate complicity in issues such as youth violence and obesity differ substantially from traditional product liability cases as the connection between social harm and companies' products becomes more tenuous. Manufacturers of violent video games (and other media content providers) are accused of contributing to the global increase in youth violence,[52] including triggering school shootings.[53] The fast-food industry has been referred to as "the tobacco industry of the new millennium."[54]

Downstream CSR has also come to include harm that *customers might cause to others* by using the product. In summer 2009, Nokia Siemens Networks was criticized for having sold network infrastructure and software solutions to the Iranian government. The government then used this technology to observe, block and control domestic communications, as well as to identify, capture, interrogate and torture dissidents.[55] In autumn 2010, an Iranian activist filed a lawsuit against Nokia Siemens Networks, Nokia and Siemens for the companies' complicity in his torture.[56] Neither the corporations nor its employees themselves arrested and tortured the activist, but Nokia Siemens Networks sold technology that enabled Iranian authorities to record telephone conversations and SMS text messages sent or received by Iranian citizens.[57]

As these examples illustrate, the link between corporations and harm becomes increasingly stretched and tenuous the further one goes from the focal corporation. Corporations are increasingly held responsible for things they have not done themselves, or caused, but to which they are *connected*.

Stretching the Value Chain

Classic concepts of responsibility assign responsibility to a person if it can be proven that there is a direct causal link between the action and harm.[58] An actor is assigned responsibility if the direct actions can be causally and proximately linked to an outcome and if those actions were voluntary and consciously performed.[59] Young refers to this as a "liability" approach to responsibility. Some early reflections on CSR that focused on the businessperson's decisions and actions illustrate this understanding.[60] Those concepts aimed to establish direct links between managers and wrongdoings.

However, in the examples above there is no direct link between MNCs and harm. Instead, the connection between MNCs and harm becomes stretched and tenuous. How can we make sense of those latest CSR demands both upstream and downstream in the value chain?

Corporations are increasingly held responsible for things they have not done themselves, but to which they are *connected*. A systemic view of CSR is proposed in this chapter. Societal issues such as obesity, youth violence and human rights violations are systemic, caused by a network. The network members under consideration do not directly cause harm, but are said to contribute to – and have the potential to mitigate – harm through their activities and interactions. Hence, responsibility does not derive from direct actions causing harm but from belonging to a network through which network members are connected to issues.

A SOCIAL CONNECTION APPROACH TO CORPORATE VALUE CHAINS

Young's[61] social connection model provides a promising approach to understanding the latest CSR demands. Contrary to the liability approach, the social connection model states that responsibility is based on the connection – direct and indirect – between actors, their activities and the (often systemic) harm produced by those activities. It understands harmdoing and injustice as the result of the interaction between numerous actors. Young's approach is based on a social connection logic, shared responsibility, a prospective perspective and a judgment of background conditions, which questions existing rules, standards and regulations.

Social connection

Instead of looking for direct causal relations between actors and harm, a social connection approach assigns responsibility based on a connection. As Young[62] argues, in the context of globally stretched business activities, CSR issues have become more complex, involving many stakeholders whose actions are interdependent. Responsibility derives "from belonging together with others in a system of interdependent processes of cooperation and competition through which we seek benefits and aim to realize projects."[63] What matters is the social connection of corporations to CSR issues and affected parties. Adopting such a social connection perspective allows for a better understanding of complex challenges such as human rights violations in conflict zones, global warming, water shortages and obesity.

These issues present difficulties under a liability understanding of CSR because it is impossible to determine precise and exclusive causal links between single actors and those issues. Social connection widens the CSR scope and the number of responsible actors. Considering the interwoven structures that connect different network members, it is obsolete to isolate responsible from non-responsible network members. Rather, all those who contribute to structural injustices by the nature and the connectedness of their actions bear a responsibility – responsibility is shared.

Shared responsibility

Determining the lines between various parties' responsibilities becomes a challenging task in global societal issues. Finding the main (or solely) responsible entity, as suggested under the liability logic, can lead to blame shifting and diffused responsibility among actors, as Young illustrates in her analysis of the sweatshop problem. However, it is also not helpful to say that all network members are *equally* responsible. Complexity of issues such as human rights violations in conflict zones or obesity requires an understanding according to which responsibility is shared among all those who contribute through their actions and linkages to specific outcomes.[64] Shared responsibility incorporates the notion that there are many actors that bear responsibility (e.g., consumers, governments, international institutions, corporations, etc.). None of them are isolated or absolved as is the case in liability CSR.

The key challenge here, however, is to define the share of responsibility of each network member. Young proposes several criteria such as power, interest, collective ability and privilege. For example, corporations often have the power to prescribe certain standards (working conditions, environmental standards) to their suppliers. Also, if a corporation gains from human rights violations, it has a greater share of responsibility than an entity that does not gain from harm (privilege). Recently, Wood[65] suggested that corporate responsibility for human rights violations along the value chain is determined by corporate leverage. If corporations have the ability to influence other members of the supply chain, they have the moral obligation to do so. This leverage-based responsibility is also consistent with the argument by Ciliberti at al.[66] According to Ciliberti et al., and others, some members of the supply chain possess relevant information (about customer preferences for example) that other supply chain members do not have. This privileged knowledge (or position) enables the so-called chain director to dominate other supply chain members, and trigger changes such as improved working conditions. Hence, the responsibility to improve worker and human rights situations is shared by the chain director (who uses his power to trigger changes), and by his business partners who conform to a code of conduct or business standards.

The idea of shared responsibility is also manifest in the fact that the solution must occur outside the specific sphere where the harm occurs. That is, in some cases the harm might occur in a specific place up or down the value chain (e.g. resource extraction). In other cases, it is the accumulation of decisions throughout the chain that triggers a problem. In such cases, a sustainable solution can only be found in the contributions of actors across the whole value chain. Global warming, for example, can be regarded as a problem to which all actors along and around a value chain contribute – even though more emissions occur in some links in the value chain than others. The solutions are not to be found in the places where the problems occur but only in coordinated initiatives that involve various network members – a classic collective action problem. Global warming can only be addressed through the joint efforts of corporations, governments, international institutions and the population in general. Consumers have a responsibility to change harmful consumption practices, governments can propel new behavioral routines through regulatory sanctions and incentives, and corporations can develop the technological knowledge necessary to reduce the emissions in the production process.

Prospective analysis

Recent CSR discussions like those on human rights violations in supply chains and on societal concerns such as obesity signal a shift from a retrospective to a prospective approach to responsibility. Social connection CSR does not deal with assigning responsibility for past incidences to obtain compensation or redistribution. Compensation and redistribution are more typical components of a liability approach to CSR.[67]

Product liability cases illustrate the compensation and redistribution mentality of a liability approach to responsibility. Flaws in Ford's gas tank design led to avoidable safety risks for customers.[68] The debate, however, only emerged *after* fatal accidents had happened.[69] Victims and relatives of victims demanded compensation. The aim of a social connection approach to CSR is different. As discussed earlier, societal challenges such as human rights violations in conflict zones or obesity are too complex to determine a culprit and demand compensation. No single actor bears a sufficiently large portion of the responsibility to render such an approach worthwhile. Instead, the aim of a social connection approach to CSR is to intervene in the complex system of networks and interdependencies in such a way that harm ceases to exist – or at least is reduced. In relation to the sweatshop debate, the primary goal of social connection CSR is to change the structures and processes that improve worker rights and to exclude systematic human rights violations in and around global supply chains.[70] In relation to downstream CSR, social connection CSR implies that the harmful side effects of products and their consumption are addressed and reduced. For example, NGOs, activists and governmental institutions are concerned about the rise of youth violence. Instead of only identifying the culprit in single incidents (such as school shootings), there is a rising global debate about how to decrease youth violence in general.[71]

Question background conditions

Finally, social connection CSR evaluates existing institutional settings in which social problems are embedded. While in traditional liability models of responsibility the institutional context is taken as given and the behavior of actors within the context is analyzed, the social connection approach claims that there are structural reasons behind existing problems of injustice. Sustainable solutions to social problems thus do not come only from the behavioral change of one or more actors connected to the problem, but rather result from a systematic analysis of the underlying driving forces of the various actors' contributions to the problem. For instance, existing audit systems used to evaluate working conditions have been criticized because many, if not most, factories cheat when the auditor comes.[72] Obviously, the systematic pressure on costs creates huge incentives for cheating, because decent working conditions would decrease the already small margins of factory owners even further. As long as suppliers are confronted with contradictory demands, they have the incentive to find the easiest (and cheapest) way out. Creating a facade for the auditor is cheaper in the short run than improving working conditions.[73] In China, for example, the authorities push for economic growth and the implementation of the Chinese labor law at the same time, which also creates tensions and contradictions.[74] Overall, as Misangyi, Weaver and Elms[75] have examined, to fight against pressing social problems, an analysis of the institutional setting in which the problematic practice is embedded is not only important for a better diagnosis of the driving forces behind the problem, but also to better understand which resources might be necessary to change the institutions that drive the problem.

Social connection CSR enables an enlarged understanding of the ways CSR upstreams and downstreams the value chain. It provides a better way of conceiving of the most recent claims in upstream CSR. While in a first move, MNCs were criticized for the working conditions in the factories of their immediate first-tier business partners,[76] demands now flow further up the supply chain and include all links of the chain.[77] As with the new enlarged understanding of upstream CSR, social connection CSR allows a responsibility enlargement downstream towards the consumer.

The requirements of Young's approach (i.e., social connection, shared responsibility, a forward looking perspective and questioned background conditions) will require a reimagining of the duties and responsibilities the various parties have for one another. An exhaustive list is beyond the scope of this chapter; and, at any rate, the nature of shared responsibility likely requires these new understandings to be cooperatively derived among the relevant parties, giving them an emergent, rather than stipulative, quality.

One new duty that can be confidently proposed is that a social connection logic will require a greater level of transparency among the connected actors. Before NGOs can approach MNCs to improve human rights situations in their value chain, for example, they need to do their homework and unveil each link in corporate value chains to show the connection between a company and an issue. It will also be helpful for critics and change agents to possess a nuanced appreciation for the constraints faced at each stage.

Social Connection and a Duty of Transparency

After being confronted with the problem of conflict minerals from the Democratic Republic of Congo, Hewlett-Packard started tracing metals used in its products to the source, developing a conflict-free smelter validation program, creating a mineral certification program and influencing policy initiatives.[78] Other electronics companies (e.g., Intel and Motorola) approach the problem similarly, surveying and visiting their suppliers to trace minerals to their source.[79] Those transparency initiatives apply a prospective perspective, which is consistent with a social connection approach to CSR. Increased transparency can help in preventing issues from happening.

A similar trend of tracing the origin of raw materials can be found in the textile industry. The Fair Labor Association established the FLA Cotton Project to investigate the possibility of tracing cotton along the entire supply chain.[80] While some companies started initiatives to trace their cotton, some clothes companies and retailers, such as Wal-Mart and The Gap, announced they would ban cotton from Uzbekistan until child labor on Uzbek cotton farms was stopped.[81]

Hence, corporations responded to rising CSR demands with transparency. Paradoxically, the extending CSR demands up and down the value chain illustrate two opposing consequences of transparency. Regarding upstream CSR, increased transparency can lead to *more* responsibility. When MNCs establish audit and monitoring mechanisms they increase their responsibility for worker and human rights violations along their supply chain as those injustices are supposed to be detected. Imagine that NGOs discover that Intel or any other electronics company with an in-depth auditing mechanism still has conflict minerals in its products. The harm of this news is higher, since it questions the effectiveness of such auditing systems.

MNCs also experience a greater burden of transparency when they disclose the list of their suppliers and sub-tier suppliers. Hewlett-Packard, Nike and other corporations list the names of some (or all) of their direct suppliers on their websites. This allows NGOs and activists to visit the suppliers, and check themselves for worker or human rights violations. Also, the publication of suppliers enables NGOs to verify certain claims such as specific supply chain programs (health and safety training, auditing procedures, correction plans). Hence, in upstream CSR, transparency can become a burden as corporations need to be sure to "walk their talk." Contradicting findings by NGOs will undermine corporations' credibility and their CSR engagement.

In contrast to increased responsibility for upstream issues, transparency can lead to *relatively less responsibility* for companies in downstream CSR issues. When fast-food companies provide information about the nutritional value in a transparent and easy-to-understand way, a portion of the responsibility for consumption shifts to the consumers themselves. This is not to say that fast-food companies have *no* responsibility. Rather, with relatively greater knowledge of what they are consenting to, consumers must bear a concomitantly greater portion of the responsibility for the effects of their behavior. However, this increased transparency does not absolve fast-food corporations from their duty to offer safe products (i.e. healthy food).

The case is similar in the tobacco industry. Warning labels on cigarette packages unequivocally communicate the dangers of smoking to consumers. The past misdeeds of tobacco companies are equally well known. Unlike an earlier time when smokers were led to believe smoking was actually beneficial to health or the dangers of smoking were systematically and univocally denied by the industry (at least in the developed world), smokers are now much more aware of the risks of smoking. Again, tobacco companies are not completely without responsibility for the use – and abuse – of this product. Rather, transparency leads merely to a shift in relative levels of responsibility from the corporation to the consumer.

Challenges to an Expanded Concept of CSR

The key challenge of a social connection model to CSR is a diffusion of responsibility that lurks behind many of the ethics problems on the corporate agenda.[82] The general problem in finding solutions and engaging in action in networks is that single network members will aim at minimizing their role in responsibility. Bandura[83] made famous the term *diffusion of responsibility*: "Where everybody is responsible no one really feels responsible."[84] Collective action provides anonymity and creates collective *ir*responsibility.[85] As discussed, there are numerous actors who are connected to an issue and are expected to take some responsibility. This leads some to disengage from the problem and to displace responsibility – a tendency which Bandura[86] defines as "obscuring or minimizing the agentive role in the harm one causes." Even though Bandura[87] discusses this mechanism on an individual level, diffusion of responsibility can also be applied to a corporate setting. Yahoo, for instance, was criticized for having provided the Chinese authorities with the identity of one of its email account holders, Shi Tao.[88] Shi Tao was arrested and sentenced to 10 years imprisonment. Yahoo used existing regulations as excuses for its (in)action and shifted responsibility to other entities –the governments in China (who made and enforced the law regarding the internet) and the United States (which provides no clear rules for US corporations being exposed to such dilemmas in difficult regulatory contexts elsewhere in the world).

Hence, some actors might acknowledge their connection to an issue but at the same time refer to others as having more responsibility due to a stronger connection to the issue. As Young[89] has highlighted, in the context of shared responsibilities, it is important not only to analyze the connectedness of a network member to the problem at stake, but also to examine what resources and power connected actors can contribute to a solution. Furthermore, she argues that those who profit more from a given situation of structural injustice can be expected to engage more with regards to the solution. While these arguments deliver some rules of thumb (e.g. The Parker Principle: With great power, there must also come great responsibility) for evaluating the scope of responsibility of various actors around a given problem, a key challenge for future research will be to spell out the concrete meaning of these rules with regards to specific problems.

Conclusions

This chapter has illustrated that there are expanding corporate responsibilities up and down the value chain. MNCs are increasingly held responsible for worker and human rights violations within (sometimes beyond) their supply chain. Also, MNCs are increasingly held responsible for how their products affect consumers and the public in general.

Those latest CSR demands cannot be understood using the prevailing liability approach to CSR. Instead, we presented a social connection approach to CSR to examine the legitimacy of those expanded CSR demands up and down the value chain. Young's social connection approach to CSR allows analyzing the responsibility demands that arise from various relationships (direct and indirect). Also, it acknowledges that issues such as human rights violations or public health are systemic, the result of a wide range of actors within a network.

While this chapter has answered some questions, such as how to make sense out of the latest CSR demands up and down corporate value chains, it also raises new questions for future research to address: How can systemic issues such as human rights or public health be jointly solved by the various actors who are socially connected? What are the concrete duties and responsibilities that derive from a social connection approach to CSR? In the future, social and environmental problems of corporations will have to be understood as systemic problems across supply chains for which systemic solutions will be required that align the engagement of various connected actors in multi-stakeholder efforts.

Notes

1   Ballinger, J. (1992), "The new free-trade heel: Nike's profits jump on the backs of Asian workers", *Harper's Magazine*, Vol. 285, pp. 46; Sethi, S.P. (1975) "Dimensions of corporate social performance: an analytical framework", *California Management Review*, Vol. 17, No. 3, pp. 58–64; Carroll, A.B. (1991), "The pyramid of corporate social responsibility", *Business Horizons*, Vol. 34, No. 4, p. 39.

2   Phillips, R.A. & Caldwell, C.B. (2005), "Value chain responsibility: a farewell to arm's length", *Business & Society Review*, Vol. 110, No. 4, pp. 345–370.

3   Appelbaum, R.P. & Dreier, P. (1999), "The campus anti-sweatshop movement", *The American Prospect*, September-October, pp. 71–78; Ballinger, *op. cit.*, p. 46.

4   Connor, T. (2002), *We Are Not Machines*, Clean Clothes Campaign, Global Exchange, Maquila Solidarity Network, Oxfam Canada, Oxfam Community Aid Abroad; Green, D. (1998), *Fashion Victims: Together We Can Clean Up the Clothes Trade: The Asian Garment Industry and Globalisation*, CAFOD, London.

5   Sethi, S.P. (2003), *Setting Global Standards. Guidelines for Creating Codes of Conduct in Multinational Corporations*, John Wiley & Sons, Hoboken, NJ.

6   Global Witness (2010), "A guide for companies: do no harm. Excluding conflict minerals from the supply chain". London, UK. Available at: www.globalwitness.org/sites/default/files/pdfs/do_no_harm_global_witness.pdf, last accessed 10 March, 2013.

7   Global Witness, 2010, *op. cit.*

8   Steinweg, T. (2010), *Driven by Corporate Social Responsibility? Top Ten Car Manufacturers: A CSR Analysis*, SOMO, Amsterdam; Steinweg, T. & Haan E.D. (2007), *Capacitating Electronics: The Corrosive Effects of Platinum and Palladium Mining on Labour Rights and Communities*, SOMO, Amsterdam.

9   Fort, T.L. & Schipani, C.A. (2004), *The Role of Business in Fostering Peaceful Societies*, Cambridge University Press, Cambridge.

10 Misangyi, V.F., Weaver, G.R. & Elms, H. (2008), "Ending corruption: the interplay among institutional logics, resources, and institutional entrepreneurs", *Academy of Management Executive Review*, Vol. 33, No. 3, pp. 750–770.

11 Smith, N.C., Palazzo, G. & Bhattacharya, C.B. (2010), "Marketing consequences: stakeholder marketing and supply chain corporate social responsibility issues", *Business Ethics Quarterly*, Vol. 20, No. 4, pp. 617–641.

12 Schrempf, J. (2012), "A social connection approach to corporate responsibility: the case of the fast-food industry and obesity", *Business and Society*, 24 July, 2012, DOI: 10.1177/0007650312449577.

13 Adams, R.J. (2005), "Fast food, obesity, and tort reform: an examination of industry responsibility for public health", *Business and Society Review*, Vol. 110, No. 3, pp. 297–320.

14 Malik, V.S., Schulze, M.B. & Hu, F.B. (2006), "Intake of sugar-sweetened beverages and weight gain: a systematic review", *American Journal of Clinical Nutrition*, Vol. 84, No. 2, pp. 274–288; Thorpe, L.E., MacKenzie, K., Perl, S., Young, C., Hajat, A., Mostashari, F., et al. (2003), One in 6 New York City Adults Is Obese. NYC Vital Signs, Vol. 2, No.7, pp. 1–4.

15 Adams, *op. cit.*; Schlosser, E. (2002), *Fast Food Nation*, Houghton Mifflin, New York.

16 Carroll, A.B. (1991), "The pyramid of corporate social responsibility: toward the moral management of organizational stakeholders", *Business Horizons*, Vol. 34, No. 4, p. 39.

17 Phillips, R. (2010), "Ethics in network organizations", *Business Ethics Quarterly*, Vol. 20, No. 3, pp. 533–544.

18   Enough Project (2010), "Getting to conflict-free. Assessing corporate action on conflict minerals", Enough Project, Washington, DC. Available at: www.enoughproject.org/files/corporate_action-1.pdf, last accessed 10 March, 2013; Schrempf, J. (2011), "Nokia Siemens Networks: just doing business – or supporting an oppressive regime?", *Journal of Business Ethics*, Vol. 103, No. 1, pp. 95–110; Global Witness, 2010, *op. cit.*.

19   Young, I.M. (2006), "Responsibility and global justice: a social connection model", *Social Philosophy and Policy*, Vol. 23, No. 1, pp. 102–130.

20   Sethi, 1975, *op. cit.*

21   Bigelow, B. (1997), "Facts on the global sweatshop", *Rethinking Schools*, Vol. 11, No. 4, p. 16; Connor, *op. cit.*

22   Appelbaum & Dreier, *op. cit.*; CBS 48 Hours (1996), "Nike in Vietnam".

23   Kernaghan, C. (1998), *Behind the Label: Made in China*, National Labor Committee, New York; Sluiter, L. (2009), *Clean Clothes: A Global Movement to End Sweatshops*, Pluto Press, New York.

24   Zadek, S. (2004), "The path to corporate responsibility", *Harvard Business Review*, Vol. 82, No. 12, pp. 125–132.

25   Phillips, *op. cit.*

26   Kahle, L.R., Boush, D.M. & Phelps, M. (2000), "Good morning, Vietnam: an ethical analysis of Nike activities in southeast Asia", *Sport Marketing Quarterly*, Vol. 9, No. 1, p. 43; Phillips, *op. cit.*; Ruggie, J. (2007), "Business and human rights: the evolving international agenda", *American Journal of International Law*, Vol. 101, No. 4, pp. 819–840.

27   Sethi, 1975, *op. cit.*

28   Sluiter, *op. cit.*

29   Harney, A. (2008), *The China Price*, The Penguin Press, New York.

30   Yu, X. (2008), "Impacts of corporate code of conduct on labor standards: a case study of Reebok's athletic footwear supplier factory in China", *Journal of Business Ethics*, Vol. 81, No. 3, pp. 513–529.

31   Moore, M. (2010), "Inside Foxconn's suicide factory", *Telegraph*, 27 May. Retrieved from: www.telegraph.co.uk/finance/china-business/7773011/A-look-inside-the-Foxconn-suicide-factory.html.

32   Hoffman, M. & Gerhardt, P. (2005), *"Diga nao ao deserto verde" – Nein Zu Grüner Wüste* [No to Green Desert], Robin Wood, Hamburg.

33   Robin Wood (2006), "Procter & Gamble comes under criticism following the displacement of Indians in Brazil". Retrieved from: www.robinwood.de/german/presse/060220en.htm, last accessed 10 March, 2013.

34   EJF (2007), *The Children Behind Our Cotton*, Environmental Justice Foundation, London.

35   Steinweg, *op. cit.* p. 2.

36   Steinweg, *op. cit.*

37   Kristof, N.D. (2010), "Death by gadget", *The New York Times*, 26 June, 2010. Retrieved from: www.nytimes.com/2010/06/27/opinion/27kristof.html?_r=0.

38   Global Witness (1998), "A rough trade: the role of companies and governments in the Angolan conflict", Global Witness, London. Available at: www.globalwitness.org/sites/default/files/pdfs/A_Rough_Trade.pdf, last accessed 10 March, 2013.

39   Global Witness (2009), "Metals in mobile phones help finance Congo atrocities", Global Witness, London. Available at: www.globalwitness.org/library/metals-mobile-phones-help-finance-congo-atrocities, last accessed 10 March, 2013.

40   Steinweg & Haan, *op. cit.*

41   Steinweg, *op. cit.*

42   Scherer, A. & Palazzo, G. (2007), "Toward a political conception of corporate responsibility: business and society seen from a Habermasian perspective", *Academy of Management Review*, Vol. 32, No. 4, pp. 1096–1120.

43   Elms, H. & Phillips, R. (2009), "Private security companies and institutional legitimacy: corporate and stakeholder responsibility", *Business Ethics Quarterly*, Vol. 19, No. 3, pp. 403–432; Fort & Schipani, *op. cit.*; Hsieh, N. (2009), "Does global business have a responsibility to promote just institutions?", *Business Ethics Quarterly*, Vol. 19, No. 2, pp. 251–273; Misangyi, Weaver & Elms, *op. cit.*

44   Ruggie, *op. cit.*, p. 10.

45   Idahosa, P. (2002), "Business ethics and development in conflict (zones): the case of Talisman oil", *Journal of Business Ethics*, Vol. 39, No. 3, pp. 227–246.

46   Boele, R., Fabig, H. & Wheeler, D. (2001), "Shell, Nigeria and the Ogoni. A study in unsustainable development: II. Corporate social responsibility and 'stakeholder management' versus a rights-based approach to sustainable development", *Sustainable Development*, Vol. 9, No. 3, pp. 121–135.

47   Amnesty International (2010), "Sudan: the Human Price of Oil", Amnesty International. Available at: www.amnesty.org/en/library/asset/AFR54/001/2000/en/82ee4ed1-dfc5-11dd-8e17-69926d493233/afr540012000en.pdf, last accessed 10 March, 2013.

48   Amnesty International (2005), "Nigeria: Ten years on: injustice and violence haunt the oil Delta", Amnesty International. Available at: www.amnesty.org/en/library/asset/AFR44/022/2005/en/63b716d6-d49d-11dd-8a23-d58a49c0d652/afr440222005en.pdf,   last accessed 10 March, 2013.

49   Crabtree, P. (2005), "Litigation onslaught threatens maker of banished ephedra pill", *San Diego Union Tribune*, 5 January, 2005, A-1; Gioia, A.G. (1992), "Pinto fires and personal ethics: a script analysis of missed opportunities", *Journal of Business Ethics*, Vol. 11, pp. 379–389; Stateman, A. (2008), "The Tylenol tampering crisis as examined 25 years ago", *Public Relations Tactics*, Vol. 15, No. 3, p. 7.

50   Gioia, *op. cit.*

51   Jolly, D. (2011), "Danish company blocks sale of drug for U.S. executions", *The New York Times*, 1 July, 2011. Available at: www.nytimes.com/2011/07/02/world/europe/02execute.html.

52   Hopf, W.H., Huber, G.L. & Weiß, R.H. (2008), "Media violence and youth violence: a 2-year longitudinal study", *Journal of Media Psychology*, Vol. 20, No. 3, pp. 79–96.

53   BBC News (2001), "Columbine families sue computer game makers", May 1, 2001. Available at: http://news.bbc.co.uk/2/hi/science/nature/1295920.stm; Haape, M. (2009), "Germany seeks answers after rampage", *Sunday Herald*, 14 March, 2009. Available at: www.heraldscotland.com/germany-seeks-answers-after-rampage-1.829159.

54   Wansink, B. & Huckabee, M. (2005), "De-marketing obesity", *California Management Review*, Vol. 47, No. 4, p. 6.

55   Rhoads, C. & Chao, L. (2009), "Iran's web spying aided by western technology", *The Wall Street Journal*, 22 June, 2009. Available at: http://online.wsj.com/article/SB124562668777335653.html

56   Dehghan, S.K. (2010), "Iranian activist sues telecoms firm over 'spying system'", *The Guardian*, August 24, 2010. Available at: www.guardian.co.uk/world/2010/aug/24/iranian-sues-nokia-siemens-networks.

57   Rhoads & Chao, *op. cit.*; Schrempf, 2011, *op. cit.*

58   French, P. (1984), *Collective and Corporate Responsibility*, Columbia University Press, New York; Honoré, T. (1999), *Responsibility and Fault*, Oxford University Press, Oxford.

59 Feinberg, J.(1970), *Doing and Deserving: Essays in the Theory of Responsibility*, Princeton University Press, Princeton, NJ; French, *op. cit.*; Honoré, *op. cit.*

60 Bowen, H.R. (1953), *Social Responsibilities of the Businessman*, Harper & Row, New York; Drucker, P.F. (1954), "The responsibilities of management", *Harper's Magazine*, Vol. 209, No. 1254, pp. 67–72.

61 Young, I.M. (2004), "Responsibility and global labor justice", *Journal of Political Philosophy*, Vol. 12, No. 4, pp. 365–388.

62 Young, 2006, *op. cit.*

63 Young, 2006, *op. cit.*, p. 119.

64 May, L. (1993), *Sharing Responsibility*, University of Chicago Press, Chicago.

65 Wood, S. (2012), "The case for leverage-based corporate human rights responsibility", *Business Ethics Quarterly*, Vol. 22, No. 1, pp. 63–98.

66 Ciliberti, F., de Haan, J., de Groot, G. & Pontrandolfo, P. (2011), "CSR codes and the principal-agent problem in supply chains: four case studies", *Journal of Cleaner Production*, Vol. 19, pp. 885–894.

67 Fletcher, G. (1999), *Basic Concepts of Criminal Law*, Oxford University Press, Oxford.

68 Gioia, *op. cit.*

69 Danley, J.R. (2005), "Polishing up the Pinto: legal liability, moral blame, and risk", *Business Ethics Quarterly*, Vol. 15, No. 2, pp. 205–236.

70 Elliott, K.A. & Freeman, R.B. (2004), *Can Labor Standards Improve Under Globalization?*, Institute for International Economics, Washington, DC.

71 CNN.com (2004), "Video game 'sparked hammer murder'", 29 July, 2004. Available at: http://articles.cnn.com/2004-07-29/world/uk.manhunt_1_violent-video-murder-simulators-killings?_s=PM:WORLD; Weber, R., Ritterfield, U. & Mathiak, K. (2006), "Does playing violent video games induce aggression? Empirical evidence of a functional magnetic resonance imaging study", *Media Psychology*, Vol. 8, No. 1, pp. 39–60.

72 Locke, R.M., Fei, Q.I.N. & Brause, A. (2007), "Does monitoring improve labor standards? Lessons from Nike", *Industrial & Labor Relations Review*, Vol. 61, No. 1, pp. 3–31.

73 Harney, *op. cit.*

74 Santoro, M.A. (2010), *Profits and Principles: Global Capitalism and Human Rights in China*, Cornell University Press, Ithaca, NY.

75 Misangyi, Weaver & Elms, *op. cit.*

76 Appelbaum & Dreier, *op. cit.*

77 Nordbrand, S. & Bolme, P. (2007), "Powering the mobile world. Cobalt production of batteries in the DR Congo and Zambia", SwedWatch.

78 Hewlett-Packard (2011), "Conflict minerals". Available at: www.hp.com/hpinfo/globalcitizenship/10gcreport/society/conflict_minerals.html, last accessed 10 March, 2013; Hewlett-Packard (2010), "HP commends enactment of conflict minerals legislation", 21 July, 2010. Available at: www8.hp.com/us/en/m/hp-news/details.do?id=572383&articletype=news_release, last accessed 10 March, 2013.

79 Enough Project (2010), "Getting to conflict-free. Assessing corporate action on conflict minerals".

80 Fair Labor Association (2010), "Cotton project report 2008–2010. Tracing the cotton supply chain". Available at: www.fairlabor.org/sites/default/files/imce/images/cottonproject_report2008-2010.pdf, last accessed 10 March, 2013.

81 Wal-Mart (2008), "Wal-Mart takes action to end forced child labor in Uzbekistan" 30 September, 2008. Available at: http://news.walmart.com/news-archive/2008/09/30/walmart-takes-action-

to-end-forced-child-labor-in-uzbekistan; The Gap (2010), "Uzbek cotton", Available at: www.gapinc.com/content/csr/html/Goals/supplychain/our_program_in_action/uzbek_cotton.html.

82 Phillips, *op. cit.*

83 Bandura, A. (1999), "Moral disengagement in the perpetration of inhumanities", *Personality and Social Psychology Review*, Vol. 3, pp. 193–209.

84 Bandura, A. (2002), "Selective moral disengagement in the exercise of moral agency", *Journal of Moral Education*, Vol. 31, p. 107.

85 Bandura, 2002, *op. cit.*, pp. 101–119.

86 Bandura. 2002, *op. cit.*, p. 106.

87 Bandura, 2002, *op. cit.*, pp. 101–119.

88 Klawitter, N. (2005), "Yahoo scandal. When the West helps China spy", *Spiegel Online International*, 17 September, 2005. Available at: www.spiegel.de/international/spiegel/yahoo-scandal-when-the-west-helps-china-spy-a-375965.html.

89 Young, 2004, *op. cit.*; Young, 2006, *op. cit.*

21 *Meta-Management of Corporate Social Responsibility*

MUHAMMAD ASIF,* CORY SEARCY,† AND
OLAF A. M. FISSCHER‡

Keywords

Meta-management, corporate social responsibility, Shell, sensemaking, integration, management systems.

Introduction

Modern corporations are powerful entities capable of significantly influencing the overall health of a society.[1] While societies can benefit from corporations in many ways; they can also be adversely affected by the activities of corporations. The examples of both types of impact are discussed widely in the literature.[2] There is a growing recognition that corporations have obligations to their stakeholders and that corporations must address the legitimate requirements of their stakeholders, including customers, regulators, suppliers, employees, and society in general.[3] To this end, literature on corporate social responsibility (CSR) has burgeoned during the last two decades.[4] This has led to an increased understanding of the concept of CSR and how it could affect the viability of a business.

While there is a broad agreement among researchers that CSR practices need to be integrated into every level of an organization,[5] and that CSR has to be anchored in a specific organizational identity,[6] the issue of integrating CSR practices into core organizational processes remains a question.[7] There is broad agreement among researchers on the need for a framework that integrates the development and implementation of CSR into the organization's strategy, structure, and culture.[8] As Campbell notes, one possible reason is that there is more normative and descriptive literature on CSR than positivist literature.[9] This highlights the need to move beyond normative realms describing the desirability of CSR actions to structured approaches for the implementation of CSR. An important requirement in this regard is that CSR implementation approaches or models should focus explicitly on developing a strategic and organization-wide program that

*   Muhammad Asif, PhD. Prince Sultan University, KSA. E-mail: muhammad.assif@gmail.com.

†   Cory Searcy, PhD. Ryerson University Canada. E-mail: cory.searcy@ryerson.ca.

‡   Prof. Olaf A. M. Fisscher, University of Twente, The Netherlands. E-mail: o.a.m.fisscher@utwente.nl.

is embedded in the organization's core infrastructure.[10] In this chapter we discuss the implementation of CSR using a meta-management approach that explicitly addresses the need to focus on the whole organization. Meta-management is a stakeholder-oriented approach to the management of business processes.[11] At its core, meta-management emphasizes the need for strategic management of business processes that integrates strategic priorities with tactical imperatives and operational tasks. The result is an integrated system for addressing stakeholder requirements. Recognizing the need to adapt to changing circumstances, continual improvement is one of the foundations of the meta-management approach.

The objective of this chapter is to elaborate the essentials of the meta-management of CSR. The development, implementation, and management of CSR are discussed using a meta-management approach. The discussion is supported by a case study of Shell. The remainder of the chapter is structured as follows. First, a concise overview of relevant literature is presented. This is followed by a discussion on the meta-management of CSR. Various elements of meta-management are discussed, including sensemaking of the organization, implementation of CSR, monitoring and continual improvement, and CSR reporting. A framework for the meta-management of CSR is presented. Meta-management of CSR is further illustrated with the example of Shell's approach to CSR. The chapter ends with a brief conclusion and recommendations for further work.

An Overview of CSR Literature

CSR has been a subject of controversy among academics due to its many different conceptualizations.[12] Carroll provided a comprehensive description of how CSR has evolved over time: the concept began to evolve in the 1950s and expanded in the 1960s and the 1970s.[13] In the 1980s and onwards there were fewer definitions, more empirical research, and fewer alternate themes. As we move into the second decade of the 21st century, a clear conceptualization of CSR is essential for effective communication and for coherent efforts in further research. Dahlsrud conducted an analysis of 37 definitions of CSR and found that five dimensions are common:[14] the environmental (natural environment), economic (socio-economic and financial aspects), social (relationship between business and society), stakeholder (stakeholder groups), and voluntary (actions not prescribed by law) dimensions.

An essential component of the CSR concept is its "stakeholder-oriented" approach.[15] Stakeholder theory has implications for the implementation of CSR in that it implies that CSR activities must be designed around key stakeholders with the overall objective of stakeholder satisfaction. Berman et al. noted that the motivation for CSR may be driven by financial benefits or by a moral responsibility to address stakeholder interests.[16] The former is an example of the instrumental perspective while the latter is an example of the normative perspective. The business case for CSR suggests that CSR practices are necessary for the growth and successful performance of a business.[17] Meta-analyses of various studies have revealed that there exists a positive relationship between CSR and financial performance.[18] These meta-studies further strengthen the business case for CSR.

The implementation of CSR has been the topic of a number of publications. Pedersen, Maon et al., and Zadek discussed the various stages of CSR implementation.[19] Zadek explained the implementation of CSR through the example of Nike – starting from categorical denial of the need for CSR initiatives to more civil actions linking the CSR initiative with broader public policy.[20] With every passing stage CSR is further institutionalized in the organizational setting. Kleine and Hauff elaborated on how to make CSR management more systematic through the development of priority areas.[21] Other researchers have emphasized that CSR must be implemented as a strategic program aimed at addressing the legitimate requirements of key stakeholders.[22] In this line of reasoning, we consider CSR as systematic organizational efforts aimed at strategically addressing stakeholder requirements; and in doing so, using a structured approach to bring various stakeholders into organizational consciousness, weaving stakeholder requirements into business processes, and doing this on a continual basis to address emerging issues. The implementation of CSR is also discussed in the literature in terms of its linkages with ISO management systems.[23] Oskarsson and Malmborg argued that the integration of management systems could be used as a means to implement CSR.[24]

However, questions remain on how the implementation of CSR may be accomplished. In particular, there is a need for research on the methods that can be used to strategically implement an organization-wide CSR program that addresses stakeholder requirements.[25] This point is particularly important because CSR practices are dependent on a number of external and internal factors, such as the financial conditions of an organization and pressure exerted by a number of different stakeholders.[26] Working in a dynamic environment characterized by various types of uncertainties, the external and internal factors that influence a CSR program are in continual flux. This highlights the need for a strategic approach to CSR that results in the development of a program that is fully functional and deeply embedded in the organization's core institutional infrastructure. An approach based on the concept of meta-management provides the structure needed to successfully design, implement, and improve a cohesive, organization-wide CSR program. Meta-management is a dynamic approach to addressing stakeholder requirements strategically,[27] integrating CSR into organizational processes, and continual improvement. Owing to these characteristics, meta-management provides a systematic means for integrating CSR into organizational processes on a continual basis.

Meta-Management of CSR

Meta-management emphasizes the stakeholder view rather than the market-based or competition-based view of the business.[28] The competition-based view of the business has an overarching focus on a limited number of stakeholders, particularly the customer. The stakeholder-based view of the business, on the other hand, suggests that customer satisfaction is only one of the *primus inter pares* objectives of the business, and business activities must be carried out in a manner that does not adversely affect other stakeholders.[29]

Meta-management in this context means integration of CSR into business processes at a high level of abstraction.[30] The three levels of meta-management are meta-modeling, modeling, and intervention – representing gradually decreasing abstraction. This is in recognition of the fact that organizational issues appear differently at each organizational level. For example, the "meta-modeling level" deals with issues such as environmental scanning, identification of stakeholders, direction setting for the organization, and development of policy. At the "modeling level" organizational priorities unfold in the form of planning and the design of CSR. In other words, this level focuses on how to realize CSR-related strategic priorities and how to design processes in a way that would yield value for key stakeholders. The development of an organization-specific business model to implement CSR is one example of activities at the modeling level. The "intervention level" deals specifically with operational issues. Meta-management, thus, ensures that CSR is implemented organization-wide.

The starting point for the meta-management of CSR is the "sensemaking" of the internal and external environment. "Sensemaking" is the cognitive process of understanding the organization and the broader environment in which it operates.[31] Sensemaking helps to highlight how the organization and the broader environment impact each other, including the nature of this impact. The detailed process of sensemaking is discussed in the following sections. An important outcome of sensemaking is an enhanced understanding of stakeholders, their requirements, and prioritization of those requirements. This provides the basis for the integration of CSR.

The organization-wide integration of CSR includes both vertical and horizontal integration. Vertical integration is the translation of organizational objectives and priorities to the tactical and operational level. Vertical integration ensures that a complete fit exists among organizational priorities, tactical processes, and operational tasks. Horizontal integration is the fit among various processes, chains, operating companies, departments, and individuals and also includes structures, systems, and competencies.[32] The purpose of integration is to make sure that CSR is implemented at all levels of the organization and is, thus, institutionalized organization-wide. At the core of meta-management is the need for continual improvement which is a never-ending pursuit for innovation, improvement, and learning from past experiences. Continual improvement needs to be organized to address both strategic and operational issues. The dynamic nature of CSR, in terms of fulfilling corporate responsibilities on a continual basis, highlights the need to acquire, assimilate, transform, and exploit knowledge. This capability, also called absorptive capacity, in turn gives rise to a dynamic capability to generate and modify new routines for improved performance. Since meta-management is a higher order approach based on learning and continual improvement at all organizational levels, it offers a dynamic capability to address emerging CSR issues. Based on learning from past experiences, this capability entails reconfiguring the existing CSR capabilities for improved CSR management.

The elements of CSR meta-management find support from the literature. "Sensemaking" has been discussed in terms of an environment understanding process,[33] and a CSR-implementation essential.[34] Literature also provides support for other CSR meta-management elements, including stakeholder-oriented business management,[35] strategic management of CSR,[36] organization-wide integration,[37] and continual improvement.[38] However, these elements have not previously been discussed in the form of an integrated framework providing a systematic approach to CSR development. The basic structure of a meta-management approach as discussed by Van Gigch and Foley,[39] and its possible application to CSR essentials as discussed in the noted publications,[40] provide the theoretical underpinning for the CSR meta-management model discussed in this chapter. The essentials of CSR meta-management are summarized in Table 21.1.

Table 21.1 Essentials of the meta-management of CSR

Essential components of the meta-management of CSR	
Sensemaking of the organization and broader environment	Sensemaking is about how business executives scan and interpret the environment in which the organization operates to understand the influence of the internal and external environment on the organization's CSR initiatives. Through sensemaking, managers develop an enhanced understanding of the organization and how CSR fits with its existing infrastructure.
Stakeholder-oriented business management	Meta-management emphasizes a stakeholder-oriented, rather than a customer- or a competitor-oriented, business management model. While the customer is clearly a key stakeholder, customer requirements should be addressed in a way that does not adversely affect interests of other stakeholders.
Strategic management	Strategic management emphasizes the development of a CSR strategy and implementation of CSR at a high level of abstraction. Its purpose is to make sure that CSR is integrated into core business processes and does not remain an isolated practice.
Organization-wide integration	Integration focuses on ensuring that CSR practices are effectively integrated throughout the organization from both a horizontal and a vertical perspective.
Continual improvement	A foundation of the meta-management approach is the dynamic process of continual improvement along the various dimensions of strategy and operation. Continual improvement must encompass both an "inside-out" and an "outside-in" approach.

The elements highlighted in Table 21.1 provide a foundation for structuring thinking and discussion about the meta-management of CSR. With those elements in mind, a framework for the meta-management of CSR is presented in Figure 21.1. The overarching purpose of meta-management is to ensure that individuals understand the *raison d'être* of the business, know their stakeholders, and incorporate their requirements through a continual improvement process. The key stages of CSR implementation are aligned with the Plan, Do, Check, and Act (PDCA) cycle of continual improvement suggested by Deming.[41] As indicated in Figure 21.1, the "plan" part of the PDCA cycle requires upfront systematic planning of CSR initiatives, developing the blueprint of the CSR program, and arranging material, informational, technical, and human resources. The planning phase of PDCA provides a basis for structuring the "do" part. The "do" phase of the PDCA cycle is focused on implementation. Throughout the implementation process, there is continuous monitoring of organizational processes and how the CSR strategy unfolds. This constitutes the "check" stage. Finally, the data collected during the "check" stage builds the foundation for further improvements, which constitute the "act" part of the PDCA cycle. The PDCA cycle, thus, provides an organization with a platform and a meta-routine for systematic continual improvement.[42]

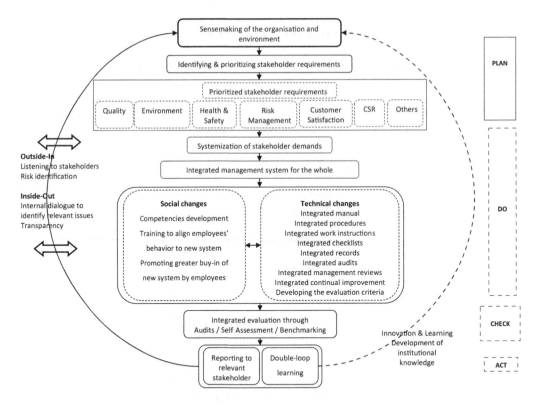

Figure 21.1 The meta-management of CSR

Briefly summarizing, the "plan" phase of the PDCA cycle includes sensemaking of the organization, CSR, and the broader environment – and development of CSR strategic plans. The "do" phase is about implementation of CSR strategic plans. This is followed by the monitoring and assessment of CSR initiatives – the "check" phase. Finally, the "act" phase is about reporting of CSR initiatives to stakeholders and learning and innovation. This is discussed in the following sections.

SENSEMAKING OF THE ORGANIZATION, ENVIRONMENT, AND CSR

The first step in the meta-management of CSR is "sensemaking" of the organization and the broader environment in which it operates. Sensemaking is defined by Weick as "placement of items into a framework, comprehending, redressing surprise, constructing meaning, interacting in pursuit of mutual understanding, and patterning."[43] Cramer et al. noted that sensemaking is about constructing meanings for CSR and its conceptualization.[44] CSR sensemaking is about understanding the organization, environment, stakeholders, how the things unfold, what is good and what is bad, the key issues and problems and how they are resolved.

The process of sensemaking starts from "environmental scanning," including both the external and internal environment. Environmental scanning is meant for identifying 1) stakeholders and issues that impact organizational strategy and business processes, 2) whether organizational strategy and business processes impact the environment and stakeholders, 3) what are the aftermaths of such impacts, and 4) how to manage such impacts using available competencies and institutional knowledge. Environmental scanning is an antecedent of the decision making process. The role of environmental scanning in decision making is evident from the literature, which shows that executives in high-performing firms scan more frequently than those of low-performing firms,[45] and from contingency theory that suggests successful decision making is based on the environmental conditions.[46]

One key component of the sensemaking process is interpretation. "Interpretation" is making inferences from data, with an emphasis on understanding the meanings of CSR. It is a cognitive process that leads to better understanding of what it means to be "socially responsible" and of "stakeholder-oriented" business management. "CSR decisions and resulting actions" are the result of environmental scanning, including the interpretation process. Figure 21.2, which builds on the notion of organizations as interpretation systems,[47] shows the essentials of the sensemaking process. An important challenge for managers is the realization of possible differences in the existing mental models and the desired approaches for CSR development, including consideration of new individual and collective CSR capabilities. Sensing the need for new capabilities and their development are critical to the development of CSR.[48]

An essential outcome of the sensemaking process is an enhanced understanding of stakeholders, their demands, and the urgency and legitimacy of their demands. Based on this outcome, managers prioritize stakeholder demands to make effective and timely use of limited organizational resources. Sensemaking and the subsequent prioritization of stakeholder requirements help in the formulation of mission and strategic plans, including development of CSR-oriented purchasing, manufacturing, and marketing strategy; and how value would be created throughout the supply chain.

IMPLEMENTATION OF CSR

Implementation constitutes the "do" part of the PDCA cycle. The meta-management of CSR implementation requires a structured approach. The essence of this approach is to consider stakeholder requirements at a high level of abstraction and then address them through continual improvement. The starting point in this regard is the systemization of stakeholder requirements. The primary focus is to link stakeholder requirements with the mainstream business management systems of the organization. Organizations implement a number of management systems to address specific requirements of their stakeholders.

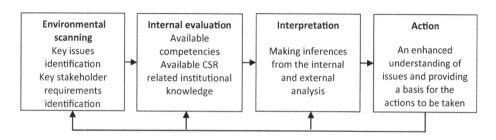

Figure 21.2 Sensemaking of the organization and the broader environmental context

ISO 9001, for instance, is a management system that helps an organization establish a sound quality management program and focuses on customer satisfaction. ISO 14001 is employed to make environmental management more systematic. Similarly, health and safety and social accountability management systems are also employed by organizations for their specific purposes. These management systems can give organizations an important starting point for systematically addressing stakeholder requirements. However, an important point to note is that standardized management systems like these are sub-systems of an overarching meta-management system for the whole organization. In the form of an integrated and overarching system for the whole organization these systems provide a structured approach to addressing stakeholder requirements.[49] The social and technical structures introduced by an integrated management system are shown in Figure 21.3

An important element in the implementation stage of CSR is the integration of CSR structures organization-wide. This means that CSR needs to be integrated throughout the organization and implemented as a strategic program that does not remain an isolated or ad hoc practice. The organization-wide integration of CSR requires vertical and horizontal integration. As noted earlier, the former is the integration across various levels of organizations to transfer organizational aims and objectives to the tactical and operational levels. The latter is the integration between processes such as purchasing, production, distribution, marketing, and the overall supply chain, operating companies, departments and individuals, and also includes structures, systems, and competencies.[50]

The institutionalization of CSR requires alignment of the social side with the technical side of the organization.[51] The mentioned management systems introduce structures to facilitate meeting stakeholder requirements. Examples of these structures include manuals, procedures, work instructions, documentation requirements, etc. These structures, however, are not sufficient on their own and need alignment along the social side of the organization. This means measures need to be taken to familiarize employees with the essentials of the CSR program. One means to carry out social alignment is training of employees. The alignment of the social side with the technical side of the organization is needed to promote buy-in of new systems and, thus, promote its institutionalization.[52] This is an important point to note because a mere focus on CSR tools and techniques such as CSR metrics, reporting tools, and standardized management systems could lead to a tools- and techniques-oriented approach to CSR that lacks employee buy-in and, thus, is not institutionalized in an organizational setting. The alignment of social and technical structures is shown in Figure 21.3.

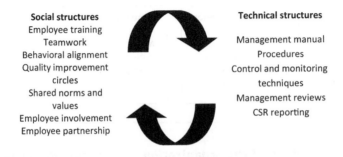

Figure 21.3 Alignment of social and technical structures

To summarize, meta-management provides a compass for the integration of CSR into business processes. This is due to its explicit focus on 1) stakeholders, 2) strategic management of CSR, 3) emphasis on organization-wide integration of CSR, 4) focus on both the social and technical sides of the organization, and 5) the need to intertwine the social side with the technical side.

CSR ASSESSMENT

An essential component of the meta-management of CSR is continual improvement along various dimensions of stakeholder requirements. This is due to the fact that stakeholders and their requirements keep changing and new stakeholder requirements emerge or gain salience. The power, legitimacy, and urgency of stakeholders changes,[53] underlining the need to incorporate stakeholder requirements continuously into business processes. The regular external environmental scanning to identify emerging issues and address them is termed as an "outside-in" approach.[54] The evaluation of a CSR program can be systematically organized through audits, self-assessment, and benchmarking or using various combinations of the three. This evaluation forms the foundation of the "check" part of the PDCA cycle.

Audits provide a retrospective perspective to the assessment of a CSR program. They are typically carried out at regular intervals and are primarily aimed at finding non-conformances. Audits usually assess a system against the clauses of a standard such as ISO 9001 and ISO 14001. Although very helpful in finding non-conformances, they are of limited usefulness in bringing improvements. To ensure independence, audits are often carried out by an external independent third party. Paradoxically, audits may marginalize the process owner who is supposed to be the ultimate beneficiary of the audit.[55] Self-assessment is carried out proactively by the process owner. Although self-assessments may lack the objectivity of an audit, they offer a powerful means for continual improvement. Due to an emphasis on the deeper involvement of the process owner, self-assessment may bring unanticipated improvements to processes. Benchmarking focuses on comparing the performance of an organization against industry best practices with the objective of finding gaps for improvements. Organizations could also use a hybrid approach consisting of audits, self-assessment, and benchmarking to bring lasting improvements to an organization. Table 21.2 provides a list of CSR-specific actions in each assessment category.

Table 21.2 Various approaches to the assessment of CSR program

Approach to evaluation	Examples of CSR-specific actions
Audit	• Evaluating the extent to which an organization complies with environmental standards, legislation, and other internal or external requirements. • Auditing suppliers for conformance with environmental and social codes of conduct. • Conducting audits of environmental and social management systems. Existing standards may be used as a starting point. • Conducting an audit of the company's CSR report.
Self-assessment	• Conducting a self-assessment of the organization's processes in an effort to improve operational performance, customer satisfaction, the ability to meet targets, the success of CSR implementation efforts, etc.
Benchmarking	• Evaluating the organization's performance over time. • Benchmarking the organization's performance against industry leaders. This could encompass CSR strategy, implementation approach, CSR reporting, CSR assessment, stakeholder engagement, the overall management system and approaches for improving organizational performance.

It is important to note, however, that caution must be exercised in the application of generic auditing, self-assessment, and benchmarking schemes. This is because CSR is highly contextual in nature.[56] There is considerable variation in terms of business type, types of stakeholders, urgency and legitimacy of stakeholder requirements, power of stakeholders, time, and geographical location. The use of standards may inadvertently promote a "minimal" or "mere conformance" approach which is against the very basic principles of CSR and its association with voluntary initiatives that go beyond mandatory requirements. Any evaluation needs to be carried out with the intent of learning and improvement, which are foundations of CSR meta-management.[57] The key point is that organizations need a mechanism to promote continual improvement along all dimensions of stakeholder requirements.

CSR REPORTING AND CONTINUAL IMPROVEMENT

CSR reporting and continual improvement constitute the "act" stage of the PDCA cycle. An essential component of CSR meta-management is reporting to relevant stakeholders. Reporting on CSR initiatives is needed for a number of reasons. First, it is needed for legitimation reasons.[58] Organizations are dependent on stakeholders for a continued supply of resources. Communicating CSR initiatives to powerful stakeholders such as regulators, customers, and society also helps provide a corporation with a license to operate. Business customers may also require evidence of CSR initiatives as a prerequisite for business transactions. CSR reporting also provides organizations with an opportunity to develop a responsible image.[59] Finally, it also shows transparency – how an organization deals with the various issues that impact its business and then communicates the same to stakeholders. An organization, thus, needs not only an "outside-in" approach to internalize and address stakeholder requirements but also an "inside-out" approach to show responsibility and transparency in its affairs. A number of methods are available to facilitate CSR reporting. The most widely used system of reporting is provided as a part of the Global Reporting Initiative (GRI).[60] The GRI provides a list of indicators along social, environmental, and economic dimensions. Using indicators mentioned in the GRI framework, CSR reporting could be carried out through annual reports, websites, letters to stakeholders, etc.[61]

The distinguishing feature of continual improvement and learning in the meta-management of CSR is that it should be "double-loop learning," which means that incorporating new improvements is carried out at the level of governing values.[62] This is different from "single-loop learning" where problems are dealt with at the operational level. In single-loop learning, governing values are not altered and therefore problems keep occurring. This also underlines that continual improvement in meta-management is pursued at both the strategic and operational levels, whereas conventional approaches focus merely at the operational level. An example of the latter is a reactive approach to some problem, which may take the form of correcting or fixing the immediate problem. Double-loop learning, however, goes beyond mere correction to focus on the causes of such problems and address these causes so that problems do not recur. In contrast to single-loop learning which could be characterized as "correction," double-loop learning could be characterized as "prevention."

Shell's Approach to CSR – a Case of CSR Meta-Management

Royal Dutch Shell is a global group of energy and petrochemical companies employing more than 100,000 people in over 90 countries. Shell's business encompasses three main areas: gas and electricity for industrial and domestic use; refined oil products such as fuel, biofuel, and lubricants; and chemical products used for plastics, coating, and insulation.[63]

Shell was selected for this research for a number of reasons. The company is very active in CSR and its reporting. Systematically managing the issue since 1997,[64] Shell is now mature and a frontrunner in CSR. The company regularly discloses its CSR initiatives to its stakeholders and the general public in its annual reports. The GRI confirmed an A+ reporting level for the information contained in the company's 2009 and 2010 sustainability reports and its 2009 report was declared a "feature report" in the GRI reports list. Shell's CSR initiatives have been discussed in several publications.[65] Availability of information about Shell's CSR initiatives was another reason for the choice of the company. An initial review of Shell's annual sustainability report[66] showed that the company employed a number of practices which are central to the meta-management approach. In brief, Shell offered a strong case for the study of its CSR practices.

In the following sub-sections, Shell is used as a case study to demonstrate the application of the key principles and framework for the meta-management of CSR. The discussion is based on publicly available information in Shell's annual sustainability report,[67] its website,[68] and web-based archives.[69] The methodology employed for this research was content analysis of the mentioned sources. Content analysis is based on finding the presence or absence of particular information in a given subject.[70] The review was carried out by reading the documents as well as electronically searching the documents using keywords. Table 21.3 provides a list of activities that are representative of CSR meta-management and how they apply to Shell. The table summarizes how the processes of CSR meta-management such as: 1) sensemaking of the organization, CSR, and the broader environment, 2) integration of CSR into organizational processes, 3) CSR assessment, and 4) CSR reporting and continual improvement unfold at Shell. Direct quotes from Shell's sustainability report are provided where insightful. Shell's approach to CSR meta-management is further discussed in the sub-sections that follow.

Table 21.3 A summary of alignment between elements of CSR meta-management and Shell's approach to CSR

Key stages of CSR meta-management	Representative CSR activities	Shell's approach / representative direct quotes
	Defining stakeholders	"[Our stakeholders] include local communities, non-governmental organizations, shareholders, investors, customers, governments, employees, media, academics, contractors and suppliers."[1]
	Engaging in stakeholder consultation and identifying their requirements	Shell actively defines stakeholders and engages with them in stakeholder dialogue. Stakeholder involvement is an important feature of corporate governance at Shell. "We have a company-wide approach for engaging with our neighbors and other stakeholders. Staff liaise closely with local communities and work with technical and management staff to address their hopes and concerns."[2] "[…] final investment decision will require … consultation with stakeholders."[3] "Our updated HSSE & SP Control Framework includes requirements for engaging stakeholders."[4]
	Defining CSR and the business case for CSR	"The Corporate and Social Responsibility Committee (CSRC) assesses our policies and performance with respect to our Business Principles, Code of Conduct, HSSE & SP standards and major issues of public concern on behalf of the Board of Royal Dutch Shell."[5] "Safety, environment and social performance are now closer to the core of our business plans and decisions."[6] "In the reorganization of our company in 2009 we embedded more sustainability related roles at the core of our operations. As a result we expect to improve our sustainable development performance and engage earlier and more effectively with our stakeholders. Sustainable development is also part of how we assess our overall business performance and reward our people."[7]
Sensemaking of the organization, CSR, and the broader environment	Developing CSR competencies	"Our people are central to the success of our business strategy. Their skills and dedication help to deliver business results and address environmental and social challenges. The reorganization of Shell in 2009 was designed to strengthen our competitiveness. It created a simpler, leaner structure with clearer accountabilities, leading to faster decision-making and a sharper focus on our customers."[8] "All staff must complete training in our Code of Conduct. Relevant staff must undergo specific training in areas such as combating bribery and corruption, and complying with competition laws. We invested in building the capabilities of local companies and workers by training them in skills needed for jobs on the project. Local people took part in our environmental, social and health studies. They also contributed their knowledge to key project decisions."[9]
	Management commitment	Shell has developed a corporate governance system to address CSR. A corporate social responsibility committee (CSRC) assesses the company's performance and business principles. The corporate governance framework provides a basis for defining management responsibilities for CSR. This is shown in Table 21.4.
	Developing measurable indicators for sustainability	Shell has developed a broad range of indicators that address the triple bottom line of sustainable development. In the environmental category these indicators relate to "greenhouse gas emissions," "flaring," "energy intensity," "acid gases and volatile organic compounds," "ozone-depleting emissions," "spills and discharges," "fresh water," and "waste disposal". Along social dimension these indicators relate to "fatalities," "illness," "injuries," "security," "gender diversity," "regional diversity," "staff forums and grievance procedures," "child labor," "contracting and procurement," "integrity," and "social investment."

Key stages of CSR meta-management	Representative CSR activities	Shell's approach / representative direct quotes
	Integration of CSR into core business processes	*"In the reorganization of our company in 2009 we embedded more sustainability related roles at the core of our operations."*[80] *"We embedded sustainable development firmly in our businesses. This means that safety, environmental and social performance are now closer to the core of our business plans and decisions."*[81] *"Sustainable development works best when it is thoroughly integrated in our business decisions at the very earliest opportunity."*[82]
	Vertical and horizontal integration of CSR	Shell's Health, Safety, Security, Environment and Social Performance (HSSE & SP) control framework delineates requirements for operations. Details follow in the text.
	Developing technical structures for CSR, including a management manual and procedures	Shell uses a number of management system standards to systematically address its stakeholder requirements. The integration of CSR into business processes is facilitated through the HSSE & SP framework, management manuals, and procedures that define how to execute the business processes.
	Developing the personnel skills needed for CSR	Shell develops employees' skills through training relating to both technical and ethical aspects. Examples of the two types of training at Shell include developing employees' job skills (technical training) and combating malpractices such as bribes and corruption (ethics oriented training). Training regarding the code of conduct is mandatory.
Implementation of CSR	Developing strategic plans for long-term CSR	Shell uses a long-term approach to address CSR. The corporate governance system of CSR is instrumental to the development, implementation, monitoring, and assessment of a CSR policy. *"Sustainability is central to the way we do business, our business principles and our long-term strategy, so we take a very far-reaching view, not a short-term view. It means for me that we help to meet the growing energy needs of the world in economically, environmentally and socially responsible ways. You can't have one without the other two."*[83]
	Managing CSR knowledge	Shell defines its CSR knowledge management in terms of 1) community knowledge gathered from extensive interaction with stakeholders; 2) knowledge support for local companies and people for environment, social, health issues; and 3) internal technical knowledge management gained from various projects.
	Ensuring transparency in CSR integration	Transparency in Shell's operations is discussed in its reports in terms of response to community complaints, revenues transparency, and whistle blowing procedures. *"Shell is a founder and board member of the Extractive Industries Transparency Initiative (EITI), an organization that works to increase revenue transparency globally. We take part in a range of national and international forums on the challenges of revenue transparency."*[84]
	Responding in case of violations and non-conformances	Shell discusses the violations and the counter-measures in terms of: • Figures about Code of Conduct violations • Figures about contracts cancelled due to incompatibility with Business Principles • Figures about joint ventures divested due to incompatibility with Business Principles • Other operations violations – such as in the Niger delta – and the counter measures taken to mitigate them

Key stages of CSR meta-management	Representative CSR activities	Shell's approach / representative direct quotes
	Monitoring of CSR initiatives	The monitoring of CSR initiatives is an essential element of the corporate governance of Shell. The CSR committee is instrumental in CSR monitoring. Details follow in the text.
	Using multiple CSR assessment methods	The company reports extensively about its regular auditing mechanism for both internal audits as well as supplier audits. However, the company does not provide any indication of other assessment methods such as self-assessment and benchmarking. The use of multiple CSR assessment methods could provide a sound base for continual improvement.
CSR assessment	Monitoring sustainable development indicators	The company monitors progress along the triple bottom line of sustainable development and reports data along environmental, social, and economic indicators. The sustainability report provides data comparisons from 2000–2009.
	Assessing adequacy of CSR integration	This is carried out through regular audits along sustainable development indicators.
	Assessing adequacy of CSR communication to stakeholders	"An External Review Committee of independent experts helps make sure our reporting is balanced, relevant and responsive to stakeholders' interests."[85]
	Assessing the overall infrastructure for CSR	Corporate governance of Shell defines the responsibilities for CSR monitoring at various organizational levels. The CSR committee makes sure that CSR is integrated into business processes.
	CSR reporting to stakeholders	It is done through formal sustainability report, the company's website, and other modes of communication.
	Determining what to report and how to report	The issues that have high impact on the strategy and environment are reported in Shell's sustainability report. The issues which have moderate impact on strategy and environment are reported on the website. The issues which have least impact are not reported.
	Engaging stakeholders to obtain feedback	Stakeholder feedback is obtained from a number of channels, including an external review committee opinion letter, a global media review, reader surveys, Shell's public policy review, socially responsible investment reports and indexes, and website hits.
CSR reporting and continual improvement	Integrating previous experiences and knowledge into current processes	"We haven't always got our approach to all of these right in the past. But we've learnt, and we're building on those lessons. For new projects we need to get it right first time by engaging early with stakeholders."[86] Details follow in the text.
	Learning and improvement along both strategy and operations	The company extensively discusses its learning and improvement initiatives along both strategy and operations. Details follow in the text.

SENSEMAKING OF THE ORGANIZATION, CSR, AND THE BROADER ENVIRONMENT

Corporate governance for CSR

Shell employs a formal corporate governance system to strategically address CSR. As shown in Table 21.4, the Royal Dutch Shell (RDS) Group has a board committee on corporate and social responsibility (the CSRC). The CSRC is responsible for overseeing the company's sustainable development efforts, including policies and standards. The committee of four non-executive directors meets four times a year. It also visits Shell facilities. In addition to the CSRC and RDS executive committee, there is the HSSE & SP Executive that is chaired by the CEO of Shell. As Shell's corporate sustainability report notes,[87] "The 'HSSE & SP Executive' reviews performance and sets priorities, key performance indicators and targets. Each business and facility is responsible for complying with Shell's safety, environmental and social requirements. They must also set out to achieve targets measured against their industry peers."

Next in this corporate governance hierarchy are the HSSE & SP global discipline teams, and HSSE & SP specialists. The global discipline teams are responsible for supporting the business in implementing company-wide standards and requirements. They share industry best practices, integrate external learning and monitor performance. The HSSE & SP specialists make up to 90% of Shell's HSSE & SP staff. They are responsible for identifying risks, implementing policies and standards, and improving sustainability performance. Business leaders from global discipline teams and the HSSE & SP specialists are accountable for delivering sustainability initiatives and for their integration into existing operations and new projects.

Table 21.4 The corporate governance of CSR at Shell (based on Shell annual report)[88]

CSR Committee	The committee reviews sustainable development, including policies and standards
RDS Executive Committee	The committee is responsible for the overall business of the company, including sustainable development
HSSE & SP Executive Committee	The committee consists of senior HSSE &SP leaders from each business. It sets strategy and reviews performance
HSSE & SP global discipline teams	The teams are responsible for: • implementation of standards and requirements • sharing best practices • integrating learning • reviewing performance
HSSE & SP specialists	The specialists ensure implementation of policies and standards at the operational level
Business leaders	Business leaders are accountable for the delivery of the specified sustainable outcomes

The important points of Shell's approach to CSR are 1) a formal corporate governance structure involving the CEO, board of directors, global discipline teams, HSSE & SP specialists, and business leaders, 2) interaction with stakeholders at every hierarchical level of corporate governance, and 3) systematic realization of strategic priorities through integrated operations.

Stakeholder-oriented business management

The stakeholder-oriented business management at Shell represents an outside-in approach – a characteristic of CSR meta-management. As shown in Table 21.3, Shell considers a broad category of interest groups in its stakeholders. The interaction with stakeholders is guided by the HSSE & SP control framework. Stakeholder dialogue is promoted during the 1) upstream operations – exploration of oil and gas; 2) downstream operations – manufacturing and supply, including operations at refineries and distribution; and 3) future investment decisions. The stakeholder dialogue involves regulators, local community, contractors, suppliers, employees, and shareholders, among others.

During the stakeholder dialogue process staff members liaise with local communities and work with technical and management staff to address their concerns. In the mid 1990s, a new coking plant by Shell at Buenos Aires, Argentina caused anxiety among local residents who had not been engaged in the earlier stakeholder dialogue. Extensive stakeholder dialogue was then carried out to address the concerns of the community. These initiatives included demonstrations of how Shell would operate; what measures it would take to ensure environmental protection and individuals' health and safety; and what mechanisms existed for risk management. Shell also stepped up its social initiatives for community welfare. According to Shell's annual report, the community welfare program has now reached more than 40,000 people through more than 100 projects that seek to improve job skills, education facilities and health care. One of its projects, "Creating Bonds," has won external recognition, including an award from the Argentina branch of the American Chamber of Commerce.[89]

ORGANIZATION-WIDE CSR INTEGRATION (IMPLEMENTATION)

Shell uses a number of management system standards to systematically address the various requirements of its stakeholders. These management systems include health and safety, environmental and quality management, and good laboratory practices, among others.[90] The HSSE & SP control framework delineates requirements for operations. The purpose of this framework and its associated manuals and standards is to ensure that environmental and social factors are integrated into the design, planning, and execution of its operations. These management manuals also ensure that social and environmental factors are taken into consideration, not only in routine operations but also in future investment decisions. This framework, thus, represents an example of strategic implementation of CSR whereby Shell's strategic directions are translated into management manuals and into operations systematically. The direct quotes provided in Table 21.3 show that management emphasizes the importance of embedding CSR in the core business processes. The HSSE & SP control framework shows how Shell carries out vertical integration of CSR into core business processes through a strategic process that cascades down the various organizational levels. However, information about horizontal integration is needed to elaborate the process by which CSR practices diffuse across departments and people.

CSR ASSESSMENT

Shell uses audits for assessment both internally as well as for supplier evaluation. Internal audits focus on the assessment of internal processes whereas supplier audits evaluate the compliance of suppliers and contractors to Shell's code of conduct. Compliance to Shell's code of conduct – determined through audits – provides a basis for conducting further business with suppliers and contractors. As the reports mention:

> *82% of the biofuels we bought by volume were from suppliers who have signed up to our sustainability clauses.*[91]

> *In 2009, we cancelled 25 contracts because of failures to adhere to our Business Principles. Of these, 18 involved violations of our HSSE standards.*[92]

Further the findings of audits are dealt with strategically and are presented to the audit and CSR committee of the board of Shell.

> *We report a summary of all helpline allegations and significant Code of Conduct violations to the Audit Committee and to the Corporate and Social Responsibility Committee (CSRC) of the Board of Royal Dutch Shell plc. In 2009, 165 violations of the Code of Conduct were reported (204 in 2008). As a result, we ended our relationships with 126 staff and contractors.*[93]

As noted earlier, CSR assessment is more effective when it is carried out through multiple channels of assessment, such as self-assessment and benchmarking, in addition to audit. Shell's report, however, mentions only conventional assessment methods – i.e., audit – and does not mention CSR assessment through self-assessment and benchmarking. This area offers potential for improvement in the future.

CSR REPORTING AND CONTINUAL IMPROVEMENT

CSR reporting

The CSR reporting system of Shell discussed in the following sections represents an inside-out approach – a characteristic of CSR meta-management. The company regularly reports its sustainability initiatives through annual reports, websites, and other means of communications. The CSR reporting is carried out in accordance with the Global Reporting Initiative (GRI) and in line with the International Petroleum Industry Environmental Conservation Association (IPIECA) guidelines. As Table 21.5 shows, the company uses a structured approach to report the issues. An analysis of Shell's 2009 sustainability report shows that the company reports its performance along social, environmental, and economic dimensions. The main features of this report are summarized in Table 21.5.

Table 21.5   The information disclosed in Shell's annual report and its purpose

Information provided in CSR report	Purpose
• Endorsement from CEO	Commitment of top management towards CSR
• Endorsement from external reviewer	Independent review and transparency
• Report provides corporate governance structure for CSR	Company commitment for a formal company-wide CSR
• Reporting criteria – what to report and how to report?	Transparency in CSR reporting
• List of sustainability indicator along with quantifiable data	Concrete measure for sustainability
• Linking CSR initiatives with the broader public policy	Commitment towards deep-rooted community initiatives
• Mention of past non-conformances and corrective actions taken in this regard – the details about Niger delta and the settlement efforts	Commitment of how companies deal with non-conformances and the transparency exercised in this process
• Supply chain management description – details about suppliers, contractors, management systems, and standards about health and safety, environment, operations, contracts cancellation due to violations, etc.	To show concrete measures taken by the company to manage the whole supply chain and also show transparency in managing along the whole supply chain

Shell's sustainability report highlights a number of measures which the company takes towards increasing transparency in its business affairs. In its 2009 annual report Shell provides a detailed description of how it dealt with the criticism of its activities in the Niger delta. This includes a separate section on security challenges, cleaning spills, financial matters, and social initiatives. It is believed that "by publishing these payments people can hold their governments accountable for how these revenues are spent."[94]

While strategic and operational non-conformances may occur, the true test of a company's corporate responsibility is how it responds in the case of transgressions and the corrective and preventive actions that are subsequently taken. Shell has been in Nigeria for over 50 years, longer than any other international energy company. In the past Shell was intensely criticized for its activities in the Niger delta, for not addressing the concerns of the local community, particularly the Ogoni tribe.[95] In 2009 Shell reached a legal settlement with the Ogoni activists. As a part of this settlement Shell will contribute to a fund meant for the education, agriculture, and small business development of people of the Ogoni tribe. Shell describes its non-conforming issues in detail in its sustainability report, including how it deals with such issues. The public reporting of past non-conformances and measures taken to address them shows a company's responsibility and transparency in its business affairs.

Reporting quantifiable indicators

The company reports its sustainability initiatives in terms of quantifiable indicators. As shown in Table 21.5, a broad list of social, environmental, and economic indicators is presented in the annual sustainability report. Publicly reported quantifiable indicators reflect a commitment to transparency and the measures which the company takes to compare its sustainability initiatives with the past and also for future target setting.

Although Shell provides elaborated information on its performance through sustainability indicators; no information is provided on integrated or cross-cutting sustainability indicators. The latter show performance along more than one dimension of sustainability and, thus, are considered more robust. This is because sustainability is a dynamic concept and changes in one dimension of sustainability may induce changes in other. The indicators that measure performance against more than one dimensions are, thus, more appealing. The eco-efficiency indicators represent one example of such indicators. The absence of cross-cutting indicators information is the area that needs improvements in future.

Organization-wide continual improvement

Continual improvement remains a strategic priority at Shell. The corporate governance framework (Table 21.4) specifies that a prime responsibility of the HSSE & SP global discipline teams is sharing industry best practices, and integrating external learning in organizational processes. The HSSE & SP executive also compares the company's performance against industry peers.[96] The corporate governance framework also highlights interaction with stakeholders for continual improvement. The continual improvement initiatives at Shell are extensively discussed in Shell's sustainability report,[97] and the terms "improve/d" or "improvement" appear in the report more than 60 times, referring to improvements along various dimensions – stakeholders, technology, strategy, and operations. This shows the broad spectrum of continual improvement at Shell as an organizational essential.

Shell's approach to CSR provides an example of how the meta-management of CSR could be organized in practice. Shell's corporate governance, organizational changes and the overall CSR management are essential elements of CSR meta-management. The available information on: 1) Shell's CSR corporate governance, 2) integration of sustainability initiatives into strategy and operations as guided by the Shell's framework, 3) an outside-in approach reflected from stakeholder-oriented business management based on extensive stakeholder dialogue, 4) an inside-out approach reflected in transparent and comprehensive public reporting, and 5) corporate-level continual improvement, provide an example of how the company addresses CSR through a meta-management approach. The CSR approach of Shell could be benchmarked by organizations who struggle for strategic and organization-wide integration of CSR and its embeddedness in core business processes. The meta-management of CSR as depicted in Figure 21.1 could also provide a means for improvement in Shell's CSR initiatives. Further research is needed on how other companies adopt a meta-management approach to CSR and what types of best practice exist regarding meta-management of CSR.

Conclusions

The growing awareness of CSR in the literature as well as in practice requires moving beyond normative realms to specific strategies and approaches for the management of CSR. Many authors have suggested that CSR needs to be integrated into organizational processes at all levels. However, the mechanisms of how to integrate are not yet clear. The aim of this chapter is to elaborate the organization-wide integration of CSR through a meta-management approach.

The concept of meta-management is operationalized through the PDCA cycle. Building on that notion, an original framework for the meta-management of CSR was presented. The "plan" stage focuses on making sense of the organization and CSR. It also includes the development of measurable indicators against which the CSR program would be assessed. Based on the "plan" stage, managers develop a CSR strategy and allocate resources for the implementation of CSR. The "do" stage is the integration of social, environmental, and other stakeholder requirements into business processes. This is facilitated through the development of an integrated management system for the whole organization to cater to the needs of stakeholders in an integrated manner. The integrated technical and social structures required for the integration of CSR into business processes are shown in the framework (Figure 21.1). Social and technical structures need to be aligned in order to promote greater buy-in by employees.

The "check" stage of the PDCA cycle focuses on CSR assessment, which could be carried out through audits, self-assessments, or benchmarking. Examples of CSR specific actions in each of these assessment categories were noted. CSR assessment paves the way for continual improvement, which is the "act" stage of CSR. The continual improvement in the meta-management of CSR differs from conventional improvements due to its explicit focus on "double-loop learning," which means that improvements are integrated into the governing values of the system, including into both strategy and operations to prevent their recurrence. The framework for the CSR meta-management also highlights an "outside-in" approach to regularly incorporate stakeholder requirements and an "inside-out" approach to communicate CSR initiatives to stakeholders and also to show transparency in the management of CSR.

The main contribution of this chapter is the elaboration of the meta-management of CSR. This chapter develops an original framework for the meta-management of CSR that is not addressed in previous publications. Given that CSR programs are highly contextual and vary widely due to factors such as type of business, stakeholders, and time, etc., a prescriptive model for CSR implementation would be inappropriate. Organizations require a CSR approach that is flexible and that may be tailored and designed to a specific business context. Meta-management provides the required model for CSR implementation. This is because meta-management does not list prescriptive requirements but rather highlights the essentials of CSR. The sensemaking, for example, requires that managers develop an enhanced understanding of the specific context in which their organization operates and then design the CSR strategy accordingly. Similarly, CSR implementation through this approach requires integration of stakeholder requirements into organization-specific business processes and organizational structures both vertically and horizontally. In other words, vertical and horizontal integration in CSR meta-management could be organized in multiple ways depending upon stakeholder requirements, organization size, type, and other contextual factors. Meta-management highlights the essentials of CSR implementation, while allowing managers the flexibility to tailor CSR essentials to their unique business contexts.

The meta-management of CSR was illustrated through a study of Shell's approach to CSR. The corporate governance of CSR, stakeholder-oriented business management, CSR reporting to stakeholders, and continual improvement at Shell could be benchmarked by other organizations. The Shell case study illustrates the value of the meta-management approach in structuring a CSR program. Systematic application of the meta-management approach will help highlight organizational strengths and weaknesses in implementing CSR and provide a basis for identifying opportunities for further work. However, it is critical to note that the meta-management approach does not guarantee excellent CSR performance in all cases. Even companies that have strong processes in place can make high-profile mistakes. It is recognized that the case study was limited in that it focused only on a content analysis of Shell's publicly disclosed documents. The study therefore explicitly relied on what Shell chose to share publicly. Additional sources of evidence, such as interviews with Shell employees, could further clarify the company's motivations, approach, successes, and failures in implementing CSR.

The framework developed in this chapter and the Shell case study provide a basis for identifying the key elements of a CSR program. Based on Asif et al.,[98] the framework, and the lessons learned from the case study, a summary of representative CSR activities is provided in Table 21.6. The table is illustrative rather than comprehensive, and any CSR program must be tailored to address unique organizational needs; nevertheless, it does highlight the wide variety of activities that may constitute an integrated CSR program. The table can therefore provide managers with a useful starting point in implementing CSR.

While this chapter makes several contributions to the literature, work remains. Future research could focus on the application of the framework in different contexts. This could include longitudinal research that evaluates the effectiveness of the meta-management approach over time. This, in turn, could provide the basis for further refinement to the elements of CSR meta-management.

Table 21.6 Meta-management of CSR (adapted from Asif et al.[99])

PDCA stage	Elements of CSR meta-management	Representative CSR activities
Plan	Sense-making of the organization, CSR, and the Broader environment	• Defining stakeholders • Conducting stakeholder consultations • Identifying stakeholder requirements • Prioritizing stakeholder requirements • Defining CSR in the context of the organization • Defining the business case for CSR • Exploring competencies for CSR at both the individual and organizational level • Conducting a strengths, weaknesses, opportunities, and threats (SWOT) analysis • Identifying the resources required for CSR • Including CSR in the mission of the organization • Including CSR in the strategic plans, including strategies for different departments and functions such as purchasing and manufacturing • Developing a business model for CSR • Developing measurable indicators for sustainability
Do	Implementation of CSR	• Securing top-management commitment • Vertically integrating CSR by translating CSR strategy into tactical imperatives and operational tasks • Integrating stakeholder requirements into the business • Developing technical structures for CSR, including a management manual, CSR procedures, work instructions, and checklists • Developing social structures for CSR, including training, teamwork, collective CSR competencies • Horizontally integrating CSR among departments, individuals, and the whole supply chain • Developing the personnel skills needed for CSR • Adhering to CSR strategic plans for realization of long-term CSR plans • Managing CSR knowledge • Ensuring transparency in CSR integration • Responding in case of transgression – responding to violations and non-conformances
Check	CSR assessment	• Monitoring of CSR initiatives • Monitoring employee behaviors necessary for CSR • Using multiple CSR assessment methods to facilitate holistic assessment and subsequent improvement • Monitoring sustainable development indicators • Conducting ongoing assessments along both strategy and operations • Assessing the adequacy of CSR integration – the extent to which a CSR decision is communicated and implemented organization-wide and/or the extent to which CSR-related changes in one department also affect others • Assessing the adequacy of CSR communication to stakeholders • Assessing the overall infrastructure for CSR
Act	CSR reporting and Continual improvement	• Determining the content and structure of internal and external reports • CSR reporting to stakeholders • Engaging stakeholders to obtain feedback • Integrating previous experiences and knowledge into current processes • Learning and improvement along both strategy and operations • Making process improvements

Notes

1   Nye, J. S. (1974), "Multinational Corporations in World Politics", *Foreign Affairs*, Vol. 53, No. 1, pp. 153–175.

2   Huff, A. S., Floyd, S. W., Sherman, H. D., and Terjesen, S. (2009), *Strategic Management: Logic And Action*, John Wiley and Sons, Hoboken, NJ; Solomon, J. (2010), *Corporate Governance and Accountability*, Wiley, West Sussex; Smith, N. C., and Lenssen, G. (2009), Mainstreaming Corporate Responsibility: An Introduction. In N. C. Smith and G. Lenssen (eds.), *Mainstreaming Corporate Responsibility*, Wiley, West Sussex; Campbell, J. L. (2007), "Why would corporations behave in socially responsible ways? An institutional theory of corporate social responsibility", *Academy of Management Journal*, Vol. 32, No. 3, pp. 946–967.

3   Freeman, R. E. (1984), *Strategic Management: A Stakeholder Approach*, Pitman, Boston; Carroll, A. B. (1999), "Corporate Social Responsibility: Evolution of a Definitional Construct", *Business and Society*, Vol. 38, No. 3, pp. 268–295; Mitchell, R. K., Agle, B. R., and Wood, D. J. (1997), "Towards a theory of stakeholder identification and salience: defining the principle of who and what really counts", *Academy of Management Review*, Vol. 22, No. 4, pp. 853–886.

4   Godfrey, P. C., Merrill, C. B., and Hansen, J. (2009), "The relationship between corporate social responsbility and shareholder value: an empirical test of the risk management hypothesis", *Strategic Management Journal*, Vol. 30, No. 4, pp. 425–445.

5   Kleine, A. and Hauff, M. v. (2009), "Sustainability-driven implementation of corporate social responsibility: application of the integrative sustainability triangle", *Journal of Business Ethics*, Vol. 85, No. 3, pp. 517–533; Maon, F., Lindgreen, A., and Swaen, V. (2009), "Designing and implementing corporate social responsibility: an integrative framework grounded in theory and practice", *Journal of Business Ethics*, Vol. 87, No. 1, pp. 71–89.

6   Nijhof, A., Bruijn, T. d., Fisscher, O. A. M., Jonker, J., Karssing, E., and Schoemaker, M. (2005), Learning to be Responsible: Developing Competencies for Organisationwide CSR. In J. Jonker and J. Cramer (eds.), *Making a Difference: Dutch National Research Program on Corporate Social Responsibilities* (pp. 57–84), Ministry of Economic Affairs, The Hague.

7   Lindgreen, A., Swaen, V., and Maon, F. (2009), "Introduction: corporate social responsibility implementation", *Journal of Business Ethics*, Vol. 85, pp. 251–256.

8   Lindgreen, Swaen, and Maon, *op. cit.*; Maon, Lindgreen, and Swean, *op. cit.*; Smith, N. C. (2003), "Corporate social responsibility: whether or how?", *California Management Review*, Vol. 45, No. 4, pp. 52–76.

9   Campbell, *op. cit.*

10 Lindgreen, Swean, and Maon, *op. cit.*; Maon, Lindgreen, and Swean, *op. cit.*

11 Foley, K. J. (2005), *Meta Management: A Stakeholder/Quality Management Approach to Whole-of-Enterprise Management*, Standards Australia Ltd, Sydney.

12 Jamali, D. (2008), "A stakeholder approach to corporate social responsibility: a fresh perspective into theory and practice", *Journal of Business Ethics*, Vol. 82, No. 1, pp. 213–231.

13 Carroll, *op. cit.*

14 Dahlsrud, A. (2008), "How corporate social responsibility is defined: an analysis of 37 definitions", *Corporate Social Responsibility and Environmental Management*, Vol. 15, No. 1, pp. 1–13.

15 Campbell, *op. cit.*; Jamali, *op. cit.*

16 Berman, S. L., Wicks, A. C., Kotha, S., and Jones, T. M. (1999), "Does stakeholder orientation matter? The relationship between stakeholder management models and firm financial performance", *Academy of Management Journal*, Vol. 42, No. 5, pp. 488–506.

17 Salzmann, O., Ionescu-somers, A., and Steger, U. (2005), "The business case for corporate sustainability: literature review and research options", *European Management Journal*, Vol. 23, No. 1, pp. 27–36; Weber, M. (2008), "The business case for corporate social responsibility: a company-level measurement approach for CSR", *European Management Journal*, Vol. 26, No. 4, pp. 247–261.

18 Margolis, J. and Walsh, J. (2003), "Misery loves companies: rethinking social initiatives by business", *Administrative Science Quarterly*, Vol. 48, No. 2, pp. 268–305; Orlitzky, M., Schmidt, F., and Rynes, S. (2003), "Corporate social and financial performance: a meta-analysis", *Organization Studies*, Vol. 24, No. 3, pp. 403–441.

19 Pedersen, E. P. (2006), "Making corporate social responsibility (CSR) operable: how companies translate stakeholder dialogue into practice", *Business and Society Review*, Vol. 111, No. 2, pp. 137–163; Maon, Lindgreen, and Swaen, *op. cit.*; Zadek, S. (2004), "The path to corporate social responsibility", *Harvard Business Review*, Vol. 82, No. 12, pp. 125–132.

20 Zadek, *op. cit.*

21 Kleine and Hauff, *op. cit.*

22 Nijhof, Bruijn, Fisscher, Jonker, Karssing, and Schoemaker, *op. cit.*; Smith and Lenssen, *op. cit.*; Solomon, *op. cit.*

23 Castka, P., Bamber, C. J., Bamber, D. J., and Sharp, J. M. (2004), "Integrating corporate social responsibility (CSR) into ISO management systems: in search of a feasible CSR management system framework", *The TQM Magazine*, Vol. 16, No. 3, pp. 216–224.

24 Oskarsson, K. and Malmborg, F. v. (2005), "Integrated management systems as a corporate response to sustainable development", *Corporate Social Responsibility and Environmental Management*, Vol. 12, No. 3, pp. 121–128.

25 Lindgreen, Swaen, and Maon, *op. cit.*; Maon, Lindgreen, and Swean, *op. cit.*; Smith, *op. cit.*

26 Campbell, *op. cit.*

27 Foley, *op. cit.*

28 *Ibid.*

29 *Ibid.*

30 Van Gigch, J. P. (1991), *System Design Modeling and Metamodeling*, Plenum Pub Corp, New York.

31 Cramer, J., Jonker, J., and Van der Heijden, A. (2004), "Making sense of corporate social responsibility", *Journal of Business Ethics*, Vol. 55, No. 2, pp. 215–222; Daft, R. L. and Weick, K. E. (1984), "Towards a model of organizations as interpretation systems", *Academy of Management Review*, Vol. 9, No. 2, pp. 284–295; Weick, K. E. (1995), *Sense-making in Organizations*, Sage Publications, California.

32 Hardjono, T. W., ten Have, S., and ten Have, W. D. (1996), *The European Way to Excellence*, European Quality Publications, London.

33 Daft and Weick, *op. cit.*; Weick, *op. cit.*

34 Cramer, Jonker, and Van der Heijden, *op. cit.*; Nijhof, Bruijn, Fisscher, Jonker, Karssing, and Schoemaker, *op. cit.*

35 Jamali, *op. cit.*; Klein and Hauff, *op. cit.*; Mitchell, Agle, and Wood, *op. cit.*; Pedersen, *op. cit.*

36 Nijhof, Bruijn, Fisscher, Jonker, Karssing, and Schoemaker, *op. cit.*; Smith and Lenssen, *op. cit.*; Solomon, *op. cit.*

37 Hardjono, ten Have, and ten Have, *op. cit.*; Lindgreen, Swaen, and Maon, *op. cit.*; Maon, Lindgreen, and Swean, *op. cit.*

38 Deming, W. E. (1986), *Out of the Crisis*, MIT Press, Cambridge, MA.; Deming, W. E. (1994), *The New Economics for Industry, Government, Education*, MIT Press, Cambridge, MA.

39 Van Gigch, *op. cit.*; Foley, *op. cit*

40 Daft and Weick, *op. cit.*; Weick, *op. cit.*; Cramer, Jonker, and Van der Heijden, *op. cit.*; Nijhof, Bruijn, Fisscher, Jonker, Karssing, and Schoemaker, *op. cit.*; Smith and Lenssen *op. cit.*; Solomon *op. cit.*; Jamali, *op. cit.*; Klein and Hauff, *op. cit.*; Mitchell, Agle, and Wood, *op. cit.*; Pedersen, *op. cit.*

41 Deming, 1994, *op. cit.*

42 Deming, 1986, 1994, *op. cit.*

43 Weick, *op. cit.*, p. 6

44 Cramer, Jonker, and Van der Heijden, *op. cit.*

45 Daft, R. L., Sormunen, J., and Parks, D. (1988), "Chief executive scanning, environmental characteristics, and company performance: an empirical study", *Strategic Management Journal*, Vol. 9, No. 2, pp. 123–139.

46 Lawrence and Lorsch. (1967), *Organization and Environment: Managing Differentiation and Integration*, Harvard University Press, Cambridge, MA.

47 Brown, J. S. and Duiguid, P. (1991), "Organizational learning and communities-of-practice: towards a unified view of working, learning, and innovation", *Organization Science*, Vol. 2, No. 1, pp. 40–57; Daft and Weick, *op. cit.*

48 Nijhof, Bruijn, Fisscher, Jonker, Karssing, and Schoemaker, *op. cit.*

49 Oskarsson and Malmborg, *op. cit.*

50 Hardjono, ten Have, and ten Have, *op. cit.*

51 Appelbaum, S. H. (1997), "Socio-technical systems theory: an intervention strategy for organizational development", *Management Decision*, Vol. 35, No. 6, pp. 452–463.

52 *Ibid.*

53 Mitchell, Agle, and Wood, *op. cit.*

54 Nijhof, Bruijn, Fisscher, Jonker, Karssing, and Schoemaker, *op. cit.*

55 Karapetrovic, S. and Willborn, W. (2001), "Audit and self-assessment in quality management: comparison and compatibility", *Managerial Auditing Journal*, Vol. 16, No. 6, pp. 366–377; Ni, Z. and Karapetrovic, S. (2003), "Perennial self-audit: model and applications", *Managerial Auditing Journal*, Vol. 18, No. 5, pp. 363–373.

56 Kleine and Hauff, *op. cit.*

57 Van Gigch, *op. cit.*

58 DiMaggio, P. J. and Powell, W. W. (1983), "The iron cage revisited: institutional isomorphism and collective rationality in organizational fields", *American Sociological Review*, Vol. 48, April, pp. 147–160.

59 Ziek, P. (2009), "Making sense of CSR communication", *Corporate Social Responsibility and Environmental Management*, Vol. 16, No. 3, pp. 137–145.

60 GRI (2006), Sustainability reporting guidelines: version 3.0. Amsterdam, GRI, The Netherlands.

61 Adams, C. and Frost, G. (2006), "Accessibility and functionality of the corporate web site: implications for sustainability reporting", *Business Strategy and the Environment*, Vol. 15, No. 4, pp. 275–287; Holder-Webb, L., Cohen, J. R., Nath, L., and Wood, D. (2009), "The supply of corporate social responsibility disclosures among U.S. firms", *Journal of Business Ethics*, Vol. 84, No. 4, pp. 497–527; Ziek, *op. cit.*

62 Argyris, C. (2007), Double-Loop Learning in Organisations: A Theory of Action Perspective. In K. G. Smith and M. A. Hitt (eds.), *Great Minds in Management*, Oxford University Press, New York.

63 Shell (2010b), Shell sustainability report 2009. Retrieved October 25, 2010, from http://sustainabilityreport.shell.com/2009/servicepages/downloads/files/all_shell_sr09.pdf

64 *Ibid.*

65 Boele, R., Fabig, H., and Wheeler, D. (2001), "Shell, Nigeria and the Ogoni. A study in unsustainable development: II. Corporate social responsibility and 'stakeholder management' versus a rights based approach to sustainable development", *Sustainable Development,* Vol. 9, No. 3, pp. 121–135; Kok, P., Wiele, T. v. d., McKenna, R., and Brown, A. (2001), "A corporate social responsibility audit within a quality management framework", *Journal of Business Ethics,* Vol. 31, No. 4, pp. 285–297; Smith, *op. cit.*

66 Shell, 2010b, *op. cit.*

67 *Ibid.*

68 Shell (2010a), The Shell global homepage. Retrieved November 4, 2010, from http://www.shell.com/

69 Shell (2013a), Shell sustainability reports: previous reports and translations. Retrieved March 15, 2013, from http://reports.shell.com/sustainability-report/2011/servicepages/previous.html.

70 Krippendorff, K. (2004), *Content Analysis: An Introduction to its Methodology,* Sage Publications, Thousand Oaks, CA.

71 Shell, 2010b, *op. cit.,* p. i

72 *Ibid.,* p. 19

73 *Ibid.,* p. 28

74 *Ibid.,* p. 20

75 *Ibid.,* p. 6

76 *Ibid.,* p. 1

77 *Ibid.,* p. 20

78 *Ibid.,* p. 4

79 *Ibid.,* p. 6

80 *Ibid.,* p.6

81 *Ibid.,* p. 1

82 *Ibid.,* p. 1

83 *Ibid.,* p. 7

84 *Ibid.,* p. 21

85 *Ibid.,* p. i

86 *Ibid.,* p. 7

87 *Ibid.,* p. 6

88 *Ibid.*

89 *Ibid.*

90 Shell (2013b), Sustainable development at Shell, HSSE and Social Performance – standards and manuals. Retrieved March 15, 2013, from www.shell.com/global/environment-society/s-development/our-commitments-and-standards/hse-manuals.html.

91 Shell, 2010b, *op. cit.*

92 *Ibid.,* p. 18

93 *Ibid.,* p. 6

94 *Ibid.,* p. 22

95 Boele, Fabig, and Wheeler, *op. cit.*; Wheeler, D., Rechtman, R., Fabig, H., and Boele, R. (2001), "Shell, Nigeria and the Ogoni. A study in unsustainable development: III. Analysis and implications of Royal Dutch/Shell Group strategy", *Sustainable Development,* Vol. 9, No. 4, pp. 177–196.

96 Shell, 2010b, *op. cit.*

97 *Ibid.*

98 Asif, M., Searcy, C., Zutshi, A., and Fisscher, O. A. M. (in press), "An integrated management systems approach to corporate social responsibility", *Journal of Cleaner Production*, DOI: 10.1016/j.jclepro.2011.10.034

99 *Ibid.*

22 *When the Social Movement and Global Value Chain Literatures Meet: The Case of Fair Trade*

NATALIA AGUILAR DELGADO* AND LUCIANO BARIN CRUZ†

Keywords

Social movements, global value chains, fair trade.

Introduction

A traditional way of analyzing the evolution of international trade is through the lens of the global value chain (GVC) perspective.[1] The vast literature on GVC provides a way to understand how different actors are integrated into diverse systems of production in the global economy.[2] Key to this approach is the notion that coordination and control of global-scale production systems can be achieved through different modes of governance. The framework proposed by Gereffi et al.[3] encompasses five modes of governance based on the degree of explicit coordination and power asymmetry between firms: market, modular, relational, captive and hierarchy.

Although the GVC perspective is valuable in illuminating the inequalities that arise from asymmetric power relationships across firms and regions,[4] it tends to overlook the complex ways in which relevant actors other than firms operate, as well as the ways in which they shape economic, social and political contexts.[5] Extending the framework described by Gereffi et al.,[6] we propose that because such structures of governance are embedded in a wide array of power relationships, they are "characterized by contestation as well as collaboration among multiple actors, including firms, state and international agencies, nongovernmental organizations (NGOs), and industry associations, each with their own interests and agendas."[7]

* PhD Student Natalia Aguilar Delgado, McGill University, 1001 Sherbrooke West, H3A 1G5 Montreal, QC Canada. E-mail: natalia.aguilardelgado@mail.mcgill.ca.

† Assistant Professor Luciano Barin Cruz, HEC Montreal, 3000 Chemin de la Côte-Sainte-Catherine, H3T 2A7, Montreal, QC Canada. E-mail: luciano.barin-cruz@hec.ca. Telephone: +1 514 340 1350.

In this regard, the social movement scholarship may help to unveil the contentious dynamic within the GVC as it sheds light on the emerging processes of destabilizing and challenging established institutions or ways of doing things.[8] A broad definition of social movements describes them as collective interests that align in the pursuit of social change.[9] In this chapter, we make use of the literature on social movements to obtain a better grasp on social change in a market surrounded by different logics and power relationships:[10] the evolution of the Fair Trade movement.[11]

The global value chain for Fair Trade products was born in the 1940s and was based on solidarity and trust between Southern underprivileged producers and Northern aware consumers. There is disagreement among scholars regarding the roots of Fair Trade; some link it to philanthropic initiatives by churches and other charitable foundations.[12] At the time, there was no corporate involvement,[13] and the logic was to create a just alternative channel for Southern producers to commercialize their products, mainly handcrafts.[14]

In recent years, with the attempt to reach more mainstream markets, different modes of governance of the global value chain for Fair Trade products,[15] as well as contradictions and challenges,[16] have emerged. While some believe that mainstreaming is the solution for leveraging the sales of Fair Trade because currently there are more consumers willing to buy these products and, by consequence, more companies eager to distribute them,[17] others fear that the solidarity message is progressively being lost in the midst of the pervasive commercial logic entailed in mainstream markets.[18]

Although the Fair Trade case has been already studied from the GVC perspective[19] or using the social movement literature,[20] rarely have there been efforts to combine both approaches. This chapter aims to fill this void by showing how the social movement literature may inform the global value chain literature, with an illustration of the case of Fair Trade. We propose that, in the last 60 to 70 years, the transformation of the governance modes of the Fair Trade global value chain can be illuminated by looking at shifts in some key characteristics proposed by the social movement literature, such as the field opportunities, the mobilizing structures and the framing processes.

The chapter is organized in the following manner. First, we introduce an overview of the social movement literature. Second, we present our framework followed by a brief presentation of Fair Trade. Third, we analyze the Fair Trade global value chain using the framework we have proposed. Finally, we highlight some challenges created by the new forms of governance adopted in recent years.

Social Movement Literature

Until the 1960s, classical studies on social movements were rooted in the assumption that activists were "flawed" people who, by choosing to involve themselves in protests or riots, reflected psychological disorders. Scholars, including Le Bon and Kornhauser,[21] studied the contagion effects of crowds on people's emotions and the idea that such effects led people to commit irrational acts. Later approaches take a new perspective on the personality of activists, assuming that they are rational actors with concrete motivations. This shift produced different types of studies that emphasize the structural and organizational aspects of social movements.[22]

Currently, the most prevalent set of studies of social movements pertains to the Political Process Model (PPM) stream. The main assumption of these studies is that grievances are given or stable in the long run[23] and thus the emergence and decline of social movements is linked to the openness of political systems.[24] The three essential notions in PPM are opportunities, mobilizing structures and frames:

> *Most political movements and revolutions are set in motion by social changes that render the established political order more vulnerable or receptive to challenge. But these "political opportunities" are but a necessary prerequisite to action. In the absence of sufficient organization – whether formal or informal – such opportunities are not likely to be seized. Finally, mediating between the structural requirements of   opportunity and organization are the emergent meanings and definitions – or frames – shared by the adherents of the burgeoning movement.[25]*

Some critiques to this approach have been put forward. First and foremost, the emphasis on the State as the source of contention is claimed to be too narrow to encompass the diversity of contemporary efforts for change.[26] Second, the lack of clarity in the conceptualization of political opportunity foresees the problems derived from "sampling on the dependent variable": if, based on the observation of movements that are currently taking place, movements are believed to emerge in favorable times and decline in less favorable ones, the argument runs the risk of becoming circular.[27] Third, the approach emphasizes explaining how, but not why, social movements occur.[28]

To overcome some of the shortcomings of PPM, scholars have proposed the incorporation of the concept of fields that assume that challengers do not encounter an external structure of opportunities but are instead constitutive elements of an arena[29] wherein participants take one another into account as they carry out interrelated activities.[30] In this renewed perspective, the contradictions between fields are responsible for creating opportunities.[31]

In this chapter, we refer to the market for Fair Trade products as a field. By understanding markets as fields, the emphasis in the analysis shifts from the act of exchange to the dynamics of the structuring forces.[32] Accordingly, dominant actors and challengers are seen as engaged in an ongoing struggle to change or to defend the social forces operating in the field.[33] By mobilizing the structures, framing the processes and seizing the opportunities created within various fields, actors build dynamic responses to existing social forces and advance their respective claims in the field. In Table 22.1, we present a summary of the key concepts derived from the stream of social movement scholarship explored in this chapter.

Table 22.1 Key concepts of the literature on social movements

Field opportunities	Mobilizing structures	Framing processes
Opportunities and constraints that emerge within the field according to the ongoing disputes in the arena[34]	Practices and structures (forms of organization) that support collective action[35]	Collective processes of interpretation, attribution and social construction that mediate between opportunity and action[36]

Social Movement Lenses for Global Value Chains

Making use of the GVC and social movement literatures, we propose a framework for the analysis of the Fair Trade field in different historical moments. The key concepts used in the framework are presented here in more detail.

As mentioned in the Introduction, the GVC framework developed by Gereffi et al.[37] incorporates five different types of governance (Table 22.2). Their proposal takes into account markets (arm's length transactions) and hierarchies (internalized activities) as opposite ends of a continuum, with intermediate modes of governance presented as modular, relational and captive networks. The key determinants for the different types of governance are reflected in the degree of explicit coordination and power asymmetry between the firms involved in the transaction.

Applied to different existing types of governance, these two elements would increase from low to high as one moves from markets to hierarchies. For instance, in captive global value chains, lead firms exert direct power on suppliers; this suggests a high degree of explicit coordination by the lead firm, which is the dominant player. The authors exemplify this mode with the case of the apparel industry until recently. In relational global value chains, both firms possess key competences, and the power balance between the firms is therefore more symmetrical. This is not the case in modular global value chains, as in markets; in these governance modes, switching customers and suppliers is relatively easy, and both suppliers and buyers have the opportunity to work with multiple partners. Table 22.2 presents further characteristics of each mode of governance.

Table 22.2 Framework for analysis of global value chains

Mode of governance	Characteristics
Markets	• Governance mechanism – price • Interaction is transactional • Information and knowledge are easily shared due to their low degree of complexity
Modular	• Relative independence of suppliers and buyers • Suppliers in modular value chains make products or provide services to a customer's specifications, even if the technology can be modulated to meet the needs of many clients • Linkages along the value chain are thicker because of the higher volume of information flow
Relational	• Mutual dependence is regulated through trust and reputation • Interaction is aimed at the long term • Dense interactions and knowledge sharing are supported by symmetrical power relationships
Captive	• Small suppliers tend to be dependent on larger, dominant buyers • High degree of monitoring and control by the lead firm • The asymmetric power relationships in captive networks force suppliers to link to their customers in ways that are specified by, and often specific to, a particular customer/contract
Hierarchy	• Vertical integration (i.e., "transactions" take place inside a single firm) • The dominant form of governance is managerial control

We propose here that the notions of mobilizing structures, framing processes and seizing opportunities from the social movement literature may provide broader lenses to analyze these different modes of governance in the global value chain (Figure 22.1). In addition, we propose to look at the field as the unit of analysis, making it possible to recognize the transformations of the analytical dimensions proposed.

Next, we turn to the illustration of the Fair Trade field using data collected from secondary sources (books, articles and websites). We show how the changes in the governance modes of Fair Trade global value chains can be illuminated by looking at the transformations in terms of field opportunities, mobilizing structures and framing processes.

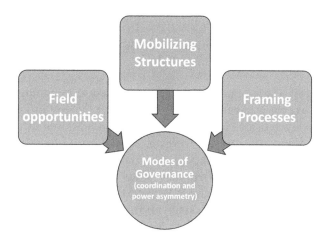

Figure 22.1 Social movements lenses for analyzing the governance of global value chains

The Fair Trade Case: Definitions and Key Players

The following definition of Fair Trade was agreed upon in December 2001 by the major Fair Trade networks FLO (Fairtrade International[38]), WFTO (World Fair Trade Organization[39]) and EFTA (European Fair Trade Association[40]):

> *Fair Trade is a trading partnership based on dialogue, transparency and respect that seeks greater equity in international trade. It contributes to sustainable development by offering better trading conditions to, and securing the rights of, marginalized producers and workers – especially in the South. Fair Trade Organizations, backed by consumers, are engaged actively in supporting producers, awareness raising and in campaigning for changes in the rules and practice of conventional international trade.*[41]

A fundamental paradox stems from this definition: Fair Trade makes use of the very markets that create injustices that harm Southern producers and workers.[42] Incorporating this hybrid logic, Fair Trade operates simultaneously as a social movement and as an alternative market structure.[43] Both commitments are illustrated in the overall goals of the movement:[44]

- To improve the livelihoods and well-being of producers by improving market access, strengthening producer organizations, paying a better price and providing continuity in the trading relationship.
- To promote development opportunities for disadvantaged producers, especially women and indigenous people, and to protect children from exploitation in the production process.
- To raise awareness among consumers of the negative effects on producers of international trade so that they exercise their purchasing power positively.
- To set an example of partnership in trade through dialogue, transparency and respect.
- To campaign for changes in the rules and practice of conventional international trade.
- To protect human rights by promoting social justice, sound environmental practices and economic security.

On the one hand, Fair Trade organizers attempt to make trading chains shorter so that producers directly receive a larger share of the profit.[45] On the other hand, as a social movement, Fair Trade advocates for changes in the conventional international trade by raising awareness among consumers. However, it is essential to acknowledge that Fair Trade is not only about cultural change; materialist objectives are also translated in international arenas.[46] Moreover, albeit the "State" is not the direct opponent of Fair Trade, multiple institutions, such as the WTO and the World Bank, exert great power in terms of macro-regulations and set the stage for international trading.

Beyond the WTO and the World Bank, Moore[47] identifies four additional groups of actors that make up the field of Fair Trade. The first consists of producers located in Southern countries. An important basis of this conception, which will be analyzed more deeply later, is that the producers initially eligible for Fair Trade were democratically organized farmer or artisan cooperatives. Presently, the concept also incorporates waged laborers on unionized plantations.[48] The second group consists of organizations in Northern countries; these organizations act as importers, wholesalers and retailers of the products produced by the first group. The third group includes umbrella bodies and organizations such as the European Fair Trade Association (EFTA), the Fairtrade Labelling Organizations International (FLO), or the World Fair Trade Organization (WFTO). These networks "bring together over 2 million Fair Trade producers and workers from more than 65 countries, 19 labeling initiatives, over 500 specialized Fair Trade importers, 4,000 World Shops and more than 100,000 volunteers."[49]

Finally, more recently a wide range of conventional organizations, typically supermarkets, have begun to engage in Fair Trade. As indicated by Moore,[50] 43,000 supermarkets across Europe and an additional 7,000 in the US and Canada stock Fair Trade products. If once these actors were not relevant to the Fair Trade field, there is now an increasing trend for such retailers to take an important part in the arena.[51] In this set of actors, we also include the consumers because the viability of Fair Trade products depends on their engagement.[52]

THE EVOLUTION OF THE FAIR TRADE FIELD

The history of the Fair Trade field has been marked by many shifts in the areas of field opportunities, mobilizing structures and framing processes; these shifts in turn reflect different modes of governance. Table 22.3 presents a summary of the history of the Fair Trade movement, which is divided into four historical phases. Each phase is extensively described in the sections that follow.

Table 22.3 Summary of the analysis of the Fair Trade case

Elements	Phase 1 1940–1950	Phase 2 1960–1970	Phase 3 1980–1990	Phase 4 2000–Current
Field opportunities	End of Second World War Rise of philanthropy	Increasing demand for alternative products	Decline in sales Stagnation of coffee prices Neoliberal reforms Certifications	CSR booming
Mobilizing structures	Loose networks – charities, churches, NGOs	Dense networks – NGOs, ATOs, World Shops	Dense networks – NGOs, ATOs, World Shops, certification bodies	Institutionalized networks – NGOs, corporations
Framing processes	Solidarity	Alternative	Fair	Ethical
Modes of governance	Relational	Relational	Relational Market	Relational Hierarchical Modular Captive

1.   Phase 1 – 1940s and 1950s: "Solidarity" trade

a) *Field opportunities*: Some authors consider Fair Trade to be rooted in the cooperative movement.[53] Others link it to the student radicalism of the 1960s through its anti-imperialism movements.[54] However, the emergence of Fair Trade is more usually linked to the philanthropic and solidarity initiatives of the 1940s and 1950s.[55] After the Second World War, churches and other charitable foundations sought ways to link impoverished communities with concerned consumers, mainly through the sale of handcrafted products.[56] For instance, in 1946, the Mennonite International Development Agency began to commercialize textile products from Puerto Rico and Jordan.[57]

b) *Mobilizing structures*: During this period, the structure of Fair Trade initiatives was very loose and sparse.[58] There were no systematic links between the crafts sold and the communities who benefited from the assistance.[59] These initial efforts were the foundation for the creation, in the 1960s and 1970s, of groups known as Alternative Trading Organizations or ATOs. There was no corporate involvement in this first phase.[60]

c) *Framing processes*: Both in Europe and in the US, the logic behind the practice of Fair Trade was that by creating this direct and "honest" alternative channel for

Southern producers to commercialize their products, solidarity development would be promoted in disadvantaged areas of the world.[61]

d) *Global value chain governance*: Long-term relationships are privileged in this chain. Price is a mechanism to guarantee the quality of life of the producers. Partnerships are oriented towards broad capacity building of small producers, not captivity.[62] In this sense, the governance mode is close to what has been established by Gereffi et al.[63] as relational.

2. Phase 2 – 1960s and 1970s: "Alternative" trade

a) *Field opportunities*: As the demand for Fair Trade slowly began to develop in Europe, opportunities for producer organizations in the South began to increase.[64]

b) *Mobilizing structures*: One of the first organizations to promote Fair Trade in Europe was Oxfam UK, an organization that has as its mission combating poverty in Southern countries. In 1964, Oxfam UK created the first Alternative Trade Organization (ATO) to facilitate the importation of crafts and commodities from Southern producers.[65] Other similar initiatives were created throughout Europe, including the creation of "World Shops"[66] in 1969 by an organization in the Netherlands.

c) *Framing processes*: From this point on, the movement was framed as "Alternative", i.e., as a challenge to the capitalist system.[67] In the early days of Fair Trade, "fair" "seemed too weak as a description of the common vision that forged these companies into a movement."[68]

d) *Global value chain governance*: Through World Shops, craft products and, in lesser volumes, coffee and tea were sold. The creation of these dedicated shops in the 1960s provided a more refined way of highlighting the injustices caused by unequal trading relationships between North and South, and a niche market of conscience-motivated consumers developed that was fed by these direct market links.[69] The chain was still based on trust and solidarity, and classified still as relational mode of governance.

3. Phase 3 – 1980s and 1990s: "Fair Trade"

a) *Field opportunities*: A process of reorientation in the alternative trade field began in the late 1980s, mainly for two reasons.[70] First, the channels that had been opened to facilitate alternative trade were repeatedly marginalized, and sales stagnated. Second, renewed emphasis on neoliberal reforms changed the political environment in which the organizations operated. For instance, advocacy groups that sought international commodity agreements on prices were less and less successful. A profound change occurred in the markets with the arrival of new commercial players and consumers who demanded higher quality goods.[71] These forces culminated in 1988, the year in which coffee prices stagnated due to the suspension of the International Coffee Agreement.[72] Additionally, by the late 1980s, a new wave of certified organic products began to expand in Europe and North America, and this tactic was used to achieve more mainstream markets.[73]

b) *Mobilizing structures*: A historical milestone of Fair Trade as we know it today was the establishment by Max Havelaar in 1988 of the first labeling initiative.[74] The Dutch Ecumenical Foundation Solidaridad had been administering grants to indigenous cooperatives. Aided by this entity, a Mexican coffee processing cooperative seeking to expand its sales was considering dealing directly with Northern transnational companies (TNCs). After their proposal was rejected because TNCs were not interested in paying premium prices, Solidaridad developed a new strategy in which a label was used to provide added value in terms of symbolic meaning. The idea of labeling fair trade products in this way spread through Europe, North America and Japan, and many other initiatives were born.[75] It was through this certification system that Southern producers had the opportunity to enter mainstream markets.[76]

c) *Framing processes*: From that point on, the movement became "Fair Trade" instead of "Alternative Trade." Once Fair Trade proposed a form of commerce operating within the traditional market but with the specific aim of obtaining a just price for producers,[77] the inclusion of corporations in the chain did not seem to significantly affect the nature of the movement.[78]

d) *Global value chain governance*: The key goal of certification was to make Fair Trade products more readily accessible to consumers by getting the products onto supermarket shelves.[79] However, even with the availability of more market-ready products and the use of labeling schemes that were open to mainstream business, there was little evidence of a major shift in corporate thinking.[80] Overall, retailers have been slow to accept Fair Trade; they have generally required convincing that there was a market for such goods before participating.[81] In that sense, retailers started to buy Fair Trade initially through arm's-length market relationships.[82] Meanwhile, the direct channels created by the World Shops and similar stores in which the governance was relational still existed.

4. Phase 4 – 2000–current: "Ethical" trade

a) *Field opportunities*: The years since 2000 have been marked by an increasing debate over the concept of corporate social responsibility (CSR).[83] With increased adoption of so-called responsible practices, companies expect to exert influence over socio-political spheres through the merchandizing of social issues.[84] As corporate actors have entered the sector, the market for Fair Trade products has increased, and the visibility of the movement has also increased.[85]

b) *Mobilizing structures*: An increasing number of certifications[86] concerning social and environmental practices have become legitimizing tools that are more often than not linked to financial performance for corporations.[87] Concerning the "unethical" use of Fair Trade labels by corporations, Mutersbaugh[88] listed three types of "fairwashing": parallel production (a company enjoys the legitimacy provided by the certification but it only dedicates a small amount of its efforts and resources to Fair Trade); dilution (attempt to reduce stringent standards); and captive certification (creation of "in-house" certification schemes). Jaffee[89] lists three different types of responses of the movement to these new developments: withdrawal, resistance and radical mainstreaming. In the first type of response, withdrawal, some groups have decided to leave the certification systems and to focus on building other alternatives. In the second type of response, some activists opted to organize initiatives to defend the integrity of the standards. An example of this is the campaign organized by the Organic Consumers Association (OCA[90]), a membership-based advocacy group focusing primarily on protecting and strengthening organic standards, to push Starbucks to purchase higher levels of fair trade-certified coffee. Finally, in the third case, some groups have begun to create alternative business models in which the initiatives are not entirely owned by the Southern workers. One example is the UK-based Divine Chocolate Ltd., 45% of which is owned by the Ghanaian cocoa producer organization Kuapa Kokoo.[91]

c) *Framing processes*: On one hand, the practice of building partnerships with "civil groups" seems to function as a guarantee of the veracity of companies claims to be socially responsible.[92] On the other hand, association with well-known brands can benefit from the image of quality associated with Fair Trade and bring it to the attention of a larger audience, thus increasing sales.[93] There is evidence suggesting that the complexity of the Fair Trade message is being lost and made subordinate to matters of quality and taste.[94] To reconcile these two interests, even if the label of Fair Trade is still maintained, the frame must be enlarged.[95] While both Fair Trade and Ethical products are oriented toward the improvement of the income and conditions of workers, the two systems attempt to do so through different mechanisms. Whereas the former implies capacity building for marginalized producers, the latter aims at ensuring fairer relationships in the supply chain, especially through higher labor and environmental standards.[96] When one considers the mobilizing structures and types of global value chain governance associated with the two systems, one could say that the framing of "Fair" is going through a transformation toward a broader notion of "Ethical".

d) *Global value chain governance*: The diversity of mobilizing structures is reflected in the governance of the global value chain. Although the relational channels managed by the World Shops still exist, with the new involvement of corporations in the global value chain three other modes are operating in parallel. First, retailers (Starbucks for example) tend to favor a modular approach to governance in which they exert greater control over the global value chain compared to market governance, but producers are still relatively independent.[97] Second, some producers (such as large fruit producer Chiquita) have been certifying their plantations, which is a typical example of vertical integration to obtain managerial control over production.[98] Third, large supermarket chains have been pressuring producers to shift to a captive mode of governance such as the one that the agro-food system is essentially working on.[99] This concern is clearly stated in Jaffee's[100] study of corporate participation in Fair Trade. One of the examples brought up by this author is the introduction of three own-brand lines of fair trade-certified coffee by Wal-Mart. At the time, there was wide repercussion among labor activists, who claimed that this was a "fair-washing" strategy. The certifying body responded by pointing out that the fair-trade certification was toward the "fairness" of the product, not of the company selling it. Another example of mainstreaming is the widespread certification of plantations, notably coffee and banana, which hinders to a great extent the possibility of strengthening the capabilities of small producers.[101] This new practice undeniably increases the scale of Fair Trade products; however, at the same time, it goes against one of the core values of Fair Trade: the empowerment of Southern communities.[102]

Discussion

The historical approach to the Fair Trade field (see Figure 22.2) presented here provides evidence that Fair Trade has evolved from a close set of producer–buyer relationships in which producers were key stakeholders[103] to a global value chain with a diversity of pathways leading to agro-food mainstream markets.[104]

In the first and second phases of the development of Fair Trade, long-term relationships were at the center of a value chain guided by the frames of solidarity and alternativeness, respectively. The Northern Foundations were the bridges between producers and consumers in a channel aimed at assuring better income to underprivileged producers. In these two phases, the mode of governance remained the same (relational), but in the second phase, it is possible to appreciate a mobilization of resources that provided the Northern traders with a better infrastructure for selling Southern products in World Shops. During that period, the framing changed slightly to highlight the inequalities produced in traditional markets.

In the third phase, some actors recognized the need for the expansion of the outlets for Fair Trade products. The process was accompanied by a new frame that evoked the idea of "Fairness", which aimed to signal that these products did not necessarily need to be sold through alternative channels to be socially desirable. In turn, certification processes were made compulsory for producers to sell in conventional market structures. However, the relational chains with World Shops still existed and were the primary outlets for these products.

Finally, in the fourth phase, a deeper involvement of corporations began to arise and, with it, a diversity of modes of governance: captive, modular and hierarchical. With respect to the first of these modes, there is evidence that some large supermarket chains are pressuring producers towards captive types of relationships in which prices are determined, not negotiated, and margins are squeezed in favor of supermarkets.[105] Other corporations have adopted an approach that favors the independence of producers but still requires some particular specifications to be met. This constitutes what is defined as a modular mode of governance and is exemplified by some coffee retailers, such as Starbucks.[106] Finally, some large corporations have adopted a hierarchical approach in which they certify a small parcel of their production but keep the rest intact, following practices guided by the logic of markets. Chiquita exemplifies this governance mode in the case of banana production.[107]

It is interesting to note that the shift in modes of governance from relational to modular, captive and hierarchical has been accompanied by changes in the mobilizing structures and framing. The entry of new actors, such as certification bodies and corporations, has encouraged the development of a new configuration of power relationships within the field. A process of de-radicalization of the frame to accommodate these new players is also evident. As shown by some of the examples cited above, the producers are progressively being marginalized in the commercialization process, which in no way translates the idea of fairness. What was once a demonstration of solidarity or an engagement with the struggle against the capitalist system through the choice of alternative channels has become a diluted notion of "ethical products." In Figure 22.2, we present the evolution of the global value chain, its modes of governance and the framing processes involved in each phase.

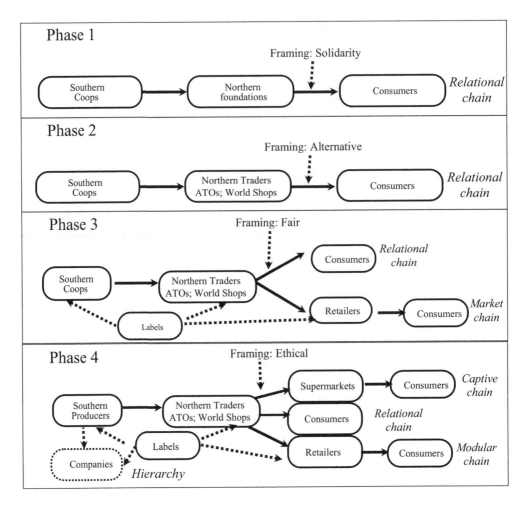

Figure 22.2 Global value chains, mobilizing structures and framing processes in the Fair Trade case

Concluding Remarks

The risk of dilution of the Fair Trade message when corporations enter the Fair Trade market is not negligible.[108] While mainstream retailers see the benefits of selling the products, they do not, with the exception of explicitly "value-driven" retailers, endorse the transformative message of Fair Trade.[109]

In practical terms, assuming that Fair Trade is able to incorporate a frame that resonates with the mainstream markets, corporations and producers have something to gain in the short term.[110] However, in the long term, the ambivalence created in the use of mainstream channels threatens key aspects of what many see as the original vision of Fair Trade,[111] and this is likely to build divisions inside the movement.[112] Other authors are more optimistic and see that mainstreaming has been accompanied both by professionalization and revitalization of the movement and an increase in political campaigning and promotional activities.[113]

Whatever may be the next chapter for the Fair Trade movement, this analysis contributes to some extent to a better understanding of its transformation. By considering the field as the unit of analysis, we emphasize the fact that different actors mobilize structures and frame claims without acting in isolation from each other. In this case, the modes of governance of the global value chain and the mobilizing structures represent the "concrete" or more objective facet of the field, whereas the field opportunities and framing processes are "abstract" or more subjective. Therefore, viewing the social movement literature elements in a field perspective not only helps us reconstruct the linkages among the actors but also helps us to understand how these elements feed each other to explain the governance modes proposed in the GVC literature.

Notes

1   Gereffi, G. and Korzeniewicz, M. (1994), *Commodity Chains and Global Capitalism*. Praeger Publishers, Westport; Gereffi, G., Humphrey, J. and Sturgeon, T. (2005), The Governance of Global Value Chains. *Review of International Political Economy*, Vol. 12, No. 1: 78.

2   Reed, D. (2009), What do Corporations Have to Do with Fair Trade? Positive and Normative Analysis from a Value Chain Perspective. *Journal of Business Ethics*, Vol. 86, No. 0: 3–26.

3   Gereffi, Humphrey and Sturgeon, *op. cit.*

4   Gereffi and Korzeniewicz, *op. cit.*

5   Levy, D.L. (2008), Political Contestation in Global Production Networks. *Academy of Management Review*, Vol. 33, No. 4.

6   Gereffi, Humphrey and Sturgeon, *op. cit.*

7   Levy, *op. cit*, p. 943.

8   Davis, G.F., McAdam, D., Scott, W.R. and Zald, M.N. eds. (2005), *Social Movements and Organization Theory*. Cambridge University Press, New York.

9   Rao, H., Morrill, C. and Zald, M. (2000), Power Plays: How Social Movements and Collective Action Create New Organizational Forms. *Research in Organizational Behaviour* 22: 237–281.

10   Davis, G.F., Morrill, C., Rao, H. and Soule, S.A. (2008), Introduction: Social Movements in Organizations and Markets. *Administrative Science Quarterly*, Vol. 53, No. 3: 389–394. Special Issue: Social Movements in Organizations and Markets.

11   Although Fair Trade can be understood as a social movement in itself, our aim is to go beyond such an understanding and show that the social movement literature may inform the literature on GVC. In order to do so, we use the case of the Fair Trade's GVC.

12   Fridell, G. (2007), *Fair Trade Coffee: The Prospects and Pitfalls of Market-Driven Social Justice*. University of Toronto Press, Toronto; Jaffee, D. (2007), *Brewing Justice: Fair Trade Coffee, Sustainability, and Survival*. University of California Press, Berkeley, CA.

13   Reed, *op. cit.*

14   Jaffee, 2007, *op. cit.*

15   Reed, *op. cit.*

16   Jaffee, D. (2010), Fair Trade Standard, Corporate Participation and Social Movement Responses in the United States. *Journal of Business Ethics*, Vol. 92: 267–285.

17   Gendron, C., Bisailon, V. and Otero Rance, A.I. (2009), The Institutionalization of FairTrade: More than just a Degraded Form of Action. *Journal of Business Ethics*, Vol. 86: 63–79; Wilkinson, J. (2007), Fair Trade: Dynamic and Dilemmas of a Market Oriented Global Social Movement. *Journal of Consumer Policy*, Vol. 30: 219–239.

18   Low, W. and Davenport, E. (2005), Postcards from the Edge: Maintaining the "Alternative" Character of Fair Trade. *Sustainable Development*, Vol. 13: 143–153.

19   Wilkinson, *op. cit.*; Reed, *op. cit.*

20   Gendron, Bisailon and Otero Rance, *op. cit.*; Friddel, *op. cit.*

21   See Goodwin, J., Jasper, J.M., and Polletta, F. (2000), The Return of the Repressed: The Fall and Rise of Emotions in Social Movement Theory. *Mobilization*, Vol. 5, No. 1: 65–83.

22   *Ibid.*

23   McAdam, D., Tarrow, S. and Tilly, C. (2001), *Dynamics of Contention*. Cambridge University Press, New York.

24   McAdam D. (1982), *Political Process and the Development of Black Insurgency, 1930–1970*. University of Chicago Press, Chicago, IL.

25   McAdam, D., McCarthy, J.D. and Zald, M.N., eds. (1996) *Comparative Perspectives on Social Movements*. Cambridge University Press, Cambridge, UK. p. 8.

26   Goodwin, J. and Jasper, J. (1999), Caught in a Winding, Snarling Vine: The Structural Bias of Political Process Theory. *Sociological Forum*, Vol. 14, No. 1: 27–54; Armstrong, E. and Bernstein, M. (2008), Culture, Power, and Institutions: A Multi- Institutional Politics Approach to Social Movements. *Sociological Theory*, Vol. 26, No. 1: 74–99.

27   Meyer, D. (2004), Protest and Political Opportunities. *Annual Review of Sociology*, Vol. 30: 125–45.

28   Poletta, F. and Jasper, J. (2001), Collective Identity and Social Movements. *Annual Review of Sociology*, Vol. 27: 283–305.

29   Ancelovici, M. (2011), Bourdieu Meets McAdam, Tarrow, and Tilly: Toward a Field Theory of Contentious Politics. Unpublished manuscript, Department of Sociology, McGill University.

30   Fligstein, N. and McAdam, D. (2011), Toward a general theory of strategic action fields. *Sociological Theory*, Vol. 29, No. 1: 1–26.

31   Armstrong and Bernstein, *op. cit.*; Ancelovici, *op. cit.*

32   Beckert, J. (2010), How Do Fields Change? The Interrelations of Institutions, Networks, and Cognition in the Dynamics of Markets. *Organization Studies*, Vol. 31: 605.

33   *Ibid.*

34   Ancelovici, *op. cit.*

35   McAdam, McCarthy and Zald, *op. cit.*

36   McAdam, McCarthy and Zald, *op. cit.*, p.2

37   Gereffi, Humphrey and Sturgeon, *op. cit.*

38   Available at www.fairtrade.net/ (Accessed on April 3 2011).

39   Available at www.wfto.com/ (Accessed on April 3 2011).

40   Available at www.european-fair-trade-association.org/ (Accessed on April 3 2011).

41   Available at www.fairtrade-advocacy.org/ (Accessed on April 3 2011).

42   Jaffee, 2007. *op. cit.*

43   *Ibid.*; Wilkinson, *op. cit.*; Gendron, Bisailon and Otero Rance, *op. cit.*

44   Redfem, A. and Snedker, P. (2002), *Creating Market Opportunities for Small Enterprises: Experiences of the Fair Trade Movement*. ILO, Geneva. p. 11.

45   Jaffee, 2007, *op. cit.*

46   Friddel, *op. cit.*

47   Moore, G. (2004), The Fair Trade Movement: Parameters, Issues and Future Research. *Journal of Business Ethics*, Vol. 53: 73–86.

48   Jaffee, 2007, *op. cit.*

49   Fair Trade Advocacy Office (FTAO). What is Fair Trade? Available at: www.fairtrade-advocacy. org/ (Accessed on April 3 2011).

50   Moore, *op. cit.*

51   *Ibid.*

52   Low and Davenport, *op. cit.*

53   Gendron, Bisailon and Otero Rance, *op. cit.*

54   Redfem and Snedker, *op. cit.*

55   Fridell, *op. cit.;* Jaffee, 2007, *op. cit.*

56   Jaffee, 2007, *op. cit.*

57   Fridell, *op. cit.*

58   *Ibid.*

59   Low and Davenport, *op. cit.*

60   Reed, *op. cit.*

61   Jaffee, 2007, *op. cit.*

62   Reed, *op. cit.*

63   Gereffi, Humphrey and Sturgeon, *op. cit.*

64   Redfem and Snedker, *op. cit.*

65   Fridell, *op. cit.*

66   In 1994, an organization called NEWS was created to coordinate the efforts of World Shops in Europe. It ceased to exist in 2008, and now this coordination is carried out by the WFTO.

67   Fridell, *op. cit.*

68   Moore, *op. cit.* p. 75.

69   Murray, D.L. and Raynolds, L.T. (2007), Globalization and its Antinomies: Negotiating a Fair Trade Movement. In L.T. Raynolds and D.L. Murray (eds), *Fair Trade. The Challenges of Transforming Globalization.* Routledge, London.

70   Fridell, *op. cit.*

71   Gendron, Bisailon and Otero Rance, *op. cit.*

72   Low and Davenport, *op. cit.*

73   Murray and Raynolds, *op. cit.*

74   Friddel, *op. cit.;* Jaffee, 2007, *op. cit.*

75   *Ibid.*

76   Redfem and Snedker, *op. cit.*

77   Low and Davenport, *op. cit.*

78   Reed, *op. cit.*

79   *Ibid.*

80   Redfem and Snedker, *op. cit.*

81   Reed, *op. cit.*

82   *Ibid.*

83   Carroll, A.B. (1999), Corporate Social Responsibility: Evolution of a Definitional Construct. *Business & Society*, Vol. 38, No. 3: 268–295; Garriga, E. and Melé, D. (2004), Corporate Social Responsibility Theories: Mapping the Territory. *The Journal of Business Ethics*, Vol. 53: 51–71.

84   Champion, E. and Gendron, C. (2005), De la responsabilité sociale à la citoyenneté corporative: l'entreprise privée et sa nécessaire quête de légitimité. *Nouvelles Pratiques Sociales*. Vol. 18, numéro 1, Fall, p. 90–103.

85   Jaffee, 2010, *op. cit.*

86 For instance, standards such as SA8000 assess the ethical standards of global supply chains, serving more as a safeguard to prevent damage to firms' reputations rather than as a tool to foster development.

87 Boiral, O. (2007), Corporate Greening Through ISO 14001: A Rational Myth? *Organization Science*, Vol. 18, No. 1: 127–146

88 Mutersbaugh, T. (2005), Just-in-Space: Certified Rural Products, Labour of Quality and Regulated Spaces. *Journal of Rural Studies*, Vol. 21: 389–402.

89 Jaffee, 2010, *op. cit.*

90 Organic Consumers Association (2011), Available at: www.organicconsumers.org/starbucks/index.cfm (Accessed on April 5 2011).

91 Divine Chocolate. Available at: www.divinechocolate.com/default.aspx (Accessed: April 5 2011).

92 Gendron, Bisailon and Otero Rance, *op. cit.*

93 Renard, M. (2003), Fair Trade: Quality, Market and Conventions. *Journal of Rural Studies*, Vol. 19: 87—96.

94 Low and Davenport, *op. cit.*

95 Redfem and Snedker, *op. cit.*

96 *Ibid.*

97 Jaffee, 2007, *op. cit.*

98 Frundt, H.J. (2009), *Fair Bananas! Farmers, Workers, and Consumers Strive to Change an Industry.* University of Arizona Press.

99 Raynolds, L., Murray, D. and Wilkinson, J. (2007), *Fair Trade. The Challenges of Transforming Globalisation.* Routledge, New York.

100 Jaffee, 2010, *op. cit.*

101 Friddel, *op. cit.;* Reed, *op. cit.*

102 Moore, *op. cit.;* Jaffee, 2010, *op. cit.*

103 Moore, *op. cit.*

104 In recent years, this sector has witnessed a large shift of power relationships in favor of retailers, creating "buyer-driven" chains, Gereffi and Korzeniewicz, 1994, *op. cit.*

105 Raynolds, Murray and Wilkinson, *op. cit.*

106 Jaffee, 2007, *op. cit.*

107 Frundt, *op. cit.*

108 Moore, *op. cit.*

109 Low and Davenport, *op. cit.*

110 Redfem and Snedker, *op. cit.*

111 Reed, *op. cit.*

112 Gendron, Bisailon and Otero Rance, *op. cit.*

113 Wilkinson, *op. cit.*

Sustainable Value Chains: Specific Sectorial and Industry Perspectives

23 Contributing to a More Sustainable Coffee Chain: Projects for Small Farmers Instigated by a Multinational Company

ANS KOLK*

Keywords

Coffee, multinationals, farmers, supply chain, sustainability, development.

Introduction

This chapter presents an empirical, practical case study on activities to move towards a more sustainable coffee chain. It examines projects for small coffee farmers in developing countries instigated by a multinational company (Sara Lee's international coffee and tea division) via its DE Foundation. The company did this as part of its overall commitment towards the mainstreaming of sustainable coffee, an objective that is still far from becoming a reality due to a variety of factors largely outside its sphere of influence. These include insufficient certified coffee on the market, lack of widespread consumer interest, and confusion related to standards of and approaches for sustainable coffee (Kolk, 2011). The chapter will first introduce the broader context of the coffee sector and the strategy adopted by the multinational enterprise (MNE), including the role of the Foundation and its approach. Subsequently, a rather practical overview will be given of five projects for small farmers in three different continents (South America, Africa and Asia), presenting basic characteristics, and discussing results, lessons and implications for MNEs and sustainable supply chains.[†]

*   Prof.dr. Ans Kolk, University of Amsterdam Business School, Plantage Muidergracht 12, 1018 TV Amsterdam, The Netherlands. E-mail: akolk@uva.nl, http://www.abs.uva.nl/pp/akolk.

†   Sonia Burgos is gratefully acknowledged for her contribution (as part of her internship at the DE Foundation) and subsequent input and feedback related to this project part of the chapter.

Background and Context

Developments on the international coffee market in the past two decades have shaped MNE activities in the coffee supply chain. The year 1989 saw the end of a regulated quota system that ensured stable prices (Gilbert, 1996; Ponte, 2002). Subsequently volatility has become inherent to the coffee market, and so has income and market vulnerability for producers. A reordering of the coffee sector took place, with trade and industry in the consuming countries gaining power to the detriment of producing-country governments, farmers and local traders. Coffee thus transformed into a more buyer-driven commodity chain (cf. Gereffi, 1999) (see Figure 23.1 for an overview of the chain from bean to cup; Kolk, 2011).

These developments focused attention on the role of the main actors on the buyer side of the chain, the large roasting and instant manufacturing companies. Non-governmental organisations (NGOs) put pressure on these large MNEs in the coffee sector to take responsibility as powerful buyers on the market, and thus as pivotal 'intermediaries'

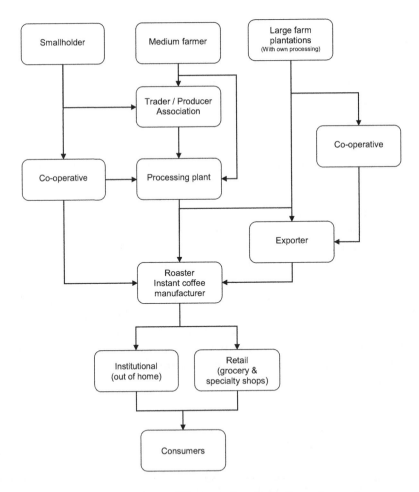

Figure 23.1 An overview of the coffee supply chain from bean to cup

Source: Adapted from Kolk (2011)

between producers and end-consumers (see Figure 23.1) (Kolk, 2005, 2011). MNEs were linked to the fate of farmers, their declining income levels, poor working conditions and social situation, and to poverty in developing countries in general as this is where coffee is grown (Oxfam, 2002). NGOs pointed to the fact that smallholders supplied 70% of the world's coffee, and that approximately 125 million people were estimated to depend on this commodity for their incomes (RIAS, 2002; UNCTAD, 2003, p. 69).

In their coffee actions, NGOs focused on the four MNEs with the largest market shares (together accounting for approximately 40% in 2000): Nestlé and Kraft (both 13%), Sara Lee (10%) and P&G (4%) (Oxfam, 2002, p. 25) (P&G sold its coffee business to Smucker's in 2008). Oxfam in particular was active, as part of a Make Trade Fair campaign, which included a report called 'Mugged: Poverty in your Coffee Cup', published in 2002, accompanied by a rating of the Big Four, in which P&G scored highest and Sara Lee lowest (see Box 1). The scores were mostly based on the price paid to farmers (70%), in which especially commitment to buy coffee with the Fair Trade label played a large role, and on support for policy alternatives (10%), financial contributions (10%) and leadership in industry-wide initiatives (10%).

BOX 1: SCORES GIVEN BY OXFAM TO THE FOUR LARGEST COFFEE ROASTERS, 2002/2003

Sara Lee – at 27% – performed abysmally. The company did little to pay coffee farmers better prices, or establish guidelines for buying coffee, or help farmers diversify into other crops.

Kraft (38%) performed poorly too, having failed in the past year to buy either Fair Trade coffee or coffee that meets internationally agreed quality standards. The company did however contribute to social development programs around the world.

Nestlé fared marginally better, at 43%, having led the industry in various international meetings and supported the efforts of the International Coffee Organisation (ICO) to solve the crisis, including buying directly from farmers. But Nestlé still refuses to buy Fair Trade coffee.

Procter and Gamble (49%) led the industry in paying farmers a decent price and had also helped lobby the US to rejoin the ICO. However, it had too few guidelines on buying coffee that would ensure at least basic standards for farmers.

Source: www.oxfam.ca/news-and-publications/news/coffee-companies-doing-little-to-help-struggling-farmers/ [last accessed 29 August 2011]

MNEs have taken steps in response, including involvement in industry activities and purchasing of coffee certified by external parties, such as Fair Trade, Rainforest Alliance and Utz Certified (hereafter referred to as Utz) (Kolk, 2011, 2012). This also applies to Sara Lee, the company on which this chapter focuses, and which moved to a rather different position compared to a decade earlier, when campaigns were waged against it.

In the Netherlands, where Sara Lee's international coffee and tea division was located,[‡] considerable pressure was exerted by Oxfam and other NGOs. They targeted Sara Lee most visibly in 2003, when the 250th anniversary of its main coffee brand Douwe Egberts (DE) was used as an opportunity to emphasise that 'there was nothing to celebrate'.

This wave of attention had a clear influence on the company, as its most well-known brand was attacked in the country where it had the largest share of the coffee market and that was home to its international headquarters. Several steps were taken, including the decision to start buying Utz-certified coffee, an active role in industry efforts to further sustainable coffee, and the creation of a Foundation in 2002 (Kolk, 2012). With an annual donation of €1.2 million from Sara Lee's international coffee and tea division (from here on, referred to as SL), this DE Foundation directly supports coffee quality improvement projects and aims to improve living conditions of small coffee producers, as we will analyse in more detail in the remainder of this chapter.[§]

Interestingly, the very organisations that initially campaigned against the company became much more positive, and moved to collaboration instead of confrontation. The Dutch NGO Solidaridad, which took the initiative for Fair Trade in the Netherlands, started to characterise the company as a frontrunner, and its coffee projects, in some of which Solidaridad participates, as best in class.[¶] Many of the projects of the DE Foundation have been presented to governments, NGOs, and industry and certification bodies as interesting examples, in view of the lessons that can be learnt from them, and the issues faced by all parties.

The Foundation and its Approach

The DE Foundation, officially established in 2002, developed from some rather loose philanthropic initiatives undertaken since 1999, towards a focus that related to SL's core activities, i.e. coffee (and later also tea), and in line with the company's intention to buy only sustainable coffee in the future. This comes to the fore in the Foundation's approach 'to further sustainability in mainstream coffee and tea production (the prevailing volumes and qualities), working in particular with small-scale producers'.[**] Sustainability is seen from a triple-bottom line perspective, encompassing economic, environmental and social aspects. This involves 'protecting and improving the natural environment'; 'safeguarding the labour rights and health of local communities'; and the promotion of 'productive, efficient and competitive' practices via projects that help small farmers 'to improve the quality of their produce', 'their income and living conditions' and other activities that can lead to 'market access with better prices'. The latter includes the objective to certify small coffee producers once that is possible, so that they might be able to obtain a higher

---

[‡]   This chapter covers the period up to 2012. In 2012, the International Coffee and Tea Division was separated from the US Sara Lee company, with an independent listing on NYSE Euronext under the name of D.E. Master Blenders 1753; this chapter also uses SL as company name as this was applicable in the period covered. There were no changes to the DE Foundation as this is a distinct entity, albeit funded by and directly linked to the International Coffee and Tea Division / D.E. Masters Blenders 1753, as implied in its name.

[§]   In the course of its existence, the scope has been extended to include small tea farmers as well. The author was independent external board member of the DE Foundation in the period 2002–2010.

[¶]   www.solidaridad.nl/files/FAQ_kortgeding_DE.pdf, last consulted on 2 September 2011.

[**]   Quotes in this and the following paragraph are taken from www.defoundation.com, accessed on 2 September 2011.

price for a better product. The standard selected for certification is Utz, similar to that followed by SL for its own sustainable coffee purchases (Kolk, 2012), although farmers in some situations decide to go for additional certifications to further improve market access.

Learning and knowledge exchange are major components for the Foundation, not only in its outreach to share insights with other parties, but also in the projects for small farmers in producing countries. This is outlined in its methodology:

We make learning easier and more effective by encouraging producers to work in groups. In participatory processes, we support producers in developing entrepreneurship by offering them knowledge on how to improve productivity, quality, production and processing efficiency. Farmer Field Schools (FFS) provide an excellent learning environment where agricultural practices are registered and compared with each other. Discussion often leads to self-initiated improvements.

Projects have focused on transferring skills related to marketing and negotiation, but also on organisational aspects such as support for the formation of cooperatives or associations, in addition to sustainable farming practices. Where possible, farmer field books have been introduced, in which participants keep records of their use of inputs and their produce. On the basis of an analysis of the data they have collected, often performed by project staff, comparisons can be made between farmers, to make informed decisions and improve practices. Training and project activities are conducted by project staff or other hired experts, or by coffee producers themselves, who have often first been trained themselves so that they can transfer knowledge and/or facilitate some of the activities, and greater numbers can be reached.

The Foundation aims for projects that last four years on average, although extensions have sometimes been given, particularly for the earliest projects. The basic idea is that 'life after the project' is taken care of from the beginning, and included in the overall set-up. The Foundation selects potential partners in a project from its own networks where possible, based on criteria related to experience and local presence and familiarity with the location involved, as these are crucial for building trust and encouraging participation by local producers. Furthermore, it uses assessments by Sara Lee's procurement organisation, Decotrade, as input for the selection of (new) projects, particularly concerning locations that might be interesting and/or crucial in terms of coffee origins and types currently available and what is needed. In this way, locations are chosen on the basis of their economic viability in relation to expected market demand. Farmers who participate in projects are not obliged to sell to the company, but Decotrade is committed to buy the coffee from them at the appropriate price – as it is Utz-certified coffee this fits with SL's policy as outlined above. In reality, Decotrade often finds that farmers from the projects sell their coffee to other parties while it would have wanted to buy it as well.

Projects for Small Farmers

Table 23.1 gives an overview of the five projects that will be discussed in more detail. While clear differences between the projects can be seen, not only in location (three different continents, four countries), but also in duration, size and number of farmers and people reached in total, there are similarities as well. These include the relatively small size of farms, considered in their local context, and the fact that producers faced serious problems when the projects started. In addition, comparable approaches and methodologies were followed, albeit adjusted to local circumstances where appropriate, and reflecting the time in which projects began and the lessons learnt up to then.

Table 23.1 Overview of five projects from the DE Foundation

	Projects				
Characteristics	*Uganda (Luwero)*	*Vietnam (Quang Tri)*	*Vietnam (Gia Lai)*	*Brazil (Serra Negra)*	*Peru (Ubiriki)*
Period analysed	2004–2010	2001–2006	2007–2009	2006–2008	2003–2008
Other phases / extensions	Phase 1: 1999–2003; Phase 3: 2011–2013			Phase 1: 2002–2005; extension: 2009	Extensions until 2012
Budget provided by DE Foundation	US$1,000,000	€645,040	€450,000	€1,083,600	€1,475,000
Budget from others		€856,960*	€200,000**		
Average farm size	0.61 ha	1 ha	2 ha (coffee and pepper)	4 ha	15 ha (of which 4.6 ha of coffee)
Products	Robusta	Arabica	Robusta	Arabica	Arabica
Farmers in project	5,000	150	800	250	300
Approximate number of people reached	30,000	1,000	4,000	1,000	1,450

*provided mainly for upgrading the processing plant by project partner Kraft Foods; **provided by Solidaridad

Source: DE Foundation project documents; DE Foundation website

Based on project documentation and, where available, other information such as masters theses, as well as interviews carried out with project managers, each project will be briefly evaluated below, particularly with an eye to generating more generic insights and implications for MNEs and sustainable supply chains. Sections will sketch some of the context, summarise economic, environmental and social outcomes as far as available (see Table 23.2), and discuss dilemmas and issues.

Table 23.2 Summary of projects' sustainability outcomes

Uganda (Luwero)	
Economic	• 19 Depot Committees (DCs) formed and 2,313 farmers (60% of certified farmers) market through the DCs • Better prices over time; participating farmers obtain 13–26% premium price above local farm gate price • Farmers get market prices from the DCs; these prices are transparently communicated by large buyers • Farmers previously sold their coffee at any price, but are now reluctant to sell their coffee to middlemen • Despite project dependency on the exporter (Ibero), the approach remains relevant because it addresses farmers' greatest challenge of obtaining access to markets • Acquisition of assets: construction of permanent housing structures, most farmers have acquired radios • Some farmers have bought motorcycles and these have created employment for the youth as they can work as taxi drivers/transporters • here is no credit access service available, but through the collective marketing initiative, coffee farming communities have adopted a savings culture within the DCs
Environmental	• Energy-saving stoves have been created in the communities, leading to savings on wood fuel and time, less smoke and soot, and a reduction of fire-related accidents in the kitchen • The trees that were planted in woodlots are well maintained and community members said that they will be harvested for timber and will always be replanted • Pupils from different schools that are supported by the NGO Plan received agricultural lessons in areas such as soil and water conservation, land preparation, recommended planting and spacing, transplanting, mulching, pruning, better post-harvest handling practices such as drying methods, recommended harvesting, and how to keep their surroundings and gardens clean • Some pupils had taken initiatives to plant trees at their homes as they obtained a thorough understanding of the benefits of trees to them, the community and future generations
Social	• 1,466 caregivers were trained in nutrition and agronomic practices and received quality inputs to boost food production • Most families can now afford adequate food supply, i.e. have more than two meals a day • 12 central nurseries were established in communities to enable caregivers to access vegetable seedlings • Chemical stores were constructed in villages to store herbicides and pesticides. That helped prevent child accidents from poisoning. • The chemical stores have been staffed with technical people (chemical experts) who were trained by Ibero to handle any chemical prescriptions within the community and its proper usage • The chemical experts work with the first aiders who were chosen by the communities and were trained to handle minor accidents at homes

Table 23.2 *Continued*

Vietnam (Quang Tri)	
Economic	• Significant increases in coffee production, prices and turnover • Coffee is sold to the major trade houses and roasters • Quality standards are brought up to par; investment in storage facilities allowed Tan Lam (the mill) to store the coffee without significant quality loss • At farm level improvements were strong, with improved efficiency of nutrient applications and stable production costs per lb of green coffee beans against rising prices for inputs and labour
Environmental	• Water use per Mt in processing was reduced by approximately 58% • Overall energy use in the factory has not changed much on per volume coffee basis, but the composition of energy sources changed. Pre-project, Tan Lam used large amounts of firewood for drying, but this has been substituted by cheaper and cleaner burning coal • Farmers increased efficiency in the use of fertiliser • Number of damage claims by farmers living downstream from the factory has reduced to zero after the waste water treatment system was implemented
Social	• Salaries have increased over the years, reflecting both inflation and improved financial performance • Payments to seasonal workers at the factory and the farm are well above the legal minimum • Living conditions for workers are more applicable to larger estates such as those found in South and Central America than to smallholder farms in Vietnam. SAI is rather vague by not further specifying what constitutes 'adequate' and 'hygienic'. The project staff's interpretation is that the workers should have similar living conditions as those of their employer for the duration of their employment. Following this interpretation, the farms all comply
Vietnam (Gia Lai)	
Economic	• Fertiliser, irrigation and labour costs were reduced by 21%, 38% and 33% respectively • At the same time a yield increase of 1.6 Mt per hectare (2007–2008) was realised • Record keeping enabled producers to take well-informed management decisions leading to more efficient production and processing management. This resulted in cost savings and increased incomes • Record keeping facilitated access to the certified/verified coffee markets for smallholders (e.g. Utz), for which record keeping is mandatory • 14 extension workers, 40 key farmers and 3 researchers have been successfully trained to become professional trainers on Participatory Agricultural Extension Methods, Good Agricultural Practices, Good Processing Practices, Entrepreneurial Skills and Certification. Key farmers are currently informally recognised as professional backups for the existing extension network • Key farmers receive the daily coffee price by mobile phone and announce that in their respective groups

Table 23.2 *Concluded*

Environmental	• Reduction in the use of chemical fertiliser, agro-chemicals, water and fuel for irrigation has beneficial effects on the environment, in particular soil, water and atmosphere (reduction of greenhouse gases) • Compost has been applied, so less fertiliser was bought • The application of the 'waste product' of processing (i.e. husks and pulp) for composting reduced CO_2 emissions, as by-products were previously generally burnt. In the medium term the technology will allow farmers to reduce chemical fertiliser applications, hence protecting soil and water resources
Social	• 7% of the target group consisted of ethnic minority families who often adhere to more traditional farming practices and are often poorer and less integrated into society • Active participation of a minority group has allowed for knowledge 'cross-pollination' between the ethnic Vietnamese and minority farmers in favour of more sustainable production and access to certified markets • Active participation of women • Training manuals developed and tested in other projects were made available for sale (at cost) through a revolving fund. Numerous farmers bought the manual on the Buon Ma Thuot Coffee Festival (December 2008) and the trading company Acom bought 3,000 copies to distribute to farmers
Brazil (Serra Negra)	
Economic	• Increase of yields and quality • Almost half of the farmers obtained Utz certification • More effective farm management
Environmental	• More responsible use of agrochemicals • Better disposal of chemical waste and its packaging
Social	• Security in the handling of chemicals and machinery • Better security measures for handling and storing agrochemicals, and for handling machinery • Social coherence has been strengthened due to participation in farmer field schools
Peru (Ubiriki)	
Economic	• Certification according to Utz, Organic and Fair Trade standards • Project farmers have lower average costs per kg of green coffee beans as well as per hectare • Higher profits per kg of coffee
Environmental	• Much higher use of organic materials, and the creation of places for compost • Use of shade management has spread, and so has replacement of seedlings after planting, pruning, aftercare of pruning, selective harvesting
Social	Higher self-esteem on the part of farmers, who experienced that they were able to help solve problems in the field, and had the opportunity to give their opinion and participate in the community

Sources: DE Foundation website and specifically for Uganda and Vietnam projects: DE Foundation final project documents; for Brazil: Silva (2009); and for Peru: Van Rijn (2008)

UGANDA (LUWERO) PROJECT

This is the region where the very first project of SL took place, which was more philanthropic in nature and started before the Foundation was created with its clearer focus and methodology. From 2004 onwards, it evolved into a much more business-oriented project on organisational development of the very small coffee farmers that were targeted, in addition to the health care, housing, nutrition and other social objectives from the first phase (for which an NGO, Plan, had been involved, but whose participation ended). Compared to other projects, the farmers in Luwero belong to the poorest coffee producers with the smallest scale. Therefore the second phase (in which the exporting company Ibero was a partner) could only succeed due to the foundations laid earlier, in terms of addressing some basic needs and building trust and an initial infrastructure.

The project worked with 5,000 small-scale farmers, scattered around the Luwero region, who produce relatively tiny amounts of coffee. Therefore, the project organisation structured the members in such a way that they could collectively market their produce, and consequently attract the interest of larger buyers and increase farmers' negotiating power. To this end, 24 Depot Committees (DC) were formed, each composed of 5–10 Producer Organizations (PO), with each PO comprising 50 members. This structure enabled farmers to sell their coffee through the DC and eliminate the middleman, to whom they used to sell their coffee for any price offered. Due to the structure put in place through the project, farmers can now wait for official prices from large buyers to be communicated to the DCs, which reflected the much higher degrees of transparency. With support from the project, producers were also encouraged to replant better coffee varieties and were taught basic sustainable farming practices.

As shown in Table 23.2, several sustainability outcomes were achieved, including collaboration between farmers and the formation of producer groups, a higher yield of coffee that is also of better quality, leading to increased prices, Utz certification (with Ibero as certificate holder), and environmental and social benefits. However, not everything was successful. The monitoring of inputs distributed to the farmers was deficient, and as a result, low quality inputs were sometimes supplied. These inputs were planting materials and livestock breeds, which were related to Plan's activities. Therefore, a lesson learnt from this project was that services and inputs should not be given for free, but rather sold at cost. This way, only the farmers that intend to use the inputs will acquire them. In addition, while the project managed to certify 46% of the 5,000 farmers, the majority of them considered that the price return was not commensurate with the effort required to acquire and maintain the certification. And although the project helped to develop a savings culture amongst the farmers, which is very appropriate for the off-season period in particular, more extensive access to financing seems to be a next step; in the current, third phase of the project, DCs are establishing contacts with banks for obtaining credit facilities.

VIETNAM (QUANG TRI) PROJECT

This second project was in a rather different setting, not only in terms of the geographical location, but also regarding farmers' literacy and market orientation. One of the partners was the former state-owned company Talaco, which bought and processed coffee from contracted producers (other project partners were Kraft Foods and the German Technical

Cooperation Agency GTZ). The technical aspects of sustainable coffee farming, via farmer field schools for instance, was pivotal. The project had several beneficial outcomes (see Table 23.2) and attracted the attention of the Vietnamese government, leading to a sector-wide, multi-stakeholder plan in 2008–2009 to roll out insights from this and other pilot projects to as many of the 500,000 farms as possible.[††]

In this specific project, market access did not present a real problem for the farmers, because it only worked with the ones who already sold to the mill in question (Tan Lam), but for the mill it was an issue vis-à-vis Western roasters. Although farmers improved quality, production and productivity (with less use of fertiliser and pesticides) with the new sustainable farming practices, the quality desired by the large Western roasters could not be provided. It should be noted that factors such as location, altitude and climate, which participants were unable to change, played a role here as well, particularly in making proper storage difficult. Decotrade initially bought some coffee from Tan Lam, but that did not last long as the quality could not meet SL standards. And while Utz certification was obtained with the support from the project, and Tan Lam managed to retain it, a better price (premium) could not be fetched due to the poor quality of the coffee. Consequently, participants did not see the price return (premium) as commensurate to the work involved in remaining Utz compliant. However, losing the certification was perceived as a loss of face for Tan Lam and therefore no option.

Farmers related to Tan Lam had to sell part of their coffee to the mill to pay for the mortgage they had on their land and for the coffee plants they had bought from Tan Lam. They sold the rest of their coffee to whoever paid most at that moment – middlemen, small traders, or any of the mills in the area. Tan Lam faced difficulties in pre-financing and in raising money for investments or for buying enough coffee to compete with other mills in the region, which put the mill in a relatively weak position. Interestingly, the farmers themselves concluded that the project had helped them sufficiently and that no extension was needed.

VIETNAM (GIA LAI) PROJECT

Building on earlier experiences in Vietnam and facilitated by relatively high numerical literacy of the farmers, this project (in a major Robusta-producing region) aimed to professionalise coffee farming and establish producer organisations, thus contributing to the sustainability of the sector. These objectives were successfully achieved through training of farmers on the different management aspects of the coffee business, from pre- to post-harvest processing and storage, as well on marketing, labour allocation, and financial and organisational aspects. The project involved different actors in the coffee value chain – farmers, exporters and authorities – which made a real difference.

While the farmers in Gia Lai obtained Utz certification to facilitate their market access, perhaps the most important learning points related to record keeping via farmer field books. For example, farmers' registration of fertiliser and pesticide usage, as well as yields, which allowed comparisons to be made with peers in the context of farmer field schools, led to more informed decision-making, and also enabled project staff to quantify the results of the project (see Table 23.2). Besides the sustainable farming tools that farmers adopted, they also started to collaborate and improved their entrepreneurial

---

[††]   www.defoundation.com/vietnam-sector-development-ended/.

skills. Another positive result of the project was that farmers overcame their distrust in cooperatives, which stemmed from the country's communist heritage. Towards the end of the project, they requested support to become organised, which has led to a follow-up project for the Central Highlands, co-funded by the DE Foundation.[‡‡]

As a consequence of the project, formal trading channels have started to predominate, with the majority of the coffee being sold to a large exporter, the Neumann Kaffee Gruppe. Neumann offered better storage for the coffee, taking over the risk of deterioration from the farmer; moreover, quality was immediately verified and prices became transparent. However, despite the advantages of selling to a larger exporter, farmers still sold part of their production to middlemen or to any other trader who would pay more. Pre-financing to acquire raw materials and inputs is, like in other projects, still an issue for farmers, for which they depend on middlemen. The Dutch Rabobank Foundation is involved in the follow-up project with an eye to easing the provision of credit to farmers.

BRAZIL (SERRA NEGRA) PROJECT

This project followed from an existing local partnership between Sara Lee do Brasil and the processing plant Quota Mille, and in the early phase a small group of farmers received farm management support on an individual basis in a rather top-down manner. The second phase, from 2006 onwards, was redesigned to be more in line with the Foundation's methodology as it had developed, in order to reach larger numbers of producers and to professionalise farm practices and improve market access. The project was successful on several counts (see Table 23.2, cf. Silva, 2009) and had a remarkable impact in the region which it helped to revitalise. This attracted considerable interest from commercial actors, local authorities and even the national media (the largest TV station, Globo, featured the project in a 25-minute documentary). Through the new sustainable farming practices taught to the farmers, quality and yields improved significantly.

Another achievement was the attainment of Utz certification by a group of smallholder producers – the project was actually pioneering in Brazil in this respect. As certification has traditionally been oriented to large producers, this was a complicated process because some of the requirements needed to be adapted to smallholder realities and capacities, and that had to be recognised by Utz and the Brazilian auditing agencies as well. However, despite all the efforts and resources dedicated to certification, the premium obtained turned out to be too small for farmers. They could get the same 'extra return' if they sold the coffee without issuing invoices (a practice adopted in 15% of the transactions) or traded it via a cooperative, which offers them some tax advantages compared to a possible premium derived from Utz certification. As a result, out of the 120 that obtained Utz, only 73 retained it by the end of the project; nevertheless, those that dropped out claimed to continue most of the farming practices learnt in the process.

It was a challenge to organise these farmers in groups in a participatory manner in the context of a very top-down culture (in which the expert tells them what to do, and the farmer listens) coupled with risk aversion and low levels of formal education (which sometimes hampered the use of farmer field books and also negatively affected project documentation activities, rather different to the Vietnamese projects). Despite a tradition of individualism, however, producers started to collaborate and participated in farmer

---

‡‡   www.defoundation.com/vietnam-central-highlands.

field schools, also due to efforts put in by project staff, resulting in higher levels of social coherence and community building. Compared to the other projects, middlemen did not play a role in this Brazilian region, as all coffee went via the mill.

PERU (UBIRIKI) PROJECT

The project in Ubiriki was started as a follow-up to a visit of Sara Lee management to Prodelsur, a processing and exporting agency (part of the Volcafe group), which saw clear opportunities for improvement in coffee quality and farm management. In contrast to other projects, support for processing was given as well, in addition to objectives related to market access and certification. The project was still ongoing when this chapter was written, and therefore no final evaluation was available. However, an impact assessment halfway through (which compared project farmers to a control group) has given insight into the positive outcomes (see Table 23.2, cf. Van Rijn, 2008). Moreover, the Sustainable Agriculture Initiative (SAI) ranked it as 'one of the best performing projects out of 12 projects worldwide and affiliated to SAI's coffee working group'.[§§]

As an outflow of the activities of the farmer field schools, producers created a new cooperative in 2004, which grew over the years. The cooperative managed to obtain certification according to Utz and several other standards, and attracted credit from banks to pre-finance coffee buying from its members. Quality improvement paid off in higher prices relative to other producers in the region, and intensive participatory efforts included attention to involving women. Extensive training and technical support, also related to representation and governance principles and methods inherent to a cooperative, was needed in this project overall, as participants had limited levels of formal education. Nevertheless, the project staff were able to introduce the use of the farmer field book, for which they often relied on dissemination via the ones who were more (technically) literate.

Despite the achievements, there were sometimes internal issues related to production, marketing, organizational structure, financial management and leadership. Regarding the latter, it is notable that in early 2011, the president of the cooperative wanted to change direction, for example by having the coffee sold locally rather than exported and by stopping certification. Interestingly, the institutional embeddedness of the cooperative, which had developed in the course of the project (e.g. with financial and trading partners), resulted in pressures that helped to build momentum for a leadership change. The president and the whole board of directors resigned, and with a newly elected management, the cooperative continues the course it had taken.

Discussion and Conclusions

This chapter has analysed steps taken by an MNE to further the mainstreaming of sustainable coffee (as an extension to Kolk, 2011, 2012). It focused on the activities of the DE Foundation, set up by Sara Lee's international coffee and tea division, particularly the

---

[§§]   www.defoundation.com/peru/. The Sustainable Agriculture Initiative (SAI), of which Sara Lee is an active member, is a platform of the food industry to promote sustainable agriculture; its coffee working group is 'one of the oldest' and 'most advanced' (www.saiplatform.org/, accessed on 2 September 2011).

projects it has carried out to help small coffee farmers in producing countries. This thus basically addressed the left side of the supply chain as shown in Figure 23.1, i.e. from smallholder to roaster. Small farmers play a large role in the sector as they supply the majority of coffee worldwide. In order to mainstream sustainable (i.e. certified) coffee, therefore, it is essential that their produce becomes certified. This is difficult, however, due to their size, spread and diversity, and the fact that certification requirements tend to be geared to large producers who have the capabilities and scale needed. Small farmers have also received much attention in the past decade as a result of public concerns about poverty and sustainability. From that perspective, a better distribution of costs and benefits, and thus value, over the whole chain is seen as necessary, and MNEs are expected to contribute here, as part of their corporate social responsibility. The activities of Sara Lee and its Foundation, discussed in this chapter, represent active steps in this context, and provide input into a practical exploration of the actual complexities, the problems and possible solutions. In the projects that focused on small farmers, intermediary actors in the chain to the MNE very often became involved as well, including producer associations, traders, processors and exporters.

To evaluate activities and achievements, different lenses can be taken. One can look, for example, at the sustainability outcomes of the projects, as the preceding section did (see also Table 23.2). In addition, a broader impact assessment framework might be used that considers the economics, capabilities and relationships, for both farmers and communities (cf. London, 2009), as included in Table 23.3. This overview shows multiple changes brought about by the projects for both groups, and also points at some possible areas of improvement. The previous section has already discussed the issues that emerged during and after the projects, alongside the results and the short and long-term implications for the various actors, especially farmers. The focus of the projects and the issues at stake directly point to a range of constraints in both value creation and value capture for such small producers (cf. London et al., 2010). These relate to financial resources, raw materials and production resources (three value creation/productivity constraints), market access, market power and market security (three value capture/transactional constraints).

Table 23.3 DE Foundation projects placed in London's (2009) framework

Small coffee producers	Communities
Potential changes in economics	
• Increased income from quality and yield improvement • Improvement of the coffee produce enabled the investment or creation of secondary income-generating activities (e.g. other crops) • Better prices due to quality improvement and premiums from certification • Lower dependence on middlemen • More transparency and less information asymmetries at the moment of trading	• Generation of new businesses as a result of farmers' new demands and needs • Income of existing businesses increases or decreases as demand for pesticides, seedlings, fertilisers and other input changes • New demand might lead to new services or better pricing • New jobs and economic opportunities • Infrastructure might be improved • New technologies might be introduced or made feasible

Table 23.3 *Concluded*

Possible areas of improvement
- High costs of Utz certification – in terms of cost-benefit in some cases it does not compensate the investments made
- Farmers are still vulnerable to coffee market fluctuations
- Lack of access to finance increases vulnerability and jeopardises projects' sustainability
- Limitations to market access if there is not sufficient organisation building

Potential changes in capabilities	
<ul><li>Sustainable farming skills, entrepreneurial skills and trading skills through training and education</li><li>Knowledge about participatory methods, organisation building and networking</li><li>Higher inclination to seek for relevant information and new developments, and better informed decision-making</li><li>Self-esteem, self-efficacy and contentment derived from results achieved and new competences learnt</li><li>Higher aspirations and goals as a result of new management skills and farming practices that led to novel opportunities</li><li>Key farmers were trained to be trainers and extension service providers, and provide first aid and chemical security</li></ul>	<ul><li>Community members have the opportunity to learn about new development and possibilities, and can get access more easily to educational opportunities and learn through information dissemination</li><li>New perceptions about and awareness of opportunities such as health care and education might lead to novel and better pronounced demands by communities to the government</li><li>Sense of dignity and respect, especially as a result of social programmes (notable in particular in the Luwero project)</li><li>At the group and community level new aspirations and goals are developed</li></ul>

Possible areas of improvement
- Retention of skilled key farmers/trainers in the project

Potential changes in relationships	
<ul><li>Increase in trust among farmers, and between farmers and project staff</li><li>Cooperation among farmers, which might lead to possible organisation building and the formation of cooperatives and/or associations</li><li>Increase in local and foreign network opportunities</li><li>The success or failure of farmers might affect their reputation and status vis-à-vis others</li><li>Possible change in the role of women in households and communities as they are also targeted in the projects</li><li>In cases where ethnic minorities were targeted, more possibilities emerged for interaction with 'dominant' ethnic groups</li><li>Some farmers had a status change to trainer, facilitator or extension service provider</li><li>Different relationships with suppliers and other actors in the chain due to higher quality of produce, certification, group formation, and better skills and knowledge</li></ul>	<ul><li>Project raised government awareness of and involvement with certain communities, and enlarged (inter)national networks</li><li>Projects in Vietnam initiated discussions and led to a project roll out that targets the whole coffee sector at the country level</li><li>More inclusion of minority groups and women in the communities</li><li>Increase in social cohesion</li><li>Higher incomes led farmers to invest more in their children's education (Vietnam), livelihood, or increased consumption</li><li>Sustainable farming practices and Utz norms improved the relationship with the natural environment (ecosystems, land, energy and water quality)</li><li>Changes in some traditional practices, leading to behavioural and cultural changes</li></ul>

Possible areas of improvement
- Reduction in dependence on extension service providers or project (partners)

If we discuss the main aspects for the small farmers in the projects, it is obvious that market access and the possibility of obtaining higher incomes have been important reasons for participation. More sustainable farming practices not only enable farmers to improve the quality of their products and consequently their competitive position, but also to increase their yields, which makes them more attractive to traders and exporters, particularly if they join forces (and thus quantities) in producer groups. Quality and quantity are the main factors when traders and exporters consider the feasibility and attractiveness of certain locations, and the logistics involved. The stronger the position of small farmers in this regard, the better it is for a reduction of their vulnerability. Another aspect of vulnerability relates to processing, one of the layers in the chain (see Figure 23.1). Farmers' cooperatives or associations that decide to own a mill and process their own coffee take a great risk on themselves. A mill requires a significant investment in terms of time and money, and also considerable technical, commercial, entrepreneurial and management skills that they might neither have in-house nor be in a position to contract. In addition, there are also risks involved in the storage and processing of the coffee. Regardless of how processing take place, however, projects have focused on strengthening the position of farmers by bringing them together in producer groups, and establishing linkages with exporters. This facilitates joint training activities and also certification, with either the cooperative or the exporter as the holder of the Utz certificate.

Another important aspect related to farmers' vulnerability is access to finance. MNEs want to help farmers improve their business by adopting more sustainable practices, but do not want to commit to or become directly involved in financing issues, which are complex and beyond their core business. Lack of access to finance (credit) puts producers in a weak position by limiting their ability to buy good quality raw materials (e.g. seedlings or coffee trees) and/or inputs such as fertiliser. In their absence, quality and yield produce will be negatively affected, producers' profits will be reduced and they will have less residual money to reinvest in their farms. Financial institutions are often inaccessible to farmers because they lack collateral for loans. This situation forces farmers to sell their products to middlemen and obtain (pre)financing from them, but these intermediaries tend either to charge high interest rates or offer low prices, thus further compromising farmers' livelihood. It is here where we see clear limits to what the private sector can do, and where government involvement and/or joint activities (e.g. via partnerships) are needed.

The tight financial situation of small farmers also influences their ability or willingness to seek certification, for example according to the Utz standard, in addition to the time and effort required to become and remain compliant. Often the premiums derived from certification are not perceived to be in line with the time and resources invested, even though customers (particularly roasting and manufacturing MNEs in the first instance) increasingly ask for certified coffee. This is all the more notable in market circumstances with higher coffee prices, which is very different from what was described earlier in this chapter for the 1990s for example. In that sense, the balance in the chain has, at least temporarily, shifted back somewhat to the producers, but this is an intricate matter that has different dimensions to it.

Certification in itself does not assure coffee quality: if the coffee is not of a quality that meets the standards required by large roasters (as was described for one of the Vietnamese projects in this chapter), farmers will not fetch the premium they may have expected. Projects that facilitate certification are of great value to small farmers, for whom attainment of certification on their own would be infeasible. However, when such a projects stops and the certification process is no longer supported, farmers may tend only to keep the certification if it makes direct economic sense to them. This added value will be less obvious in a situation when coffee prices are high due to market shortages (possible exacerbated by speculative trading). In this situation, Fair Trade, for example, has had difficulties obtaining sufficient certified coffee despite its normally higher (fixed) prices, as farmers prefer to sell it to middlemen instead, to profit from market conditions and generate a higher income from their produce.[¶¶] Still, for farmers, this approach may mean that short-term economic considerations are traded off against longer term (potential) benefits. If prices go down again, non-certified coffee is likely to become less beneficial than certified coffee, and farmers without certification will face a competitive disadvantage, which increases their vulnerability.

Certification is an issue that requires further careful consideration by both researchers and practitioners. This concerns the pure costs involved (related to the acquisition of the appropriate skills and knowledge, compliance and control systems, and auditing), and who will have to bear them, one-off and periodically. Attention must also be given to ways of keeping the process manageable and accessible for small farmers more broadly, given that standards are often rather complex and not really designed for them. Moreover, there are multiple standards, with different requirements and (market) peculiarities, which complicates matters not only for producers but also for consumers, and for all the actors in the chain in between (Kolk, 2011). A simplification and streamlining of the diversity of labels and approaches appears to be needed. However, steps in the direction of 'complementarity' require a major breakthrough towards collaboration rather than (implicit) competition.[***]

Still, the fact that producers sometimes have their coffee certified according to multiple standards may point the way, although convergence rather than ongoing diversity appears to be necessary. How such an approach to certification can be extended to small farmers in a relatively cost-effective and easy manner will be a major challenge, but a crucial one. This also applies to novel ways of accessing finance which are in line with local contexts, characteristics and conditions. Partnerships between multiple actors are likely to be a main route for steps ahead, as well as practical insights on the complexities of actually implementing more sustainable farming practices for small producers, including certification. It is here that the activities examined in this chapter seem to have made a clear contribution, even though the scale has been limited.

[¶¶]   The decision by Fair Trade to allow traders, subject to several conditions in time and percentages of volumes, to buy non-certified coffee and sell it as certified (see www.maxhavelaar.nl/nieuws/fairtrade-international-introduceert-koffie-actieplan and www.fairtrade.net/single_view1.0.html?&cHash=4a8942a3af&tx_ttnews[tt_news]=220, last accessed 4 September 2011) caused a great stir in the media, for example in the Netherlands, in 2011. It led one of its proponents, who launched a Fair Trade chocolate brand in the Netherlands, to declare the label 'dead' (Van de Keuken, 2011). This adds to broader criticism of Fair Trade, also from other long-standing advocates (e.g. Haight, 2011).

[***]   In February 2011, the organisations behind the main standards (Fair Trade, Rainforest Alliance/Sustainable Agriculture Network and Utz Certified) issued a joint statement, under the guidance of the ISEAL alliance (the global association for social and environmental standards) of which they are all members. This seems to have put an end to the public exposure of disagreements since the organisations 'publicly acknowledged their aligned mission' (www. isealalliance.org/news/historic-joint-statement-fairtrade-sanrainforest-alliance-utz-certified, last accessed 3 September 2011). How the 'market competition', which they stated to welcome 'as long as this is "healthy competition"', can be reconciled with the convergence and simplification that seems necessary, is unclear, however.

References

Gereffi, G. 1999. International trade and industrial upgrading in the apparel commodity chain. *Journal of International Economics*, Vol. 48: 37–70.

Gilbert, C.L. 1996. International commodity agreements: An obituary notice. *World Development*, Vol. 24, No. 1: 1–19.

Haight, C. 2011. The problem with Fair Trade coffee. *Stanford Social Innovation Review*, Summer: 74–79.

Kolk A. 2005. Corporate social responsibility in the coffee sector. The dynamics of MNC responses and code development. *European Management Journal*, Vol. 23, No. 2: 228–236.

Kolk A. 2011. Mainstreaming sustainable coffee. *Sustainable Development*, doi: 10.1002/sd.507.

Kolk, A. 2012. Towards a sustainable coffee market? Paradoxes faced by a multinational company. *Corporate Social Responsibility and Environmental Management*, Vol. 19: 79–89.

London, T. 2009. Making better investments at the base of the pyramid. *Harvard Business Review*, Vol. 87, No. 5: 106–113.

London, T., Anupinid, R. & Sheth, S. 2010. Creating mutual value: Lessons learned from ventures serving Base of the Pyramid producers. *Journal of Business Research*, Vol. 63: 582–594.

Oxfam. 2002. *Mugged. Poverty in your Coffee Cup*. Washington: Oxfam International.

Ponte, S. 2002. The 'Latte Revolution'? Regulation, markets and consumption in the global coffee chain. *World Development*, Vol. 30, No. 7: 1099–1122.

RIAS. 2002. Identification and assessment of proposals by the international private coffee sector regarding the poor income situation of coffee farmers. Utrecht: Rabobank International Advisory Services.

Silva, F. 2009. *Viabilidade economico-financera da certificação Utz Certified em um grupo de cafeicultores familiares na região da Mogiana*. São Paulo: Fundação Instituto de Administração MBA Gestão e Empreendedorismo Social.

UNCTAD. 2003. Economic development in Africa. Trade performance and commodity dependence. Geneva.

Van de Keuken, T. 2011. Havelaar. *Het Parool*, 30 July, p. 29.

Van Rijn, F. 2008. *A socio-economic impact study of the DE Foundation coffee project Peru*. Wageningen: Wageningen University, Department of Social Sciences, MSc thesis development economics.

24 Corporate Social Responsibility in the Bank Value Chain

BERT SCHOLTENS*

Keywords

Banks, banking industry, corporate social responsibility, production.

Introduction

This chapter investigates how corporate social responsibility (CSR) may connect to the value chain in the banking industry. Banks have a small direct impact on sustainable development because of the low resource intensity of their production processes.[1] However, their indirect impact is substantial as banks facilitate economic activity.[2] Wood argues that CSR can be regarded as a set of structural categories integrated in an open-systems model of a firm.[3] An open system takes in resources from and emits outputs into its larger environment. As such, CSR connects with the harms and benefits that result from a corporation's interactions with its larger environment, including the social, cultural, political, economic, legal, and natural dimensions.[4] Dyllick and Hockerts discuss how social, environmental, and ethical issues can be integrated at the business level and why it is crucial for the development of a corporation to account for these issues.[5] Hart et al., Van Tulder et al. and Mefford[6] further theorize on the economic rationale for a sustainable supply chain based on production, finance, and marketing theories.[7] Babiak and Trendafilova find that both strategic and legitimacy motives play a role in the adoption of environmental management practices, with strategic motives dominating the more institutional pressures.[8] Roth and Jackson provide a framework to analyze strategic determinants of service quality and performance in the banking industry.[9] They find that generic operations capabilities affect quality and performance, that quality and innovations can be directly observed and imitated, that investments in people are critical to success, that market conduct influences the generic capabilities of banks more than performance, and that total factor productivity tends to be negatively correlated with service quality. However, they do not account for environmental, ethical, and social conduct and performance.

*   Professor Bert Scholtens, Energy and Sustainability Centre, University of Groningen, Faculty of Economics and Business, Department of Economics, Econometrics and Finance, PO Box 800, 9700 AV Groningen, The Netherlands. E-mail: L.J.R.Scholtens@RUG.NL. Telephone: + 31 503637064.

We depart from the framework of Roth and Jackson[10] and amend it for an application to financial intermediaries, which basically is a service-oriented industry, whereas most of the theory focuses on production-based industries. We show how financial intermediaries operate and point out how CSR connects with their operations. We provide an overview of the conduct and performance of a group of internationally operating banks in industrialized countries to illustrate our ideas.

The structure of this chapter is as follows. We first elaborate on what banks actually do. Then, we connect CSR to the activities and the value chain of the banks. Next, we provide empirical evidence about international banks' CSR. We end with our conclusion.

What Do Banks Do?

In order to be able to investigate how CSR connects with the value chain of banks, it is essential to know exactly what banks do and where and how they create value for society. In this respect, it is key to analyze what banks actually do. We will rely on Scholtens and Van Wensveen and provide different perspectives.[11]

Transactions in kind have to be paid for. In most economies, the payments system affects the greater part of these transactions. Because of the asynchronous pattern of most expenditure and income, lending and borrowing requirements occur. But why is it that we need banks, brokers, insurance companies, etc., to satisfy our financial needs instead of direct transfers between surplus and deficit households? Boyd and Prescott characterize financial intermediaries as follows. They borrow from one subset of agents in the economy and lend to another, thereby diversifying both sides of their balance sheet.[12] They generally deal with borrowers whose information may differ from their own and they produce costly information on the attributes of would-be borrowers. They also issue claims with state-contingent payoffs which differ from the claims of ultimate borrowers. Gerschenkron sees bank prominence in the economic development of industrializing countries as a consequence of their economic backwardness.[13] Scarcity of human capital and real capital within these economies creates a role for banks.[14] This contrasts with the views of Gurley and Shaw[15] and Goldsmith,[16] in which financial intermediation fulfills an important role in economic development. In their view, specialized financial institutions emerge to smoothen the functioning of the economy.[17] Financial intermediaries have evolved in the course of history and many origins can be traced. Modern intermediaries not only have roots in goldsmiths, as many textbooks would have us believe, but in merchants, manufacturers, money-changers, tax-farmers, scriveners, and notaries as well.[18]

As to financial intermediation, a distinction has been made between self-finance, direct finance, and indirect finance.[19] Self-finance occurs when expenditure takes place by spending units with balanced budgets. This type of finance is called internal finance. Expenditure which is undertaken by deficit spending units requires external finance. External finance can be divided into direct finance and indirect finance. Direct finance involves lending by surplus households to deficit households. The deficit households can issue direct debt. The surplus households may buy and hold this debt (financial assets) as direct securities. With indirect finance, intermediaries like banks or markets can step in. They take in debt and credit and will restructure this into standardized (and potentially tradable) assets.

Financial intermediation is generated by economic units specializing in the production of financial goods and services. Financial and non-financial firms can be distinguished by the tendency of the former to acquire predominantly financial assets with the attracted funds, whereas the latter obtain mainly real assets.[20] Draper and Hoag differentiate intermediation from any other economic activity by its information content: intermediaries will arise to occupy a 'shell' when there is value in producing and processing information and in restructuring firms' securities.[21] Financial assets are tradable claims on future money and, thus, are future purchasing power for real goods and services.

Financial intermediation is the transformation of (contingent) financial claims with respect to four characteristics: maturity, risk, scale, and location. This is because the claims on the intermediary and its assets can differ regarding the properties and volumes along these four characteristics. Financial transformation is the key economic function of the financial intermediary. Due to its transformation function the financial intermediary assumes risk itself. Without assuming the risk that evolves from financial transformation, there would be no economic rationale behind the existence of financial intermediaries. Later on in history, regulation has evolved to mark this special position. As to maturity transformation, the duration of the financial titles, either on- or off-balance, differs from that of the liabilities. As to financial risk transformation, it should be noted that the risk of the titles the intermediary collects or receives (deposits, premiums, savings, etc.) differs from the risk of the projects in which it invests or for which it lends. The latter risk will generally be higher. As to transformation of scale and location, the composition of the (contingent) claims on the financial intermediary usually also differs substantially from its own claims. Banks keep capital as a buffer. But given their business, they are highly leveraged and have to be very protective of their reputation to ensure that the public maintains its trust in the bank. Thus, the specialization in financial risk management in fact is the main reason why financial intermediaries emerged, specializing in information production and processing and trying to reduce transaction and agency costs.

Financial intermediaries satisfy the portfolio preferences of borrowers who wish to expand their holdings of real assets and the portfolio preferences of lenders who wish to hold (part of) their net worth in financial assets. Financial intermediaries may issue claims on themselves and use the proceeds to purchase other financial assets.[22] The assets of financial intermediaries are the obligations of the borrowers; their liabilities are the assets of the lenders. The financial assets and liabilities of financial intermediaries are financial instruments. These are contracts which differ in important characteristics such as the nature of the owner and issuer of the contract, the duration, liquidity, and marketability of the instrument, and the level and character of the yield. Advice with respect to the portfolios of lenders and borrowers is another product of financial intermediaries. The advice and the financial instruments usually make up a packaged deal. Examples are brokerage, trust operations, underwriting, correspondent services, and the making of payments. Intangibility is an important characteristic of many these activities. Of course, various financial intermediaries may opt for different combinations of these basic products and/or may specialize in specific segments of the value chain.[23]

In the economic literature there seems to be little disagreement about what financial intermediation is and what financial intermediaries do. In part, this results from the fact that the literature hardly provides definitions of this class of economic activities.[24] However, there are different opinions about which functions are of the greatest importance.

This leads to multiple classifications of the activities of financial intermediaries, which may be a reason for the diversity in explanations of financial intermediation. Two main approaches of these classifications can be observed where macroeconomic elements are the distinguishing feature. In the first, authors such as Black, Hart and Jaffee, and Smith[25] concentrate on asset transformation and brokerage activities of financial intermediaries. Their classification concentrates on the indirect finance function of intermediaries. Indirect finance can involve risk for intermediaries (asset transformation) or it can be risk-free (pure brokerage). In the financial transformation activities of economic units, money and demand deposits are treated as special assets, fulfilling an important role though not a characteristic one. Implicitly, the accounting system appears to be a by-product of indirect financing activities of the financial intermediary. In the second approach, authors such as Klein, Sealy and Lindley, Fama, and Goodhart[26] regard the operation of the payment system as the heart of financial intermediation. Here, location and maturity transformation is the central function of the intermediary.

Financial intermediation can be defined as the propagation of financial products, goods as well as services, that may satisfy the financial needs of economic subjects. The activities of financial intermediations can be classified as follows:

1. The demand and supply of financial assets and liabilities, such as deposits, equity, credit, loans.
2. The administration of an accounting system, e.g. giro, cheque transfer, electronic funds transfer, settlement, clearing.
3. The matching of the preferences of borrowers and lenders, i.e. pure brokerage.
4. The demand and supply of non-tangible assets and liabilities, such as collateral, guarantees, advice, custody.

We focus on financial intermediaries and define them as the institutions that specialize in financial transformation. They transform (contingent) financial titles with respect to maturity, risk, scale, and location. For example, maturity transformation is undertaken in particular by savings and mortgage banks and by pension funds. Risk transformation is undertaken especially by commercial banks and insurance companies. Scale transformation is carried out by investment funds and by almost all types of banks. Transformation with respect to location is undertaken by investment banks in particular and by all internationally operating intermediaries. A particular financial intermediary may perform more than one transformation function and may engage in various financial activities. The financial intermediary usually is a multi-product firm, providing financial transformation along various dimensions and to different degrees.

Financial activities combine characteristics of both goods and services. Goods are objects which are appropriable and, therefore, transferable between economic units. Bonds and equities can be seen as examples of financial goods. Services, however, are not objects which can be transferred. For example, skilled investment bankers can provide specialist services, but they cannot dispose of the actual skills themselves because these cannot be transferred of their own. According to Hill (p. 318), a service is the change in the condition of a person or good which is brought about as the result of the activity of some other economic unit with the prior agreement of the former person or economic unit.[27] Thus, one must distinguish the process of production of a service and the output of that process. The process is the activity which affects the person or the good belonging to an economic unit. The output itself is the change in the condition or good affected.

To investigate the activities of financial intermediaries, two general methods can be used. The first method examines the value added by the financial industry by concentrating on national income and product accounts. It views financial intermediaries as resource-using institutions producing loans, advice, accounting services, etc. Here, inputs are capital, labor, and operating costs. Outputs are accounts and transactions. The second one is concerned with the 'technical' output of the individual firm, such as credits, advice, and depository facilities. It views the borrowing and lending of funds to others to gain a profit as the primary business of financial intermediaries. Their outputs are loan volumes and their inputs are the costs of these funds.

National income and product accounts use the concept of value added, i.e. the subtraction of inter-firm purchases from total sales. When trying to compute the value added of the financial industry two complications arise. First, a large part of the financial firm's product is not sold for an explicit price. Instead implicit charges are made in this industry. Thus, the income earned on lending and investing deposits is not fully paid to the owners of the deposits. The imputed price is, for example, total interest received on loans and investments minus the interest paid to the depositors. Therefore, the system of national accounts (SNA) would need to measure gross products originating in the financial sector as the imputed services charged plus the explicit services charged minus inter-firm purchases. However, interest charged can also be seen as a transfer payment between borrowers and lenders or as a payment for financial services rendered. The former means that intermediary services are not productive and, hence, interest is a reward to depositors.[28] The latter implies that interest is a payment to the community, the depositors, or the borrowers for rendered services.[29]

The second complication concerns the ultimate economic effect of the financial product. For example, consider the ownership of bank deposits. Deposits owned by business households imply an imputed bank product to be an intermediate purchase by these households which cancels out in the consolidated SNA.[30] Bank deposits owned by private individuals can be interpreted as the purchase of final goods. An increase in their consumption of financial products will result in an increase in GDP. Treating financial services as intermediate products, as for example the United Nations suggests, is based on the assumption of a closed economy. Once this assumption is relaxed, the treatment of financial services as intermediate products seems inappropriate. In an open economy, financial services rendered to non-residents are final products from the perspective of the residents of the supplying country. As a result, the GDP of countries active in the export of financial services is understated.

Various assumptions must be made to integrate financial production in the SNA.[31] Questions to be answered are: Are all the imputed benefits of financial services enjoyed by depositors? Do borrowers receive services over and above borrowing costs which would otherwise not be counted as 'product' (e.g. payment services, investment advice)? Does the usage of deposits depend on the distribution of imputed benefits? Do prices need to be deflated by an index of interest rates or consumer prices? How should external effects be accounted for? A drawback in measuring the nominal output of banking services on a SNA basis is the lack of a strict economic calculus for allocating the value of gross bank output between intermediate and final sales. More general criticism on national accounting, especially when international comparisons are involved, is also relevant:[32]

neither the kind nor the quality of production is expressed in the SNA; it is just monetary values that are accounted for. Studying the development of value added confronts us with the index problem: the composition of production and consumption changes in time. Furthermore, informal production is not accounted for. In international comparisons, denominations in various national currencies have to be expressed in one currency. Due to exchange rate fluctuations, changes in value added may differ from those in the original denomination and we face transaction, translation, and economic exposure. In the SNA, services rendered to non-residents represent final products, whether the customers are business enterprises or not. Furthermore, the way assumptions are applied in setting up the SNA differs between countries.

The second approach used to measure the operations of the financial industry is based on a microeconomic perspective. Here, the production and the intermediation approach can be distinguished.[33] Under the production approach, depository financial institutions are producers of services associated with individual loan and deposit accounts. These services are produced with labor and capital. Here the number of the various accounts is the output definitions. Total costs exclude interest costs. The intermediation approach views depository institutions as producers of services related directly to their financial intermediating role.[34] They collect deposits and purchase funds to intermediate these into assets. Deposits, labor, and capital are inputs. In this case, the various (monetary values of the) volumes of assets are output measures. Total costs include interest expenses. Clark and Hannan offer a review of this cost literature.[35] It appears that brokerage, lending, and borrowing are included in most indicators of financial firm output. The supply of non-tangibles and of payment accounts is frequently neglected. Composite output measures are also used. However, Kim demonstrates that composite measures fail to provide a proper representation of intermediating technology and, therefore, disaggregate cost functions will be necessary for studying the output of the financial firm.[36]

In all, the literature on financial intermediation offers no consensus on how one ought to view the production of financial services. Three issues are of importance here. The first is the problem of measuring the production of the financial industry. The second is the multi-product character of most financial intermediaries. The third is the inability to classify the products of a financial intermediary as inputs or as outputs of its financial operations. The first two issues have been countered by various methodological solutions, leading to various outcomes. However, they do not appear to be crucial for the information of a theory of financial intermediation. Nevertheless, they are relevant challenges which must be dealt with when evaluating the efficiency of financial firms. The third issue seems to be of a much more serious character. Two opposing types of reasoning can be distinguished by the way in which they view the output of the financial firm. In a technical sense, output is a set of financial goods and services to the firm's clients. In an economic sense, however, output is value added by the firm. Technical outputs are not necessarily economic outputs. If one is interested in the economic foundations of financial intermediation, these technical issues are primarily instrumental. From an economic point of view, it is important that the value added by providing the intermediary services is greater than the costs of the services being offered.

Risk Management (Credit Risk, Liquidity Risk, Market Risk, Interest Rate Risk, Operational Risk)					
Human Resource Management					
Technology Management					
Marketing	**Sales**	**Products**			**Transactions**
Advertising	Acquisition	*Funding*	*Lending*	*Services*	Payment
Branding	Account management	Deposits	Credits	Accounts	Trading
Support	Offering	Securitization	Structured products	Assets	Clearing & Settlement
	Multichannel	Markets	Securities	Capital	Custody
			Markets	Issuance	
				Advisory	

Figure 24.1 Generic banking value chain

Source: in part derived from Lammers et al.[37]

Figure 24.1 gives a stylized view of the value chain in the banking industry. This scheme is based on Lammers et al. and on Roth and Jackson.[38] Given the perspective of corporate social responsibility, we are especially interested in the value activities from the banks' products and transactions; the sales and marketing of the value chain is quite similar to that elsewhere. With products and transactions, value creation is both in the input and in the output character. This is primarily due to the intermediate character of financial products. For example, with deposits, the bank offers a means to its customers to safely store and manage funds. This is creating value for the customer. But it also creates value for the bank as the deposits are used as inputs in the lending (asset management) process. However, then, the output of the bank (the loan) is an input of the borrower. In essence, the risk transformation processes of the bank are what create the value in this production chain. The value added is related to the type and quality of the bank's risk management which primarily is based on the quality of its human capital and technology management.

Banks as organizations have different ways to organize and manage the operations and specialists have evolved who focus on particular segments of the bank's value chain. Given the purpose of this chapter, we concentrate on the banking industry's value chain as a whole and investigate banks' corporate social responsibility.

CSR and the Value Chain of the Banking Industry

Although banks may have a small direct impact on sustainable development because of the low resource intensity of their production processes,[39] their role as a financial intermediary implies that they may have a much larger indirect impact. Figure 24.1 is a general value chain of the banking industry and we will try to relate each part to corporate social responsibility. We briefly discuss how the different elements of the value chain connect with CSR.

SALES AND MARKETING

Although this may create financial value, CSR value is unlikely to be derived from sales and marketing. To the contrary, many people are quite skeptical about banks telling them that they do good. Here, the recent experience with the financial crisis has done substantial harm to banks' reputation. The banking industry traditionally has had a credibility problem[40] and this has been aggravated by the credit crisis. With sponsoring, volunteering, and community involvement, the banks usually try to create social value and at the same time try to realize financial value. In part, this is goodwill, in part, this is employee recognition and loyalty. Both strategic (especially labor market) and institutional factors play a role here. From a strategic perspective, the intermediary tries to create a comparative advantage in labor and capital markets by signaling that it is responsible and so is a nice place to work and is an institution that is less prone to risk than non-responsible banks. Institutional factors are the peer pressure and media attention that 'force' banks to engage in responsibility matters. However, there is the danger of 'greenwash' where banks communicate that they are green but do not show (or are unable to show) what they actually do in this respect and how it matters for the people and the planet. They should account for the investments being undertaken in this respect and for their performance regarding some key performance indicators. However, so far, banks have not succeeded in producing a credible metrics about their own CSR. Moreover, greenwash is a clear example of irresponsible conduct. There appears to be a thin line, and in several respects even a slippery slope, between reporting and marketing expressions and greenwash. If the (suggested) claims by the bank about its performance or its products are not true and cannot be proven, this may backfire and will impact the bank's reputation.

FUNDING

As for CSR of bank deposits, responsible funding can mean that banks make the banking and payment system accessible for households who thereby can save on storage and security costs. Especially in the least-developed countries and in the lower social classes, having access to banking services is very important to arrive at social and economic development. Hermes et al. provide a critical reflection of the positive and less positive effects of microfinance.[41] Traditionally, bank services are provided by bricks-and-mortar affiliates, but internet banking has opened a new window of opportunities. The risk, however, is that people who are physically or mentally challenged face additional handicaps in internet banking. A responsible bank will take care of these weak and poor customers too and, here, the availability of a multi-distribution channel network is what distinguishes more responsible from less responsible banks. A bank that only relies on the internet is much less responsible as it rations (excludes) socially vulnerable groups from its services. Furthermore, bank branches may add value to the empowerment of local communities. The price of financial services will play a role too, but offering depository facilities is crucial for people's economic development and social well-being as it offers them the opportunity to participate in the economy against minimal transaction costs.

Since the 1930s banks have increased their securitization of assets. As the financial crisis has shown, transparency is key in this part of the value chain. There is therefore a clear connection with CSR via governance. As most (ultimate) investors are wholesale, price does play a dominant role, in contrast to retail deposits.

Regarding bank capital, several responsibility issues are at stake, especially longevity, durability, governance, and transparency. Capital can only truly perform the function of being a solid buffer if it can keep its value. This is a major drawback for banks whose capital to a large extent is made up of shareholder capital, as the value of equity moves up and down with the stock market. If the bank has other sources of capital as well (like retained earnings), this will improve the buffer function and sustain the bank in operating its main economic and social functions. Mutual banks and cooperatives do not face the problem of unexpected devaluations of their capital base but can be hampered in their growth strategies when their members have a limited capital base. The financial crisis has also shown that many non-listed banks failed and being a mutual or a cooperative is certainly not a guarantee for keeping a bank's head above water. Governance and transparency of the bank are important with respect to responsibility, as it is essential to guarantee that the decision-making process is sound and appropriate and that stakeholders have an outlet for their ideas and complaints.

Another important feature regarding the banks' liabilities is that they should know the origin of the money they take in: who is it who they actually facilitate with their services? Of course, there are a lot of legal requirements here too, for example anti-terrorism laws, but first and foremost it counts that the money can be trusted and especially that the client can be trusted. This is as important on the liabilities side of the balance sheet as it is on the asset side.

LENDING

The banking laws of a country usually forbid banks to lend for particular illegal activities. Banking ethics go beyond what is required by the law. Here, the information production and processing of the banks plays a crucial role as it will screen the lender and the lender's projects. As to screening, there can be positive and negative screening. Negative screening implies that the bank refrains from particular lenders and/or activities. In the case of positive screening, a bank picks the best firms regarding social, environmental or ethical criteria or it selects the firms that perform above a particular threshold level. In banking, it is mostly negative screening that is being practiced. Banks exclude industries that are regarded as problematic and that lack public acceptance, even though the industries do not perform illegal activities. Here, gambling is a case in point, as in most jurisdictions it is legal but in most cultures it is suspect.

Positive screening is difficult in a competitive market, as it results in losing market opportunities. Screening can result in 'redlining', where particular housing blocks or neighborhoods are denied access to banking services. This can be irresponsible from a social perspective and from a bank perspective as well. Negative screening can be related to particular industries where there are moral objections, such as financing the exploitation of women via prostitution. Thus, a bank will have to decide (and explain the motives for its decision) which economic activities it finances and which ones it does not invest in.

In the lending process, banks will want to account for efficient use of resources in the production process and they will try to help and advise the customer to arrive at a good business plan and see it through to implementation. The lender also will want to account for the external effects of production as environmental, social, and ethical risks will affect the value of the firm – especially through the risk factors – and thereby that of the bank loan.

An issue of responsibility that in fact is related to both the asset and the liabilities side is that of the long-term commitment of the bank to its customer. Where there is a long-term relationship, the bank can help manage the client over the business cycles as the horizon of the (more responsible) bank's services goes beyond that of individual products. Thus, it may, or may not, see a firm through a period of stress. Where the relationship is on a fiduciary and not on a transaction basis, such behavior can make the economy and society more robust. Here, a responsible bank can really make a difference. In addition, there are cases where a bank could create value for the customer by not selling a product. For example, the customer applies for a mortgage where interest and amortization is too high, and which they may have trouble meeting. Even if the bank could then resell the house, which would mean that the value for the bank is kept, it could decide not to make the loan in order to protect the customer. A bank that puts the interests of its customer first would not sell such a mortgage.

SERVICES AND TRANSACTIONS

With banking services, it counts that the bank adds value to the client and, thereby, to society. By performing the key functions of the intermediary efficiently, a bank can do so. In addition, through specialization, the bank also reduces social and environmental costs. In a barter economy, people would use a lot of time and resources to trade and to reach the same level of welfare. However, there also will be rebound effects, as the money that is saved from engaging in costly barter trade may be spent elsewhere on products and this will certainly have a social and environmental impact. Access as such to financial services is a very valuable option for all households and an important driver of economic and social development. Here, we find that private and investment banks in particular have concentrated mostly on the wealthy, whereas, traditionally, mutuals and cooperatives have tried to serve groups who were deprived of access to banking services. Later on, with increasing economic welfare, in most developed countries the services and customer basis has become much broader for these different types of banks.[42] Given that many services of the banks relate to transactions, the provision of payment and advisory services has both private and social benefits and impact. This also has been an important reason to regulate the financial industry.[43]

In all, we find that throughout the whole value chain of the banking industry there are numerous connections with CSR. In this respect, we want to stress the elephant in the room that is very often ignored. Furthermore, we want to point out that the direct environmental and social impact of bank activities usually is limited. Because of its role as a financial intermediary, the indirect effects can be very substantial, as banks can help projects to happen and can help mitigate the external effects. Thus, especially within the lending process, a lot of responsibility issues appear to play a role. First there is the decision whether or not to grant credit for a particular project. Here, ethical dilemmas and negative and positive screening can have an impact. Second there is the broad social and environmental impact of projects themselves. Here, the banks can help restructure projects and help account for the external effects. Given that there is a continuing relationship between bank and customer, these two issues are of an ongoing nature.

Example of CSR Performance

In this section, purely as an illustration, we will assess the CSR of some internationally operating banks; we will not investigate their economic impact. We refrain from relying on CSR ratings. This is because it is not clear exactly how ratings agencies arrive at their assessment and because there are some flaws in the ratings, as described by Chatterji et al.[44] They examine how well KLD ratings provide transparency about past and likely future performance. They conclude that the 'concern" ratings are fairly good summaries of past performance. They also find that firms with more concerns have more pollution and regulatory compliance violations in later years. Furthermore, they find that the strengths do not accurately predict pollution levels or compliance violations. In addition, it appears that both strengths and concerns in the ratings are significantly positively correlated. Instead, we will try to provide a more transparent approach.

The approach chosen here is based on Viganò and Nicolai, Bijl and Scholtens, and Scholtens:[45] Bijl and Scholtens report CSR performance of 32 banks, Viganò and Nicolai include 17 banks in their analysis, while Scholtens investigates 153 insurance companies. We report CSR in the banking industry in 2005 on the basis of Bijl and Scholtens.[46] To investigate the CSR policies of banks, we assess both social and environmental indicators. Although rating agencies pay a great deal of attention to corporate governance and compliance issues, we will not include these in our assessment. This is because all banks listed on a stock exchange already have to comply with various regulations.[47] In contrast, we are much more interested in how banks take account of their social responsibility in a proactive manner. Therefore, we assess bank policy with respect to items that are strictly voluntary, rather than items for which legal requirements are set up. In doing this, we follow Geoffrey Heal's definition of CSR, namely the internalization of external effects in the strategy and conduct of the firm.[48] We will also 'check' whether the banks we assess are within the investment universe of so-called sustainable indices. These indices check – mostly in some proprietary manner – whether firms are 'sustainable' and, if so, allow them in their investment universe on which they base their real-time stock market indices.

We use four groups of indicators about a bank's social responsibility: 1) codes of ethics, sustainability reporting, and environmental management systems; 2) environmental management; 3) responsible financial products; 4) social conduct. These groups reflect the different areas that are relevant for sustainable development at the firm level. Furthermore, it is more directly related to this concept than the framework used by Viganò and Nicolai,[49] who look into CSR instruments and community activities, voluntary activities, organization and resources, and CSR performance. As to our group 1, by adopting codes, publishing sustainability reports, and by implementing an environmental management system, we suppose that a bank commits itself to socially responsible behavior. How a bank actually does take care with regard to environmental issues can be based on its environmental policy and/or the management of its supply chain. Transparency about environmental performance allows us to assess how a bank operates in this respect. Taking care of the environment also is reflected in the ways in which banks account for environmental risks. The supply and development of 'green' or socially responsible financial products is another means by which a bank can signal its commitment to sustainable development. Here, there is a wide range of potential products, for example socially responsible investing, financial products aimed at reducing energy use and greenhouse gases, and microcredit (finance for the poor and deprived). Fourth is social conduct. Here, we assess a bank's internal and external social commitment. The former relates to the ways in which it deals with its workforce. The latter relates to its attitude and behavior with regard to society, for example, community involvement, volunteering, sponsoring. We relate our results to the inclusion or exclusion of banks in so-called sustainability indices. We also check with the Dow Jones Sustainability and the FTSE4Good index, which are worldwide indices. The Domini 400 Sustainable Index (DSI) is an index for the US and we check whether US banks are included in this DSI. The same applies for European banks with respect the European Ethibel Sustainability Index (ESI).

In 2005, the Scandinavian banks did not publish a separate sustainability report, whereas all others did. The first to do so were Barclays, UBS, and Rabobank. Thirteen banks signed the Business Charter for Sustainable Development of the International Chamber of Commerce. Double that amount signed the UNEP Statement by Financial Institutions on Sustainable Development. Twenty-one banks adopted the Equator Principles and Global Compact. Eight (European) banks contributed to the report 'Who Cares Wins'. Furthermore, in 2005, only Unicredit Group had achieved EMAS certification. At that time, fifteen banks had ISO 14001 certification. When we summarized the performance of the banks on codes, reporting, and systems, we found that Credit Suisse and HSBC performed best.

Most banks had transparent quantitative objectives with respect to their sustainability policy. Only Bank of Montreal, Nordea, Credit Agricole, Svenska Handelsbanken, Bank of Tokyo Mitsubishi, and Mizuho provided qualitative objectives. As to the environmental goals, it appears that most banks had qualitative goals in 2005. Quantitative environmental goals were stated by the US and British banks, Deutsche Bank, and Credit Suisse. Banca Intesa and Mizuho Financial Group were the only banks that did not provide an explicit environmental policy. Furthermore, none of the Japanese banks nor Intesa and Nordea had an explicit sustainable supply chain policy. All banks, with the exception of Mizuho and BSCH, accounted for environmental risk in their credit policy. US, Dutch, Belgian and Australian banks, as well as Barclays and Société Générale, excluded particular sectors from lending and investing. Only 25% of the banks adopted the OECD guidelines, whereas more than 80% of the banks adopted those of the World Bank. Summarizing the performance of the banks on environmental management, we observed that Barclays, Deutsche Bank, National Australian Bank, and Rabobank performed best.

Two thirds of the banks in our sample offered socially responsible investing in 2005. Socially responsible saving appeared to be a typical Dutch product. Two thirds of all banks offered responsible loans. European banks in particular included microcredit in their portfolios. Environmental advisory services were a facility of all North American banks. One third of the banks had climate-related products. Among others, the North American and the Spanish banks offered other socially responsible products. The Dutch Rabobank offered all socially responsible financial products. Other well-equipped banks were ABN Amro, Credit Suisse, JP Morgan Chase, and Royal Bank of Canada.

As to the social conduct of the sample of international banks, almost all of them were active with respect to sponsoring local communities and NGOs, and were associated with community involvement in 2005. All banks had a code of ethical conduct. Furthermore, the vast majority of the banks offered training and education facilities and had diversity and equal opportunity employment policies in place.

Figure 24.2 shows the overall CSR score for each bank in 2005. This is somewhat arbitrary as it gives equal weight to every item although there is no a priori reason to do so. Figure 24.2 reveals that Rabobank had the highest score in 2005. ABN Amro, Barclays, and HSBC were the runners-up.

Lastly, we relate CSR performance to the inclusion in one of the four sustainability indices in 2005. It is quite remarkable that weak performers in our metrics, like CIBC and BSCH, were included in the global indices, whereas a strong performer like JP Morgan Chase was not. Furthermore, the number one bank in 2005, Rabobank, was not included in any index at all. This was because it is a cooperative bank and not listed on the stock exchanges. Thus, we establish a substantial discrepancy between our assessment of banks' CSR policies and the rating industry's assessment. As the latter is not public and transparent, we cannot comment on the exact reasons behind this discrepancy.

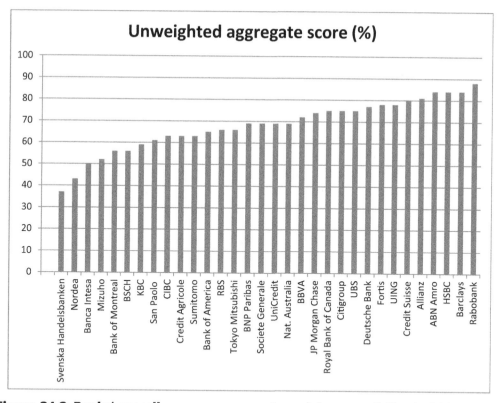

Figure 24.2 Banks' overall score on corporate social responsibility in 2005

Source: Bijl and Scholtens[51]

Conclusions

We have analyzed what banks do and why they do it, and tried to find out how this might connect with their corporate social responsibility. Banks engage in financial risk transformation. They are risk managers and produce and process information. As such, they reduce information and agency costs. They help firms and households to connect with the real economy and to manage their business and transactions more efficiently. This basically is banks' economic and societal value and it is how they gain their private benefits. As intermediaries, they can affect the size and direction of economic development and this has traditionally been one of the reasons for widespread financial regulation. Although, as a service industry, banks may have a relatively small social and ecological footprint, they can have a huge impact because of their economic role as a financial intermediary.

We have found that in the bank's value chain CSR can relate to all elements: sales and marketing, funding, lending, and services and transactions. We observed that throughout the value chain there are numerous connections with CSR. However, the direct environmental and social impact appears to be small, because the production process of a bank in itself hardly involves any material flows and human capital of a bank is usually above average. The indirect environmental and social impact can be much bigger as banks help numerous economic projects become a reality, and can have an impact on the actual implementation of these projects. Accounting for external effects is a key issue here. In this respect, the time horizon used by entrepreneurs and the banks will play a role; many environmental and social problems result from the fact that in the project's assessment these are not well aligned with the socially optimal time horizon and there is a differential between private and social costs and benefits.

As for banks' corporate social responsibility, we suggest that the elephant in the room, very often ignored, is the provision of credit and deposit facilities and the provision of the payment system. These already have an enormous impact on human, social, and economic development. Because of its role as a financial intermediary, the indirect effects can be substantial as a bank can help enable projects to happen and mitigate external effects. Thus, a lot of responsibility issues appear to play a role. First, there is the decision whether or not to grant credit for a particular project. Here, ethical dilemmas and negative and positive screening can play a role. Second, there is the broad social and environmental impact of projects. Here, the banks can help restructure projects and help account for the external effects. This suggests that, in order to assess CSR in the value chain of the banking industry, one has to account for the real economic effects as well, and not only consider the social and environmental issues involved in banking. In the microfinance literature this is done by considering the outreach of banks.[50] It would be straightforward for CSR rating agencies to include this in their assessment of more conventional banks as well.

It appears that measuring banks' CSR is problematic, because it is not clear what banks actually do. Furthermore, there is no generally accepted definition of CSR and a valid CSR metric is still lacking. We think it is important that banks make progress on this and arrive at a metrics that is transparent and that can signal their CSR performance. We argue that apart from conventional ethical, environmental, governance, and social issues, banks need to account for their economic impact as well. Without the appropriate

CSR metrics, and given widespread skepticism about bankers, it will be very difficult to arrive at credible claims about bank CSR.

In all, we conclude that the banking industry could make an important difference when it comes to changing course to a more sustainable development of society. We argue that, in order to assess and manage this, a more standardized and transparent CSR metric would be very helpful. However, a metric in itself will not be sufficient to ensure improved CSR performance of banks – this is in the joint hands of banks, management, employees, customers, society, and government.

Table 24.1 Framework to assess international banks' CSR

Group	#	Indicator	Operationalization	Source
1. Codes of ethics, sustainability reporting and environmental management systems.	1	Sustainability report	Year of first report; yes (1) or no (0)	Bank's website
	2	ICC Business Charter Sustainable Development	Adopted (yes/no)	Bank's website, ICC, sustainability reports
	3	UNEP FI	Adopted (yes/no)	www.unepfi.org and www.unpri.org
	4	Equator Principles	Adopted (yes/no)	www.equatorprinciples.com
	5	Global Compact	Adopted (yes/no)	www.unglobalcompact.org
	6	'Who Cares Wins'	Participated in publication (yes/no)	Who Cares Wins statement (www.unepglobalcompact.org)
	7	Certified environmental management system	EMAS	Website and sustainability reports
	8	Certified environmental management system	ISO 14001	Website and sustainability reports
2. Environmental management	9	Environmental policy	Environmental policies (yes/no)	Website and sustainability reports
	10	Supply chain management	Policies on sustainability (yes/no)	Website and sustainability reports
	11	Quantitative environmental management targets	Yes or no	Website and sustainability reports
	12	Transparency of environmental performance	Quantitative or qualitative	Website and sustainability reports
	13	Environmental risk management in lending policy	Yes or no	Website and sustainability reports
	14	Exclusion of specific sectors	Yes or no	Website and sustainability reports
	15	World Bank guidelines environmental risk management	Adopted (yes/no)	Website and sustainability reports
	16	OESO guidelines environmental risk management	Adopted (yes/no)	Website and sustainability reports
3. Responsible financial products	17	Socially responsible investing	Yes or no	Website and sustainability reports
	18	Socially responsible saving	Yes or no	Website and sustainability reports
	19	Sustainable financing	Yes or no	Website and sustainability reports
	20	Microcredit	Yes or no	Website and sustainability reports
	21	Environmental advice services	Yes or no	Website and sustainability reports
	22	Climate products	Yes or no	Website and sustainability reports
	23	Other sustainability products	Yes or no	Website and sustainability reports

Table 24.1 *Concluded*

4. Social conduct	24	Sponsoring	Sponsoring of community activities and other NGOs (yes/no)	Website and sustainability reports
	25	Community involvement	Donations and volunteering (yes/no)	Website and sustainability reports
	26	Training and education	Yes or no	Website and sustainability reports
	27	Diversity and opportunities	Yes or no	Website and sustainability reports
	28	Feedback from employees	Yes or no	Website and sustainability reports
	29	Business ethics	Code of conduct (yes/no)	Website and sustainability reports
5. Indices	30	Dow Jones Sustainability Group Index	In DJSGI (yes/no)	DJSI World Constituent Data
	31	FTSE4Good	In FTSE4Good (yes/no)	FTSE4Good Global Index Constituent data
	32	Domini Social Index	North American bank in Domini Social Index (yes/no)	DSI Constituent Data
	33	ESI Europe	European bank in ESI Europe (yes/no)	ESI Europe constituent data

Source: Bijl and Scholtens[52]

Notes

1   Kolk, A., Walhain, S., and Van de Wateringen, S., 2001. Environmental reporting by the Fortune Global 250: Exploring the influence of nationality and sector. *Business Strategy and the Environment*, Vol. 10: 15–28.

2   King, R.G., and Levine, R., 1993. Finance and growth: Schumpeter might be right. *Quarterly Journal of Economics*, Vol. 108: 717–737.

3   Wood, D.J., 2010. Measuring corporate social performance: A review. *International Journal of Management Review*, Vol. 12: 50–84.

4   *Ibid.*; Lindgreen, A., and Swaen, V., 2010. Corporate social responsibility. *International Journal of Management Review*, Vol. 12: 1–7.

5   Dyllick, T., and Hockerts, K., 2002. Beyond the business case for corporate sustainability. *Business Strategy and the Environment*, Vol. 11: 130–141.

6   Hart, S.L., Milstein, M.B., and Caggiano, J., 2003. Creating sustainable value. *Academy of Management Executive*, 17: 56–69; Tulder, R. van, Wijk, J. van, and Kolk, A., 2008. From chain liability to chain responsibility. *Journal of Business Ethics*, Vol. 85: 399–412; Mefford, R.N., 2011. The economic value of a sustainable supply chain. *Business and Society Review*, Vol. 116: 109–143.

7   See also Lankoski, L., 2009. Cost and revenue impacts of corporate responsibility: Comparisons across sustainability dimensions and product chain stages. *Scandinavian Journal of Management*, Vol. 25: 57–67; Carroll, A.B., and Shabana, K.M., 2010. The business case for corporate social responsibility: A review of concepts, research and practice. *International Journal of Management Review*, Vol. 12: 85–105.

8   Babiak, K., and Trendafilova, S., 2011. CSR and environmental responsibility: Motives and pressures to adopt green management practices. *Corporate Social Responsibility and Environmental Management*, Vol. 18: 11–24.

9   Roth, A.V., and Jackson III, W.E., 1995. Strategic determinants of service quality and performance: Evidence from the banking industry. *Management Science*, Vol. 41: 1720–1733.

10 *Ibid.*

11 Scholtens, B., and Wensveen, D. van, 2000. A critique on the theory of financial intermediation. *Journal of Banking and Finance*, Vol. 24: 1243–1251.

12 Boyd, J.H., and Prescott, E.C., 1986. Financial intermediary coalitions. *Journal of Economic Theory*, Vol. 38: 211–232.

13 Gerschenkron, A., 1962. *Economic Backwardness in Historical Perspective*. The Belknap Press of Harvard University Press, Cambridge, MA.

14 *Ibid.*

15 Gurley, J.G., and Shaw, E.S., 1955. Financial aspects of economic development. *American Economic Review*, Vol. 45: 515–538; Gurley, J.G., and Shaw, E.S., 1960. *Money in a Theory of Finance*. The Brookings Institution, Washington, DC.

16 Goldsmith, R.W., 1969. *Financial Structure and Development*. Yale University Press, New Haven/London.

17 See Fry, M.J., 1995. *Money, Interest, and Banking in Economic Development*. John Hopkins University Press, Baltimore. King, R.G., and Levine, R., 1993, Finance and growth: Schumpeter might be right, *Quarterly Journal of Economics*, Vol. 108: 717–737.

18 See Kindleberger, C.P., 1993. *A Financial History of Western Europe* (second edition). Oxford University Press, New York and Oxford.

19 Gurley and Shaw, 1955, *op. cit.*

20 Tobin, J., 1987. Financial intermediation. In: J. Eatwell, M. Milgate and P. Newman (eds.), *The New Palgrave, Money*. MacMillan, London and Basingstoke: 157–174.

21 Draper, D.W., and Hoag, J.W., 1978. Financial intermediation and the theory of agency. *Journal of Financial and Quantitative Analysis*, Vol. 13: 595–611.

22 Leland, H.E., and Pyle, D.H., 1977. Information asymmetries, financial structure and financial intermediation. *Journal of Finance*, Vol. 32: 371–387.

23 Jacobides, M.G., 2005. Industry change through vertical disintegration: How and why markets emerged in mortgage banking. *Academy of Management Journal*, Vol. 48: 465–498.

24 Draper and Hoag, *op. cit.*

25 Black, F., 1975. Bank funds management in an efficient market. *Journal of Financial Economics*, Vol. 2: 323–339; Hart, O.D., and Jaffee, D.M., 1975. On the application of portfolio theory to depository financial intermediaries. *Review of Economic Studies*, Vol. 41: 129–147; Smith, B.D., 1984. Private information, deposit interest rates, and the 'stability' of the banking system. *Journal of Monetary Economics*, Vol. 14: 293–317.

26 Klein, A., 1973. The economics of security divisibility and financial intermediation. *Journal of Finance*, Vol. 28: 923–931; Sealy Jr., C.W., and Lindley, J.T., 1977. Inputs, outputs, and a theory of production and cost at depository financial institutions. *Journal of Finance*, Vol. 32: 1251–1266; Fama, E.F., 1985. What's different about banks? *Journal of Monetary Economics*, Vol. 15: 29–39; Goodhart, C.A.E., 1987. Why do banks need a central bank? *Oxford Economic Papers*, Vol. 39: 75–89.

27 Hill, T.P., 1977. On goods and services. *Review of Income and Wealth*, Vol. 23: 315–338.

28 Fixler, D., and Zieschang, K.B., 1991. Measuring the nominal value of financial services in the national income accounts. *Economic Inquiry*, Vol. 29: 53–68.

29 Arndt, H.W., 1984. Measuring trade in financial services. *BNL Quarterly Review*, Vol. 149: 197–213.

30 Mackara, W.F. 1975. What do banks produce? *Monthly Review, Federal Reserve Bank of Atlanta*, Vol. 60, No. 95: 70–74.

31 Towey, R.E., 1974. Money creation and the theory of the banking firm. *Journal of Finance*, Vol. 29: 57–72; Arndt, *op. cit.*; Fixler and Zieschang, *op. cit.*

32 Arndt, *op. cit.*

33 Clark, J.A., 1988. Economies of scale and scope at depository financial institutions: A review of the literature. *FRB Kansas City Economic Review*, Vol. 73, No. 8: 16–33.

34 *Ibid.*

35 Clark, J.A., 1984. Estimation of economics of scale in banking using a generalized functional form. *Journal of Money, Credit, and Banking*, Vol. 16: 53–68; Hannan, T.H., 1991. Foundations of the structure-conduct-performance paradigm in banking. *Journal of Money, Credit, and Banking*, Vol. 23: 68–84.

36 Kim, M., 1986. Banking technology and the existence of a consistent output aggregate. *Journal of Monetary Economics*, Vol. 18: 181–195.

37 Lammers, M., Loehndorf, N., and Weitzel, T., 2004. *Strategic Sourcing in Banking - A Framework*. *ECIS 2004 Proceedings*. Paper 87. http://aisel.aisnet.org/ecis2004/87

38 Lammers et al., *op. cit.*; Roth and Jackson, *op. cit.*

39 Kolk et al., op. cit.

40 Kindleberger, *op. cit.*

41 Hermes, N., Meesters, A., and Lensink, R.M., 2011. Outreach and Efficiency of Microfinance Institutions, *World Development*, Vol. 39: 938–948.

42 Kindleberger, *op. cit.*

43   Goodhart, *op. cit.*

44   Chatterji, A.K., Levine, D., and Toffel, M.W., 2009. How well do social ratings actually measure corporate social responsibility? *Journal of Economics and Management Strategy*, 18: 125–169.

45   Vigano, F., and Nicolai, D., 2004. *CSR in the European Banking Sector: Evidence from a Sector Survey*, Rhetoric and Realities: Analysing Corporate Social Responsibility in Europe; Bijl, L., and Scholtens, B., 2007, Duurzaamheid bij internationale topbanken. *Kwartaalschrift Economie*, 4: 377–393; Scholtens, B., 2011. Corporate social responsibility in the international insurance industry. *Sustainable Development*, Vol. 19: 143–156.

46   Bijl and Scholtens, *op. cit.*

47   Jaworski, W., 2007. *Use of Extra-financial Information by Research Analysts and Investment Managers*, European Centre for Corporate Engagement, Maastricht/Rotterdam.

48   Heal, G., 2008. *When Principles Pay. Corporate Social Responsibility and the Bottom Line*. Columbia Business School.

49   Viganò and Nicolai, *op. cit.*

50   Hermes et al., *op. cit.*

51   Bijl and Scholtens, *op. cit.*

52   *Ibid.*

25 Sustainability in Value Chains: Empirical Evidence from the Greek Food Sector

GEORGE MAGLARAS,* MICHAEL BOURLAKIS,†
AND CHRISTOS FOTOPOULOS‡

Keywords

Sustainability, food value chain, value outcomes, Greek agri-food sector.

Introduction

Considerable academic and industry interest has been devoted to the issue of sustainability in recent years. Sustainability is defined as a development that meets the needs of the present but also takes into account the needs of future generations.[1] In the literature, sustainability is operationalized with the triple bottom line approach which suggests that sustainability consists of three components: the natural environment, society and economic performance. The term *sustainability* has recently appeared in the literature of management and operations.[2] This organizational sustainability posits that the positive effects on natural environment and society could be accompanied by long-term economic benefits and competitive advantage for firms.

The significance of sustainability is high in all industries for maintaining the appropriate living conditions for future generations, and managers have to respond to these demands with highly sustainable products and processes.[3] Nevertheless, practitioners are adopting sustainable practices quite slowly.[4] The implementation of a sustainable mode of operation needs different approaches across different industries.[5] Regarding the food industry and the food value chain, in particular, the limited attention paid to sustainability issues in the past resulted in recent food crises and hence, sustainability is now a necessary condition of the operation of any food supply chain.[6] In addition,

* George Maglaras, University of Western Greece, Department of Business Administration in Food & Agricultural Enterprises, Seferi 2, Agrinio, 30100, Greece. E-mail: geomag@cc.uoi.gr. Telephone: +30 6942292945.

† Professor Michael Bourlakis, Brunel Business School, Brunel University, Elliot Jaques Building, Uxbridge, Middlesex, UB8 3PH, United Kingdom. E-mail: Michael.bourlakis@brunel.ac.uk. Telephone: +44 01895 265427.

‡ Professor Christos Fotopoulos, University of Western Greece, Department of Business Administration in Food & Agricultural Enterprises, Seferi 2, Agrinio, 30100, Greece. E-mail: chfotopu@cc.uoi.gr. Telephone: +30 210 2776960.

the significance of sustainability issues varies across the different value chain members.[7] Scholars have shown increased interest in the sustainability concept and this is evident in the number of relevant published papers.[8] In order to cope with the sustainability issue, researchers have proposed a large number of frameworks for measuring sustainability performance.[9] However, there is a lack of studies that empirically implement those frameworks and their relevant identified sustainability indicators in order to measure the performance of firms and value chains on sustainability outcomes.[10]

The food sector is highly significant for the Greek economy[11] and it is also highly fragmented, with most business being small and medium-sized enterprises.[12] Major international manufacturers (e.g., Vivartia group, FAGE S.A., Nestlé Hellas S.A., MEVGAL S.A., Creta Farm, Hellenic Quality Foods, Pindos and others) and retailers also operate in the Greek food sector, but national companies still command a strong presence.[13] Sustainability initiatives in Greece have proved insufficient to lead the changes necessary to respond to the future environmental, social and economic issues.[14] In particular, the Greek agri-food sector presents various sustainability problems (e.g., increased waste and use of fertilizers),[15] which may also burden other Mediterranean countries.[16] In fact Mediterranean countries such as Greece, Italy, Spain and Portugal are adopting sustainability regulations later than the northern European countries and they frequently have lower standards.[17] Thus, sustainability issues may arise more easily. Unfortunately, sustainability in Greece is not very high on the business agenda.[18] Hence, slow progress is being made on issues such as sustainability in waste.[19] We should also take into consideration the structural characteristics of the Greek food chain (e.g., the average size of farms is small, the average number of plots per farm is large) that reveal its traditional character.[20] These characteristics, along with economic problems that small producers may face, do not favor investments in sustainable operations and thus, sustainability is a real challenge for the Greek food chain.[21]

This chapter focuses on these issues and aims to assess the performance of the key members of the Greek food value chain regarding specific sustainability outcomes. By measuring the same sustainability outcomes for all key chain members we assess the sustainability issue as a whole and give compatible information, allowing performance comparisons. The chapter is organized as follows. First, following an introduction to the concept of sustainability in value chains and the food sector in particular, we specify our aims and objectives. Next, a section on the methodological approach employed is presented whilst another section analyzes the key findings. Towards the end of the paper, the managerial implications and research limitations are discussed, followed by a concluding section.

Sustainability in Value Chains

Various environmental issues (e.g., pollution and waste) have evolved into big global issues (e.g., climate change).[22] Our way of producing and consuming is unsustainable and it must be replaced by a more sustainable pattern.[23] As a result, the need for environmentally friendly operational strategies is growing.[24] Moreover, sustainability is a highly complex concept and companies face many problems when trying to implement it in their operations. Normally, companies are not able to define the term and translate it to specific requirements for sustainable development.[25] However, companies have attempted to respond to environmental issues and business performance is often evaluated in parallel with sustainability outcomes.[26] According to Handfield et al.[27] the sustainability concept has been used the sustainability concept has been used as a framework for examining management practices and has started to influence decision making in the field of business operations only recently. In addition, there is a link between value chain activities and company's operations regarding sustainability issues. As a result, managers should change their way of thinking and their practices according to the needs of sustainable development.[28]

In today's dynamic business environment, competition no longer takes place between individual firms, but between entire value chains.[29] The pressures from environmental and social issues are becoming increasingly crucial in the public agenda; they have attracted the attention of practitioners and they have increased the general interest in managing products in a sustainable way.[30] The environmental and social aspects of sustainability often require solutions beyond the organization's boundaries and include integrated business processes in a network of companies. As a result, the way value chain activities are managed could impact on sustainability practices followed. Chain activities, including packaging, warehousing, working conditions and energy usage, could be managed in a way that positively affects the natural environment but they can also have a long-term impact on the economic performance and the corporate reputation of an organization.[31]

Sustainability in Food Chains

Even though sustainability is analyzed in relation to environmental, economic and social aspects, it is evident that different industries and thus, different value chains will face different sustainability issues.[32] The food value chain is a chain with many unique characteristics relating to food safety, food quality and complexity.[33] Food products are produced in a complex system of processes along the value chain.[34] Complexity has an obstructing role in the struggle towards sustainability.[35] In a typical food value chain the number of actors may be large, as will be the number of raw material sources. In addition, transactions are frequently taking place at arm's length.[36] As a result, the implementation of holistic sustainability strategies relating to the whole value chain becomes a difficult issue and it is also difficult to detect which are the possible underperforming value chain actors in sustainability outcomes. Hence, it would be interesting to examine differences in sustainability outcomes between companies that participate in value chain activities of different food chains.[37]

These differences in sustainability activities can be examined against key value outcomes (indicators) found in the relevant literature. According to Lee et al.[38] the importance of value outcomes depends on the position of the organization in the chain. There is no relevant work in the appropriate value literature and the concept of value outcome is perceived as being similar to performance within the value literature (e.g., Lindgreen and Wynstra[39]). Thus, the sustainability value outcomes can be discussed in relation to supply chain performance indicators, and in the next paragraphs we provide some key sustainability issues that a food value chain may face.

Specifically, the operations of the food industry may have an impact on the environment, and the literature presents waste as one of the most frequent food value chain sustainability issues.[40] In fact, pollution itself is characterized as a form of waste.[41]

According to Hanfield et al.,[42] there is a link between value chain activities and a firm's performance in relation to sustainability issues. As a result, operational issues are a significant source of waste generated by the value chain.[43] Reducing waste could result in significant efficiencies[44] and some of the positive outcomes could be economic (for shareholders) and environmental (for the public).[45] Past literature has focused primarily on the economic impact of waste on chain operations.[46]

According to Handfield et al.,[47] sustainability does not have an impact on firms' search for quality. On the contrary, an operational strategy that is focused on quality is more likely to allow the successful implementation of a more sustainable value chain strategy.[48] According to Carter and Rogers,[49] high product quality could be the result of sustainability initiatives at chain level. However, high quality of products cannot be achieved unless the whole value chain is operating towards this sustainable objective.[50] In addition, Keeble et al.[51] state that quality is a key sustainable performance indicator and Ilbery and Maye[52] note that food chains are using quality as a means to address consumers' environmental anxiety. Similarly, Maloni and Brown[53] report that a responsible (in terms of protecting the environment) food chain should seriously consider the element of quality. As a result, the chain should pay great attention to product quality to obtain the title of a "sustainable value chain."[54]

A crucial aspect of quality in every food value chain is the concept of product conservation time. In the literature, this is usually referred to as "product shelf life."[55] We have avoided this term since it refers to packaged and ready-to-eat foods and to the length of time a packaged food will last without deteriorating.[56] In the case of a value chain, not all tiers deal with ready for consumption foods (e.g., breeders). Thus, different chain members have a different view of product conservation time and it is highly linked to the amount of waste that a value chain produces.[57]

In this vein, product conservation time is interrelated to food packaging, which is one of the key processes in the value chain.[58] Packaging contributes to the safe transportation of products in the value chain, to the better storage of products and to the marketing success of the product.[59] Good quality packaging could positively impact the economic performance of value chain members.[60] According to Heller and Keoleian,[61] packaging is an important sustainability issue and this is confirmed in numerous papers in the relevant literature.[62]

Another element highlighted in the sustainability literature is food traceability,[63] which is mandatory for every value chain since it allows its members to acquire information regarding the product flows. This information is crucial in the case of a food crisis for managing the product recall action.[64] Unfortunately, value chains face difficulties in the implementation of chain-wide traceability systems, as traceability is implemented separately between each value chain member. Traceability also deals with social sustainability since it aims to protect human health by maximizing the safety of food products.[65]

In a food value chain, the storage and delivery processes are of primary concern.[66] According to Lewis,[67] value chains should transport products while meeting sustainability requirements. Similarly, Gerbens-Leenes et al.[68] and Darnall et al.[69] argue that transportation links between value chain members impact sustainability, the environmental element in particular. In addition, the literature confirms the relationship between storage/delivery conditions in a value chain and sustainability elements.[70]

Aims and Objectives

The literature presents a large number of frameworks and indicators that help value chain managers adopt the principles of sustainability and improve the chain's sustainability value outcomes.[71] However, the examination of the various aspects of sustainability is a quite unique process according to the specific environmental, social and economic pressures that different value chains may face.[72] Sustainability issues may also differ between companies of the same business sector.[73] As a result, the various frameworks presented in the literature are highly specific and produce highly specific information that lacks generalizability and makes comparisons difficult. Caratti et al.[75] argue that there is lack of comparable and reliable information on sustainability performance. Moreover, and contrary to the large number of frameworks, Maloni and Brown[76] argue that empirical studies should examine if the firms are actively producing sustainability value outcomes. Similarly, Kolk[77] posits that there is a need to evaluate the firms' actual sustainability value outcomes rather than their sustainability policies. However, the empirical examination of the value chains should be done from a holistic perspective and not separately for each stage of the value chain.[78] Towards this notion, Handfield et al.[79] posit that any attempts to increase sustainability outcomes should be integrated into all the value chain stages.

This chapter will illustrate the degree of sustainability with which the Greek food value chain operates by using a number of sustainability value outcomes. We will focus on the key value chain members of the Greek food value chain (breeders, growers, growers' associations, manufacturers, wholesalers, importers, exporters and retailers) and we will investigate each category separately by comparing the value outcomes of the firms dealing with different food products. In our extended food value chain we included the following products: dairy, fruit, meat and vegetables. The evaluation of sustainability outcomes will be done in two stages: the first will evaluate the Greek food value chain as a whole and the second will evaluate each value chain category separately. By using a small number of sustainability value outcomes applicable to all food value chains and to all value chain stages, we can obtain insights regarding their sustainable performance compared to other similar value chains or value chain members. The current study will analyze sustainability issues in the Greek food value chain and will address the following research questions:

- Are there any differences in various sustainability value outcomes between various firms?
- Are there any firms that excel or underperform in their sustainability value outcomes?

Methodology

In order to examine these issues, we used a number of quantitative and qualitative value outcomes related to value chain sustainability. For this reason, we conducted a survey by using a structured questionnaire. According to Anderson and Narus,[80] this method is appropriate in cases of value assessment and it has been widely used in the past in similar studies.[81] The value outcomes were evaluated for every member of each food value chain and for the food value chain as a whole. The questionnaire used had two distinct sections. The first one included questions for the value outcomes of a food value chain regarding sustainability issues. The respondents were asked to evaluate their firm as a member of the food value chain in specific sustainability value outcomes. In total, six items were used for the assessment of sustainability value outcomes: waste, quality of products, product conservation time, consistency in the traceability system used, storage and delivery conditions, and the quality of the firm's product packaging. These outcomes were assessed using a seven-point Likert-type scale (1 = Very satisfying value outcome to 7 = Very unsatisfying value outcome), except for waste, which was assessed as a percentage (%) of the total turnover of a firm. The second section included the demographics of the food value chain members.

We chose to include firms from four key food sectors of the Greek food industry: dairy, fruits, meat and vegetables. The selection of these four food value chains is based on their high significance in the Greek food chain. These are the largest sectors in the Greek food value chain in terms of total number of companies involved, employment and production at upstream level (both primary production and manufacturing). In addition, they share big similarities within the downstream level (wholesale, retail) of the food chain.[82] We examined four members/stages of the Greek food value chain: breeders/growers/growers' associations, manufacturers, wholesalers/importers/exporters, and retailers. Since most of the firms in the Greek food value chain are SMEs, the appropriate respondent to our questionnaire was the general manager or the owner of the firm. Interviews were conducted by means of a Computer-Aided Personal Interviewing system (CAPI) and a total of 1,042 responses were obtained via a telephone survey and 1,015 questionnaires were analyzed. Table 25.1 provides the number of firms in every key food chain stage and their core product.

Results/Analysis

PROFILE OF THE RESPONDENTS' FIRMS

The profile of the respondent firms and their characteristics are illustrated in Table 25.2. Specifically, 16.16% of the sampling firms were first tier suppliers of the food value chain (breeders/growers/growers' associations), 22.96% of the firms were food manufacturers, 43.45% of the firms were in the wholesaling/importing/exporting business and 17.44% of the firms were retailers. The breeders and growers were family-based companies. The growers' associations operated with 28 employees on average whilst the rest of the chain members had various numbers of employees. Retailers employ the highest number of people (89). On average, the level of turnover was between €500,000 and €1,000,000 for the growers' associations and the manufacturers while wholesalers/importers/exporters had the highest average turnover (> €1,000,000). Growers' associations had the biggest warehouses and retailers the smallest and all the examined firms used trucks for their operations. The breeders/growers/growers' associations were grouped together as they showed similar behavior regarding their sustainable operational practices and because they are all first tier suppliers.

Table 25.1 Firms examined and key food products involved

Firm Food product	Breeders/growers/ growers' associations	Manufacturers	Wholesalers/ importers/exporters	Retailers	Total
Fruits	44	54	163	49	310
Dairy	35	75	70	49	229
Meat	47	79	104	20	250
Vegetables	38	25	104	59	226
Total	164	233	441	177	1015

Table 25.2 Profile of the respondent firms

Type of firm N = 1015 (% of the chain)	Breeders/growers/ growers' associations N = 164 (16.16%)		Manufacturers N = 233 (22.96%)	Wholesalers/ importers/ exporters N = 441 (43.45%)	Retailers N = 177 (17.44%)
	Breeders/ Growers N = 45	Growers' Assoc. N = 119			
Number of employees (mean)	Family-based	28	41	23	89
Turnover (more frequent responses in relevant groups, in Euros)	40,000–50,000[a]	500,000–1,000,000	500,000–1,000,000	> 1,000,000	200,000–500,000
Size of warehouses (in sq.m.) (mean)	N/A (61.6)[b]	3,587	2,488	1,747	610
Number of trucks (mean)	5[c]	4	6	6	3

[a] Annual income [b] Farm size in hectares [c] Number of agricultural trucks

VALUE OUTCOMES FOR FOOD CHAIN SUSTAINABILITY

Table 25.3 provides a summary of means and standard deviations for the six value outcomes regarding sustainability issues in the Greek food value chain. We obtained the average score in each value outcome for every member (i.e., breeders/growers/growers' associations, manufacturers, wholesalers/importers/exporters and retailers) and for the food value chain as a whole. The average value outcomes indicate that the food industry had moderate product wastage rates that represented almost 6% of the turnover. The respondents were very satisfied with the storage and delivery conditions (average score: 1.69) and quite satisfied with their quality (2.20). Since we were examining a food value chain, consistency in the traceability system used was expected to be higher than the average of 2.13. Product conservation time had the worst score (3.56) of all the examined value outcomes, followed by quality of packaging (2.93). The average scores for breeders/growers/growers' associations of our sample were similar to the scores for the whole chain.

The results showed that food manufacturers were operating in a quite sustainable way. They had scores of below 2 in three out of the six value outcomes examined (consistency in the traceability system used, storage and delivery conditions and quality of packaging). However, conservation time was the main sustainability issue where manufacturers were not satisfied with the value outcome (3.11). The average scores for wholesalers were quite similar to those of the whole value chain, whereas retailers showed low sustainability value outcomes for packaging (4.01), product conservation time (3.84) and traceability (2.51).

Table 25.3 Average sustainability value outcomes of the Greek food value chain and its members

Value outcome	Waste[a] Mean (SD)	Quality of product[b] Mean (SD)	Product conservation time[b] Mean (SD)	Consistency in traceability system used[b] Mean (SD)	Storage & delivery conditions[b] Mean (SD)	Quality of product packaging[b] Mean (SD)
Chain member						
Food value chain mean	5.72 (6.30)	2.20 (2.05)	3.56 (2.16)	2.13 (1.68)	1.69 (1.09)	2.93 (2.34)
Fruit (N = 44)	6.76 (6.83)	2.50 (2.04)	3.23 (2.03)	2.39 (1.90)	2.05 (1.14)	2.66 (2.28)
Dairy (N = 35)	5.05 (6.49)	3.11 (2.99)	4.11 (2.34)	2.51 (2.15)	1.77 (1.19)	2.94 (2.33)
Meat N = 47)	5.18 (6.29)	1.94 (1.76)	3.96 (2.15)	2.28 (1.79)	1.45 (0.72)	3.89 (2.71)
Vegetables (N = 38)	6.11 (8.06)	2.11 (1.81)	3.74 (2.31)	2.24 (2.01)	1.97 (1.39)	2.21 (1.76)
4 chains mean (N = 164)	5.86 (6.98)	2.38 (2.19)	3.74 (2.20)	2.35 (1.93)	1.80 (1.13)	2.97 (2.39)
Fruit (N = 54)	8.17 (8.15)	1.76 (1.37)	3.15 (1.84)	1.93 (1.56)	1.78 (1.11)	1.87 (1.26)
Dairy (N = 75)	3.76 (4.46)	2.56 (2.56)	2.79 (1.90)	1.91 (1.57)	1.47 (0.79)	1.80 (1.26)
Meat (N = 79)	5.74 (7.24)	1.68 (1.30)	3.49 (2.40)	1.81 (1.52)	1.53 (0.92)	2.15 (1.78)
Vegetables (N = 25)	7.82 (9.98)	2.76 (2.49)	2.76 (2.13)	1.72 (1.28)	1.68 (0.90)	1.40 (0.71)
4 chains mean (N = 233)	5.83 (7.22)	2.10 (1.98)	3.11 (2.10)	1.86 (1.52)	1.58 (0.93)	1.89 (1.43)
Fruit (N = 163)	7.32 (6.21)	2.13 (1.80)	3.85 (1.84)	2.24 (1.53)	1.82 (1.20)	2.89 (2.24)
Dairy (N = 70)	4.15 (3.19)	2.77 (2.56)	2.93 (1.76)	1.87 (1.42)	1.54 (1.14)	2.67 (2.29)
Meat (N = 104)	3.74 (4.03)	2.03 (1.91)	3.14 (2.30)	2.00 (1.56)	1.56 (0.99)	3.04 (2.40)
Vegetables (N = 104)	6.56 (7.46)	2.58 (2.40)	2.88 (2.07)	1.89 (1.39)	1.65 (1.12)	3.06 (2.49)
4 chains mean (N = 441)	5.80 (5.99)	2.32 (2.12)	3.31 (2.04)	2.04 (1.49)	1.67 (1.13)	2.93 (2.34)

Row groups (left side labels): Breeders/growers/growers' associations (Fruit N=44 through 4 chains mean N=164); Manufacturers (Fruit N=54 through 4 chains mean N=233); Wholesalers/importers/exporters (Fruit N=163 through 4 chains mean N=441).

Table 25.3 *Concluded*

Retailers	Fruits (N = 49)	5.77 (3.42)	1.63 (1.29)	3.96 (2.23)	2.20 (1.62)	1.80 (1.06)	4.35 (2.65)
	Dairy (N = 49)	2.96 (2.23)	1.67 (1.31)	3.53 (2.04)	2.24 (1.88)	1.63 (0.95)	3.57 (2.63)
	Meat (N = 20)	6.30 (9.33)	3.20 (2.65)	3.95 (2.40)	3.35 (2.43)	1.70 (0.80)	3.95 (2.44)
	Vegetables (N = 59)	7.68 (6.78)	2.29 (2.15)	3.95 (2.10)	2.69 (2.08)	2.02 (1.36)	4.10 (2.50)
	4 chains mean (N = 177)	5.97 (6.09)	2.04 (1.86)	3.84 (2.14)	2.51 (1.97)	1.81 (1.12)	4.01 (2.57)

[a] % of turnover [b] Seven-point Likert scale (lower values indicate higher value outcome)

DIFFERENCES IN SUSTAINABILITY VALUE OUTCOMES BETWEEN FIRMS

One of our objectives was the investigation of possible differences in the sustainability value outcomes for each chain member and for different products. For this reason, Analysis of Variance (ANOVA) was employed in order to determine whether any significant score differences existed between firms of different products. We chose ANOVA for our analysis because it is a widely used statistical method for this kind of investigation and many examples can be found in the relevant literature where appropriate metrics are analyzed for value chain operations.[83] Table 25.4 illustrates significant differences in the sustainability value outcomes for various members, with wholesalers demonstrating most differences in value outcomes (i.e., waste, quality of product and product conservation time). Two sustainability value outcomes (i.e., storage and delivery conditions, consistency in traceability system used) did not show any significant differences. Regarding the first one, the results indicate that all chain members examined are very careful during the transportation of products. However, the results also indicate that there are common trends regarding traceability that firms follow regardless of the food chain.

Table 25.4 **Differences in sustainability value outcomes between firms**

	Waste[a] ANOVA F-Statistic[c] (Sig.)	Quality of product[b] ANOVA F-Statistic[c] (Sig.)	Product conservation time[b] ANOVA F-Statistic[c] (Sig.)	Consistency in traceability system used[b] ANOVA F-Statistic[c] (Sig.)	Storage & delivery conditions[b] ANOVA F-Statistic[c] (Sig.)	Quality of product packaging[b] ANOVA F-Statistic[c] (Sig.)
Breeders/growers/ growers' associations (N = 164)						4.108 (0.01)
Manufacturers (N = 233)		4.119 (0.01)				
Wholesalers/ importers/ exporters (N = 441)	5.294 (0.00)	2.662 (0.05)	6.739 (0.00)			
Retailers (N = 177)	3.158 (0.03)	4.632 (0.00)				

[a] % of turnover [b] Seven-point Likert scale (lower values indicate higher value outcome) [c] $p < 0.05$

Breeders/growers/growers' associations expressed significantly different value outcomes only in the case of quality of product packaging. Table 25.3 presents the differences in the means of firms dealing with each product category. The results showed a significantly low level of quality of product packaging in the case of meat breeders (3.89). A moderate level value outcome for packaging was presented only the vegetables growers/growers' associations showed a moderate value outcome for packaging (2.21). The combined results of Table 25.3 and Table 25.4 clearly show that the quality of packaging is better in the case of growers/growers' associations and worse in the case of breeders. This indicates that some food safety and thus health issues may arise for breeders due to bad packaging.

Food manufacturers showed significant differences in the quality of product. In particular, manufacturers of fruit and meat products had significantly better outcomes (1.76 and 1.68 respectively) than manufacturers of vegetables and dairy products (2.76 and 2.56 respectively). The difference is a significant one and these quality problems for dairy and vegetables manufacturers could have an impact on sustainability elements by incurring economic losses and creating waste, and may even raise food safety issues.

Wholesalers/importers/exporters was the firm category with the biggest number of respondents (N = 441) and presented the most significant differences in the sustainability value outcomes. Regarding waste, the firms dealing with meat and dairy products showed low levels of product wastage (3.74 and 4.15 respectively) and had significantly different outcomes than vegetable and fruit firms (6.56 and 7.32 respectively). These results are probably related to the fact that meat and dairy firms have more options for further using their low quality meat and dairy parts (e.g., for processed meat products, ice creams, etc.). In addition, these parts can be processed in conditions of high (pasteurization) or very low (frozen meat) temperature in order to be preserved. These conditions can not be as easily applied to fruit and vegetables without damaging the product. Quality of products was another sustainability issue in which wholesalers/importers/exporters showed significant differences. Dairy firms had the worst score in product quality (2.77) and then followed the moderate product quality level of dairy breeders and dairy manufacturers. It is worth mentioning that wholesalers/importers/exporters were not very satisfied with the quality of their products (all average scores > 2). Dairy products are quite perishable and low quality could result in safety issues and product recalls. Product conservation time was the primary problem for this category, especially for the fruit wholesalers/importers/exporters (3.85). The firms dealing with vegetables and dairy products had lower scores (2.88 and 2.93 respectively) but the respondents are clearly not satisfied with their value outcome.

Retailers showed differences in the outcomes of waste and product quality. Dairy firms had by far the best score for waste (2.96) and this may be related to the market practice of returning dairy products (especially milk) to manufacturers. By contrast, retailers selling vegetables had the worst score (7.68), which represents a significant amount of turnover and equates to large economic losses. Fruit and dairy retailers evaluated the quality of their products quite highly (1.63 and 1.67 respectively) while meat retailers showed a very bad score for this value outcome (3.20). This result suggests that the meat value chain is quite vulnerable and there are significant problems in its operations.

SUSTAINABILITY VALUE OUTCOME ANALYSIS PER AVERAGE CHAIN MEMBER

The previous results illustrated the differences in sustainability value outcomes for various firms. We investigated further the differences between firms dealing with different food products and the members' average results. To show these differences, we employed a T-test analysis and the results are presented in Table 25.5.

In the examined group of breeders/growers/growers' associations, only the meat and vegetable firms showed significantly different value outcomes in sustainability issues. In particular, meat firms had a better score in storage and delivery conditions (1.45 compared to the category average of 1.80). By contrast, meat firms showed much poorer quality of packaging than the category average (3.89 compared to category average of 2.97). In addition, vegetable growers and growers' associations had a much better than average packaging value outcome (2.21), which means that the primary vegetable producers offered more standardized food products than the average member.

Moreover, the results showed that dairy manufacturers had lower waste than other firms in the category (3.76 compared to the category average of 5.83). In addition, meat manufacturers evaluated better the quality of their products (1.68 in comparison to the category average of 2.10). Moreover, vegetable manufacturers enjoyed better packaging than average (1.40 compared to the category average of 1.89).

Wholesalers/importers/exporters provided most of the cases of food chain members that had significantly different sustainability value outcomes than the average chain member. Regarding waste, fruit firms showed higher levels of product wastage than the other food wholesalers/importers/exporters (7.32 compared to the category of average 5.80). On the other hand, meat and dairy firms showed that they could handle waste more effectively and they had better than average scores (3.74 and 4.15 respectively). The other significant differences that were detected concerned product conservation time. Firms dealing with fruit evaluated it as worse than average (3.85 compared to the category average of 3.31). This could mean that they dealt mainly with fresh fruits which are vulnerable to environmental conditions. By contrast, vegetable wholesalers/importers/exporters had better scores in product conservation time than the average (2.88), which may indicate that the specific firms mainly dealt with frozen vegetables that could be better preserved.

Finally, dairy retailers showed better scores in the case of waste as well. More specifically, their score for waste was 2.96 whilst the category average was 5.97. The retailers selling fruit evaluated the quality of their products as better than the category's average (1.63 compared to 2.04). Our sample mostly included small retailers trying to compete with bigger players by focusing on the quality of their fruits and not on the cost issues.

Table 25.5 Sustainability value outcome analysis for firms compared to average chain member

		Waste[a] Mean (T-test)[c]	Quality of product[b] Mean (T-test)[c]	Product conservation time[b] Mean (T-test)[c]	Consistency in traceability system used[b] Mean (T-test)[c]	Storage & delivery conditions[b] Mean (T-test)[c]	Quality for product packaging[b] Mean (T-test)[c]
Breeders/growers/ growers' associations	Fruit (N = 44)						
	Dairy (N = 35)						
	Meat (N = 47)					1.45 (t = -3.379)	3.89 (t = 2.334)
	Vegetables (N = 38)						2.21 (t = -2.663)
	4 chains mean (N = 164)					1.80	2.97
Manufacturers	Fruit (N = 54)						
	Dairy (N = 75)	3.76 (t = -3.005)					
	Meat (N = 79)		1.68 (t = -2.855)				
	Vegetables (N = 25)						1.40 (t = -3.465)
	4 chains mean (N = 233)	5.83	2.10				1.89
Wholesalers/importers/ exporters	Fruit (N = 163)	7.32 (t = 2.163)		3.85 (t = 3.773)			
	Dairy (N = 70)	4.15 (t = -3.019)					
	Meat (N = 104)	3.74 (t = -3.756)					
	Vegetables (N = 104)			2.88 (t = -2.148)			
	4 chains mean (N = 441)	5.80		3.31			
Retailers	Fruit (N = 49)		1.63 (t = -2.217)				
	Dairy (N = 49)		2.96 (t = -6.494)				
	Meat (N = 20)						
	Vegetables (N = 59)						
	4 chains mean (N = 177)	5.97	2.04				

[a] % of turnover [b] Seven-point Likert scale (lower values indicate higher value outcome) [c] $p < 0.05$

Discussion, Implications for Practitioners and Research Limitations

The results of our study revealed that the Greek food value chain was not very successful in dealing with the sustainability issues examined. The worst value outcome was related to product conservation time. This is not a surprising result since managing perishable food products is a very challenging task. However, the fact that breeders/growers/ growers' associations have the worst outcome in this sustainability issue could mean that conservation time is not adequately managed at the very beginning of the value chain operation and as a result it puts pressure on the chain members until the food reaches the final consumer. Waste was as much as 6% of the average firm's turnover, which is a significant loss of revenues. Part of the problem could be the moderate results of the packaging outcome, which indicated that food was treated more as a commodity rather than being processed with value added activities. The outcomes of quality and traceability also required improvements.

Breeders/growers/growers' associations seem to suffer from moderate value outcomes that caused the whole value chain to underperform. The results revealed significant and large differences in specific value outcomes between the primary producers. For example, meat breeders had a very satisfying outcome for storage and delivery conditions but at the same time they noted bad packaging practices. A possible explanation could be the traditional character of the Greek food value chain, which treats products as commodities. Hence, value adding activities such as packaging in the early stages of the value chain are neglected.

The results showed that manufacturers operated in a sustainable way. In addition, the average value outcomes show that manufacturers play a key role in improving the sustainable operation of the Greek food value chain. Thus, they showed some cases of best practice such as the low levels of waste (dairy manufacturers) and the high quality of packaging (vegetable manufacturers). Food manufacturing is the top manufacturing activity in the Greek economy[84] and it could use its expertise, know-how and ability to support other small value chain members, such as the primary producers.

The value outcomes for wholesalers/importers/exporters were very close to the outcomes of the food value chain as a whole. The combined results of the average scores, the ANOVA analysis and the T-test revealed that dairy and meat wholesalers/importers/ exporters showed high value outcomes, particularly for product wastage, quality and conservation time. The fact that the dairy sector includes some of the largest food companies in the country (e.g., Vivartia group, FAGE S.A., Nestlé Hellas S.A., MEVGAL S.A. and others)[85] could mean that they exercise better control over their distribution channels in sustainability issues.

Retailers had low scores for consistency in the traceability system used, and this is disappointing. The results were divided in two groups: the group of fruit and dairy retailers operated in a more sustainable way and the group of meat and vegetable retailers operated in a less sustainable way. Their differences were particularly related to the amount of product wastage and the quality of products. The poor results of the meat chain could be explained by the fact that the Greek consumers buy meat mainly from local butchers that disregard sustainability issues.[86] In the case of vegetables, waste and quality had low value outcomes and this could indicate that retailers were supplied with vegetables of poor quality.

The results of our study could be of particular importance to managers, practitioners and industry professionals. In general, firms dealing with fruit and dairy products had better sustainability value outcomes. On the other hand, firms that were members of the vegetable value chain had worse sustainability value outcomes. This means that the members of the vegetable value chain should implement improvement programmes in order to get better value outcomes in key areas of sustainability. The results showed that the whole Greek food value chain needs to improve its sustainable operations. These improvements should be based on the practices of the firms that excel on specific value outcomes in each value chain member category. In general, the results showed that sustainability is an underdeveloped area in the Greek food value chain. This could be the reason for significant food scandals in the past (e.g., contamination of Greek yoghurt).[87] Although, it would be of great value to examine scandals and debates in the Greek food sector, it is beyond the scope of this chapter. However, the results revealed a significant problem in the Greek food chain – first tier producers are disconnected from the rest of the chain and this creates sustainability problems along the whole food chain. This result is of great importance for all members of the food value chain because it creates problems in the creation and transfer of value from the primary producers towards the downstream food chain members. As a result a value problem is created in the very beginning of the food value chain and this is where the practitioners should focus.

The comparative analysis revealed the differences between firms dealing with various products and it provides insights regarding sustainability issues where every company should focus its efforts. Ideally, firms should follow the practices of high-performing companies. Thus, the results of the ANOVA and T-test analysis could be used as benchmark points and could guide companies towards achieving better sustainability value outcomes. Moreover, our study revealed sustainability successes and failures related to specific members and possible value outcome gaps were revealed. Modifications in the value chain strategy could enable firms to reach the value outcomes of their category champions.

Members of each category did not show any differences in the traceability issue, indicating similar practices in each category. In addition, an increase of packaging quality, especially for the upstream value chain members, is essential for the reduction of many sustainability problems that could occur before the food reaches the final consumer (e.g., waste, economic losses, food safety). Managers should also pay attention to quality since it could be the source of economic losses and it could also be related to risks and to potential increased vulnerability of the whole chain.

There are a few limitations of this study. The most important one is the relatively small number of sustainability value outcomes that were used. Also, we should note the relative large number of wholesalers/importers/exporters in our sample. In fact, it has been very challenging to guarantee equal representation for all categories in our sample. Nevertheless, we are confident that our survey has provided a balanced analysis of the Greek food value chain. Because we invited the respondent firms to self-evaluate their firm's perceived sustainability value outcomes, it is possible that the results suffer from respondent bias because we invited the respondent firms to self-evaluate their sustainability value outcomes. However, a similar approach has been followed by several studies in the past and resulted in the generation of very insightful findings.[88] Future studies may also take into consideration the opinion of non-firm respondents in order to further validate the results. Moreover, our sample included many small retailers and this could have negative results regarding the evaluation of the sustainability value outcomes for this group. Finally, our study examined only four key sectors of the Greek food chain: dairy, fruit, meat, vegetables. Although these sectors are very significant in the Greek food value chain, future work could consider other sectors too and illustrate their strengths and weaknesses.

Generalizing our results should be done with caution. The sustainability issues raised above refer to the Greek food value chain and could give useful insights for food value chains dominated by small and medium-sized enterprises. But it would be interesting to examine also food value chains where larger firms operate, and detect possible differences between the results. The examination of sustainability may differ according to the characteristics and specifically the environmental, social and economic pressures that each business sector may face.[89] Thus, the examination of possible differences in sustainability outcomes between different sectors could give interesting insights. Similarly, countries with different characteristics than Greece in terms of environmental, social and economic conditions may need to be examined under different perspectives using different sustainability indicators. In addition, the current Greek financial crisis should be taken into consideration when examining the sustainability of the Greek food value chain. As we previously noted, the Greek food value chain as a whole performs poorly in key sustainability outcomes. It is possible that managers focus their efforts on achieving short-term economic results and thus, long-term sustainability issues are undermined. Future research should also examine the role of the financial crisis in the sustainability outcomes of value chains. However, the overall poor sustainability value outcomes of the Greek food value chain could be attributed to the weak regulations characteristic of the Mediterranean countries.

Conclusions

In our chapter, we evaluated the sustainability value outcomes of the Greek food value chain and examined the differences between the value outcomes of various members of the chain according to four food product groups. It is clear that many improvements are required in this chain in order for it to become more sustainable. Firms dealing with vegetables had clearly the worst scores in sustainability indicators and members should modify their strategy according to the successful sustainable practices of fruit and dairy firms.

There was no member that excelled in the sustainability value outcomes and overall, the issues of product conservation time, traceability and packaging demand great improvements. Food manufacturers presented rather good scores in sustainability operations. Similarly, best practices can be transferred for waste (dairy firms), quality of products (meat firms) and packaging (vegetable firms). Wholesalers/importers/exporters should treat their products more carefully during distribution in order to decrease product wastage. Finally, the low performance of retailers in sustainability issues endangered the total value outcome of the whole food value chain.

The last point is of great importance. In our chapter we examined the perceived performance of the key value chain members in sustainability outcomes. In this way, managers may obtain insights regarding the sustainability issues in which they underperform and thus, they could find ways to improve them. However, other food chain members may further harm the three elements of the triple bottom line approach.[90] Consequently, managers should also take into consideration the performance of the upstream and downstream value chain members in order to examine sustainability under a holistic approach and implement sustainability strategies for the entire food value chain. Hence, the process of evaluating a value chain's sustainability as a whole should result in compatible information.[91] Different industries have potentially different and unique value chains[92] and comparing sustainability value outcomes may demand a different approach even for companies of the same business sector.[93] However, the use of a common group of sustainability indicators such as the ones used in our study allows comparisons and may possibly detect weak links in the sustainability value outcomes of a value chain. Thus, the various sustainability frameworks should be specific according to the environmental, social and economic priorities of every value chain but should also have a common denominator that could allow useful comparisons to be made.

Notes

1   Seuring, S. & Müller, M. (2008), "From a literature review to a conceptual framework for sustainable supply chain management", *Journal of Cleaner Production*, Vol. 16, No. 15, 1699–1710.

2   Carter, C. R. & Rogers, D. S. (2008), "A framework of sustainable supply chain management: moving toward new theory", *International Journal of Physical Distribution and Logistics Management*, Vol. 38, No. 5, 360–387.

3   Wognum, P. M., Bremmers, H., Trienekens, J. H., van der Vorst, J. G. A. J. & Bloemhof, J. M. (2011), "Systems for sustainability and transparency of food supply chains: current status and challenges", *Advanced Engineering Informatics*, Vol. 25, No. 1, 65–76.

4   Maloni, M. J. & Brown, M. E. (2006), "Corporate social responsibility in the supply chain: an application in the food industry", *Journal of Business Ethics*, Vol. 68, 35–52.

5   Maloni & Brown, *op. cit.*

6   Wognum, Bremmers, Trienekens, van der Vorst & Bloemhof, *op. cit.*

7   Gerbens-Leenes, P. W., Moll, H. C. & Uiterkamp, A. J. M. S. (2003), "Design and development of a measuring method for environmental sustainability in food production systems", *Ecological Economics*, Vol. 46, 231–248.

8   Seuring & Müller, *op. cit.*

9   Gerbens-Leenes, Moll & Uiterkamp, *op. cit.*

10   Carter & Rogers, *op. cit.*; Maloni & Brown, *op. cit.*; Gerbens-Leenes, Moll & Uiterkamp, *op. cit.*; Handfield, R. B., Walton, S. V., Seegers, L. K. & Melnyk, S. A. (1997), "Green value chain practices in the furniture industry", *Journal of Operations Management*, Vol. 15, No. 4, 293–315.

11   ICAP Hellas (2007a), *The Greek dairy sector*, ICAP Hellas, Athens; ICAP Hellas (2007b), *The Greek meat sector*, ICAP Hellas, Athens; ICAP Hellas (2007c), *The Greek canned fruit and vegetables sector*, ICAP Hellas, Athens.

12   Matopoulos, A., Vlachopoulou, M. & Manthou, V. (2007), "Exploring the impact of e-business adoption on logistics processes: empirical evidence from the food industry", *International Journal of Logistics: Research and Application*, Vol. 10, No. 2, 109–122.

13   Bourlakis, M. & Bourlakis, C. (2001), "Deliberate and emergent logistics strategies in food retailing: a case study of the Greek multiple food retail sector", *Supply Chain Management: An International Journal*, Vol. 6, No. 3/4, 189–200; Menachof, D., Bourlakis, M. & Makios, T.

(2009), Tracing the order lead-time of grocery retailers in the UK and Greek markets, *Supply Chain Management: An International Journal*, Vol. 14, No. 5, 349–358; Tatsis, V., Mena C., Van Wassenhove, L.N. & Whickler, L. (2006), E-procurement in the Greek food and drink industry: drivers and impediments, *Journal of Purchasing and Supply Management*, Vol. 12, 63–74.

14   Manoliadis, O., Tsolas, I. & Nakou, A. (2006), "Sustainable construction and drivers of change in Greece: a Delphi study", *Construction Management and Economics*, Vol. 24, 113–120.

15   Islam, S.M.F., Papadopoulou, H. & Manos, B. (2003), "Ecological sustainability in Greek agriculture: an application of energy flow approach", *Journal of Environmental Planning and Management*, Vol. 46, No. 6, 875–886.

16   Gerakis, A. & Kalburtji, K. (1998), "Agricultural activities affecting the functions and values of Ramsar wetland sites of Greece", *Agriculture, Ecosystems and Environment*, Vol. 70, 119–128.

17   Vogel, D. (2003), "The Hare and the Tortoise revisited: the new politics of consumer and environmental regulation in Europe", *British Journal of Political Science*, Vol. 33, No. 4, 557–580.

18   Kassolis, M.G. (2007), "The diffusion of environmental management in Greece through rationalist approaches: driver or product of globalization?", *Journal of Cleaner Production*, Vol. 15, 1886–1893.

19   Den Boer J., Den Boer, E. & Jager, J. (2007), "LCA-IWM: a decision support tool for sustainability assessment of waste management systems", *Waste Management*, Vol. 27, 1032–1045.

20   Chalikias, M. S., Kyriakopoulos, G. & Kolovos, K. G. (2010), "Environmental sustainability and financial feasibility evaluation of woodfuel biomass used for potential replacement of conventional space heating sources. Part I: Greek case study", *Operational Research*, Vol. 10, No. 1, 43–56.

21   Lekakis, J. (2000), "Environmental policy-making in Greece: examining the interaction of bureaucratic and academic cultures", *Journal of Environmental Policy & Planning*, Vol. 2, 69–86.

22   Gerbens-Leenes, Moll & Uiterkamp, *op. cit.*

23   Lewis, H. (2005), "Defining product stewardship and sustainability in the Australian packaging industry", *Environmental Science & Policy*, Vol. 8, No. 1, 45–55.

24   Handfield, Walton, Seegers & Melnyk, *op. cit.*

25   Lewis, *op. cit.*

26   Gerbens-Leenes, Moll & Uiterkamp, *op. cit.*

27   Handfield, R., Walton, S. V., Sroufe, R. & Melnyk, S. A. (2002), "Applying environmental criteria to supplier assessment: a study in the application of the Analytical Hierarchy Process", *European Journal of Operational Research*, Vol. 141, No. 1, 70–87.

28   Handfield, Walton, Seegers & Melnyk, *op. cit.*

29   Horvath, L. (2001), "Collaboration: the key to value creation in supply chain management", *Supply Chain Management: An International Journal*, Vol. 6, No. 5, 205–207.

30   Seuring & Müller, *op. cit.*

31   Carter & Rogers, *op. cit.*

32   Maloni & Brown, *op. cit.*

33   Aramyan, L., Ondersteijn, C., VanKooten, O. & Lansink, A. O. (2006), "Performance indicators in agri-food production chains". In C. Ondersteijn, J. H. M. Wijnands, R. B. M. Huirne & O. Van Kooten (eds.), *Quantifying the Agri-Food Supply Chain* (pp. 47–64): Springer; Van der Vorst, J. G. A. J. (2006), "Performance measurement in agri-food supply chain networks. An overview". In C. Ondersteijn, J. H. M. Wijnands, R. B. M. Huirne & O. VanKooten (eds.), *Quantifying the Agri-Food Supply Chain* (pp. 13–2): Springer.

34   Gerbens-Leenes, Moll & Uiterkamp, *op. cit.*

35   Wognum, Bremmers, Trienekens, van der Vorst & Bloemhof, *op. cit.*

36   Wognum, Bremmers, Trienekens, van der Vorst & Bloemhof, *op. cit.*

37   Maloni & Brown, *op. cit.*

38   Lee, Ch. Y., Seddon, P. & Corbitt, B. (1999), "Evaluating the business value of internet-based business to business electronic commerce". *Proceedings of the 10th Australasian Conference on Information Systems*, pp. 508–519.

39   Lindgreen A. & Wynstra, F. (2005), "Value in business markets: What do we know? Where are we going?", *Industrial Marketing Management*, Vol. 34, 732–748.

40   Maloni & Brown, *op. cit.*

41   Handfield, Walton, Sroufe & Melnyk, *op. cit.*

42   Handfield, Walton, Sroufe & Melnyk, *op. cit.*

43   Darnall, N., Jolley, G. J. & Handfield, R. (2008), "Environmental management systems and green supply chain management: complements for sustainability?", *Business Strategy and the Environment*, Vol. 17, No. 1, 30–45.

44   Sarkis, J. (2001), "Manufacturing's role in corporate environmental sustainability", *International Journal of Operations & Production Management*, Vol. 21, No. 5/6, 666–686.

45   Handfield, Walton, Seegers & Melnyk, *op. cit.*

46   Gunasekaran, A. & Kobu, B. (2007), "Performance measures and metrics in logistics and supply chain management: a review of recent literature for research and applications", *International Journal of Production Research*, Vol. 45, No. 12, 2819–2840; Shepherd, C. & Günter, H. (2006), "Measuring supply chain performance: current research and future directions", *International Journal of Productivity and Performance Management*, Vol. 55, No. 3/4, 242–258; Gunasekaran, A., Patel, C. & Tirtiroglu, E. (2001), "Performance measures and metrics in a supply chain environment", *International Journal of Operations and Production Management*, Vol. 21, No. 1/2, 71–87; Neely, A., Gregory, M. & Platts, K. (1995), "Performance measurement system design: a literature review and research agenda", *International Journal of Operations and Production Management*, Vol. 25, No. 12, 1228–1263.

47   Handfield, Walton, Sroufe & Melnyk, *op. cit.*

48   Angell, L. C. & Klassen, R. D. (1999), "Integrating environmental issues into the mainstream: an agenda for research in operations management", *Journal of Operations Management*, Vol. 17, No. 5, 575–598.

49   Carter & Rogers, *op. cit.*

50   Darnall, Jolley & Handfield, *op. cit.*

51   Keeble, J. J., Topiol, S. & Berkeley, S. (2003), "Using indicators to measure sustainability performance at a corporate and project level", *Journal of Business Ethics*, Vol. 44, No. 2, 149–158.

52   Ilbery, B. & Maye, D. (2005), "Food supply chains and sustainability: evidence from specialist food producers in the Scottish/English borders", *Land Use Policy*, Vol. 22, No. 4, 331–344.

53   Maloni & Brown, *op. cit.*

54   Seuring & Müller, *op. cit.*

55   Aramyan, L. H., Lansink, A. G. J. M. O., Van der Vorst, J. G. A. J. & Van Kooten, O. (2007), "Performance measurement in agri-food supply chains: a case study", *Supply Chain Management: An International Journal*, Vol. 12, No. 4, 304–315; Van der Vorst, *op. cit.*

56   Aramyan, Lansink, Van der Vorst & Van Kooten, *op. cit.*

57   Heller, M. C. & Keoleian, G. A. (2003), "Assessing the sustainability of the US food system: a life cycle perspective", *Agricultural Systems*, Vol. 76, No. 3, 1007–1041.

58   Handfield, Walton, Seegers & Melnyk, *op. cit.*

59 Lewis, *op. cit.*

60 Tracey, M., Lim, J. S. & Vonderembse, M. A. (2005), "The impact of supply-chain management capabilities on business performance", *Supply Chain Management: An International Journal*, Vol. 10, No. 3, 179–191.

61 Heller & Keoleian, *op. cit.*

62 Carter & Rogers, *op. cit.*; Darnall, Jolley & Handfield, *op. cit.*; Maloni & Brown, *op. cit.*; Lewis, *op. cit.*; Heller & Keoleian *op. cit.*; Handfield, Walton, Sroufe & Melnyk, *op. cit.*; Sarkis, *op. cit.*; Handfield, Walton, Seegers & Melnyk, *op. cit.*

63 Wognum, Bremmers, Trienekens, van der Vorst & Bloemhof, *op. cit.*

64 Dabbene, F. & Gay, P. (2011), "Food traceability systems: performance evaluation and optimization", *Computers and Electronics in Agriculture*, Vol. 75, No. 1, 139–146.

65 Wognum, Bremmers, Trienekens, van der Vorst & Bloemhof, *op. cit.*

66 Dabbene & Gay, *op. cit.*

67 Lewis, *op. cit.*

68 Gerbens-Leenes, Moll & Uiterkamp, *op. cit.*

69 Darnall, Jolley & Handfield, *op. cit.*

70 Carter & Rogers, *op. cit.*; Maloni & Brown, *op. cit.*; Heller & Keoleian, *op. cit.*; Keeble, Topiol & Berkeley, *op. cit.*

71 Carter & Rogers, *op. cit.*; Gerbens-Leenes, Moll & Uiterkamp, *op. cit.*

72 Maloni & Brown, *op. cit.*; Gerbens-Leenes, Moll & Uiterkamp, *op. cit.*

73 Gerbens-Leenes, Moll & Uiterkamp, *op. cit.*

74 Gerbens-Leenes, Moll & Uiterkamp, *op. cit.*

75 Caratti, P., Ravetz, J., Alvarez, M. & Schade, W. (2005), "Bringing Sustainable Development vision into evaluation practice: a 'flexible framework' toolkit for assessing and benchmarking sustainability performance of European regions", *EASY-ECO Conference*, Research Institute for Managing Sustainability, 15–1 7 June, Manchester.

76 Maloni & Brown, *op. cit.*

77 Kolk, A. (2004), "A decade of sustainability reporting: developments and significance", *International Journal of Environment and Sustainable Development*, Vol. 3, No. 1, 51–64.

78 Heller & Keoleian *op. cit.*

79 Handfield, Walton, Seegers & Melnyk, *op. cit.*

80 Anderson, J. C. & Narus, J. A. (1998), "Business marketing: understand what customers value", *Harvard Business Review*, Vol. 76, No. 6, 53–65.

81 Molnar, A. & Gellynk, X. (2009), "Performance imbalances in the chain: EU traditional food sector". *APSTRACT: Applied Studies in Agribusiness and Commerce*, 3; Chow, W. S., Madu, C. N., Kuei Ch., Lu, M. H., Lin, Ch. & Tseng, H. (2008), "Supply chain management in the US and Taiwan: an empirical study", *Omega*, Vol. 36, 665–679; Lai, K., Ngai, E. W. T. & Cheng, T. C. E. (2004), "An empirical study of supply chain performance in transport logistics" *International Journal of Production Economics*, Vol. 87, 321–333.

82 ICAP Hellas (2007a), *op. cit.*; ICAP Hellas (2007b), *op. cit.*; ICAP Hellas (2007c), *op. cit.*

83 Greer, B. & Ford, M. (2009), "Managing change in supply chains: a process comparison", *Journal of Business Logistics*, Vol. 30, No. 2, 47–63; Kahn, K., Maltz, E. & Mentzer, J. (2006), "Demand collaboration: effects on knowledge creation, relationships, and supply chain performance", *Journal of Business Logistics*, Vol. 27, No. 2, 191–221.

84 Matopoulos, Vlachopoulou & Manthou, *op. cit.*

85 ICAP Hellas (2007a), *op. cit.*

86 Krystallis, A., Chryssochoidis, G. & Scholderer, J. (2007), "Consumer-perceived quality in 'traditional' food chains: the case of the Greek meat supply chain", *Appetite*, Vol. 48, 54–68.

87 Van Kleef, E., Houghton, J. R., Krystallis, A., Pfenning, U., Rowe, G., Van Dijk, H., et al. (2007), "Consumer evaluations of food risk management quality in Europe", *Risk Analysis,* Vol. 27, No. 6, 1565–1580.

88 Tan, K. C. (2002), "Supply chain management: practices, concerns and performance issues", *The Journal of Supply Chain Management*, Vol. 38, No. 1, 42–53; Gunasekaran, Patel & Tirtiroglu, *op. cit.*

89 Gerbens-Leenes, Moll & Uiterkamp, *op. cit.*

90 Darnall, Jolley & Handfield, *op. cit.*

91 Gerbens-Leenes, Moll & Uiterkamp, *op. cit.*

92 Maloni & Brown, *op. cit.*

93 Gerbens-Leenes, Moll & Uiterkamp, *op. cit.*

26 *Standardizing Sustainability: Certification of Tanzanian Biofuel Smallholders in a Global Value Chain*

HENNY ROMIJN,* SANNE HEIJNEN,† AND
SAURABH ARORA‡

Keywords

Biofuels, sustainability, standardization, certification, governance, global value chains.

Introduction

This chapter documents a case study about sustainability certification of Tanzanian smallholder farmers in a global chain for biofuel feedstock supply for a European airline. The certification project was initiated in the context of recent policy measures adopted by the EU and its member states to promote the use of biofuels. These measures, accompanied with growing public concern about climate change and oil shortages in the last decade, prompted a barrage of biofuel promotional activities by corporate and non-profit actors in the EU and beyond.

The effects of these rampant efforts were soon to be felt, and by 2007–8, many actors in the EU (and elsewhere) had begun to voice serious concerns about the sustainability of biofuels. In particular, it had become clear that Europe would only be able to meet a small part of its biofuel targets from feedstocks cultivated domestically.[1] This gave rise to the question where the bulk of the non-EU supply was to come from, and under what conditions this biomass would be cultivated. The first estimations about devastating greenhouse gas emissions, ecosystem annihilation and human displacement from large biofuel plantations on cleared peatlands in Indonesia and Malaysia began to reach the general public.

*   Associate Professor, School of Innovation Sciences, Eindhoven University of Technology, Postbus 513, 5600MB, Eindhoven, The Netherlands. E-mail: h.a.romijn@tue.nl. Telephone: +31 40 2474754.

†   Ph.D researcher, Copernicus Institute, Utrecht University, Heidelberglaan 2, 3584CS Utrecht. The Netherlands, e-mail: s.heijnen@uu.nl. Telephone: +31 30 253 7628.

‡   Assistant Professor, School of Innovation Sciences, Eindhoven University of Technology, Postbus 513, 5600MB, Eindhoven, The Netherlands. E-mail: s.arora@tue.nl. Telephone: +31 40 2474754.

Around this time, the Dutch Environment Minister, Mrs Jacqueline Cramer, put together a committee of policy and academic experts tasked with the formulation of adequate social and environmental sustainability criteria for the cultivation and utilization of biofuels. The idea was that these criteria could act as a base for designing guidelines and standards for governing biofuel production and use, particularly for biomass imported from faraway places where formal institutions of social and environmental governance are either weak or work according to free market principles. The Cramer Criteria were adopted by the Dutch standardization institute (NEN) as the basis for drafting a national biofuel standard. This process eventually culminated in a biofuel sustainability norm, NTA8080/81,[2] a first version of which became operational in 2010.

A Dutch entrepreneur with a Tanzanian subsidiary, procuring Jatropha oilseeds from smallholder farmers for bio-kerosene production, soon showed interest in obtaining certification under NTA8080/81. The entrepreneur formed a consortium to carry out the certification pilot project, which included the NEN and a technical university as partners. We analyse the practice of this project to govern Jatropha cultivation by Tanzanian smallholders, from its inception in January 2010 to May 2012, primarily from the viewpoint of the main university participants in the consortium. The project is scheduled to end in June 2013, so we document an unfinished story and cannot draw any conclusions about the project's final outcomes. However, the story allows us to draw some important lessons about multi-actor certification processes as 'gathering[s] in tension of multiple, sometimes contradictory realities'.[3]

The chapter is structured as follows. We begin with an overview of the literature on governance in global value chains. This is followed by a general description of the standards and protocols under study. The actual process of the certification pilot study is documented in two subsequent sections. A final section provides some concluding remarks.

GOVERNING FOR SUSTAINABILITY IN GLOBAL VALUE CHAINS

Governance has long been a central concern of the global value chain (GVC) literature.[4] Governance was initially viewed as the exercise of power by lead firms in imposing their product and process requirements on suppliers in buyer-driven chains, such as those for clothing garments, or product characteristics on buyers in supplier-driven chains, such as those for personal computers.[5] This 'driven-ness' approach was refined by Gereffi and co-authors, who proposed that GVC's could be governed in one of five different modes: market, modular, relational, captive and hierarchy.[6] Only in the hierarchy mode can GVC governance be equated with the exercise of power by lead firms. As expected, the market mode is associated with arm's-length transactions that according to Gereffi et al. are not governed by power of the lead firms.[7] Power asymmetry between chain actors increases as one moves from the market mode to the hierarchy mode of governance. Furthermore, attributes of the products exchanged and firms' capabilities in a chain play a role in defining its mode of governance. For instance, the market mode is characterized by low informational complexity, high supplier capabilities and relatively low switching costs to new partners, while the hierarchy mode is associated with high informational complexity and low capabilities among suppliers.

The foregoing approaches to GVC governance have been criticized on a number of counts.[8] Of particular relevance for our purposes is the criticism that both the driven-ness and mode of governance approaches tend to sideline the process through which the product performance and quantity requirements of buyer firms are translated into product and process standards, and how the standards are enacted by different actors through certification schemes or otherwise. It is in standard-setting and implementing (certification) processes of 'governance in practice' that different socio-technical realities of buyers, suppliers and any third party certification/standardization bodies collide with each other.

Recent work in GVC governance, focusing on agricultural commodities, has begun to study the exchange between multiple realities as (sustainability) standards and certification protocols are created and implemented in specific socio-geographical settings.[9] Building on conceptual insights from Science, Technology and Society (STS) studies, these scholars highlight how the objective and unified front-end of sustainability standards, exhibited and 'sold' to the consumers of certified agro-commodities, masks the messy world of the same standards and commodities in the making. In the latter world, standardization and certification are argued to be always unfinished processes riddled with unequal relations of power between different actors. Despite the unequal relations, however, no single actor is able to simply impose its desired standards on other actors, but rather compliance has to be worked out through multiple translations, that is, mutual adjustments made by different actors in order to gradually align their interests with each other. Furthermore, in this STS-inspired work, standards are viewed as ontological entities that attempt to make the 'realities that they claim to describe'.[10] And while they help reshape practices on a farm, and in an office or a factory, the standards themselves are often adapted and adjusted to better suit local conditions. These mutual adjustments are geared towards the production of a situation in which the localized standards and certification protocols come to accurately describe the actual practices and conditions they refer to.[11]

We make two interrelated contributions to this emerging literature on standardization and sustainability certification in GVCs. First, while most studies have focused on efforts of different actors in implementing standards and monitoring for compliance during certification, we study the prior process in which certification protocols are designed and piloted in the field. This standard-setting process has been termed as the legislative phase, as opposed to the later executive (implementing the standards) and judicial (monitoring and assessing compliance) phases, of governance in practice.[12] The legislative phase appears too early in the whole standardization and certification procedure to have an ontological effect in terms of remaking local realities and practices (of farmers). Rather the legislative phase is characterized by flexible standards and protocols which are, in principle, still open to 'official' modifications in rulebooks. In the following discussion, we map how some of these modifications were produced, paying specific attention to the coming together in friction of different actors' interests and practices. This analysis also constitutes our second contribution to the recent GVC governance literature, which largely has focused on how 'users' of the standards and protocols reject or comply with them in everyday practice, leading to the relative neglect of the study of modifications made to the standards by (or in collaboration with) the standard-setters themselves.

THE STANDARD AND THE PROTOCOLS

The Dutch standardization institute's biofuel sustainability norm NTA8080/81 follows the Cramer Criteria, which consist of six core themes:[13] greenhouse gas balance; competition with food production and/or supplies of local energy, medicines and building materials;

biodiversity effects; economic effects; social well-being effects; and environmental effects. The first three themes concern issues that are specifically important for energy supply from biomass sources, whereas the remaining three specifically address the people, planet and profit (triple P) dimensions of sustainability. Assessing the performance of biomass energy along these dimensions requires the traceability of the relevant biomass streams to their point of origin, and validating the conditions under which the biomass energy is being produced. In NTA8080/81, the Cramer Criteria have been redefined into the following nine core sustainability principles:

1. The greenhouse gas balance of the production chain and application of the biomass is positive.
2. Biomass production is not at the expense of important carbon sinks in the vegetation and in the soil.
3. The production of biomass for energy shall not endanger the food supply and local biomass applications (energy supply, medicines, building materials).
4. Biomass production does not affect protected or vulnerable biodiversity and will, where possible, strengthen biodiversity.
5. In the production and conversion of biomass, the soil and soil quality are retained or even improved.
6. In the production and conversion of biomass, ground and surface water are not depleted and the water quality is maintained or improved.
7. In the production and conversion of biomass, the air quality is maintained or improved.
8. The production of biomass contributes towards local prosperity.
9. The production of biomass contributes towards the social well-being of the employees and the local population.

Certification of smallholders in the Jatropha value chain from Tanzania requires: (a) implementation of a monitoring and control system to ensure that all Jatropha seeds have been grown in line with the above sustainability principles; and (b) setting up an organizational structure that enables certification of the smallholders as a group, since they are too small and resource-poor to be certified individually.

The Dutch entrepreneur's interest in certification predominantly was fuelled by the fact that it had just struck a deal with a subsidiary of the Dutch national airline (S-KLM for short) for supplying Jatropha oil, which is one of the few known suitable feedstocks for bio-kerosene. S-KLM had been deputed by its mother company to develop the airline's sustainable biofuel feedstock sourcing. S-KLM foresaw the implementation of the EU's Renewable Energy Directive under which certain requirements would be posed that all imported biofuel feedstocks into the EU would have to meet. S-KLM agreed to pay a handsome price for the pure Jatropha oil supplied by the Dutch enterprise, which sources its feedstock from its Tanzanian Jatropha subsidiary, an oil processor, which in turn obtains its oilseeds from thousands of smallholder farmers cultivating Jatropha plants as hedges around their food-crop plots and homesteads in rural Tanzania.

Amidst all the upheaval about unsustainable practices on biofuel plantations, this dispersed small-scale hedge arrangement seemed to hold out the promise of becoming a truly attractive business model. It seemed to avoid direct competition with food production for land and did not destroy any valuable ecosystems through direct or indirect land use change. In fact, in the majority of cases, the Jatropha oilseeds came from long-existing hedge stock, because Jatropha had been a well-known plant in Tanzania for decades. It was widely used in the socialist Ujamaa period to resolve land disputes through demarcation of land boundaries at a time when many rural people were on the move due to the government's forced resettlement in Ujamaa villages.[14] For smallholders, sale of the Jatropha seeds brought in a small amount which, although perhaps not exceeding 1% of their annual income, could pay for the school fees of a child.

The Dutch entrepreneur set up a consortium to bring the certification project to fruition. In addition to the entrepreneur (the project leader), the Dutch standardization institute (NEN), the Tanzanian Jatropha subsidiary, S-KLM and one of the Netherlands' technical universities were enlisted. The consortium filed a proposal with NL Agency, an agency of the Dutch Ministry of Economic Affairs and received a subsidy under the Ministry's Importation of Sustainable Biomass scheme towards the end of 2010. The project got underway on 1 January 2011 (see Figure 26.1 for a schematic representation of its organization), and is supposed to run until mid-2013. During the final six months of the project, at least 5,000 smallholders should be officially audited and certified. In the first two years (2011–12), various preparatory activities were to be carried out by the project consortium to enable the eventual auditing by an independent certification agency. The following story highlights some key encounters during this preparatory trajectory up to May 2012.

CERTIFICATION PHASE I: THE FEASIBILITY STUDY

The first six months of the project consisted mainly of a feasibility desk study to identify any binding constraints which could prevent the value chain from meeting one or

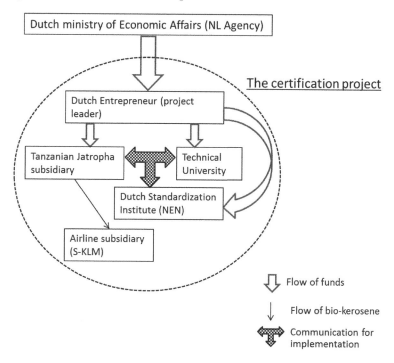

Figure 26.1 Organization of the certification project

more of the six core Cramer Criteria themes. An important part of the feasibility study was to come up with reliable estimates of greenhouse gas (GHG) emission reductions achieved with Jatropha bio-kerosene. However, none of the existing GHG calculation tools, not even the EU's own tool, Biograce, facilitated a GHG lifecycle assessment for Jatropha. Ultimately the project team had to design a 'pathway' for hedge Jatropha on their own, using sparse data from existing studies about Jatropha in combination with some assumptions from the palm-oil pathway in Biograce. The outcomes of the emission reduction estimations thus remain subject to an unknown margin of error. Estimations were produced for a variety of scenarios, using different combinations of assumptions concerning the fossil fuel baseline, by-product emission allocation, extent of carbon stock change due to land use change, level of emissions from conversion of pure Jatropha oil into bio-kerosene, and the amount of fertilizer given to the farmers as a compensation for the nutrients removed from their soils by harvesting Jatropha seeds (further details below). The estimated GHG emission reductions ranged from more than 100% (mainly due to assumed favourable carbon sequestration rates in newly planted Jatropha) to a mere 33% (as would occur in a setting of net carbon stock loss when older non-Jatropha hedges would be cut down to make way for Jatropha hedges). Agreement among the different project members was never reached about which GHG scenario should be used as a baseline for S-KLM.

Part of the GHG controversy emanated, literally and figuratively, from the ground in Tanzania. The process of pressing oil out of Jatropha seeds leaves a considerable residue called seedcake. The seedcake is still rich in (hard-to-extract) oil, and contains nutrients and minerals that the plant has absorbed from the soil. Hence, in order to meet the NTA8080/81 requirement of avoiding reduction of soil fertility, the nutrients should be replenished. In sub-Saharan smallholder agriculture, soil nutrient depletion is already a severe problem. The seedcake, if returned to the farmer, acts as an organic fertilizer. The Tanzanian Jatropha subsidiary is aware of this but does not see a practicable way to take the seedcake back to the farmers' plots because the farmers are spread out across a terrain of hundreds of square kilometres, and the rural road infrastructure is very poor. Renting dedicated trucks for transporting the bulky seedcakes back to the farmers would be too costly. Instead, the project team analysed the GHG effects of providing the farmers with an occasional dose of mineral fertilizer. As mineral fertilizer is compact and lightweight, it would be easier and cheaper to handle. But as a fertilizer it is less valuable than the seedcake and has a negative effect on the GHG emission balance of the Jatropha oil value chain. This latter effect was estimated by the university team: if quantities of nitrogen and potassium similar to those removed through Jatropha cultivation are replenished, the emission reductions from pure Jatropha oil chain (up to the point of delivery in Rotterdam port) would fall well below the minimum requirements of the EU's renewable energy directive. This finding led the project consortium to prepare two separate feasibility study documents: the uncomfortable estimates have only made it into a 'private' version of the document that has not been circulated outside the consortium. Presumably it is hoped that certification auditors will not pick up on the issue when they read the 'public' version.

While this research was underway, it also became clear that returning the seedcake to the farmers would not be in the interest of the Tanzanian subsidiary for other reasons. The seedcake still has substantial energy value and can be pressed into pellets and briquettes for use in urban areas where these products find a ready market. The proceeds from these seedcake products constitute a valued source of additional revenue for the subsidiary. Furthermore, in GHG assessments for the EU's renewable energy directive, emissions associated with replacing traditional cooking fuels can be subtracted from the emissions produced when utilizing Jatropha seeds for biokerosene, thereby improving the GHG performance of the Jatropha oil chain. In view of the problematic GHG results detailed above, this constitutes a major advantage of utilising the seedcake for energy purposes. At the same time, however, this use of the seedcake comes at the expense of further soil nutrient depletion of smallholders' land, threatening the sustainability of their livelihood.

Despite encountering many such issues and some nagging concerns over expected high costs of sampling and auditing large numbers of smallholders, the consortium decided to move ahead with preparatory field activities for certification from mid-2011.

CERTIFICATION PHASE II: BASELINE STUDIES IN THE FIELD

There has always been a clear difference in vision between 'people on the ground' and between policymakers and academics, and that is no different this time. (Manager, Tanzanian Jatropha subsidiary)

This phase consisted predominantly of the collection of certain baseline data from the smallholders, required by the NTA8080/81 for monitoring purposes. It was at this point that the university researchers participating in the project first got in touch with the Jatropha subsidiary's manager in Tanzania to verify the number and location of the smallholders that the company sources seeds from. According to the NTA8080/81, water, air and soil samples had to be collected from a specified number of smallholders. This is necessary to enable future group certification, after the formation of smallholder cooperatives. The original project document, drafted less than a year earlier, had foreseen a manageable total of 5,000 smallholders in two regions, to be organized into two cooperatives of 2,500 members each. According to the NTA8080/81 requirements, this situation would require baseline water, air and soil samples to be taken from at least the square root of the number of members per cooperative, i.e. a minimum of 50 smallholders per cooperative. However, the response from the Tanzanian subsidiary's manager indicated that reality on the ground had moved ahead of the original plan:

We have expanded into several new regions. I believe we are now sourcing from around 57,000 farmers. The exact number is not known because the administration by the local collection centres is not exact and many farmers are not yet officially registered with us as suppliers. Many people who come to sell seeds are not the farmers, it's mostly children and old people, they could be farmers' relatives but they could also be unrelated poor vulnerable groups. Therefore I think we need a different division for the cooperatives, and we also have to review the number of members per cooperative. The original plan does not make sense anymore ... it is infeasible to audit the square root of the members of each cooperative, and then having to take samples from them on an annual basis! This will become a completely unmanageable undertaking. (E-mail excerpt, from Tanzanian subsidiary's manager to university team leader, 21 May 2011)

There were other reasons for apprehension on the part of the project implementers. The NTA8080/81 text spoke of the requirement to form homogeneous cooperatives in terms of climatic conditions, water availability, soil type and agricultural practices. On this, the manager wrote:

> *Another problem that I foresee is the heterogeneity of the soils and water availability. In Mi—*
> *there is kichanga soil and there is no water source, hence no irrigation. In contrast, in Mb—*
> *where we are active now, there is Tifutifu soil and people can regularly use water from a*
> *nearby river. These are big differences in what is considered to be one and the same region.*
> *The other regions have again quite different soils and climate variations. There is a lot of local*
> *and regional variability – and we are talking of vast sourcing areas, spanning hundreds of*
> *square km, some are over 600 km away from our processing site. The NTA8080 requirement*
> *of homogeneity of soil and climate within each cooperative group can only be met if we form*
> *very small cooperatives of a few hundred farmers each, but that is absolutely no option for the*
> *reasons I already indicated [too many cooperatives]. Please ask NEN to relax this requirement.*
> *(E-mail excerpt, from Tanzanian subsidiary's manager to university team leader, 21 May 2011)*

The standardization institute (NEN), however, responded by asking for proper scientific evidence before considering any relaxation of their norm requirements. The university team then had to trace detailed soil maps for Tanzania (ultimately located at the FAO), and superimpose on these the approximately 2,000 smallholders who had already been registered in a central database with their GPS coordinates, in the absence of any physical addresses in rural Tanzania. The pictures that ultimately could be produced with the help of a specialist from Wageningen University were still rather primitive, as they could not go beyond a resolution of blocks of 20 square km and covered only one sub-region of the sourcing area. The maps showed great soil diversity in Tanzania, and smallholders within one and the same region were seen to be located on several different soils. The NEN was ultimately satisfied with the maps and relaxed its homogeneity assumption, but the amount of effort involved in getting this one obstacle removed was considered enormous by the university team.

The university researchers meanwhile began to assess the implications of the changed number of smallholders (57,000 instead of the original 5,000) to be included in the project. The new numbers required samples to be taken from about 10 times the number of farmers specified in the original plan. These concerns were aggravated by reports coming in from the field regarding the actual work involved in the sampling (more on this below). Furthermore, the NTA8080/81 text gave rise to many questions about how to operationalize the water, air and soil sampling and analysis procedures. The university team was unsure if they would find laboratories in Tanzania that would have the capacity and capabilities to execute the analyses. Taking thousands of samples back to the Netherlands was obviously too difficult and expensive to consider.

The foregoing discussion illustrates the collision between Tanzanian agrarian realities and the context in which the NTA8080/81 norm was designed. Although the designers of NTA8080/81 had taken care to consult different stakeholders, this obviously did not include African smallholders. The norm design was done in several rounds, with possibilities for feedback and suggestions from an interest group, the so-called Committee of Experts, constituted by Dutch environmental and fair trade foundations, governmental representatives and the private sector, in order to ensure broad support for the eventual outcomes through a participatory process. But the Dutch designers of the norm did not, or could not, consider the institutional complexities of scientific and agrarian realities in different parts of the world. The scenario of a biofuel value chain built on tens of thousands of smallholders without physical addresses, who are cultivating plots of 0.5–2 acres each, was not conceived by NTA8080/81's designers. The so-called 'inclusive' group certification option allowed by NTA8080/81 clearly does not work for this type of production system.

Ultimately, the main hurdle in the way of feasible operationalization turned out to be the requirement of soil samples taken and analysed from the square root of the number of cooperative members on an annual basis. Although the water sampling requirements in the NTA 8080/81 were similar to this, and equally tenuous in principle, the lack of surface water close to smallholder plots and groundwater levels of at least several metres deep finally convinced the NEN to relax its requirement of water sampling. The logic of measuring the Biological Oxygen Demand (BOD) in the water, in any case, was ludicrous for Tanzania. BOD is useful for monitoring *excess* nutrient supply, a requirement inspired by the nitrogen-surplus situation in the Netherlands with its huge pig population. In contrast, as noted above, sub-Saharan African soils widely suffer from nutrient *depletion* problems.

The soil management (and associated sampling) requirements presented challenges of a different order. The overwhelming majority of Tanzanian smallholders farm organically, if only because they cannot afford to buy expensive mineral fertilizers and chemical pesticides. In general, their Jatropha plants do not displace food production because Jatropha yields much lower value than common staple foods such as maize, beans, cowpeas or cassava. The few (larger) farmers who tried to introduce mini-plantations during the initial Jatropha hype, about five or six years ago, have long since uprooted the shrubs in disappointment and frustration.[15] Thus there is very little land use change to speak of. Currently, among Tanzanian smallholders, Jatropha largely survives as a wind-break hedge, an anti-erosion device, pen for farm animals, grave marker, land dispute settlement mechanism, and privacy-yielding hedge around homesteads.[16] Labour, water, animal manure or any other major resources are first allocated for food production, while Jatropha is treated as a residual crop. Thus, in broad terms, the smallholders satisfy the NTA8080/81 Principle 5, which states: *'In the production and conversion of biomass the soil and soil quality are retained or improved.'* The only problem is some localized nutrient mining due to the Jatropha seed removal, but this is something that other actors further down the value chain have to address (e.g., by returning seedcakes to the farms, see above). The main problem with the soil requirements in the NTA 8080/81 is, then, that the smallholders simply do not have the means to prove their organic practices according to the demands of a European standard with its specific and rigid interpretation of what constitutes 'adequate scientific proof'. This case exemplifies the nature of unequal power relations operating in the certification process, due to which only some actors' knowledge and practices are considered legitimate and scientific.

The experiences with NTA8080/81's cumbersome and often superfluous provisions, as discussed above, may be considered as cases of 'excess governance' by the standard. These provisions seemed to serve no purpose except that of satisfying EU and Dutch bureaucratic requirements. The project also encountered the opposite problem of 'governance deficit'. For instance, NTA8080/81 did not require collection of samples from a control group of farmers who have not been cultivating Jatropha. Without this control group, it is difficult to separate any ecological impact of Jatropha cultivation from other factors that produce similar impacts. In particular, soil fertility deterioration may not be limited to Jatropha growers alone. However, the NEN was unconvinced of the need for control samples and during one of the project progress meetings, the collection of control samples was even flagged as a waste of the university's allotted budget.

The foregoing analysis of the coming together in tension of different realities may be depicted in a schematic diagram, as shown in Figure 26.2. The upper half of the figure represents the official NTA8080/81 requirements, while the lower half of the figure schematically depicts Tanzanian smallholder reality with which the NTA8080/81 norms were confronted. Missing or deficient governance cases are placed on the left side of the figure, while cases of excess governance are on the right. In the 'middle ground', where governance was felt to be feasible and operable, the norm requirements were subjected to major translation efforts involving brainstorming in Tanzania, remedial research to identify acceptable ways forward, and perhaps most importantly, significant improvisation in the field.

As the fieldwork for the collection of baseline data in Tanzania proceeded, many newer instances of excess and deficient governance were encountered. Due to lack of space, we only discuss some key issues below. Before doing so, however, we first home in on some problems that fell in the intermediate category of 'legitimate governance provisions' of NTA8080/81 (see Figure 26.2). The list given here is not exhaustive. These problems were experiences where prolonged discussion and mutual adjustment by the parties in the Netherlands and Tanzania were eventually able to produce a compromise.

- **Where to measure soil quality?** The NTA8080/81 emphasized that adverse effects on food production must be avoided, but the Jatropha hedge is obviously located *beside* the food plot or even some distance away from it. The university team ended up taking samples from both food plots and under Jatropha hedges, since the NEN was unaware of the requirements that would be posed by the auditors. This was laborious and expensive.

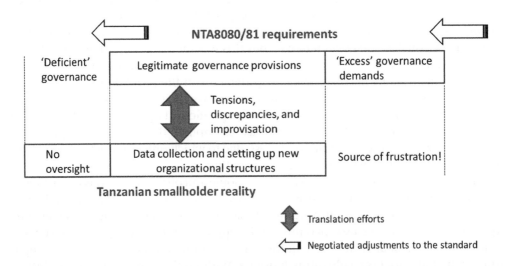

Figure 26.2 NTA8080/81 sustainability standard meets Tanzanian smallholder reality

- **How deep to dig for the soil samples?** Again, the NTA8080/81 did not provide adequate guidance. NEN indicated that this must be determined locally. But for assessing the soil quality of a food plot, one should not go deeper than 40 cm in order to obtain meaningful estimates of e.g., soil carbon, whereas a depth of 40 cm is barely sufficient for determining effects from deep Jatropha roots on the soil under the hedge. At the same time, the sample results from the food plot and hedge must be mutually comparable and this is only possible if the same soil depth is used for both. A compromise depth of 50 cm was decided upon for all samples, but this is obviously a coarse rule of thumb.
- **How to dig?** Soil probes were recommended, but they were found to be useless in stony ground. Heavy-duty shovels, pick axes and pangas were required to get into some Tanzanian soil, but that meant obtaining rough, 'disturbed samples' – another unavoidable problem that would reduce the reliability of soil quality data.
- **Where to analyse?** A local laboratory was contracted for the analysis of almost 440 soil samples that needed to be processed. The first results that came back revealed values that were outside theoretically possible ranges, and the laboratory had to be requested to re-analyse everything. About 8 months later, the final values for some of the key nutrients had still not been delivered. By this time it had become obvious that the laboratory was not equipped to handle large numbers of samples. The future scenario of certifying 60,000 odd smallholders who are supplying to the Tanzanian Jatropha subsidiary acquired nightmarish proportions.
- **How to deal with 'illegitimate' target groups?** As already forewarned by the Tanzanian subsidiary's manager, the main seed suppliers proved to be children and elderly people. Does this, then, involve child labour? This is the inevitable question asked by European parties, and absence of proof to the contrary usually stands firmly in the way of any certification involving labour standards. The Cramer Criteria, on which NTA8080/81 is based, likewise include a clause which forbids the use of child labour. Information from interviews with the 2,300 database farmers seemed to indicate that their children were indeed attending school. But school timings are limited to the morning hours, so the children can help out on the farm after school. Of course, this could also include picking, peeling and selling Jatropha seeds. Such farm work by children is a sheer necessity for many poor farming families. Is this child labour, or not? The auditors have yet to reach a verdict on this.

We move on to the problems with deficient or missing governance by NTA8080/81. The NEN was rather uninterested in taking up these issues, even though they were found to constitute major gaps in sustainability oversight according to the university researchers, who argued that these gaps could easily undermine the future credibility of the standard. Here is a sample of these issues:

- **Neglected key shortages of minor minerals**: Significant removals of calcium and magnesium from local biomass production systems can occur due to frequent harvesting of woods and/or crop seeds. Scientific research in Eastern African settings has shown that this can have an adverse impact on local soil productivity.[17] However, NTA8080/81 does not require their measurement and monitoring. It only asks for the measurement of macro nutrients, basically potassium, nitrogen and phosphorus, and of soil organic carbon (SOC).

- **No requirement to measure soil moisture content**: This non-requirement was a huge oversight since some biofuel crops, including Jatropha, are known to be water hungry (an observation made also by some farmers in our study area) and hence could affect water availability for adjoining food crops.
- **No need to measure toxic effects from Jatropha by-products**: The NEN argued that the NTA8080/81 is solely meant to capture the sustainability of 'production units' in the Jatropha oil supply chain. This meant that any by-products emanating from oil production could remain unscrutinized. Bizarrely, NTA8080/81 prescribes in great detail the monitoring of soil, water and air effects on smallholder plots, even where these can be expected to be minimal, whilst completely disregarding any similar effects after the seeds have left the smallholder plots. In view of persistent reports about the high toxicity of Jatropha, especially due to *phorbol esters*,[18] this was deemed a particularly unacceptable omission in the NTA8080/81 by the university team and their Tanzanian collaborators.

Yet the most serious problems arose from the *'excess governance demands'* depicted in the right-hand side of Figure 26.1. The requirement to register all smallholders in a database with their GPS details turned out to be expensive, with the average cost per farmer exceeding €4 for the initial 5,000 farmers included in the certification project. This is due to the time-consuming nature of the registration process, which has to be done on location in remote rural areas, to take proofs such as photos of the hedges, and measure the hedge length and width. On top of these costs there would be annual soil sample analysis. As stated before, the number of farmers from whom baseline soil samples were taken had to be at least 100. The costs of this initial baseline sampling and analysis amounted to around €4,500 for laboratory costs, while additional amounts were spent for the labour and transport involved in the collection of the samples. Since a substantial number of these farmers are to be re-analysed on *an annual basis* to meet the NEN's requirement of monitoring, these costs were deemed to be prohibitive for the prospective cooperatives. It is also worth noting that these were the approximate costs of certifying the first 5,000 farmers only, which supply a mere 11–12% of the oil processor's estimated break-even level of oil production (source: Tanzanian subsidiary's manager). The other 88–89% would presumably still need to be certified later, *without* any subsidies from NL Agency or assistance from the technical university. Furthermore, according to NTA8080/81, a certification auditor would need an average of three hours to audit one smallholder (*excluding* travelling time and costs). Overall the cost of certification was estimated to exceed the benefits (for the value chain) by a large margin. The benefits, to recap, consisted primarily of market access to the EU aviation sector which paid a more attractive price than would be achievable on local markets. But, clearly, despite its provision of group certification, the NTA8080/81 did not cater to the needs, or appreciate the realities, of thousands of smallholders in Tanzania.

As the financial and logistical consequences of certification became clearer, the university team along with the Tanzanian subsidiary's manager began to explore ways to reduce costs. First, they suggested replacing a part of the sampling with estimations based on calculations of nutrient removals due to seed harvesting, and limiting primary soil measurements to once in five years. But the NEN was unwilling to modify prescribed NTA8080/81 procedures without consulting the Dutch Council of Accreditation, RvA (a body that supervises the quality of procedures used by the NEN and other standardization institutions in the Netherlands). The accreditation council was extremely reluctant to get drawn into such operational issues and referred the NEN to the European Cooperation for Accreditation (ECA), of which the Dutch accreditation council is a member. The ECA had recently drawn up a guide document for group certification, which was duly sent to the NEN. This rather bulky document revealed that the NEN's NTA8080/81 did not meet all of ECA's group certification guidelines, and that it would have to comply with these guidelines by mid-2013. This discovery did not bide well for the project. At the time of writing, the NEN was still trying to find out from the Dutch accreditation council how it can or should interpret the ECA group certification guidelines.

Concluding Remarks

Despite being unfinished, the story of the certification process documented above allows us to draw some general lessons about sustainability standards and their implementation in global value chains. It is clear that standard design and operationalization by bodies such as the NEN cannot foresee the issues encountered during implementation, especially in other parts of the world. The institutional and ecological complexity of realities such as those of the Tanzanian smallholders cannot be reduced to guidelines and protocols of a 'universal' globally applicable standard. This is true even for standards, such as the NTA8080/81, designed in a participatory process on the basis of widely accepted sustainability principles that were formulated with the intention of protecting poor and vulnerable people and environments.

The irreducibility of complex realities to standards and norms paves the way for ontological effects produced by standards that attempt to make the realities so as to accurately describe them. The pilot stage of the certification process studied by us is perhaps too early to witness such ontological effects. We have focused instead on the adjustments made and attempted on the 'official' standard itself as it is confronted with the real world of growers and processors in a part of Tanzania. As a result of these adjustments, that were often resisted by the powerful actors in the certification project, the standard may have become more aligned with the local realities encountered. But other frictions, both similar to and different from the ones discussed in this chapter, are bound to crop up as this 'adjusted' standard moves to new locales and encounters other social and material realities.

Perhaps a way of reconciling the heterogeneity and complexity of the world is to reject the idea of universal standards beyond the level of broad core principles, instead opting for regional or niche standardization.[19] With niche standardization, it may be possible to take better account of socially and geographically bounded realities, such as those of Tanzanian smallholders growing Jatropha as a hedge. A niche standardization strategy would be better positioned to serve the certification's intended purpose (fostering 'social' and environmental sustainability), although care still has to be taken not to exclude the poorest farmers from reaping the benefits of the sustainability of their existing practices, a sustainability they cannot afford to prove 'scientifically'.

On a final note of caution, within and beyond the confines of the certification, the sustainability of smallholders' existing practices is not something given or unchanging. Farmers may respond to high demand for biofuels created by European subsidies and mandatory fuel mix requirements by cultivating crops such as Jatropha on lands that were hitherto used for cultivating food crops. Alternatively, in their attempts to increase yields, they may start using greater amounts of water and (organic) fertilizers on Jatropha, diverting these scarce resources away from food and fodder production. Biofuels therefore are inherently risky technological 'solutions' to climate change, which can jeopardize poor peoples' food security in Tanzania and many other parts of the global south, with or without sustainability certification.

Acknowledgments

The project described in this chapter received financial support from the Sustainable Biomass Programme of NL Agency, Netherlands Ministry of Economic Affairs (www.agentschapnl.nl/en/programmas-regelingen/sustainable-biomass).

The chapter also forms an output from the research programme 'Biofuels: Sustainable Innovation or Gold Rush?' at Eindhoven University of Technology, financed by the Netherlands Organisation for Scientific Research (NWO) under its Responsible Innovation programme (www.nwo.nl/nwohome.nsf/pages/NWOA_73HBPY_Eng).

Notes

1   Bindraban, P. et al. (2009), 'Can biofuels be sustainable by 2020? An assessment for an obligatory blending target of 10% in the Netherlands'. Netherlands Environmental Assessment Agency, Bilthoven.

2   NTA8080/81 refers to a set of two documents: (a) NTA8080, the Dutch Technical Agreement describing the requirements for sustainably produced biomass for energy applications to be applied at organizations that wish to sustainably produce, convert, trade, or use biomass for energy generation or as transportation fuel; and (b) NTA8081, the description of the accompanying certification scheme, which specifies the 'rules' to enable certification against the requirements of the NTA8080. For more information, see www.sustainable-biomass.org/publicaties/3892.

3   Moreira, T. (2011), 'Healthcare standards and the politics of singularities: Shifting in and out of context', *Science, Technology and Human Values,* published online, doi: 10.1177/0162243911414921, p. 11, citing Law, J. (2004), *After Method: Mess in Social Science Research,* Routledge, London, p. 97–100.

4   For a literature review, see Gibbon, P., Bair, J. and Ponte, S. (2008), 'Governing global value chains: An introduction', *Economy and Society,* Vol. 37, pp. 315–338.

5   Gereffi, G. (1994), 'The organization of buyer-driven global commodity chains: How US retailers shape overseas production networks'. In G. Gereffi and M. Korzeniewicz (eds.), *Commodity Chains and Global Capitalism,* Praeger Publishers, Westport, CT, pp. 95–122.

6   Gereffi, G., Humphrey, J. and Sturgeon, T. (2005), 'The governance of global value chains', *Review of International Political Economy,* Vol. 12, pp. 78–104.

7   *Ibid.*

8   Gibbon, Bair and Ponte, *op. cit.;* Muradian, R. and Pelupessy, W. (2005), 'Governing the coffee chain: The role of voluntary regulatory systems', *World Development,* Vol. 33, pp. 2029–2044.

9   Bain, C. and Hatanaka, M. (2010), 'The practice of third-party certification: Enhancing environmental sustainability and social justice in the Global South?' In V. Higgins and W.

Larner (eds.), *Calculating the Social: Standards and the Re-configuration of Governing*, Palgrave MacMillan, Basingstoke, pp. 56–74; Bain, C., Ransom, E. and Worosz, M. (2010), 'Constructing credibility: Using technoscience to legitimate strategies in agrifood governance', *Journal of Rural Social Sciences*, Vol. 25, No. 3, pp. 160–192; Berndt, C. and Boeckler, M. (2011), 'Performative regional (dis-)integration: Transnational markets, mobile commodities and bordered north-south differences', *Environment and Planning A*, Vol. 43, pp. 1057–1078; Konefal, J. and Hatanaka, M. (2011), 'Enacting third-party certification: A case study of science and politics in organic shrimp certification', *Journal of Rural Studies*, Vol. 27, pp. 125–133; Loconto, A. (2010), 'Sustainably performed: Reconciling global value chain governance and performativity', *Journal of Rural Social Sciences*, Vol. 25, No. 3, pp. 193–225; Ouma, S. (2010), 'Global standards, local realities: Private agrifood governance and the restructuring of the Kenyan horticulture industry', *Economic Geography*, Vol. 86, pp. 197–222.

10   Busch, L. (2011), 'Food standards: The cacophony of governance', *Journal of Experimental Botany*, Vol. 62, pp. 3247–3250, p. 1; Timmermans, S. and Epstein, S. (2010), 'A world of standards but not a standard world: Toward a sociology of standards and standardization', *Annual Review of Sociology*, Vol. 36, pp. 69–89.

11   cf Callon, M. (2007), 'What does it mean to say that economics is performative?' In D. MacKenzie, F. Muniesa and L. Siu (eds.), *Do Economists Make Markets? On the Performativity of Economics*, Princeton University Press, Princeton NJ, pp. 311–357; Callon, M. (2008), 'Economic markets and the rise of interactive *agencements*: From prosthetic agencies to habilitated agencies'. In T. Pinch and R. Swedberg (eds.), *Living in a Material World*, MIT Press, Cambridge, MA, pp. 29–56.

12   Tallontire, A. (2007), 'CSR and regulation: Towards a framework for understanding private standards initiatives in the agri-food chain', *Third World Quarterly*, Vol. 28, pp. 775–791.

13   Cramer, J. et al. (2006), 'Criteria for sustainable biomass production'. Final report of the Project Group 'Sustainable production of biomass'. Dutch Energy Transition Taskforce, The Hague.

14   Source: A. van Peer, bio-energy consultant. Personal communication, 13 October 2011.

15   GTZ (2009), 'Jatropha Reality-check: A field assessment of the agronomic and economic viability of Jatropha and other oilseed crops in Kenya'. Endelevu Energy, World Agroforestry Centre, Kenya Forestry Research Institute.

16   van Eijck, J.A.J. and Romijn, H.A. (2008), 'Prospects for Jatropha biofuels in developing countries: An analysis for Tanzania with Strategic Niche Management', *Energy Policy*, Vol. 36, No. 1, pp. 311–325; NL Agency (2010), 'Jatropha assessment. Agronomy, socio-economic issues, and ecology'. Utrecht.

17   Lulandala, L.L.L. and Hall J.B. (1990), 'Nutrient removals in harvesting of Leucaena hedgerows at Mafiga, Morogoro, Tanzania', *Forest Ecology and Management*, Vol. 35, pp. 207–216; van Hook, R.I., Johnson, D.W., West, D.C., and Mann, L.K. (1982), 'Environmental effects of harvesting forests for energy', *Forest Ecology and Management*, Vol. 4, pp. 79–94.

18   Makkar, H.P.S., Becker, K., Sporer, F. and Wink, M. (1997), 'Studies on nutritive potential and toxic constituents of different provenances of Jatropha curcas', *Journal of Agricultural and Food Chemistry*, Vol. 45, pp. 3152–3157; Gübitz, G.M., Mittelbach, M. and Trabi, M. (1998), 'Exploitation of the tropical oil seed plant Jatropha curcas', *Bioresource Technology*, Vol. 67, pp. 73–82.

19   Epstein, S. (2007), *Inclusion: The Politics of Difference in Medical Research*, University of Chicago Press, Chicago.

27 *Sustainability in Humanitarian Organisations*

IRA HAAVISTO* AND GYÖNGYI KOVÁCS†

Keywords

Humanitarian organisation, humanitarian supply chain, sustainability, supply chain design, content analysis.

Introduction

The raison d'être for humanitarian aid is to help people in need, the beneficiaries. The two beliefs guiding humanitarian operations are, first, that *"those affected by disaster or conflict have a right to life with dignity and, therefore, a right to assistance"*; and second, that *"all possible steps should be taken to alleviate human suffering"*.[1] Although the objective of humanitarian operations is to provide aid to a society, relatively little attention has been paid to the sustainability of humanitarian operations. The focus in humanitarian operations has rather been on (the lack of) aid effectiveness.[2] Facing this criticism and trying to please donors, humanitarian organisations are striving to improve their operational efficiency through a focus on cost and time efficiency and by increasing the transparency of their operations. Some aspects of sustainability, such as environmental responsibility, ethics and longevity, have not been in focus in the humanitarian context on the operational level, but this is slowly changing as humanitarian organisations embrace the agenda of climate change adaptation pioneered by the United Nations Development Programme (UNDP).[3]

Several large donors (USAID, ECHO and DFID[4]) nowadays require humanitarian organisations to consider the longevity of programmes and the persistence of their impact. However, other aspects of sustainability have not yet been emphasised from the donor side, nor in the strategy or operational planning of humanitarian organisations. In spite of this attention to longevity and impact persistence from the donor side, disaster relief operations have been criticised for not expanding their view to encompass the overall supply chain design[5] and for not considering the long-term implications of

* PhD Candidate Ira Haavisto, HUMLOG Institute, Hanken School of Economics, P.O.Box 479, 00101 Helsinki, Finland. E-mail: ira.haavisto@hanken.fi. Telephone: + 358 40 7352 761.

† Professor Gyöngyi Kovács, HUMLOG Institute, Hanken School of Economics, P.O.Box 479, 00101 Helsinki, Finland. E-mail: kovacs@hanken.fi. Telephone: + 358 40 3521 421.

delivering aid. Important supply chain design questions in terms of sustainability could be, for example, the choice between using local or global suppliers, or choice of modes of transportation.

Sustainability, particularly in terms of social impact, for instance the restoration of livelihoods, is part of the overall raison d'être of humanitarian aid and the organisations involved with providing it. Humanitarianism builds on the principles of humanity, neutrality and impartiality, which together are sometimes seen as the cornerstones to define the "humanitarian space", and amongst which humanity is aimed at relieving suffering wherever it is found.[6] There are, of course, different schools and perspectives on humanitarian aid, and overall, humanitarian aid is a highly politicised issue. Nonetheless, the principle of humanity to relieve suffering can be seen as coming with an objective of positive social impact, which is an important aspect of sustainability. Yet little attention has been paid to other aspects of sustainability in humanitarian operations. At the same time, different aspects of sustainability have serious implications on the long-term effectiveness of aid. It is little understood how humanitarian organisations consider various aspects of sustainability in their operations. The aim of this chapter is therefore to increase the understanding of sustainability in humanitarian organisations. Particular attention is paid to how sustainability is operationalised in the humanitarian context, hence the operational focus on logistics and supply chain management in the analysis.

Annual reports of the largest humanitarian organisations are analysed to capture different aspects of sustainability. The operational focus of the analysis helps in identifying not just how sustainability aspects are discussed but also, how they are implemented. On the other hand, this also restricts the analysis to disaster relief, albeit questions of development aid are taken up to the extent to which they impact on sustainability in humanitarian organisations. Due to the operational focus, much attention is paid to performance measurement and also to supply chain design.

Sustainability in Humanitarian Organisations

Weerawardena et al.[7] define sustainability in the non-profit sector overall as maintaining operations, or more precisely "being able to survive so that it [the organisation] can continue to serve its constituency". On the other hand sustainable development is defined by the United Nations as "meeting the needs of present without compromising the ability of future generations to meet their own needs".[8] In this study we adopt the United Nations definition of sustainability.

The main difference between humanitarian organisations and companies is their very raison d'être. While a company's goal is to make profit for its shareholders, the goal of humanitarian organisations is most often to save lives,[9] decrease human suffering[10] and contribute to development.[11] All of these goals have a link to longevity. Yet in spite of recent donor requirements to consider the long-term implications of humanitarian programmes, humanitarian organisations have not yet experienced much stakeholder pressure in other aspects of sustainability such as electricity usage, fuel consumption, or even supplier selection criteria.

The lack of corresponding stakeholder pressure can be identified when studying the strategies of humanitarian and development organisations through the lens of the Global Reporting Initiative (GRI). The GRI promotes economic, environmental and social sustainability and provides a reporting framework to manage and monitor sustainability aspects in the operations of an organisation. The GRI and other environmental standards such as ISO (e.g. standard 14031 of the International Organization for Standardization) can be used by companies and other types of organisations. However, when looking at GRI reports from 2010, it appears that there is a lack of implementation of this sustainability standard in the non-profit sector. Out of 2,032 GRI reports in the year 2010, only 57 were from non-profit organisations, of which only three were published by humanitarian organisations. Oxfam GB, Caritas del Peru and World Vision Australia reported on their operations according to the GRI standard, which means by default that environmental aspects are considered in the organisations and that there is an environmental strategy in place in the organisation.[12]

Though few, the recent GRI reports of humanitarian organisations indicate a slight change towards the incorporation of various aspects of sustainability in the agendas of humanitarian organisations. In 2005 no humanitarian organisation reported according to GRI, compared to three in 2010.[13] Furthermore, organisations are encouraged to integrate the causes and consequences of climate change in their agenda[14] pioneered by the UNDP.[15] Humanitarian organisations are starting to take some aspects of sustainability into consideration but have yet to also embrace the challenge of "greening" in their operations, and more specifically in their supply chains,[16] and hence extend their view on sustainability beyond the principle of humanity.

ASPECTS OF SUSTAINABILITY IN SUPPLY CHAIN MANAGEMENT

Two views stand out when it comes to sustainability in the humanitarian context.[17] First, questions of longevity and long-term development raise a *holistic view* of humanitarian supply chains. Such a view would require taking a view beyond the mission, organisation or even the supply chain and on to society. Approaching the impact of aid on the societal level is embedded in the very concept of aid effectiveness that is often used in the macro-economic sense to measure the effect of aid overall on livelihoods and economic growth.[18] The second view also extends the focus beyond the humanitarian organisation to its supply chain, and in particular, to supply chain strategy and *supply chain design*. Investigating these two views, Kovács and Spens[19] cite five aspects related to the sustainability of aid: 1) bridging the gap between disaster relief and long-term development and managing the transitions between these; 2) supply chain design for preparedness, and with an exit strategy; 3) community-based supply chain design; 4) greening humanitarian supply chains; 5) and local, regional vs. global sourcing and capacity building. Thus overall, there are multiple aspects of sustainability to consider in the humanitarian context:[20] for example, the concept of sustainability can be applied in relation to sustaining an operation, i.e. maintaining aid through continuous funding (financial continuity) and/ or coordinating it with development activities (long-term development). Interestingly, humanitarian and development activities are usually considered in isolation, even though disasters often take place in countries in which development organisations, and development aid, is already present (e.g. the 2008 cholera outbreak in Zimbabwe, the 2010 Haiti earthquake). Therefore it is crucial to view (humanitarian) disaster relief activities as interlinked with development ones. But the longevity of aid, i.e. its long-term effects on society, is of importance even if disaster relief is not delivered on top of development activities (e.g. the 2011 Japan earthquake).

Taking the holistic view, the limited link between disaster relief and development programmes becomes apparent. This is due to the involvement of different organisations in humanitarian as opposed to development programmes, which pursue different mandates and have diverging operational scopes. There are, however, good examples as well; for example the International Alliance Against Hunger between the World Food Programme, the Food and Agriculture Organisation and the International Fund for Agricultural Development has been established precisely to consider the long-term effects of aid and the interrelations between humanitarian and development activities. The idea of this alliance is to contribute to food security overall and to continue development through the distribution of seeds along with (emergency) food aid. The alliance supports an extension of the view of humanitarian aid as being short term to linking it with longer-term development activities, hence considering the longevity and long-lasting effects aspects of sustainability.

Such a more long-term perspective also links disaster relief to reconstruction and rehabilitation – in the humanitarian sector known as the concept of LRRD, linking relief, rehabilitation and development – as well as to prevention through learning, and preparedness for further disasters to come, as embodied in the disaster relief cycle proposed by UN/ISDR in 2003[21] that was later adopted across humanitarian organisations. Learning and preparedness can occur on the regional level, in particular for cyclical disasters such as cyclones (a good example is how Bangladesh has reduced the number of people killed by cyclones over the years[22]), or within an organisation. As for the latter, Gatignon et al. evaluate the learning of the International Federation of Red Cross and Red Crescent Societies (IFRC) over a series of disasters in terms of key performance indicators related to the effectiveness of a programme (e.g. average number of families served per day), time efficiency (e.g. order lead time) as well as operational costs.[23] The case is directly linked to the preparedness of the IFRC through regional pre-positioning.

Preparing for future challenges is another aspect of preparedness. Global challenges for humanitarian supply chains extend to the preparedness for the effects of climate change, urbanisation and security issues.[24] Climate change adaptation requires a different set of approaches in preparedness than the actual response to a disaster, requiring a change of lifestyles but also changing support systems to facilitate adaptation mechanisms. Urbanisation, on the other hand, increases the vulnerability of people to disasters as it exposes them to disasters while reducing their coping strategies.[25] What is more, urbanisation has been linked to climate change as a result of climate change-related migration, but also discussed as a trigger of climate change.[26]

The other view focuses on supply chain strategy and *supply chain design*. Supply chain design can consider sustainability from the angle of community development through local sourcing, capacity building and engagement of beneficiaries. Thus, Kovács et al. present a case of community-based supply chain design where beneficiaries become active members of the reconstruction supply chain.[27] Community-based supply chain design can even incorporate aspects of peace-building,[28] but more generally, it contributes to beneficiary empowerment, helping to ensure community ownership of the reconstruction process, as well as to the local economy in general. This approach not only sources materials locally but also involves beneficiaries in decision-making and even as a workforce in the humanitarian supply chain.[29]

One way to empower the beneficiary in decision-making is through vouchers and cash components. This approach allows beneficiaries to purchase their own items, thus reducing the need for imports that would impact negatively on the local economy, cost more to organise and contribute to transportation emissions. Generally, if feasible, the more local solution seems to combine aspects of sustaining the local economy with cost-efficiencies as well as eco-efficiency. Overall, community-based approaches to supply chain design enable humanitarian organisations to hand over a programme to the community. Hence sustainability can also be understood as designing the humanitarian supply chain in a way that facilitates its continuation in the region after humanitarian organisations have left (in other words, a sustainable exit strategy).[30]

Researchers have begun to pay more attention to effects on the sustainability of the supply chain by looking at supply network design.[31] If a network is built in a way where hubs are geographically far apart, the supply chain automatically requires emission-intense transportation and the choice of transportation mode becomes secondary from a sustainability perspective. To transform a supply chain into being more sustainable might require some redesigning.

Ways to re-plan the supply chain are geographical decisions such as where to locate manufacturing, warehouses with pre-positioned goods and distribution centres.[32] Humanitarian hub systems exist at national and also international level. Apart from typical network analysis for locating hubs that focuses on the aspects of closeness to supply vs. demand, routing possibilities and intermodal possibilities, facility location decisions in humanitarian aid also need to consider the disaster proneness of a hub location.[33] The locations of current hub systems (e.g. the global United Nations Humanitarian Response Depots, UNHRDs, or IFRC's regional logistics units) are based on these principles and enable humanitarian organisations to pre-position stock, ranging from water purification tablets and high energy biscuits to shelter equipment, which can then quickly be moved into disaster areas. However, such pre-positioning does not take the overall effect (e.g. on transportation emissions) into account, even though it emphasises closeness to beneficiaries.

Access to the beneficiary is an important problem in the humanitarian sector which has to do with the urgency of the disaster.[34] Actually, a precondition for the success of any kind of humanitarian operation (whether disaster relief or development activities) is access of aid and relief to the affected area and to the beneficiaries.[35] Under conditions where the beneficiaries are not accessible (because of damage to the infrastructure, for example), the only possible mode of transportation might be air transportation, i.e. airplanes or helicopters. Neither of these is very environmentally friendly, nor are they cost-efficient.

From a supply chain strategy perspective, humanitarian supply chains have traditionally been viewed as highly agile.[36] However, a combination of lean and agile supply chain strategies can be found in IFRC's supply chain design with a decentralised structure of regional warehouses that decrease the distance to beneficiaries (with a focus on the lean concept of time efficiency while preparing for an agile response) and an emphasis on regional if not local sourcing (focusing on the economic sustainability of the community whilst reducing transportation costs and emissions).[37] The example shows not just a combination of lean with agile performance measures but also the impact on economic, social and environmental sustainability. Lean and green have often been mentioned in combination;[38] here, though, closeness translates also into sustaining the local economy through local sourcing.[39] What is more, Vinodh found an existing relationship between agile manufacturing and sustainability[40] – something to consider for humanitarian supply chains as well. (Even though humanitarian organisations typically act as logistics service providers[41] without their own manufacturing, there are examples in which they actually set up manufacturing sites, e.g. for winterised tents for victims of the Pakistan earthquake.)

A lack of consideration of sustainability is not unique to humanitarian supply chains. Carter and Easton criticise supply chain management overall for a tradition of stand-alone thinking without considering larger, more long-term aspects of sustainability.[42] Interestingly, while environmental and social aspects of "logistics social responsibility" have been operationalised, according to Carter and Easton, it is the economic aspect that has been neglected.[43] The missing link is thus between ecological and social aspects of sustainability and the impact on supply chain performance – sustainability being conceptualised as a space that considers all three aspects (social, economic and environmental) from a triple bottom line perspective.

SUSTAINABILITY IN OPERATIONAL PERFORMANCE

The performance of a humanitarian operation is bound to the aid effectiveness requirements of donors.[44] Effectiveness here does not refer to the organisation alone but needs to consider aid effectiveness in terms of social welfare, livelihoods and economic growth.[45] Several large donors require performance reporting from their implementing humanitarian organisations.[46] The reporting consists of programme assessment of on-going programmes and of monitoring and evaluation requirements at the end of a programme. The required reporting does not only entail operational data but also other measurements on the societal level. For example, a common measurement of the overall success of a humanitarian operation is a decrease of the crude mortality rate of beneficiaries in the receiving society. That said, such impact is difficult to measure and even more difficult to attribute to a particular programme or organisation. Other, more programme-related indicators depend on the scope of the programme itself but can be, for example, the overall amount of delivered supplies.

Whilst donors require more holistic performance reporting of humanitarian operations, supply chain performance in the humanitarian sector is still often defined as financial and volume-related performance.[47] Operational performance could refer to final output and operational impact, but this holistic perspective is not much considered in performance measurement of humanitarian operations. Previous research on performance in a humanitarian setting suggested measuring it as *output, resources, flexibility*[48] or as *customer service, financial control and process adherence,*[49] whilst Blecken et al. argue that in relief supply chains donation-to-delivery time, the output and resources should be measured.[50] Although Beamon and Balcik refer to output as well,[51] their suggested measurements of *population coverage* and *order fulfilment rate* are fairly narrow and do not reflect the overall impact of aid. None of the above suggested performance indicators take any aspects of sustainability into consideration.

Just as sustainability and performance can, for humanitarian organisations, be interpreted and measured in multiple ways. Figure 27.1 summarises the various aspects of sustainability into four perspectives:

1. Societal perspective (overall aid impact)
2. Programme perspective
3. Beneficiary perspective
4. Supply chain perspective

In doing so, Figure 27.1 portrays how the sustainability aspects could be accounted for in the performance of humanitarian response.

The first, *societal perspective*, makes a macro-economic assessment of the overall impact of aid. Important sustainability aspects that belong to this perspective are social welfare, livelihoods, economic development and climate change mitigation. Social welfare can be measured as a function of an individual welfare or as an aggregated measurement, such as life expectancy or income per capita. Livelihoods again refer to the societies, individual households or the individual's ability to support themselves. The aspect of livelihood further comprises the capabilities, assets and activities required for a means of living, and is seen as sustainable when it can cope with and recover from stress, such as emergency or other external disturbance.[52] Furthermore, the aspect of livelihood is seen as sustainable when it can maintain (or enhance) its capabilities now and in the future.[53]

The third aspect in the societal perspective is economic development, which is a traditional measurement of the development of a society or country, and can be measured, for example, as GDP. Poverty measures are also included here, such as the percentage of the population living on a dollar or less a day. The fourth aspect, climate change mitigation, is often used as a term for the reduction of greenhouse gas emissions that are the source of climate change.[54] Climate change itself is a change in the state of climate due to "natural internal processes or external forcings, or to persistent anthropogenic changes in the composition of the atmosphere or in land use" as defined by the IPCC.[55] The aspect of climate change mitigation in Figure 27.1 is used as a more comprehensive term and refers to a country's or a society's capability to lessen their own impact on climate change and to be prepared and to therefore have the prospect of preventing the impact of possible hazards resulting from climate change. Mitigation can be measured as, for example, hazard-resistant construction as well as improved environmental policies and public awareness.[56]

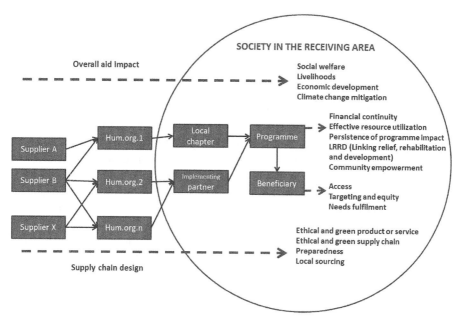

Figure 27.1 Four perspectives on sustainability

The second perspective portrays sustainability from the viewpoint of a defined aid programme. This *programme perspective* is important, as humanitarian organisations typically organise their activities under various programmes. Also funding is often granted for specific programmes (projects or disasters); rarely do organisations receive overall funding to run their operations. Sustainability aspects included in this perspective are financial continuity, effective resource utilisation, persistence of programme impact, LRRD (linking relief, rehabilitation and development) and community empowerment.

The aspect of financial continuity refers to the possibility of a programme continuing to serve the society or beneficiaries in need. If a programme's funding is cut or is short lived, the long-term objectives of a programme might not be met. Effective resource utilisation again can be measured as social or environmental responsibility, as a programme should not use resources such as workforce in a manner that does harm to the local market in the long run, and neither should resources such as supplies or assets be deployed without appropriate usability rates. Resource utilisation furthermore includes asset maintenance and asset disposal. The aspect further consists of coordination and resource sharing amongst organisations, which according to Long and Wood takes a great deal of effort, not least because each organisation has its own operating methods and goals.[57]

The persistence of programme impact refers to the long-term impact of a programme. Can the objectives of a programme be met even after the actual end of the programme? Is, for example, a medical clinic able to continue serving the society even after the programme has ended? From a sustainability perspective the aspect refers to the persistence of a programme and its activities, services or interventions, and the persistence of resulting changes for individuals or the aided society.[58] The aspect further refers to well-planned exit strategies and hand-over of programme activities to the local community (or other).

The aspect of LRRD is an acknowledgment of the gap between humanitarian response and development aid. If long-term effects of aid (not only lifesaving effects) are sought for with humanitarian relief supplies, the continuation of humanitarian aid projects is much needed.[59] From a sustainability perspective, any action taken in the immediate response phase of disaster relief should furthermore keep in mind what effects (and possible harms) the actions have for recovery and the long-term development of the society. Since the main priority in an immediate relief phase is to save lives, sustainability aspects might easily be overlooked.

Community empowerment is an aspect of sustainability in the sense that programmes with deep community involvement (active role in planning and decision-making) are seen to have a positive result on the long-term impact of the programme. Community involvement can also be seen through the sustainability sense, as beneficiaries can be hired as a workforce in active programmes, which might subsequently boost economic development in the local community. The effects of community empowerment on programme impact are nevertheless not always positive. The effects depend on the type of programme and the type of involvement.[60]

The third perspective, the *beneficiary perspective*, includes the sustainability aspects of access, targeting and equity, and needs fulfilment. Access refers to the opportunity for supplies to meet the beneficiary, or more precisely, to meet the beneficiaries' need with the right supplies or services at the right time in the right place.[61] Without this match there cannot be any impact of the humanitarian response.[62] Targeting and equity again refers to the correctness of the needs assessment (who is in need?) and the even coverage of that target group.[63] Needs fulfilment here is a function of how well the beneficiary needs have been served overall. Oloruntoba and Gray[64] have questioned the aspect of needs fulfilment and rather talk about customer service; however, the notion of beneficiaries as customers remains disputed due to the lack of purchasing power of beneficiaries.[65]

The last perspective on sustainability in Figure 27.1 is the *supply chain perspective*, with the aspects of ethical and green product or service, ethical and green supply chain, preparedness, and local sourcing. The aspect of ethical and green product or service refers to the actual items or services delivered to the beneficiary where, for example, a non-disposable product might cause more harm than good. On the other hand, the aspect of ethical and green supply chains is related to supply chain (and network) design. This aspect includes questions on how long the transportation routes are, where hubs and warehouses are located, which transportation mode is used, and also social responsibility questions such as how labour issues and health and safety questions are considered throughout the supply chain.

Local sourcing is also an aspect of both social and environmental responsibility. Local sourcing can have a positive impact on the economic situation in the region and can be seen as an action of community empowerment[66] and consequently as mentioned above have a positive impact on the long-term impact of humanitarian response. Other positive implications of local sourcing are that it reduces the response time[67] and can contribute to cost decrease in the supply chain. Shortened response time has, however, a direct effect on transportation emissions, hence becoming a question of sustainability. Due to a potential positive impact of local sourcing on the long-term impact of a programme, the current trend in humanitarian logistics is towards favouring local sourcing whenever possible.[68]

Method

A content analysis of humanitarian organisations' annual reports was conducted to increase the understanding of the various aspects of "sustainability" in these organisations. Content analysis is mostly used to assess websites, annual reports or corporate responsibility reports[69] but has also been used in supply chain management research to look at issues such as modal choice,[70] logistics education,[71] research approaches in logistics,[72] the content of journals[73] and job advertisements.[74] The unit of analysis of content analysis in supply chain management research varies from an article to a job advertisement. Our content analysis uses annual reports as the unit of analysis. The annual reports were chosen as the source of data since they often include missions and goal statements and descriptions of current and previous programmes and operations. The annual reports are used as the source in understanding whether the organisations view logistics and/or sustainable operations as an important part of the total operations. While the annual reports are not necessarily a direct reflection of what occurs in the field, they do express the view of the organisations want to portray to external stakeholders.

The sampling strategy was to identify large humanitarian organisations for the content analysis. Large organisations were identified by the total sums in emergency donations they raised from donors through appeals in 2010. As the sampling followed funding appeals for humanitarian relief operations (not long-term development aid programme funding appeals), the resultant sample mainly included organisations with a focus on disaster relief. Nonetheless, one needs to keep in mind that the mandates of humanitarian organisations vary, and that several of them are active in disaster relief as well as in development aid.

The final sample of 12 consisted of 11 humanitarian organisations and one UN agency:

- CARE USA
- Caritas
- Disasters Emergency Committee (DEC)[75]
- International Federation of Red Cross and Red Crescent Societies (IFRC)
- International Rescue Committee (IRC)
- Médecins sans Frontières (MSF)
- Mercy Corps
- Oxfam GB
- Save the Children (annual report of 2009)
- United Nations Children's Fund (UNICEF)[76]
- World Food Programme (WFP)
- World Vision International (WVI)

Other UN agencies were not included because many of them did not have any annual report. The 2009/10 income of the selected organisations ranged from €2,880 million (UNICEF) to £3.5 million (Disasters Emergency Committee).

Content analysis can be used to classify latent as well as explicit content, and to analyse textual data on a qualitative as well as quantitative basis.[77] Keyword searches (with the keywords "logistic*", "supply chain", "sustainab*" , "green", "climate change") were used to identify and quantify relevant data. Boolean characters were used to extend the search, e.g. "logistic*" was used to find "logistics" as well as "logistical", "sustainab*" to find both "sustainability" and "sustainable". Since the study is exploratory, keywords where chosen to get an overall understanding of whether the concept of sustainability was at all represented in the annual reports. To use the terminology from Figure 27.1 would have limited the results since the performance categories are too specific.

However, a further analysis of latent content was necessary even for the quantification, as some keywords were used for alternative meanings as well, e.g. when the term "green" was used as for the colour of green, not relating to ecological values. Keywords that were found several times in the same sentence were only counted as one. A rigid coding scheme was applied with definite, independent, and mutually exhaustive categories in the coding, so as to ensure objectivity and transparency. Independent and mutually exhaustive coding categories are also important for the validity of the content analysis.[78] However, only one coder was used, hence inter-coder reliabilities cannot be computed. On the other hand, keyword searches in content analysis do not result in coding discrepancies, hence there was no need to use several coders.

Findings

The annual reports of the selected organisations varied in structure and depth. What is noteworthy is that the annual reports (also sometimes called annual reviews) vary in length from 3 pages (WVI) to 112 pages (MSF). The length of the report thus impacts on the number of times a keyword is mentioned in the content analysis. Nevertheless, the very appearance or non-appearance of some keywords in the annual reports (see Table 27.1) lends to the interpretation of their importance to the organisation.

Table 27.1 Results from the content analysis

Organisation	"logistic*"	"supply chain"	"sustainab*"	"green"	"climate change"
CARE USA	0	0	0	0	4
Caritas	1	0	1	1	9
DEC	3	0	0	0	0
IFRC	4	1	2	0	3
IRC	0	0	0	0	0
Mercy Corps	0	0	0	0	0
MSF	9	0	4	0	0
OXFAM	2	0	3	1	26
Save the Children	0	0	0	0	0
UNICEF	1	2	4	0	2
WFP	7	0	1	1	0
WVI	0	0	0	0	0
Number of times mentioned	**27**	**3**	**15**	**3**	**44**
Number (and %) of organisations mentioning	**7 (58.3%)**	**2 (16.7%)**	**6 (50%)**	**3 (25%)**	**5 (42%)**

From a supply chain perspective, it is quite revealing how few organisations talk about their supply chain in their annual reports, even if they discuss logistics. This may reflect their operational view on the discipline. At the same time, even though climate change adaptation has been on the humanitarian agenda since 2008/9, only 42% of organisations discuss climate change at all. Sustainability and greening are talked about even less, which again may reflect the importance of the climate change agenda over any other sustainability dimensions.

The analysis of latent content sheds some light on the interpretations of these statistics. "Logistics" was most discussed in the light of partnerships with logistics service providers, logistical training, in relation to transportation, but also in terms of pre-positioning in hubs. Logistical challenges were mentioned in relation to particular disasters such as flash floods and earthquakes. "Supply chain" was discussed in fewer dimensions, related to sharing expertise (e.g. in training or capacity building) and the integrity of the organisation. Pre-positioning and training (especially capacity building) are related to a holistic view on sustainability, with the ideal to reduce and mitigate the impacts of disasters. At the same time, they are also linked to sustainable supply chain design and contribute to the speed and effectiveness of disaster relief.

"Sustainability", when mentioned, was related to very diverse aspects of the concept, surprisingly including even the aspect of financial continuity of development programmes. Mostly, sustainability was used to denote long-term economic, equitable and social recovery and development, the long-term assurance of livelihoods, and even sustainable health care. The following quote serves to illustrate this point: "A sustainable and safer future has also been the focus in rebuilding houses" (Caritas). All this can be summed up under the umbrella of long-term development, and the long-term impact of aid. UNICEF made explicit links between recovery and the Millennium Development Goals; other links were made to equity but also to gender and resilience: "It also means recognising the critical role women play in producing and preparing food, and investing in their capacity to claim their rights to develop equitable, sustainable and resilient solutions" (Oxfam).

WFP viewed greening as an essential strategy to ensure food security: "At the same time, poor rural families in Tajikistan needed help achieving household food security, which led to a happy marriage between WFP's new green initiative and the agency's long-standing food-for-training programmes" (WFP), which indirectly refers to activities of the International Alliance Against Hunger. Apart from this view, however, greening was rarely discussed, and usually referred to greenhouse gases and climate change. Thus one could see UNDP's climate change agenda as an important driver of greening initiatives in humanitarian organisations.

Climate change was, however, also linked to the increasing number of disasters: "The focus on preparedness reflects the reality that natural disasters are on the rise, in many cases linked to climate change" (UNICEF), to the extent that climate change modules were introduced in disaster risk reduction programmes. There is some consensus around the following statement: "Climate change has enormous economic repercussions for developing countries, through its impact on agriculture and livelihoods, and through increased natural disasters" (here by Oxfam); but even the EU is warned of climate change-related disasters in the future: "Climate change is altering disaster patterns and EU member states need to consider the possibility that they too may need to call on outside assistance in the future" (IFRC). Climate change adaptation is also highlighted: "Mitigating the impact of climate change on vulnerable communities has long been central to our work" (IFRC). Whilst this shows a strong community focus, it does not relate to community-based supply chain design.

On the other hand, climate change adaptation shapes the disaster relief landscape towards strategies to mitigate the potential impact of disasters, as expressed in the following quote: "The next phase of the campaign brings together the on-going challenge of climate change with the need to invest more in small-scale agriculture in developing countries" (Oxfam). Also, Caritas has started to reorientate its focus to main challenges in the humanitarian context: "The United Nations says the economic cost of natural disasters in 2010 was $109 billion, three times that of the previous year. It warned that this may come to look benign unless we tackle climate change, environmental degradation and the growth of slums in cities" (Caritas).

The challenges mentioned here reiterate Suarez' focus on coping strategies for climate change[79] as well as the double challenge of climate change and urbanisation.[80] Out of the sample organisations, five organisations directly mention climate change in their annual reports. Three of these five discuss climate change mitigation.

Other aspects of sustainability (Table 27.1) covered in the annual reports were financial continuity and persistence of programme impact that were part of the programme dimension. Sustainability as an LRRD aspect was discussed by one organisation. Sustainability as an aspect of livelihoods was also discussed by one organisation. Furthermore, sustainability from an environmental aspect was discussed by the WFP.

Regardless of a relatively good coverage of operational aspects in the annual reports (logistics were mentioned by almost 60% of the organisations), sustainability as a supply chain dimension with aspects such as ethical and green products, ethical and green supply chains and local sourcing was not discussed in any of the reports.

Conclusions

The concept of sustainability is highly diffuse, especially in the humanitarian sector where the mission of sustainable development of societies has not yet translated into sustainability aspects considered in humanitarian operations. In the corporate sector, too, supply chain management has been criticised for a lack of holistic thinking in terms of its possible negative impacts.[81] The same applies to humanitarian supply chains – where arguably, holistic thinking is even more necessary. Overall, a first perspective on sustainability relates to the embeddedness of humanitarian supply chains in society and nature. Taking this perspective, it is of essence that the long-term effects of aid are considered on local economies, the society and the environment, which were all related to the holistic view on sustainability in humanitarian operations.

Our analysis shows that humanitarian organisations are indeed concerned about the long-term sustainability of their operations, and discuss their impact on livelihoods, social recovery, sustainable health care and development overall. That said, little attention has been paid to greening their operations, even though climate change adaptation is on their agenda. In other words, climate change adaptation is considered for the livelihoods of beneficiaries, in the search of coping and mitigation strategies, but there is no direct link to green supply chain management on behalf of humanitarian organisations. Sarkis et al. list a number of barriers to greening the humanitarian supply chain, which can be summed up in the notion that "[The] goal [is] to help people, [the] environment [comes] second at best".[82] The stakeholders of humanitarian organisations have also not put greening on the agenda, in spite of all the debate about climate change and even the Copenhagen summit. Such a lack of environmental considerations could be seen already in the lack of GRI reports of humanitarian organisations.

Also, in spite of repeated considerations of the livelihood and the community of beneficiaries, there was no link to supply chain design that would build on this community. Local sourcing was, however, mentioned, and there was considerable training and capacity building in the field. Pre-positioning addresses closeness to beneficiaries – closeness can be more effective and improve time and cost-efficiencies – and reduces environmental impact.

In summary, humanitarian organisations could implement more sustainability strategies but as long as stakeholders do not identify them as important it is unlikely that humanitarian organisations will consider them in their supply chain design.

Limitations and Further Research

This chapter aimed to increase the understanding of sustainability in humanitarian organisations. Even though sustainability was discussed and categorised at the operational level and linked to performance, the limited results of the content analysis make it necessary to extend the research to use other methods in order to assess the performance measures related to each aspect of sustainability more in detail. For example, interviews with humanitarian organisations, and also with donors, could enhance the understanding of sustainability in the humanitarian context. Extending the content analysis to include documents other than annual reports may also lead to further findings. Furthermore, a focus on different stakeholders' (donor, organisation, beneficiary) perspectives on sustainability could be valuable. Further research could also focus on the possibility of measuring the sustainability aspect of the humanitarian operational performance.

Humanitarian organisations will have to consider sustainability aspects in all levels of their actions, from mission to operations. This will be challenging unless they recognise and understand different aspects of sustainability. An understanding of how to translate overall missions and strategies of sustainability into operations and how to measure the sustainability of operations will be needed. The performance framework summarising the sustainability aspects presented in this chapter strives to portray categories of overall missions related to operational performance. This categorisation should be helpful to understanding not only the various aspects of sustainability but also their interrelation and impact. This understanding is useful for humanitarian organisations in the planning and implementation of their operations but also for donors in policy planning, programme execution, and in programme monitoring and evaluation.

Notes

1   SPHERE (2011), *Humanitarian Charter and Minimum Standard in Humanitarian Response*, 3rd edn., The Sphere Project, Practical Action Publishing, Bourton on Dunsmore, UK.

2   Burnside, C. & Dollar, D. (2000), "Aid, policies and growth", *American Economic Review*, Vol. 90, No. 4, pp. 847–868; Moyo, D. (2009), *Dead Aid: Why Aid Is Not Working and How There Is a Better Way for Africa*, Allen Lane, London; Rajan, R.G. & Subramanian, A. (2008), "Aid and growth: What does the cross-country evidence really show?", *The Review of Economics and Statistics*, Vol. 90, No. 4, pp. 643–665.

3   United Nations Development Programme (UNDP, 2010), "UNDP in action 2009/2010: Delivering on commitments", at www.undp.org/publications/UNDPaction2010/pdf/wUNDPinAction-E-full.pdf, accessed November 2010.

4   USAID (2012), *Compliance & Oversight of Partner Performance*, U.S. Agency for International Development, at www.usaid.gov/compliance, accessed May 2012; Humanitarian Aid and Civil Protection Department of the European Commission, (ECHO 2010), "Rules and procedures applicable to property, supply, works and service contracts awarded within the framework of humanitarian actions Financed by the European union", Version October 2010; EuropeAid (2012), "Practical Guide to Contract procedures for EU external actions", at http://ec.europa.eu/europeaid/prag/document.do, accessed January 2012.

5   Kovács, G., Matopoulos, A. & Hayes, O. (2010), "A community-based approach to supply chain design", *International Journal of Logistics Research and Applications*, Vol. 13, No. 5, pp. 411–422.

6   Tomasini, R. & van Wassenhove, L. (2009), *Humanitarian Logistics*, Palgrave Macmillan, UK.

7   Weerawardena J., McDonald R. & Mort G. (2009), "Sustainability of nonprofit organizations: An empirical investigation", *Journal of World Business* , Vol. 45, pp. 346–356, *cit. from* p. 347.

8   WCED (1987), "Report of the World Commission on Environment and Development" (The Brundtland Report), United Nations World Commission on Environment and Development, UN publication A/42/427.

9   Beamon, B.M. (2004), "Humanitarian relief chains: Issues and challenges", *Proceedings of the 34th International Conference on Computers and Industrial Engineering*, San Francisco, CA; Kovács, G. & Spens, K.M. (2007), "Humanitarian logistics in disaster relief operations", *International Journal of Physical Distribution and Logistics Management*, Vol. 37, No. 2, pp. 99–114.

10 International Committee of the Red Cross (ICRC, 2010), "The ICRC: Its mission and work", at www.icrc.org/eng/assets/files/other/icrc_002_0963.pdf, accessed November 2010.

11 UNDP, *op. cit.*

12 Global Reporting Initiative, "Sustainability Disclosure database", at http://database. globalreporting.org/search, accessed May 2012.

13 *Ibid.*

14 Haavisto, I. & Kovács, G. (2012), "Measuring sustainability in humanitarian operations", *Proceedings of the Joint EUROMA / P&OM World Conference 2012*, Amsterdam.

15 UNDP, *op. cit.*

16 Eng Larsson, F. & Vega, D. (2011), "Green logistics in temporary organizations: A paradox? Learnings from the humanitarian context", *Supply Chain Forum: An International Journal*, Vol. 12, No. 1, pp. 128–139; Sarkis, J., Spens, K.M. & Kovács, G. (2012), "A study of barriers to greening the relief supply chain". In: G. Kovács & K.M. Spens (eds.), *Relief Supply Chain Management for Disasters: Humanitarian, Aid, and Emergency Logistics*, IGI Global, Hershey, PA.

17 Kovács, G. (2011), "So where next? Developments in humanitarian logistics". In: M. Christopher & P. Tatham (eds.), *Humanitarian Logistics*, Kogan, London, UK, pp. 249–263.

18 Doucouliagos, H. & Paldam, M. (2005), "The aid effectiveness literature. The sad result of 40 years of research", Denmark: University of Aarhus, Working Paper No. 2005–15.

19 Kovács, G. & Spens, K.M. (2011a), " Humanitarian logistics and supply chain management: The start of a new journal", *Journal of Humanitarian Logistics and Supply Chain Management*, Vol. 1, No. 1, pp. 5–14.

20 Kovács, *op. cit.*

21 Safran, P. (2003), "A strategic approach for disaster and emergency assistance," *5th Asian Disaster Reduction Center International Meeting and the 2nd UN-ISDR Asian Meeting*, Kobe, Japan.

22 Tatham, P.H., Oloruntoba, R. & Spens, K. (2012), "Cyclone preparedness and response: An analysis of lessons identified using an adapted military planning framework", *Disasters*, Vol. 36, No. 1, pp. 54–82.

23 Gatignon, A., van Wassenhove, L.N. & Charles, A. (2010), "The Yogyakarta earthquake: Humanitarian relief through IFRC's decentralized supply chain", *International Journal of Production Economics*, Vol. 126, No. 1, pp. 102–110.

24 Kovács, G. & Spens, K.M. (2011b), "Trends and developments in humanitarian logistics: A gap analysis", *International Journal of Physical Distribution and Logistics Management*, Vol. 41, No. 1, pp. 32–45.

25   Suarez, P. (2009), "Linking climate knowledge and decisions: Humanitarian challenges", *The Pardee Papers No. 7* (December 2009).

26   IPCC (2007), "Climate change 2007: Impacts, adaptation and vulnerability", at www. meteotrentiNo. it/clima/pdf/rapporti_meteo/IPCC_Impacts_Adaptation_and_Vulnerability. pdf, accessed October 1, 2010; Kalnay, E. & Cai, M. (2003), "Impact of urbanization and land use of climate change", *Nature,* No. 423, pp. 528–531; Ziska, L.H., Gebhard, D.E., Frenz, D.A., Faulkner, S., Singer, B.D. & Straka, J.G. (2003), "Cities as harbingers of climate change: Common ragweed, urbanization, and public health", *Journal of Allergy and Clinical Immunology*, Vol. 111, No. 2, pp. 290–295.

27   Kovács, Matopoulos & Hayes, *op. cit.*

28   Anderson, M.B. (1996), *Do no Harm: Supporting Local Capacities for Peace through Aid*, Collaborative for Development Action, Inc., Cambridge, MA.

29   Kovács, Matopoulos & Hayes, *op. cit.*

30   *Ibid.*

31   Mangan, J., Lalwani, C. & Butcher, T. (2008), *Global Logistics and Supply Chain Management*, John Willy and Sons, Wiltshire.

32   *Ibid.*

33   cf. Balcik, B. & Beamon, B. (2008), "Facility location in humanitarian relief", *International Journal of Logistics: Research and Applications*, Vol. 11, No. 2, pp. 101–121; Rawls, C.G. & Turnquist, M.A. (2010), "Pre-positioning of emergency supplies for disaster response", *Transportation Research Part B: Methodological*, Vol. 44, No. 4, pp. 521–534.

34   cf. Tatham, P., Haavisto, I., Kovács; G., Beresford, A. & Pettit, S. (2010), "The logistic cost drivers of disaster relief". In: T. Whiteing (ed.), *Towards the Sustainable Supply Chain: Balancing the Needs of Business, Economy and the Environment, LRN 2010 Conference Proceedings*, Leeds/ Harrogate, UK, pp. 650–659.

35   Mancini-Roth, D. & Picot, A. (2004), *"Humanitarian Negotiation: A Handbook for Securing Access, Assistance and Protection for Civilians in Armed Conflict"*, Henri Dunant Centre for Humanitarian Dialogue, Geneva. At: http://hdcenter.org./publications/; accessed April 4, 2010.

36   Oloruntoba, R. & Gray, R. (2006), "Humanitarian aid: An agile supply chain?" *Supply Chain Management: An International Journal*, Vol. 11, No. 2, pp. 115–120.

37   Gatignon, van Wassenhove & Charles, *op. cit.*

38   cf. King, A.A. & Lenox, M.J. (2001), "Lean and green? An empirical examination of the relationship between lean production and environmental performance", *Production and Operations Management*, Vol. 10, No. 3, pp. 244–256.

39   cf. Jahre, M. & Spens, K. (2007), "Buy global or go local – that's the question". In: P. Tatham (ed.), CD-ROM *Proceedings of the International Humanitarian Logistics Symposium*, 19–20 November 2007, Faringdon, UK.

40   Vinodh, S. (2010), "Improvement of agility and sustainability: A case study in an Indian rotary switches manufacturing organization", *Journal of Cleaner Production*, Vol. 18, No. 10/11, pp. 1015–1020.

41   Jensen, L-M. (forthcoming), "Humanitarian cluster leads: Lessons from 4PLs", *Journal of Humanitarian Logistics and Supply Chain Management,* Vol. 2, No. 2.

42   Carter, C.R. & Easton, P.L. (2011), "Sustainable supply chain management: Evolution and future directions", *International Journal of Physical Distribution and Logistics Management*, Vol. 41, No. 1, pp. 46–62.

43   *Ibid.*

44   Haavisto & Kovács, *op.cit.*

45   Doucouliagos, H. & Paldam, M. (2005), "The aid effectiveness literature. The sad result of 40 years of research", University of Aarhus, Denmark, Working Paper No. 2005–15.

46   Haavisto & Kovács, *op. cit.*

47   Blecken, A., Hellingrath, B., Dangelmaier, W. & Schulz, S.F. (2009). "A humanitarian supply chain process reference model", *International Journal of Services Technology and Management*, Vol. 12, No. 4., pp. 391–413; Beamon, B.M. & Balcik, B. (2008), "Performance measurement in humanitarian relief chains", *International Journal of Public Sector Management*, Vol. 21, No. 1, pp. 4–25.

48   Beamon & Balcik, *op. cit.*

49   Schulz, S.F. & Heigh, I. (2009), "Logistics performance management in action within a humanitarian organization", *Management Research News*, Vol. 32, No. 11, pp. 1038–1049.

50   Blecken et al., *op. cit.*

51   Beamon & Balcik, *op.cit.*

52   Youn, H., Jaspars, S., Brown, R., Frize, J. & Khogali, H. (2001), "Food-security assessments in emergencies: A livelihoods approach", HPN paper No. 36.

53   Régnier, P., Neri, B., Scuteri, S. & Miniati, S. (2008), "From emergency relief to livelihood recovery: Lessons learned from post-tsunami experiences in Indonesia and India", *Disaster Prevention and Management*, Vol. 17, No. 3, pp. 410–429.

54   United Nations Office for Disaster Risk Reduction (UNISDR) at www.unisdr.org/files/7817_UNISDRTerminologyEnglish.pdf, accessed 19 Mar 2013, p.6.

55   Intergovernmental Panel on Climate Change (IPCC, 2012) [Field, C.B., Barros. V., Stocker. T.F., Qin. D., Dokken. D.J., Ebi. K.L., Mastrandrea. M.D., Mach. K.J., Plattner. G.K., Allen. S.K,. Tignor. M. & Midgley. P.M.], *Managing the Risks of Extreme Events and Disasters to Advance Climate Change Adaptation*, Cambridge University Press, Cambridge, p. 5.

56   UNISDR, *op. cit.*

57   Long, D.C. & Wood, D.F. (1995), "The logistics of famine relief", *Journal of Business Logistics*, Vol. 16, No. 1, pp. 213–229.

58   Schröter, D., (2010), "Sustainability evaluation checklist", at www.wmich.edu/evalctr/wp-content/uploads/2010/06/SEC-revised1.pdf, accessed June 2012.

59   Voluntary Organisations in Cooperation in Emergencies (VOICE, 2006), "Focus: Linking Relief, Rehabilitation and Development (LRRD)", *VOICE out loud* No. 4, December 2006.

60   Hughes, K. (2009), "The evolution of fully flexible supply chains". In: J. Gattorna and friends (eds.), *Dynamic Supply Chain Alignment. A New Business Model for Peak Performance in Enterprise Supply Chains Across All Geographies*, Gower Publishing, Farnham, Surrey, UK, pp. 85–95; Davidson, C.H., Johnson, C., Lizarralde, G., Dikmen, N. & Sliwinski, A. (2007), "Truths and myths about community participation in post-disaster housing projects." *Habitat International*, Vol. 31, No. 1, pp. 100–115.

61   Kovács, Matopoulos & Hayes, *op. cit.*

62   Tatham, P., Haavisto, I., Kovács, G., Beresford, A. & Pettit, S., *op. cit.*

63   Balcik, B., Iravani, S. & Smilowitz, K. (2010), "A review of equity in nonprofit and public sector: A vehicle routing perspective", *Wiley Encyclopedia of Operations Research and Management Science*, JohnWiley & Sons.

64   Oloruntoba, R. & Gray, R. (2009), "Customer service in emergency relief chains", *International Journal of Physical Distribution and Logistics Management*, Vol. 39, No. 6, pp. 486–505.

65   Pettit, S. & Taylor, D. (2007), "Humanitarian aid supply chain assessment: A preliminary consideration of the relevance of lean supply chain concepts to humanitarian aid supply

chains". In: Á. Halldórsson & G. Stefánsson (eds.), *Proceedings of the 19th Annual Conference for Nordic Researchers in Logistics*, NOFOMA 2007, 7–8 June 2007, Reykjavík, Iceland, pp. 881–894.

66   cf. Long & Wood; Jahre & Spens *op. cit.*

67   cf. Gatignon, van Wassenhove & Charles; Balcik, Iravani & Smilowitz

68   Jahre & Spens, *op. cit.*; Kovács & Spens (2011b), *op. cit.*

69   Jose, A. & Lee, S.-M. (2006), "Environmental reporting of global corporations: A content analysis based on website disclosures", *Journal of Business Ethics*, Vol. 72, No. 4, pp. 307–321.

70   Cullinane, K. & Toy, N. (2000), "Identifying influential attributes in freight route/mode choice decisions: A content analysis", *Transportation Research Part E*, Vol. 36, No. 1, pp. 41–53.

71   Gravier, M.J. & Farris, T.M. (2008), "An analysis of logistics pedagogical literature: Past and future trends in curriculum, content, and pedagogy", *International Journal of Logistics Management* Vol. 19, No. 2, pp. 233–253.

72   Craighead, C.W., Hanna, J.B., Gibson, B.J. & Meredith, J.R. (2007), "Research approaches in logistics: Trends and alternative future directions", *International Journal of Logistics Management* Vol. 18, No. 1, pp. 22–40; Spens, K.M. & Kovács, G. (2006), "A content analysis of research approaches to logistics research", *International Journal of Physical Distribution and Logistics Management* Vol. 36, No. 5, pp. 374–390.

73   Miyazaki, A.D., Phillips, J.K. & Phillips, D.M. (1999), "Twenty years of JBL: An analysis of published research", *Journal of Business Logistics*, Vol. 20, No. 2, pp. 1–20.

74   Rossetti, C.L. & Dooley, K.J. (2010), "Job types in the supply chain management profession", *Journal of Supply Chain Management*, Vol. 46, No. 3, pp. 40–56; Kovács, G., Tatham, P. & Larson, P.D. (2012), "What skills are needed to be a humanitarian logistician?" *Journal of Business Logistics*, Vol. 33, No. 3, pp. 245–258.

75   Disaster Emergency Committee (DEC) is an umbrella organizations for Actionaid, Age UK, British Red Cross, Cafod, Care International UK, Christian aid, Concern Worldwide, Islamic Relief, Merlin, Oxfam, Save the Children, Tearfund and World Vision.

76   CARE (2011), "Live, Learn, Earn, Lead – Care USA Annual Report 2010", www.care.org/newsroom/publications/annualreports/index.asp, accessed January 2012; Caritas (2011), "Caritas Internationalis Annual Report 2010", www.caritas.org/resources/CaritasAnnualReport10.html, accessed January 2012; Disasters Emergency Committee (2011), "DEC Annual Report and Accounts 2010–11", www.dec.org.uk/sites/default/files/files/Annual%20Reports/DEC_AR_2010%E2%80%9311_v6.pdf, accessed January 2012; International Federation of Red Cross and Red Crescent Societies (IFRC, 2011), "International Federation of Red Cross and Red Crescent Societies Annual Report 2010", www.ifrcmedia.org/assets/pages/annual-report/resources/IFRC-Annual-report-2010-English.pdf, accessed January 2012; International Rescue Committee (IRC, 2011), "International Rescue Committee – From Harm To Home – Annual Report 2010", www.rescue.org/sites/default/files/resource-file/2010/annual-report_us.pdf, accessed January 2012; Oxfam International (2011), Oxfam Annual Report 2009–2010", www.oxfam.org/sites/www.oxfam.org/files/oxfam-international-annual-report-2009-2010.pdf, accessed January 2012; Médecins sans Frontières (2011), "MSF Activity Report 2010", www.doctorswithoutborders.org/publications/ar/MSF-Activity-Report-2010.pdf, accessed January 2012, Mercy Corps (2011), "2010 Annual Report A Crisis Is Just The Beginning", www.mercycorps.org/sites/default/files/2010_annual_report.pdf, accessed January 2012; Save the Children (2011), "Save the Children Annual Report 2009 – Revitalizing Newborn and Child Survival", www.savethechildren.org/atf/cf/%7B9def2ebe-10ae-432c-9bd0-df91d2eba74a%7D/stc-annual-report-2009.pdf, accessed January 2012; United Nations Children's Fund (UNICEF, 2011), "Annual Report 2010 – United for Children", www.unicef.org/lac/UNICEF_Annual_

Report_2010_EN_052711.pdf, accessed January 2012; World Food Programme (WFP, 2011), "Fighting Hunger Worldwide", http://documents.wfp.org/stellent/groups/public/documents/communications/wfp220666.pdf, accessed January 2012; World Vision International (WVI, 2011), "World Vision International 2010 Review", www.wvi.org/wvi/wviweb.nsf/8D286BEE 77C06222882578D50018B69C/$file/World_Vision_International_2010_Annual_Review_-_English.pdf, accessed January 2012.

77 Guthrie J., Petty, R., Yongvanich, K. & Ricceri, F. (2004), "Using content analysis as a research method to inquire into intellectual capital reporting", *Journal of Intellectual Capital*, Vol. 5, No. 2, pp. 282–293; Kripendorff, K. (2004), *Content Analysis: An Introduction to its Methodology, 2nd edn.* Sage Publications: Newbury Park, CA.

78 Krippendorff, *op. cit.*

79 Suarez, *op. cit.*

80 Kalnay & Cai, *op. cit.*

81 Carter & Easton, *op. cit.*

82 Sarkis, Spens & Kovács, p. 204.

Index

Bold page numbers indicate figures, *italic*
    numbers indicate tables.